volume **1**

The West
A Narrative History

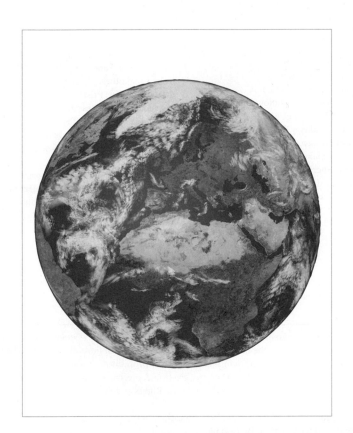

A. Daniel Frankforter

The Pennsylvania State University

William M. Spellman

University of North Carolina, Asheville

PEARSON

Prentice
Hall

Upper Saddle River, New Jersey 07458

Library of Congress Cataloging-in-Publication Data

Frankforter, A. Daniel.
   The West : a narrative history / A. Daniel Frankforter, William M. Spellman.—2nd ed.
      v. cm.
   First ed. has subtitle: Culture and ideas.
   Includes bibliographical references and index.
   ISBN-13: 978-0-13-605634-8 (combined, v. 1 and 2)
   ISBN-10: 0-13-605634-2 (combined, v. 1 and 2)
   ISBN-13: 978-0-13-605820-5 (v. 1)
   ISBN-13: 978-0-13-605822-9 (v. 2)
   1. Civilization, Western—History. I. Spellman, W. M. II. Title.
   CB245.F7 2009
   909'.09821—dc22

2008021280

VP/Publisher: Priscilla McGeehon
Executive Editor: Charles Cavaliere
Editorial Assistant: Lauren Aylward
Media Project Manager: Tina Rudowski
Marketing Manager: Laura Lee Manley
Marketing Assistant: Athena Moore
Managing Editor (Production): Lisa Iarkowski
Project Manager: Marianne Peters-Riordan
Senior Operations Specialist: Mary Ann Gloriande
Senior Art Director: Maria Lange
Interior and Cover Designer: K&M Design
AV Project Manager: Mirella Signoretto
Cover Illustration/Photo: Dagli Orti/Picture Desk, Inc./Kobal Collection; Albrecht Duerer, "Self-Portrait."

1500. Oil on Panel. 26 1/4" × 19 1/4" (66.7 × 49 cm). Alte Pinakothek, Munich. SCALA/Art Resource, NY
Cartographer: Pristine Graphics
Director, Image Resource Center: Melinda Patelli
Manager, Rights and Permissions: Zina Arabia
Manager, Visual Research: Beth Brenzel
Manager, Cover Visual Research & Permissions: Karen Sanatar
Image Permission Coordinator: Fran Toepfer
Composition/Full-Service Project Management: Heather Willison/S4Carlisle Publishing Services
Printer/Binder: Quebecor Printing

Credits and acknowledgments borrowed from other sources and reproduced, with permission, in this textbook appear on pages 394–395.

Pearson Education LTD., London
Pearson Education Singapore, Pte. Ltd
Pearson Education, Canada, Ltd
Pearson Education–Japan
Pearson Education Australia PTY, Limited

Pearson Education North Asia Ltd
Pearson Educación de Mexico, S.A. de C.V.
Pearson Education Malaysia, Pte. Ltd
Pearson Education, Upper Saddle River, New Jersey

10 9 8 7 6 5 4 3 2 1
ISBN-13: 978-0-13-605820-5
ISBN-10:   0-13-605820-5

Brief Contents

Contents

Part 1 Departure 2

1 The Birth of Civilization

4

KEY|QUESTION: How do environments shape human communities and human
communities alter environments?

2 The Rise of Empires and the Beginning of the Iron Age **32**

KEY|QUESTION: Does civilization promote unity or intensify divisions among
peoples?

Part 2 The Classical Era 2000 B.C.E. to 30 C.E.   60

Part 3 The Division of the West
300 to 1300 178

7 The West's Medieval Civilizations   **180**

8 The Emergence of Europe   **208**

9 Europe Turns Outward   **236**

13 Reformation, Religious Wars, and National Conflicts   354

Maps

KEY|QUESTIONS

Preface

The Western civilization course, which was invented for American students, has evolved as students' educational needs have changed. Toward the end of the nineteenth century, when the traditional literature-based curriculum centered on Greek and Latin classics yielded to a new system of elective courses offered by a rapidly growing number of specialized academic departments, the Western civilization course was introduced to provide a foundation on which to erect a coherent program of study. At many schools the course became the centerpiece of a "general education program" that served as a required introduction to college for all students.

During the twentieth century, as thinking about higher education evolved, different rationales were offered for Western civilization courses and for general education requirements. Some instructors have presented these courses as essential instruction for novice scholars in a body of knowledge that all educated persons must have. In the environment created by the great wars that shaped much of the twentieth century, the Western civilization course was often perceived as training for citizenship and the defense of democracy. The history of the West was represented as the story of the rise of a rational and free way of life that was humanity's supreme achievement and universal aspiration—a precious legacy that had to be guarded against the forces of barbarism.

All of this was radically questioned during the 1960s. Many American schools abandoned the idea of general education and compulsory course requirements. In light of the growing specialization and professionalization of academic fields, faith in the unity of knowledge and the existence of a body of information with which every educated person should be familiar seemed naive. Given the complexity and diversity of intellectual life, academic reformers swept aside general education programs and insisted that students should be free to pursue their personal interests and define the contents of their own educations.

In this environment the Western civilization course was singled out for special criticism. It was accused of promoting provincialism and narrowmindedness by elevating European-American history to the status of universal history—the story of Earth's premier "high civilization." The realities of the emerging global community, it was argued, compelled the development of a new paradigm for higher education, one that did not "privilege" the West or represent its history as progress toward freedom and rationality. New courses in World civilization were proposed to take its place.

The critics of Western civilization courses make valid points—at least with respect to the way these courses have sometimes been conceived and taught. The Western civilization course has, at times, promoted Euro-American triumphalism and perpetuated colonialist attitudes, cultural intolerance, and racism. However, the fact that a subject can be badly taught does not suggest that it should never be taught. Any national history can degenerate into propaganda and be used to foster jingoism. The fault is less with the subject than with a loss of objectivity in its presentation.

Students at American colleges and universities are—regardless of their ancestral ethnic backgrounds—immersed in a culture deeply indebted to Europe and the

Mediterranean region. Other parts of the globe have made undoubted contributions to the culture of what is largely an immigrant nation, but these influences integrate with the values and institutions of a trans-Atlantic civilization that, for want of a better term, is invariably described as "the West." Despite this, most students begin their undergraduate careers with very little knowledge of the roots of their way of life. Those who come from American public schools have repeatedly been taught something of their national history, but they seldom have had more than a cursory exposure to its background. Their lack of understanding of the historical processes that shaped the West makes it difficult for them to situate the American experience in a global context. Having an inadequate knowledge of themselves, they are handicapped in their efforts to comprehend others. Far from narrowing their perspective, a course in Western civilization—which helps American students grasp how and why they have come to be what they are—can help them understand how and why other peoples have developed differently. Such understanding is essential if students are to appreciate other cultures, sympathize with their struggles, and value their integrity.

Approach

The West: A Narrative History is a unique text in its field in that it was conceived and developed as a brief introduction to the history of the West. The text is not a reduced version of a larger study, but a fully realized project in its own right. It defines *West* in the broadest terms as encompassing all the cultures that trace at least some of their ancestry to the ancient Mediterranean world. The text consistently reminds its readers of the links between the people who have come to define the West and those in other regions of the world.

In this respect as well, *The West: A Narrative History* distinguishes itself from many of the textbooks currently available for teaching courses in Western civilization. These books begin with brief treatments of ancient Mesopotamian and Egyptian civilizations and then largely abandon the Middle East. When they reach the medieval period, they mention the rise of Islam but leave students with the impression that Islam is an alien, non-Western phenomenon. This obscures the fact that both Christians and Muslims built on the same cultural foundations—Hebraic religious tradition and Hellenistic philosophy and science—and both borrowed significantly from the civilizations of India and the East. The importance of the help that the Muslim world gave medieval Europe in reclaiming the legacy both regions shared from the ancient era is often slighted; with the rise of the Ottoman Empire, Islam usually disappears from the narrative (except for brief references to later European encroachments on Ottoman territory).

Such minimal treatment of Muslim history poorly prepares students to understand the current international political situation and to evaluate critically common "Western" assumptions about what is, somewhat inaccurately, called "the East." The future of much more than the West may depend on Western civilization's Euro-American and Middle Eastern heirs re-examining their history of interaction and divergence and developing a deeper understanding of how much they have in common.

Organization

The volume of tourist traffic flowing through historical sites and the existence of a History Channel on TV prove that the public at large finds the past innately interesting for its own sake. Undergraduates, however, are often afflicted with "presentism," the assumption that the past is an alien land—a curious, but irrelevant realm. To encourage them to relate the experiences of long-vanished peoples to their own lives, each chapter of *The West: A Narrative History* begins by posing a "key question," a question of broad scope or general significance that is raised by something in the period the chapter treats. The chapter is not an essay on the question, and the chapter does not propose a definitive answer to the larger issue it asks students to ponder—though the problems it raises are reconsidered at the end of each chapter. The "key question" feature provides a springboard for wide-ranging class discussions of questions that have no simple answers. Debating the issues raised by the "key question" essays helps students discover for themselves that the past is more intriguing (and knowledge of its history more useful) than they may have realized.

Each chapter is equipped with features to assist its readers in grasping its structure and design. Quotations from primary sources, at the head of each chapter, introduce the chapter's theme—which is elaborated by the brief "key question" essay that follows. The topics covered in the chapter are then listed, and the text of the chapter is divided into sections and subsections with headings that make its content easy to outline. The text contains ample maps, illustrations, and timelines. Each chapter also has a sidebar that deals with an individual whose life illustrates something about the era the chapter discusses. The narrative unfolds chronologically and avoids shifting back and forth in time—something that many students claim makes a text confusing and difficult to understand. Politics often provides the skeleton of the story, but the traditional "names, dates, and battles" are fleshed out with materials from social, economic, and intellectual history. Attention is paid to segments of society (for example, women, slaves, and peasants) whose contributions sometimes receive insufficient recognition in survey courses. To help students grasp the overall design of the book, it is divided into eight parts that group related chapters. Numerous illustrations and maps, with detailed captions, supplement the primary narrative. A set of review questions, which can be used either for class discussion or written assignments, concludes each chapter, and an extensive list of resources that students can explore on their own is provided at the end of the text.

Changes to the Second Edition

In response to edifying comments and helpful suggestions from reviewers across the country, we have improved the book's organization and narrative flow and updated or enhanced the coverage of several important topics. We have also changed the book's subtitle to *A Narrative History* because it more accurately reflects the basic goal we set out to achieve when we embarked on this project—to provide students with a clear, concise, and provocative examination of civilization in the West.

Introduction
- Completely revised, the Introduction now examines "the West" in light of globalization. It offers an expanded discussion of the concept of "civilization."

Chapter 1
- A new "key question" focuses attention on relations between the environment and culture.
- The chapter provides an expanded discussion on the origins of agriculture and the rise of civilization on the Eurasian continents.

Chapter 2
- A new "key question" has been added on the dynamics of civilization—unity versus conflict.
- Expanded discussion is provided of the Bible and history.
- Increased coverage is offered of the roles of women.

Chapter 3
- Increased coverage is provided of Minoan civilization.
- Discussion of the values of classical civilization has been significantly revised.
- Expanded description is provided of Athens.

Chapter 4
- Coverage of military history has been clarified.
- Improved analysis is provided of the positive and negative aspects of Hellenic civilization.
- More emphasis is placed on Greece's ties with the Near East.

Chapter 5
- A new "key question" explores developments that undermine popular governments.
- Increased coverage is provided of the consequences of the Peloponnesian War.
- Expanded treatment is given of Alexander and the Hellenistic era.

Chapter 6
- A new discussion is offered of Augustus's strategy for ruling Rome.
- Treatment of Marcus Aurelius is expanded.
- Discussion of the political influence of the Roman military has been expanded.

Chapter 7
- A new "key question" examines the limits of religious freedom.
- Expanded discussion is provided of the status of women.
- Coverage of Byzantium and Islam has been increased.

Chapter 8
- A new "key question" focuses on the transmission of classical culture to medieval Europe.
- Increased coverage is offered of the Benedictines.
- Expanded discussion is provided of the manorial economy and agricultural innovations.

Chapter 9
- Updated discussion is provided of the concept of feudalism.

Chapter 10
- A new "key question" examines the ability of societies to confront change.
- Increased coverage is offered of religious heresies.
- Discussion of the artistic movements of the High Middle Ages is increased.

Chapter 11
- Expanded discussion is provided of medieval philosophers.
- Improved coverage is provided of military developments.
- More material is given on the Avignonese papacy and the resolution of the Great Schism.

Chapter 12
- Increased coverage is provided of the motives behind European exploration.
- Enhanced discussion is offered of the impact of European colonization.
- Updated analysis is given of the Ottoman Empire.

Chapter 13
- A new "key question" explores the rationales for war.
- Coverage of the Reformation has been increased.
- Increased coverage is given of the English Civil War.

Chapter 17
- Expanded analysis is provided of the French and American Revolutions.

Chapter 18
- To improve the narrative flow, Chapter 18 (formerly Chapter 19) examines industry and society in nineteenth-century Europe, while Chapter 19 (formerly Chapter 18) examines political, intellectual, and artistic developments during this same period.

Chapter 19
- Expanded discussion is offered of Marx and Engels.

Chapter 21
- Expanded discussion is offered of scientific racism.

Chapter 23
- Improved coverage of the Spanish Civil War and expanded treatment of Nazi theories of racism is provided.

Chapter 25
- Now entitled "Decolonization and the Cold War," this significantly revised chapter devotes more coverage to the end of European empire. It also includes a new section on domestic life in Western Europe after the war, with a special emphasis on the rise of American-style consumer culture, the rise and fall of the welfare state, and the place of the EU in world politics.

Chapter 26
- Significantly revised, the final chapter includes new consideration of demographic changes in Europe, the consequences of new immigration on Europe's domestic politics, and relations between Islam and the West.

In addition, this second edition of *The West* has been enriched with new maps and illustrations, a substantially revised and expanded "Suggested Readings," and a crisp and elegant full-color design.

Support Materials

The West: A Narrative History comes with an extensive package of support materials for teachers and students.

For Instructors and Students

MyHistoryLab for *The West* offers instructors and students a state-of-the-art, interactive solution for Western civilization and can form the basis for administering an online course.

Features of MyHistoryLab

Instructor Resources
- Textual documents from the Primary Source DVD
- Images and captions from the Primary Source DVD in PowerPoint presentations
- Lecture Outline PowerPoint presentations
- Classroom-response system PowerPoint questions for *The West*
- Animations
- Maps from the text in PDF format
- Map Outlines
- The Prentice Hall Atlas of World History in PDF format
- Test-Item File

Student Resources
- Complete ebook for *The West*
- Chapter pretests

- Personalized study plans which include review material for items missed on the pretests
- Flash cards of key terms
- "How to Read Primary Source" interactive tutorial

MyHistoryLab is available via an access code. Contact your Pearson/Prentice Hall representative for details or visit www.myhistorylab.com.

Primary Source: Documents in Western Civilization This is both a rich collection of textual and visual documents—many never before available to a wider audience—and an indispensable tool for working with sources. Extensively developed with the guidance of historians and teachers, this DVD-ROM includes over 800 sources in Western civilization history—from cave art, to text documents, to satellite images of Earth from space. All sources are accompanied by headnotes and focus questions, and are searchable by topic, region, or theme. In addition, a built-in tutorial guides students through the process of working with documents. Please refer to the back of the book for a complete listing of sources. The DVD can be bundled with *The West* at no charge. Please contact your Pearson representative for ordering information.

An abridged two-volume print version of *Primary Source: Documents in Western Civilization* is also available. Please contact your Pearson representative for more information or to receive an examination copy.

For Instructors
- **Instructor's Resource Manual and Test-Item File**

This supplement provides chapter outlines, detailed chapter overviews, discussion questions, lecture strategies, and essay topics. The test-item file contains over 1,200 multiple-choice, true-false, map, and essay questions, organized by chapter.

- **Test Manager**

This is a computerized test management program for Windows and MacIntosh environments. The program allows instructors to select items from the test-item file to create tests. It also allows for online testing.

- **Instructor's Resource Center (www.prenhall.com)**

Text-specific materials, such as the Instructor's Manual, the test-item file, PDF files of all the maps from *The West*, and PowerPoint™ presentations, are available for downloading by adopters.

For Students

- **CourseSmart Textbooks Online.**

This is an exciting new choice for students looking to save money. As an alternative to purchasing the print textbook, students can subscribe to the same content online and save up to 50% off the suggested list price of the print text. With a CourseSmart eTextbook, students can search the text, make notes online, print out reading assignments that incorporate lecture notes, and bookmark important passages for later review. For more information, or to subscribe to the CourseSmart eTextbook, visit www.coursesmart.com.

- **Study Guide (Volumes One and Two).**

The study guide provides students with chapter outlines, map questions, and practice tests.

 - **The Prentice Hall Atlas of Western Civilization, Second Edition.**

This popular atlas includes over 100 full-color maps, drawn by Dorling Kindersley, one of the world's most respected cartographic publishers. Copies of the Atlas can be bundled with *The West* for a nominal charge. Contact your Pearson sales representative for details.

- **Lives and Legacies: Biographies in Western Civilization, Second Edition.**

Extensively revised, *Lives and Legacies* includes brief, focused biographies of 60 individuals whose lives provide insight into the key developments of Western civilization. Each biography includes an introduction, prereading questions, and suggestions for additional reading.

Titles from the renowned **Penguin Classics** series can be bundled with *The West* for a nominal charge. Please contact your Pearson Arts and Sciences sales representative for details.

Acknowledgments

The only names that appear prominently on books are those of their authors. However, all books—particularly textbooks—are communal projects to which many people contribute their skills and expertise. The authors wish to acknowledge the debt they owe to all who have assisted them in bringing this project to completion, particularly the following individuals. Charles Cavaliere, executive editor at Pearson/Prentice Hall, sponsored this edition of the text and assumed the added responsibility of serving as its developmental editor. He deserves credit for many aspects of its design, its special features, and its supplements. Special thanks is owed to Jonathan S. Perry of the University of South Florida for the detailed reviews that guided the revision of Volume One, and John M. Cox of Florida Gulf Coast University, who provided major assistance with the preparation of Volume Two. Guy Ruggiero of Pristine Graphics redesigned and redrafted the maps. Credit for the book's attractive appearance belongs to Maria Lange, senior art director. Lauren Aylward, editorial assistant, took on many daunting assignments with grace and aplomb, while production editors Heather Willison and Marianne Peters-Riordan brought all the strands together to create the volume you hold in your hands.

A useful, accurate textbook owes much to the scholars who agree to review its contents from the perspective of their fields of specialization. Their willingness to take time from their own research and writing to enhance the value and utility of a textbook is a service to their profession that rarely receives the acknowledgment that it deserves. Their contributions to this project are hardly repaid by this brief expression of gratitude:

Stephen J. Andrews, *Central New Mexico Community College*

Thomas Behr, *University of Houston*

Beverly Blois, *Northern Virginia Community College*

April Brooks, *South Dakota State University*

Gregory Bruess, *University of Northern Iowa*

Laurel Carrington, *St. Olaf College*

Sara Chapman, *Oakland University*

John M. Cox, *Florida Gulf Coast University*

Peter L. DeRosa, *Bridgewater State College*

James Halverson, *Judson College*

Mark Herman, *Edison Community College*

L. Edward Hicks, *Faulkner University*

Charles Hilken, *St. Mary's College of California*

David Hudson, *California State University, Fresno*

Gary J. Johnson, *University of Southern Maine*

Sara L. Kimble, *University of Northern Iowa*

Christine J. Kooi, *Louisiana State University*

Jennifer M. Lloyd, *State University of New York at Brockport*

John W. Monroe, *Iowa State University*

Sean Moran, *Oakland University*

Michael G. Paul, *University of South Florida*

Jonathan S. Perry, *University of South Florida*

Mary Pickering, *San Jose State University*

Stuart Semmel, *University of Delaware*

Larissa J. Taylor, *Colby College*

William B. Whisenhunt, *College of DuPage*

Andrew D. Wilson, *Keene State College*

Note on Dates and Spelling

Dates

Human beings struggle to orient themselves in a featureless sea of time. For much of their history the heavens have served as their primary clock. The Hebrew Bible claims that the Creator placed two "lights" in the sky, one to govern the day and the other the night. This sounds simpler than it turns out to be in practice, for the two lights divide time into cycles that are difficult to coordinate. Earth's journey around the Sun, which determined the annual revolution of the seasons, took 365.2424 days. The moon's revolution about Earth took 29.53059 days. A year could be divided approximately into 12 months by charting the waxing and waning of the moon—but only very approximately. The lunar year passed weeks faster than its solar partner; therefore, months originally associated with one season gradually drifted into another.

As ancient peoples improved accuracy in measuring the movements of the heavenly bodies, they devised a variety of increasingly sophisticated methods for computing calendars that better coordinated months and seasons. The Egyptians favored a year divided into 12 equal, 30-day-long months to which they annually added 5 days to complete the year. This still fell about 6 hours short of the actual length of the solar year, and as the centuries passed, those 6 hours accumulated, causing months gradually to slide from one season to another. The Babylonians devised a calendar based on cycles of 19 years—a combination of 7 years of 13 months and 12 years of 12 months. This was close, but still short enough to fall behind by several weeks each century. Julius Caesar drew on the best astronomical information of his day to decree a year of 12 months (some 30 and others 31 days long) with an additional "leap" day added every 4 years. This Julian Calendar was an improvement, but there was still a small discrepancy that eventually made a noticeable difference. In 1582 Pope Gregory XIII ordered a leap of 11 days (declaring that the day after October 4 be October 15) to synchronize months and seasons and added another refinement to calendar calculations. In the Gregorian calendar, leap years were to occur every four years but be omitted for years that marked centuries divisible by 400 (e.g., 2000). This, the calendar most widely in use today, is still several seconds out of sync with the Earth's orbit about the sun.

Not only did ancient calendars differ on how to calculate months and supplemental days, there was also no consensus on when a year began. The cycle of seasons disposed people to look on Spring, the season of rebirth, as the appropriate time to declare a new start. Therefore, in the northern hemisphere, March was often favored as the first month of the year. A memory of this survives in the names still used for some months: September, October, November, December—7th, 8th, 9th and 10th months (counting from March). About a century and a half before the birth of Christ the Romans decided to begin their year on January 1, the date on which their chief executives, the consuls), took office. The custom lapsed in many places during the Middle Ages and did not begin to win general acceptance until about 300 years ago.

The lack of a universal standard for measuring years and of agreement on when the year began made life difficult for ancient record keepers. A common strategy for keeping track of things was to associate an event with some memorable person or unusual development. For example: "This happened in the 8th year of the reign of King Sed, 17 years after the great famine." Greeks and Romans sometimes created "eponymous" offices and named each year for the person who held that office that year. For example: "In the year of the *praetor maximus* Livius Aurelianus." This system required public records offices to keep long and growing lists of names.

The modern way to chart a path through time is to choose a fixed point from which to count the sequence of years. The Jewish calendar begins with the date of the Creation of the world—calculated from information provided by the genealogies recorded in the Hebrew Scriptures. The Muslim calendar begins with an event in the Prophet Muhammad's life, an act that marked the birth of the *umma*, the community of Islam. As Christianity acquired status as the dominant faith of the region that had been the Roman Empire, the birth of Christ gained appeal as the pivot point of history. Dionysius Exiguous (c. 500–560) is said to be the first scholar to propose dating events from what he assumed (erroneously) to be the year in which Jesus of Nazareth was born. About a century and a half later, his system was popularized by the best historian of the day, an English monk named Bede (672–735), as a method for dating events both before and after Jesus' birth. This led to the custom of designating years as either B.C. ("before Christ") or A.D. (*anno Domini*, "in the year of the Lord")—e.g., "457 B.C." (457 years "before Christ") or A.D. 457 ("in the year of the Lord 457"). Writers today, who wish to be sensitive to the fact that not all their readers may share the Christian faith, use B.C.E. and C.E., which can be read as "Before the Common [or Christian] Era" and the "Common [or Christian] Era."

These dating conventions mean that years are counted down from the most remote eras to the birth of Christ and up to the present time from the birth of Christ. Thus in the pre-Christian or Common Era events become more recent as numbers grow smaller (i.e., 132 B.C.E. is earlier than 32 B.C.E.) and post-Christian events become more recent as numbers grow larger (i.e., 32 C.E. is earlier than 132 C.E.). Counting back from the birth of Christ, the 3rd century B.C.E. would begin in 201 and end in 300 (i.e., the 3rd century B.C.E. is the 200s). Counting forward from the birth of Christ, the 12th century would begin in 1101 and end in 1200 (i.e., the 1100s).

Spelling

Human beings are capable of making a wide range of sounds, and they have used their extensive vocalization skills to construct a myriad of different languages. Some are fairly monotone. Others are almost musical, using differences in pitch to indicate meanings. Some favor soft, mellifluous tones, while others emphasize harsher sounds. There are even languages that employ percussive, clicking noises that non-native speakers may find impossible to reproduce.

Writing systems invent symbols to represent the sounds of speech. Because not all languages use the same sounds, however, it can be difficult to write a language using a symbol system that has been developed for a different kind of speech. Letters may have to be combined in odd ways to suggest unique sounds (e.g., "kw"), "diacritical" marks may be added to indicate how a sound should be made (e.g., á, ä, or â), or entirely new symbols may have to be invented to supplement those that are normally sufficient. An added complication derives from the fact that a number of ancient languages were written only with consonants. Readers were expected to infer vowel sounds for themselves from context. A modern scholar who wishes to translate (and transliterate) these languages for English readers must make an educated guess as to what the sounds originally intended may have been. For instance, the seventeenth-century English translators of the Bible thought that the Hebrew consonants for God's name should be supplied with vowels and read as "Jehovah," but modern scholars generally prefer "Yahweh." The two English words render the same word in Hebrew, but they do not look much alike.

Linguists have devised sophisticated rules to promote consistency in moving from one writing system to another, but different traditions and customs have prevailed at different times and in different academic environments. For instance, because "c" in English can be pronounced like "s" or "k," a Greek name that begins with a hard consonant (kappa) might be spelled with either a "c" or a "k." British scholars might prefer one spelling of the name while Americans choose another. Classicists may favor one and historians another. Students must, therefore, be prepared to be flexible when they confront variant spellings in different texts.

About the Authors

A. Daniel Frankforter is Professor of History at the Pennsylvania State University, where he has taught for nearly four decades. His undergraduate work was in the history of ideas and philosophy at Franklin and Marshall College. He earned a Master of Divinity degree from Drew University, did graduate work at Columbia University and the University of Göttingen, and completed master's and doctoral degrees in medieval history and religious studies at Penn State. His research has focused on the medieval English Church and on the evolving role of European women throughout the medieval period. His articles on these topics have appeared in such journals as *Manuscripta, Church History, The British Studies Monitor, The Catholic Historical Review, The American Benedictine Review, The International Journal of Women's Studies,* and *The Journal of Women's History.* His books include *A History of the Christian Movement: An Essay on the Development of Christian Institutions, Civilization and Survival, The Shakespeare Name Dictionary* (with J. Madison Davis), *The Medieval Millennium: An Introduction, The Western Heritage,* brief edition (with Donald Kagan, Stephen Ozment, and Frank Turner), *The Heritage of World Civilizations,* brief third edition (with Albert Craig, William Graham, Donald Kagan, Stephen Ozment, and Frank Turner), an edition and translation of Poullain de la Barre's *De L'Égalité des deux Sexes,* and *Stones for Bread: A Critique of Contemporary Worship.* Over the course of his career he has developed 15 courses dealing with aspects of the ancient and medieval periods of Western civilization, Judeo-Christian studies, and gender issues. His work in the classroom has been acknowledged by the Penn State Behrend Excellence in Teaching Award and the prestigious Amoco Foundation Award for Excellence in Teaching Performance.

William M. Spellman is the Dean of Humanities at the University of North Carolina, Asheville. He is a graduate of Suffolk University, Boston, and holds a PhD from the Maxwell School of Citizenship and Public Affairs at Syracuse University. He is the author of *John Locke and the Problem of Depravity* (Oxford, 1988); *The Latitudinarians and the Church of England, 1660–1700* (Georgia, 1993); *John Locke* (Macmillan, 1995); *European Political Thought, 1600–1700* (Macmillan, 1997); *Monarchies, 1000–2000* (Reaktion Press, 2000); *Extraordinary Women of the Medieval and Renaissance World* (Greenwood Press, 2000); co-authored with Carole Levin et al.; *The Global Community: Migration and the Making of the Modern World, 1500–2000* (Sutton, 2002); *A Concise History of the World Since 1945* (Palgrave, 2006); and *Migration and the Nation State* (Reaktion Press, forthcoming).

Introduction

The Nature of History

History is not a natural phenomenon—something like gravity or the cycle of a plant's life. People "make" history in two ways: (1) by their actions in the present, and (2) by what they think about the past. Without the former, of course, there would be no past for historians to study. However, the present is also important to historians, not only because it becomes the past, but because it influences how they view the past. Each of us comes into a world that we did not make, and each of us is forced to live in circumstances that we, as individuals, cannot entirely control. A desire to understand the foreordained conditions that provide the context for our lives is often what makes us curious about the past. We want to know the origins of the problems, institutions, and values that are important to us—and even when we study remote eras or cultures that have no immediate or obvious ties with our own, we tend to interpret them in light of our concerns, assumptions, and experiences.

Before people become engaged in the study of history, they sometimes assume that history is a straightforward, objective narrative of dates, facts, and figures—and that, like most things that leave little room for imagination and intuition, it is "cut and (literally) dried." History can, of course, be badly written and taught so as to meet the lowest of expectations. But because historians write about the past from the perspective of the present, their work often stirs up strong feelings and invites controversy. It has a personal dimension for both its writers and its readers. Curiosity about ourselves plays a role in determining the books we choose to read or the topics we are drawn to research. We may identify ourselves and our issues with figures and events from the past and sit in judgment on what previous generations thought and did. Even the most rigorous scientists cannot entirely escape viewing the world through lenses shaped by their educations and life experiences.

The influence of the present on perceptions of the past makes any given historian's work a source of information on two sometimes widely separated eras—the one about which the historian writes and the one the historian writes in. For example: Edward Gibbon's *The Decline and Fall of the Roman Empire* is one of the most famous (if not one of the most read) works by an English historian. This immensely detailed description of Rome's decline rests on a mountain of evidence that Gibbon mined from the physical and literary remains of the ancient world. But it is also thoroughly imbued with the intellectual assumptions of Gibbon's own eighteenth century, Europe's "Age of Enlightenment." Gibbon ended his long narrative with a short and succinct summary of its conclusions: "In the preceding volumes of this History I have described the triumph of barbarism and religion. . . ."[1] Most European intellectuals of Gibbon's generation be-

---

[1] Edward Gibbon, *The Decline and Fall of the Roman Empire*, vol. II (Chicago: Encyclopedia Britannica, Inc., 1952), p. 592.

lieved that reason held the key to understanding and solving all of humanity's problems and that rational thinking would inevitably spread—promoting knowledge of science and sweeping away every trace of supernaturalism. Rome, Gibbon argued, had been brought down by the opposite trend. It fell victim to the growth and convergence of two kinds of irrationality, ignorance and superstition—by which Gibbon meant German barbarism and the Christian religion, respectively.

Gibbon's argument appeared convincing at the time, and his study seemed destined to become the last word on its subject. But a century later the story of Rome's fall looked quite different to Russian-born and educated historian Michael Ivanovich Rostovtzeff (1870–1952). He lived at a time when the theories of Karl Marx had great influence. Marx believed that economic activities and class struggles were the engines that drove historical evolution, and in mid-life Rostovtzeff had witnessed an event that seemed to support Marx's theses. A popular revolution overthrew Russia's inept tsar and aristocracy and established a classless, but brutally oppressive, society in the historian's homeland. Something similar, Rostovtzeff believed, was what had destroyed first the Roman Republic and then the Roman Empire. He wrote:

> So long as Rome was fighting for pre-eminence in the ancient world, the division of classes within the state remained in the background or at least did not cause bloodshed. As soon, however, as she became mistress of the world, the power of 'the best men', the *optimates* or aristocracy, was assailed by the citizens in general. . . . [W]hen the empire was forced, after nearly two centuries of peace and tranquillity, to defend itself against enemies from without[, the] time called for a great display of enthusiasm. But the rich could not be roused from their indifference; and the poor, seeing the helplessness and weakness of their betters, and deprived of all share in their idle and indolent contentment, were filled with hatred and envy. [2]

The reasons Rostovtzeff gives for Rome's fall in the fifth century might serve almost as well as an explanation for the decline of tzarist Russia in the early twentieth. The fact that what seems important to historians in their own day often looms large in their view of the past does not mean that historians have no objectivity and simply write themselves into their narratives. It does, however, help us understand why history is never definitively written, but is always in the process of being rewritten. As time passes, newly evolving social contexts create new perspectives from which to view the past, and new perspectives suggest new ways of framing questions. Because people tend to see what they look for and ignore things they do not value, new questions prompt new discoveries. The modern feminist movement illustrates this dynamic. For centuries historians thought they could adequately explain the past by focusing only on the activities of men—and usually only a very few "great men." By demonstrating the importance of women to contemporary societies, feminism alerted historians to the necessity of understanding their activities in earlier periods. If the present could not adequately be understood without examining the

---

[2]Michael Rostovtzeff, *Rome* (NY: Oxford U. Press, 1960), pp. 321 & 323.

roles of women, neither could the past. This realization has resulted in the discovery of information that has caused many narratives to be rewritten.

The involvements, commitments, and loyalties that individuals embrace as fundamental to their identities can make them passionate about the past. They may, for instance, come to resent injustices that have been done to a specific category of people and write history to vindicate the importance of that group—to reveal its previously ignored contributions and to accord it what they regard as its due dignity. An Irish-American author, who is proud of his lineage, writes a book to explain *How the Irish Saved Civilization* (Thomas Cahill, 1995). Or an advocate for the peoples of the "developing world" writes to correct what he regards as a deliberate effort to conceal their historical significance (Martin Bernal, *Black Athena: The Afroasiatic Roots of Classical Civilization*, 1987). Advocacy for a cause is not necessarily bad. But if passions run too high, a historical inquiry can become an inquisition. Much history has been written to justify or convict, to claim credit for or to blame, to vindicate or to indict one party or another. It is up to its readers to decide how useful (or entertaining) this is, and it should not be allowed to get in the way of the primary reason for studying history: to understand.

The Divisions of History

Attempts are made to grasp human history as a whole, but broadly generalized surveys rest on a myriad of narrowly focused studies. There are political histories, gender histories, economic histories, intellectual histories, national histories, and numerous other kinds of approaches to the past. Different scholars have different preferences and vigorously debate the merits of different ways to develop narratives about the past.

One of the hottest arguments raging today concerns the legitimacy or usefulness of focusing attention specifically on a field defined as Western civilization. Many scholars believe that this implicitly continues a tradition of historiography that unfairly exalts European societies over the cultures of other peoples. And the current international political climate has made arguments about Western civilization especially intense. Hatred of "the West" (the European and American so-called "first world") is emerging as the major political problem of the twenty-first century. It has motivated appalling acts of terrorism and prompted a violent reaction—a "war on terrorism." The world—especially the academic world—seems increasingly to be divided between extreme critics (e.g., post-colonialists and post-modernists) and extreme defenders (e.g., Eurocentrists) of "the West." Each tars the other with a broad brush that makes orderly, fruitful discussion difficult.

The sins alleged to be the legacy of Western civilization are many: colonial exploitation, slavery, sexism, racism, heartless capitalist manipulation, wasteful consumption, and environmental degradation. There is no denying that Europeans, Americans, and their cultural kin have been guilty of these things, but it is less certain that all of these transgressions against humanity are innately or uniquely "western." A kind of racism justified by physical features was uncritically accepted by many eighteenth- and nineteenth-century Europeans, but many societies throughout history have drawn a sharp line between themselves and groups with characteristics (e.g., linguistic, cultural, and physical) that allegedly defined them as inferior "others." Imperialism, slavery, and abuse of women long predate the rise of European powers and can be found in many cultures around the globe. As for capitalism, China may have preceded Europe in its invention, and environmental degradation began with the technologies that supported Earth's first civilizations. What the West may not always get due credit for is its effort to promote the moral sensitivities, the self-critical attitudes, and the rational and scientific discourses that have been used to combat imperialism, slavery, sexism, racism, abusive capitalism, and ecological devastation.

Some students will be surprised to learn that courses in Western civilization are a relatively new idea and that they are an American innovation. They first appeared in the early twentieth century and were designed to lay a common foundation on which to build a coherent college education. Their content and design was profoundly influenced by the political environment of the first half of the twentieth century—particularly the First and Second World Wars. Americans and their European allies fought these bloody struggles in the belief that they were sacrificing themselves to save the world from tyranny. Wars create extreme conditions that can degrade patriotism into chauvinism, and scholars are not immune to their effects. At times Western civilization has been taught in ways that implied that it was the only true civilization—the goal toward which all other peoples should aspire and the standard by which their cultures should be judged. The triumphalism that accompanied this view of the West encouraged the belief that the West was innately superior and self-generating—that it owed little or nothing to inventions and ideas

The arrogance with which some Western nations have dealt with weaker countries is illustrated by this magazine cover from 1911. It asserts that the people of Morocco should yield gratefully to paternalistic dominance by France and the imposition of France's concept of civilized life. Abraham Lincoln's Emancipation Proclamation, however, is an icon for more enlightened behavior by Western powers, which have been in the forefront of movements to end social evils such as slavery.

borrowed from others. Its alleged native genius supposedly gave it a right to world leadership if not world domination.

The study of history is almost inevitably corrupted by the prejudicial assumptions and ethical blind spots of each generation that engages in it. This is certainly true of the ways in which Western civilization has sometimes been studied and taught. But things change, and the heirs of a tradition are free to correct the errors of its founders. Some people believe, however, that the whole enterprise should be abandoned. They insist that the current environment of globalization makes a focus on Western civilization obsolete and that world history should take its place. Others argue, however, that exploration of the world might best begin with an examination of one's own culture. Students at American colleges and universities are—regardless of their more or less distant ethnic backgrounds—products of a society that is still deeply indebted to Europe and the Mediterranean region. Other parts of the globe have made definite contributions to the life of what is largely an immigrant nation, but these influences are integrated with the values and institutions of what has been called, for lack of a better term, "the West."

Many students bring some knowledge of their nation's political and social history to college, but they have had few opportunities to consider that history in a larger context. One approach (and only one) that they might take to broadening their understanding is to situate the American experience in the older European-Mediterranean tradition before beginning to explore that tradition's links with, and indebtedness to, other regions of the world. Study of one's own culture need not inevitably lead back to oneself. It can equip an exploring intellect for the challenge of discovering meaningful patterns within the flux of information that is generated by an increasing complex and ever expanding global community.

Where Is "the West"?

One problem with the study of Western civilization is the slippery nature of the term *west*. It is hard to define or pin down just what historians mean when they speak about "the West." "West" is, after all, a direction, not a place. Dictionaries define it as the opposite of Earth's rotation (the English word *west* derives from a word that means "evening"). This makes "the west" relative to the point of view of the person who watches the sun set. Because this could be a source of confusion for navigators, geographers have arbitrarily fixed a line—the "prime meridian," running north-south through an observatory in Greenwich, England—to separate east from west. Therefore, technically most of the British Isles, a small portion of France, Spain, and a bit of the African continent are in "the west" while the rest of Europe and Africa are in "the east." This meaning of west is not very useful for historians. China, after all, is west of Japan and both these countries are west of the United States, but neither is thought of as part of what most people mean when they speak about "the West."

At first glance it might seem odd that books dealing with Western civilization begin in the Middle East and only slowly work their way across the Mediterranean to Europe and the Atlantic. But west and east are not simply geographical terms. They have always also had cultural implications. The Bible's Book of Genesis begins the human story in a garden that God plants "in the east"—the place where the sun rises being the appropriate symbol for "beginning." Similarly, the west has long been associated with death and ending. For these reasons, graves and places of worship (including medieval Christian churches) have often been oriented to the path of the sun.

The antagonism that developed between Christians and Muslims during the European Middle Ages created a "West" that was Christendom, a region under Christian control. During the sixteenth century, explorers made "the West" the "New World." For nineteenth-century Americans "the West" became a frontier, a wild land to be explored and tamed. During the Cold War of the second half of the twentieth century, "the West" indicated a political alliance—a block of states that opposed the communist east. Most people today think of "the West" as a term for countries that are, or once were, closely linked with those of western Europe. But this is not always an easy identity to determine. "The West" spans the globe, for it includes Europe, the United States, Canada, New Zealand, and Australia. But does it include the Catholic, Spanish- and Portugese-speaking nations of South America? Does it include English-speaking South Africa? Should it include post-communist Russia? Should it include Turkey, a majority Muslim state that has applied for membership in the economic alliance called the European Union? Should it include modern China because China has passionately embraced the "western" ideologies of capitalism and Marxism?

Confusion about the definition of "the West" today is not solely the result of the spread of its civilization. It also reflects the way in which that civilization has come into existence. Culturally speaking, "the West" did not give birth to itself. It is the child of many parents, and it has always existed in the context of diverse cultures exchanging goods and ideas over immense distances. The modern world has been compared to a "global village," but to greater and lesser degrees "the West" has always been part of a global community. It may too rarely acknowledge—or even realize—its debts to other civilizations, and at times it has drawn sharp distinctions between itself and cultures it viewed as "other" (and, by implication, inferior). But it has usually remained open to change and to learning from those with whom it comes in contact.

What Is Civilization?

If the definition of western creates problems for courses in Western civilization, so does the definition of civilization. The word's Latin root (*civis*) means "citizen," the resident of a city (*civitas*), and the common assumption is that urban institutions are central to civilizations. Civilizations are also said to be characterized by bureaucratic governments, stratified social systems, long-distance trade, and specialized technologies such as metal working and writing. Descriptions of this kind are, however, not very informative, for they merely assert that civilization appears when people begin to do what are thought of as civilized things. They do not explain what makes a behavior civilized, and the lists of civilized behaviors they propose are not definitive. This approach to defining civilization also begs the question of which and how many civilized attributes a people must manifest in order to be considered civilized. The Inca of ancient Peru, for example, had urban institutions, monumental architecture, and metal working, but no writing system. Did the absence of literacy mean they were not civilized?

Civilization is a tricky term, for its use sometimes implies a judgment about a society. There are ethical and aesthetic dimensions to civilized living. Despite romantic myths about "noble savages," people who live civilized lifestyles have often been regarded (or have regarded themselves) as superior to people who have not made the kind of progress that civilization supposedly represents. Not to be civilized is to be primitive, backward, and even barbaric—all emotionally charged descriptors.

Cultural relativists challenge the assumption that one society can legitimately be judged by the standards of another. They particularly object to the long tradition of historical writing that assumes the superiority of "western" (European-based) civilization, but it seems unduly contentious to question the value of civilization itself. The humane values articulated by great thinkers from many of the world's civilizations would seem to provide a scorecard by which all societies can justly be evaluated. If torture, slavery, human sacrifice, and cannibalism are authentic, indigenous practices of a society, does that make them acceptable—or do there seem to be ethical lines that no humane person should cross? There are, of course, costs to civilization that have to be weighed against its benefits, and a painful gap often yawns between the problems that civilization causes and the technologies it invents to deal with its effects. Civilization also offers no surefire way to prevent people from behaving barbarously, and it has in fact often helped human beings magnify their inhumanity.

Arguments about the relative merits of the so-called "high civilizations" versus "simple cultures" might benefit from contemplating what both forms of social organization have in common. They are best understood not as opposing conditions, but points on a continuum. Civilization is simply an elaborate form of the cultural behavior that is an innate characteristic of human beings and (to a lesser degree) the higher primates. The goal of that behavior is the preservation and enhancement of life. How that goal is best achieved depends very much on the context in which a population operates. The best outcome for the global community may not be to impose one way of life or set of institutions on everyone, but to find a way to reconcile diversity with a set of universal human values.

The West

Part 1
Departure
Prehistory to 1000 B.C.E.

The Earth from Space.

During the last half of the twentieth century, technology gave Earth's inhabitants their first opportunity to literally step back and view their home world in its totality. What they saw might prove to be the universe's rarest treasure: a planet that sustains a complex of delicately modulated systems without which the fragile phenomenon called life would not exist. Humanity has only just begun to unravel the mysteries of the great "blue marble" that gave it birth, for it has had relatively little time to explore its habitat. Earth is approximately 4.5 billion years old. The current human species did not appear until about 150,000 years ago, and it has been experimenting with civilization for, at most, 5,000 years. It is an infant species that has more energy than wisdom. To continue to thrive, it needs to grow in judgment and understanding. It has, however, no teacher other than itself and no choice therefore but to learn from experience. History is its classroom.

	ENVIRONMENT AND TECHNOLOGY	SOCIETY AND CULTURE	POLITICS
C. 4,500,000,000 B.C.E.	Earth's origin		
C. 4,000,000 B.C.E.	Hominid evolution begins	AUSTRALOPITHECINES	
C. 2,500,000 B.C.E.	Pebble tools	Lower Paleolithic era *Homo habilis*	
C. 1,600,000 B.C.E.	Pressure-chip tools	*Homo erectus*	Hunter–gatherer tribes
C. 200,000 B.C.E.	Migration out of Africa	Middle Paleolithic era Neanderthals *Homo sapiens sapiens*	
C. 130,000 B.C.E.	Composite tools	Upper Paleolithic era	
C. 30,000 B.C.E.	Cave painting Sculpture		
C. 10,000 B.C.E.	Agriculture Farming and herding	Neolithic era	Settled life: villages
C. 3500 B.C.E.	Centers of population density Irrigation Metal working Writing	Bronze Age	city-states, in Sumer
C. 3000 B.C.E.	Salinization of the Sumerian region		Unification of Egypt (3100 B.C.E.) Sumerian monarchy (3000 B.C.E.) Egypt, Old Kingdom (2700 B.C.E.) Egypt, Middle Kingdom (2025 B.C.E.) Sumer's fall (2004 B.C.E.)
C. 2000 B.C.E.	Domestication of the horse		Indo-European migration (2000 B.C.E.) Amoritic Babylon (1800 B.C.E.) Egypt, Hyksos invasion (1630 B.C.E.) Hittite Empire (1600 B.C.E.) Egypt, New Kingdom (1550 B.C.E.)
C. 1200 B.C.E.	Smelting and forging of iron	Iron Age	Sea Peoples invasion (1230 B.C.E.)
C. 1000 B.C.E.			Kingdom of Israel (1000 B.C.E.)

Topics in This Chapter

The Evolution of Prehistoric Cultures • The Archaic States • The Origin of Civilization
in Mesopotamia: Sumer • The Rise of Civilization in Egypt

1 The Birth of Civilization

And God blessed them and God said unto them, Be fruitful, and multiply, and replenish
the earth, and subdue it: and have dominion over the fish of the sea, and over the fowl
of the air, and over every thing that moveth upon the earth . . . And unto Adam he said,
. . . cursed is the ground for thy sake; in sorrow shalt thou eat of it all the days of thy
life; thorns also and thistles shall it bring forth to thee . . .

—The Book of Genesis 1:28; 2:17–18 (Standard Version)

KEY | Question

**How do environments shape human communities and human communities
alter environments?**

For thousands of years the human species was migratory. Men and women survived by hunting and gathering the foodstuffs that nature spontaneously provided. When supplies were exhausted in one area, they moved to another. About 10,000 years ago, some people began what
became a nearly universal shift from hunting and gathering to farming and herding. This forced
them to stay in place for longer periods of time and to confront the challenges that come with
settlement—everything from the construction of durable buildings to the engineering of new
social relationships. In a few exceptional locales environmental conditions and evolving food-
producing technologies contributed to the growth of unprecedented population density. The
informal, personal relationships that structure tribes and villages were insufficient for the management of the large settlements that began to appear. As societies grew more complex,
some communities established the institutions, created and improved the technologies, and
built the monuments that have customarily been regarded as signs of civilization.

The world's first civilization flourished some 5,000 years ago on the plains of southern
Iraq in a land called Sumer. Among the many achievements of the ancient Sumerians was the

Sumerian Artifact   This gold-encased wooden object was found in 1927 by excavators working near the ancient Sumerian city of Ur. Lively imaginations linked it with the biblical story of Abraham and Isaac and named it, "Ram Caught in a Thicket."

invention of writing. The documents they produced make them the first people who were able to leave behind a record of their reflection on the human condition—on the conundrum summarized by the biblical quotes that head this chapter. People "subdue" nature and alter the environment in which they live, but nature resists and compels them to adapt to its changing realities. The result is an endless interplay between human actions and the contexts in which humans act.

From the perspective of the natural world, the construction and maintenance of a civilization may be humanity's most radical act. Civilization's pioneers, the Sumerians, lived in large city-states ruled by kings, the most famous of whom is the quasi-legendary king of Uruk, Gilgamesh. His deeds are celebrated in what may be the earliest extant literary narrative, *The Epic of Gilgamesh*. This ancient poem describes its hero's superhuman efforts to subdue the Earth. In passing, it also reflects on the costs as well as the benefits of such behavior. Gilgamesh's subjects admired his strength, wisdom, and beauty. They boasted of the monsters he killed, the protection he offered them, the great walls and temples he built to foster their pride in their city, and his dangerous journeys to bring them treasures from foreign lands. But these good things came at a high price. Gilgamesh's ambitious projects compelled his people to sacrifice their sons to his wars and their daughters to his lusts.

Sumerian monarchies maintained order in large communities, coordinated labor on monumental public works, and helped ensure security and prosperity. But while they enhanced lives in some ways they limited them in others. They subordinated ties of family and kinship to hierarchies of class and institutionalized authority. They confiscated wealth, impressed labor, and limited freedoms. This enabled them to marshal unprecedented resources with which they literally redesigned their world. They altered humanity itself by altering the physical and mental environments in which human beings come to self-awareness. The assumption of such power entailed responsibilities of which they were only dimly aware and led to consequences they could not anticipate. In this, they resemble most people past and present. As you reflect on civilization's history, consider how the human struggle to survive by subduing the Earth alters the natural and cultural environments that, in turn, influence human actions.

The Evolution of Prehistoric Cultures

The human story has traditionally been divided into two phases. History is said to begin with the invention of writing and the accumulation of documents. Prehistory is the pre-literate era that preceded the innovation of writing systems. The division between the two periods is arbitrary and imprecise. Civilization can exist without writing, and people created and preserved vast amounts of information in oral traditions long before they began to write. When writing finally appeared, it was a very long time before it was used for any but a few narrowly specialized functions.

Humanity's prehistory is vastly longer than its recorded history. Hominids, the biological family to which human beings belong, may have evolutionary roots that go back 7,000,000 years. The modern human species, *Homo sapiens sapiens*, has existed for about 195,000 years. Anthropologists divide the immensely long prehistoric era into periods called Stone Ages, so designated because most of what is known about them has been inferred from the study of the stone implements that are their chief surviving artifacts. The characterization of the prehistoric eras as Stone Ages may, however, be somewhat limiting. It is, after all, likely misleading to judge an entire culture on the basis of only one of its products, particularly when that product may not reflect that culture's most sophisticated work. Stone is a difficult medium, and prehistoric people doubtless produced other—and possibly more elaborate—things from more tractable materials such as wood, leather, and fibers. Had more specimens of these crafts survived, we might have greater appreciation for the inventiveness of these peoples and the complexity of their cultures.

The Paleolithic Era   The **Paleolithic ("Old Stone") era** begins with the first evidence of hominids that displayed characteristically human cultural behavior (e.g., tool use), and it continues through the retreat of the last Ice Age (about 10,500 years ago). Tool use is not unique to the human species. Various kinds of animals and birds use and even make tools, but none relies on tools to the extent that humans do. Tools helped Paleolithic peoples support themselves by hunting and gathering. As hunters and gatherers, they had a passive relationship with their environment. They were dependent on whatever resources nature spontaneously offered them. Hunter-gatherer economies can be organized in different ways, and environmental conditions would have created differences among prehistoric societies. Locales with a rich variety of foodstuffs would have well rewarded gathering, while others, such as Arctic regions, would have increased dependence on hunting. In some modern aboriginal communities, gathering is often a female specialization and hunting an activity dominated (although not exclusively) by males. Scholars have speculated about the distribution of power between males and females in Paleolithic communities, but theories about prehistoric gender relations are more abundant than evidence to support them.

Our modern human species may have begun either as a single population arising in Africa or as the result of simultaneous development in several regions. About 30,000 to 40,000 years ago, signs of cultural activity exploded just as *Homo sapiens sapiens* was emerging as Earth's sole surviving member of the family *Hominidae*, which, like other families of animals, once had many branches. What happened to the other hominids—particularly the Neanderthals with whom *Homo sapiens sapiens* coexisted for a long time—is unknown. Some authorities believe that the modern human species exterminated the Neanderthals; others claim that the two species interbred and that *Homo sapiens sapiens* absorbed the Neanderthal line.

The people who lived in Europe as the Paleolithic era drew to a close were evolving increasingly complex cultures, as evidenced by the highly refined, specialized tools they produced. But their true breakthrough was the creation of a new genre of artifacts—things that modern scholars describe as art. The difference between an art object and a tool is not a simple contrast between a utilitarian instrument and an ornament. A tool can have aesthetic features, and an art object can be used for more than the pleasure of contemplation. Paleolithic sculptors and painters may have been less motivated by aesthetic impulses than by a hope that their works of art would help them manipulate magical or religious powers. The key distinction between a tool and an art object lies in art's symbolic functions. Human intellectual capacity took a great leap forward once people began to see things not just as themselves, but as symbols—as representations of something more or other than themselves. Higher level thinking rests on the ability to perceive and manipulate symbols.

What Paleolithic artists intended to symbolize by their work is uncertain. Scholars have, for instance, puzzled over the meaning of the numerous female figurines that have been found at Paleolithic sites from Europe to Siberia. Most of these follow a fairly standard design: an obese, pregnant female torso with full breasts. Some scholars claim that these images are evidence for a prehistoric mother-goddess cult. Others believe that this reads too much into them. Rather than serving as symbols of something as intellectually complex as religious belief, they may have been simple fertility amulets or charms to ensure safety in childbirth. Equally puzzling are the pictures that Paleolithic people began to paint on the walls of caverns about 30,000 years ago. The tradition they began continued for 15,000 years. Cave paintings were not decorations for places where people lived. They are found in deep caverns that were sometimes difficult and dangerous to access. There is evidence that rituals took place in some of the painted caves, but no one knows the purpose of the art or of the ceremonies that might have been associated with it. When cave paintings first began to come to light in the nineteenth century, scholars assumed that they were products of hunter magic—symbols used for ritual enactments that were intended to ensure successful hunts. But then it was noticed that the kinds of animals that Paleolithic people ate were rarely depicted. Some caves also seem to have been organized thematically—assigning different species of animals to different places. Cave artists lavished their greatest skill on realistic descriptions of animals. They rarely treated human figures, but they frequently covered walls with abstract shapes, hand prints, patterns of

Prehistoric Painting of Multiple Animals, Chauvet Cave, Ardèche Gorge, France   When the first prehistoric painted caves were discovered in the nineteenth century, many people assumed that they were hoaxes. But scientific analysis has proven that they are genuine, and new ones continue to come to light. The Chauvet Cave was only discovered in 1994, and analysis of its contents has only begun. Portions of the cave have not been entered so as to preserve the ancient floors, which are littered with prints and detritus left by animals and ancient peoples. The paintings come from a wide span of time, but some may date as far back as 28,000 B.C.E.

dots, and clusters of lines. Some scholars speculate that cave art was linked with cycles of myths and legends that have long been forgotten.

The Paleolithic era phased into the **Neolithic** ("New Stone") at roughly the same time in perhaps seven different places around the world. The cultural innovations that marked the transition suggest that people were responding to a need to increase their food supplies. As the last Ice Age's glaciers retreated, the global climate became warmer and wetter, sea levels rose, the tundras favored by herd animals shrank and shifted northward, and plant and animal species redistributed themselves. Those stressed communities that could not migrate to the shrinking regions where their old way of life was still possible had to figure out how to wring more sustenance from their changing environment. This inched some of them toward the brink of civilization.

The Neolithic "Revolution"   As one of the Stone Ages, the **Neolithic era** is associated with the emergence of a particular kind of stone implement. In earlier periods, tools were manufactured by pressure chipping—by nicking flakes from pieces of flint, quartz, or obsidian (volcanic glass) to make instruments with sharp edges. Neolithic toolmakers worked tougher kinds of stone by grinding them into shape, but theirs was not the most important new technology of the New Stone Age.

The Neolithic has been described as a revolution, but some scholars object to this, pointing out that although the era had a revolutionary outcome, it was not the product of a revolutionary discovery. There is no disputing the fact that the Neolithic era witnessed a major lifestyle change that had wide-ranging implications for human development, for Neolithic people traded a passive relationship with nature for an active one. Instead of simply harvesting what nature spontaneously provided, they intervened in nature's systems to compel their environments to produce what they wanted. They ceased to rely exclusively on hunting and gathering, and began to farm and herd. Herding and farming revolutionized the context for human life, but they were not new ideas or inventions. Herders and farmers simply exploited what Paleolithic people had long since learned about the life cycles of plants and animals. Nomadic gatherers sowed seeds before they left a region to ensure a crop when they returned, and hunters, who sometimes trapped animals before killing them, knew that some species would feed and breed in captivity.

It did not take a stroke of genius to turn a hunter-gatherer into a farmer-herder. It did, however, take strong motivation, for farming did not make life easier. Farming probably required longer and more arduous labor than hunting and gathering. Farmers had a less varied and healthy diet. They staked their survival on fewer resources, and they ran a greater risk of disease from contact with domesticated animals and the wastes that accumulate when people remain in one place for an extended period of time. Anthropological evidence even suggests that the transition to farming reduced life spans. Why, then, was farming so widely adopted?

Farming offered one obvious advantage. It increased the yield of food from a finite amount of land. If climate change or population growth made it difficult for a people to feed themselves, they had to go on the offensive—that is, to force nature to yield more than it would on its own.

PEOPLE IN CONTEXT   The Iceman

The study of prehistory usually yields generalizations about groups of people, whereas historical records often preserve specific information about unique individuals. On September 19, 1991, hikers in the Alps, on the border between Austria and Italy, made a discovery that constitutes a rare exception to this rule. They stumbled across the corpse of a male who died about 3300 B.C.E. Because his remains (possibly the oldest known human mummy) had survived frozen inside a glacier, the media quickly dubbed him "the Iceman." He was 5' 4" tall and was in his early to mid-40s when he died. His clothes, weapons, and a few other possessions were preserved with his body: an axe with a copper head and yew-wood handle, a flint-bladed knife, a pouch filled with materials that may have been a fire-starting kit, an unfinished bow of yew wood (which is longer than its owner was tall), and a quiver with 14 arrows (two of which were finished with stone points and feathered shafts). He wore a fur cap, a vest of pelts stitched together, a leather loincloth, a leather belt, fur leggings, a cloak woven of grasses, and what appear to have been snow shoes—with bearskin soles and deer-hide upper portions. He used an insulating layer of grass as socks. His body bore 57 tattoos, and he sported an ornament or talisman suspended on a leather thong—a doughnut-shaped disk of white marble.

Chemical analyses of his remains suggest that he grew up in a region near a modern village called Feldthurns and that he probably never ranged more than about 40 miles from

his childhood home. The partially digested remains of a meal he had ingested about eight hours before his death were recovered from his gut. He had dined on meat (probably venison), some vegetable matter, and grain—einkorn, a form of domesticated wheat that is not native to Europe. Pollen grains consumed with his food were from trees that bloom in March and April, indicating the season when he died. He did not die from natural causes. A flint arrowhead about an inch long was lodged about three inches under his left shoulder near his lung. It traveled upward into his body, missing organs but severing blood vessels. He was involved in a fight before his death. Signs of bruises and cuts remain on his hands and chest, and there are traces of blood from four other people on his clothes and weapons. The shaft of the arrow that mortally wounded him had been pulled out. However, he may have done that himself, for he apparently died alone. His possessions were not looted, so he may have killed whoever shot him or escaped his enemy. He seems carefully to have stowed his equipment before lying down beside it to bleed to death or die of exposure. No one retrieved his body for burial. Perhaps he had been wandering alone or was the only survivor of an ill-fated hunting party. If he had friends and relatives who searched for him, they never found him, and his fate remained unknown for over 5,000 years.

The Iceman This manikin is a scholarly reconstruction of the appearance of the Bronze Age man whose mummy was found in the Alps in 1991.

Question: What do the Iceman's possessions and physical remains reveal about his environment and the cultural adaptations that helped him deal with the challenges it posed?

The agricultural economy that the Neolithic era pioneered has worked extraordinarily well for humanity. Some 500,000 years ago, Earth's hominid population may have numbered no more than a million. At the start of the Neolithic era, about 6 million people were spread around the globe. For eons population growth was moderated by plagues, wars, and famines, and it was not until the eighteenth century that the human species could boast a billion members. Another two centuries brought it to 6 billion, and there may be 9 billion humans by the mid–twenty-first century. Given that Earth's resources are limited and its environment is showing signs of stress, humanity may well be undone by its own success.

Prelude to Civilization   Farming appeared first where nature made it easiest. Pioneering farmers looked for fields that they could clear of undesirable vegetation, soil that they could work with simple tools, and a climate in which grains flourished. The thick forests of central and northern Europe, with their damp, heavy soils, were too challenging to till and lacked the desired indigenous species of plant life. The semi-arid grasslands of Asia Minor and the Middle East were, however, ideal, and many of the domesticated species on which Western agriculture came to depend (wheat, barley, pigs, sheep, goats, and cattle) were native to that region (see Map 1–1).

The earliest agricultural settlements appeared about 10,000 years ago. Most of them probably combined hunting and gathering with farming. (Some Native Americans still pursued this lifestyle in the nineteenth century.) The biblical city of Jericho, which appeared about 8400 B.C.E., is the oldest known continuously inhabited settlement in the world. By 7300 B.C.E., it had about 2,000 residents and was partially protected by a dry-stone wall equipped with a circular tower about 30' high. Whether the wall was meant to defend against human aggressors or flash floods is uncertain. The tower could have been used for observation or for exposure of corpses. (Some cultures retrieve the bones of their dead for burial after carrion-eating birds have stripped away the deceased's flesh.) During the eighth millennium, the people of Jericho collected skulls, which they coated with plaster and painted to represent flesh and hair. These artifacts suggest a cult of ancestor worship, but no one can be certain what inspired them.

Many early agricultural sites have been found in Syria and Palestine and in neighboring Anatolia (Asia Minor or modern Turkey). The most remarkable of these may be Çatalhöyük in central Turkey. It flourished for about 1,400 years (c. 7400 to 6000 B.C.E.), and at its peak it sprawled over 33 acres and was home to about 8,000 people. From a distance it probably looked like a huge adobe building, a cluster of 1,000 mud-brick houses. Each house was architecturally independent. Although each house had its own walls, these abutted those of its neighbors. There were a few open spaces in the town, which separated sections of settlement and provided dumping grounds for refuse, but there were no streets. People traveled over the roofs of buildings and used ladders to access their interiors.

Most houses at Çatalhöyük featured a large room for living space and one or more smaller storage rooms. They were furnished with mud-brick benches or sleeping platforms, woven floor mats, baskets, and various wooden and pottery vessels. Tools were made from obsidian. People clothed themselves with fur, leather, and cloth woven from plant fibers and animal hair. They wore jewelry made from bone and seashells,

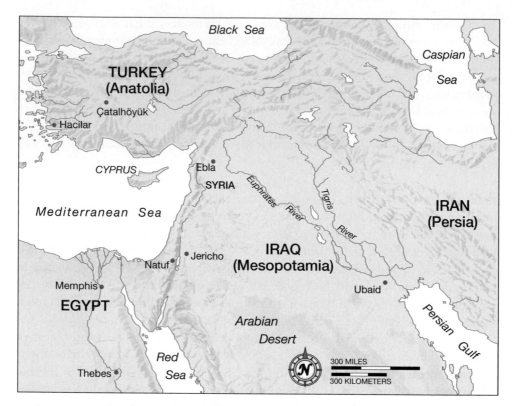

Map 1–1   Early Agricultural Settlements   This map shows some of the earliest significant settlements and archaeological sites in the Middle East. The first civilizations arose along the Tigris, Euphrates, and Nile Rivers, but as the map indicates, that is not where the earliest farming communities were found.

Question: Why did the places where agriculture was first practiced not produce the first civilizations?

and figurines depict them wearing elaborately styled hair. The bodies of many of their dead were interred beneath the floors of homes where people continued to live. The remains of as many as 62 people have been identified from excavation of a single house site. Sometimes skulls were retrieved from previously buried bodies, and at least one plastered skull, similar to those found at Jericho, has come to light.

Many of the buildings excavated at Çatalhöyük are elaborately decorated. Domed ovens were standard features of each house. The walls of houses, soiled by soot from the fires that burned in these ovens, were frequently replastered and painted. Horns, skulls, and claws of cattle and wild beasts were embedded in walls. Bulls, leopards, vultures, and bears are common artistic motifs, and there are scenes that represent mass hunts or group baiting of wild animals. Human and animal figurines have been recovered, many of which have been mutilated, presumably for ritual purposes.

Some houses were a bit larger or more lavishly decorated than others. Some graves were a bit more richly equipped than others, but there is little evidence that the population of the town was divided into classes on the basis of wealth or privilege. No communal structures—that is, places for group activities—have been found. Although Çatal-höyük was tied into a wide-ranging trade network, its households appear to have been economically autonomous. Each may have produced what it needed for its own members, and there is not much evidence of specialized labor. The town was not fortified, and thus far archaeologists have found no evidence that it was presided over by kings, priests, or a warrior caste. Doubtless there were communal feasts and ritual celebrations that helped to integrate the community and enable so many people to live together in such close quarters. Çatalhöyük was a large, long-lived, and apparently stable settlement, but was it a truly civilized community or only an imposing agglomeration of households?

The Archaic States

Pottery appeared during the early seventh millennium in conjunction with the Neolithic lifestyle. Things made of fired clay were too heavy and fragile to be of much use to the Paleolithic era's nomadic hunters and gatherers, but pottery vessels were invaluable for the Neolithic's settled agricultural communities. They provided safe storage for the grains that were staple foods, and they facilitated the cooking that made these grains easier to consume. The invention of pottery was also a great boon for modern archaeology. Pottery can survive burial for eons, and shifting pottery styles and designs provide evidence that archaeologists use to establish chronologies for cultures and date the sites they excavate.

Civilization dawned as people added metals to their repertoire of stone and pottery artifacts. Nuggets of copper were being beaten into tools and ornaments as early as 7500 B.C.E., but it was not until about 5500 B.C.E. that copper began to be smelted from ore and cast in molds. Pure copper was too soft to make durable tools, but when it was alloyed with tin or arsenic, it became a much more serviceable metal called bronze. The technique was developed in Anatolia, and by 4000 B.C.E. it had spread throughout the Middle East.

Societies that were indisputably complex enough to be classed as civilizations arose in Sumer and Egypt well before 3000 B.C.E. Similar transitions to civilization took place somewhat later at other places around the globe. The Harappan civilization of the Indus River Valley emerged about 2500 B.C.E., and city-states ruled by the Shang Dynasty flourished along China's Yellow River sometime after 1800 B.C.E. A society capable of erecting monumental buildings was thriving on the coast of Peru as early as 2000 B.C.E., and the Olmecs pioneered civilization in Mesoamerica about 1500 B.C.E. The fact that peoples who lived on the Eurasian continent (in Egypt, Mesopotamia, India, and China) took the lead in founding civilizations may be explained by natural advantages they enjoyed. Compared to other parts of the world, Eurasia had a much greater abundance of native species of plants and animals (e.g., kinds of wheat, barley, rice, sheep, goats, oxen, horses, etc.) that could be domesticated. Unlike Africa and the Americas, Eurasia also has an east-west horizontal axis, which means that its people and species can easily diffuse throughout wide regions without having to adapt to extreme changes in climate and environment. Eurasians had the resources needed to support civilizations and unusual ease in sharing the domesticated species, inventions, and ideas that stimulated the development of civilizations.

The Origin of Civilization in Mesopotamia: Sumer

At first glance, it seems surprising that Earth's first civilization should have arisen in one of its more hostile environments. Average summer temperatures on the Mesopotamian plain hover around 104°F and may soar to 120°F or more. There is little rainfall, and no natural barriers offer protection from the windstorms and floods that sweep the flat, open landscape. Resources are few. The region has no stone, no metal ores, and no trees sturdy enough to provide lumber. However, it did have an abundance of deep, rich soil deposited and continuously renewed by the annual flooding of the Tigris and Euphrates Rivers. Many of the primal civilizations (e.g., Sumer, Egypt, India, and China) sprang up along flooding rivers. Once the Sumerians developed irrigation systems, water from their rivers unleashed the unique fertility of their land. The Sumerian farmer may have got 20 seeds back for every one that he sowed—two to four times what a Roman or medieval farmer earned thousands of years later (see Map 1–2).

Map 1–2   The Fertile Crescent   The arc of agriculturally productive land where civilization first took root is called the *Fertile Crescent*. Farmers in its eastern portion (Mesopotamia—Greek for "between rivers") relied on irrigation and the annual floods of the Tigris and Euphrates Rivers. Those inhabiting its center section (the Mediterranean coast) had enough rainfall to sustain their crops. The Nile's floods and irrigation ensured the productivity of the crescent's western segment.

Question: Would geography have facilitated contacts between the two primal civilizations or encouraged them to develop in isolation?

During the Neolithic era, farmers flourished in the Iranian highlands east of the Tigris River, but they were slow to move down onto the hot, dry Mesopotamian plain and confront its many environmental challenges. The Tigris River ran fast through a relatively deep channel that made its waters difficult to tap for use in irrigation. Early settlers preferred the banks of its partner, the shallower, slower-moving Euphrates. But it, too, presented them with problems. The sluggish Euphrates dropped silt that formed levees along its banks and raised its bed above the level of the surrounding countryside. The river sometimes broke through these levees, turning wide stretches of contiguous land into swamp. Its floods might carve new channels that altered its course, and these inundations came at an inconvenient time each year—in April, when grain crops were ripening. Skillful engineering and massive labor were needed to trap flood waters in reservoirs for distribution when and where they were needed during the growing seasons. However, once the Sumerians found solutions to these problems, their homeland was able to produce enough food to support a population of unprecedented density.

The Predynastic Era   We do not know where the Sumerian people originated or when they settled the lands north of the Persian Gulf. Language often provides a clue to a people's background, but in this case linguists can offer historians no help. Sumerian is not related to any known tongue.

The Sumerians probably entered Mesopotamia from the east, from the Zagros Mountains. Although they dominated the earlier periods in the history of the region, they were not alone. Sumer's population was multi-ethnic and multilingual. Settlers were drawn to southern Mesopotamia by the abundant foodstuffs that could be harvested from the marshes that lined the banks of the rivers and the coasts of the Persian Gulf. Agricultural villages appeared near the rivers as early as 6500 B.C.E., and by 6000 B.C.E. irrigation was enabling farmers to move farther out onto the plains. Pioneers in the region would have relied on a mixture of farming, herding, hunting, and gathering. Myths and archaeological evidence identify Eridu, near the site of the later and more famous Ur, as one of the area's earliest cities (c. 5400 B.C.E.).

During the early stages in Sumer's development, new kinds of settlements spread across the southern Mesopotamian plain. They were larger than Neolithic villages, and each boasted a major building, the construction and maintenance of which required a larger workforce and a more sophisticated supervising authority than was characteristic of a simple village. Given that most of the dwellings in these communities were about the same size, there is little evidence of significant differences in wealth or of occupational specialization. Clans may have owned land communally, and councils of elders may have provided government. The investment that these communities made in their public buildings suggests, however, that privileged social classes were appearing. The great structures they erected were probably temples, and temples of such size and grandeur usually indicate the presence of powerful priesthoods.

Sumerian city-states reached their full development between 3600 and 3000 B.C.E. The first to achieve some kind of regional dominance may have been Uruk (or Erech), home to the epic hero, Gilgamesh. Uruk owed its influence, at least in part, to its two great temples, one raised to the sky god Anu and the other to the goddess of fertility and war, Inanna. (The earliest known specimens of writing have been retrieved from the ruins of her shrine.) Uruk, like the dozen or so other urban centers that sprang up in Sumer during the fourth millennium B.C.E., grew by absorbing neighboring villages. At its peak it numbered about 50,000 inhabitants. Scholars have speculated about the motives that drove the Sumerians to congregate in cities. For a long time it was assumed that the creation and management of irrigation systems must have encouraged centralization of populations, but recent archaeological discoveries suggest that the expansion of irrigation systems actually followed the rise of cities. Sumer's cities were heavily fortified. Uruk, for instance, was encircled by six miles of defensive walls. Given that legends suggest that the threat of war was never far from the Sumerians' minds, they may have clustered together for protection.

The Dynastic Eras   Archaeology provides most of what is known about the early phases in Sumer's development, but a new source of information appeared when the Sumerians invented writing toward the end of the fourth millennium B.C.E. About the year 2100 B.C.E., a scribe compiled a list of the names of all the kings who were believed to have reigned in Sumer. Although buildings identifiable as palaces have not been found dating much before 2500 B.C.E., the Sumerian "king list" claimed that there were kings reigning in Sumer for about 240,000 years before a great flood nearly obliterated humanity. The Sumerian flood legend lies behind the Bible's account of Noah's ark, but there is no geological evidence for a universal flood. When Sumerian myth-makers imagined an event that would sweep the world clean and serve as a beginning point for their era, they naturally imagined a flood. Floods often swept across Sumer and forced its people to rebuild their lives literally from the ground up. The kings listed before the flood have impossibly long reigns of tens of thousands of years and are figures of myth and legend. The existence of some of the kings who are named after the flood can be documented. The earliest of these is Enmebaragesi, king of Kish (c. 2600 B.C.E.). Lavishly equipped graves at Ur, which are assumed to be those of royal men and women, also date to his era.

As villages grew into cities, several things may have fostered the development of monarchy. Sumer's early urban households, like those of villages, were economically self-sufficient and, therefore, fairly autonomous. But city life would have eroded their independence. Informal meetings of heads of families suffice to run small settlements, but not large cities—particularly when crises demand swift action. The records suggest that Sumer's cities were engaged in a perpetual struggle for supremacy. This must often have created military emergencies that left little time for groups to debate what to do. Success favored those who submitted to the authority of a single leader. After a crisis passed, such a leader might have surrendered his powers and returned to private life. (The Bible's Book of Judges suggests that the early Hebrew tribes had leaders of this kind.) But if one emergency followed quickly on the heels of another, people would come to depend on a permanent leader. The result would be enthronement of a king and possibly a **dynasty** (i.e., a family with a hereditary right to rule). Religion contributed to the authority and legitimacy of a Sumerian king, but unlike the Egyptians, the Sumerians seem not routinely to have deified their rulers. The king was generally believed to have a special relationship with the gods, but not to be a god himself. The story of the great king Gilgamesh centers on his futile search for immortality and his efforts to come to terms with the inevitability of death.

City Life   The security of a city required negotiation with heavenly as well as earthly powers. Priesthoods may have dominated Sumer's cities before dynasties of kings were permanently established. When modern scholars first began to delve into Sumer's history, they thought that Sumerian cities were religious communes in which everyone worked on temple estates and survived on rations doled out from temple granaries. Most authorities now believe, however, that this was an illusion created by the fact that most of the surviving documents come from temple archives. They provide insights into the organization and conduct of only one of Sumer's institutions, not the whole of its urban life.

Sumerian cities were complex societies, not hives of temple slaves. Artisans, merchants, priests, and government officials lived in cities, as did many farmers who commuted to the countryside to work their fields. Temples and kings had large estates, but much property remained in private hands. Title to this private land was often held by kinship groups rather than individuals, and it could be sold only with the consent of all the members of the family that had title to it. The prejudice against selling land away from the family was so strong that sellers sometimes adopted buyers to make the transaction more socially acceptable and legally secure. Personal property was passed down through the male line, and all a man's sons shared equally in his estate. Women, however, could own, buy, and sell land and testify in court cases. Monogamous marriage was the rule, but divorce and remarriage were possible. Women as well as men were impressed into labor gangs to carry out communal projects such as clearing irrigation ditches and building walls. The rations they received in exchange for their toil were smaller than those of the men with whom they worked.

Urban economies were complex systems to which farmers, traders, artisans, and various kinds of professionals all contributed. Some families prospered more than others, and class divisions and social stratification eventually became a fact of life. An aristocracy entrenched itself at the top of society, but it did not succeed in blocking social mobility. A few men from obscure backgrounds even became kings. Slave markets were supplied by war captives and persons who fell into debt. Slavery was taken for granted in this first civilization as it was in almost all of those that followed it until the modern era, but it was not essential to the Sumerian economy. Slaves usually worked as household servants, for it was hard to prevent their running away if they were sent out into the fields to do agricultural work.

By modern standards, Sumerian cities were uncomfortable. The tens of thousands who were sheltered behind the walls of a large town might be crammed into an area equivalent to about 20 football fields. Given that stone had to be imported, everything was constructed of mud brick. Major public edifices were sometimes protected with expensive facings of fired brick or sheets of copper. Their walls might be decorated with mosaics made from cones of colored clay set in plaster. With the exception of sacred structures, most buildings were only one or two stories high. They clustered along narrow (seldom more than nine feet wide) streets that followed no plan or pattern of organization. The expense of fortifying a town made space within it precious, so there were few open areas. Houses were jammed together and fronted directly on the street. They had few doors or windows on their outside walls and depended on interior courtyards for light and ventilation. This enhanced their security and cleanliness. The column of dust that was raised as the 50,000 or so residents of a city (and their animals) trod its unpaved streets must have been visible for miles. Homes were minimally furnished. Possessions were few and clothing simple. Men and women wore similar skirts or kilts and cloaks woven of wool.

Cities were unhealthy, for they had no sewers. Wastes were dumped into streets for animals to scavenge, and drinking water was drawn from the same streams and canals into which refuse was discarded or allowed to drain. One of the byproducts of civilization's urban lifestyle is epidemic disease. Dense human populations (particularly those that live in close association with domesticated animals) create ideal conditions for the spread of parasites and infectious agents. Trade and war also help disease spread quickly among population centers.

The most imposing features of a Sumerian city were its fortifications and its temples. Mud-brick walls encircled the greater cities, and temples soared above all other urban structures. Each city chose a deity as its special patron and provided him or her with lavish accommodations. Sumerian gods were assumed to want the same things that human beings crave: shelter, food, leisure, and amusement. Temples were literally homes for the gods, and their sacred images were cared for like living things. They were provided with changes of clothing, meals, and entertainment.

The Sumerians believed that a god's residence should be elevated above the ordinary human plane. Before 3000 B.C.E., lofty terraces were being built to serve as foundations for temples. Builders then began to layer terraces on top of terraces to create pyramidal structures called **ziggurats** (from an ancient Babylonian term meaning "pinnacle"). A ziggurat was an artificial mountain, a solid structure on whose top a temple perched. The largest ziggurats covered about two acres and may have been as tall as a seven-story building. Given that they were made of fragile, sun-dried bricks, considerable engineering skill was needed to stabilize them. They required constant maintenance, for fundamentally they were huge piles of dirt whose cores were weakened by the moisture they absorbed from the soil beneath them. Today they are so badly ruined that experts can only speculate about their original appearances.

Sumerian Trade and Industry   Sumer produced surpluses of grain that it traded for things that were not locally available. The merchants who dealt in goods from abroad did not necessarily make long journeys to obtain them. Items could reach Sumer's markets simply by being passed from hand to hand across great distances. Lapis lazuli, a blue stone used for jewelry, came from northern Afghanistan some 1,500 miles from Sumer. Carnelian, a red stone, was mined in equally remote India.

Sumerian artisans made skillful use of the materials merchants imported. They created splendid jewelry from beaten gold or silver and semiprecious gems. They carved statues from blocks of stone brought from distant quarries. They built furniture and musical

The Ziggurat of Ur   This is an artist's recreation of a ziggurat built by the city of Ur about 2111 B.C.E. Only the lowest level of the building survives, so the sketch represents an archaeologist's informed guess at the appearance of the intact structure.

instruments from rare woods and decorated these objects with subtle inlays. They wove garments from wool and linen for both domestic and foreign markets. (Cotton was not available to the Mediterranean world until the seventh century B.C.E., when an Assyrian king imported cotton plants from India to ornament his palace garden.) Sumerians knew how to make glass, and by 3000 B.C.E. their potters were using wheels to throw vessels. The Sumerians may have pioneered uses for the wheel; by 3500 B.C.E., they were replacing sledges with wheeled carts. The most distinctive Sumerian artifact was a small, but exquisitely carved, object called a cylinder seal. This was an engraved cylinder that was rolled across a clay tablet to imprint a design that served its owner as a signature.

Writing, Religions, and Intellectual Life   The challenge of managing Sumer's cities and their economies inspired the most famous Sumerian invention: writing. Fortunately for historians, the Sumerians wrote on tablets made from their country's most abundant, inexpensive, and durable material—mud. Many of these tablets, some sun-dried and some fired, have survived burial in the soil for thousands of years. As such, they are history's first true documents.

The earliest specimens of writing come from Uruk and may date as far back as 3500 B.C.E. Although they have not yet been deciphered, they support the theory that writing was invented by accountants. As early as 8000 B.C.E., people began to make small clay tokens whose size, shape, or design represented quantities of various commodities. By assembling piles of these tokens, a merchant or warehouse manager could keep track of how many, and what kinds of, items he or she had in stock. Frequent collection and distribution of things made it almost impossible to remember what one had on hand without some method for keeping and updating records. Eventually it dawned on some accountants that it was easier to draw pictures of their tokens than to make models of them. Some of the early tablets from Uruk have rows of lines beside these drawings that may indicate numbers. The evidence suggests therefore that writing was not first intended (or used) to preserve the words of scholars and poets, but it was inspired by the mundane needs of businesspeople. It was a long time before Sumerian scribes produced anything but business ledgers. Given the fact that only a small minority of people ever learned to read in the ancient world, most works of literature and learning were preserved, transmitted, and experienced as oral traditions.

Busy scribes were driven to speed up their work by making their writing systems more efficient. Because it took time to draw realistic pictures of objects or tokens, scribes began to strip these images down to a few essential lines. This made writing easier but reading more difficult. The meaning of simplified signs was not always self-evident. People had to be taught what each one represented. In addition to the invention of a more efficient script, speed and clarity were improved by reforming the physical act of writing. The Sumerians had nothing like paper, and given that most of the documents they produced were intended only for short-term use, they needed an inexpensive medium. Mud for making tablets was free and readily at hand, but linear drawings were difficult to make on mud tablets. Inscribed lines gouged furrows that had jagged edges and ended in messy clumps. It was cleaner and faster to poke a stylus (a reed) into a clay tablet than to push or pull it across one. Poking produced a triangular indentation instead of a line, but a quick series of jabs could create a clump of wedge-shaped impressions that approximated one of the older linear symbols. The triangular indentations with which the Sumerians covered their tablets constitute a script that modern scholars call **cuneiform** (from *cuneus*, Latin for "wedge").

The cuneiform writing system is complex, for its symbols can represent both objects and prominent sounds in the words for objects. The latter function allowed scribes to begin to think of writing as a method for recording what they heard rather than depicting what they saw. Once writing was viewed as a way to represent speech, its use spread to record anything that could be thought. Early cuneiform employed about 1,200 signs representing things and the syllables used to sound out the words of spoken language. Scribes steadily reduced the number of these signs, but the Sumerians never developed a true alphabet (a set of symbols for a language's elemental sounds). That was the achievement of Semitic-speaking Canaanites who lived in Palestine about 1600 B.C.E. The Phoenicians transmitted this invention to the Greeks and ultimately to us. The short list of symbols in the alphabet "democratized" writing by making it much easier to learn. Cuneiform was a script, not a language. Therefore, it could be—and was—adapted to record many tongues. It spread widely throughout the ancient Middle East and remained in use into the first century C.E.

Writing made history in every sense of the word. For the first time, thinking beings could leave an enduring, precise record of their thoughts. Most ancient cuneiform tablets are the byproducts of mundane transactions, but some record myths, legends, laws, proverbs, medical texts, astronomical charts, mathematical calculations, scientific treatises, dictionaries, letters, poems, and prayers. Knowledge of the development of Western literature and thought begins with the cuneiform legacy. It has been particularly enlightening for biblical scholars, for much of the material in the opening chapters of Genesis (the first book in the Bible) harks back to Sumerian or Mesopotamian sources.

The Sumerians worshiped gods who incarnated the powers of nature. They believed that although the gods were analogous to human beings, they were beyond human understanding. The wisest course, therefore, was not to try to understand them, but to curry their favor by offering them gifts and praise. The Sumerian pantheon numbered about 3,600 gods and goddesses, but only a few were of major importance—most notably: Anu, a remote high god; Inanna (also called Ninhursaga or Ishtar), a war and fertility goddess; Enlil, a storm god; and Enki, the god of the fresh waters that imparted life to Sumer's arid land. Myths depict Sumerian gods as all too human. They schemed, lied, loved, formed and broke alliances, sought revenge, and held grudges. The politics of heaven resembled those of a Sumerian city-state. Gods could be bribed, and they resorted to threats and influence peddling. A god who did a favor for another god—or a human being—expected something in return. When struggles broke out among the gods, the fates of the cities allied with them hung in the balance.

The major modern Western faiths all posit a connection between religion and ethics. They claim that how people treat one another has transcendent importance and that the deity they worship demands justice and judges their conduct. The Sumerians, by contrast, did not sense a moral principle at the base of reality. They believed that gods were interested primarily in themselves and were restrained by neither reason nor morality. Gods could, however, be swayed by offerings and magic spells. To guard against misfortune, therefore, it was important to try to anticipate what the gods might be intending to do. The Sumerians saw the world as filled with omens. All kinds of things (the livers of sacrificial animals, flights of birds, patterns of smoke, deformed births, etc.) hinted at what the gods were about, and it was a priest's profession to interpret these coded messages and recommend responses to them.

Some Sumerian myths taught that people should not hope for much from life. The gods were said to have created humanity for the sole purpose of laboring to keep their altars piled high with offerings. People were the slaves or the "cattle" of the gods. In practice, this meant that most men and women could expect to spend their lives in an unending struggle to win favor with heavenly, as well as earthly, powers. Ultimately, everyone suffered the same fate: death followed by a lingering, shadowy existence in the underworld. In *The Epic of Gilgamesh*, Enkidu, Gilgamesh's friend, has a deathbed vision of the underworld, a place where even kings and priests languish in darkness with nothing to eat but dust and clay.

The Mesopotamian environment may help to explain this gloomy outlook. Sumer was wealthy but insecure. The flooding rivers on which it depended periodically threatened to rout its people and destroy the monuments of its civilization. Violent storms swept the countryside. Epidemics and plagues decimated cities. Nomadic raiders pressed in on every side. Power struggles raged within and between cities, and innocent people were caught up in tumultuous events that were beyond their control or understanding. Even a superhuman hero like Gilgamesh was advised to yield to fate and to aspire to no more from life than enjoyment of its simple, transient pleasures—food, drink, friends, family, and sex.

Sumer's History   Sumer's cities probably began as independent settlements, but as they grew, they started to compete with one another for dominance. The king list claims that Eridu was the first state to achieve supremacy and that leadership passed to Kish after the great flood. The struggle went on, for the featureless plain that the Sumerians occupied provided no natural boundaries for a stable state and little encouragement for political centralization.

The Sumerian cities were subsumed into what has been called history's first empire by a man who called himself Sargon or "Rightful Ruler" (2371–2316 B.C.E.). He came from Akkad, a Semitic-speaking district on Sumer's northern border. Legend claims that he was a self-made man of obscure origin—allegedly abandoned as an infant and found floating in a basket on the Euphrates. (Similar stories were later told about the founders of other states, the Hebrews' Moses and Rome's Romulus and Remus.) Sargon rose to power in Kish, won sway over Sumer by defeating its high king (at that time, the ruler of Uruk), and then went on to build an empire that extended from the Persian Gulf up the Euphrates and across the caravan stations of northern Syria to the Mediterranean and Asia Minor. The site of the city he founded as the seat for his government has yet to be located, but it was near ancient Babylon (and modern Baghdad), a locale that remained politically important for millennia because of the communication links it commanded. The flow of information was such, however, that Sargon could not have exercised much direct control over the far-flung peoples who had submitted to him to greater or lesser degrees. The primary concern of his government may have been to exploit the trade routes that coursed through the lands over which he claimed jurisdiction. The soldiers he maintained for this purpose have been said by some to constitute history's first standing army. Sargon doubtless hoped that family ties would consolidate his government, and he assigned key posts to relatives—some of whom were women. His daughter Enheduana supervised the great temples of the cities of Ur and Uruk as their high priestess. Some of the hymns that she wrote have survived. They are the earliest literary compositions to which an author's name can be attached.

Sargon's empire collapsed following the death of his great-grandson about 2200 B.C.E. It may have been economically undermined by a three-century-long drought that began about 2100 B.C.E. Following a period of confusion, leadership of the region passed to the kings of the Third Dynasty of Ur. They presided over the last creative phase in Sumer's history (2112–2004 B.C.E.).

By the time that King Ur-Nammu founded Ur's third dynasty, the Sumerians had been a literate people for nearly a thousand years. Ur's kings were aware of the antiquity of their culture, and they assumed responsibility for preserving its legacy. They re-

Head of Sargon the Great   This foot-tall, bronze bust is usually said to be a portrait of the Akkadian king, Sargon, dating to about 2300 B.C.E. It was found in the ruins of the ancient city of Nineveh. Originally the eye sockets would have been filled with colored stones. The piece is highly stylized and may have been intended to represent the ideal of a king more than the features of an individual.

built temples, collected ancient documents for safekeeping in their archives, and presided over a kind of Sumerian renaissance. In 2004 B.C.E., however, they were defeated by Elamite tribes, who invaded from southern Iran. The region fragmented politically, opening the way for Amorites, nomadic tribes native to the deserts west of Sumer, to spread throughout Mesopotamia. The Amorites who settled in Akkad founded the famous ancient city of Babylon, gradually restored order in Mesopotamia, assimilated Sumer's cuneiform culture, and rescued what they could from Sumer's fall.

The fall of a civilization that had endured for nearly 2,000 years cries out for an explanation. Many things could have happened. As governments age, they may develop rigid bureaucratic structures that resist adapting to changing conditions. States also fail when they cannot find leaders with talents equal to their responsibilities. Divisions between rich and poor (or other kinds of class conflicts) can destabilize societies, or shifting trade routes, military struggles, and natural disasters might pose ruinous economic challenges.

In addition to these problems, Sumer may have been the victim of an environmental disaster of its own making. Sumer depended on irrigation, and irrigation can degrade farmland. The minerals dissolved in irrigation water are left behind in the soil when that water evaporates. Ground water also contains minerals that are drawn to the surface. If these "salts" are not flushed out (which was hard to do on Sumer's flat, poorly drained terrain), the ground slowly becomes poisonous to plant life. The effect was mitigated by the new soil that the flooding rivers laid down, but as the years passed, the region suffered. Farmers developed strategies to deal with the changing conditions. They planted less wheat and more barley, for barley is more tolerant of salted soil than wheat. But the combination of declining harvests and political confusion may eventually have encouraged a critical mass of people to seek better conditions elsewhere. The fall of a civilization is not likely to have a single, simple explanation, but it is worth reflecting for a moment on the possibility that humanity's first civilization may inadvertently have engineered an ecological disaster that doomed it to destruction.

The Rise of Civilization in Egypt

At the start of the second millennium, the Middle East underwent wrenching transitions. Sumer disappeared. Small cities that had arisen in Palestine declined, and the first phase in the history of Egypt, the West's other premier civilization, also came to an end.

The Egyptian Environment   The Egyptians dealt with environmental conditions similar to those that confronted their Sumerian neighbors. It seldom rained in Egypt. Temperatures often hovered around 100°F, and permanent settlement of a large population would not have been possible without an annually flooding river that renewed fertile fields and supplied water for irrigation. An ancient Greek historian aptly described Egypt as "the gift of the Nile." Where the river's floods reached, Egypt was a "black land," formed by deposits of rich silt. A dramatically different "red land," an utterly barren desert, began where the river's reach ended and stretched to the horizons.

The Nile's bounty was so generous that prehistoric Egyptians were slow to take up agriculture. Along the river's banks plants and wildlife flourished, and nature needed little encouragement to meet human needs. As early as 5000 B.C.E., Egyptians had domesticated sheep, cattle, goats, barley, and wheat. But for over a thousand years, herding and farming simply supplemented hunting and gathering. Villages fully dependent on agriculture may not have appeared much before 3500 B.C.E., and no great feats of irrigation engineering were needed to support them. The Nile, unlike the Tigris and Euphrates, flooded predictably and at a convenient time for farmers. It rose in late summer following the harvest. Then it dropped a fresh layer of silt and saturated fields just in time for replanting. The Egyptians measured the flood's rise at their southern frontier, and the volume of water helped them predict how large the harvest would be. The floods of the Tigris and Euphrates were a mixed blessing for the Sumerians. They were essential for survival, but sometimes destructive, for Sumer occupied a vast flat land that offered no protection from surging rivers. The Egyptians, on the other hand, had little to fear from the Nile's flood, for much of Egypt was sheltered in a valley, whose walls kept the Nile's waters confined to natural flood plains.

The Nile rose in Uganda and flowed north toward the Mediterranean as if it were descending a huge staircase. When the river spilled over the edges of the higher steps, it created rapids or cataracts. Egypt's southern boundary was marked by what was, from the Egyptians' perspective, the First Cataract. From there to the Mediterranean—about 700 miles—there was no more white water. The Egyptians did not need roads to tie their country together. Given that the Nile Valley is only about 12 miles across at its widest, no one was ever far from the river. The river made trade and communication easy. Its current carried vessels north, and when boats raised their sails, prevailing winds pushed them south. The Nile provided such convenient transport that the Egyptians were slow to utilize wheeled vehicles.

Nature protected as well as provided for the Egyptians. On both sides Egypt's borders were defended by cliffs and deserts. The country was politically unified for over 1,300 years before it suffered a major foreign invasion. Metal ores and good building stone were also to be found in close proximity to Egypt's agricultural land. Wood was scarce, but it was easily imported by sea from the coast of Palestine. Egypt's generous environment may partially explain why many of its myths and legends seem to express more contentment with the human condition and more hope for life beyond death than some of Sumer's religious texts.

Egypt's Political Development   Nature divided Egypt into two distinct regions. The largest part of the country was Upper (up-river) Egypt, the long, narrow valley described previously. Lower (down-river) Egypt was the broad delta that accumulated where the Nile emptied into the Mediterranean. Lower Egypt was a flat, swampy land much like Sumer, and it was the part of Egypt most exposed to the outside world. Mediterranean sailors used its ports, and coastal routes linked it by land with Libya to the west and the Sinai to the east.

Settlement patterns help to explain why Egypt became a united country early in its history and was politically more stable than Sumer. Sumer's broad, featureless plain allowed people to cluster in fortified towns surrounded by farmland. Sumerian settlements, having originated as separate city-states, cherished independence, competed with one another, and resisted unification. Much of Egypt's productive land, by contrast, was confined to a narrow valley, which in many places was no more than two miles wide. Because lateral expansion was limited, Egyptians did not cluster in large cities. That would have forced many of them to make long commutes to their fields. This, together with the relative security from invasion their country enjoyed, encouraged the Egyptians to distribute themselves evenly in small villages throughout the valley. Patterns in the delta were probably different, but archaeological information from that part of Egypt is sparse. A damp environment and deep deposits of silt have worked against preservation and excavation of the earlier stages of human habitation.

Political divisions did exist in Egypt. The Nile Valley is composed of a series of flood basins, and long before the dawn of history, each of these was claimed by a tribe. Struggles among these tribes gradually led to the formation of separate kingdoms in Upper and Lower Egypt, and about 3100 B.C.E. a king of Upper Egypt conquered the delta. Egypt, therefore, became a unified country about the time when the first evidence for monarchies appeared in Sumer's city-states.

The writing of history was an invention of the ancient Greeks. After Alexander the Great conquered Egypt in 332 B.C.E., the country's Greek rulers charged scholars with organizing the records of Egypt's past. They grouped the names of the people who had ruled Egypt from its unification to its Greek occupation into 31 dynasties and dated events in Egypt's history by the reigns of its rulers. Although the ancient list of royal families is now known not to be entirely reliable, modern historians still use the numbers the Greeks assigned to Egypt's dynasties. In terms of historical development, Egypt's past can be divided into three major eras or "kingdoms" and a number of relatively brief periods of transition.

Early Dynastic Period (3100–2700 B.C.E., Dynasties I–II)   A clue to Egypt's origin as a unified state was found at the site of ancient Hierakonpolis in 1897—a palette (a ritual object used for grinding pigments) with inscriptions commemorating the victories of a ruler called Narmer (or Scorpion). On one side Narmer wears the crown of Upper Egypt and on the other the crown of Lower Egypt. If Narmer unified Egypt and launched its first dynasty, he can be called its first pharaoh. However, that title was not used until about 1400 B.C.E. It evolved because ancient peoples believed that naming something invoked its presence. The awe Egyptians felt for their ruler, who was literally the incarnation of a god, encouraged the custom of referring to him indirectly as pharaoh ("great house").

Key Events in Sumerian and Egyptian History	
SUMER	**EGYPT**
Predynastic Era (5300–3000 B.C.E.)	3500 B.C.E., agricultural villages appear 3100 B.C.E., unification of Egypt
Dynastic era (3000–2004 B.C.E.) monarchy appears	Early Dynastic Period (3100–2700 B.C.E.) Old Kingdom (2700–2200 B.C.E.) 2550 B.C.E., pyramids at Giza
Sargon's empire (2371–2200 B.C.E.)	First Intermediate Period (2200–2025 B.C.E.)
III Dynasty of Ur (2112–2004 B.C.E.)	Middle Kingdom (2025–1630 B.C.E.)

The early dynasties ruled from Memphis on the border between Upper and Lower Egypt. Memory of the delta's and the valley's origins as separate kingdoms survived, and pharaohs wore a double crown: the red circlet with a hooded cobra of the delta laid over the valley's white conical cap.

The institutions, artistic styles, and theologies that evolved early in Egypt's history established conventions that endured for 2,000 years. What began as a remarkably inventive society grew increasingly conservative as respect for tradition restrained the impulse to innovate. This may have been an effect of Egypt's rigorously centralized government. Pharaohs were worshiped as manifestations of an eternal god, and their courts were the chief markets for the products of Egypt's artists and intellectuals. Court taste favored repetition of symbols and images that by their unchanging nature expressed the pharaoh's timeless essence. Innovation may also have been inhibited, oddly enough, by the invention of writing. In modern societies writing stimulates development by facilitating communication and data collection. For ancient peoples, however, writing was an arcane and arduously acquired skill that few possessed. The mysterious markings that scribes made seemed magical. Many modern people share this primitive inclination to trust whatever is "in print" (or, worse, on the Web), and the word *scripture* ("writing") still connotes something holy—something that has authority and cannot be changed.

Archaeologists can trace the gradual development of Sumer's cuneiform writing system, but Egyptian **hieroglyph** ("sacred writing") has no comparable ancestry. Hieroglyphs began to appear about 3100 B.C.E., and a fully developed script quickly evolved. Egypt had trade contacts with Sumer, and Sumerian writing may have given the Egyptians hints that helped them quickly create a script of their own. Both the Sumerians and Egyptians based their writing systems on pictographs. As Sumerian scribes developed cuneiform's efficient clusters of wedge-shaped impressions, these early images became unrecognizable, but Egypt's hieroglyphs never lost their pictographic quality. Egyptian scribes did not inscribe clay tablets. They wrote with brushes and ink on a paper-like material made from the papyrus reeds that grew along the Nile. They had no difficulty making linear drawings. Hieroglyphs always remained in use for monuments and holy texts, but by 2000 B.C.E. a faster cursive script (called demotic) had been developed for ordinary documents.

The Old Kingdom (2700–2200 B.C.E., Dynasties III–VI)   The heart of ancient Egypt's civilization was its monarchy. The Egyptians believed that their pharaoh was their primary link with the supernatural powers on which life depended. He was an incarnate god whose power was absolute (in theory, if not always in practice). Egypt and all its people belonged to him, but he was not supposed to be a self-serving tyrant. He had a vital communal function. The Egyptians viewed the world as a dynamic place, a realm of order threatened by chaos. The pharaoh's task was to preserve *ma'at* ("justice"), the balance among competing forces that preserved a stable world order. His authority was so sweeping that Egypt, unlike many ancient kingdoms, did not develop a code of laws. Pharaoh's will was all the law that Egypt needed.

Pharaohs governed Egypt with the help of an elaborate bureaucracy. Some 2,000 titles have been identified for officials of the **Old Kingdom**. The pharaoh had to employ a horde of royal agents, for he had many functions. He was responsible for the religious ceremonies

King Menkaure and Queen Kamerernebti II   This regal couple from Egypt's IV Dynasty reigned about 2490 B.C.E. Their dress is simple, barely concealing their perfect bodies. The pharaoh sports a false chin beard, a mark of his rank. His rigid posture—facing forward, hands at sides, one foot advanced—illustrates one of the conventions of ancient Egyptian sculpture. The touch his queen gives him may not indicate affection. The inheritance customs of the early dynasties are uncertain, but some pharaohs may have claimed their thrones through marriages with important princesses—possibly their half-sisters. The queen's gesture might signal the king's legitimacy. *King Menkaure (Mycerinus) and Queen. Egyptian, Old Kingdom, Dynasty 4. Reign of Menkaure, about 2490–2472 BC. Egypt, Giza, Menkaure Valley Temple. Greywacke. 142.2 × 57.1 × 56.2 cm (56" × 22 1/2" × 21 3/4"). Harvard University-Boston Museum of Fine Arts*

that placated the gods and regulated the cycles of nature. On a practical level, he handled defense, dispensed justice, oversaw planning for the Nile's flood, coordinated food production and distribution, erected buildings, provided patronage for artisans, handled long-distance trade, supervised public works projects, and oversaw the army of scribes who audited all this activity.

Egypt was highly centralized but minimally urbanized. Most Egyptians lived in small villages. For administrative purposes, the country was subdivided into units of local government called nomes (22 in Upper Egypt and 20 in Lower Egypt). In theory, all the land belonged to the pharaoh, and he could impress all his subjects into labor gangs to work for him. Actual slavery, however, may not have been all that common in the Old Kingdom. In the ancient world, slaves were often foreigners captured in wars, and the Old Kingdom was not very active in military campaigning in foreign lands.

The tombs of the Old Kingdom's pharaohs are the best surviving testimonials to their power. The investment that the Egyptians made in tombs throughout their history can create the mistaken impression that they were a grim people preoccupied with death. In reality, their preparations for death attest to their love of life. Egyptian burial practices were meant to guarantee that the deceased would continue to enjoy life's pleasures beyond the grave. So similar and so close were the worlds of the living and the dead that the Egyptians believed that support from this side of the tomb was important for happiness on the other. The dead were assumed to need all kinds of things. Supplies were buried with them, and they tried to arrange for a steady stream of offerings to flow in perpetuity across the altars of their funerary temples.

The Egyptian outlook on both life and death was more positive than the view described in some Sumerian texts. The Sumerians, on their exposed plain, were engaged in a constant struggle with one another and the seemingly arbitrary forces of nature. Life in the rich Nile Valley was easier and safer. The Sumerians conceived of the universe as a chaotic battleground for quarrelsome, incomprehensible gods, but the Egyptian universe was a realm in which a god, the pharaoh, was physically present and laboring to maintain balance and order. The eternal, unchanging nature of things caused death to be viewed as an event in life rather than an end to life. Experience with the dead tended to confirm this. The Egyptians did not waste agricultural land on cemeteries. They buried their dead in the deserts that bordered the Nile's flood plains—usually on the western frontier, the direction the sun took on its daily descent to the underworld. The desert's arid sands dehydrated corpses and shielded them from decay. Nature's reluctance to reclaim the physical remains of the departed may have inspired the Egyptian conviction that physical preservation of the dead was important. The methods the ancient Egyptians developed for embalming their dead imitated nature's technique. Bodies were gutted and the internal organs mixed with spices and sealed in jars. The corpse was then thoroughly dried, wrapped in bandages to preserve its shape, and dipped in pitch. The English word *mummy* derives from an Arabic word for tar or bitumen.

It was more difficult to provide a secure grave for a corpse than to preserve it from decay. Tomb construction evolved as the Egyptians experimented with ways to prevent bodies buried in desert sands from being exposed by the wind or dug up by animals. At the dawn of the dynastic eras, flat, rectangular structures made from bricks were being used to stabilize mounds of dirt over graves. This kind of a tomb is called a *mastaba* (from an Arabic word for a bench). Corpses could be interred in the ground beneath *mastabas,* but rooms were also created within them to house coffins and grave offerings. Royal tombs conformed to this pattern until about 2650 B.C.E., when the pharaoh Djoser, the second king of the Old Kingdom, departed from tradition. The result was a monument so impressive that later generations assumed that its architect, Imhotep, had been a god. Imhotep first built a *mastaba* for his employer, but then he began to tinker with its traditional design. He enlarged it, and then he piled levels of masonry on top of it to create a solid building resembling a square, six-layered wedding cake. Imhotep's "step pyramid" (a pyramid whose layers are not angled or filled in to create smooth sides) is the world's first monumental stone building. Around it was erected a model city in stone and the whole complex was enclosed within a wall a mile in circumference.

Djoser launched a fad for pyramid construction that lasted for centuries. The ruins of about 110 pyramids have been identified in Egypt, but the greatest are the earliest— those erected during the Old Kingdom. What pyramid designers strove to create was a soaring structure that rose at a steep angle. This was hard to do, for as any child who builds a sand castle at the beach discovers, gravity causes the sides of a steep mound to sheer off. By 2550 B.C.E., the Egyptians had developed engineering techniques that enabled them to erect what is still the world's most massive stone structure: the Great Pyramid at Giza.

The Great Pyramid, which was probably built for the pharaoh Cheops (or Khufu), is the supreme example of its kind. It anchors a sprawling complex of smaller pyramids, tombs, temples, and other monuments on the western bank of the Nile near modern Cairo. The statistics of the Great Pyramid are staggering. It covers 13 acres, rises to a height of 481 feet, and is constructed of 2,300,000 blocks of precisely cut and fitted stone. Some of the blocks of granite used for its interior chambers weigh 50 tons and were brought from quarries 500 miles away. Surveyors oriented the building precisely on a north-south axis and kept its sides in perfect alignment. When the Greek historian Herodotus visited the pyra-

Djoser's Step Pyramid   Great Pyramid at Giza

The First Pyramid and the Greatest Pyramid   Most pyramids, like the first, were solid structures raised over subterranean tombs, or they had one small interior chamber. The Great Pyramid at Giza was not only the largest but it also had the most complex internal design. This has variously been interpreted as the result of changing plans or even the use of the building while it was under construction for purposes of astronomical observation. The straight passages leading directly to the primary chambers would not have done much to deter tomb robbers. No inscriptions or paintings have been found within the pyramids.

mid 2,000 years after it was built, he was told that it took only 20 years to complete. A modern authority has estimated that it might have been finished in as few as five.

Whatever the pyramids were built to contain was looted in antiquity, and what they symbolized for the ancient Egyptians is uncertain. Egyptian mythology envisioned the creation of the world as an island emerging from the waters of primal chaos. Pyramids may have represented this island, where life began, or their shape might have been meant to recall the slanting rays of the sun, the path that the pharaoh's spirit took as it returned to the heavens after his death.

The most mysterious thing about the pyramids may be the motive that persuaded the Egyptians to undertake the physically and logistically daunting labor of constructing them. They are sometimes dismissed as the work of megalomaniacal tyrants who enslaved thousands to build monuments to their personal glory. Pyramids were, however, not the work of slaves, and they may have done more than exalt an individual. A pharaoh could use only one tomb, but some pharaohs built more than one pyramid. This suggests that the process of building may have been as important as the end product.

Early Egypt did not have to fend off many invaders, but its creation was not bloodless. Texts praise pharaohs for being great warriors. Some led armies into the deserts to discipline nomads or up the Nile to intimidate Egypt's Nubian neighbors. Some fought to maintain internal order. The Old Kingdom was a relatively new monarchy that was attempting to do something that had never been done before—to consolidate a huge territorial nation. Pyramid building might have contributed to this. Great projects can strengthen a leader by inspiring awe for his power, and pharaohs may have used their construction to keep their subjects occupied at times when they might be inclined to cause trouble. Agricultural work is seasonal, and during the months when Egypt's fields required little tending, its idle men probably had a tendency to brawl. Pharaohs may have forestalled this by occupying their subjects on great projects that were sources of both employment and communal pride. Egypt certainly built pyramids, but pyramids may also have built Egypt.

First Intermediate Period (2200–2025 B.C.E., Dynasties VII–X) The Old Kingdom continued for about 500 years. No one is sure why its centralized government ultimately lost control and allowed regional strongmen to begin fighting among themselves. A severe drought afflicted much of the Middle East about the time that both the Old Kingdom and Sargon's Mesopotamian empire fell. The drought may have depressed Egypt's economy, but the pharaohs of the Old Kingdom also may inadvertently have created the situation that contributed to their fall. Unless central governments moved their local officials from time to time, these men built regional power bases that increased their independence. But as governments took on greater responsibilities, a need for efficiency prompted them to leave experienced men at their posts for longer periods. The clever governor trained his son in the duties of his office and arranged for the boy to succeed him. If a family managed to do this for several generations, it acquired a kind of hereditary right to its office and enough local support to assert its independence if its royal overlord showed signs of weakness. The last pharaoh of the Old Kingdom lived to a great age, and his failing powers may have given Egypt's governors the opportunity they were waiting for.

The collapse of the Old Kingdom was followed by a period of political upheaval, internal warfare, and economic hardship called the First Intermediate Period. By then Egypt may have had over one million inhabitants, and it did not function well when divided against itself. Famine stalked the land, and confidence in the pharaoh was shaken. But the confusion was not entirely detrimental to Egypt's civilization. The destruction of the Old Kingdom's authoritarian government freed Egyptian society to evolve. When the country's unity was finally restored by the pharaohs of the Middle Kingdom, cultural creativity flourished with renewed vigor.

KEY QUESTION | Revisited

The belief that primitive societies thrive without disturbing nature is a romantic fantasy. Any hiker who has tried to "tread lightly on the land" and visit the wilderness without altering it knows how difficult that is. Nature is constantly adjusting to what its resident species consume, do, and produce. Prehistoric peoples changed the world around them by hunting and gathering. They drove some species toward extinction and encouraged the proliferation of others. The goal of a successful organism may not be to avoid having any impact on nature but to strike a sustainable balance with nature. This is difficult, for history and personal experience teach that actions have unintended, unpredictable consequences, particularly when they affect the complex symbiotic systems that make up the world of nature.

The people whose increasingly elaborate cultural activity culminated in the rise of the first civilizations exploited the potential of unique, but similar, environments—arid regions with annually flooding rivers. A major part of their strategy for adapting to these challenging environments was to adapt the environments to meet their needs. The result was acceleration of the cycle of action and reaction between communities and their contexts that continues throughout history.

Some of the most significant steps in the early stages of this process may have been taken in complete ignorance of what was happening. Civilization rests on the economic foundation laid by agriculture, and agriculture depends on the availability of domesticated species of plants and animals. The domestication of wheat, the staple food of the ancient world, may have come about largely by accident. Grains of wheat are the seeds of a kind of grass. In nature, grasses perpetuate themselves by scattering their seeds to the wind. This favors species in which ripened seeds are loosely tethered to a plant's stalk and can easily be blown free. Human gatherers may have begun to harvest grains by shaking their seeds into baskets, but it would have been difficult for them to avoid a lot of loss. When gatherers invented simple sickles for cutting clumps of grasses, their harvests improved. But they had most success collecting the seeds of plants that did not easily break loose and drift away. Planting these seeds encouraged the genetic evolution of a kind of wheat with seeds firmly attached to stalks. This is a domesticated species, for it is ill-adapted to survive on its own. Its reproduction depends on a human harvester gathering and planting its seeds. The ease and minimal loss with which such wheat could be harvested encouraged the ancient harvester to serve the plant that served him.

Environment for human beings is a context shaped by both nature and culture. The West's early civilizations created a previously unknown physical environment through technologies such as irrigation, agriculture, and metal working. The cities and states they built were not only new kinds of spaces in which to live; they constituted challenging new intellectual and social environments. The Sumerians and the Egyptians acted, and were acted upon, in ways that were similar and ways that were different. But each experienced the same thing: As they changed the world, the world changed them. To be civilized is to grasp a tiger by the tail and pin hopes for survival on the ability to cope with the consequences.

Review Questions

1. How did Paleolithic and Neolithic societies differ?
2. How did the first civilizations differ from the prehistoric cultures that preceded them?
3. Does environment explain why civilization appeared first in Sumer and Egypt?
4. How and why did Egypt's political evolution differ from Sumer's?
5. How and why did the Egyptian outlook on life and death differ from the Sumerian view?
6. What is the relationship between environment and civilization?

Please consult the Suggested Readings at the back of the book to continue your study of the material covered in this chapter. For a list of documents on the Primary Source DVD-ROM that relate to topics in this chapter, please refer to the back of the book.

2 The Rise of Empires and the Beginning of the Iron Age

You march forth to take your enemy's land, and he comes to take yours.

—**Mesopotamian Proverb**

KEY | Question

Does civilization promote unity or intensify divisions among peoples?

The word **civilization** and its cognates (civility, for example) conjure thoughts of peaceful, orderly behavior. Civilized persons, unlike barbarians, are supposedly possessed of self-control, rationality, and respect for life and standards of justice and decency. The history of civilization is, however, largely a history of wars and other atrocities waged by and among civilized peoples. This is puzzling, but when civilization is viewed as the most highly developed form of the cultural behavior on which the human species has pinned its survival, it becomes less so. Human beings do not just live their lives. They think about living them. They make themselves objects to themselves and describe themselves to themselves. This creates something called a personal identity. By locating a person in a context, it gives meaning to life and seems so essential to an individual's survival that people will go to great lengths to defend it.

A civilization shapes a people's view of "the right way to live," and it seems so natural that it is often difficult for persons from one civilization to appreciate the alternatives offered by another. All a leader may need to do to mobilize a people for war is to claim that their "way of life" is threatened by the "barbarism" of an alien culture.

But civilized life is a complicated phenomenon. The identity a civilization provides may unite millions of people on one level while simultaneously dividing them into groups with differing interests and concerns on others. In complex societies people acquire complex identities based on such things as wealth, occupation, gender, education, religion, ancestry,

Ramses II This statue from Egypt's Abu Simbel temple of an enthroned pharaoh, Ramses II (r. 1279–1213 B.C.E.), projects a sense of the majesty and power of the god-kings who presided over the ancient seats of civilization.

and so on. People can, therefore, feel tugged in contrary directions by their civilized lifestyle. Whether the values that unite them are strong enough to counter the tensions that divide them depends to a very large extent on their historical situation.

Individuals acquire their sense of identity as they become aware of how they resemble some people and differ from others. Unfortunately, people often tend to view persons different from themselves with suspicion, contempt, and hostility. One's identity is fundamental to one's sense of worth, and sometimes the mere existence of other lifestyles may seem to call into question the validity of one's own. A single difference (over a religious belief, for example) may be enough to set people who have everything else in common at one another's throats. The lives of small, scattered hunter-gatherer bands and farming villages may not have been much disrupted by this human tendency. But civilizations, the supreme products of the human capacity for invention and imagination, maximize potentials both for cultural differences and human contacts. They mobilize large populations and have often sought unity, stability, and self-affirmation through imperialism—that is, by imposing their way of life on others.

During the second millennium B.C.E., rulers in both Egypt and Mesopotamia began to use military force to build empires. This opened the way for a blending of cultures that produced sophisticated, cosmopolitan societies. But it also increased the risk of instability by raising questions about legitimate political authority and personal identity. Empires have always been easier to create than to maintain.

The Transition States

In 2004 B.C.E. the Third Dynasty of Ur was overthrown by the Elamites, tribesmen whose homelands lay east of the Tigris River. The Elamites were ill-equipped to maintain Sumer's urban institutions, and as the heartland of the West's first civilization declined, other groups took advantage of the political confusion. The Assyrians established the nucleus for a new state on the upper reaches of the Tigris River, but the immediate future lay with the Amorites. These nomadic tribes from the western deserts spread throughout Mesopotamia and Syria. Some of them settled in Akkad, north of Sumer, founded the city of Babylon, and gradually came to control much of the Middle East.

Babylon   The Babylonian empire was largely the work of the city's sixth king, Hammurabi (1792–1750 B.C.E.). He was about 25 when he inherited his throne, and he devoted the first 30 years of his reign to wars of conquest. At its height, Hammurabi's Babylon held sway from the Persian Gulf to northern Assyria. This was not a large state in comparison with later empires, but its population was diverse and hard to pacify. Hammurabi is memorable for his novel approach to dealing with this problem. He issued a common set of rules for all his subjects. That is, he published what is often said to be history's first code of laws, called the **Code of Hammurabi**. Fragments of earlier legal texts survive from the reign of the founder of Ur's Third Dynasty, Ur-Nammu, but they are probably records of decisions in particular court cases, not general principles meant to guide the administration of justice. Hammurabi's code, which contains almost 300 clauses, was much more ambitious and may have had a different purpose. Unlike modern legislation, it was not a set of statutes that lawyers cited when arguing cases. It was probably intended to provide judges with examples of the kinds of decisions the king wished them to make when dealing with various categories of disputes. By superseding local customs and establishing a common standard for justice throughout the empire, the king's law helped break down some of the cultural barriers that separated his subjects.

Hammurabi's laws provide historians with their first detailed description of an ancient Mesopotamian society. Hammurabi's code made separate provisions for three types of people: aristocrats, free commoners, and various kinds of dependents and slaves. People's legal rights were determined by their class standing. An injury done to an important person was more harshly punished than the same injury done to a less significant individual. Because ancient societies were not prepared economically or organizationally to maintain prisons, punishments took the form of fines, mutilations, and executions. Hammurabi's concept of justice followed the principle that the Bible succinctly characterizes as "an eye for an eye, a tooth for a tooth." It was not always easy, however, to make "the punishment fit the crime," and Hammurabi's attempts to establish exact equivalencies sometimes sought justice by mandating what are, from the modern perspective, unjust acts. For example, a builder who erected a house that fell down and killed its owner's son was punished by the execution of his own son. The boy might well have questioned the justice of this decree, but Hammurabi probably never thought about that. In his world sons were the property of their fathers. Fathers could sell them into slavery and lose them in property disputes.

Hammurabi's code gives significant space to property and family law. It spells out principles governing land ownership, rights of renters and tenants, and responsibilities for the maintenance of communal facilities such as irrigation systems. Some of its precepts would be judged enlightened by modern standards. It assumes that governments have responsibility for protecting environmental resources. The state was also to regulate money lending to prevent abuse of debtors, set fair standards for workers' wages, and protect the quality of consumer goods.

Hammurabi's code is especially noteworthy for the protection it offered the poor and the weak. It said that husbands could not abandon wives who were barren or ill without providing for their support. It gave women rights to property of their own and allowed them to run businesses—so long as they did not neglect their domestic duties. It granted wives the power to initiate divorce and reclaim their dowries, but it also enforced a sexual double standard. It allowed husbands to have sex outside of marriage, but it harshly punished adulterous wives. Babylonian society was patriarchal, and men were anxious to ensure that the children they raised were their own. The only way to do this was to limit the freedom of women.

In addition to women, the law protected slaves, another vulnerable segment of the population. Some slaves were war captives, but some were members of citizen families. A man could discharge his debts by selling his wife, his children, and himself. Slavery was, however, not inevitably permanent. A person could be enslaved for a specific term. A slave could also own property, go into business for himself, and earn the price of his freedom.

The rights Hammurabi's people had in theory no doubt exceeded those they had in practice, for it is unlikely that Hammurabi had the governmental machinery to enforce his laws and hold all his judges accountable. Public officials were legally liable for doing their duty. They were even supposed to compensate victims if they failed to find and punish thieves and murderers. However, given the difficulty modern governments

Hammurabi's Code The seven-foot-tall stele (pillar) of black marble on which Hammurabi's famous laws are inscribed was found in the ruins of the ancient Persian city of Susa. It may originally have been set up as a boundary marker for Hammurabi's Babylonian state and later carted off as loot by Persian conquerors. *Stele of the Law Code of Hammurabi, from Susa (modern Shush, Iran). c. 1792–1750 BCE. Basalt, height of stele appx. 7" (2.13 m), height of relief 28" (71.1 cm). Musee du Louvre, Paris. RMN/Reunion des Musees Natioaux/Art Resource, NY*

have in meeting such high standards of justice, Hammurabi may have been legislating pious hopes.

In addition to progress in law and government, Babylonian intellectuals made significant advances in science—particularly astronomy and the mathematics needed to study the heavens. They used both decimal (base 10) and sexagesimal (base 60) systems. The latter survives in the conventional division of circles into 360 degrees and of hours into 60-minute segments of 60 seconds each. Babylonians did not distinguish astrology from astronomy. Their belief that celestial events influenced life on Earth may indeed have inspired their commitment to recording precise measurements of the movements of the heavenly bodies. The data they collected were used for centuries and greatly improved the accuracy of calendars.

Hammurabi's empire began to fall away shortly after his death, but his dynasty held on to Babylon for another 150 years. About 1595 B.C.E. the city fell to a group of northern raiders called the Hittites. They came to loot, not conquer. After they retreated to their base in Asia Minor, the Kassites moved down from the Zagros Mountains to occupy Babylon, Akkad, and Sumer. They ruled the lower Euphrates for the next 600 years and conscientiously guarded the region's cultural legacy. They restored temples, built libraries, and spread knowledge of cuneiform and its literary treasures.

Egypt's Middle Kingdom (2025–1630 B.C.E., Dynasties XI–XII) Central government was reestablished in Egypt a few years before the fall of Ur's Third Dynasty and survived almost to the sack of Babylon by the Hittites. The pharaohs of this **Middle Kingdom**, contemporaries of Hammurabi's dynasty, presided over an era of prosperity and creativity. Many of the buildings they erected were torn down and replaced by grander structures by their successors, the rulers of the New Kingdom, but the Middle Kingdom's literary achievements proved more enduring.

The Middle Kingdom was founded by a warrior from Thebes in Upper Egypt. The pharaohs of both the Middle Kingdom and the New Kingdom claimed descent from Amun-Ra, the sun god of Thebes, and they preferred Thebes to Memphis, the Old Kingdom's seat near the juncture of the valley and the delta. The pharaohs of the Middle Kingdom seem to have cultivated a somewhat less remote image than their predecessors. The literature of the period calls them the shepherds of their people and praises them for defending the poor and equitably enforcing justice. They invested less in grandiose tombs and more in what might be described as economic development. They extended their power up the Nile into Nubia. They sponsored trading expeditions to distant lands. They dug canals to improve transportation and created reservoirs and irrigation systems that greatly expanded the agricultural productivity of the Fayum, an oasis in northwestern Egypt.

Historians have learned less from the monuments of the Middle Kingdom's pharaohs than from the private tombs of their officials. These are fairly numerous, suggesting that wealth was more widely distributed during the Middle Kingdom than in earlier eras. More people could afford to follow pharaoh's example and invest in tombs, and they even appropriated sacred texts that had previously been reserved for pharaohs. The cult of Osiris, the god of the dead, and his goddess wife Isis flourished during the Middle Kingdom and remained popular well into the Christian era. Osiris was a vegetation deity who, like the crops in Egypt's fields, died to be reborn with Isis's assistance. Each year, the inundation of the Nile restored life to Egypt, and Osiris and Isis promised worshipers a similar victory over death.

Because the Egyptians believed that in death they would want and need everything they had enjoyed in life, they stocked their tombs with their favorite possessions. Tombs were also well supplied with pictures and sculptures, for representations of things, like things themselves, were thought to have power to nurture the dead in their afterlives. Sometimes boxes filled with dolls representing servants at work were added to a tomb's equipment. They look like children's toys, but they had the serious adult purpose of supplying the deceased's needs for all eternity. They now provide invaluable information about the kinds of ordinary daily activities that usually go unrecorded.

The Middle Kingdom was remarkable for its literary productivity. Mythological and theological works, administrative tracts, letters, medical and mathematical treatises, and a great deal of less formal material survive from the era. The Egyptians were fond of morally edifying tales and proverbs, and they had an appetite for practical advice on how to get ahead in this world. The sages of the Middle Kingdom advised modesty, hard work, loyalty, and deference to superiors. They praised acts of charity and cursed officials who abused their offices and exploited the poor. They also warned young men to be especially careful in their dealings with women. The love poetry that survives from the era suggests that such advice may have been more readily given than heeded.

Second Intermediate Period (1630–1550 B.C.E., Dynasties XIII–XVII)

The Middle Kingdom had a strong government that cultivated a reputation for justice and worked hard to promote prosperity. It gave Egypt about four centuries of peace and stability before it was undone by a development that it understandably failed to anticipate. For eons, Egypt's location and terrain had protected it from foreign invasion, but now the defense these things provided was suddenly revealed to be inadequate. The delta was invaded and occupied by a people whom the Egyptian records simply describe as Hyksos ("foreigners"). These were bands of Semitic warriors who may have had links with the Amorites. It was their military technology and not their political connections, however, that enabled them to rout the numerically superior Egyptians.

The Egyptians of the Middle Kingdom had fallen behind in the development of military technology—thanks in part to their environment. Egypt had little need for wheeled vehicles drawn by animals. Simple sledges sufficed for men to drag things to the banks of the Nile, and the river provided most of the transport the country required. Some draft animals were used. Old Kingdom farmers plowed with teams of oxen. Donkeys served as pack animals, but horses may not have reached Egypt much before the end of the Middle Kingdom. (Horses had been domesticated in the Ukraine late in the fourth millennium, but they were not in widespread use in Mesopotamia until the second millennium.) The horse had greater speed and stamina than the ox or donkey, but it was more difficult to train and much more expensive to feed. By 1600, however, warriors from Asia Minor were demonstrating how useful horses could be on the battlefield. Archers who sped about in light, horse-drawn chariots could devastate companies of foot soldiers–cutting them down before they got within striking distance with their lances, spears, and clubs. Egypt's simple hordes of warriors were no match for Hyksos charioteers on the battlefield.

The Hyksos crossed the Sinai Peninsula, occupied Lower Egypt, and established their capital at Avaris in the eastern delta. Much of Upper Egypt remained in the hands of Egyptian chiefs who paid tribute to the Hyksos. Several generations passed during which the Egyptians learned to copy the weapons and tactics of their invaders. Finally, a leader emerged from Thebes who helped them begin the struggle to evict the Hyksos and reclaim their country (c. 1550 B.C.E.).

The Hyksos interlude taught the Egyptians that isolationism was a luxury they could no longer afford. Reasoning that the best defense is an offense, pharaohs developed a new interest in the outside world. They embraced expansionism and sent their armies into Nubia and Palestine to begin conquest of an empire.

Imperial Egypt: The New Kingdom (1550–1075 B.C.E., Dynasties XVIII–XX)

With the return of independence and unity, Egypt entered the period in its history known as the **New Kingdom**. Many of the New Kingdom pharaohs were warlords, and their conquests brought ancient Egypt to the pinnacle of its wealth and power. Thutmose I (1504–1492 B.C.E.), the third ruler of the eighteenth dynasty, led armies east to the Euphrates and farther south into Africa than Egyptians had previously ventured.

The New Kingdom produced some pharaohs who were great generals and some who did not fit the newly militarized image of their office. One of these was a woman. Six women are believed to have governed ancient Egypt at some point in its long history. Some served as regents who ruled during the minority of a male heir. Others were the last surviving members of their dynasties. The most significant were Egypt's last pharaoh, the famous Cleopatra VII, and a woman of the eighteenth dynasty named Hatshepsut (1478–1458 B.C.E.). The daughter of one pharaoh and the widow of another, Hatshepsut began her reign as regent for a stepson. She then shunted him aside, asserted a hereditary right of her own to the throne, and ruled Egypt for 20 years. Because the pharaoh's role was understood to be male, images of Hatshepsut conformed to tradition by depicting her wearing male dress and the pharaoh's false beard. The queen's chief ally was a man of obscure origin named Senenmut. He was her spokesman, the steward of her properties, and the supervisor of her many building projects. The most significant of the latter was her great mortuary temple at Deir el-Bahri, opposite Thebes, set against the cliffs of the western Nile Valley. Egypt had never seen anything like it—a series of ascending colonnades and terraces on which gardens

Mortuary Temple of Hatshepsut   The pharaohs of the eighteenth dynasty began the custom of separating their burial place from their mortuary temples. Hatshepsut's temple of terraced gardens and colonnades was a novel design. It marked the entrance to what became the customary burial place of the New Kingdom pharaohs. Tombs, such as pyramids, that were highly visible were open invitations to looters. By carving cave tombs into the walls of the Valley of the Kings, concealing their entrances, and providing the site with guards, the pharaohs hoped to provide themselves with a more secure final resting place.

were planted. For her burial, the queen may have prepared several tombs in the valley behind her temple. Her father, Thutmose I, was the first of the 62 pharaohs who were ultimately interred in what came to be called the Valley of the Kings. The location was probably chosen to provide greater security for royal tombs, the contents of which constituted an irresistible temptation for looters. Hatshepsut's multiple tombs may have been intended to throw grave robbers off the track. As it turned out, she had good reason to be concerned for the safety of her resting place. It is not clear how her reign ended, but following her death, an attempt was made to erase her name from her monuments and thus deny her the immortality they were erected to assure. Her burial place, like most of the other royal graves, was looted in the ancient era, but her remains appear to have been rescued and stowed without a coffin or treasures in the tomb of one of her servants. If forensic evidence confirms that the mummy now housed in the Cairo national museum is hers, she was an overweight woman who died in middle age—afflicted with diabetes and cancer.

Hatshepsut's successor, Thutmose III (1458–1425 B.C.E.), was a vigorous military man. He fought 17 campaigns to secure his hold on Palestine and Syria, and he brought all of Nubia under Egypt's control. The pharaoh was also something of a scholar. He collected plant specimens while on his military expeditions. He studied ancient literature, and he may have done some writing of his own. One of his strategies for consolidating his empire was to imbue the client kings who ruled its foreign provinces with enthusiasm for Egypt and its culture. The pharaoh took hostage the sons of kings he conquered and sent the boys to Egypt to be educated. By the time they returned home to inherit their fathers' thrones, they were thoroughly indoctrinated. Some of the New Kingdom's later pharaohs married foreign princesses to confirm treaties, and these women introduced alien cultural influences into Egyptian society at the highest level. Not until late in Egyptian history, however, did a pharaoh condescend to send an Egyptian princess abroad to marry a foreign ruler.

Egypt was managed by an army of bureaucrats that had to be closely supervised. Some reported to the pharaoh's chief wife, the high priestess of some of the state's most important temples, and others were directly accountable to the pharaoh. Vigilant attention was needed to preserve the empire. With the possible exception of Nubia, the Egyptians did not plant colonies abroad. Instead of occupation, they relied on periodic military expeditions to maintain the loyalty of native princes who governed as Egypt's clients.

The Amarna Period   The New Kingdom reached a pinnacle of power and prosperity during the reign of Thutmose III's son, Amenhotep III (1390–1352 B.C.E.). He made major additions to ancient Egypt's most imposing temple complexes, the shrines of the Theban god Amun-Ra at Karnak and Luxor. Egypt's temples were not churches designed to accommodate congregations of worshipers. They were private residences for the gods whose statues were enshrined in their innermost chambers. The pharaoh delegated his responsibility to tend the images of the gods to priests who maintained an elaborate round of daily rituals. From time to time, a sacred idol was taken out of its temple and carried in procession so that it could be seen and worshiped by the masses. Temples were branches of government, and their granaries provided a pharaoh with reserves of food for distribution to his subjects in time of need.

Wealthy priesthoods could occasionally threaten to impinge on the power of a pharaoh. By the end of his reign, Amenhotep III appears to have had reservations about the growing strength of the temple of Amun-Ra. Holding an endowment amounting to about a quarter of Egypt's arable land, its priests had immense resources at their disposal. Suspicion of the ambitions of Egypt's established priesthoods seems to have influenced the thinking of Amenhotep's son and successor, Amenhotep IV (1352–1338 B.C.E.), and motivated him to take a bold step. He closed many of the temples, confiscated their properties, and announced that henceforth Egypt would exclusively worship a new god—the Aten (the disk of the sun)—to whom only the pharaoh and his family were said to have direct access. In 1348 B.C.E. the pharaoh changed his name to Akhenaten ("Beloved of the Sun") and began construction of a new capital called Akhetaten ("Horizon of the Sun"). Akhetaten or **Amarna** (Tell el-Amarna, the modern name for its site) was situated between Thebes and Memphis on land that had no previous religious associations. It was strategically located opposite a cleft in the eastern walls of the Nile Valley through which the Aten's worshipers could glimpse the first signs of dawn, the daily rising of their god. The great temple at Amarna was not a dark sanctuary concealing a remote god. It was open

Akhenaten and Nefertiti Worship the Aten   This panel depicts the pharaoh Akhenaten, his wife Nefertiti, and their children worshiping the Aten. The royal family shared in the divinity of their god in that they were the unique mediators between him and Egypt's people. The sun disk of the Aten soars above them, and its descending rays end in hands bestowing blessings. Note the curiously distorted profiles, a characteristic of the art of the Amarna period.

to the heavens. Its god was depicted as a bright sun whose descending rays ended in open hands, a symbol of the blessings the sun generously bestowed on Egypt. The Aten was not a mysterious, hidden god but a power that everyone experienced.

Little is known about the theology of the Aten cult, for few of its monuments have survived. But given the spiritual powers it reserved to the pharaoh and his family, most scholars doubt that it was a true monotheism. It may have been an innovative attempt to revive and update the pharaoh-centered faith of the Old Kingdom.

Devotion to the Aten did not extend far beyond court circles, but it was sincere and powerful enough to inspire new artistic visions. One of the most famous of all Egyptian sculptures is a bust of Akhenaten's beautiful wife Nefertiti that was found in the ruins at Amarna. It realistically depicts the regal elegance of a queen, but much of the art of the Amarna period was expressionistic. Like some modern schools of art, it distorted forms to create graceful linear compositions. So odd are the jutting chins and protruding bellies that characterize the style's treatment of the human form that some people have speculated that it was intended to flatter a pharaoh whose body was misshapen by a glandular disease. It may be simplistic, however, to assume such a literal motive for the art of a faith that set out to transform so many of Egypt's traditions.

Akhenaten may have vowed never to leave the confines of his beautiful new city, and his preoccupation with his new religion may have caused him to neglect the management of his empire. Some 350 clay tablets inscribed in cuneiform with the Akkadian language

■ ■

PEOPLE IN CONTEXT King "Tut"

I n 1922 British archaeologist Howard Carter realized every Egyptologist's fantasy. He discovered the intact tomb of an Egyptian pharaoh—the only one known to have survived into the modern era. The richness and elegance of the treasures found in the tomb of the pharaoh Tutankhamun, which include a 250-pound gold coffin, amaze visitors who view them in the Cairo Museum. (The pharaoh's mummy has been returned to his tomb for respectful reburial.) Staggering as the treasures of "King Tut's" tomb are, they only hint at the potential magnificence of Egyptian royal burials. The tomb Carter found was a small one that had been hastily furnished for a young, unnoteworthy king. Its occupant's insignificance may explain why his grave survived. Shortly after his funeral, attempts were made to loot his tomb, but they were foiled before the raiders did much damage. According to packing inventories found in the tomb, thieves made off with about half of the jewelry buried with the king, but some 5,400 items of various kinds were left in place. The tomb's entrance was then covered by debris from the excavation of another, larger tomb, and it was forgotten until Carter stumbled across it.

The Pharaoh Tutankhamun This magnificent gold bust (inlaid with lapis lazuli, obsidian, and turquoise) was created to serve as a mask for the pharaoh's mummy.

Tutankhamun, whose original name was Tutankhaten, may have been the son of Akhenaten by Kiya, a junior wife. If so, he was wed to his half-sister, Ankhesenpaaten, Akhenaten's third daughter by his primary queen Nefertiti, and he succeeded to the throne when he was 8 or 9 years old. Being too young to rule, Egypt was governed by a regency headed by Nefertiti's father Ay, who bore the title "God's Father." The new government returned to Thebes from Amarna, eschewed the Aten cult, revived the worship of the traditional sun god, Amun-Ra, and appropriately revised the pharaoh's name to Tutankhamun. The young man matured to a height of 5'6" and may have been athletic. He was probably trained for war, for he was buried with a horde of military equipment: 50 bows, 2 swords, 8 shields, 2 daggers, slingshots, and 6 chariots. Up until the time of his sudden death at the age of 18 or 20 (c. 1323 B.C.E.), he appears to have been in good health. He had sired no heir, but his young wife had had a miscarriage and a stillborn child (remains were buried with him).

It was far from unusual for a man to die young in the ancient world, but at one point archaeologists thought they had evidence that Tutankhamun had been murdered. A bone fragment within his skull (spotted by X-ray) appeared to have been caused by a blow to the back of his neck, something unlikely to be the result of an accident. It is now believed, however, that the fragment was a byproduct of the embalming process. The king's left thighbone is also broken, but it is uncertain whether that occurred while he was alive (perhaps leading to complications and death) or whether it was damage caused by rough handling of his mummy.

Murder conspiracies were fed by events that unfolded in the wake of Tutankhamun's death. His widow, Ankhesenpaaten, knew that she would quickly be remarried to confer legitimacy on an heir to her former husband's throne. Some remarkable letters have come to light in the archives of Suppiluliuma, ruler of the powerful Hittite empire based in Asia Minor. Scholars cannot be certain, but most believe that the correspondence was that of Ankhesenpaaten. She wrote to ask for the hand of one of Suppiluliuma's sons. Apparently under pressure to accept a husband she considered unworthy, she declared her determination never to wed one of her "servants." She urged the Hittite ruler to respond quickly, for she was uncertain how long she could hold out. Suppiluliuma was understandably suspicious, but he eventually sent a son named Zananza on the road to Egypt. The prince and his entourage were killed before they arrived, and Egypt's young queen was compelled to marry one of her "servants," her husband's former regent, Ay. Ay was in his sixties, and he may have been father to Nefertiti, Akhenaten's wife and Ankhesenpaaten's mother. If so, the young widow was forced to marry her grandfather. Ay survived on the throne for only three or four years. He may have been killed by a powerful general named Horemheb. Nothing more is recorded of the fate of his reluctant wife, and her tomb has never been found.

Question: How can religious belief in the divinity of pharaohs be reconciled with the ways in which the throne was passed from one person to another in ancient Egypt?

that was used for international diplomatic correspondence have been discovered at Amarna. Many contain appeals for help from client rulers, which suggests that trouble was developing in the eastern portion of Egypt's empire. The end of Akhenaten's reign is obscure, but it is likely that the old priesthoods joined forces with disgruntled military officers against their unconventional pharaoh. The identity of his immediate successor is uncertain. All the children of his chief wife, Nefertiti, were female. His male heirs may have been sons by minor wives who were wed to Nefertiti's daughters.

By 1336 B.C.E., a boy named Tutankhaten had been proclaimed pharaoh. He was controlled by a conservative political faction that was set on obliterating the cult of the Aten and returning Egypt to its traditions. The young pharaoh's name was changed to Tutankhamun (to honor Egypt's former high god), and the court returned to Thebes. Amarna, a city that had housed 20,000 people, was abandoned and dismantled. It had existed for only about 25 years. Fortunately for archaeologists, many of its inscribed stones were carted off for use in later buildings. Some 12,000 of them have been discovered at Karnak—pieces that help make up what is doubtless the world's most unwieldy and historically important jigsaw puzzle.

The three pharaohs who followed Tutankhamun were self-made men. Ay had been one of Akhenaten's most powerful officials. He was succeeded by a general named Horemheb, and at his death Ramses, another military man who rose through the ranks, became pharaoh. Ramses founded the nineteenth dynasty, which restored the glory and stability of the New Kingdom and guided Egypt through its final years as a powerful, independent nation. Ramses I's son, Seti, was a vigorous campaigner, and Seti's son, Ramses II, was both a warrior and ancient Egypt's most prolific builder. About half of ancient

Egypt's extant monuments were constructed during his reign (1279–1212 B.C.E.), one of the longest in Egypt's history. Ramses II did his best to ensure the future of his dynasty by fathering (with the aid of a large harem) about 160 children. However, by the time he died, threats to the power of his successors were materializing on the horizon.

Egyptian Society   No matter what happened abroad, Egypt's internal stability was rarely threatened. Life changed little from generation to generation. Security, a reliable economy, and the overwhelming authority of pharaohs moderated the development of the kinds of tensions that stressed societies in Mesopotamia and elsewhere. In theory, all Egyptians were on the same legal footing. They were the pharaoh's slaves. In practice, some families had opportunities for education and for government service that gave them advantages over others.

Most ancient Egyptians were peasants who lived in simple rural villages near the fields they farmed. Their ephemeral settlements have largely disappeared without a trace, making it difficult for archaeologists to find evidence to illuminate ordinary life. However, remains of villages that housed the artisans who worked on royal tombs have survived. They were in arid regions close to desert cemeteries, and their founders sometimes used their tomb-building and ornamenting skills to enhance their domestic environment. Although these communities served a unique class of specialized laborers, they give some impression of how most Egyptians lived. Villages were laid out in an orderly fashion. Some had walls to protect their residents from robbers. Houses were flat-roofed, rectangular structures constructed of mud brick and coated with painted plaster. They clustered closely together to shade narrow streets from Egypt's glaring sun. They contained five or six rooms, and their flat roofs provided additional living space—a cool place to sit or sleep after the sun went down. Furnishings were few. Villages maintained community shrines and cemeteries, but each home also had an altar dedicated to the worship of its household gods. The great temples served the state's gods. Each locality had its own patron deities and each family its own ancestral cult. Clothing was simple, and people sometimes dispensed with it entirely. The Egyptians valued bodily cleanliness. Soap had not yet been invented, but they scrubbed themselves with various compounds and applied unguents to protect their skin from the sun. They reduced the sun's glare by outlining their eyes with dark makeup (like some modern athletes). They shaved or plucked most body hair and wore wigs that were easy to clean and keep free of vermin. Males were circumcised.

Warlike peoples tend to exalt the status of males and to value sons more highly than daughters, but thanks to the protection that nature provided, Egypt was a fairly secure place. This seems to have fostered a milder form of patriarchy than found in other ancient societies. Egyptian men and women of the same class had nearly identical legal rights. Both could inherit, purchase, and sell property. Both could enter into contracts, make wills, and bring suits in court. Pharaohs had harems, but ordinary people were monogamous. Marriage was a private arrangement. The state did not impose regulations, but couples sometimes drew up contracts to define the terms of their relationship. A household's possessions were considered communal property, and divorce could be initiated by either a husband or a wife. People traced their ancestry through both maternal and paternal lines and inherited estates from both parents. Some Egyptians may have practiced brother–sister marriages, but evidence for this is sparse. Most documented examples come from the royal family and were motivated by its unique concern for establishing clear hereditary rights to the throne. The princes and princesses who married were usually half siblings, a pharaoh's son and daughter by different wives.

Women were associated with domestic environments and occupations. Artists painted women white and men brown to indicate that the former led sheltered lives in the home while the latter worked outside, exposed to the elements. Egyptians cherished their homes, and the home's female caretaker was highly respected. When Egyptian men composed epitaphs for their tombs, they often waxed sentimental about their mothers and bragged about both their matrilinies and patrilinies. The ancient Mediterranean world was, in general, not kind to women, but Egyptian women had a better lot in life than their sisters elsewhere.

The Indo-Europeans and the Clash of Empires

During Egypt's Second Intermediate Period (c. 1590 B.C.E.), as the country came under Hyksos domination, new peoples migrated into the Middle East and caused considerable upheaval. They were part of a vast movement that spread the **Indo-European** family of languages from Ireland to Iran and India. The Indo-European mother tongue no longer exists, but the distribution of its various offshoots suggests that it originated somewhere north of the Black Sea. People from this region began to migrate outward about 2000 B.C.E., and almost everywhere they went, their language dominated. It evolved to become the speech of the ancient Greeks, Romans, Persians, and Indians—and, ultimately, most modern Europeans and Americans (see Map 2–1).

The Hittites   An Indo-European people called the Hittites founded the most powerful of the Middle East's new states. Their base was in north-central Anatolia, but their influence was felt much farther afield. They sacked Babylon in 1595 B.C.E. but were prevented from immediately expanding into Syria and Mesopotamia by the Hurrians of Mitanni, a country north of Assyria. The Mitannians dominated Syria and northern Mesopotamia from about 1500 to 1360 B.C.E. and skirmished with the empire-building pharaohs of the early New Kingdom. About 1360 B.C.E. the Hittites defeated them. The Hittites then turned their attention to challenging Egypt's Middle-Eastern empire.

The contest between the Hittites and the Egyptians culminated in a battle that Ramses II fought in 1286 B.C.E. at a place called Qadesh. The pharaoh's monuments claim it as a great victory for Egypt, but it appears to have been a draw. At any rate, the rapprochement between the Egyptians and Hittites that followed Qadesh probably had little to do with the battle's outcome. The fall of the Mitannian Empire had liberated the Assyrians, a people who lived along the upper reaches of the Tigris River, and they had begun to pose a threat to the Hittites. The Hittites made peace with Egypt to avoid being caught between two enemies and dispatched a princess to Egypt to become one of Ramses' many wives.

Map 2–1   The Seats of the Ancient Middle-Eastern Empires   Many states appeared in the Fertile Crescent, and from time to time one would attempt to bring the others under its control and create an empire.

Question: How might the geography of the Middle East influence the region's military history?

The Hittites adapted cuneiform to write their language and assimilated the civilization they found already established in the Middle East. They lived in isolated, self-sufficient villages and established few cities apart from their heavily fortified capital, Hattusas. Theirs was a warlike society that was well mobilized to support a large, expensively equipped army. Their king shared power with a council consisting of the heads of his subjects' chief families, and their government was plagued by coups, assassinations, and disputed successions.

The Invasion of the Sea Peoples   The Hittite empire collapsed about 1200 B.C.E. in the wake of events that also forced Egypt to retreat from its empire. Seafaring raiders attacked the coasts of the Mediterranean from Asia Minor to Libya. They were a polyglot band of pirates whom the Egyptians lumped together as the **Sea Peoples**. The invasion of the Sea Peoples was a mass migration that swept up different elements as it spread. It may have been triggered by the collapse of some small states in Greece and expanded as a growing crowd of refugees undermined and overwhelmed one community after another. Incursions into the Egyptian delta began in 1207 B.C.E. and continued for over 20 years. The Egyptians were not enthusiastic open-sea sailors nor adept at dealing with naval invasions. The Hittites were less exposed to attack from the sea, but they failed to cope with the waves of dislocated peoples who flooded across their borders. Famines may also have hampered the efforts of the established states to defend themselves. There is evidence that a prolonged drought afflicted much of the Mediterranean world at the end of the thirteenth century. A shift in military technology may also have played a role in the decline of the older empires. They had become heavily dependent on light chariots bearing archers to rout disorganized throngs of foot soldiers who fought with clubs and spears. But the invaders were armored men equipped with round shields, two-edged swords, and javelins. They may have developed a tactic for charging and disabling horse-drawn chariots. Whatever the causes, the result was widespread disruption and resettlement.

Assyria's Opportunity   The indigenous peoples who profited most from the confusion created by the Sea Peoples' invasion were the Assyrians, a Semitic folk who occupied the upper reaches of the Tigris River. Their difficult hilly homeland on the fringes of Mesopotamian civilization was under constant pressure from hostile tribes that dwelt in the mountains on its eastern and northern borders. The threat these people posed may explain the militarism that took hold of Assyrian society.

The fall of the Mitannian Empire (c. 1360 B.C.E.) removed the chief obstacle to Assyria's expansion, but the Assyrians advanced slowly. To the south they confronted the powerful Kassites of Babylon. In the west they faced the Aramaeans, desert nomads who were seeking places to settle. Their old enemies in the northern and eastern mountains remained a problem. On top of all this, Assyria wrestled with internal political problems that finally caused its drive toward empire to falter late in the thirteenth century.

Assyria languished until Tiglath-Pileser I ascended the throne in 1114 B.C.E. He subdued Babylon and drove through northern Syria to the coast of the Mediterranean. After his death in 1076 B.C.E., Assyria entered another period of decline. Its march toward empire resumed in the ninth century B.C.E., when it won control of most of Mesopotamia and Syria. A glorious new city called Nimrud was built south of the old Assyrian capital at Nineveh, and the ruins of the palace that Ashurnasirpal II (883–859 B.C.E.) built in Nimrud were among the first sites to be explored by the European adventurers who pioneered the science of archaeology in the nineteenth century. The great stone slabs covered with cuneiform inscriptions and bas-reliefs that formed the palace's walls were widely disbursed and can be seen in many European and American museums.

Disputed successions to the throne inaugurated another period of decline for Assyria in the late ninth century B.C.E. In 745 B.C.E. a general, Tiglath-Pileser III (745–727 B.C.E.), seized power and built an empire that extended from the Persian

The Assyrian Army Besieges a City   This bas-relief depicts Assyrian warriors battling their enemies, a task at which the Assyrians were notoriously adept. Note the weapons and shields, the prominence of foot soldiers, and the way chariots appear to be used.

Gulf north to Armenia and west to the Mediterranean coast and the borders of Egypt. In 722 B.C.E. the throne was usurped by Sargon II, who founded the last and greatest Assyrian dynasty. His grandson, Esarhaddon (681–669 B.C.E.), brought the empire to its height in 671 B.C.E. by conquering Egypt.

Egypt's Fading Glory   Egypt's New Kingdom began to decline following the raids of the Sea Peoples, and as local strongmen broke free of the central government and set up petty states, the country's vulnerability to invasion increased. Nubia, which had so often been invaded by Egypt, turned the tables on its old adversary. Nubian kings drove down the Nile, and by 727 they had become the pharaohs of a reunited Egypt. The Nubians then overreached themselves by invading Palestine in an effort to regain Egypt's former empire. This prompted an Assyrian counteroffensive that drove the Nubians from Egypt. The Assyrians then tried to govern Egypt with the help of native client rulers, but these men were chronically unreliable. The Assyrian kings, Esarhaddon and his successor, Assurbanipal (668–630 B.C.E.), repeatedly sent armies into Egypt to reassert their authority. Their empire was, however, overextended militarily, and they had pressing problems elsewhere that prevented them from consolidating their hold on Egypt.

By 655 B.C.E. the governors of Sais, a city in the delta, had restored Egypt's unity and independence. The Saite pharaohs sought allies and trading partners abroad and opened their country to the outside world. Foreigners established merchant colonies in Egypt and served the pharaohs as mercenary soldiers. The Saite dynasty tried to bolster its legitimacy (and maybe counter the influence of the alien cultures to which it had exposed its homeland) by restoring archaic Egyptian practices. Artists and architects resurrected the styles of the Old and Middle Kingdoms, and there was a literary renaissance. Egypt's destiny, however, was to be absorbed into a succession of empires: Persian, Greek, Roman, and finally Muslim.

Assyria's Culmination   Assyria relied on brute force and psychological intimidation to build and hold its empire, and its most significant cultural contributions were in the area of military science. Assyria maintained a standing army consisting of specialized units: infantry, cavalry, chariots, scouts, and engineers (to level roads, bridge rivers, and construct siege equipment). Progress in metallurgy made iron weapons and armor increasingly common, and breeders produced horses large enough to be ridden into battle. Most ancient armies were little more than armed mobs, but the units of the Assyrian army supported one another in the field and were trained to execute battle plans. Support structures were also devised to keep large armies well supplied during sieges and on the move.

An increasing supply of iron weapons may have contributed something to Assyria's success. During the eleventh century B.C.E. iron ceased to be an exotic metal and came into more general use in parts of the Middle East. Unlike copper, iron was seldom found in nature in a pure state—although meteors provided some highly prized specimens. The metal was so rare that it was sometimes set in gold and used as jewelry. Iron ore was much more plentiful than the copper and tin ores used to make bronze, but it was more difficult to smelt and forge into implements. Copper and tin melted at lower temperatures and could be cast in molds to create useful objects. But air had to be forced into furnaces to achieve the temperatures needed to smelt iron, and the resulting metal was too brittle for use. It had to be converted into steel by repeated heating, cooling, and hammering to combine it with carbon and to shape it. The first people to figure out the processes for working iron may have lived in Armenia. The Hurrians of Mitanni were using some iron as early as 1500 B.C.E. After the Mitannian Empire fell, its Hittite successor became known for iron production. One of the treasures found in Tutankhamun's tomb was an iron-bladed dagger that was probably a gift from a Hittite king. Hittite iron production was, however, limited. Not until about 900 B.C.E. did iron begin to become plentiful and cheap enough to equip large numbers of soldiers. The Assyrian military may have been the first to use it extensively, but soldiers were not the only people whose lives were affected by the new metal. Iron is plentiful, and iron implements were relatively inexpensive compared to bronze. Some peasant farmers began to acquire metal tools and to explore what these could do to make farming easier and more productive.

Assyrian emperors did not rely solely on well armed, elaborately equipped, and efficiently drilled armies to achieve victory. They resorted to terrorism to frighten their opponents into submission, and their monuments proudly catalogued the atrocities they committed: heads lopped off, eyes gouged out, limbs severed, skin flayed from living bodies, and the mass slaughter of women and children. Such treatment was not designed to win the loyalty and love of the peoples whom the Assyrians conquered, and their empire was plagued by revolts and rebellions. Some regions were pacified by deporting and scattering entire populations. This was the fate of the Bible's famous "ten lost tribes of Israel."

The creation and preservation of the Assyrian empire thoroughly militarized Assyrian society. Militarization sometimes promotes a kind of hyper-masculinization of a culture that makes life difficult for women. This is reflected in Assyrian law codes. Assyrian laws were more concerned with property rights than human freedoms, and they lavishly recommended mutilations and executions as punishment for all kinds of transgressions. The law declared women to be the property of their fathers and husbands, and a woman who dishonored the man who was responsible for her was fortunate if she lost only her ears, nose, or fingers. Some female offenders had their breasts ripped off. Because a man could get in serious trouble if he had contact with women belonging to another man, he needed to be able to recognize the status of each woman he met. Assyrian law, therefore, ordered respectable women to veil their faces whenever they left their homes and punished any prostitute who tried to hide behind a veil. The custom of requiring women to cover their faces when in public was widespread in the ancient world, and it is still enforced to greater and lesser degrees in some Middle-Eastern countries.

Assyrian civilization reached its height under the warlike, but cultivated, Assurbanipal (668–630 B.C.E.). He was a scholar and an aesthete as well as a general. He could read the long-dead Sumerian language and had a passion for collecting ancient texts. He searched his empire for documents and created a huge library at Nineveh. Some 30,000 tablets have been recovered from its ruins.

Things deteriorated rapidly during the reigns of Assurbanipal's two sons. The garrisons that had to be maintained throughout the empire to keep watch over its hordes of resentful subjects imposed a fatal drain on the empire's manpower, and this was probably a factor in its sudden collapse. The end came quickly after the Chaldaeans, an Aramaic-speaking tribe, seized Babylon and began to negotiate with their eastern neighbors, the Medes, an Indo-European people who had settled in Iran. In 612 B.C.E. the Chaldaeans and the Medes joined forces against Assyria and sacked Nineveh. By 610, the Assyrian empire was only a memory, and the Chaldaeans had become the rising power in the Middle East. The Chaldaean empire proved to be short-lived (612–539 B.C.E.), and it is remembered today primarily because of the role it played in biblical history. The Chaldaeans conquered Judah, destroyed Jerusalem and its temple, and forced the Jews into exile. The crisis created by the loss of their land and temple inspired the Jews to focus on the compilation of the Hebrew scriptures as one of several strategies they used to preserve the memory of their past, the rules of their cultic life, and their identity as a people.

The Bible and History

No ancient peoples have had a greater influence on what Western civilization became than a tiny group to whom the great Mesopotamian and Egyptian empires paid scant attention. All three of the West's major religions (Judaism, Christianity, and Islam) trace their origins, at least in part, to the sacred literature of a people who are known variously as Hebrews (from a Semitic term for nomad), Israelites (from Israel, the northern part of their territory), and Jews (from Judah, the region around their sacred city, Jerusalem).

The ancient Israelites' concept of divine power contrasted with the views prevalent in the ancient world. Over time, the Israelites came to embrace a monotheistic faith, but more original than their belief in one god was how they conceived that god. Most ancient peoples equated gods with forces of nature and assumed that gods were simply part of the created order. The gods may have designed and constructed this world, but they did not create existence itself. The God of the ancient Hebrews was different. He was the transcendent Creator who was the source of everything that was. He was not subject to time and space, the dimensions of the reality He called into being. He was the Other, an omnipotence beyond mere existence.

The exalted nature of Israel's God removed Him from the realm of ordinary human experience. He could be known, therefore, only if and where He chose to manifest Himself. The Israelites argued that as the Creator of nature, God was not revealed by the cycles of nature. The things of nature follow fixed laws. They are not free, whereas the Creator is absolute freedom. He is nature's master, not its prisoner. The suitable place for Him to reveal Himself, therefore, is in the kinds of phenomena where free wills manifest themselves—in the events of history. Because God is beyond all compulsion, however, He is no more a prisoner of history than of nature. He does not appear in all history, but only in the history He chooses to use. The ancient Israelites believed that God had elected their history as the vehicle for His self-revelation. This was what they meant by claiming that they were God's "Chosen People." God did not value them more than others, but for reasons He did not explain He invited them to become His human partners and to have a history that was to disclose Him to the world.

Many ancient cultures thought of time as an eternal, repetitive cycle of days and seasons. It went nowhere and had no significance. Most people had little awareness of time as a sequence of unique, significant events—of time as history. The Israelite conception of God fostered a different view of life's temporal context. It implied that the passage of time was a kind of journey filled with meaningful adventures and learning experiences that served to bring people a greater awareness of their Creator.

This journey, the Israelites believed, did not truly get underway until long after the world had been created. They did not think of themselves as one of the world's first (or even ancient) peoples. They traced their origin to a covenant (compact) that God made with a man named Abram ("honored father"), who was renamed Abraham ("father of many") as a sign of God's pledge to make him the founder of a nation. The Israelites were the "children of Abraham," descendants of a landless man who was born into a world that had long been occupied by other peoples.

The stories of Abraham and the creation of the Chosen People begin in the twelfth chapter of Genesis, the first book of the Bible. For the earlier chapters, which provide background for this event, the Israelites drew on the general religious mythology that circulated throughout the ancient Middle East. These chapters, with their stories of gardens of paradise, snakes, floods, arks, and heaven-scaling towers, derive from the myths of the Sumerians and Babylonians. There is little historical information in this material, but then the histories of most peoples begin with myths and legends. The Israelites recycled and transformed the tales provided by their cultural environment to explain their understanding of their mission in history and their God.

Sacred Myth and History   The Bible purports to derive, at least in part, from the experiences of a real people, the ancient Israelites. For generations scholars have sought to test this thesis by analyzing the Bible's narratives and comparing them with other ancient records. Because this undertaking has implications for the cherished convictions of both believers and nonbelievers, it has always excited great controversy.

The Bible claims that Abraham was an Aramaean nomad whose family came from "Ur of the Chaldaeans." Ur was gone long before the Chaldaeans appeared, but at the time when this text was written, the Chaldaeans ruled the Mesopotamian heartland where the Israelites believed their founding father's family had originated. After the collapse of the Third Dynasty of Ur in 2004 B.C.E., there was significant migration of Aramaean tribes into northern Mesopotamia, where the Bible locates Abraham at the start of his story. But no one can be certain if Abraham was a real individual or only a symbol representing the origin of a people and their unique sense of identity and destiny.

The Bible describes Abraham and his people as having virtually nothing on which to build a significant future. Their weakness was key to their mission. Any success they might have would obviously be due to God's strength and not their own. For several generations they remain *apiru* (Hebrews), landless nomads, a people who "dwell in tents." They wander about Syria, Palestine, and the Sinai following Abraham and his heirs, the patriarchs Isaac, Jacob, and Joseph. Archaeological evidence suggests that the Sinai was more hospitable to herders during parts of the second millennium than at other times, and Egyptian records from the fifteenth century B.C.E. document the presence of nomads in that region.

The Bible says that Joseph, the last of the patriarchs, persuaded a pharaoh to allow his people to settle in the "land of Goshen," a district on the border between Egypt's delta and the Sinai. If there is any truth to this, the Egyptian pharaohs who were most likely to welcome *apiru* immigration were Hyksos. The Hyksos, like the *apiru*, were Semites, and they may have wanted help with their occupation of Egypt. The Bible says that Joseph's people remained in Egypt for over 400 years, but it says nothing about these centuries.

The Middle-Eastern Empires of the Iron Age

THE MIDDLE EAST	EGYPT	BIBLICAL NARRATIVE
2004 B.C.E., Ur falls	MIDDLE KINGDOM (2025–1630 B.C.E.)	
BABYLONIAN EMPIRE Hammurabi (1792–1750 B.C.E.) {Indo–European migration}		Abraham and the Patriarchs
	SECOND INTERMEDIATE PERIOD (1630–1550 B.C.E.) {Hyksos invasion of Egypt}	
{1595 B.C.E., Hittites sack Babylon} Kassites occupy Babylon		Sojourn of the Israelites in Egypt
MITANNIAN EMPIRE (–c. 1360 B.C.E.) Hittite Kingdom	NEW KINGDOM (1550–1075 B.C.E.) Thutmose I (1504–1492 B.C.E.) Hatshepsut (1478–1458 B.C.E.) Thutmose III (1458–1425 B.C.E.) Amenhotep III (1390–1352 B.C.E.) Akhenaten (1352–1338 B.C.E.) {The Amarna Period} Tutankhamun (1336–1327 B.C.E.) Ramses II (1279–1212 B.C.E.)	The Exodus and Moses'
HITTITE EMPIRE (–c. 1200 B.C.E.) {1286 B.C.E., Qadesh} 1230 B.C.E., invasion of the Sea Peoples		Entrance into Canaan The era of Judges
		The Kingdom Saul (1020–1000 B.C.E.) David (1000–961 B.C.E.) Solomon (961–922 B.C.E.) ISRAEL and JUDAH
Ashurnasirpal (883–859 B.C.E.) Tiglath-Pileser III (745–727 B.C.E.) Esarhaddon (681–669 B.C.E.) Assurbanipal (668–630 B.C.E.) 612 B.C.E., Nineveh falls CHALDAEAN EMPIRE (612–538 B.C.E.) PERSIAN EMPIRE	Nubian pharaohs (–c. 656 B.C.E.) Saitic Dynasty (–c. 655–525 B.C.E.)	Israel falls, 721 B.C.E. 587 B.C.E., Judah falls The Exile

Abraham's descendants did not begin to become a distinct people with a unique identity, according to the Bible, until a man called Moses (the root of Egyptian names such as Thut-moses, "Son of Thut") led them out of Egypt. This event, which is called the **Exodus**, is described in some passages as a dramatic flight from a pursuing Egyptian army that drowned in the Sea of Reeds. There is no report of such a catastrophe in the Egyptian records. Some scholars have tried to connect Moses with the court of Akhenaten and to ground Hebrew monotheism in the cult of the Aten. Others favor a later date for the Exodus, during the reign of Ramses II (1279–1212 B.C.E.). All that the Bible says is that there was a change of dynasty that brought a new pharaoh to power, and he set the Hebrews to making bricks to build the cities of Pithom and Ramses. During the period of the New Kingdom, the residents of Egypt's eastern borderlands would have been impressed into service to construct the forts and depots (the Bible's "store cities") that were part of the empire's new military infrastructure.

The Hebrews who fled Egypt allegedly tried to break into the agricultural districts of southern Palestine, but were repulsed and forced to resume the nomadic life of their ancestors in the desert. Joshua, Moses' successor, finally led them across the Jordan River, past the city of Jericho, and into a land occupied by an urbanized people called the Canaanites. A likely time for desert tribes to breach Canaan's frontier defenses would be about 1230 B.C.E., when raids by the Sea Peoples were drawing defenders away from the inland borders to protect the coasts. Some Sea Peoples established themselves permanently in the region. The Bible knows them as the Philistines, the powerful enemies of the Hebrews. The Egyptians paid close attention to events in Palestine, and the first extra-biblical reference to a people called Israel is found on a monument erected by the pharaoh Merneptah in 1207 B.C.E. Merneptah, successor to Ramses II, defended Egyptian territory from incursions of invaders, and he claimed (erroneously, as it turns out) to have virtually exterminated Israel.

Although some biblical passages describe the Hebrews' invasion of Canaan as a war of conquest, examination of the details suggests something less dramatic. The Hebrews did not occupy any cities or claim the agriculturally rich Jordan Valley. They scattered into the mountains between the valley and the coast, and spent generations scratching out a precarious existence. They are said to have formed a loose federation of 12 tribes that was led, from time to time, by charismatic figures called judges. They were culturally backward folk, and although they survived, their existence was tenuous.

Archaeological evidence suggests an even less dramatic tale. Instead of a horde of people under single leadership spreading from Egypt and across the Sinai into Canaan, it implies that around 1100 B.C.E. small villages that relied heavily on herding appeared in the central hill country of Palestine. These were populated by people who had long lived on the margins of the Canaanite city-states. The Bible's description of the Jews as descendants of a single man who moved together through the Sinai to Egypt and ultimately left Egypt to claim Canaan as their "Promised Land" may well be an oversimplification—an effort by later generations to construct a story of origin for their people, a story that supported the sense of mission and political agendas of later generations.

Palestine   Urban settlement began very early (c. 7000 B.C.E.) along the eastern edge of the Mediterranean. The region had sufficient rainfall to support farming, and its rough terrain encouraged the formation of small city-states rather than large territorial kingdoms. The richest district was a strip of coast west of the Lebanese Mountains called Phoenicia. The Phoenicians, the West's first notable seafarers, derived their wealth from trade, for their ports (Tyre, Sidon, and Byblos) were ideally situated to mediate exchanges of goods between Mesopotamia and Egypt. Phoenicians were shipping wood from the Lebanese Mountains to treeless Egypt as early as the start of the Old Kingdom. They also trafficked in copper and manufactured a scarlet dye that was so costly that its color came to be identified with royalty. So many sheets of Egyptian papyrus passed through Byblos that the port's name became the Greek word for book (*biblos*), the source of the English word Bible.

The Phoenicians were explorers as well as traders. They traveled the length of the Mediterranean, colonized the coast of North Africa, and ventured onto the Atlantic. They may have reached Britain and, if a report in an ancient Greek history is accurate, circumnavigated Africa. They were the chief agents for diffusing the civilization that was evolving in the ancient Middle East throughout the Mediterranean world. Their influence lives on, for the Greeks adapted their letter forms and alphabet, and transmitted these things to the Romans and ultimately to the modern West.

In the biblical account, the Israelites who settled in the mountains between the Jordan Valley and the Mediterranean coast were less concerned with the Phoenicians than with the Philistines (who occupied the coast west of Jerusalem) and the Canaanites. The Canaanites were related to the Amorites who founded Babylon, and their urbanized culture was much more advanced than that of the Israelites. The Bible says that the Israelites had to trade with them to obtain metal implements, for they did not know how to make these things for themselves. Disillusionment with their inferior status finally convinced the Israelites that they needed to make changes in their way of life so that they could be like all the nations. This, they believed, required them to submit to the authority of a king.

The Bible says that religious leaders were reluctant to change tradition but finally agreed to appoint the Israelites' first king, a man named Saul (c. 1020–1000 B.C.E.). Saul's reign was not successful, and after Saul died in battle with the Philistines, his crown passed to an ambitious general named David (c. 1000–961 B.C.E.). David is said to have united the Israelite tribes, conquered Canaan, and created a state with its capital at Jerusalem. The new kingdom allegedly won international respect and grew extremely wealthy during the reign of David's son, Solomon (c. 961–922 B.C.E.). This was a time when small states like Solomon's might have flourished. The great empires of the Egyptians and Hittites had fallen, and no new superpower had yet appeared to threaten the independence of Palestine.

The Bible describes Solomon as a mighty ruler, but historians caution that no archaeological evidence confirms the Bible's picture of David's or Solomon's kingdom. An inscription mentioning the "House of David" has been found. Although it dates to about a century and a half after David's generation, there is no trace of great buildings or a great city at the site of Jerusalem. Some scholars believe that the first important Hebrew kingdom appeared north of Jerusalem in the territory the Bible calls Israel. Its capital was at Shechem. After this kingdom collapsed, the southern state, with its cult and political center at Jerusalem, may have rewritten history to magnify its own importance.

The Bible's narrative, however, describes a Hebrew state that, like Egypt, was a double monarchy: a northern kingdom of Israel and a southern kingdom of Judah. The Bible says that the ten northern tribes of Israelites refused to accept Solomon's heir and declared their independence under a king of their own. Solomon's dynasty retained only the smaller and more rural Judah. Both kingdoms were caught up in the international conflicts that accompanied the rise of the Assyrian empire. In 721 B.C.E. Assyria overwhelmed Israel and deported its people. Israel's ten tribes were "lost" in that they were scattered throughout the Assyrian empire. The tiny kingdom of Judah managed to outlast the Assyrian Empire, but it succumbed to the Assyrians' successors, the Chaldaeans. In 587 B.C.E. the Chaldaeans destroyed Jerusalem and deported its people. This began the **Exile**, the period that was, after the Exodus, the most theologically significant in Hebrew history (see Map 2–2).

Exile was intended to extinguish a people's identity, but the Jews escaped this fate. They were helped by the fact that for some of them the Exile was relatively brief. In 539 B.C.E. Cyrus the Great defeated the Chaldaeans, established the Persian Empire, and permitted a few Jews to go back to Jerusalem to rebuild its temple. Jerusalem was rarely independent of the empires that subsequently rose and fell in the Mediterranean world, but its continuing existence provided an anchor for Jewish identity.

A major thing that enabled the Jews to preserve their identity was the creation of the Hebrew Scriptures. The first five books, called the **Torah** (Law), probably assumed their present form during the Exile. Court scholars, who worked for the kings of Israel and Judah, had recorded several versions of the ancient oral traditions of their people, and these were integrated into a single narrative by Jewish scribes or rabbis (teachers) working during the Exile. They, of course, viewed the Hebrew past from the perspective of Judah. According to the Book of Ezra, the Jews who returned to Jerusalem were the first to hear a reading of the Torah. Its stories of Abraham and his descendants reminded them that it was a relationship with their God—not their land—that made them a people. This belief has helped them survive millennia of exile, *diaspora* (Greek for "scattering"), and persecution to become the only ancient people who have maintained their identity into the modern era.

The Biblical Faith

The land of Israel did not make the Jews a people, but its loss was a challenge to their faith. They believed that David's kingdom had been given to them in fulfillment of the promises that God made to Abraham. The loss of this "Promised Land" might have been taken as a sign that God had abandoned them, or that He was too weak to keep his promises, or that He was untrustworthy. Meditating on the experience, however, helped religious leaders, whom the Jews called prophets, articulate some of the Bible's most profound insights into the human condition.

Map 2–2   Ancient Palestine   Although some scholars are skeptical, the Bible credits the establishment of the ancient Hebrew state to the second of Israel's kings, David. He is said to have conquered and united the Canaanite city-states and linked the Jordan Valley with a strip of coast bordered by Phoenicia in the north and the territory of the Philistines in the south. Following the reign of his son and successor, Solomon, the state he built allegedly split into rival kingdoms called Israel and Judah.

Question: Does geography support or provide grounds for questioning the Bible's description of the reigns of David and Solomon?

A twentieth-century philosopher has characterized the seventh and sixth centuries B.C.E. as the **Axial Age,** a crucial turning point for world civilizations. During these years, major religious leaders appeared in several parts of the world and changed how people thought about social relationships and the meaning of life. Greece produced the first philosophers. Zoroaster led a religious reform in Persia. Confucius and Lao-tzu taught in China. Buddha emerged from India, and a number of Hebrew prophets added their books to the Bible.

The Hebrew prophets were not prophets in the sense of fortune tellers. The Bible affirms the reality of human freedom and responsibility. If the future could be foretold, freedom would be an illusion. The Hebrew prophets operated like modern political commentators. Their mission was to explain the religious significance of contemporary events, and their predictions for the future were based on the lessons of history. For them, the loss of the Promised Land was part of a divine plan. God had given the Jews a law to explain how He wanted them to treat one another and honor Him. Instead, they had tried to placate Him, like a pagan god, with ritual and sacrifice. But what He demanded was justice and care for the poor and weak. The Jews had lost their land, the prophets claimed, because they had ceased to do God's will. But their situation was not hopeless, for God was more than a judge who punished transgressors. He was a faithful and merciful Father who somehow reconciled the requirements of justice (recompense and punishment) with those of love (mercy and forgiveness). The Bible's claim that human communities are accountable to transcendent standards of justice and charity sank deep into Western consciousness. Although Western societies have fallen far short in pursuit of this vision, they have never lost a sense of obligation to it.

KEY QUESTION | Revisited

Thanks to human ingenuity in finding multiple ways to adapt to environments (and to the new environments adaptation continually creates), human communities and cultural identities are of nearly infinite variety. As civilization spread and diversified in the ancient Middle East, drives for unity and order struggled with tendencies to disrupt and divide. Small political entities gave way to ever larger ones, and governments faced the challenge of wielding authority over great landmasses inhabited by diverse peoples. The states that appeared in ancient Mesopotamia and Egypt were the first to confront issues of this kind, and they developed a number of strategies for dealing with them. The most common plan was to impose order from above and to use the threat of force to suppress divisive tendencies. The need for efficiency in a world with relatively primitive means of travel and communication encouraged concentration of power in the hands of a monarch. But poor communications made the effective exercise of centralized authority difficult. It was hard for a king to know what was happening when he was not present in person to observe. To compensate for this, rulers sought to awe their subjects into obedience. The means they used to elevate themselves above the common herd of humanity were designed to persuade their people that their power was of supernatural origin and reach. But ideas about the accountability of monarchs to something beyond themselves also began to circulate in the ancient world. Egyptian pharaohs were responsible for maintaining *ma'at*. Babylonian emperors enforced laws decreed by their gods, and Hebrews inched their way toward faith in a humane principle of transcendent justice as the source of all things. Such beliefs could be used to justify the efforts of an individual civilization to expand the range of its dominance, or they could promote respect for diversity in the belief that all civilizations fell short of the ideal enshrined in the concept of civilization itself.

Review Questions

1. What challenges faced Hammurabi in consolidating his empire? How did he try to meet them?
2. How did religion and geography interact to unite Egypt and build its empire?
3. What strategies did the Assyrians employ to build and hold their empire?
4. What lessons about the construction of a viable society are taught by the biblical account of the rise, fall, and restoration of the Hebrew kingdoms?
5. Which of the strategies employed by the ancient empire builders was most successful? Why?
6. Is civilization one thing, or is it many?

Please consult the Suggested Readings at the back of the book to continue your study of the material covered in this chapter. For a list of documents on the Primary Source DVD-ROM that relate to topics in this chapter, please refer to the back of the book.

Part 2
The Classical Era 2000 B.C.E. to 30 C.E.

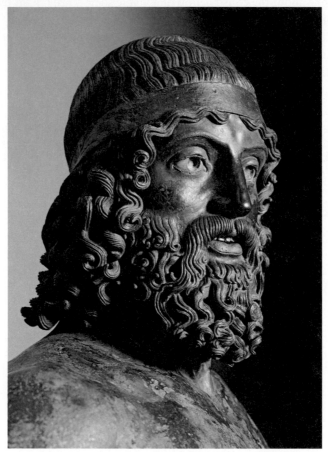

Head of a man, from a bronze statue by the Athenian sculptor Phidias (c. 450 B.C.E.)

■ Many of the characteristics that distinguish Western civilization first emerged clearly during the era when the Greeks and the Romans dominated the Mediterranean world. Their moment in history therefore became the West's classical period. Western peoples are not, and have never been, a homogenous group with a single outlook, and they do not all honor, nor have they ever honored, identical institutions or sets of values. But certain ideas or attitudes have repeatedly surfaced in their societies and provided continuity for their history. A major Greco-Roman legacy was a faith in humanity itself—in reason, science, and human intellect as adequate tools for understanding the world and coping with its challenges. Associated with this was the assumption that ethics and morality have a basis in nature—a belief that has inspired noble concepts of human rights and drives to organize just societies. Respect for the past has paralyzed some peoples, but the West's recurring bouts of enthusiasm for its classical period have inspired innovation and renewal.

TIMELINE

	ENVIRONMENT AND TECHNOLOGY	SOCIETY AND CULTURE	POLITICS
C. 2000 B.C.E.	Sea-faring ships Linear A script	Bronze Age Minoan Crete	Merchant-princes
C. 1800 B.C.E.	Linear B script	Mycenaean Greeks	Bureaucratic administration
C. 1230 B.C.E.	Geometric-style pottery	Aegean Dark Age	
C. 1200 B.C.E.		Iron Age	
C. 750 B.C.E.	Phoenician alphabet Social engineering Hoplite infantry	Greek Archaic era Etruscan expansion Rome founded Homer and Hesiod	Greek colonization *Polis* Spartan mobilization (650 B.C.E.)
C. 500 B.C.E.	Ionian natural science Black-figure pottery Red-figure pottery Doric and Ionic architecture	Hellenic era Sophist philosophers Athenian theater Socrates	Athenian democracy (510 B.C.E.) Roman Republic founded (500 B.C.E.) Persian Wars (492–479 B.C.E.) Delian League (477 B.C.E.)
C. 400 B.C.E.		Herodotus Thucydides Plato Aristotle	Peloponnesian War (432–404 B.C.E.) Philip of Macedon (359–336 B.C.E.) Alexander (336–323 B.C.E.)
C. 300 B.C.E.	Urban planning Alexandrian science The museum Euclid	Hellenistic era Pastoral and lyric poetry novels	Seleucid and Ptolemaic kingdoms
C. 200 B.C.E.	Roman legion Roman engineering: roads Latifundia	New Comedy	Punic Wars (264–202 B.C.E.) Roman civil war (133–30 B.C.E.)
C. 100 B.C.E.		Cicero Jesus of Nazareth Golden Age, Roman poetry Virgil, Horace, Ovid	Julius Caesar (100–44 B.C.E.) Octavian Augustus (63 B.C.E.–14 C.E.) Roman Empire founded (30 B.C.E.) Julio-Claudians (30 B.C.E.–68 C.E.)
C. 100 C.E.		Silver Age, Roman poetry	
C. 200 C.E.			Flavians (69–96 C.E.) "Good Emperors" (96–180 C.E.) Severans (193–235 C.E.) "Barracks Emperors" (235–285 C.E.)

3 Aegean Civilizations

I would rather be a humble servant plowing fields for the owner of a tiny farm than the greatest lord in the kingdom of the dead.

—Achilles, *The Odyssey*

KEY | Question

When does civilization in the West become "Western" civilization?

On his way home from the Trojan War, a Greek king named Odysseus paid a visit to the mouth of the underworld to consult the ghost of Achilles, a friend who died in that war. Achilles, who had been the greatest of Greece's heroes, used the occasion to explain the facts of death to Odysseus. He said that he would rather occupy the lowest station in the land of the living than the highest post in the world of the dead. Achilles' passion for life and faith in the value of earthly existence, which are implied by this remark, help to explain the achievements of the Greeks. The civilization they founded on the shores of the Aegean Sea transformed the ancient world, and it continues to influence the modern world. People still adapt the Greeks' architecture, imitate their sculpture, debate the theories of their philosophers, use their scientific vocabulary, and even go to the theater to be entertained by their playwrights.

The influence of the ancient Greek thinkers and artists has been so pervasive that some historians claim that the Greeks were the founders of Western civilization. Others caution that the Greeks did not develop in a vacuum—that they had close ties with Middle-Eastern states and borrowed much from them. A controversial school of contemporary scholars has gone so far as to claim that most of Greek civilization was derived from Egypt and Africa.

The Mask of Agamemnon   This gold mask was discovered in a grave at the ancient Greek city of Mycenae. Heinrich Schliemann, who excavated Troy, found it in 1876 and leapt to the unwarranted conclusion that it represented Agamemnon, leader of the Greek army in Homer's *Iliad*.

Advocates for all these positions make their cases by listing specific things that the Greeks are said either to have borrowed or to have originated. Arguments of this kind are not very persuasive, for a civilization is more than its component parts. The debate does, however, illustrate how difficult it is to draw hard and fast lines across the continuum of history, and it is a healthy corrective to the belief that Western civilization developed in isolation and entirely from its own intellectual resources.

The ancient Greeks' experience with civilization demonstrates how complex the interaction between people and environments can be. People inhabit two worlds simultaneously: one constructed by nature and one created in their minds. What they make of the former depends to a great extent on how they frame the latter. Different people react differently to similar sets of challenges and opportunities, and explanations for their behaviors are rooted in the mysteries of human psychology.

Greek history illustrates the role that imagination and creativity play in the human struggle for survival, for nature provided the Greeks with few resources. The Greek mainland was small (about the size of the state of Louisiana) and poor. It had no rivers like the Nile or Euphrates and no fields as productive as those of Egypt or Mesopotamia. Greek farmers could work only about 18% of their country's mountainous terrain. Greece's forests were depleted in prehistory, and even the seas off its coasts were not particularly rich in fish. The success the Greeks had in building a civilization under such circumstances proves that environmental resources alone are not enough to explain the rise of a great culture. The Greeks made extraordinary use of what they were given by their homeland, but they also profited from contacts with older civilizations. The fame of Greek civilization should also not obscure the fact that the role the Middle East played in the formation of "the West" did not end with the arrival of the Greeks.

Minoan Mentors

What has long been regarded as the West's most influential ancient civilization appeared in the Aegean, the part of the Mediterranean that is bound by the island of Crete on the south, Asia Minor on the east, and the Greek peninsula on the west and north. It was the work of a people who called themselves Hellenes, but who are better known as Greeks, the name the Romans gave them.

The Greeks were introduced to civilization by the inhabitants of ancient Crete. Archaeologists have named them Minoans after Minos, a legendary king of Crete. What they called themselves is unknown, for the documents they left us have not yet been deciphered. Scholars speculate that their language was related to one of the Semitic tongues of the Middle East. If so, significant elements in their population may have migrated from that region.

Minoan Civilization   Crete was inhabited as early as 7000 B.C.E., but the kind of monumental architecture that often signals the presence of a civilization did not appear until about 2000 B.C.E. Crete's great buildings, unlike those of Mesopotamia and Egypt, were not temples or tombs. They were palaces for merchant-princes, rulers whose major interest was trade, not conquest. Minoan civilization was forgotten until the ruins of the largest of these structures were discovered at a place called Knossos in 1899. No one knows whether the ruler of Knossos presided over all of Crete or was only one of several Minoan

Map 3–1   The Bronze-Age Aegean World   Two distinct but related civilizations (the Minoan and the Mycenaean) arose in the Aegean region between 2000 and 1200 B.C.E. Both were maritime powers whose wealth derived from Mediterranean trade.

Question: How would you expect Minoan civilization to differ from Mycenaean civilization given that the Minoans lived on an island and the Mycenaeans on the mainland?

princes. His court was certainly magnificent. The multistoried palace at Knossos had about 300 rooms arranged around its great courtyards—as well as lavishly decorated reception halls, ceremonial staircases, workshops, warehouses, and well-engineered ventilation, drainage, and sewage disposal systems. The fact that it was not fortified suggests that its owner enjoyed mastery of the sea and had no fear of invasion (see Map 3–1).

Seafaring funded Minoan civilization. Egypt had an insatiable appetite for northern products such as wood and olive oil (the all-purpose lubricant, fuel, and the chief source of fat in the ancient world's grain-based diet). Peoples such as the Minoans and Phoenicians, whose island and coastal homes oriented them to the sea, were eager to serve the Egyptian market. Minoan merchants were active in Egypt as early as the Middle Kingdom (2100–1700 B.C.E.), and Egypt greatly influenced Minoan culture.

Minoan trade supported the aristocrats who lived in palaces, such as Knossos on Crete's northern coast and Phaistos on its southern rim. It also enabled the residents of the towns scattered about Crete and on neighboring islands to erect comfortable homes. Little is known about its impact on the Minoan peasantry, for few traces of their villages survive.

Like other ancient peoples whose economic activities required them to maintain inventories of goods, the Minoans invented a system of writing. Crete's scribes may have been inspired by Egyptian hieroglyphs, but by 1800 B.C.E., they had evolved a distinctive script of their own. Scholars have named it Linear A to distinguish it from a later version, **Linear B**, that the early Greeks adapted for writing their language. Both scripts were drawn (using traced lines rather than cuneiform's imprinted wedges) on clay tablets and both were probably used exclusively for the purpose of compiling economic records. Because Linear A cannot yet be read, most of what we know about Minoan civilization comes from the study of its ruined buildings.

The frescoes that decorated the walls of homes and palaces provide windows into the Minoan world, for Minoan art was realistic. It described plants, animals, landscapes, and a variety of human activities. The paucity of military scenes in paintings and of weapons in graves has led some scholars to conclude that the Minoans were not a warlike people. No society that depended on the dangerous profession of long-distance trade could, however, have been indifferent to the martial arts, and myths and archaeological remains suggest that human sacrifices may have featured in Minoan religious ritual.

Minoan frescoes depict a slender, graceful, and athletic people. The men of Crete, like those of Egypt, wore short kilts. Female court costumes featured floor-length skirts and tight fitting bodices that left the breasts bare. Women are prominent subjects of a few frescoes, and Minoan religion featured a goddess, a young woman associated with snakes and birds. Some people claim that this is evidence that Minoan society was dominated by women, but many communities have honored a few privileged females and venerated goddesses while denigrating ordinary women. Minoan religious symbolism was also not exclusively female. Bulls represented the male element in what was doubtless a fertility cult. The horns of bulls decorated the walls of the palace at Knossos, and some frescoes depict young men and women engaged in a form of bull fighting that may have had religious significance. Recently what is believed to be a Minoan temple has been discovered, but the paucity of such sites suggests that Minoans may more commonly have worshiped at sacred places under the open sky, in caves, and at shrines in their homes.

Minoan History   Minoan civilization belonged to the Bronze Age and evolved in distinct stages. During the Early Minoan Period (2600–2000 B.C.E.), Crete developed its trade. The Minoans clustered into urban settlements and built their first palaces during the Middle Minoan Period (2000–1600 B.C.E.). The Late Minoan Period (1600–1125 B.C.E.)

The Minoan Bull-Leapers   This much reconstructed fresco from the palace at Knossos illustrates what may have been a sport, a religious ritual, or an illustration of a myth. The participants leaped at charging bulls, grabbed their horns, and somersaulted over their backs. Similar frescoes have been discovered in a palace in the Egyptian port of Avaris. New Kingdom Egypt had close commercial ties with the Minoans.

emerged in the wake of a disaster that caused widespread destruction on the island. Because there was no change in Minoan culture, the damage was probably the result of a natural catastrophe, such as an earthquake, and not a foreign invasion.

About 1450 B.C.E., the scribes working at Knossos switched from Linear A to Linear B. The significance of this change became clear in 1952, when a young British scholar proved that Linear B recorded an early form of Greek. The use of Greek at Knossos suggests that warriors from the mainland conquered and occupied Crete. About 50 years later the whole island was again devastated by the hand of either man or God, and Minoan civilization began to fade from memory. The Minoans may have sowed the seeds of their own destruction by introducing the Greeks of the mainland to seafaring, trade, and civilization.

The Mycenaeans, Greece's First Civilization

The Greeks created two quite different civilizations. The one for which they are famous is the second, their Hellenic or "classical" civilization. Their first, which flourished from about 1600 to 1200 B.C.E., modeled itself on the Minoan example. Historians have named it for Mycenae, a city in the northeastern Peloponnese (the southern portion of the Greek peninsula) that Homer's *Iliad* says was ruled by Agamemnon, the leader of the Greeks in the Trojan War.

Origin of the Greeks   The ancestors of the Greeks were part of the great wave of migration that spread Indo-European languages from the Atlantic Coast to the Indian Ocean. They entered the Greek peninsula from central Europe between 2100 and 1900 B.C.E. and displaced its earlier inhabitants, villagers with cultural ties to Asia Minor. They were a warlike people with strongly patriarchal customs, and as nomadic herders from the northern plains, they had no maritime experience. Their language even lacked a word for sea.

The Greeks' appearance in the Aegean world roughly coincided with the rise of Minoan civilization on Crete. There is no evidence that the Minoans ever ruled the Greek mainland, but mythology suggests that the early Greeks were overawed by Crete's superior culture. The myth known as "Theseus and the Minotaur" narrates the adventures of a prince of Athens who was sent to Crete as human tribute. He negotiates a labyrinth, a maze that King Minos built to hold the Minotaur (Minos-bull), a beast born of a union between a bull and Minos's wife. Theseus kills the monster and escapes—with the help of Minos's daughter. The story suggests that the primitive Greeks knew that bulls featured in Minoan religious sacrifices and that Minoans erected mysterious buildings, such as the maze-like palace at Knossos, a "labyrinth," so-called because it was decorated with a sacred symbol, a double-headed axe called a *labys*. Another Greek myth claimed that in infancy the god Zeus had been hidden on Crete to prevent his father from killing him. When he grew up, he overthrew the older deities and established the reign of the Greeks. This may preserve a faint memory of the transition from Minoan to Mycenaean dominance in the Aegean.

The Mycenaean Kingdoms   Mycenaean civilization was the invention of mainland kingdoms that were tiny versions of the great states of Egypt and Mesopotamia. Mycenaean kingdoms had centralized governments administered by elaborate bureaucracies, and they were intensely militaristic. Their palaces were citadels into which besieged populations could retreat. Their art featured battle scenes. Their leaders were buried with weapons, armor, and chariots, and their merchants trafficked in armaments. The Mycenaeans had inherited a warlike disposition from their nomadic Indo-European ancestors, and Greece's environment did little to moderate it. The country's mountainous terrain hampered political unification, and competition for its scarce resources and commercial opportunities sparked vicious rivalries among its inhabitants.

Mycenaean kings were, like the Minoan rulers, merchant-princes. The professions of merchant and warrior were closely allied in the ancient world, for traders who ventured far from home had no protection other than what they provided for themselves. They were heavily armed, and only opportunity distinguished them from pirates. When they encountered the strong, they traded. When they met the weak, they looted.

The earliest evidence for the wealth and power of Mycenaean kings comes from offerings found in shaft-graves dating from about 1600 to 1500 B.C.E. Later, the Mycenaeans constructed imposing *tholoi* to house their dead. *Tholoi* were vaulted masonry chambers (shaped like bee hives) that were mounded over with soil and used for multiple burials. The **tholos** at Mycenae is 50 feet in diameter and 40 feet high. Young

The Lion-Gate at Mycenae   The gate that provided entrance to the citadel at Mycenae was formed from huge blocks of stone and decorated with a tympanum depicting two lions guarding a pillar, a motif found in Middle-Eastern art.

monarchies sometimes bolster their authority by acts of conspicuous consumption intended to overawe their subjects. *Tholoi* were probably shrines for the worship of royal ancestors. Unlike the later Greeks, the Mycenaeans seem not to have built temples. The fortress-palaces, which began to rise about 1400 B.C.E., were constructed of huge, irregularly shaped stone blocks that were fitted together like pieces of a puzzle. So monumental were their remains that later Greeks concluded that these "cyclopean" structures were the work of the Cyclopes, an extinct race of giants.

The reception rooms of the Mycenaean fortresses were decorated with frescoes and tiled floors and had furnishings made from exotic woods and precious metals. Like Minoan palaces, the Mycenaean royal residences housed the workshops, warehouses, and scribal offices essential to the livelihood of a merchant-prince. Mycenaean scribes developed Linear B, a writing system based on the Minoans' Linear A. Two major collections of their tablets have been found. One, as previously mentioned, is from Knossos. The other is from Pylos, a fortress on the southwestern coast of the Peloponnese (the mainland's southern peninsula). The 1,200 Linear B tablets from the archives of Pylos owe their survival to the destruction of the people who wrote them. Pylos fell to an attacker about 1200 B.C.E., and the flames that consumed the palace baked the fragile clay tablets in its scribes' offices into durable tiles.

The only things found on the Linear B tablets are inventories of supplies, but these reveal a great deal about Mycenaean life. Ration lists suggest that wheat and barley bread were the staples of the diet. Workers were also issued wine and figs. Meat is not often mentioned, but some must have been available. Many animals had to be slaughtered to produce the quantities of leather that palace craftsmen used to manufacture armor. Some agricultural products, particularly olive oil and honey, were cultivated for export. The 400 bronze smiths that Pylos's king employed would have turned out far more weapons than he needed, so he must have been an arms dealer. About 600 women were attached to the palace to weave linen and woolen cloth. The Pylos documents mention many specialized professions and list titles for numerous kinds of bureaucrats. The peasants who inhabited the kingdom's 200 villages may have been semi-free laborers who were legally dependent on a military aristocracy. Slaves, a byproduct of war, were plentiful. Most were female, for the males of defeated communities were usually slaughtered.

The Aegean Dark Age

Pylos was destroyed and abandoned about 1200 B.C.E., and within a few decades all the Mycenaean kingdoms had collapsed. Linear B, which was known only to the scribes who served the Mycenaean kings, was forgotten, and a Dark Age (an era without literacy) descended on the Aegean. Not until commerce revived in the eighth century B.C.E. did the Greeks again sense a need for writing. About 800 B.C.E. they adapted the Phoenician script for their own use.

Homer and the Fall of Mycenae   Although literacy disappeared from the Aegean with the Mycenaeans, an oral tradition preserved some memory of their existence and inspired the composition of the *Iliad* and the *Odyssey*, the first major pieces of Greek literature. Tradition attributes both these epic poems to a certain Homer, who supposedly flourished about 700 B.C.E., but stylistic features suggest that they may not have been the work of one man. The *Iliad* is the story of a quarrel between two Greek leaders, Agamemnon and Achilles, which took place in the tenth year of a Greek siege of Troy, a city in northwestern Asia Minor. The *Odyssey* catalogues the adventures of Odysseus, one of their companions, on his way home from the Trojan War. Both poems purport to narrate events from the Mycenaean era, but they read back into that period the conditions of the later and more primitive Dark Age.

It was once assumed that Homer's stories were entirely fictional, but in 1871 Heinrich Schliemann, a brilliant self-taught German archaeologist (who made a fortune in the California gold rush as a banker) discovered the site of Troy. His excavations there and on the mainland of Greece uncovered evidence for several Trojan wars and for the great Greek kingdoms that could have fought them. Scholars dispute which of Troy's battles may have given rise to the tales collected in the *Iliad,* but Troy's location explains why the Greeks would have fought a Trojan War. Troy commanded the entrance to the Hellespont, the waterway by which Greeks imported grain from the Black Sea. If anything could have persuaded the Mycenaean kings to set aside their differences and wage a joint expedition against a foreign power, it was a threat to their food supply. Troy was sacked sometime after 1250 B.C.E., not long before the Mycenaean kingdoms themselves began to fall. If the destruction of Troy was the last proud achievement of the Mycenaean era, stories about it would have come, during the Dark Age, to represent the glories of an increasingly mythic past.

A spate of fortification building on the mainland of Greece suggests that around 1250 B.C.E. the Mycenaean governments sensed a need to strengthen their defenses. Historians once postulated that the Mycenaeans confronted a second wave of Indo-European migration from the north, an invasion by primitive tribes that spoke the Dorian dialect of Greek. But no archaeological evidence confirms a Dorian presence in Greece until after the Mycenaean decline. An attack from without is not the only explanation for a civilization's fall. Internal problems can also bring it down. By the thirteenth century the Mycenaeans were struggling with overpopulation, declining agricultural production, and costly, unwieldy bureaucratic administrations. Under these circumstances, the fall of one shaky kingdom could have initiated a domino effect that brought them all down. As refugees flooded from a collapsing state into the territory of its neighbor, that neighbor would be pushed over the edge and its people would join a swelling tide of refugees. Greeks seeking new homes probably triggered the invasions of the Sea Peoples who descended on the coasts of Egypt and Palestine in the late thirteenth century. At this time Greeks also occupied the Aegean islands and the coast of Asia Minor.

The Homeric Era   The Mycenaean collapse cleared the way for the Greeks to reinvent themselves, but almost five centuries passed before the outlines of their great Hellenic, or classical, civilization emerged. These transitional centuries were not devoid of achievement. Iron came into widespread use. Pottery painters began to develop a distinctive and historically informative art. Religious traditions changed. New weapons and battlefield strategies were introduced. Novel political and social institutions appeared, and colonization scattered Greek cities throughout the ancient world.

Mycenaean trade, industry, and agriculture had been centrally managed by royal agents. Once these officials passed from the scene, a much simpler economy emerged. It centered on the village and the household. This is the world that Homer (or the school of poets he represents) knew and projected onto the Mycenaean past. It was far less wealthy than its Mycenaean predecessor. Few of its settlements had as many as a thousand residents, and the decline of trade in the Aegean meant that each community had to produce almost everything it needed for itself.

Conditions were difficult during the Dark Ages but not unpromising. A reduced population lessened competition for farmland, and an economy of self-sufficiency minimized class differences based on wealth and access to imported luxuries. The collapse of centralized political authority allowed local governments to flourish. The chieftains who headed these were called kings, but they were far less powerful than Mycenaean royalty. The simple equipment they took to their graves suggests that the economic gap between them and their followers was not great. The Homeric king was a first-among-equals in a band of military companions. He fought at the side of his men and shared their way of life.

Homeric society was dominated by warrior bands that were only nominally subservient to a hierarchy of regional overlords. The leaders of these bands constituted a hereditary aristocracy, but it was a working aristocracy. A king and his nobles defended their people and enriched them by raiding their neighbors' territory. The monarch's office passed to his son, but only if his men considered the heir to be competent. A leader was accountable to a warrior code that demanded demonstrations of strength, courage, and honor. He was expected to inspire his men by his superior prowess in battle and in the hunts and athletic competitions that proved his readiness for the rigors of combat.

A Homeric king's income consisted of locally produced consumable items (olive oil, grain, and wine). It made no sense to hoard such things, for they deteriorated in storage. However, if they were invested as social capital—that is, distributed among his followers—they returned rewards in the form of increased loyalty. Noblemen were supposed to be openhanded and hospitable, and to strive to outdo one another in the giving of gifts. A chief had to be as generous with time and patience as with property. The aristocratic warriors he led enjoyed freedom of speech in his councils and expected him to be capable of eloquent oratory. Men of less distinguished ancestry and reputation were, of course, required to show deference to their betters.

The works of Homer occupied a place in Greek society comparable to that of the Bible in the Christian communities of the medieval and early modern West. Most Greeks, regardless of their social status, identified with Homer's *aristoi* ("best men," aristocrats). Lineage and famous ancestors were important, but good bloodlines were not enough. Individuals were expected to earn respect through their achievements. The ideal man had to be both competent and handsome—a harmony of muscle, bone, brain, and spirit that excited the envy of the gods. The greatest of men could, in myths at least, become deities themselves.

The Hellenic Era

As things settled down in the Aegean world, trade revived and population increased. The Dark Age drew to a close, and the vague outlines of a new Greek civilization appeared. Its fundamental institutions were quite different from those of the Mycenaean era.

The Archaic Period (750–500 B.C.E.)   Population did not have to increase much before pressures on the limited resources of the Aegean environment caused social problems. Division of land among heirs reduced many farms to tiny plots that could not support families. This forced their owners either to become dependents of more prosperous neighbors or to sell their land and relocate. Both options transformed Greek society by concentrating land in fewer hands and widening class divisions. This caused political unrest, and many Greeks chose to leave the Aegean for new homes elsewhere. Emigration expanded trade networks, and entrepreneurs began to venture forth looking for new markets. City-states in the homeland eased their population crunch by sponsoring colonies, but they did not exploit their colonies for their own benefit. Each colony was independent and self-governing, and many were in locations that gave them opportunities to grow larger and richer than their mother cities (see Map 3–2).

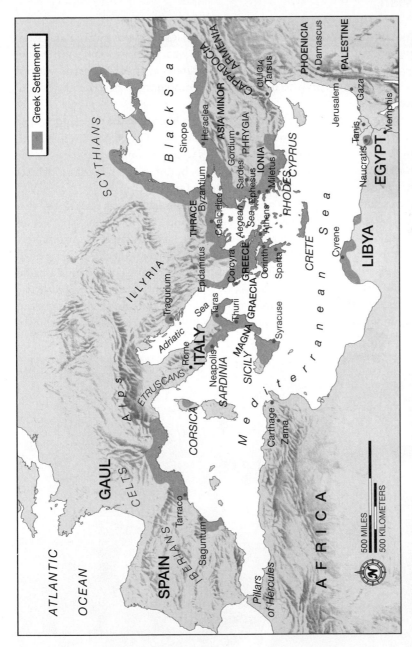

Map 3–2 Greek Territories of the Hellenic Period About 750 B.C.E. the Greeks began a colonization movement that spread them around the Black Sea and the Mediterranean. They looked for unoccupied harbors that could be developed as ports, and they prospered by trading with native peoples in the hinterlands.

Question: Why were the Greeks able to create a coherent civilization, given that their cities were so widely scattered?

PEOPLE IN CONTEXT   Hesiod, The Uncommon Common Man

Homer may not have been a real person, but the poet Hesiod, whose work dates from the same period as the *Iliad* and *Odyssey*, probably was. He is especially intriguing, for while Homer, like most ancient authors, concentrated on the aristocratic warrior class, Hesiod was a common man who used his uncommon gifts to describe the lives of people like himself.

Hesiod is credited with two major poems: *Theogony*, a history of the Greek gods, and *Works and Days*, a description of the annual round of labor on a Greek farm. In the latter, Hesiod speaks in the first person about what he alleges to be personal experiences. Some scholars think that this may have been a literary device, but, if so, that does not detract from the accuracy of the picture of rural life that Hesiod paints.

Works and Days takes the form of an open letter to Hesiod's brother Perses. The two men had fought over the division of their father's estate, and Hesiod claimed that Perses bribed the judges to obtain the larger share (which he then squandered by mismanagement). Hesiod's letter is a species of "wisdom literature," a version of the collections of proverbs and secular sermons that were popular throughout the ancient Middle East and that made their way into the Bible as the books of Proverbs and Ecclesiastes. *Works and Days* lectures farmers and the agents of government on their duties and singles judges out for special attention. Hesiod warns that authorities who take bribes risk divine punish-

Hesiod's *Theogony*   This painting from an ancient Greek vase depicts Hesiod's story of the birth of the goddess Athena. She emerges fully grown and armored from Zeus's head, which the god Hephaestus is shown splitting open with an axe.

ment, for there is a moral order in the universe that holds rulers accountable—a natural standard of justice to which human laws must conform. This was a conviction he unknowingly shared with his contemporaries, the Hebrew prophets.

Hesiod believed that justice was simply common sense. People should pay their debts, honor their obligations, and deal fairly and generously with one another. He also insisted that there was no substitute for hard work, that idleness was a personal disgrace and an offense to the gods. The small-property-holders whom he addresses are assumed to have a few slaves or hired hands, but they sweat in their fields alongside their servants. Hesiod saw in the work of these ordinary men the kind of nobility that Homer praised in the feats of aristocratic warriors. His definition of the good man is the self-sufficient individual whose unrelenting labor keeps his barns filled. Such a man, the poet warned, chooses a wife with care. Hesiod valued women as resources, not companions. He claimed that females were by nature deceitful, lazy, wasteful, and the source of most of mankind's problems. A man had to take a wife, for he needed children to care for him in his old age. But Hesiod advised the potential bridegroom to choose his fiancée not for her sex appeal but for her ability to pull a plow.

Hesiod was, in short, the champion of the frugal householder who kept a constant eye on the bottom line. The poet accused the upper classes of living off the backs of men like himself, but he was blind to his own exploitation of slaves and hired men. He advised that they be fed only enough to enable them to do a day's work. Hesiod was the spokesman for an emerging yeoman class that was destined to play a major role in shaping Hellenic civilization.

Question: Why might Greece, at the start of the Classical era, have produced a poet with interests like Hesiod's when Egypt and the Middle East did not?

■ ■ ■ ■ ■ ■ ■ ■

Between 750 and 500 B.C.E., Greeks scattered colonies around the Black Sea, across Sicily and southern Italy, and along the coasts of Asia Minor, France, Spain, and parts of North Africa. They preferred sites where they could maintain contact with the sea. Although they generally avoided places occupied by other maritime peoples, some long-established nations, such as Egypt, welcomed Greek merchants and gave them land on which to build.

Greek colonists were exposed to alien cultural influences, but they resisted assimilation. The Greeks divided humanity into two categories: those who spoke Greek, and "barbarians" whose unintelligible babble sounded like "bar-bar-bar." They saw themselves as scattered members of a single culture and jealously guarded their Greek identity. Pan-Hellenic ("all-Greek") religious shrines (e.g., Apollo's oracle at Delphi) and festivals (e.g., the Olympic Games) helped maintain ties among them and spread Hellenism (Greek culture) far beyond the Aegean. Many of classical civilization's major artists and intellectuals were citizens of the colonies, not the Greek mainland.

The Greeks who spread throughout the world during the Archaic era took with them a unique institution called the **polis** (plural: *poleis*). *Polis* is often translated as city-state, but that captures only part of the word's meaning. The *polis* created the environment that nurtured Hellenic civilization. *Polis* is the root of the word *politics*, but a *polis* was much more than a political entity. It was an experiment in social engineering that used art, religion, education, sport, and entertainment—as well as governmental authority—to create model citizens.

Classical civilization embraced a philosophical point of view centered on the human being. It saw the world as a rational, humane place amenable to understanding and control. It taught that human beings were open-ended creatures who had the power and duty to invent themselves. The *polis* provided a means to this end. Most *poleis* were small states situated in sparse, competitive environments. Unlike the wealthy, populous kingdoms of the Middle East that could afford to squander manpower, *poleis* needed all their residents to contribute their best. Their small size also encouraged activism, for individuals were not lost in a mass of humanity. The impact they had on their communities was visible. This created a curious linkage in the Greek mind between what are often contrary drives: individualism and community spirit.

The Hoplite Infantry   Military technology powerfully influenced the development of the *polis*. The Dark-Age battles that Homer describes were free-for-alls, simultaneous single combats fought by heavily armored champions who were carried about a battlefield in chariots. A horde of men from a chief's household accompanied him to war, but they did not fight in organized units. True infantry was an Assyrian invention of the eighth century. When it spread to Greece at the end of the Dark Age, it became uniquely lethal.

The Greek infantry soldier was called a **hoplite**—from his *hoplos,* a shield shaped like a round, shallow bowl that was his most distinctive piece of equipment. A hoplite was a foot soldier who was laden with about 70 pounds of equipment (about half the body weight of an average male in the ancient world). He had a helmet and breast plate, was armed with a thrusting spear and a short sword, and carried his *hoplos* on his left arm. The *hoplos* was made of wood and leather and was about three feet in diameter. It was carried on the left arm to protect its bearer's left side and shelter his neighbor's right. Hoplites fought shoulder to shoulder in a tightly packed company called a phalanx. A phalanx was eight ranks deep, and only the men in the front lines could wield their weapons. Men in the rear ranks used their shields to push into the backs of the men in front of them. Their strategy was to pool their strength, their weight, and the momentum of their charge so as to deal a crushing blow to their opponent's formation. Tactics were simple. Armies charged each other, smashed together, and the phalanx that first broke exposed its scattered men to slaughter.

Hoplite battles were intended to be brief and murderous. They relied more on strength, endurance, and courage than on skill with weapons. There was no room for fancy sword play, but any man who hoped to survive had to stay in peak physical condition and learn to control himself. Sports and athletic activities were not mere entertainments for the Greeks. They provided the physical training that prepared a man for the military duties of citizenship and preserved his life. The males of a *polis*

Warriors in Hoplite Armor   This carving illustrates opposing soldiers in battle, each with hoplite equipment.

were liable for military service from their teenage years until the age of 60, and they could expect to be called into the field at frequent intervals. Because the strength of a *polis* literally depended on the physical condition of its men, the *polis* provided public facilities for training, made physical education part of their upbringing, and inspired them with art that celebrated the perfectly developed male body. The uniquely Greek custom of exercising in the nude spread after Homer's day and accompanied the rise of the *polis*. The Greeks themselves were not certain why this practice began, but it was consistent with the pressure the *polis* put on its men to demonstrate that they were keeping themselves in physical condition for combat. The gymnasiums in which people train today take their name from *gymnos*, a Greek word meaning "naked."

Hoplite Culture   As the Greeks came to rely on their new infantries, the balance of power shifted in their communities. Infantry armies depend on numbers for their strength, and the small circle of aristocratic families that had traditionally monopolized military power and political leadership could not provide all the manpower that they required. A *polis* needed every man who was competent to serve. Competence was determined by health, strength, and money. Simple governments were not equipped to collect taxes with which to finance armies. They expected their subjects to pay for their own arms and training. Only the rich could afford horses and chariots, but these were no longer all that important. Hoplite equipment was within the reach of men of moderate means, and they had good reason to invest in it. If their *polis* relied on them for its defense, it could not deny them some political recognition.

Service in the hoplite infantry enfranchised the male residents of a *polis*. Furthermore, because hoplite warfare put all soldiers on roughly the same footing, it promoted social egalitarianism. It turned the *polis* into a kind of military fraternity, a brotherhood of men who shared the bond of a common battlefield experience. The link the *polis* established between citizenship and soldiering also fueled intense patriotism and, like modern sports competitions, heightened rivalry among city-states. Greek *poleis* found it hard to coexist peacefully, and they often had more to fear from one another than from foreign invaders.

The militarized environment of the *polis* put women at a major disadvantage. The aristocratic women in Homer's epics are respected, influential people. There were some constraints on their activities, but they enjoyed freedoms that most *poleis* denied to women from their citizen families. Because women lacked the upper-body strength that would have enabled them to serve as hoplites (and earn citizenship), men regarded them as inferior creatures. They were declared unfit for public life and confined to their homes. A citizen woman had the same legal status as her children, but unlike her sons, she was a life-long dependent.

The legitimacy of children was extremely important, for citizenship in a *polis* was hereditary. The only way fathers could be sure that their offspring were their own was to limit the contact their wives had with other men. A woman's primary duty was to marry and produce the heirs that would perpetuate her husband's *oikos* (household). This was crucial, for a *polis's* strength depended on preserving the *oikoi* that provided its fighting men. Poor women had no choice but to go out in public and work to earn money to support their families, but their better-off sisters were confined to special quarters in their homes and expected to be as invisible as possible. A woman could visit family members, go to the neighborhood well to draw water, and attend some religious festivals, but she did not take part in social gatherings with her husband and his friends. Indeed, her husband may not have thought of her as a companion. Men often delayed marriage until they were about 30 years old and financially established. Their brides were usually girls just past puberty who were half their ages.

Men were seldom at home and invested little in making their homes impressive or comfortable. They spent their time out of doors or in the public facilities that were a *polis's* chief source of civic pride—its temple precincts or its *agora*, a place to conduct commercial and political business. A man had no opportunity to make female friends outside his family circle. When he desired female company, he turned to *hetairae*, professional entertainers who ranged from simple prostitutes to highly educated women who could engage a man in witty repartee and serious discussion. These women were usually slaves or foreigners. They entertained at *symposia* (drinking parties), feasts for male guests only that offered a citizen his primary opportunity for relaxed social interaction with his peers.

The Rise of the Mainland Powers

There were hundreds of *poleis* scattered throughout the Mediterranean and along the shores of the Black Sea. It is difficult to generalize about them, but we can gain insight into how *poleis* operated by examining the two quite different city-states that dominated political life on the Greek mainland.

Sparta   The Spartans possessed the most intimidating army in Greece. They created it by doing what the citizens of a *polis* were supposed to do. They decided what they wanted to be and then ruthlessly implemented a program of social engineering to achieve their goal.

The Spartans' ancestors were Dorian-speaking tribes that wandered into the Peloponnese during the Dark Age and settled along the Eurotas River. They expanded their territory by making war on their neighbors, and late in the eighth century they overran the plain of Messenia (the old Mycenaean kingdom of Pylos). This drastically changed the context for Spartan life. The war made Sparta the largest state on the mainland, but it left the Spartans outnumbered perhaps seven to one by people whom they had enslaved. The Spartans concluded that they would not survive unless they created a standing army that was so powerful it could frighten the *polis's* resentful *helot* (slave) population into submission. That meant that every male Spartan had to commit to becoming a superb, full-time soldier.

Legends claim that a sage named Lycurgos devised the system that kept Sparta in a state of permanent, total military mobilization. Sparta had to ensure that each of its citizens automatically accepted the lifetime of harsh discipline and regimentation that turned him into a professional soldier. It did so by making sure that it never entered his mind to be anything else. His training began at birth. State officials examined each newborn, and only those infants that were strong were allowed to live. Because all males were destined to serve the state as full-time soldiers, the state had to support them. Each boy was assigned a *kleros*, a farm worked by slaves, to maintain him, and the state did not invest in raising boys who could not fight.

At the age of 6 or 7, a boy left home and reported to a military camp. The army played a larger part in rearing him than did his family. He was taught basic literacy and subjected to trials that made him strong, courageous, and indifferent to hardship. At the age of 20 he saw front-line service. If he acquitted himself well in battle until the age of 30, he was granted full citizenship. Those who failed to measure up were publicly humiliated and shunned.

For most of his life, a Spartan lived in barracks as a member of a 15-man mess unit called a *sussition*. A man's mess mates were closer to him than were his family members. He was expected to marry and sire children, but he could not set up a household and live openly with his wife until he received his full citizen privileges. This created unique opportunities for Spartan women. Because their husbands were rarely at home and a man's time was taken up with military duties, women had both freedom and responsibility. Sparta could not afford, like other *poleis*, to confine women to their homes, and the interests of the state dictated that they be given much better treatment than most Greek women received. To ensure that they grew up to give birth to healthy children, Spartan girls were fed well, given physical training, and not married until they were fully mature at age 18.

The Spartan system produced the best army in Greece for the simple reason that the Spartans were the only Greeks who could devote all their time to training and physical conditioning. Most *poleis* were defended by part-time citizen militias, but the Spartans had a professional army. Sparta's primary weakness was the difficulty it had in maintaining its population. Birthrates were low, and the harsh conditions of Spartan life increased mortality.

The Spartans paid a high price for their system, but it gave them a tremendous sense of pride. They did not marry foreigners and kept a careful eye on visitors to make sure that outsiders did not spread alien ideas that caused citizens to question the Spartan way of life. The *polis's* economy ensured social stability by preventing the development of a gap between rich and poor. Some trade was necessary, but a primitive medium of exchange using iron bars kept it to a minimum. Each Spartan had his *kleros* to guarantee him a living wage. Private property existed, but the flaunting of wealth was discouraged. The Spartans boasted of their coarse food, rough attire, and indifference to comfort and luxury. Their educations taught them obedience to authority and tradition, and discouraged inquiry and speculation.

The Spartan *polis* had what the Greeks called a mixed constitution: that is, a government that combined aspects of different political systems. The monarchical element was represented by two royal families from whose princes the Spartans chose their kings. Spartan kings had little civil authority. Their chief function was to serve as commanders in the field. Sparta was a kind of all-inclusive aristocracy. Its chief organ of government was a council called the Gerousia. It was composed of 28 men over the age of 60 who held office for life. The Gerousia set policies that were implemented by five executives called *ephors*. The democratic element in the system was represented by a popular assembly to which all full citizens belonged. It elected the members of the Gerousia and the *ephors*, but had very limited powers. It met primarily to be advised of government decisions. It could ratify or reject proposals put to it, but it could not debate or suggest alternatives. Sparta also had a *krypteia*, a secret police corps that terrorized the *helots* and eliminated potential troublemakers.

Sparta had reason to be proud of its achievements. It was more stable than most *poleis*, and the other Greeks were in awe of its military might. But Spartan success came at a cost. By refusing to evolve and by turning their backs on the outside world, the Spartans lived through one of the most creative periods in Western history without being touched by it. In an era of unprecedented artistic and intellectual activity, the Spartans, with the exception of a few early poets, produced no great thinkers, authors, or artists. They focused exclusively on military matters and prided themselves on ignoring most of the things for which Greek civilization became famous. Worse, their decision to halt development, ignore change, and pin their survival on a single strength ultimately proved fatal.

Athens The *polis* that is most associated with the achievements of Hellenic civilization is Athens, an Ionian-speaking community on the plain of Attica in the upper portion of the Greek peninsula. By the end of the Dark Age, its Mycenaean monarchy ("one-man rule") had been replaced by an aristocracy ("rule by the best," by those of elite lineage). Its chief organ of government was the Council of the **Areopagus**, a committee of leaders from aristocratic families. The council's mandates were enforced by three officials called *archons*, and it occasionally convened a popular assembly to publicize its edicts. At this stage in its development Athens resembled Sparta, but the two *poleis* steadily diverged. Sparta halted its economic and social evolution at this point by absorbing all its men into a single class and training them for the same profession. Athens allowed an unregulated economy to create divisions and tensions within its society, and these propelled further political development.

The citizens of Athens were not supported by the state. They had to earn their own livings. As trade began to revive in the eighth century B.C.E., new sources of wealth enabled some commoners to prosper, and they acquired the means to force the landed aristocracy to share its power with them. This delivered Athens into the hands of an oligarchy ("rule by the few"), a government dominated by the rich as well as the well born. Athenians who did not have large estates or commercial interests were at a serious disadvantage economically and politically. Each year, they had to raise enough grain on their small farms to feed their families and, if they hoped to accumulate any savings to fall back on, some surplus for sale. In years when harvests were poor, they could not make ends meet. They had to borrow from the rich and pledge to pay back their loans out of next year's crop. In effect, they mortgaged a portion of their labor for the following year and bound themselves to work their land for someone else's benefit. Over the long haul, the poor tended to dig themselves so deeply into debt that they were enslaved. Societies that allow wide gaps to develop between the few rich and the many poor flirt with disaster. The poor resent their condition, and when a leader appears to mobilize them, they have the strength of numbers to foment revolution. Revolutions are often begun by a member of the privileged class who rallies the people and uses them to drive his competitors from the city. This leads to a form of government the Greeks called tyranny ("rule by an individual who seizes power").

During the seventh century, many *poleis* passed into the hands of tyrants. The leading families in a *polis* were highly competitive and inclined to feud. When their fights threatened to destabilize a community, the lower classes often rallied behind a *tyrannos* ("a ruler who takes control by force") in an effort to restore order. Some tyrants abused their authority and oppressed their subjects. But if a tyrant was wise, he remembered the source of his power and courted the people by doing things that improved their lives. He funded buildings, festivals, and programs that provided jobs, promoted civic pride, and enhanced the reputation of his *polis*. In the process, he might encourage the growth of popular government. That, at least, was the Athenian experience.

In 632 B.C.E. the aristocrats of Athens thwarted an attempted coup by a popular Olympic victor named Cylon. He raised a private army and seized the Acropolis, the citadel at the heart of Athens. He hoped that the Athenian masses would join him, but they were not ready. The aristocrats put Cylon down, but the crisis alerted them to the danger they faced.

In 620 B.C.E. the Council of the Areopagus asked an elderly aristocrat named Draco to improve the enforcement of justice in Athens. Athens was governed by vague oral traditions that were subject to manipulation by powerful individuals, and rather than looking to the state for help, men often waged vendettas to punish those who wronged them. These private wars could easily get out of hand, and Draco sought to create a credible alternative to them. His plan was to publish a code of law and make neutral state officials responsible for enforcing a standard of justice that applied equally to everyone. Our word *draconian* ("extremely severe") derives from the harsh punishments that Draco decreed for even minor offenses. He may have hoped that fear would inspire respect for the novel idea of rule by law.

Legal reforms were a good thing, but they did not address the economic problems that were the chief source of discontent in Athens. In 594 B.C.E. the politicians in Athens took the remarkable step of granting a man named Solon absolute authority to reorganize the *polis*. Solon began by abolishing the debts of the farmers who had become enslaved agricultural laborers. This got both the rich and the poor out of what had become a mutually unprofitable situation. By cancelling their debts, Solon freed poor peasants to sell the small farms that could not sustain them, and he provided them with alternative forms of employment. He promoted trade, made loans to small businesses, and invited foreign craftsmen with valuable skills to settle in Athens. The rich were compensated by the opportunity this gave them to increase their estates and turn the land to more profitable uses. Poor farmers grew grain. They needed it to feed themselves, and it was the only crop that brought them a rapid return on the little capital they had to invest. Grain did not grow all that well in Attica, but olives and grapes did. It made more sense to import grain and devote Athenian land to the production of olive oil and wine for export. These were, however, capital-intensive crops. Only the rich could afford the decades that it took to bring an olive grove or a vineyard into production. Solon's reforms cleared the way for wealthy investors to convert Attica from minimally profitable grain production to valuable export crops and for Athens to become a thriving manufacturing center.

Solon also implemented political reform. He reserved archonships, the *polis's* most prestigious offices, to candidates from the wealthiest strata of society. Men who could afford hoplite armor qualified for lesser offices, and the poor (who had no equipment but who rowed the city's warships) were allowed to vote in the popular assembly and serve on juries. To help the assembly assert its authority, Solon created the **boule**, a council of 400 representatives chosen from the four tribes into which the Athenian electorate was divided. It prepared the agenda for meetings of the assembly.

Solon's reforms were well conceived, but they did not improve people's lives quickly enough to head off support for tyranny. In 560 B.C.E. a well-known military hero named Peisistratus won control of Athens. He cultivated the masses who had lofted him to power by providing loans for the poor, promoting trade, financing public works projects to provide employment, and sponsoring festivals. He commissioned a definitive edition of Homer's works for the city's archives, and his support for rites honoring the popular rural god Dionysus marked the dawn of one of the glories of Athenian civilization: the theater (see Chapter 5).

When Peisistratus died in 527 B.C.E., his sons Hippias and Hipparchus succeeded him. In 514 B.C.E. two men who had a personal grudge against Hipparchus tried to assassinate him and his brother. Hippias escaped, but fear turned him into a ruthless, suspicious dictator. In 510 B.C.E. the Alcmaeonids, an aristocratic family that Peisistratus had driven into exile, enlisted Spartan aid and forced Hippias to flee Athens. The Alcmaeonids' leader, Cleisthenes, became the city's next tyrant.

Cleisthenes set out to destroy the political machines on which the power of his aristocratic opponents was based by reforming Athens' electoral system. Each Athenian citizen inherited membership in a tribe through which he exercised his rights. These tribes were under the thumbs of the great families that had long dominated Athenian politics. Cleisthenes minimized their influence by limiting the four original tribes to religious functions and transferring their political duties to ten new and differently constituted tribes. Attica was divided into *demes* (counties or townships), and each of the new tribes was made up of *demes* from every region of the country. This meant that great landlords, who had always voted in tribes filled with their local dependents and retainers, now had to vote with strangers over whom they had no power. Cleisthenes may have gerrymandered the system for the benefit of his family, but it had the long-term effect of freeing up individuals to vote as they pleased. Aristocratic advantage was further diminished by the practice of filling many offices by casting lots. Each tribe chose 50 of its members by lot to serve on a new 500-member *boule* that led the assembly and oversaw state finances.

The assembly governed Athens, but it met only occasionally. When it or the *boule* was not in session, the aristocratic Council of the Areopagus was likely to assume power by default. Cleisthenes forestalled this by creating the *prytaneis* ("presider"). He divided the year into ten equal segments, each of which was assigned to one of the tribal committees that composed the *boule*. For the tenth of the year entrusted to it, each 50-man committee met daily as the *prytaneis*, the body that "presided" over Athens. Each day during their term, the members of the *prytaneis* cast lots to determine which of them would serve as Athens' chief executive that day.

The army was also reorganized to reflect the principles by which the state was to be governed. Each tribe provided a company for the army, and the soldiers elected their own leader, their *strategos* ("general"). Because soldiers much prefer to follow officers who have earned their trust, generals, unlike civilian leaders, could serve consecutive terms. The board of ten *strategoi* was able, therefore, to provide some continuity for Athens' government.

Finally, according to tradition, Cleisthenes instituted a special vote called an **ostracism** to prevent anyone from overthrowing the system he had established. From time to time the Athenian electorate was asked to take *ostraca* (fragments of pottery used as ballots) and scratch on them the name of any man suspected of posing a danger to the city. No trial was held, but if an individual garnered 6,000 votes, he was immediately exiled for ten years.

Cleisthenes's reforms launched Athens on an experiment with a radical version of an untested form of government that the Greeks called democracy ("rule by the *demos*," the people). All laws and major policy decisions were made by the people themselves, not by a small group of their representatives. The use of lots to select men for office meant that any individual, regardless of his talents and experience, had a chance of finding himself charged, if only briefly, with major responsibilities. Small villages could operate informally on similar principles, but Athens was no village. History was to prove if the unprecedented trust the Athenians placed in the masses was justified.

The Persian Wars: Crucible of a Civilization

The larger world did not stand still while Greek civilization reorganized itself in the Aegean. In the wake of Mycenae's collapse and the invasions of the Sea Peoples, successive empires rose and fell in the Middle East. The Assyrians built on the ruins of the Hittite and Egyptian empires. In 614 B.C.E. the Assyrians fell to the Chaldaeans, and in 539 B.C.E. Chaldaean Babylon surrendered to Cyrus the Great (r. 559–530 B.C.E.), founder of a gigantic Persian Empire that ultimately stretched from Egypt to the borders of India and the Himalayan Mountains.

Ionia and Marathon   In 547 B.C.E. Cyrus conquered the wealthy kingdom of Lydia in central Asia Minor and pushed on to the Aegean to subdue Ionia, a coastal district occupied by Greek cities. More important campaigns elsewhere and palace coups subsequently distracted him and his immediate successors from further adventures in the Aegean. In 499 B.C.E. the Ionian city of Miletus organized a rebellion that prompted the Persian emperor, Darius I (r. 522–486 B.C.E.), to return to the Greek world. Miletus asked the *poleis* of the mainland for assistance. Sparta refused, but Athens sent help. Athens was dependent on imported grain, and it feared that Persian control of the Hellespont might endanger its access to supplies from the Black Sea. The Athenians also worried that Darius might restore their exiled tyrant Hippias, who had fled to his court. The Greek rebels had some initial successes, but after they drove the Persians from the former Lydian capital at Sardis, their alliance fell apart. Darius then counterattacked, recovered Ionia, and inflicted a horrible punishment on Miletus as a warning to the Greeks.

In 492 B.C.E. Darius decided to make sure that a hope of support from the mainland never again tempted the Ionian cities to rebel. He demanded that the Aegean submit to Persia. Many of the Greek *poleis*, mindful of Miletus's fate, yielded, but Athens and Sparta refused. In 490 B.C.E. Darius's fleet landed an army of 20,000 men on the plain of Marathon about 20 miles north of Athens. Some Athenians wanted to surrender, but the *strategos* Miltiades persuaded the assembly to fight. A champion runner was dispatched to Sparta to ask for help, but the Spartans claimed that a religious festival prevented them from offering immediate assistance. The tiny *polis* of Athens (led by its new, untested democratic government) was left almost entirely alone to confront the superpower of its day (see Map 3–3).

Map 3–3 The Persian Wars   The first of the Persian Wars was an attack from the sea on the plain of Marathon. The second involved a Persian army that was too large to be ferried across the Aegean. This map shows the routes taken by Xerxes' soldiers and the navy that accompanied them. (Stars mark the sites of major battles.)

Question: What advantages and disadvantages did each of these strategies offer for invaders of the Greek mainland?

Miltiades's army may have been half the size of the Persian force, but the battle on the plain of Marathon gave his hoplites a chance to prove that Greek training and discipline could compensate for inferior numbers. Greek sources claim that 6,400 Persians, but only 192 Greeks, died at Marathon. Whatever the statistics, the losses persuaded the Persians to withdraw. The delighted, but stunned, Athenians credited their victory to the patriotic morale generated by democracy, and like the Spartans, their confidence in the program of their *polis* soared.

Thermopylae and Salamis   The loss at Marathon angered the Persians far more than it hurt them, but a rebellion in Egypt and other problems prevented Darius from continuing the war. It fell to his son and heir, Xerxes (r. 486–465 B.C.E.), to determine the Persian response. In 484 B.C.E. Xerxes began to make highly visible plans for a massive assault on the Aegean. This had the intended effect of persuading a number of *poleis* to submit voluntarily, but 31 states pledged to cooperate in defending the mainland. Prospects for their success were not good. The Persian army was huge—perhaps a quarter of a million men. Even the sacred oracles to whom the Greeks turned for advice were intimidated and did not offer much encouragement.

The Greeks wisely chose to take their stand at Thermopylae, a narrow strip of beach in northern Greece that had mountains on one side and the sea on the other. The Persians had to pass through Thermopylae to reach their targets in Greece, but its confines prevented their great army from spreading out and using the advantage of its numbers. If the Greeks' navy prevented Persia's ships from landing soldiers behind the Greek lines, the allies could halt Persia's advance, and this alone might have forced Xerxes to retreat. Sanitation problems spread disease in large armies unless they stayed on the move.

The Greek allies mustered a mere 7,000 men to face the Persians at Thermopylae, but with the help of their commander, the Spartan king Leonidas, they repelled the Persians' assaults for three days. The battle was lost when a Greek traitor guided a troop of Persians through the mountains to a position behind Leonidas's lines. Realizing that his position was untenable, Leonidas dismissed most of his men. He, his 300 Spartans, and a handful of allies chose, however, to stay and fight to the death. Their willing self-sacrifice turned Thermopylae into a moral victory and made them the most celebrated heroes in Greek history.

The Greek army fell back to the Isthmus of Corinth, the land-bridge between northern and southern Greece. The plan was again to halt the Persian advance by blocking a narrow pas-

Spartan Warrior   Art objects from Sparta are rare finds, and this is one of the most famous. It dates to the early fifth century B.C.E. It has been called "Leonidas," after the famous Spartan commander at the battle of Thermopylae, but there is no proof that he was the intended subject.

sage. This had failed at Thermopylae, but the Spartan generals who commanded the army saw no alternative. Athens, which lay north of the Isthmus, was abandoned to the enemy. Its women and children were ferried to various islands, and its men took to their ships and watched as the Persians burned their city.

In 482 B.C.E. the Athenian voters had made a remarkably intelligent decision that now saved their homeland. A rich vein of silver was discovered in the state mines, and the assembly had to decide what to do with the profits. Some politicians courted popularity by proposing that the money be shared among the citizens, but Themistocles, the first non-aristocrat to rise to prominence in the young democracy, persuaded the

---

The Rise of Hellenic Civilization

THIRTEENTH CENTURY

1250 B.C.E., sack of Troy
1200 B.C.E., fall of Mycenaean
Civilization
Dark Age

EIGHTH CENTURY

776 B.C.E., first Olympic victor
750–700 B.C.E., Homer
750 B.C.E., Greek colonization begins
700 B.C.E., Hesiod
Hoplite warfare develops
Poleis appear

SEVENTH CENTURY

Spartan system established
Athenian system evolves:
632 B.C.E., Cylon's coup
620 B.C.E., Draco's law
614 B.C.E., Assyrian Empire falls

SIXTH CENTURY

594 B.C.E., Solon's constitution
560–527 B.C.E., Peisistratus tyranny
539 B.C.E., Chaldaean Empire falls
510 B.C.E., Cleisthenes exiles Hippias
Cyrus founds the Persian Empire
Democracy established

FIFTH CENTURY

499 B.C.E., Miletus rebels
492 B.C.E., Persian Wars: Darius
484–479 B.C.E., Persian Wars: Xerxes

voters to prefer their public to their private interest. He convinced them to use the money to expand their navy and make Athens a major sea power. The Spartans wanted the Athenians to use their navy to prevent the Persians from outflanking the Greek defenses on the Isthmus of Corinth, but Themistocles saw no advantage to Athens in sending its ships to protect the Peloponnese, which was Spartan territory. Because prospects for success on land were dismal, as Thermopylae had proved, he decided to risk everything on a battle at sea. Themistocles lured the Persian navy into the straits between Attica and the island of Salamis, and his smaller, faster ships, which were operating in familiar waters, outmaneuvered and sank many of the Persian transports. Xerxes could not afford to lose the navy that was his communications link with his empire. He chose to go home but to leave behind an army, under a general named Mardonius, to continue the fight.

Mardonius went into winter camp at Plataea, west of Attica, and prepared to resume the campaign the following spring. The Greeks used the time to amass the largest army they had ever assembled, and in the spring of 479 B.C.E. they took the offensive. Pausanias, the Spartan regent for the heroic Leonidas's infant heir, commanded the allied army. When he drove through the Persian line and killed Mardonius, the leaderless Persians scattered. The Greeks were again amazed to discover that they had succeeded against all odds. The conclusion seemed obvious: Their institutions were superior to all others, and there was no limit to what they might do.

KEY QUESTION | Revisited

The Greeks' victories over the Persians persuaded them that there was a wide gap between their civilization and that of their opponents. The Greek historian Herodotus (c. 484–425 B.C.E.), who wrote the first history of the Persian Wars, claimed that the Greeks won because they were free men fighting for their homeland, while the Persians were the dispirited subjects of an autocrat. The war had been a contest between freedom and slavery, and Greek liberty had proved its superiority.

There were obvious contrasts between Persia's empire and Greece's city-states, but there were also ties between the Greek and Persian worlds. The Mycenaean kingdoms had closely resembled and borrowed much from their Middle-Eastern neighbors. Many of the Greeks who fled their collapse settled in the Middle East, strengthened trade ties between the Aegean and the Middle East, and adapted Middle-Eastern technologies (such as writing and infantry warfare) as they emerged from their Dark Age. Trade with Egypt and the Middle East was extremely important to both the Mycenaean and the Hellenic civilizations, and Greek artists and intellectuals drew inspiration from, and had great respect for, the Middle East's older civilizations. There is no doubt that the Greeks were original and that they ultimately changed the course of civilization throughout the ancient world, but the long-popular assumption that they created a "West" that was independent of—and opposed to—an "East" can certainly be challenged.

Review Questions

1. What were the similarities and differences between the Minoan and Mycenaean kingdoms and those of Egypt and the Middle East? Do environments help to explain these?
2. Might people who live in a Dark Age be more open to cultural innovation than those who inhabit a fully civilized period? Why?
3. How did the Hellenic *poleis* differ from the Mycenaean kingdoms?
4. What explains the differences between the *polis* systems of Athens and Sparta?
5. What impact did the military have on the development of Hellenic civilization?
6. How did the Persian Wars affect the way the Greeks viewed themselves and their relationships with other peoples?

Please consult the Suggested Readings at the back of the book to continue your study of the material covered in this chapter. For a list of documents on the Primary Source DVD-ROM that relate to topics in this chapter, please refer to the back of the book.

4 The Hellenic Era

The monuments of the society that we have created are so great that future generations will be as awed by our achievements as are our contemporaries.

—**Pericles**

KEY | Question

What did the Greeks contribute to the development of modern civilization?

In the winter of 431 B.C.E., an Athenian politician named Pericles delivered a speech in which he made the following points:

1. We Athenians are grateful to our ancestors for creating a free country and bequeathing it to us;
2. Our greatness derives from our unique form of government, a democracy in which everyone is equal before the law;
3. We value people for their abilities, not their social class;
4. We do not despise the poor, but only men who do not try to better themselves;
5. We do not interfere in a man's personal affairs, and we are tolerant of one another;
6. We do not let our private goals and ambitions keep us from fulfilling our public responsibilities;
7. We obey our elected officials, our laws, and the unwritten standards that govern morality and human rights;
8. We enjoy an abundance of good things and relish our pleasures;
9. But our cultivated lifestyle does not make us soft;
10. Our society is open, for we are confident in the loyalty and courage of our people and do not need to resort to covert plotting;

Temple of Poseidon This temple to Poseidon, Greek god of the sea, stands on cliffs overlooking Cape Sounion, five-and-a-half miles south of Athens. Dating to about 444 B.C.E., it is in the same style as the famous Parthenon in Athens.

11. Our selfless generosity wins us friends abroad;
12. And each one of us enjoys freedom and independence.

This ancient speech could be delivered today in the United States Senate. Indeed, Pericles would find much that seems familiar were he to visit one of the modern Western capitals. Most are filled with buildings, monuments, and sculpture in a style he would recognize. He would not be surprised by the scientific orientation of the modern world, for he witnessed the rise of theoretical science. References to history would not confuse him, for the study of history was pioneered by men he knew personally. He might even attend a performance of a drama that he had previously seen in Athens.

Pericles' speech celebrated the virtues of what has come to be known as "classical" civilization. The adjective implies that his Hellenic (Greek) civilization set the standards for the West. Hellenic societies were, however, far from perfect. They were plagued by wars, internal conflicts, and injustices (particularly in their treatment of women and slaves). Despite their stated commitment to reason, moderation, and self-control, they were capable of senseless, self-destructive acts and emotional excesses. Their moment of glory was brief, and the West may owe some of its weaknesses as well as its strengths to them.

Persian Wars as Catalyst

The defeats the Persians suffered at Salamis and Plataea hardly crippled Xerxes' empire, and the Greeks assumed that Persia had by no means given up hope of conquering the Aegean. The most pressing business of the mid-fifth century, therefore, was to evict the remaining Persians from Greek territory and to organize a defense that would prevent their return.

Sparta's Retreat   The Greek **poleis** had worked together to repel Xerxes' invasion, and they could defend the Aegean only if they continued to cooperate. No one knew, however, how to structure a permanent alliance. The Spartans had the best land army, and the Athenians were the strongest naval power. The military resources of both cities were needed, but neither *polis* trusted the other.

The immediate advantage was with the Spartans who had routed the last of Xerxes' forces at Plataea. The Athenians were temporarily homeless, for the Persians had burned Athens and leveled its walls. Sparta argued that Athens should not rebuild its defenses lest the Persians reoccupy the city and use it against the Greeks. They pointed out that Sparta's villages were unfortified, for Spartan men were all the "walls" Sparta needed. Themistocles saw things differently. He dragged out discussions with the Spartans while the Athenians hastily rebuilt their ramparts.

Pausanias, the Spartan general who had triumphed at Plataea, commanded the allied forces as they pursued the retreating Persians. But power apparently went to his head. The allies accused him of behaving like a Persian despot, and Sparta recalled him and convicted him of treason. When Pausanias sought sanctuary in a temple in order to avoid execution, the Spartan authorities—acting on a suggestion from his mother— bricked up the building's doors and windows and left him to starve.

The Spartans needed their men at home to guard against slave rebellions. Long-term, distant commitments of their soldiers made them nervous. As the Persian threat retreated, the Spartans returned to their accustomed isolation and left foreign affairs to Athens. Thanks to Solon's reforms, Athens had become a populous *polis* that was dependent on trade, and as a naval power, it was better equipped than Sparta to sweep the Persians from their outposts in the Aegean. Themistocles might have been the logical choice to be Pausanias's successor, but his increasing arrogance and a suspicion that he was engaging in foreign intrigues led the Athenian electorate to ostracize him in 471 B.C.E. He fled to Argos and finally found refuge in the Persian empire—and employment as a provincial governor!

Athens' Advance   In 477 B.C.E. the *poleis* that believed that a permanent defense had to be organized to protect the Aegean from Persia sent delegates to a conference on the island of Delos. The result was the formation of the **Delian League**, a military alliance that at its height numbered about 150 members. Athens dominated the league, but the league's treasury was headquartered on Delos, neutral territory sacred to all the Ionian Greeks.

Cimon, son of the Miltiades who had won the battle of Marathon, assumed leadership of the league's navy and did such a good job of pushing the Persians back that by 468 B.C.E. some members of the Delian League concluded that the organization had served its purpose. Cimon, however, used force to prevent them from withdrawing. The league had become too important to Athens to be allowed to disband. Cimon had urged the allies to supply him with money rather than men and ships, and their contributions had built what was fundamentally an Athenian navy. The Delian League was transformed into an Athenian Empire, and in 454 B.C.E. its treasury was moved to Athens. League money was even diverted from military programs to fund the construction of Athens' famous temples.

Cimon fell from power in 462 B.C.E. He was an aristocrat, and Athens' aristocrats tended to be pro-Spartan. (They equated Spartan discipline with the Homeric virtues of their presumed ancestors.) When Sparta asked Athens for help in putting down a slave revolt, Cimon persuaded the reluctant assembly to allow him to lead four thousand Athenians into the Peloponnese. They no sooner arrived than the Spartans changed their minds and ordered them to leave. The humiliated electorate promptly ostracized Cimon.

The political situation in Athens changed as the city used the resources of the Delian League to build its navy. The hoplite infantry, which was recruited from a relatively prosperous class, had been the original driving force behind the Athenian democracy. But the increasing prominence of the navy shifted power to the poorer element in the Athenian population, the men who rowed the state galleys. Athens' new generation of politicians, the most successful of whom was Pericles (c. 490–429 B.C.E.), cultivated this larger electorate. From 461 B.C.E. until his death, Pericles held the office of *strategos* and used his position to prod, manipulate, and lead his city first to the pinnacle of power and then to defeat.

The Parthenon and the Athenian Acropolis   Athens sprang up around the Acropolis, a rock-bound height that served the plain of Attica as a natural fortress. As the city grew rich and powerful, it adorned the Acropolis with monuments, the most famous of which was the *Parthenon*, a temple dedicated to the goddess Athena, Athens' patron deity.

The Peloponnesian War

Hellenic civilization was the product of a society that was almost constantly at war—more often with itself than with a foreign enemy. The Greeks' victories in the Persian Wars increased the threat of internal conflict by polarizing the Aegean world. Athens developed a maritime empire, and Sparta responded by expanding its league of Peloponnesian cities. This division of the Greeks into opposing armed camps set them up for civil war (see Map 4–1).

Precursor to Civil War   Great wars often begin with small conflicts. The first round in what was initially an undeclared war went to Athens. Corinth, the *polis* that occupied the narrow isthmus that connects northern and southern Greece, was Athens' major commercial competitor and Sparta's chief ally. Athens dominated the Aegean, but Corinth had access both to the Aegean and, through the Gulf of Corinth, to the Greek colonies in the western Mediterranean. About 460 B.C.E., Corinth's northern neighbor, the small *polis* of Megara, made a deal with Athens that allowed the Athenians to use Pegae, Megara's small port on the Gulf of Corinth. Corinth viewed this as a threat to its western trade.

Map 4–1   Competing Alliances: Athens (Delian League) and Sparta   This map illustrates the polarization of the Aegean region that developed in the wake of the Persian Wars.

Question: How did geography influence the formation of the Greeks' political alliances?

Corinth invaded Attica in 459 B.C.E. The attack failed, but it prodded the Athenians into making an important addition to their city's fortifications. Athens had sprung up around the Acropolis ("upper-town"), an outcropping of rock that served Attica as a natural citadel. The Acropolis was some four miles inland from the sea, and Athens' commerce passed through a small coastal port called the Piraeus. The obvious strategy for an invading army was to encircle Athens, cut its link to the sea, and starve it into submission. To prevent this, the Athenians built a fortified corridor (the Long Walls) to connect their capital with its port. So long as the Athenian navy ruled the sea and supplied the city through the Piraeus, land-based armies had little hope of taking Athens.

■ ■

PEOPLE IN CONTEXT Aspasia, the Woman Behind the Great Man

The love of Pericles' life was his mistress, Aspasia, one of the few women who seem to have influenced Athenian politics. Unlike Sparta, Athens encouraged immigration to promote economic development, and it allowed its population to explode. However, as the city grew richer, more powerful, and more democratic, its citizens became jealous and protective of their privileges. In Pericles' day, about 50,000 of Attica's free male residents were citizens and about 25,000 were classed as metics (resident aliens). Metics could not own land, but many of them prospered as craftsmen and merchants. Their families lived in Athens for generations without acquiring citizenship. The sons of metic women who married Athenian citizens had always inherited citizenship from their fathers. But in 451 B.C.E. Pericles persuaded the assembly to limit citizenship to men whose mothers and fathers both came from citizen families. Pericles' motive probably had less to do with Athens' metics than with the dangerous alliances that were created by intermarriage of Athenian aristocratic families with nobles from other *poleis*. Whatever the law's purpose, it made Athens a more closed society and backfired on Pericles.

Pericles married a close relative who bore him two sons, but the union did not last. He divorced his wife and, a few years later (c. 445 B.C.E.), took up with Aspasia, a *hetaira* from Miletus. She lived with him for well over a decade (possibly until his death). After plague carried off Pericles' two older boys, his only surviving male child was a son that Aspasia bore him. To save his *oikos* (his lineage), Pericles had to plead with the assembly to give him an exemption from the law he had sponsored and to grant citizenship to Aspasia's son.

Pericles' bond with Aspasia was (or became in legend) a love match. Athenian gossips circulated the shocking rumor that he kissed her each morning when he left for work and again at evening when he came home. Such affection was considered a sign of an unmanly passion that made him vulnerable to manipulation by his foreign lover. In later years, she was even blamed for pushing him to take the actions that caused the **Peloponnesian War**.

Aspasia was a convenient target for Pericles' opponents, and accurate information about her is difficult to disentangle from their xenophobic and misogynistic propaganda. She was born in Miletus about 470 B.C.E. and may have come to Athens about 450 B.C.E. with an older sister who had married an exiled Athenian aristocrat. Pericles' decree doomed any hope she may have had for a marriage that would have placed her on the same footing as a citizen-wife. Some

Aspasia Greek artists in Pericles' day did not make portraits—especially of women. But sculptors in later generations depicted famous people, such as Aspasia, as ideal types. This bust hints at the beauty and intelligence of one of the few women whom history recalls from an era of great men.

sources refer to her as Pericles' concubine. Some maintain that she was a *hetaira*, a professional entertainer, and some simply call her a whore.

In comic plays from the period, Aspasia is a vamp, a seductress who uses sex to manipulate men. But elsewhere she is described as a highly educated, intelligent woman who taught rhetoric and held her own in debates with the city's philosophers. Several of Socrates' students remarked on his friendship with her and testified to her skill as a conversationalist and speech writer. If she was Pericles' most influential advisor, he might have done worse.

After Pericles' death, Aspasia was taken up by another of Athens' leaders, and his political career profited from her advice and connections. No one knows when or where she died, but unlike most Greek women of her generation, she was not forgotten. For good or ill, she—a foreigner and a woman—had helped to shape Athens' destiny.

Question: What does Aspasia's story imply about attitudes toward women in Pericles' Athens?

Athens' foreign policy in this era reflected the city's growing self-confidence and willingness to take risks. The most audacious decision the Athenian assembly made was to dispatch a fleet to Egypt to assist rebels who were trying to force the Persians out. The campaign bogged down, and in 453 B.C.E. the Persians cornered and obliterated the Athenian expedition.

The two hundred ships that Thucydides, an Athenian historian, says his city lost in Egypt sobered Athens, and in 451 B.C.E. the conservative politician Cimon returned to power and negotiated a five-year truce with the Peloponnesian League. At the same time, Callias, Cimon's former brother-in-law, seems to have come to an agreement with Persia. If so, it was not publicized, for a formal peace with Persia would have undercut the rationale for the Delian League. When the truce ended and a rebellion erupted among some of Athens' allies, Sparta seized the opportunity to invade Attica. Athens then abandoned most of its mainland holdings outside of Attica, and in 445 B.C.E. the two Greek superpowers signed the Thirty Years' Peace—a commitment that proved to be overly optimistic.

The Peloponnesian War   The Thirty Years' Peace gave the Athenians an opportunity to concentrate on trade contacts with the *poleis* of Italy and Sicily. This worried Corinth and Syracuse, a Corinthian colony that was the largest of the Sicilian *poleis*. Tensions increased in 433 B.C.E. when Corcyra, a Corinthian colony on an island off the western coast of Greece, quarreled with Corinth and asked for Athenian help. The ships Athens sent to observe developments intervened in a battle between Corinth and Corcyra, and this prompted Corinth to charge Athens with committing an act of war. Athens exacerbated the situation by ordering Potidaea, a *polis* in Chalcidice (the northern Aegean), to dismantle its defenses. Potidaea was a Corinthian colony, and Athens feared that if war broke out, it might provide the enemy with a base for attacking shipping through the Hellespont and cutting off supplies of grain to Athens. When Potidaea resisted Athens' order (with Corinthian encouragement), Athens had to undertake a lengthy, expensive siege of the city.

As the international situation heated up, the Athenians concluded that they had two options. They could back down, or they could mount a show of force that frightened their enemies into retreating. Pericles preferred the latter strategy and persuaded the assembly to take an action that some of his contemporaries later claimed caused the Peloponnesian War. As a warning to others, Athens closed the ports of its empire to merchants from Megara. This devastated Megara, for it cut off most of its trade.

Corinth appealed to Sparta, and Sparta summoned a meeting of the Peloponnesian League. Fighting did not immediately break out, for factions in both Sparta and Athens were opposed to war. The decision, however, was not left to the superpowers. Sparta's ally Thebes attacked Athens' ally Plataea, and that forced the two great cities to act.

Civil wars are among the most senseless of conflicts, for by squandering the resources of a country, they undermine both victor and vanquished. The Peloponnesian War was a particularly hopeless struggle, for neither combatant knew how to deal with the military strength of the other. The Athenian navy could not harm the Spartan infantry, and the Spartan army could not attack Athens' ships. Pericles assumed that once Sparta understood that it could not deal Athens a lethal blow, Sparta would give up. His trust in the fundamental rationality of human conduct proved to be misplaced.

The War's First Phase   Pericles' strategy for winning the war was to refuse to fight it on the enemy's terms. He talked the Athenians into abandoning the defense of Attica and retreating behind the walls of their city. Thanks to the Long Walls and Athens' control of the sea, Athens could outlast any Spartan siege. Initially, things played out as Pericles predicted. Sparta led an army into Attica and found nothing for it to do but chop down olive trees and uproot vineyards. Sparta's army was shown to be impotent against Athens, but instead of concluding what Pericles took to be self-evident (that is, that the war was unwinnable), Sparta refused to give up.

Pericles' strategy severely tested the discipline of the democracy, for it was as costly to individual citizens as it was to the state. Men were asked to stand idly by while an enemy torched their farms and taunted them with charges of cowardice. The resolve of the Athenian electorate was further tested in the second year of the war when plague spread through the crowded city. About a third of its inhabitants died. Among them were Pericles' elder sons and then Pericles himself.

As time passed and sacrifices mounted, emotion replaced reason in the deliberations of the Athenian assembly, and Athens' democracy began to deteriorate as voters were swayed by the self-serving rhetoric of **demagogues**. Calls for restraint were equated with treason as politicians fanned the flames of jingoism in their attempts to sway the citizenry. Still, the city was slow to lose its moral compass. In 428 B.C.E. four *poleis* on the island of Lesbos declared their intention to secede from Athens' empire. Athens' refusal to engage the Spartans might have led them to conclude that Athens would not fight. If so, they seriously miscalculated. Athens descended on Lesbos in force and quickly retook the island. In a fit of vindictive passion the assembly then dispatched a ship with an order directing the commander on Lesbos to slaughter his captives. Overnight, Athenian tempers cooled and consciences awoke. The assembly reconvened the next day, rescinded its decree, and managed to get word to Lesbos just in time to prevent genocide. The event provides a marker for measuring the effects of prolonged war on the ethics of a democracy. At the time of the Lesbos revolt, the Peloponnesian War was young, and its brutality had not yet lessened the Athenians' respect for the value of human life. Twelve years later, the situation was different. In 416 B.C.E. Athens ordered the tiny island of Melos to join its alliance. When Melos refused, Athens invaded, slaughtered its men, and enslaved its women and children. This time there were no second thoughts and no last-minute reprieves.

In 425 B.C.E. Athens scored a coup. A storm forced an Athenian fleet into the bay at Pylos, which had been abandoned since the fall of its Mycenaean kingdom over seven centuries earlier. Demosthenes, the admiral in charge, recognized the strategic importance of the site and decided to occupy it. The Spartans soon discovered his presence and sent an army to evict him. However, relief forces arrived from Athens and surprised and trapped 420 Spartans on an island in the bay. Sparta, fearing the loss of so many men, promptly sued for peace. But no Athenian politician was willing to urge moderation on an assembly that had a taste of victory. Athens sent enough men to Pylos to overwhelm the blockaded Spartans, and 292 of them were taken alive.

The capture of Spartan hostages at Pylos emboldened the Athenians to abandon Pericles' strategy and pursue the war on land. They attacked Thebes, Sparta's major ally in northern Greece, and were soundly trounced. An even greater loss followed in Chalcidice, where a Spartan general organized an uprising that cost Athens control of key ports on the crucial Hellespont grain route. The panicky assembly blamed the loss on an Athenian admiral named Thucydides and banished him. Posterity is grateful, for Thucydides devoted his enforced leisure to writing an extraordinary history of the war that preoccupied his generation.

Athens' ardor for war cooled. In the spring of 423 B.C.E. it endorsed a temporary cessation of hostilities. Two years later, Nicias, an Athenian general, negotiated a treaty that was supposed to end the war. Athens promised to withdraw from Pylos and Sparta from Chalcidice. Both states pledged to maintain the peace for 50 years. The treaty was a de facto defeat for Sparta, and several of its allies refused to sign. When ports in Chalcidice declined to submit to Athens, Athens refused to give up Pylos.

Interlude in Sicily   The treaty did not resolve the issues that had caused the war, so it was not likely to hold. Athens should therefore have proceeded with caution. Instead, it committed itself to a campaign on the distant island of Sicily. The chief advocate for the ill-advised expedition was Alcibiades (c. 450–404 B.C.E.), Pericles' nephew and one of the philosopher Socrates' students. Nicias, the elder statesman who had negotiated peace with Sparta, opposed it, but Alcibiades was the more appealing politician. Young, rich, handsome, intelligent, and totally unprincipled, he carried the day. The best that his opponents could do was to persuade the assembly to split command of the expedition among Alcibiades and two older generals, one of whom was Nicias. The night before the fleet sailed, many sacred images were vandalized in Athens. This blasphemy had to be punished lest the gods turn against the city, and the finger of suspicion pointed at a group of young rowdies led by Alcibiades. A ship was sent to Sicily to bring him home for trial. Rather than risk conviction, Alcibiades chose to defect to

Sparta. Nicias was left with responsibility for a campaign he had opposed, and the project's sponsor, Alcibiades, began to plot with the Spartans to bring about its failure.

Athens had committed about 25,000 men and 250 ships to the invasion of Sicily, but this was not enough. Nicias claimed that twice as many were needed, and he urged the assembly to allow him to withdraw. It chose instead to send him more troops. The Spartans countered by dispatching a general to organize the defense of Syracuse, the great Sicilian city that Nicias was besieging. Syracuse's navy first trapped the Athenian fleet in its harbor. Then Syracuse's army outflanked and began to encircle the Greek camp. Seeing that the situation was hopeless, Nicias ordered his men to scatter and try to save themselves. All of them (some 40,000) were captured. Nicias was executed, and his men were either enslaved or herded into a quarry and left to die from thirst and exposure. The loss of the army rendered Athens defenseless, but the city was unaware of that fact until a visitor to the port of the Piraeus casually mentioned the disaster to his barber.

Sparta could not pass up the opportunity presented by Athens' vulnerability. While Alcibiades moved through the Aegean urging members of the Athenian empire to revolt, Sparta established a fort on the edge of Attica as a retreat for runaway Athenian slaves. Some 20,000 defected and helped the Spartans lay Attica under permanent siege.

The War's Final Phase   Athens' fortunes had sunk suddenly and dramatically, but the city refused to give in. The war dragged on for another eight years and was finally ended by the intervention of Persia. The Spartans decided that they had to meet the Athenians on their own turf (metaphorically) by taking to the sea, and Persia financed the fleets with which Sparta pursued Athens' navy. Alcibiades may have arranged this, but when news of the hyperactive young man's affair with the Spartan king's wife leaked out, he fled Sparta for Persian territory. There he tried to make a deal that would allow him to return to Athens. The Persians were willing to offer Athens assistance, for it was to their advantage to help the Greeks destroy one another. All that was needed, Alcibiades said, was for Athens to replace democracy with a form of government that Persia regarded as more reliable. The Athenian elite promptly staged a coup that disenfranchised most of the *polis's* citizens. But when news of this reached the sailors of the fleet, they threatened to mutiny and elected new generals—one of whom was Alcibiades! Democracy was restored, and under Alcibiades' leadership the Athenians won several victories. However, suspicion of further double dealing prompted Athens to exile Alcibiades in 406 B.C.E. and replace him with incompetent admirals whose blunders assured the city's defeat.

In 404 B.C.E. Lysander, the Spartan admiral, destroyed the Athenian navy, blockaded Athens, and starved it into submission. Sparta allowed Athens to survive, for it wanted to block the expansion of Athens' ambitious neighbor, Thebes. But Sparta ordered the Athenians to tear down the Long Walls and limit their fleet to a mere dozen ships. Athens' days of military glory were over, but the city's fame as a cultural center endured.

Sparta profited little from its victory, for it was poorly equipped by tradition, experience, and manpower to lead the Aegean world. It also alienated the Greeks by ceding Ionia to Persia as repayment for its war debt. Persia, for its part, continued to fund the Greeks' internecine quarrels. Rebellions erupted against Sparta, and in 371 B.C.E.

Thebes, led by a brilliant general named Epaminondas, defeated Sparta and ended its hegemony. Thebes declined following Epaminondas's death a few years later, and without a dominant *polis* to maintain order, local wars proliferated. The Greeks continued to tear at the fabric of their civilization.

Only a little more than a century separated the victory at Marathon (490 B.C.E.) from the confusion that attended Sparta's fall (371 B.C.E.). From the military perspective, that century was bloody, wasteful, and disastrous. Surprisingly, however, the carnage did not impede the work of artists and intellectuals. In the midst of the tumult, they created the artistic and literary monuments that made these years a classic era in Western civilization.

Intellectual and Artistic Life in the *Polis*

Traditional wisdom held that the world was a product of divine forces and that the causes of things were mysteries hidden in the minds of gods. The explanation for earthly phenomena lay, therefore, in a realm that human beings could not explore. During the sixth century B.C.E. some Greek thinkers from Ionia began to question such beliefs. They demystified the world and conceived of it as an orderly place governed by intelligible principles that could be discovered by observation and rational analysis. For centuries people had collected data about the world in order to improve their ability to manipulate things, but the Greeks went further. They invented science, the disinterested search simply for an understanding of how things worked.

The rationality of the Greek mind should not be overemphasized, for Greek culture had its dark side. The Greeks believed that there were mysteries and truths that could be grasped only through intuition, feeling, or divine revelation. They invented potent myths and symbols that still engage our imaginations. They were capable of bloody deeds. They cultivated trances and ecstatic experiences, and they thrilled at stories of mutilation, incest, and cannibalism. They believed in magic, rituals, spells, visions, dreams, omens, and oracles, and they bowed before inexplicable forces they called fate or chance. Classical civilization was not a simple or even self-consistent phenomenon.

From Myth to Philosophy and Science   The *Iliad* and the *Odyssey*, which were composed in Ionia in the mid-eighth century B.C.E., belong to the most ancient of literary genres—the hero epic, the story of people who are larger than life. During the seventh and sixth centuries B.C.E., the Greeks began to produce a different kind of poetry—lyrics, short songs inspired by the personal feelings of real individuals. These intimate and sometimes confessional poems mark a shift of interest among the Greeks from fantasies about the past to the real situations people face in the present. The greatest lyric poet of the archaic period (750–500 B.C.E.) was an aristocratic woman named Sappho (fl. c. 600 B.C.E.), a native of the island of Lesbos. Only fragments of her work survive, but her passionate love songs were so exquisitely constructed that they joined Homer's epics as standard texts in ancient Greece's schools.

The lyric poets' interest in the real world was shared by their contemporaries, the first thinkers to seek rational alternatives to the mythic view of nature. Greeks called these people philosophers, "lovers of wisdom." They set aside stories about the gods and proposed natural explanations for natural phenomena.

Thales (fl. c. 550 B.C.E.), from the Ionian city of Miletus, pioneered the field of metaphysics, the search for the fundamental principles of existence. He was fascinated by the fact that things around us are constantly changing, yet the world remains a stable, permanent place. How, he wondered, could change and permanence, which are opposites, coexist in the same system? That the world maintains a balance between them suggested to Thales that there was a more fundamental reality, a single "substance" ("something standing under"), that controlled them. Such a substance had to be able to exist as a solid, a liquid, and a gas, for all these states are found in nature. Thales knew only one thing that fit the bill: water. He concluded, therefore, that everything that exists is a form of water. Things hold together because their contrasts are more apparent than real. In actuality, only one thing exists, a watery substance that naturally assumes different states of being.

Thales' followers, the **Monist** ("single principle") philosophers, taught that change was only a shift among the states that are natural to the one eternal substance that underlies all things. They disagreed, however, about the identity of that substance. Anaximander (c. 611–546 B.C.E.) objected that nothing we could experience with our senses (such as water) was complex enough to account for the variety of things found in nature. He postulated, therefore, that the ultimate substance was "the indefinite," a material that is never directly perceived in its pure essence, but only as it manifests aspects of itself in particular things. His successor, Anaximenes (d. c. 500 B.C.E.), was not convinced. He pointed out that an unknowable substance offered no better explanation for the world than an unknowable god. To explain anything, Anaximenes said, the ultimate substance had to be something identifiable. He proposed air. Just as the "breath of life" sustains the human body, he theorized that air maintains and activates the universe.

The problem with these theories was that they were unverifiable. This led some thinkers to suspect that their premise was incorrect. The Monists had begun by asking how opposites like change and permanence coexist, but what if change and permanence do not exist? What if only one of them is real and the other is an illusion?

Heracleitus of Ephesus (fl. c. 500 B.C.E.) argued that permanence was the illusion. Things that change more slowly than we do appear permanent to us, but in actuality everything is constantly changing. Being is analogous to a flowing river, and no one, he pointed out, can step into the same river twice. If we need to imagine a primal substance for the world, we should envision it as fire, pure energy. Parmenides of Elea (fl. fifth century B.C.E.) came to the opposite conclusion, for he regarded change as an illogical concept. Change implies that something new has come into being. There are only two ways this could happen, and neither is possible. If a change comes from what already exists, there is nothing new and therefore no change. If a change comes from something that does not exist, then nothing has created something, which is absurd. Nothing is the absence of being, not a kind of being with the power to cause something else to be. Therefore, Parmenides insisted the universe must be an inert solid. Empty space in which movement might take place cannot exist. Emptiness is nothingness, and nothingness means nonexistence.

The Classical Era	
POLITICS	**ARTISTS AND INTELLECTUALS**
[600–500 B.C.E.**]**	
Solon (c. 638–c. 559) Peisistratus (fl. c. 560) Cyrus the Great (c. 600–530) Cleisthenes (fl. c. 507)	Sappho (fl. c. 600) Thales (c. 640–546) Anaximander (611–547) Anaximenes (d. c. 528) Pythagoras (d. c. 497) Aeschylus (525–456)
[500–400 B.C.E.**]**	
Miletus's rebellion (499–494) Darius invades Greece (492) Xerxes' campaign (484–479) Peloponnesian War (431–404) Pericles (490–429)	Heracleitus (fl. c. 500) Parmenides (fl. c. 500) Hecataeus (fl. c. 550–480) Sophocles (496–406) Empedocles (493–433) Protagoras (d. c. 421) Euripides (485–406) Herodotus (480–425) Socrates (469–399) Democritus (460–347) Hippocrates (460–377) Thucydides (460–399) Aristophanes (450–385) Plato (429–347)
[400–300 B.C.E.**]**	
Thebes defeats Sparta (371) Philip of Macedon (r. 359–336) Alexander the Great (r. 336–323)	Aristotle (384–322)

The rigorous logic of Heracleitus and Parmenides led to dead-end conclusions and a description of the world that defied common sense. The **Pluralist** ("multiple things") philosophers therefore hoped that by reconciling the arguments of these two thinkers, they might find a logically coherent explanation for the natural world that was consistent with ordinary experience. The Pluralists claimed that changing configurations of a number of different, but permanent, components create the world we experience. Empedocles of Agrigentum (fl. c. 450 B.C.E.) suggested that everything that exists is a product of the interaction of four fundamental elements ("irreducibles"): earth, air, fire, and water. The elements themselves never change, but their combinations do. Democritus of Abdera (c. 460–370 B.C.E.) felt that a few elements were insufficient to explain the great diversity of things found in the world. Like the Monists, he believed that only one substance existed, but that it existed in the form of discrete atoms ("indivisibles"). These were innumerable, eternal bits of a material that had only primary characteristics (size, shape, and location). All secondary attributes (such as color and odor) were mere impressions created by interactions among the atoms. Human beings and all they experience were the result of shifting agglomerations of atoms.

Democritus reduced the universe to a mechanism: a swirl of physical objects that randomly come together and split apart. This implied that existence has no meaning, but it encouraged the development of science by suggesting that mathematical measurements of physical changes might suffice to explain everything. A century earlier, Pythagoras, a contemporary of the Ionian Monists, had proposed something similar. Pythagoras concluded from the mathematical relationships that exist between sounds (pitches) and physical objects (lengths of plucked string) that mathematics provided the key to unlocking the mysteries of the universe.

Greek science developed these portentous theories largely by intuition and imagination, but speculation alone could carry science no further. Unless hard data could be found to confirm the existence of Empedocles' elements and Democritus's atoms, they were no more helpful in explaining the universe than were the gods. Two thousand years passed before the West invented instruments that could gather the information needed to test the ancient Greek hypotheses. Consequently, thinkers ended this line of inquiry and turned their attention to questions of a different kind.

Medicine   Greek science tended to trust rational argument more than observation and to be abstract and theoretical, but it also made advances in applied fields—particularly medicine. Hippocrates of Cos (c. 460–377 B.C.E.), Democritus's contemporary, acquired such a reputation as a healer that modern physi-

Ideal Humanity   The scientific and artistic interests of the Greeks converged in the production of the *kouros,* a free-standing statue of a nude youth. The sculptors of these works sought to depict the essence of real, if idealized, humanity: the male athlete at the peak of his development, devoid of all concealment, ornament, or artifice. The rigid standardized posture of these statues abstracted them from time and place. They represented male existence, not an individual man caught in a particular moment or action. The rigid posture was also doubtless influenced by the conventions of Egyptian painting and sculpture.

cians take a vow to honor the principles he allegedly established for the conduct of their profession. Almost no dependable information survives about him, but about 300 B.C.E. Greek scholars collected a body of medical literature that they claimed stemmed from his school. It influenced the practice of medicine for over two millennia.

Much ancient healing relied on spells and charms, but the Hippocratic tradition was relatively free of superstition. It sought natural causes for physical problems, relied on observation to diagnose them, and sought to cure them with drugs, surgery, and changes in diet and regimen. The treatment it offered was primitive, but its method had merit. Medicine did not make much more progress until the early modern era, when the microscope and advances in chemistry began to provide new clues to the mechanisms of disease and human physiology.

History   The invention of history was another sign of the Greek's preoccupation with science. The word *historia* ("inquiry") originally meant an investigation by a judge (a *histor*) into the facts of a dispute. A *histor* became a historian when he broadened his inquiry and searched for explanations for larger events.

It may seem odd to speak of the invention of something like history. Because human beings have memories, it is obvious that they have always been aware of the past. Early civilizations even compiled annals and lists of the names of kings or other officials and dated events by assigning them to years in the reigns of certain rulers or priests. The peoples of Egypt and the Middle East had accumulated much more of this material than the Greeks, whose civilization was comparatively young. But it was the Greeks who turned records of this kind into history by looking for patterns that made the past meaningful. Most of their neighbors dismissed history's panorama as transitory and meaningless or as a byproduct of mysterious struggles among the gods. Parts of the Hebrew Bible foreshadow history, but there, too, the past was of interest primarily as a revelation of God's will. Greece's historians, like its philosophers, were curious to see how far they could go in explaining the world in purely human terms.

History developed from geography. The Greeks of the archaic era were traders and colonizers who needed accurate information about foreign lands. Anaximenes, the Monist philosopher, was also a cartographer. He produced a map of the world, and one of his contemporaries was ancient Greece's first great cultural geographer, Hecataeus of Miletus (fl. c. 500 B.C.E.). Hecataeus believed that information of all kinds (topography, climate, plants, animals, religions, customs, and institutions) was needed to make foreign lands intelligible. (Hippocratic physicians agreed—maintaining that hard environments produced hardy people and that rich lands undermined both strength and character.) Herodotus of Halicarnassus (480–425 B.C.E.), the "father of history," began as a geographer building on the work of Hecataeus.

At a time when literate people were few and manuscripts rare, authors like Herodotus made their livings by giving lectures and public readings. They resembled Homeric bards and were regarded as entertainers. But what Herodotus offered his audiences was something different from Homer's epics. Poetry was the traditional medium for sacred myth and serious literature. Even secular leaders like Athens'

Solon wrote poems to explain their political agenda. But Herodotus composed prose. Anaximenes was the first major thinker from whom we have a few lines of prose. Prose signaled science's break with sacred myths and legends. Herodotus learned much about storytelling from Homer, but his use of prose declared his intention to depart from the epic tradition and view the past from the perspective of the new secular science.

Herodotus began by writing ethnographical studies in the style of Hecataeus— sketches of life in exotic locales like Egypt and Babylon. But when he visited Athens, he found the theme that transformed descriptive geography into history. The Athens Herodotus experienced was fresh from its victories over the Persians and riding the crest of a wave of self-confidence. The city's heady environment persuaded Herodotus that, thanks to the Greeks and particularly the Athenians, the world was on the brink of a glorious new age. He decided to try to explain how this had come about and suspected that the answer was to be found in a study of the Persian War. The war had pitted the might of a despotic empire against the will of a free people, and freedom had proved invincible. The Greek victory had changed the world by revealing for the first time what a free society could achieve.

The generation that had fought the Persian War was dying out by the time Herodotus arrived in Athens, and his history of it appeared during the early years of the Peloponnesian War. He may have wanted to remind his readers of what their ancestors had achieved by working together, but he probably did not expect this to divert them from their current path. Herodotus suspected that events were not entirely under human control. Individuals certainly affected what happened, but chance also played a role, as did a mysterious force that maintained a cosmic balance in the universe. Some outcomes seemed fated no matter what people did: Wealth and power undermined themselves; fortune and happiness did not last forever.

The era that invented history produced two of the West's greatest historians. Herodotus was about 20 years old when his future Athenian colleague, Thucydides (460–399 B.C.E.), was born. The two men not only worked in the same field; they treated complementary subjects. Herodotus told the story of the "good" war that launched Greece's Golden Age, and Thucydides narrated the sad tale of the willful conflict that frittered away Greece's opportunities. There were differences in their approaches to their common subject. Herodotus was not overly credulous. He went out of his way to check information and find reliable sources. Sometimes he warned his readers that they should not assume that he believed every story that he felt obliged to tell. He was, however, a religious man who trusted in omens and who felt that human agency alone could not explain history. For Thucydides, history was simply an account of human decisions and their consequences.

Thucydides was an aristocratic Athenian who was deeply immersed in his city's political and intellectual life. An intuitive sense of the importance of the time and place in which he found himself inspired him to do something that had never been done before: to record history as it unfolded. He had time and opportunity, for a few years after the Peloponnesian War began the Athenians blamed him for losing a battle and exiled him for 20 years.

Thucydides claimed that the proper subjects for a historian were politics and war, and he rigorously excluded everything else from his narrative. He believed that events could be explained as the outcomes of decisions that individuals made and that these decisions were rooted in the intelligence and character of their authors. No gods or mysterious powers intervened. An element of chance affected how situations played out, but chance was not a mystical force (a providence, fate, or destiny). Chance entered in because the human ability to anticipate developments and plan for every possible contingency is limited. Thucydides viewed human beings as fundamentally rational agents who are motivated by self-interest. Pursuit of power is part of their nature, and the strong always dominate the weak. The study of history has much to teach, he insisted, because human nature does not change. We learn about ourselves by analyzing the motives of our predecessors and the consequences of their actions. What ultimately counts is developing the skill we need to bring about the outcomes we want.

Philosophy, Psychology, and Politics

Natural scientists and physicians work by observing phenomena and collecting and rationally analyzing data, but Greek thinkers of Thucydides' generation wrestled with the troubling discovery that what is observed depends, in part, on the observer. They knew that the unaided human senses (their primary scientific instruments) could deceive them. They concluded, therefore, that to learn more about the world, they had to learn more about themselves. In the interim between the Persian and Peloponnesian Wars (the 470s and 460s B.C.E.), Greek philosophers shifted their attention from the external world of the senses to the internal world of the human psyche. They began to analyze thought itself—to work out the mechanics of logic, explore the emotions, and ask themselves what "truth" meant. Some wondered if such a thing existed.

The earlier Greek philosophers, who focused their attention on the natural world, are called the "**pre-Socratics**." This suggests that the Athenian thinker Socrates (469–399 B.C.E.) was responsible for the major shift that took place in philosophy's focus, but philosophy's reorientation actually began with his teachers, professional educators called Sophists. Sophists taught public speaking and the arts of persuasion, valuable skills in a democracy. Their study of the uses of language led them to explore how the mind forms concepts and opinions and caused them to wonder what words like *justice, virtue,* and *truth* really signify.

Relativism was in the air that Socrates breathed. Colonization and trade had brought the Greeks into contact with all kinds of people, and the knowledge that alternative cultures existed was causing some Greeks to question their traditional values and institutions. Furthermore, the Sophist sellers of oratorical training claimed that truth, if it was even knowable, was irrelevant. A skillful speaker could make weak causes appear strong and black look white. There were no absolute standards or values, for as Protagoras (493–421 B.C.E.), one of the leading Sophists, succinctly put it, "Man is the measure of all things." One person sees things one way, and another sees them differently. Both are "right," for no one can rise above his or her individual perspective and grasp pure, objective truth. We might prefer one opinion to another, but only because it is useful or consistent with our preconceptions, not because it is true.

This radical skepticism had alarming implications. It undercut the possibility of shared values and objective standards and justified selfish individualism. If everything is simply a matter of personal opinion, how can people justify the laws and values that make it possible for them to form communities? How can they maintain a *polis*? The Greeks valued the individual, but believed that individuals were formed by community life. Citizenship in a *polis* made them what they were, and citizenship implied a duty to subordinate self-interest to the common good.

Socrates devoted himself to the search for an alternative to the relativism and skepticism of the Sophists. Because he never wrote anything, we know him today only through the reports of others—and those reports differ significantly. The most elaborate descriptions of his conversations (he would not have said "teachings") are dialogues penned by his devoted pupil Plato (c. 429–347 B.C.E.). These are imaginative recreations, not verbatim reports, and it is likely that they tell us more about Plato than Socrates.

In Plato's dialogues, Socrates is an ingenious debater who spends his life forcing people to justify their beliefs. He delights in revealing the absurd and contradictory implications of the commonsense opinions held by his fellow Athenians. He is adept at demolishing belief systems and unwilling to propose anything to take their place. Some people, like Plato himself, were devoted to Socrates for liberating them from sterile complacency and teaching them how to think; others considered him a nuisance or a threat to the beliefs on which the *polis* was based.

In the wake of the Peloponnesian War, the Athenians struggled with humiliation and self-doubt, and they had little tolerance for intellectual gadflies. Citizens of a democracy are responsible for what their government does. When it flourishes, they congratulate themselves; but when it blunders, they look for scapegoats on whom to place the blame. Socrates' habit of questioning the legitimacy of traditional values made him a convenient target. He may indeed have had little respect for democracy, a form of government guided by the kinds of commonly held opinions he delighted in demolishing. Socrates was indicted, tried, and convicted on a charge of corrupting the youth of Athens by undercutting their faith in the gods and the wisdom of their elders. This was a capital offense, but Athens, having made its point, was not eager to put a defenseless old man to death. Socrates was given an opportunity to flee, but he insisted on being executed. He told his friends that having been protected by Athens' laws all his life, he could not reject the authority of those laws just because they were now inconvenient. His death was perhaps his ultimate attempt to refute relativists and skeptics. It implied that rational people have an innate obligation to something more than personal self-interest.

Plato, Socrates' ardent disciple, was determined to justify belief in the existence of truth, and he thought he found the evidence he needed in the way our minds organize the things we perceive. When we encounter a thing, we assign it to a class of objects. A collie does not look much like a dachshund, but somehow when we see either of these animals (even the first time), we know that it is a dog. Plato believed that this was only possible if all the members of a class had something in common that our minds recognize—a defining reality that he called a form or an idea. Their form or idea makes them what they are even if it manifests itself somewhat differently in each individual. Plato claimed that the forms are eternal and exist apart from the particular things that we experience. We recognize dogs because our minds are born with some previous experience of "dogness," of the pure ideal that makes a dog a dog. Plato noted that our knowledge of a class of things becomes more accurate as we study more individuals belonging to that class. By combining multiple examples, we discover the higher category of being that each individual only partially represents. What is true of individual objects is also true of individual ideas. They, too, fit into categories, and those categories compose a hierarchy of increasingly abstract ideas. The class of dogs, for instance, is subsumed in the class of animals, and the class of animals, in higher and higher classes until we arrive at the ultimate idea—all-encompassing Truth. Plato's theory—that the world of sense experience is less real than a realm of pure intelligibility (which is accessible only to the mind)—has a mystical aspect that has long appealed to religious thinkers. Some of them have equated his ultimate Idea, which intuits all things, with what they mean by divinity.

Plato was born after the Peloponnesian War began, and the Athens he knew was a *polis* that labored, and finally broke, under the strains of that campaign. The great experiment with democracy that Athens had conducted was not an unqualified success. In the opinion of scholarly aristocrats, such as Plato and Thucydides, democracy tended to degenerate into mob rule. The ideal state that Plato conceived in his youth, therefore, was not a democracy like the one that had executed his beloved teacher Socrates. Plato hypothesized instead that power ought to be entrusted only to persons who had the knowledge and self-control to use it wisely. The best form of government was one that vested all authority in individuals whom nature had especially equipped to rule. When citizens of democratic societies (like Plato) lose confidence in themselves, they tend to look for a savior, a person with extraordinary gifts that will supposedly enable him or her to do for the people what the people have failed to do for themselves. The young Plato pinned his hope for the future on such saviors, and he even tried (and failed) to educate one. As he aged, he came to doubt that any individual could be trusted to use power disinterestedly. In his last work, he turned his attention from his earlier efforts to model an ideal state to drafting what he hoped would be a practical set of laws for a real community—one populated by people who struggle to reconcile their private desires with their obligations to society.

Among Plato's students was a youth named Aristotle (384–322 B.C.E.), who was destined to join him in the ranks of the West's greatest intellects. Unlike Plato, Aristotle was not an Athenian and not from an aristocratic family. His father was a physician who served the king of Macedonia. At about the age of 17 Aristotle came to Athens to work in Plato's school, the Academy. He remained there for 20 years, leaving only on Plato's death, when leadership of the school passed to Plato's nephew. About 335 B.C.E. he returned to Athens to found a school of his own, the Lyceum. He remained there until a year before his death, when a deteriorating political situation caused him to move to the nearby island of Euboea.

There were differences between Aristotle and Plato, but given their long association, these things should probably not be overemphasized. Aristotle followed Plato in believing that our knowledge of the world is the result of our ability to recognize the universal ideas or forms that are partially realized in individual things. He departed from his master, however, in rejecting the thesis that the ideas have a separate existence in a realm of their own. This disagreement reflected the differing intellectual preferences of the two men. Plato was drawn to the study of mathematics. He relied primarily on reason to develop explanations for the things that interested him. Consequently, he saw the world in terms of static abstractions. Aristotle, too, was intrigued by the processes of rational thought. He was the first to articulate the rules of logic that govern valid arguments. But Aristotle preferred to reason from information obtained by observation. His standard method was to collect and describe specific specimens and then propose general theories to explain their attributes. Like a modern scientist, he amassed data and looked for hypotheses that could make sense out of the information that he had collected. Consequently, he had a more dynamic view of the world than Plato. He saw it as an evolving place in which things strove to realize their innate potential—that is, to become rather than simply to be.

Aristotle believed the universe to be a coherent system of things moving toward ends or goals. Because motion cannot be perceived or defined without a fixed point of reference, he argued that the universe had its origin in what he called a "prime mover"—an unmovable reality that inaugurated the motion (or change) that characterizes existence. Christian theologians were later to find his argument for an "unmoved mover" a persuasive proof for the existence of the Bible's creator God. Aristotle was fascinated by every aspect of nature and human behavior. He brought order to the information he gathered by dividing it into separate fields or disciplines, and he produced treatises on everything from biology, zoology, and psychology to ethics, politics, poetics, logic, and metaphysics. The result was a vast amount of data organized and fit into a logical framework of explanation. Later generations of scholars were so impressed that many of them came to regard Aristotle's opinions as definitive.

Aristotle was, however, very much a man of his time, and reason did not prevent him from absorbing the common beliefs and prejudices of his day. He, for instance, thought that there was abundant evidence in nature for the inferiority of females. The male, he argued, was the human prototype. Females were produced when something went wrong with the processes of conception and gestation. The result of their failure to reach completion, Aristotle claimed, was the birth of a kind of diminished and castrated male, the physically weaker and intellectually inferior creature known as a woman. Its limitations necessitated its subordination to men and justified its exclusion from public life. What was true of women was also true of some categories of men. Aristotle agreed with Plato that human beings could reach their full potential only by participating in the life of a *polis*. But participation was possible and appropriate only for men rich enough to afford the leisure time needed for education and public service. Aristotle, like Plato and others of the post-Peloponnesian War generation, was no fan of the kind of radical democracy with which Athens had experimented.

The Arts and Politics   The Greeks practiced all the arts known to us and some that we no longer regard as fine arts. The influence of the remnants of their architecture and sculpture has been and remains incalculable, but their achievements in other media are harder to assess. We know that they produced skilled painters. Athens had a state art collection, which it displayed in a public gallery on the Acropolis. Fragmentary mosaic copies of a few paintings exist. But because none of the original work has survived, no one knows what it was like. Greek music and dance are also lost. The Greeks experimented with musical notation systems, but did not succeed in developing and standardizing an adequate one. Sculptors and vase painters depicted dancers, but it is difficult to infer choreography from frozen images. The texts of some ancient tragedies and comedies have survived, but words were only part of the experience of Greek theater. It was a multifaceted art that combined dance, music, costuming, and conventions of acting that are hard for us now to imagine.

Much Hellenic art was public art. That is, it was meant to educate and inspire citizens, to impress a *polis's* allies, and to intimidate its enemies. There was, however, an art that served private collectors: pottery painting. The Greeks turned the decoration of pottery into high art. Their jars, bowls, and cups were in demand throughout the ancient world, and they provide us with invaluable pictorial documentation of Hellenic society.

The Minoans and Mycenaeans produced sophisticated pottery decorated in multiple colors with naturalistic figures, but it was replaced during the Aegean Dark Age by a novel "geometric" style. Geometric pottery, as its name implies, featured bands of repetitive, abstract figures. It was an art that celebrated order and control, the preoccupations of a world struggling to rebuild. About 700 B.C.E., black-figure pottery appeared. Its images were painted in black glaze against a red background of fired, unglazed clay. Red-figure ware, the pinnacle of the Greek potter's art, emerged in the second half of the sixth century B.C.E. Its practitioners achieved greater realism by painting backgrounds in black

Red-Figure Pottery   Pottery painting is not usually regarded as a high art today, but it was much respected in the ancient world. This hydra (a container for water) was signed by one of the pioneer Athenian red-figure artists, Phintias (c. 525 B.C.E.). It depicts a teacher of a musical instrument called a lyre instructing a student. It is, therefore, a valuable historical document as well as a work of art.

glaze and letting the color of unglazed pottery represent the ruddy skin tones of their human figures. The drafting skills of the great pottery painters were extraordinary. Although they worked on curved surfaces, they were able to give figures volume, substance, and convincing proportions. They provide us with more intimate knowledge of the lives of the Greeks than we have for most other ancient people.

Greek sculptors worked in wood, stone, and bronze, and also assembled monumental figures from sheets of ivory and gold. Much of what they made survives today only in Roman copies. The principles of classicism (balance, restraint, simplicity, and harmony of proportions) are clearly apparent in their work (particularly in their treatment of their favorite subject, the human form). They did not record the idiosyncrasies of their models but created ideal human types. Males were more commonly represented than females. Greek science, as noted previously, maintained that the perfect human form was male. Female figures were usually clothed, but males were nude. Perfection was a matter of essence, not decoration or other enhancement.

The consummate examples of Greek architecture are temples. Greek temples were not analogous to modern churches, synagogues, or mosques, for they were not built to house worshiping congregations. They sheltered images of gods and goddesses and provided storage space for sacred treasures. Public religious ceremonies were held at outdoor altars, for which a temple's façade provided a backdrop.

Greeks practiced multiple religions simultaneously. Families maintained household shrines and venerated sacred objects inherited from their ancestors. Many individuals sought initiation into mystery cults whose secret rituals and teachings promised them spiritual support. Magicians cast spells to promote fertility or to curse enemies. Trust in omens and oracles was widespread. Greece's official pantheon consisted of relatives and courtiers of Zeus, an Indo-European sky-deity associated with Olympus, a mountain on Greece's northeastern frontier. The "Olympians" were the household gods of the state, the guardians of the *polis*, and their temples celebrated the principles on which it was founded.

Unlike the soaring complexity of a Gothic cathedral, a Greek temple was not meant to inspire a sense of transcendent mystery. Its purpose was to confirm the Greeks' belief that the world was fundamentally intelligible. The principles of a temple's construction—its stout pillars supporting horizontal lintels and a low-pitched roof—were meant to be immediately obvious and reassuring. Its symmetry, balance, and proportion reflected the stability and rationality that was fundamental to the order of nature.

Hellenic architects created three styles. The earliest, the Doric, featured sturdy, fluted pillars with plain, flat capitals and no bases. The pediments on the façades of its temples were filled with statuary. The second style, the Ionic, was inspired by the elegant arts of the Middle East. It was light, refined, and highly decorated. Its pillars were slender columns with bases and capitals sculpted to resemble curved ram's horns. The third style, the Corinthian, spread in the wake of the Peloponnesian War and reflected values associated with the decline of *poleis* and the rise of empires. Corinthian buildings were imposing and florid. Their pillars had capitals resembling sheaves of acanthus leaves (a plant common to the Mediterranean region).

Some Greek temples had no roofs or pillared façades. They were amphitheaters. Drama (comedy as well as tragedy) was a sacred ceremony, and actors had the status of

The Greek Architectural Orders   This drawing represents the three styles of ancient Greek architecture. The Doric was the earliest and simplest and the Corinthian the latest and most grandiose. Although Greek temples were often constructed from a pure, white marble, they, like the statues of the era, were frequently painted. They might, therefore, have appeared somewhat garish to the modern eye.

priests. The Greek plays were staged to honor Dionysus, the inebriated god of the vineyard. His intoxication represented the power of the irrational—of ecstacy, inspiration, and feeling.

Theater's conventions evolved from rural holidays that featured dancing and singing. The tyrant Peisistratus may have introduced these celebrations to Athens. He is alleged to have established the **Great Dionysia,** a spring festival for which the plays that survive were written. The theater was not a mere entertainment. It was a civic duty. Everyone was expected to attend. Wealthy citizens were honored publicly for funding productions. Hundreds of men and boys took part as singers and dancers, and prestigious prizes were awarded to the playwrights who won the audience's favor. Theatergoing was serious, arduous business. During the four days of the Great Dionysia, Athenians sat through 16 or more plays. Each playwright who won a slot at the festival had to create enough plays to fill the bill for an entire day.

Because Dionysus was attended by satyrs (men with the loins and legs of goats), hymns to him were called tragedies ("goat songs"). Originally, these took the form of dithyrambs, anthems sung and danced by choruses. Drama, as we know it, was allegedly born in the sixth century B.C.E. when a poet named Thespis made dialogue possible by separating a soloist from the chorus. (The modern term for actor, *thespian*, honors his memory.) Early Greek plays devoted a great deal of space to choruses and were written so that one or two actors could perform all the parts. Later plays reduced the role of the chorus, but authors of tragedies never employed more than three actors. The rules governing comedy were less strict. All performers were male, and because they wore masks and elaborate costumes, men could play women and take multiple roles as different characters. Masks were functional as well as traditional. Plays were staged in huge amphitheaters that seated thousands. Superb acoustical design meant that a trained actor's voice could be heard without difficulty, but many in the audience were seated so far from the stage that they could not have seen facial expressions and subtle gestures. Actors had to be magnified to make them visible. They performed on elevated stages above the level where the chorus danced and sang. Padded costumes, elevator shoes, and large masks enhanced their stature, but these ponderous outfits forced them to move carefully and to use choreographed, stylized gestures. They could not stage convincing fights or engage in violent action. Incidents of this kind took place offstage and were described to the audience by speeches from the actors or chorus. Scenery and props were limited, and Greek audiences (like Shakespeare's) were expected to use their imaginations to supply sets for the action.

The oldest complete plays we have from the ancient Greek theater are those of Aeschylus (525–456 B.C.E.), a veteran of the battle at Marathon. (It was this service to his *polis* and not his literary achievement that he ordered recorded on his tombstone.) Aeschylus was 26 when his first tragedy was produced. He continued to write throughout his long life, creating a total of 80 or 90 plays. Among the seven that survive is our only nearly complete bill for a day in the Athenian theater, the *Oresteia*, a trilogy (cycle of three plays) staged at the Great Dionysia in the year 458 B.C.E. Aeschylus's earliest extant play is unusual in that it treats a historical event (the Persian War). Playwrights customarily chose themes from sacred mythology. Aeschylus's dramas have long choruses, and his characters and plots deal with clashes of ideas more than with the behavior of realistic people. His gods harshly punish men who overstep human bounds, and the society he describes is preoccupied with codes of honor and duty to blood kin.

Sophocles (496–406 B.C.E.), Aeschylus's younger contemporary, was a member of the Athenian democracy's second generation, and his was a different mental universe. He was a politically active aristocrat, a friend of Pericles, who served as treasurer of the Delian League. Despite a busy public life, he found time to write 123 plays. Seven survive, some of which (particularly *Oedipus Rex* and *Antigone*) are perennial favorites with modern audiences. Sophocles reduced the role of the chorus, wrote compelling dialogue, and created characters that undergo psychological transformations. He was intrigued by competing moral obligations and by the fact that people never have enough information to know how the decisions they make will turn out. He pondered the relationship of society's laws to the higher obligations intuited by ethically sensitive individuals. He claimed that the moral order of the universe holds us accountable for the consequences of our actions—whether they are intended or not.

Euripides (485–406 B.C.E.), the youngest of Athens' three great tragedians, was socially and intellectually an outsider. His family was not prominent, and he did not hold major public offices. The Athenians had a love-hate relationship with his work. He wrote 92 plays, but won only five first prizes. The Greeks admired his poetry but found his plays troubling. Euripides' characters are psychologically complex, and his plots explore, but do not always resolve, morally ambiguous situations. In the year in which the Athenians voted to slaughter the people of Melos, for instance, Euripides produced a play about the Trojan War that described the brutalization of Troy's women by Greece's "heroes."

Euripides' work highlights the function of theater in the life of the Athenian *polis*. No modern state periodically suspends its activities and gathers all its citizens together for a week of theater. Why did Athens? Perhaps the answer lies in the importance of education to a democracy. Popular government requires an informed electorate—voters who are trained to think about serious issues and make sound judgments. Modern democracies use free public schools, newspapers, and electronic media to equip their citizens to govern themselves. None of these was available to the ancient Athenians, but the theater was. The theater regularly brought the Athenians together for a crash course in the problems posed by ethical dilemmas and the complexity of decision making. It created safe opportunities for the masses to vent—and learn to deal with—passionate feelings. Because each play was intended to be staged only once, its author wrote with the concerns of the moment in mind. Although most dramas were set in Greece's mythic past, playwrights chose stories with themes that had contemporary relevance and often made their connections with living issues pointedly obvious. Actors might wear masks with the faces of prominent politicians, name people in the audience, and refer to current events.

The topical relevance of Greek theater is most obvious in comedies, for the rules governing comedy were much more liberal than those for writing tragedy. Comedy was, however, as serious in its intent and function as tragedy. The only plays that survive to give us a sense of what comedy was like during the golden age of Greek theater are by Aristophanes (488–380 B.C.E.). He wrote about 40 comedies, 11 of which are extant.

Comedy derives from a word meaning "phallic song," a clear indication of its roots in fertility rituals. Not surprisingly, therefore, Aristophanes' plays feature broad humor, parody, and crude sexual references. His actors wore costumes that were padded to accentuate sexual characteristics, and what they did on stage might shock even the most sophisticated of modern audiences. While provoking hilarity, Aristophanes also prodded his audiences to think about serious issues, the most compelling of which for his generation was the Peloponnesian War. The hero of *The Acharnians* is a country bumpkin who, disgusted by the war, makes a separate peace with Sparta. In *Peace* the gods are asked why they inflict war on mankind, and they claim that they have nothing to do with it—that men make war and can stop whenever they want to. *Lysistrata*, a romping farce, proposed that the women of Athens and Sparta force their men to stop fighting by staging a sexual strike. Complications arise as the women discover that they find it as hard to do without sex as their men. Aristophanes concluded the play with a serious proposal for an exchange of territories to end the conflict. He also warned the Athenians of the continuing threat posed by Persia and reminded them of their cultural solidarity with other Greeks.

KEY QUESTION | Revisited

The speech that the historian Thucydides puts in the mouth of Pericles (which is referenced at the start of this chapter) reflects the confidence of a dynamic society at a pinnacle of its development. Pericles evidently had superb political skills. Athens was governed by a direct democracy, a system in which the masses made all decisions. The risk of such a system was that its electorate would be whipped about by emotional appeals and persuaded to make radical shifts of policy on momentary whims. But for decades Pericles (for good or ill) kept Athens committed to consistent goals. So great was his influence that historians have dubbed the period in which Athens reached the height of its power the "Age of Pericles." His fellow citizens were basking in the glow of their victories over Persia and their successful imperialistic ventures, but they had also suffered losses. His speech was a funeral oration for fallen soldiers, an address to a community of mourners who wanted to be assured that those who had died did so for a good cause. That cause, Pericles argued, was the defense of a unique and unprecedented way of life—a set of values and institutions that made Athenian society a model of justice and probity for the world.

There was much to admire about Pericles' Athens. The thinkers and artists of the Hellenic era, most of whom had ties to Athens, set in motion ideas that transformed the Mediterranean world and profoundly influenced subsequent civilizations. Indeed, the history of civilization in the West has been studded with renaissances, eras of cultural development stimulated by renewed interest in the art and literature of the classical era. The virtues of Athens, which Pericles listed, are worthy of emulation, but the splendor of the city's achievements should not obscure acknowledgment of its failings. Valuable things are learned from what goes wrong as well as what goes right.

There was a dark side to Greek civilization. Athens' prosperity rested on the twin pillars of slavery and imperialistic exploitation. The devotion of its famous intellectuals to reason and clear thinking did not prevent some of them from concluding that women were congenitally inferior creatures and that some men were naturally superior to others and therefore entitled to more privileges. Superstition was rampant, as was belief in witchcraft and participation in religions that cultivated emotional excess and violent behavior.

Readily apparent also is the fact that as Pericles' Athens grew stronger, it also became a more arrogant and closed society. Admission to the privileged rank of citizen was limited, and the democratic electorate endorsed aggressive actions that pushed Greece into the great disaster that was the Peloponnesian War. A popular theme of the tragic playwrights was *hybris*, the arrogant overconfidence that success creates and that leads ultimately to destruction. The Greeks knew the risks and dangers of the paths they chose, but one lesson their history teaches is that knowing that a behavior is self-destructive is often not enough to motivate people to abandon it.

The Greeks' interest in rationally examining the environments created by nature and human cultures produced considerable self-awareness. Greek writers analyzed both the strengths and weaknesses of their civilization. They were intensely proud of being Greeks, but that did not prevent them from admiring—indeed standing in awe—of some "barbarians." Egypt particularly intrigued them, and many Greek intellectuals would have freely acknowledged that they built on legacies from the older cultures of the Middle East and were stimulated by continuing contact with them. The Greeks were not solely responsible for what the West has become. The enduring influence of Greek philosophy, for instance, owes much to the uses to which the West's religions, which originated in the Middle East, have put it. The dynamism and creativity of Western civilizations spring from a multiplicity of sources.

Review Questions

1. Was civilization invented by the Greeks or passed to them?
2. How did Mycenaean Greek civilization differ from Hellenic civilization?
3. What contributed to the development of the *polis*?
4. Was Athens' experiment with democracy a success or a failure?
5. What does Greek history suggest about the influence of wars on civilization?
6. Was there a common theme or interest in the science, art, and literature of the Hellenic era?

Please consult the Suggested Readings at the back of the book to continue your study of the material covered in this chapter. For a list of documents on the Primary Source DVD-ROM that relate to topics in this chapter, please refer to the back of the book.

5 The Hellenistic Era and the Rise of Rome

No one is so incurious or indifferent as not to want to understand how the Romans (in less than fifty-three years) conquered, and how they now govern, practically the whole inhabited world—an accomplishment that has no historical precedent.

—Polybius

KEY | Question

What circumstances are likely to undermine governments by the people?

Greek intellectuals tended to feel superior to non-Greeks, but Polybius (c. 201–120 B.C.E.) was an exception. He admired the Romans even though they repeatedly invaded his home-land, defeated its armies, and in 168 B.C.E. carted him and a thousand of his fellows off to Rome as hostages. In Rome he was treated more as a guest than a prisoner and was admitted to the highest levels of Roman society. Publius Cornelius Scipio Aemilianus Africanus Numantinus (185–129 B.C.E.), whose imposing name catalogued his aristocratic connections and professional achievements, became his friend, and for 16 years Polybius enjoyed an insider's view of the workings of the Roman Republic.

Polybius's acute awareness of Greece's political problems contributed to his respect for his captor-hosts. The Greeks were better at the arts of war than those of peace. About 130 years before Polybius's birth, Alexander the Great had distracted the Greeks from fighting among themselves by turning their attention to the conquest of the Persian Empire. He led them on a triumphant march from the Aegean to Egypt and east to the Indus River Valley. At Alexander's death, his great empire came apart, and the Greeks returned to making war on one another.

The Romans shared Indo-European ancestry and many other things with the Greeks. Their civilization developed more slowly, but Polybius believed that they would ultimately

The Winged Victory of Samothrace   This statue of Nike, goddess of victory and daughter of the titan Pallas, was found on the Aegean island of Samothrace in 1863. The sculptor of this acknowledged masterpiece of Hellenistic art is unknown. *Nike of Samothrace. 3rd–2nd BCE. Helleninstic marble statue. H.: 328 cm. Inv.: 2369. Musee du Louvre/RMN Reunion des Musees Nationaux, France. SCALA/Art Resource, NY*

solve problems that had defeated the Greeks. Romans did not just conquer lands; they held on to them. In Polybius's day, they had no philosophy, science, art, or literature that compared to the products of Greek civilization (which they were eagerly assimilating), but Polybius thought that the world had much to learn from Rome's political and military institutions. Time has vindicated his faith. Rome created the largest and most long-lived empire the West had yet seen, and centuries after its fall, its memory continued to influence the course of Western societies. Leaders as different as feudal kings, medieval popes, French philosophers, Russian czars, German kaisers, and American revolutionaries have all laid claim to Rome's legacy.

The stability and longevity of Rome's empire was a hard-won prize for which the Romans paid dearly. The Romans began their climb to world domination by throwing off monarchy and embracing a form of government they called a Republic. It was not a direct democracy, such as Athens had established, but it gave significant power to its citizenry. The Romans developed a passionate affection for their republican system, and their patriotic military service in its defense led ultimately to the acquisition of a territorial empire. Administration of an empire proved, however, to be difficult for the Republic, and the methods the Romans devised simply set them up for a century-long civil war. Peace was not achieved until a skillful leader persuaded the Romans that submission to his monarchical leadership was essential to save their Republic. As the republican trappings of his system fell away, Rome became an openly autocratic Empire. The Empire limited freedoms but it delivered a long period of relative peace and prosperity.

As you reflect on Rome's history, consider the challenges that face democracies and republics as they try to reconcile the inherent inefficiency of government by the masses with a state's need for a swift and decisive executive.

The Hellenistic Era

The Peloponnesian War (432–404 B.C.E.) had no real winner. Athens yielded to Sparta, but Sparta collapsed under the burdens of victory. Sparta owed its military preeminence to a unique social system that enabled it to field the only full-time professional army in Greece. The lengthy Peloponnesian conflict neutralized that advantage by professionalizing the armies of many Greek *poleis*. Thebes finally dispelled the myth of Spartan invincibility by routing Sparta's armies in fair fights, but Thebes failed to fill the leadership vacuum left by Sparta's decline. Greece's *poleis* formed leagues and alliances, and fell to fighting among themselves. War became a major Greek industry—producing hordes of mercenaries who found employment at home and abroad.

This dismal situation convinced some Greeks that their compatriots were incapable of self-government. Men as different as the philosopher Plato (c. 429–347 B.C.E.), the soldier-historian Xenophon (c. 435–354 B.C.E.), and the Athenian orator Isocrates (436–338 B.C.E.) advocated some form of monarchy. Their hope was that an individual with a unique genius for leadership would unite the Greeks and protect them from their ancient enemy, Persia.

Macedonia Takes Control   When people decide that they need a savior, candidates for the job appear. Greece's savior emerged from an unexpected quarter, from the semibarbarous kingdom of Macedonia on the northern rim of the Greek mainland. The Macedonians were a tribal people who had not taken to life in *poleis* and who had even backed the Persians against their fellow Greeks in the Persian Wars. In the mid-fifth century B.C.E., however, Macedonian kings decided to Hellenize their subjects. They established a capital at Pella and ornamented their court with artists, craftsmen, and intellectuals imported from the more advanced Greek states. Men as distinguished as Athens' tragic playwright Euripides and the philosopher-scientist Aristotle entered their service. Despite this, Macedonia remained a rough, politically volatile country. The hereditary chiefs of its tribes were powerful, and coups and battles shortened the lives of its kings. Eight men ascended Macedonia's throne during the first four decades of the fourth century B.C.E.

In 360 B.C.E. King Perdiccas III died in battle, and his brother, Philip II (r. 360–336 B.C.E.), won the ensuing struggle for the crown. Philip spent two or three years of his youth as a hostage in Thebes which gave him a chance to observe Greek politics at close hand and to acquire training in the best Greek military techniques. Philip used what he had learned to transform the Macedonian army and unite his kingdom's tribal factions.

During the 350s B.C.E. some *poleis* sought Philip's help in their wars with their neighbors, and this gave him an excuse to intervene in the affairs of the Greek states. As one war led to another, the Athenian orator Demosthenes (384–322 B.C.E.) tried to rally opposition to Philip in the name of defending democracy, but in 338 B.C.E. the Macedonian army won a decisive victory over Athens and Thebes at Chaeronea. Further resistance seemed futile, so most of the mainland states accepted Philip's invitation to a peace conference to be held at Corinth in 337 B.C.E. At the meeting, Philip persuaded the Greeks to join him in an attack on Persia, but on the eve of this campaign he was assassinated. His son, Alexander (who may have been implicated in his murder), seized the Macedonian throne.

Alexander (III) the Great   Alexander was not cast in the mold of his father. Philip was a brute of a man who enjoyed physically and psychologically intimidating others. Alexander, who had the slight build of a runner, was distinguished by will and nervous energy more than muscle. His youthful appearance was enhanced by his habit of shaving, a custom that spread as his reputation grew. Alexander (r. 336–323 B.C.E.) was only 20 years old when his father died, but he had considerable military experience. He commanded the elite cavalry unit in Philip's army that carried the day for the Macedonians at the crucial battle of Chaeronea.

Alexander assured the Greeks that he intended to lead them in the Persian War his father had proposed, but he had to delay its start. He was not the only man with a claim to Philip's throne, and his survival was uncertain. Young, untried rulers face tests to their authority, and Alexander spent the first year of his reign eliminating potential rivals and fighting for control of his kingdom. Anti-Macedonian Greeks confidently anticipated his failure and began to scheme against him. This ended when he suddenly descended on Thebes, the rebels' ringleader, and destroyed the city. Similar acts of terrorism might have forced the Greeks to cooperate temporarily, but Alexander knew that he could not hold them against their will once he and his army were locked in combat with Persia far from home. The Greeks would inevitably rebel and isolate him in enemy territory. His survival, therefore, depended on inspiring them with genuine enthusiasm for him and his campaign.

Alexander left Greece, never to return, in the spring of 334 B.C.E. His army was ludicrously small for the task he set. He had about 37,000 men, but over 23,000 of these were Greek allies whose loyalty was doubtful. The core of Alexander's army consisted of 12,000 Macedonian infantrymen and 1,800 cavalry, most of whom were more closely tied to their hereditary chiefs (Philip's contemporaries) than to their young king.

Alexander was ahead of his time in understanding what skillful management of public relations can do for a ruler. At the campaign's start, he made a side trip to Troy to sacrifice at what was said to be the grave of Achilles, the hero of the *Iliad*. He wanted the Greeks to link the war on which they were embarking with him with the epic victory their Homeric ancestors had won over Greece's first eastern enemy. Alexander also began the development of something like the modern press corps. It consisted of a troop of scholars, headed by Calisthenes (the nephew of Alexander's boyhood tutor, Aristotle), whose job was to build enthusiasm for the campaign by providing the homeland with reports of its progress and descriptions of the exotic locales it discovered.

Alexander desperately needed a quick victory that would assure his men that he could deliver what he promised. The Persians might have defeated him by retreating. If they had drawn him deep into their territory, his soldiers would have grown increasingly fearful until they panicked, turned on him, and fled home. The Persians chose instead to give Alexander exactly what he had to have. They made a stand at the Granikos River in western Asia Minor (334 B.C.E.).

Alexander understood that he would have no second chances in this war. Only by appearing utterly self-confident and invincible could he distract his men from the odds they faced. At the first hint of failure, they were likely to lose heart and desert him. Therefore, he threw everything he had into every engagement. He commanded the most dangerous posts in each battle and performed heroic acts that inspired his men to comparable feats. The strategy worked, but it placed an all but unbearable burden on Alexander. The king's injuries mounted as the war progressed. He was often ill. The hardships of the march sapped his strength, and the stress of command tested his will.

At Granikos the ferocity of Alexander's attack swept the Persians from the field, but Alexander resisted the temptation to pursue them. He slowed the pace of the march and spent a year exploiting his victory, building the morale of his men, and picking up allies. It was the spring of 333 B.C.E. before he reached the Taurus Mountains and crossed from Asia Minor into Syria. The Persian emperor, Darius III (r. 336–330 B.C.E.), was eager to confront him, but faulty intelligence led the Persian army astray. By the time Darius found Alexander, impatience may have been clouding the emperor's judgment. At the Issos River on the Syrian coast he committed himself to a battle on a narrow field where he could not deploy his superior numbers. Alexander struck the center of the Persian line, and when Darius pulled back, his men panicked and fled (see Map 5–1).

Darius retreated from Issos in disarray, but Alexander did not go after him. Alexander could not risk proceeding inland, for the Persians controlled the sea. If Darius's navy had invaded the Aegean, Alexander would have had to go home to defend Greece. Because Alexander had insufficient ships with which to challenge the Persians at sea, the only way he could neutralize their fleet was to take all of the ports from which it oper-

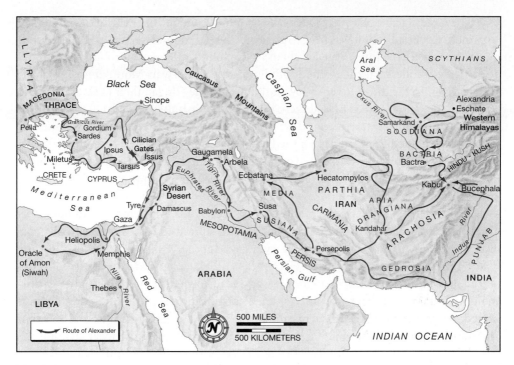

Map 5–1 Alexander's Adventure   Alexander led one of history's most extraordinary military campaigns. After winning the Persian Empire, the prize for which his men had signed on, Alexander persuaded them to march farther and farther east into territory unknown to the Greeks. He was preparing to invade China when he died and was rumored to have had a plan for the conquest of the western Mediterranean as well.

Question: Does Alexander's route suggest that he had a rational strategy for building an empire or that he was simply wandering about?

ated. This required arduous sieges of city after city until the whole coast as far as Egypt was in Greek hands.

By July 331 B.C.E., Alexander was finally free to leave Egypt and strike inland to challenge Darius. Darius wisely waited for Alexander to come to him and chose a battlefield that gave him all the advantages. The Persians dug in at **Gaugamela**, an arid plain north of Babylon. It provided ample space for them to maneuver and forced the Greeks to camp in a place that had no water. Despite the Persians' superior numbers and position, the Greeks triumphed at Gaugamela, but they were never entirely sure how. Dust and poor communications prevented anyone from having an overview of the battle.

Darius's army may have been too large for its own good. At any rate, it was thrown into confusion by Alexander's attacks, and Darius had to flee once again. Babylon submitted. The Greeks claimed the imperial treasury at Susa and made their winter camp at the Persian capital, Persepolis. The following spring, Alexander renewed the campaign. When Darius ordered another retreat, his disgruntled officers assassinated him.

The Greeks had done what they set out to do—conquer the Persian Empire. Most assumed, therefore, that it was time to go home, but Alexander persuaded them to continue the war a little longer. He led them farther and farther east into unknown territory. They wandered through the foothills of the Himalayan Mountains and finally descended into the Indus River Valley. At that point, they dug in their heels and refused to go on. Alexander agreed to lead them home, but only if they vowed: (1) to fight their way back through new territory, and (2) to return a year later to resume their conquests. The Greeks battled their way down the Indus River to the Indian Ocean and then endured a brutal march across the wastes of the Gedrosian Desert. A remnant of the army staggered back to Babylon, where Alexander threw himself into organizing his conquests and planning future campaigns.

Alexander did not have the manpower to occupy his huge empire and hold it by force. He had to induce his non-Greek subjects to submit to him voluntarily. His plan was to bolster his legitimacy in their eyes by adopting Persian court customs and adding Persian soldiers to his army. His Greeks and Macedonian followers strongly objected, but in the end Alexander got his way. He also tried to interfere as little as possible with the lives of his new subjects. The Persian Empire was composed of districts called *satrapies*. Their borders were drawn to respect the ethnic identities of their inhabitants. Alexander appointed a native governor (who knew the local customs) to handle each *satrapy's* civil affairs, a Greek to deal with its fiscal administration, and a Macedonian to provide for its defense. This gave the residents of a *satrapy* at least one leader with whom they could identify and made it difficult for any single official to take over a *satrapy* and use it against the central government.

Alexander demanded extraordinary things of himself, and he finally exhausted his physical resources. On May 29, 323 B.C.E., following an all-night drinking bout with his officers, he fell ill. His fever rose. He sank into a coma, and on June 10, 323 B.C.E., he quietly died. There were rumors that he had been poisoned, but no evidence of foul play was uncovered. Fevers were

Portrait of Alexander   No one can be certain of the accuracy of ancient portraits, for they were often idealized for purposes of propaganda or meant to represent a type of person rather than an individual. Alexander's statues broke with the conventional representation of a king by depicting him as a beardless youth rather than a mature man. This bust dates to the late fourth century B.C.E., the same century as Alexander's death.

common in swampy Babylon, and Alexander's arduous lifestyle must have sapped his strength and weakened his resistance.

The Hellenistic Environment   Alexander was only 32 when he died, and he was not the kind of man who cared to think about mortality. Death surprised him before he had provided himself with a successor. Alexander's primary emotional attachments were homosexual. He delayed marriage, and he had no children by mistresses. In 327 B.C.E. he had wed an Iranian princess named Roxane, and after returning to Babylon, he had also married one of Darius's daughters. Both women may have been pregnant at the time of his death. The Persian princess did not long outlive Alexander, but Roxane made him the posthumous father of a son, Alexander IV. Alexander's generals declared themselves regents for the infant, dispatched him to Macedonia to be raised, and set about carving up his empire. This inaugurated a period of shifting alliances and bloody conflicts. By 317 B.C.E. the surviving generals had disposed of Alexander's son, wife, and mother, and the outlines for a lasting division of his empire had emerged. The Aegean and the Macedonian throne went to Antigonus the One-Eyed (d. 301 B.C.E.). **Seleukos** (c. 358–280 B.C.E.), governor of Babylon, claimed the Persian heartland, and **Ptolemy** (d. 285 B.C.E.), one of Alexander's boyhood friends, made himself pharaoh of Egypt. Ptolemy also highjacked Alexander's body and enshrined it in a mausoleum in Alexandria, a great port in the Egyptian delta that Alexander had founded.

Alexander's empire did not survive, but his imperial conquests had lasting significance. They marked the end of the Hellenic (Greek) period and the beginning of the Hellenistic (Greek-like) phase in Western civilization. Greeks had always avoided mixing with "barbarians" (non-Greeks), but Alexander believed that a blending of peoples and cultures was essential for the survival of his empire. He promoted intermarriage between his men and his eastern subjects, and he was willing to learn from the peoples he conquered and to adapt to their expectations.

The garrisons that were posted throughout Alexander's empire grew into Greek towns that spread Hellenic culture as far east as India. It is debatable how much influence the Greeks had on indigenous peoples, but these peoples clearly influenced the Greeks. As thousands of Greeks migrated to the new towns that had been founded in the wake of Alexander's armies, they became a more cosmopolitan people. Their widening view of the world even affected their language. Its grammar and syntax simplified, and its vocabulary grew much richer as it assimilated words from other tongues. The result was a flexible new *koine* ("common") Greek that was so adaptable that it became the international medium of communication. When the Romans added the eastern rim of the Mediterranean to their empire in the first century B.C.E., they found Greek so well established that they used it rather than imposing Latin on their subjects. Many Romans were bilingual, and the early Christians (even those who were born Jews) wrote their New Testament in *koine* Greek instead of the language of the Hebrew scriptures.

The Hellenistic era witnessed the decline of the *polis*, the institution that had nurtured Hellenism. This signaled a significant change in the environment for civilized life in the Mediterranean world. Small, self-governing city-states had failed to maintain order in the Greek world. As they succumbed to the builders of empires, political power shifted from their citizens to the bureaucrats who administered those empires. The Hellenistic era preferred professionals to citizen-volunteers. This was not necessarily bad, for the highly trained specialists who served Hellenistic rulers were extremely competent and able to plan and execute great projects. They laid out orderly cities and equipped them with magnificent temples, monuments, baths, theaters, and arenas. They built sewage systems. They constructed aqueducts to convey fresh water over great distances. They organized police forces, regulated commerce and food supplies, and generally made urban life far more comfortable, clean, and secure than it had ever been.

Hellenistic communities were as prosperous as they were well run. Alexander returned to circulation a great deal of gold that had been sealed away in Persia's coffers, and the consolidation of large territorial states by his successors made trade easier and promoted economic growth.

There was, of course, a cost for the comforts of the new societies. As governments grew larger and specialists assumed responsibility for more governmental functions, the power of popular assemblies and elected officials declined. A citizen's vote meant little to a huge, centrally managed state, and it had no use for his amateur military service or advice. Even his labor was not all that important, for wars replenished the supply of inexpensive slaves who did much of society's essential work.

Hellenistic Civilization

The subjects of the Hellenistic states were prosperous and well cared for, but they were pawns of forces beyond their control. For those who came from *poleis* proud of their democratic traditions, this required some emotional adjustment. The Hellenic *polis* affirmed the worth of the individual by demanding much from him, but a Hellenistic empire reduced the individual to a replaceable cog in the machinery of a great state. The world of the *polis* was human in scale and amenable to control, but empires rendered their subjects small and impotent.

The art and literature of the Hellenistic era reflect the period's new sociopolitical environment. Theater flourished, but playwrights steered clear of political issues and focused on entertainment. Aristophanes, the master of Hellenic Old Comedy, used laughter to make people think, but Hellenistic **New Comedy** was the ancient world's equivalent of a television "sit-com." It relied on stock characters and plots that were as silly as they were predictable. Persons who wanted comparable entertainment at home turned to the era's new literary genre, the novel. The most popular novels were erotic romances set in exotic places or idealized bucolic locales. They conjured up fantasy worlds and provided escapist entertainment for literate urbanites.

Hellenistic architecture and visual arts, like the era's literature, appealed to emotion more than to intellect. Buildings grew large and imposing. The first skyscraper (a 400-foot-tall lighthouse) was erected on an island in the harbor of Alexandria. The city of Ephesus on the coast of Asia Minor built a temple to Diana that was almost five times the size of Athens' Parthenon, the largest of the mainland's Hellenic temples. The port of Rhodes erected a bronze statue of the sun god that may have been 120 feet tall, about the height of America's Statue of Liberty. Sculptors developed incredible technique that imparted stunning realism to their work, and they expanded their range far

Laocoön and His Sons   Unlike their Hellenic predecessors, Hellenistic sculptors sought to convey drama, complexity, emotion, and movement in their work. This literally writhing statue depicts an episode from Homer's *Iliad*, the destruction of the priest Laocoön and his sons. Laocoön tried to thwart the will of the gods by persuading the Trojans not to drag into their city the wooden horse the Greeks had mysteriously left on the battlefield.

beyond the Hellenic era's idealized male athletes. They sought out subjects that were novel and emotionally stirring: portraits of individuals, erotic female nudes, cute children and animals, persons suffering the ravages of age and poverty, and men and women in the throes of death or extreme passions. The human ideal, the art of the democratic *polis*, lost some of its relevance for the subjects of the Hellenistic empires. They lacked the political freedoms that gave dignity and meaning to *polis* citizenship and made Hellenic ideals worth striving for. What they wanted was art that dispelled boredom and affirmed the values of uniqueness and individuality that the imperial context threatened.

Most schools of Hellenistic philosophy focused on developing "philosophies of life" that were designed to help individuals come to terms with their new cultural and political environment. The most popular of these urged people to distance themselves in some way from the world around them. Zeno (335–263 B.C.E.), the founder of the Stoics, preached acceptance of the inevitable. He maintained that everyone had a preordained place in the universe's unalterable, rational system. Fulfillment lay in doing the duties of one's station while cultivating an emotional detachment that preserved inner peace. Stoics warned that people could not control what happened to them but claimed that they could control their emotional responses to life's vicissitudes. Zeno's contemporary, Epicurus (341–270 B.C.E.), believed that everything that existed (including the human soul) was the result of random, temporary conjunctions of atoms and that nothing, therefore, had meaning or permanence. Because lasting achievements were impossible, life's only purpose, he concluded, was the enjoyment of pleasure. However, true pleasure was not ecstasy and sensual indulgence, but tranquility, a state undisturbed by extreme emotions of any kind. Individuals who retreated from the world to "cultivate their gardens" had the best chance of achieving happiness, for they avoided situations that might stir the emotions. The followers of Diogenes of Sinope (c. 400–325 B.C.E.) were called Cynics ("dogs"). Diogenes claimed that fulfillment derived from self-sufficiency, and self-sufficiency was achieved by minimizing one's needs and obligations. The Cynics were likened to dogs because, like animals, they spurned all social conventions and freely and openly did whatever came naturally. Diogenes lived in the street, expressed contempt for authority, and performed intimate bodily functions in public. The Cynics, Epicureans, and Stoics all agreed that individuals had no mastery over the world; the best they could do was to master themselves. This was a far less ambitious assessment of human potential than the visions that had inspired the social engineers of the Hellenic *poleis*.

Hellenistic Greeks still had confidence in the superiority of their civilization, and their desire to explore and to learn only grew as their empires broadened their horizons and stimulated their curiosity. Hellenistic monarchs provided unprecedented patronage for intellectuals—particularly the Egyptian dynasty founded by Alexander's friend, Ptolemy I (r. 323–285 B.C.E.). The Ptolemaic pharaohs established a library in Alexandria and set the goal of obtaining a copy of every important book. They dispatched agents abroad in search of rare volumes. They funded translations (including one of the Hebrew scriptures), and they even searched the baggage of travelers entering Egypt, hoping to find interesting texts. The result was a collection that may have numbered a million items.

A research institute was attached to Alexandria's library. It was called the Museum, the home of the Muses (the nine female deities who, according to the poet Hesiod, preside over the arts). Some of the Museum's scholars devoted their lives to refining the library's collection and building on its contents. They compiled dictionaries and catalogues, and wrote commentaries on classic texts. What their work lacked in originality, it made up for in quantity. A certain Didymus of Alexandria is said to have written 3,500 books—not one of which survives!

Pedantry did not characterize all the work at the Museum. Some of its scholars pioneered new literary genres. The most popular of these was a sophisticated pastoral poetry that romanticized rural life and reveled in obscure, learned references. The Museum was especially noted for encouraging progress in the sciences and mathematics. Euclid (fl. c. 300 B.C.E.) wrote the text that has made his name synonymous with geometry, and Archimedes of Syracuse (c. 287–212 B.C.E.) laid the groundwork for calculus. Eratosthenes of Cyrene (c. 270–194 B.C.E.) calculated Earth's circumference with remarkable accuracy. Hipparchus of Nicaea (c. 160–125 B.C.E.) made precise calendar calculations. Aristarchus of Samos (fl. c. 275 B.C.E.) advanced the theory that Earth was a globe that rotated on an axis and revolved around the sun, but for the next 1,500 years, most astronomers supported the contention of a non-royal Ptolemy of Alexandria (fl. c. 130 C.E.) that the sun revolves around Earth. The Hippocratic medical texts were edited at the Museum, and some of its physicians conducted important anatomical research. Herophilius of Chalcedon (fl. c. 270 B.C.E.) mapped the sensory nerves and identified the brain as the center of a nervous system. Although capillaries were too small to be seen by the naked eye, Erasistratus of Ceos (fl. c. 260 B.C.E.) hypothesized that veins and arteries were connected, a prelude to the discovery of blood circulation and the function of the heart.

Alexandrian technicians and engineers produced marvelous gadgets that ranged from useful pumps and astronomical instruments to amusing toys (one of which was a working model of a steam turbine). To the modern mind, the most puzzling thing about all of this activity is that so little of it found practical application. The fact that Hellenistic society was slave-based may have something to do with this. Its educated classes were not motivated to think of ways to make work easier, and its workers had little freedom to innovate.

The Origin of Rome

Hellenistic civilization spread to, and was spread by, the Romans. The Latins (Rome's founders) took to it readily, for they had much in common with the Greeks. Both peoples had Indo-European ancestry, and their languages were related. They settled in their respective homelands at about the same time (c. 1900 B.C.E.), and their cultures evolved in similar environments. The Greeks, however, got off to an earlier and faster start, for they had the stimulating advantage of close contacts with the civilizations of the Middle East.

The Italian Environment   The Aegean Sea and its many islands facilitated communication between Greece and the Middle East, but Italy faced west. Like the Greek mainland, Italy is a mountainous peninsula. All its major agricultural plains and most of its natural harbors are on its western coast, and the Apennine mountain chain forms a spine along its eastern edge that makes access from the Adriatic Sea difficult.

The Greeks planted Naples (Nea-polis, "New Town") and other colonies in Campania, Italy's southwestern plain, in the mid-eighth century B.C.E. At the same time, the Etruscans, a people whose origin has been much debated, built prosperous city-states on the plain of Etruria (Tuscany) north of the Tiber River. The Latins took their name from the small plain of Latium ("flat land") that lay between Campania and Etruria. North of Etruria and the Apennines was the great basin of the Po River. It was inhabited by Celtic tribes and considered by the Romans to belong to Gaul more than Italy (see Map 5–2).

The Kingdom of Rome   The Romans were aware that their Latin ancestors had lived in Latium for a long time before they established the city of Rome, but they knew little about them. Homer's epics provided the classical world with what it assumed to be its earliest history, so the Romans looked to Homer to supply them with a past. Because Romans were not Greeks, they sought an ancestor from the *Iliad*'s other nation, the Trojans. The attention of Roman myth-makers centered on a Trojan prince named Aeneas, who escaped Troy's fall. After several adventures, he allegedly landed on the plain of Latium and married Lavinia, daughter of the native king, Latinus. Thirteen generations of their descendants reigned over Latium before

Map 5–2 The Rise of Rome The Apennine Mountains form a crescent-shaped wall running the length of the Italian peninsula. They impede access to Italy from the east and cradle the three western agricultural plains (Campania, Latium, and Etruria) where urban communities first appeared in Italy. The ancient Romans considered the Po Valley north of the Apennines part of Gaul, not Italy.

Question: Did Rome's location inevitably make it the seat of a great empire, or was its location inconvenient for an imperial capital?

Rome's founders, the twins Romulus and Remus, were born to a Latin princess and Mars, the Latins' god of war. The city that Romulus founded (and that bore his name) was said to have begun as a rough frontier post populated by outcasts and women abducted from the surrounding region. Although this colorful myth of Rome's origin is fanciful, it nonetheless contains some truth.

The traditional date for Rome's founding is April 21, 753 B.C.E. Archaeological evidence confirms the existence of several primitive villages on the hills next to the Tiber in the mid-eighth century B.C.E. and suggests why the Latins might have planted them there at that time. Rome came to occupy the first spot inland from the coast (about 20 miles) where the Tiber River narrowed enough to be easily bridged. In the mid-eighth century B.C.E., when the Greek and Etruscan civilizations that flourished on either side of Latium developed trade routes converging at the Tiber crossing, the Latins hastened to occupy this corner of their territory.

Seven kings are said to have reigned over Rome from 753 B.C.E. to 509 B.C.E. They ruled in tandem with an aristocratic council called the Senate (*senex*, "elder"). Most of the stories told about the monarchy are legends, but some historical information can be gleaned from them. Etruscan names are recorded for two of Rome's kings, and it is unlikely that the Romans would have invented a memory of a time when outsiders ruled their city if this had not been the case. There is ample evidence of Etruscan influence on Roman institutions and customs, but this does not necessarily imply Etruscan occupation of Rome. The Romans may have chosen Etruscan leaders to strengthen commercial or political ties with Etruria.

The Etruscans   Much that was unique about Rome can be traced to the Etruscans, but the Etruscans themselves remain something of a mystery. Their language is not related to any known tongue and, apart from words whose meaning has been provided by ancient Latin authors or can be inferred from context, it is largely untranslated. Most surviving specimens are short inscriptions. Etruscan cities developed very quickly (possibly in response to the trade that was increasing between Italy and the eastern Mediterranean in the eighth century B.C.E.). Etruria had a benign climate, fertile fields, and accessible deposits of metal ores. The skills of its gold and bronze workers were second to none. Etruscan traders had much to offer, and they took to the sea to compete with Greek and Phoenician merchants.

Stories circulated in the Greek and Latin worlds about the luxury and permissiveness of Etruscan society. The Greeks were shocked by the freedom enjoyed by Etruscan women, and the Romans, who wrested austere livings from small plots of poor land, insisted that the Etruscans' self-indulgent custom of feasting twice a day was evidence of their moral laxity. Some Etruscans were undeniably rich, for they built expensive subterranean chamber-tombs that replicated their lavishly furnished homes and banqueting halls. The favorite design for a sarcophagus was a dining couch with an effigy of the deceased reclining on its lid—at ease in festive clothes, wine cup in hand. Etruscan graves have yielded some of the finest specimens of pottery, jewelry, and bronze work to survive from the classical era.

The Etruscans may have been connoisseurs of life's pleasures, but wealth did not make them soft. They dominated Italy until the mid-fifth century. Their decline was caused, at least in part, by the failure of their independent city-states to cooperate in countering competition from the Greeks. The Greeks planted colonies on both sides of Etruria and battled the Etruscans for control of the sea.

The Romans owed many of their political symbols and social customs to the Etruscans, but it was in the area of religion that they were most aware of their debt.

An Etruscan Couple   This sarcophagus from the sixth century B.C.E. depicts what are probably an Etruscan husband and wife resting at ease on a dining couch. Greeks and Romans often reclined while eating. In early Rome, however, women sat while men reclined. Although a Roman woman of the republican era had more freedom than her Greek sister, neither may have enjoyed as much independence as a contemporary Etruscan lady. *Sarcophagus of a married couple on a funeral bed. Etruscan, from Cerveteri, 6th BCE. Terracotta. Lewandowski/Ojeda. Musee Lourve, Paris, France. RMN Reunion Des Musees Nationeaux/Art Resource, NY*

Throughout Rome's history, colleges of priests perpetuated ancient rituals and sacrifices of Etruscan origin. Romans saw omens everywhere and studied them before undertaking any project. They were especially in awe of the presumed skills of Etruscan diviners and soothsayers. Long after the Etruscan civilization disappeared, the Romans preserved Etruscan as a dead language used primarily in arcane religious rites. A similar fate was, of course, one day to befall Latin.

The Roman Republic

Rome made significant progress under the leadership of its later kings, one or more of whom had ties with the Etruscan city of Tarquinia. The Romans drained the swampy lowland that separated the hills on which they lived to create the Forum, a place for markets and assemblies. They built the largest temple in Italy on the Capitoline hill, and archaeological evidence suggests that they enjoyed a rising standard of living.

Kings may not deserve all the credit for early Rome's progress, for they operated under the watchful eye of the city's Senate. Relations between the monarch and the aristocratic families represented in the Senate must often have been strained. Few of Rome's kings (including the city's founder) were said to have died peacefully in their beds, and eventually the Senators decided to dispense with kings and govern the city themselves.

The Roman Revolution   Legends blame Sextus, the aptly named son of King Tarquinius Superbus (Tarquin the Proud), for the fall of his father's throne. In 509 B.C.E. Sextus supposedly raped a virtuous Roman matron named Lucretia, a deed that so infuriated the Romans that they drove out the Tarquins and vowed never again to submit to a king. The story may be fanciful, but the revolution was real.

The republic that the revolutionaries established to govern Rome was not a democracy. It limited political privileges to the male members of the city's "**patrician**" families. Early Rome was a federation of extended families, and for reasons that even the Romans could not explain, citizen families were divided into two classes: the noble patricians and the common **plebeians**. In the early republic, only the former could hold political offices and priesthoods.

Family was such an important determiner of status that each Roman male needed three names to indicate the place he occupied in the social order. His first name was one of a few common names used only by close friends. His second identified his *gens*, the great clan to which his paternal ancestors belonged. His third indicated his birth family. If his achievements were notable, the city might commemorate them by granting him a fourth name. The winner of a war in Africa, for example, bore the ponderous name Publius Cornelius Scipio Africanus.

A Roman *familia* included not only immediate blood kin but all the dependents of a household—including slaves. The male head of a *familia*, the *paterfamilias*, had

TABLE 5–1   The Greek and Roman Pantheons

GREEK GODS	ROMAN EQUIVALENTS	
Zeus	Jupiter	The Greeks and Romans both were Indo-
Hera	Juno	European people, so it is not surprising that their
Athena	Minerva	state religions were similar. However, few of their
Apollo	[Apollo]	gods and goddesses had Indo-European ancestry.
Artemis	Diana	Zeus or Jupiter (Deiw-pitar, "Father of the Bright
Hephaestus	Vulcan	Sky") had impeccable Indo-European credentials,
Aphrodite	Venus	but some of his children (Apollo, for instance)
Ares	Mars	had Middle-Eastern origins.
Demeter	Ceres	Comparable gods did not always have the same
Poseidon	Neptune	significance for Greeks and Romans. Mars, for
Hades	Pluto	example, loomed large in the Roman pantheon as
Hestia	Vesta	the god who brought victory in war. Ares, his Greek
Hermes	Mercury	double, was a far less respected deity, a symbol of
Dionysus	Bacchus	the negative passions that spark conflict.

absolute authority over all its members. His sons never outgrew his power, and he could, if he wished, order their execution.

Some of Rome's plebeian families were as ancient as (and richer than) their patrician superiors. The Senate expected them to contribute their men to its army, but it refused to allow them any role in government. Not surprisingly, they refused to accept this, and a "struggle of the orders," the challenge they mounted to the patrician monopoly of political power, dominated the early history of the republic. The plebeians were able to force concessions from the Senate because the patrician Senate needed plebeian help to defend the city. Whenever the Senate balked at the demands of the plebeians, they threatened a military strike. These confrontations usually ended in compromises that, over the course of two centuries, forged a complex constitution for the republic.

In 471 B.C.E. the plebeians set up an assembly of their own headed by ten magistrates called tribunes. In 451 B.C.E. they won acceptance of the Twelve Tables, a law code establishing a common standard of justice for all citizens. In 445 B.C.E. marriage between patrician and plebeian families was legalized, and elective offices began to be opened to plebeian candidates. In 287 B.C.E. the Hortensian Law made plebiscites (votes by the people) binding on all Romans. This granted legislative authority to the people, but the result was hardly a triumph for democracy. The effect of the new laws was to permit intermarriage between wealthy patrician and plebeian families and to create a complicated system of checks and balances that allowed these wealthy families to dominate the republic.

The republic's complex organization was designed to prevent any individual from acquiring enough power to reestablish monarchy. All elected magistrates served terms of only one year, and they were forbidden to seek immediate reelection. The duties of the chief executive were shared by two consuls—the expectation being that each would keep the other in check. The consuls' authority over soldiers in the field (their *imperium*) was absolute, but their power in the city was limited. To prevent them from seizing control of Rome, their armies were strictly forbidden to cross the *pomerium*, the city's sacred boundary. If the Senate wished to honor a general, it showed its trust by suspending this rule and granting him a "triumph" (permission to parade his men through the city).

The diffusion of power in Rome made alliances necessary and encouraged influence peddling and a system of patronage. The poorer citizens needed the support and protection of those who were richer and more powerful. A patron advertised his importance by parading through the streets accompanied by a crowd of his clients. They gave him political clout, for they voted as he commanded or risked losing his support. (The secret ballot was not introduced until 139 B.C.E.) No poor man could marshal enough votes to be elected to an office, and if he had, he could not have afforded to serve. The republic's magistrates were not paid, and they were expected to fund the costs of their offices from their private fortunes. A man who wanted a major office also had to spend years pursuing it. The *cursus honorum* ("path of honors") decreed a sequence of lower offices that a man had to win before he qualified to run for higher ones.

The Roman Republic was so far from what most people today would regard as an equitable government that one wonders why the Romans were so attached to it. They, of course, did not have the advantage of a modern perspective and did not feel deprived of rights they had never imagined. But they also had a good reason to be proud of their republic. It won them an empire.

The Republic Acquires an Empire   At the start of the fifth century B.C.E., Rome was a tiny, landlocked city-state that had no obvious potential to become an imperialistic power. Its survival was threatened by enemies that attacked from every direction: Etruscan, Greek, Latin, and Celtic. Time and again, however, the Romans rose to the challenge and built on their victories by generous treatment of those whom they defeated. The republic annexed some territory and garrisoned some places with military colonies, but it created more allies than subjects. One by one, Italy's city-states (some eagerly and others lacking alternatives) joined Rome in a federation. They retained control over their domestic affairs, but submitted to Rome's foreign policy and contributed to its armies. The rights some allies were given to trade with Rome, to migrate to Rome, and to marry Romans helped spread Roman customs and language and create a common culture for Italy.

Rome's consolidation of Italy was viewed with suspicion by the western Mediterranean's other major power, the Carthaginian empire. While the Greeks were planting their colonies in Sicily and Italy in the mid-eighth century B.C.E., their seafaring competitors, the Phoenicians, were colonizing the Mediterranean's southern rim. Their chief outpost, the North African city of Carthage, emerged as the administrative center of a self-sufficient empire that closed the southwestern corner of the Mediterranean to outsiders. The primary threat to the Carthaginians came from the Greeks on the island of Sicily. Carthage believed that it had to hold the western end of Sicily to protect its sea lanes (see Map 5–3).

Sicily was perpetually at war. Its Greek *poleis* fought among themselves and with the Carthaginians, and Syracuse, the largest Greek city on Sicily, sought to unite the island under its control. In 265 B.C.E., the Romans added to the confusion by acceding to a request from the Sicilian city of Messana for military assistance. (Messana commanded the narrow strait between Sicily and Italy through which Italy's shipping passed.) Carthage and Syracuse were both alarmed by Rome's intervention in their sphere of influence, and the situation quickly escalated into a major conflict called the First Punic (Phoenician) War (264–241 B.C.E.). The war dragged on because Carthage and Rome were incompatible military powers. Carthage fought at sea with its navy, and Rome campaigned on land with its army. Neither made much progress until Rome built a navy and set out to meet Carthage on its own terms. Carthage finally decided that the war was not worth its cost, and it ceded Sicily to Rome in exchange for peace.

The Romans had not set out to conquer Sicily, but the war convinced them that they had to hold the island to prevent anyone from using it as a base for invading Italy. Because their interests in Sicily were primarily defensive, they declared it a military

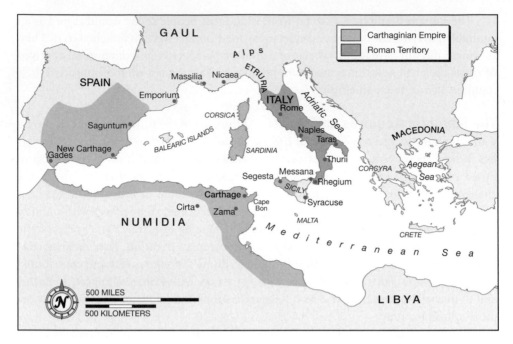

Map 5–3   Rome and Carthage   The lines drawn on maps seem to imply that the Romans and Carthaginians controlled large blocks of contiguous territory, but such was not the case. Borders were vague, jurisdictions overlapped, and governmental power was more effectively imposed in some places than others.

Question: Does the map support Rome's belief that Carthage was a threat to its security?

province and turned it over to a Roman general. This first province in what was to become a Roman Empire altered the politics of the republic in unanticipated ways. Rome refused to shoulder the expense of maintaining its army in Sicily and ordered its commander to raise the funds he needed from the Sicilians themselves. This gave him an opportunity to loot the province and return to Rome much richer than when he left. He could then pour his new wealth into a campaign to win more offices and honors. As Rome's leaders discovered the advantages a provincial governorship gave a man in the game of Roman politics, the republic's foreign policy began to change.

By expanding into Spain, Carthage recovered from the First Punic War much more quickly than Rome expected. Its leading general, Hamilcar Barca (c. 270–228 B.C.E.), believed that things were not settled between his people and the Romans, and his suspicions increased in 238 B.C.E., when Rome ordered Carthage to surrender the island of Sardinia. Rome may only have wanted to make sure that Carthage could not use Sardinia to attack Italy, but by annexing Sardinia, it confirmed Carthage's fear that Rome was bent on its destruction. Hamilcar Barca's son, Hannibal (247–182 B.C.E.), inherited his father's belief that war with Rome was inevitable. The Romans, for their part, felt fairly secure. Control of the seas around Italy gave them confidence that if war came, it would be fought on Carthaginian territory.

When the Second Punic War (218–202 B.C.E.) broke out, the Romans dispatched their armies to Spain and Sicily to confront Hannibal and his forces. But Hannibal was not where they expected to find him. When Publius Cornelius Scipio, the Roman commander of the Spanish expedition, landed to take on supplies on the coast of Gaul, he was shocked to discover that Hannibal had already departed Spain with an army of 30,000 men (and 60 famous elephants), crossed Gaul, and was heading over the Alps into northern Italy. Scipio sent his soldiers on to Spain while he hastily returned to Italy to patch together another army, but the ease with which Hannibal routed him gave the Romans their first hint at the danger they faced. Hannibal won every major battle the Romans risked giving him (except the last). He devastated Italy and slaughtered its men. But Rome refused to admit defeat, and the war dragged on for 14 years. Hannibal had made a serious miscalculation. He had expected Rome's Italian allies to defect and join him, but most remained loyal to Rome. If Italy's cities were subjects of a Roman Empire, they were not eager to seize the chance Hannibal gave them to escape their subjugation.

Rome finally defeated Hannibal by refusing to fight him in Italy while opening new fronts against the Carthaginians elsewhere. One Roman army dogged Hannibal's tracks in Italy and harassed his rearguard. Another overwhelmed his bases in Spain and his allies in Sicily, and a third finally took the war to North Africa. In 204 B.C.E. Hannibal was forced to pull his men out of Italy and take them home to defend Carthage. He fended off the Romans for two more years, but he was finally defeated by Scipio "Africanus," the son of the Scipio who had tried (and failed) to stop him when he first entered Italy. Carthage surrendered, and Hannibal fled to the Middle East, where ultimately he committed suicide to avoid capture by Rome's agents.

Carthage was allowed to survive—stripped of most of its territory and ships, and burdened with a huge war indemnity. Rome annexed Spain but ceded much of North Africa to Numidia, its ally in the war with Hannibal. The western Mediterranean was now indisputably Roman territory, but only portions of it were directly administered by Rome (which still had no plan for organizing an empire).

The Second Punic War had exhausted the Romans, but they leaped immediately into new campaigns in Greece. In 215 B.C.E. Philip V of Macedon (r. 221–179 B.C.E.) had allied with Hannibal because he was afraid that Rome might use its naval bases at the mouth of the Adriatic to invade his realm. A war with his Greek neighbors prevented him from sending help to Hannibal, but that made no difference to Rome. Rome declared war on Philip in 200 B.C.E., and three years later he surrendered. Curiously, Rome annexed no territory but contented itself with liberating the Greek city-states from Macedonian control. So long as the Greeks were disunited and fighting among themselves, they posed no threat to Rome.

When a warring Greek faction invited the Seleucid emperor, Antiochus III (r. 223–187 B.C.E.), to come to its aid, Rome sent its armies back to Greece. Antiochus beat a hasty retreat. The Romans pursued him across the Aegean, and in 188 B.C.E. he yielded most of Asia Minor to Rome. Rome fought two more wars with Macedonia and the Greeks, and in 168 B.C.E. it tried to pacify Greece by taking a thousand prominent Greeks hostage (the historian Polybius among them). In 148 B.C.E. Rome finally turned Macedonia into a province, and in 146 B.C.E. Rome sacked the city of Corinth and put down the last of the Greek rebellions. In the same year, a Third Punic War (149–146 B.C.E.) ended with the obliteration of Carthage. Rome emerged as the dominant power in the Mediterranean world, but its imperial territory did not yet have an imperial government.

The Stress of Success   Rome's republican institutions were barely adequate for a city-state, and they were certainly not designed for the responsibilities of a vast empire. The new lands that Rome had acquired altered life for both the rich and the poor in ways that did neither class much good. Lax oversight of the provinces meant that most of the profits from the empire went into the pockets of military governors who used them to corrupt republican politics. The custom developed of giving a Roman magistrate a provincial command at the end of his year-long term in office. This prevented him from scheming to stay in power by getting him out of the city. But it also gave him a chance to recoup his finances and return to Rome with enough money to run for another office that would bring him another governorship. Because it was virtually impossible for an outsider to break into this system, about 50 families appropriated much of the empire's wealth and monopolized the republic's offices.

As the few rich grew richer, the empire's new provinces impoverished many of the soldiers who had conquered them. The Hannibalic War devastated Italy's farms, and long terms of military service prevented many men from caring for their land. When Rome's farmer-soldiers finally returned home, many lacked the capital to rebuild their farms and those who had the money found that the kind of farming they could do was no longer profitable. Grain was the small farmer's cash crop, but the Italian market was flooded with cheap grain from the provinces. Small domestic producers could not compete and had to sell out to wealthy investors who could afford to convert the land to more profitable uses. Rich families consolidated huge blocks of land and created **latifundia**, plantations that produced commercial crops (such as olives, wine, and cattle) for the international market. These *latifundia* provided no employment for the Roman farmer whose land they absorbed, for Rome's wars created an excess of cheap slaves. As slaves took over much of the agricultural work, rural freemen had little choice but to flood into cities like Rome. The government distributed bread to keep them quiet, and they earned handouts by joining the armies of clients with which the great families fought their political battles.

The situation was so corrupt that by the middle of the second century B.C.E. even wealthy Romans feared that the republic might collapse. There were calls for reform, but two things made changing the system difficult. No one was sure what would work, and no one wanted anyone else to get credit for a program that did work. Matters came to a head in 133 B.C.E., when Tiberius Gracchus (168–133 B.C.E.), a tribune, proposed confiscating the excess from anyone who had appropriated more than 320 acres of what was designated as public land, dividing the surplus into small farms, and giving these to the poor. The office of tribune had been created to protect the plebeians, and each tribune had the power to block legislation that he thought was not in the people's interest by standing up in the assembly and saying *veto* ("I forbid!"). When Tiberius presented his land redistribution proposal, its opponents induced another tribune to cast a veto. Tiberius, however, was prepared for this. He persuaded the assembly to throw the man out of office—on the theory that he had not used his powers for the purpose for which they had been granted. Land reform passed, but at the cost of destroying one of the crucial checks and balances of the Roman constitution. If the mob could instantly depose any politician who displeased it, the republic would degenerate into mob rule. When Tiberius's opponents finally ran out of legal ways to counter his maneuvers, they simply murdered him.

Tiberius's land redistribution plan was implemented, but it failed. Like many reforms, it addressed the symptom of a problem while ignoring its causes. It did nothing to change the situation that had forced small farmers off their land in the first place. Returning them to the land only set them up to fail again.

The strategy Tiberius invented to pass his reform program had a greater impact on the republic than did the reform itself, for it caused a new division in Roman politics. The **populares** ("people's party") sought power, as Tiberius had, by championing ideas that appealed to the mob. The **optimates** ("aristocrats") defended the prerogatives of the Senate by affirming Rome's conservative traditions. Neither party had a platform of proposals designed to cure the ills of Roman society. Each was defined by the method it used for gaining political advantage.

In 123 B.C.E. Tiberius Gracchus's younger brother, Gaius (159–121 B.C.E.), took up the *populares*' cause and made considerable headway until the *optimates* again employed force to destroy a rival politician. Rome's next leader, Gaius Marius (157–86 B.C.E.), learned a lesson from the fate of the two Gracchi that profoundly affected the course of Roman history. He concluded that to survive in the Roman political arena, a man had to have an army at his back.

In 107 B.C.E. Marius won a consulship by promising to bring a war with Numidia to a speedy conclusion. He proposed beefing up the army by dropping the traditional property qualification for service. This was welcomed by the impoverished Roman masses who had no jobs and no prospects, for it gave them a chance to vote themselves military careers. The soldiers Marius created in this way were, however, more his than Rome's. To secure their own continued employment, they were determined to keep him in office. Marius's reform turned Rome's army into a political machine that, contrary to tradition, won one consulship after another for its general.

Rome's Civil War

No one could compete with a man like Marius without building an army comparable to his, so every Roman politician who hoped to stay in the game set about winning a military command. That meant that aspiring politicians needed wars, for armies were

PEOPLE IN CONTEXT Cornelia, Mother of the Gracchi

In theory Roman women, like Greek women, were subject to male authority, but in practice they had much more freedom. Roman girls could attend school, and Roman women were not confined to their homes. They followed politics and sometimes demonstrated in the streets to push for legislation they wanted. Women from prominent families were well-known public figures who exercised considerable influence. The most respected of these from the republican era was the Gracchi brothers' mother, Cornelia. Roman women bore only one name, the feminine spelling of their father's *gens*. (All of a man's daughters had the same name.) Cornelia (c. 180–105 B.C.E.) was the daughter of Publius Cornelius Scipio Africanus, the victor in the Second Punic War. The husband to whom Scipio gave her (at age 12) was a distinguished Roman considerably her senior, Tiberius Sempronius Gracchus. The marriage was fruitful. Cornelia bore him 12 children, alternating boys and girls. Only three survived to adulthood: Tiberius, Gaius, and their sister Sempronia (who married a Scipio to reaffirm the links between her parental families).

Mother of the Gracchi   This statue is of a woman from the era of Rome's Empire, not the Republic. But its design follows a convention believed to have been established by the lost republican-era statue of Cornelia (i.e., depicting Roman matrons seated in chairs).

After her husband's death in 154 B.C.E., Cornelia chose to remain a widow and declined a proposal of marriage from the pharaoh of Egypt. She devoted herself to the education of her sons and was said to have fired their political ambitions by telling them that she was ashamed to be known as Scipio's daughter rather than the Gracchi's mother. Given their bloody fates, she may have come to regret her words. Ancient historians cited letters (the authenticity of which modern scholars doubt) that she wrote to Gaius, urging him to moderate his radical politics. She was so well known and admired that her sons could score points with their audiences simply by mentioning her in their speeches, and her popularity was such that she became the first Roman woman, other than a priestess, to whom the republic erected a statue. The bronze effigy has disappeared, but its inscribed base survives. We know what it looked like, for statues honoring other women took it as their model. It is hard to imagine such a monument being raised in Athens, where, according to Pericles, the best women were those who were totally invisible.

Question: What explains the fact that women were more liberated in the Roman republic than in the Athenian democracy?

■ ■ ■ ■ ■ ■ ■

only justified when there were wars. After years of being slow to acquire provinces, Rome's foreign policy changed. Its leaders began to look for lands to conquer as a means to the ultimate conquest: Rome itself.

Sulla   In 88 B.C.E. Sulla (138–78 B.C.E.), one of Marius's officers, revealed the danger at the heart of the new power politics. He raised an army and marched on Rome to force the Senate to legitimate his command. After a profitable campaign in Asia Minor, Sulla retook Rome, assumed dictatorial powers, and executed thousands of citizens. Although Sulla used the *populares'* strategy to win control of Rome, he was an *optimate* reformer. He believed that Rome's difficulties had been caused by *popularis* demagogues, and to prevent any more of them from appearing, he emasculated the popular assembly and restored the traditional dominance of the Senate.

Sulla's reform was as unrealistic as the Gracchan land redistribution scheme. The Senate could not defend the empire with magistrates who were hobbled by the traditional restraints of the republican constitution. A government in which every office changed hands every year lacked continuity and could not successfully wage lengthy foreign wars. Almost immediately, therefore, the Senate began to appoint "special commanders" to deal with its more difficult problems. What made a command "special" was its freedom from the legal limitations imposed on the regular magistrates. Ambitious men immediately recognized that the fastest route to power was not through the old *cursus honorum* but via a series of special commands.

The first of the great special commanders was Pompey (106–48 B.C.E.), a young *optimas* who was one of Sulla's supporters. His conservative credentials persuaded the Senate that he could be trusted, and his loyal service lulled the Senators into granting him one special command after another—culminating in a commission to sweep pirates from the Mediterranean. This warranted a massive army and navy, which Pompey used not only to suppress piracy but to extend the empire in the east to the borders of Egypt. The Senate ultimately awoke to the possibility that it had created another Sulla, and the only strategy it could think of to block him was to make more like him. The Senators decreed special commands for Crassus (115–53 B.C.E.), reputedly Rome's richest man, and an ambitious and talented blue blood named Julius Caesar (100–44 B.C.E.).

When Pompey returned from the east in 62 B.C.E., he surprised everyone by leaving his army behind. He was a conservative man who would have been content simply to be showered with lavish praise for his services to the republic. The Senators chose instead to try to bring him down. They delayed the grants of land he requested as retirement pay for his veteran soldiers in an attempt to undermine his troops' loyalty to him. The Senators also concluded, somewhat prematurely, that they could handle Pompey on their own and that they had no further need for Crassus and Caesar. This had the effect of forcing Pompey, Crassus, and Caesar to bury their differences and join forces to defeat the Senate. In 59 B.C.E. they formed an alliance called the First **Triumvirate** ("rule by three men").

The First Triumvirate   Together, Pompey, Crassus, and Caesar were invincible, but they had no common objective for the use of their power. Each man had a private agenda that reflected his suspicion of his allies. Because Pompey's army made him the dominant member of the triumvirate, Crassus and Caesar wanted assignments that would enable them to build up comparable forces. Crassus set out to conquer the Parthian Empire, a great Iranian state on the eastern edge of Rome's territory, and Caesar stirred up trouble with the Gauls in northern Europe. Caesar pushed Rome's frontier to the Rhine River and the English Channel and whipped up enthusiasm in Rome by publishing an account of his campaigns (*The Gallic Wars*). Pompey, who stayed in Rome, was distrustful of both his colleagues, and the Triumvirate unraveled after the Parthians killed Crassus in 53 B.C.E. The Senate concluded that Pompey, an *optimas*, was a lesser threat to its interests than Caesar, a *popularis*, and it joined with Pompey in an attempt to end Caesar's career.

The situation came to a head in 50 B.C.E. Caesar's term as governor of his provinces expired, and the Senate refused to extend his command of his army. Caesar then marched on Rome and Pompey, and many of the Senators fled to Greece where large numbers of Pompey's troops were quartered. Although Caesar's army was much smaller and short of supplies, it went in pursuit, and in June, 48 B.C.E., Caesar routed the Senatorial forces at the battle of Pharsalus. Remnants of Pompey's army scattered to Africa and Spain, and Pompey sought refuge in Egypt, the only Mediterranean state still outside Rome's empire. Fearing Caesar's retribution, the Egyptians killed Pompey, embalmed his head, and sent it to Caesar as a token of their friendship. Caesar then invaded Egypt to avenge Pompey's murder. Egypt owed its survival as an independent country to the skill with which its young queen, Cleopatra VII (69–30 B.C.E.), a descendant of Alexander's general Ptolemy, handled Caesar.

Cleopatra   In the popular imagination Queen Cleopatra VII of Egypt, mistress to both Julius Caesar and Mark Antony, has become a seductress whose beauty men found irresistible. However, the most reliable of her portraits suggest that she was not remarkably handsome. The formalized example shown here was probably executed during her lifetime. The legend of her beauty may in large part be a product of misogyny—of the assumption that a woman's only power and appeal derive from her sexuality.

It took some time for Caesar to clean out pockets of resistance, but by 45 B.C.E. he was master of Rome. Caesar was a good historian, and he probably concluded from his study of recent events that a republic could not govern an empire. Rome's urban mob had neither the wisdom nor the right to rule the world, and there was no way (given the primitive means of communications that were available) to enfranchise all the free men of the empire. Because monarchy was the only form of government efficient enough to run a large state in the ancient era, Caesar probably planned to establish kingship of some kind. That, at least, is what the Senate suspected, and to prevent it, some 60 Senators mobbed him at a meeting on March 15, 44 B.C.E. (the ides of March), and stabbed him 23 times.

Brutus and Cassius, the plot's leaders, had no plan to replace Caesar. They saw themselves as reformers who were defending the republic, and like previous reformers, they mistook a symptom for a cause. They assumed that Caesar was the problem and that when he was removed, the republic would automatically thrive. It was the republic's inadequacy, however, that had brought Caesar to power. His death did not correct that. It simply created a vacuum to be filled by a new Caesar.

The man best poised to succeed Caesar was his popular second-in-command, Mark Antony (c. 83–30 B.C.E.). Antony's plan was to stage a showy funeral for Caesar and distract Caesar's men until their desire to avenge themselves on the Senators abated. If they remained under his control, the Senate would be forced to rely on him for protection and he would be Rome's master. The problem with Antony's strategy was that Caesar had an heir. Caesar had no son, but he had adopted a nephew, Octavian (63 B.C.E.–14 C.E.), to carry on his name. Octavian was only 18 when Caesar died, and he had little military or political experience. But when he charged into Rome demanding vengeance for the murder of his "father," Caesar's soldiers cheered. The Senate was perversely delighted. Even though Octavian was vowing to punish the senatorial assassins, the Senate granted him a military command. It assumed that he was too young to be a threat and that his mere existence would divide Caesar's men and set them to fighting among themselves. Octavian was too smart for that. As soon as he had something to offer, he joined forces with Antony and Lepidus (d. 13 B.C.E.), another of Caesar's officers. They formally established the Second Triumvirate, a legal joint dictatorship, and in 42 B.C.E. they defeated the armies of Brutus and Cassius at Philippi in Greece.

The Second Triumvirate

The triumvirs had assumed dictatorial powers allegedly to restore the republic, but they were in no hurry. After Philippi, they divided up responsibilities for governing the empire. Antony's military reputation made him the dominant member of the triumvirate, and he awarded himself the best assignment. He headed east to prepare an invasion of Parthia. A successful Parthian campaign would provide him with a huge army with which he hoped in the end to sweep the other triumvirs aside. Octavian remained in Italy and oversaw efforts to track down rebel armies led by Pompey's sons. Lepidus governed Africa until 36 B.C.E., when Octavian placed him under house arrest (which continued until Lepidus's death 24 years later).

Octavian was a poor general but a superb politician, and when Antony committed a public relations blunder, Octavian moved in for the kill. Like Julius Caesar before him, Antony struck up a relationship with Egypt's Cleopatra. It was personal. (He fathered three of her children.) But it was also a sensible strategic alliance between two level-headed rulers. Antony needed Egypt's support for his invasion of Parthia, and Cleopatra extracted a promise of land in exchange for her aid. Octavian, however, convinced the Romans that the unpopular eastern queen had used her sexual wiles to captivate Antony—as she had previously captivated Caesar—and that Antony had become her pawn and the instrument through which she intended to rule Rome.

Octavian's charges would have had little effect if Antony's attack on Parthia had succeeded. But when it failed, Octavian made his move. In 32 B.C.E. he persuaded the Italians to swear a personal oath of loyalty to him and to support him in attacking Antony—allegedly to save the Roman Republic from overthrow by Cleopatra. The opposing armies again met in Greece, but they had little enthusiasm for the fight. The issue was decided by a sea battle off the western coast of Greece at Actium (31 B.C.E.). Antony and Cleopatra retreated to Egypt where they committed suicide rather than submit to Octavian.

Octavian's victory confronted him with the challenge that had cost Caesar his life—the responsibility for creating a stable government for Rome's empire. Octavian had already publicly eliminated the option of monarchy, for he had risen to power by promising to restore the republic. His ingenious strategy for reconciling what Rome wanted with what Rome needed was to create an "invisible monarchy,"

Greece and Rome, 750 B.C.E.–31 B.C.E.	
GREECE	**ROME**
750 B.C.E., colonization movement	750 B.C.E., foundation of the city of Rome
510 B.C.E., Cleisthenes and Athens' democracy	509 B.C.E., Roman Republic founded
492–479 B.C.E., Persian Wars	"Struggle of the Orders"
432–404 B.C.E., Peloponnesian War	Rome fights in Italy
336–323 B.C.E., Alexander the Great	
323 B.C.E., Antigonids, Seleucids, Ptolemies (Zeno, Epicurus, Euclid)	
	287 B.C.E., Plebiscite established
(Archimedes)	264–241 B.C.E., First Punic War
	218–202 B.C.E., Second Punic War
200–196 B.C.E., Rome's war with Philip V of Macedonia	
190 B.C.E., Rome defeats Antiochus and occupies Asia Minor	
(168 B.C.E., Polybius deported to Italy)	
	146 B.C.E., Corinth and Carthage sacked
	133 B.C.E., Tiberius Gracchus's tribunate
	123 B.C.E., Gaius Gracchus's first tribunate
	107 B.C.E., Marius's first consulate
	88 B.C.E., Sulla's first march on Rome
	67–61 B.C.E., Pompey expands empire in the east
	60 B.C.E., First Triumvirate
	45 B.C.E., Caesar defeats Pompey (d. 48 B.C.E.)
	43 B.C.E., Second Triumvirate
	31 B.C.E., Octavian defeats Antony

an imperial administration masked by a republican façade. By allowing the Romans to indulge the illusion of living in a republic, he was able to subject them to a monarchy. Sometimes governments increase their power by seeming to repudiate the very things that they are doing. Citizens of modern republics and democracies need to keep that in mind.

KEY QUESTION | Revisited

Imperialism and monarchy have largely fallen out of fashion in the modern West, and Americans generally view some form of government by the people as the only reliable guarantor of what they hold to be God-given, inalienable freedoms. Americans have, from time to time, felt that it is the obligation of their country to defend democracy and spread it around the globe.

Government by the people may, however, not always be a people's highest priority. A potential conflict can arise between two things that citizens want from government: they want protection for individual liberties, but they also want security for person and property. If circumstances force them to choose between these things, history suggests that the desire for safety often wins out. The Greeks' experiment with democracy led to an era of civil war and chaos that ended in foreign occupation. The Romans repeatedly tinkered with their republic in an effort to make it work, but in the end they sacrificed the reality of government by the people for its illusion. For many Romans the price must have seemed worth paying. The imperial administration that took over from Rome's quarrelsome republic unified Europe, North Africa, and much of the Middle East and maintained something like world peace for over three centuries.

An autocracy can provide a more efficient response to a crisis than a government that depends on numerous people reaching consensus about what to do. Given that efficiency can mean the difference between life and death in wartime, people may willingly sacrifice liberties to achieve it. Consequently, wars—particularly long ones—are dangerous for democracies. The struggle for victory usually drives them to increase the power and reduce the number of their leaders.

The size of a state has also often been a factor in determining the success or failure of a citizen-run government. Consensus is usually easier to reach in small communities than large ones, and citizens of small communities develop emotional bonds that sometimes inspire them to remarkable acts of self-sacrifice in defense of their homeland. Such was the experience of Athens in the Persian Wars, as well as the behavior of the Romans in the early days of their republic. In the ancient world, however, when the scale of social life grew beyond a certain point, government by the people tended to falter and to allow autocracy to take its place. Given the limited means of communication then available, an autocratic hierarchy provided the only efficient way to govern a large area. Orders could quickly be sent down from the top, but it was difficult for opinions to be gathered up from the bottom. In this respect the modern world is different. It is often said that communications technologies have shrunk the world and made it the equivalent of a global village. If so, can great territorial states now be successfully and permanently governed by the masses, or are governments by the people still fated, when pressured by war and conflict, to surrender to small coteries of powerful leaders?

Review Questions

1. What were Alexander's strategies for conquering an empire and for making that conquest permanent?
2. What do the arts, sciences, literatures, and philosophies of the Hellenistic empires imply about the sociopolitical environments these empires created?
3. Why did the discoveries and inventions of Hellenistic scientists have so little impact on their world?
4. How did Rome's republican system of government differ from Athens' democracy?
5. Did Rome intentionally build an empire, or was its empire an unintended consequence of its attempts to defend itself?
6. Why was the Roman Republic unable to manage its empire?

Please consult the Suggested Readings at the back of the book to continue your study of the material covered in this chapter. For a list of documents on the Primary Source DVD-ROM that relate to topics in this chapter, please refer to the back of the book.

6 Rome's Empire and the Unification of the Western World

[Octavian Augustus] seduced the military with gifts, the civilians with cheap food, and everyone with the benefits of peace. Then he gradually took over the functions of the Senate, the magistrates, and the law itself. The prominent men who had survived [the civil war] found that the best way to prosper politically and financially was slavishly to support him.

—Tacitus

KEY | Question

Do people prefer order to liberty?

In 1937 a skillful feat of engineering recovered fragments of the Altar of Peace (*Ara Pacis*), a first-century monument that lay buried beneath a sixteenth-century Roman *palazzo*. It had been erected about 9 B.C.E. to commemorate the *pax Romana* ("Roman peace") that descended on the Mediterranean world after Octavian's victory over Antony and Cleopatra. The altar stood on a platform open to the sky, and it was surrounded by a wall on which carvings depicted Octavian (63 B.C.E.–14 C.E.) and his family in a religious procession. Its style so brilliantly synthesized Greek idealism and Roman realism that it inspired artists for centuries.

Near the end of his life, Octavian published a testament cataloguing his services to Rome. In addition to bringing peace, he noted that he had used his personal fortune to see the state through fiscal crises. He had rebuilt the city of Rome and entertained its residents with races and games. He had provided free food during famines. He had reduced the size of the army while expanding the empire, securing its frontiers, and maintaining its internal order. But the achievement of which he said he was most proud was the restoration of Rome's republican government.

Portrait of a Roman Woman Portraits on planks of wood, such as this one, were commissioned to cover the faces of mummies. Their style may be a little rough, but they can be compelling in the way they capture the individuality of their subjects. *Dagli Orti/Picture Desk, Inc./Kobal Collection*

In truth, Octavian had not restored the republic. He had used republican rhetoric to engineer Rome's transition to monarchy. At the time, few objected, for it seemed safe to trust him with overwhelming power. Few thought about what might happen when that power passed to other hands. Within a few years, the historian Tacitus (c. 55–120 C.E.) and other members of the senatorial class were so disillusioned that they even denigrated the peace the emperors created for Rome. It was purchased, they said, at the cost of the republican liberties that they had long enjoyed (and abused). Tacitus claimed that the victim sacrificed on Octavian's Altar of Peace was freedom.

Just societies aspire to reconcile the freedom of the individual with the desires of the group for security and stability. This is difficult. Too much freedom leads to chaos, and too much control to tyranny—and fear of one may bring on the other. Octavian rescued Rome from a century-long civil war and established a peace that brought undeniable benefits. There was, however, a cost. As you examine the history of imperial Rome, reflect on what it implies about the problem of balancing liberty against the risk of anarchy.

The Augustan Era

The Roman Republic was able to conquer an empire, but not to rule one. The republic's strategy for heading off tyranny was to divide power among its magistrates. This risked disorder, for men often yielded to the temptation to use the resources of their offices to fight among themselves for supremacy. A monarchy, which set one man far above all others, promised more stability, but the Romans equated monarchy with servitude. They were so attached to the image of themselves as free citizens (not subjects of a king) that they clung to their faulty republic—even though it condemned them to a century of recurrent civil war.

An Invisible Monarchy   When Octavian returned to Rome from his eastern campaigns in 29 B.C.E., he was hailed as the savior of his country. He knew that its salvation would be short-lived unless fundamental changes were made in its political institutions, but he was acutely aware of the danger of making any changes that might be interpreted as threats to the republic. Suspicions of monarchical ambitions had cost Julius Caesar and Mark Antony their lives.

Rome's immediate need for a leader strong enough to restore order bought Octavian a period of grace. For eight years, he provided a legal basis for his authority by monopolizing one of the consulships, but this was risky. It looked suspiciously like a step toward monarchy. In January, 27 B.C.E., he secured his position by threatening to give it up. He convened the Senate and offered to surrender all his powers and fully restore the republic. There was no risk that the Senate would accept his offer. The Senators realized that things would fall apart if he loosed the reins of power. So instead, they thanked him for his services to the republic by granting him a title—Augustus ("majestic")—and prevailed on him to continue as consul and accept a ten-year term as governor of 18 of the empire's 28 provinces. The army had been split up and posted to trouble spots in the provinces, most of which, coincidentally, were the ones assigned to Octavian.

As the holder of **imperium** *maius* ("supreme military authority"), the new Augustus was Rome's *imperator* ("emperor"). This was an ancient republican term for a victorious general, not a monarch, but Augustus preferred to use a civilian title that the grateful Romans had lavished on him to recognize his record of public service: *princeps civitatis* ("first of citizens"). All of Augustus's titles were republican in origin, but they, like his adopted family name, Caesar (the origin of Kaiser and Tsar), soon came to signify regal authority.

Augustus believed that the Romans would tolerate a *principate* (a government in which one man had the power to keep things on track) if it brought the blessings of peace and if its prince honored their republican traditions. He scrupulously avoided anything that looked monarchical. His home on the Palatine Hill was a typical upper-class residence. (Parts of it have survived.) He wore ordinary civilian dress, and he claimed that his togas (the garments that symbolized Roman citizenship) were home-spun by his wife, Livia, and daughter, Julia. He did not surround himself with armed men or throw his weight around needlessly. He wandered the streets, entered into the fray of elections, solicited votes for candidates he backed, took part in debates, and treated his senatorial colleagues as equals.

Augustus's stated affection for republican tradition was not entirely insincere. He shared as much power as he thought he safely could with the Senate and the republican magistrates. He reduced the Senate from 1,000 to about 600 members and filled its ranks with experienced men of good reputation. His preference was for members of Rome's old families, but the civil war had taken a toll on these. They were dying out and a new aristocracy with roots in other Italian cities and the provinces was in the making. The reconstituted Senate had real responsibility. It managed the treasury, served as a kind of supreme court, and had the power to legislate. Augustus assembled a small company of trusted Senators and magistrates to serve as his personal advisors, and during his sometimes lengthy absences from Italy, the Senate was left to manage (or mismanage) on its own.

In 23 B.C.E. Augustus increased his republican cover by resigning the office of consul. His successive terms were unpopular, for they violated tradition and kept other men from enjoying the prestige of the office. Thereafter, he based his authority on his privileges as an honorary tribune and the periodic renewal of his provincial governorships. From time to time, he also held the office of censor, which allowed him to create Senators and "equestrians" (Rome's second highest social class), and he served as *Pontifex maximus*, the head of the state religion. Throughout his career he was careful to make sure that his powers derived from republican offices or precedents. By skillfully combining and prolonging these, he exercised mastery over Rome. His example suggests that the greatest danger to a modern republic with separated branches of government may not be an overt attack on its constitution, but a covert strategy that quietly and behind the scenes amasses privileges and bits of authority.

Octavian Augustus   Octavian Augustus, unlike Julius Caesar, was not a soldier or talented general. His skills were political, and he was a master of propaganda. He claimed that his goal was the restoration of the Roman Republic, and he carefully avoided any of the trappings of monarchy. This statue depicts him as a good republican citizen. He wears the toga Roman men donned on formal occasions. He has no crown or jewelry, and he carries nothing more threatening than a scroll.

Reorganization   The republican cloak that shrouded Augustus's monarchy rendered it officially "invisible," and this allowed his fellow Romans to submit to it without sacrificing pride or patriotism. Even those who understood what was happening were inclined to play along with Augustus. The benefits of his administration were obvious but alternatives to it were not. On several occasions the Senate and the people of Rome begged him to take charge and see the state through an economic or political crisis.

The Augustan peace owed a great deal to Augustus's military reforms. Since the days of Marius, Rome's politicians had repeatedly involved its armies in their power struggles, and the empire's military had grown to immense size. At each stage in the civil war, the victor had added his defeated opponents' legions to his own. The army of which Augustus took command after Antony's fall was more than twice as large as the one that he estimated Rome could afford, and he was eager to shrink it for other than fiscal reasons. A smaller army meant fewer threats from fewer generals. Augustus appropriated Egypt as his personal domain and used its wealth to retire about 300,000 men. This reduced the standing army from 60 to 28 legions.

Augustus limited the legionnaires' opportunities to intervene in Rome's politics by posting them to camps along the frontiers. An elite troop of about 4,500 men, the Praetorian Guard, was created to maintain order in Italy. Its name derived from a term for the loyal soldiers who guarded the tents (*praetorii*) of republican generals. In later years, the Praetorian Guard's proximity to the city of Rome tempted it to intervene in the empire's politics, but Augustus hoped that by professionalizing military service he could eliminate some of the motives that previously had politicized Rome's armies. Legionnaires signed on for tours of duty lasting from 16 to 20 years. They were paid according to a fixed scale and could earn promotion from the ranks to the officer corps (although the higher commands were reserved for men from the Senatorial and equestrian classes). In short, Rome's defenders became state employees and no longer were dependent on their generals for their pay and retirement benefits.

Augustus's military reforms helped to consolidate, as well as pacify, the empire. His 28 legions enrolled about 160,000 men—just barely enough to maintain Rome's 4,000-mile-long frontier. To back up the legions (membership in which was limited to Roman citizens), Augustus created auxiliaries, companies of men recruited from the provinces. The legions and auxiliaries together provided about a quarter of a million men to protect and police a population of about 100 million. Auxiliaries were less well paid than legionnaires, but a term of honorable service earned citizenship for the veteran of an auxiliary unit and qualified his sons to join the legions. The army thus provided entry into Roman society for provincials.

Cities were central to the administration of the empire, for its primitive systems of communications meant that most government had to be local government. The army literally built Rome's famous network of roads to facilitate its movements. Augustus began to extend the roads beyond Italy to the headquarters he established for the legions in the provinces. Many of these new military camps became permanent cities that assumed responsibility for administering the districts in which they were located, and they helped to spread Latin language and culture—particularly in the west. The eastern half of the empire already had many cities, but much of the west (particularly in Spain,

North Africa, and trans-Alpine Europe) was still rural territory divided among tribes. Augustus sponsored about 100 colonies, many of which were settled by his veterans. Part of a soldier's pay was banked for him so that when he retired at about the age of 40 he had a nest egg with which to begin a new career. Many men invested in farms and businesses in the provinces in which they had served.

The Roman Empire became a kind of federation of city-states. Each of its urban centers operated within parameters set by the central administration, but each also accommodated local customs. The schools that towns supported and the opportunities for political participation they provided helped to Romanize the provincial elites and foster their loyalty to the empire. As these elites learned Latin and Greek, the empire's upper classes acquired a common culture. The cities in which they lived were similar, no matter where they were located. Each had temples, arenas, theaters, schools, monuments, baths, and public buildings, many of which Augustus and his successors funded. Each had its councils of local leaders. Romanization spread widely, but in many places classical civilization was only a thin veneer over native cultures that outlasted the empire.

Augustus turned the republican hodgepodge of territories into a coherent empire. He redrew the boundaries of provinces and standardized their governments. He reduced corruption by establishing fixed rates of taxation and by appointing state officials, rather than private contractors, to collect and audit taxes. He waged campaigns to extend the empire to what he believed were defensible frontiers. In the east he set up a string of client kingdoms dependent on Rome. In the west he suppressed resistance in Spain and the Alpine region and extended Roman territory in the Balkans north to the Danube Valley. He planned to cross the Rhine and conquer more of Germany, but he failed in his attempt. In 9 C.E. the Germans ambushed and exterminated three legions. Augustus recovered enough to hold the line and maintain order, but the historian Tacitus grumbled about the emperor's heavy-handed methods. The peace in some provinces, Tacitus said, was only the quiet of a man-made desert (see Map 6–1).

Augustus's administrative reforms also helped to turn Rome's diverse holdings into a true empire. The republic had largely been run by amateurs who improvised ad hoc policies to govern its provinces. But Augustus created an imperial bureaucracy of salaried, specially trained professionals to manage the empire. Wealthy Romans often relied on well-educated freedmen and slaves to run their plantations and political offices, and Augustus followed a similar practice when staffing the administration of the empire. Service in the government gave some men, who were legally or socially handicapped, considerable power over people who were otherwise their superiors. Senators and equestrians were enlisted to oversee a growing list of government services. They supervised grain and water supplies, police forces, courts, treasuries, public entertainments, and construction projects.

Moral Regeneration   Augustus, like many Romans, believed that Italy had been able to build the empire because of the unique strength and virtues of its people—their **Romanitas**. It was vitally important, therefore, to preserve Italy's traditions and cultural dominance. This was not a new idea. The Roman Senate had from time to time sought

Map 6–1 Augustus's Empire   Under Augustus Rome completed its encirclement of the Mediterranean, but the empire had not yet reached its full extent. His successors added territory in Britain, Germany, Central Europe, and the Middle East.

Question: Were there natural geographic boundaries for Rome's empire?

to limit the spread of eastern religions that it viewed as detrimental to Roman character, and Italy had supported Augustus in his fight with Mark Antony because Mark Antony was seen as having succumbed to evil eastern influences.

To guarantee Italy's supremacy and the continued integrity of Roman culture, Augustus believed he needed a large pool of disciplined, patriotic upper-class Romans from which to recruit a staff for governing the empire. The civil war had devastated the citizen population, and Rome's upper classes preserved their fortunes by limiting the number of their offspring. Augustus tried to solve the manpower problem by passing laws aimed at strengthening families, increasing birthrates, and restoring commitment to traditional values. He financially penalized women below the age of 50 and men younger than 60 who failed to marry early and remarry promptly when widowed or divorced. Bachelors and sterile couples were heavily taxed, and families with three or more children were given honors and preferential treatment by the government. Adultery for women and for men who had affairs with married women became a crime against the state, punishable by fine, exile, or death. Temples were restored and archaic patriotic ceremonies revived as part of a program to promote patriotism and civic virtue.

Augustus's social legislation was a failure. He and his family even failed to set a good example for others. He sired only one child, a daughter named Julia, and her flagrant immorality ultimately drove him to exile her to a remote island.

Latin High Culture

The arts played a part in Augustus's program for the moral and patriotic regeneration of his fellow citizens, and Roman literature reached the pinnacle of its development during his reign. Ironically, given Rome's condemnation of eastern influences, Romans did not produce much in the way of art, literature, or serious thought until they were stimulated by contact with the Greeks during the last century of the republican era. As Rome's armies moved east, Rome was flooded with looted objects and trade goods that Italian craftsmen eagerly imitated. Much classical Greek statuary survives today only in Roman copies. Influential upper-class Romans, such as the Scipios who led the city during the First and Second Punic War, were infatuated with all things Greek. They learned Greek, dressed as Greeks, bought Greek furniture and slaves, and sat at the feet of Greek philosophers. Some Roman intellectuals and politicians insisted that Greeks were effeminate, untrustworthy, and otherwise lacking in the stalwart virtues of *Romanitas*, but Rome thoroughly succumbed to the blandishments of Hellenistic civilization.

Romans followed the Greeks more closely in some fields than in others. They also adapted what they copied and made some original contributions of their own. This is most evident in architecture. The Romans shared the classical taste for symmetrical designs, but their buildings were often larger and more complex than those of the Greeks. They added curves—arches and domes—to the linear elements (columns and lintels) characteristic of Hellenic buildings. They invented concrete and used it to construct new kinds of imposing but graceful structures. Sulla built Rome's first major building (a temple) in the Greek style. Pompey and Caesar added a few more, but when Augustus came to power, his empire's capital still had few notable buildings. He set about changing that—claiming in the end that he found Rome a city of brick and left it a city of marble.

Related to architecture was the Romans' unique gift for engineering. They drove arrow-straight roads across rough terrain, tunneled through mountains, and created immense systems of aqueducts to supply their cities with lavish amounts of water. Over 200,000 gallons a day eventually flowed into Rome to supply its fountains and baths. A leisurely daily bath was an indispensable ritual of civilized life for a Roman, and Roman cities were equipped with luxurious public bathing facilities.

Latin literature was pioneered by comic playwrights. Twenty-one plays by Plautus (c. 254–184 B.C.E.), an Italian, and six by his successor, a former Carthaginian slave named Terence (c. 195–159 B.C.E.), have survived. Both men imitated Greek models, but Terence's work was the more refined. Plautus served a Roman appetite for farce and slapstick, as serious playwrights with literary pretensions were not much in demand.

The authors of the early republican period were handicapped by the immaturity of the Latin language. The first Romans to try their hands at prose writing wrote in Greek. Cato the Elder (234–149 B.C.E.), a Senator remembered primarily for his political activities, attempted a history of Rome in Latin. It has been lost, but a book he wrote on agriculture survives to provide us with our earliest extended specimen of Latin prose.

Latin poetry began to flourish in the middle of the first century B.C.E. as Romans be-came acquainted with the work of Greeks associated with Alexandria's Museum. Among the best and earliest extant examples are the poems that Catullus (c. 85–54 B.C.E.) penned to describe his passionate, stormy, and disillusioning affair with the promiscuous wife of a prominent Roman politician. Lucretius (c. 94–55 B.C.E.), the republican era's other ma-jor poet, chose a more serious theme for his work. He wrote to convince his countrymen that Epicurean materialism provided escape from the stress and anxiety of the wars that plagued his generation. He claimed that the universe was nothing more than bits of mat-ter randomly colliding in empty space and that when people came to understand this, they would lose their fear of death and the gods and begin to behave rationally. Reason would persuade them of the wisdom of avoiding strong feelings—the pleasurable as well as the painful—by distancing themselves emotionally from a world that was essentially random and meaningless.

At about the same time when Romans were discovering Greek poets, they were in-troduced to Greek philosophy. In 155 B.C.E. Athens dispatched a number of its promi-nent teachers to Rome as ambassadors. The traditional values of Roman culture disposed the Romans to reject philosophies that flirted with atheism and religions that undercut moral rigor. In 186 B.C.E. the Senate outlawed the worship of Dionysus (Bac-chus), a cult associated with orgiastic excesses. In 173 B.C.E. it banished Epicurean philosophers for teaching what it regarded as self-indulgent quietism. The Greek phi-losophy that most appealed to the Romans was Stoicism, and Rome produced two of the best known Stoic authors: Epictetus (b. c. 50 C.E.), a Greek slave, and Marcus Aure-lius (r. 161–180 C.E.), an emperor (both of whom wrote in Greek). Stoics provided a ra-tionale for the traditional Roman virtues of duty and self-discipline. They taught that the world is a great material organism animated by a rational principle. Because it is a rational system, all of its parts serve essential purposes in the functioning of the whole. Individual freedom is, therefore, an illusion. Peace of mind comes from realizing this—from accepting the duties of one's station knowing that everyone (from emperor to slave) is on the same footing. All obey necessity. The only thing within their power is their attitude toward life, and the only real evils are the painful emotions (such as anger, frustration, disappointment, and jealousy) that are aroused when the world cannot be made to serve one's personal desires. Reason frees the virtuous individual to serve the community dispassionately and disinterestedly.

Because republican politicians had to solicit support from voters and sway the thinking of popular assemblies, they were attracted to the study of rhetoric, the art of persuasive speaking pioneered by Greek philosophers. The oratorical skills of Cicero (106–43 B.C.E.) helped him overcome the handicap of undistinguished ancestry, earn a consulship, and serve as one of the Senate's leaders during the era of the First and Second Triumvirates. Cicero was less an original thinker than a popularizer of Greek philosophy. He favored the Stoics and maintained that the infighting that plagued the republic would end if men allowed themselves to be guided by the rational laws that Stoics claimed governed nature. A rational society would grant uniquely talented people (such as Cicero) special privileges and elevate them to positions of leadership no matter what their family backgrounds. Cicero claimed that, from time to time, the republic needed a **princeps**, an extraordinary citizen whose natural charisma, wisdom, and moral authority equipped him to guide the Senate and the popular assemblies in discharging their respective duties. To his dismay, Cicero discovered that a *princeps* might not be all that rational and benevolent. He attacked Mark Antony in a series of fiery speeches, and when the Second Triumvirate came to power, Antony murdered him and exhibited his head and right hand (the orator's instruments) on the speaker's platform in the Forum.

Greeks were certainly capable of the kind of viciousness that Mark Antony displayed, but only the Romans turned slaughter into entertainment for the masses. By the Hellenistic era, most towns had arenas and theaters in which to stage public spectacles. The Greek and Roman religious calendars were replete with festivals celebrated with games. But where the Greeks had a passion for athletic competitions, the Romans loved to witness the shedding of animal and human blood.

The politicians of the Roman Republic competed for office by bribing the voters with lavish games, and this was one of the many traditions Augustus honored. When he totted up his services to Rome, they included sponsorship of 18 gladiatorial combats involving 10,000 men and 3,500 animals. Later emperors outdid him. Tens of thousands of men and beasts were offered up during holidays that sometimes continued for months. Exotic animals were imported at great expense simply to be destroyed. To find men to kill, jails were emptied of criminals, slaves purchased, and captives taken in war. Contests between odd pairings of animals (a bear versus a bull, for example) or men with different weapons were invented to prevent the slaughter from becoming routine and boring.

Some of Rome's educated elite (including a few emperors) despised the games, but they knew that it was politically unwise to insult the masses by expressing contempt for the public's entertainment. The delight Romans took in witnessing bloodshed and death might tempt a modern American to look down on them, but no Roman was ever able to relish the kind of elaborate atrocities that Hollywood simulates. Contemporary audiences excuse their appetite for mayhem by pointing out that what they spend billions of dollars to watch is not real. But if the Romans had had special effects artists at their disposal, they too might have been content with make-believe. The real question is why such spectacles appeal to anyone in any age.

Art and Augustan Propaganda   The Golden Age of Latin literature dawned with Augustus's empire. The leading authors of his day helped promote his reforms, but their propagandistic works were inspired by sincere belief in his vision of Rome's strengths and his faith in its destiny. They were deeply grateful for the Augustan peace and brimming with patriotic enthusiasm. They shared Augustus's faith that cultivation of the sturdy agrarian virtues that had enabled their ancestors to win an empire would equip them to lead the world into an era of peace and plenty.

Virgil (70–19 B.C.E.) was Rome's greatest poet. His father, a northern Italian landowner, wanted him to practice law. His work, however, came to the attention of one of Augustus's close associates, a wealthy equestrian named Maecenas (c. 63–8 B.C.E.) whose patronage freed Virgil to pursue his writing. Virgil's earlier poems, *Eclogues*, were mostly romanticized descriptions of the Italian countryside and the simple pleasures of

The Altar of Peace The altar Augustus commissioned to express gratitude for the end of the civil war was surrounded by a wall on which a religious procession (featuring members of Augustus's family) is depicted. It is a masterpiece both of classical sculpture and Augustan propaganda. The public ceremony it celebrates is very much an idealized family affair. The women have their heads modestly covered, the toga-clad males wear wreaths indicating honor and public service, and they have produced children who are being raised in traditions of Roman patriotism and piety.

rural life. He followed these with the *Georgics*, patriotic poems giving thanks for the Augustan peace and celebrating the yeoman farmer, the type of hard-working citizen that Augustus claimed was the source of Rome's strength. Virgil's greatest project, one he did not live to finish, was the *Aeneid*, the story of the Trojan prince Aeneas, the legendary founder of the Roman people. Virgil intended the *Aeneid* to provide Rome with an epic account of its origin comparable to the *Iliad* and the *Odyssey*, and to tie the story of Rome's founding into Homer's mythic history. The poem justified the Roman Empire by claiming that the gods destined the Roman people to rule the world and establish universal peace. That was why the gods endowed the Romans with *Romanitas*, their characteristic virtues of self-sufficiency, strength, courage, devotion to duty, patriotism, and simple piety. Virgil's description of Rome's past was Augustus's vision for Rome's future.

The second major poet of Rome's Golden Age was Horace (65–8 B.C.E.), a freedman's son who saw military service in the civil war. Virgil recommended him to Maecenas, who gave Horace a rural estate on which to live and write. Horace worked on a smaller scale than Virgil (producing satires, odes, epistles, and hymns,) but joined Virgil in exhorting the Romans to practice the hardy, sober virtues that Augustus championed.

Augustus was less pleased with the third of the Golden Age's great poets, Ovid (43 B.C.E.–17 C.E.). Ovid's prolific output dealt largely with sensuous subjects that appealed to the dissolute young aristocrats whom Augustus was trying to reform. Among his works was a textbook for seducers, *The Art of Love*, which was especially likely to offend the *princeps*. Scarcely less titillating were some of the 250 or so tales he retold in *Metamorphoses*, a kind of encyclopedia of classical mythology. In 8 C.E. Ovid's involvement (with Augustus's granddaughter) in a sexual scandal led to his banishment to a remote, barbarous town on the shores of the Black Sea. His pleas for forgiveness went unanswered, and he died in exile.

The greatest prose writer of Augustus's generation was the historian Livy (59 B.C.E.–17 C.E.), who produced a monumental survey of Roman history from the city's founding to his own day. The 35 of its 142 books that survive constitute a virtually unique source of information relating to Rome's early development. Like the poets, Livy was an advocate for the Augustan virtues. He believed that history's purpose was to teach moral lessons, and his history was filled with tales of Roman valor, self-control, piety, patriotism, and moral rectitude. For centuries, schoolteachers have used Livy's inspirational stories in their struggle to turn unruly children into disciplined adults.

Order and Continuity: The Dynastic Option

Augustus avoided assassination, gave Rome over 40 years of stable government, and died in his bed at an advanced age. He knew that the empire needed someone like him to oversee it. However, because Rome was still officially a republic, it had no provision for appointing a successor to carry on his work. An invisible monarchy had to be passed on secretly. This was not hard to do, for Romans were not particular about the line that separates public from private authority.

In the testament Augustus wrote to review his life's work, he gave an accounting of his private expenditures on behalf of Rome. On several occasions, he had distributed 400 or more sesterces to at least a quarter of a million men. During famines, he had fed Rome at his own expense. He had spent 400 million sesterces to settle veterans from the army, and he had donated 150 million sesterces to the public treasury. Given that a laborer's daily wage was about four sesterces and that Augustus by no means impoverished his heirs, his fortune must have been staggering. By using it to fund public services, Augustus blurred the distinction between government agents and his personal servants. This created confusion between his household and the state bureaucracy that allowed the latter to pass to his heirs when they inherited the former. The easiest way to perpetuate his invisible monarchy was to make it the hereditary property of his family.

Augustus's popularity and the length of his reign helped smooth the path for his heir. By the time he died, there were few Romans left who had experienced life under the old republic and who had painful memories of the civil war. The Romans did not want to return to the past, but they were not ready to repudiate their republican traditions and acknowledge the new political reality. This meant that they, in effect, surrendered to Augustus's heirs, for they could not control the choice of their monarch until they admitted that they had a monarchy. Hereditary systems of succession are risky. An heir may not be qualified to handle his inheritance, or a ruler may fail to produce an heir. Augustus's family confronted Rome with both problems.

The Julio-Claudians   Augustus's only child was his daughter Julia, and his hopes for an heir were pinned on the two grandsons she gave him. When both these boys died, he had to make an arrangement that displeased all concerned. He compelled his estranged stepson Tiberius, the son of his wife Livia and her first husband (Claudius Nero), to divorce a wife he loved, marry Julia, and assume the duties of heir. Because Augustus was a Julian by adoption and Tiberius a Claudian by birth, historians refer to Rome's first imperial dynasty as the Julio-Claudians.

Augustus owed much of his success to his ability to cultivate the fantasy that he was only a first among equals in the game of republican politics. On his deathbed he reportedly asked a group of friends, "In life's farce have I acted my part well?" Tiberius (r. 14–37 C.E.) initially tried to follow Augustus's example, but Tiberius was a moody man who lacked Augustus's patience and ability to connect with people. He was soon loathed by both the masses and the Senators.

In 26 C.E. he left Rome and took up permanent residence on the island of Capri in the Bay of Naples. By now the imperial bureaucracy was so well entrenched that Rome's imperator could ignore the Senate and popular assemblies and run the empire from any location he chose. This humiliated and infuriated the Senators, whom Tiberius disliked as much as they disliked him. He characterized them as "men eager to be slaves." To be fair, Augustus had put the Senators in the difficult position of having responsibility without power, and they reasonably feared being set up to take the blame for things that were beyond their control. Having few alternatives, they took up their pens and vented their frustrations by writing histories. Modern readers need to keep in mind that the descriptions of Rome's emperors in these sources are far from objective.

If Tiberius failed at public relations, he succeeded at government. He surrounded himself with good advisors and trained specialists, paid close attention to the administration of the provinces, reduced their taxes, built roads, economized by cutting back on Rome's gladiatorial games, and racked up a huge surplus in the imperial treasury for his successor.

Tiberius's only son died in 23 C.E., and his heir was a grandnephew, Gaius Caesar. He is better known by the childhood nickname his father's soldiers gave him when he strutted about their camp in a tiny military uniform: Caligula ("Little Boots").

Caligula (r. 37–41 C.E.), who is remembered as one of Rome's worst emperors, began well. He returned to Rome, was deferential to the Senate, courted the Roman populace with games, and recalled exiles. Then something went terribly wrong. Some historians believe that a serious illness disturbed his already precariously balanced mind. He was frenetic, high strung, given to insomnia, and plagued by insecurities. Many of the outlandish stories about him that are found in hostile senatorial histories defy belief. If Caligula was mad, there may have been a logic to his insanity. His extreme behavior makes some sense if it was an attempt to force the Romans to recognize that their republic was a farce and that they had become the subjects of rulers similar to the god-kings of Egypt, Persia, and the Hellenistic East.

Caligula made the mistake of alienating those closest to him, and disaffected officers of the Praetorian Guard murdered him, his wife, and his only child (an infant daughter). The Praetorians then elevated his uncle, Claudius, to the throne.

Claudius (r. 41–54 C.E.) was a bookish man who studied with the historian Livy and wrote on subjects ranging from Etruscan history to the alphabet. He was just what the faltering empire needed. Although the strength of the imperial bureaucracy and sheer momentum had carried Rome through Caligula's years of mismanagement, inertia would not preserve order indefinitely. Rome needed a conscientious leader, and Claudius had the right qualifications. He was a well-educated workaholic who enjoyed the details of administration. He had extensive knowledge of Roman law, which he put to work in the courts. He financed new colonies and public works—the most important of which was the rebuilding of Ostia, the port (at the mouth of the Tiber River) that served the city of Rome. He authorized the campaign that added Britain, which Julius Caesar had twice invaded but never conquered, to Rome's empire.

Claudius's fourth and last wife was his niece, Agrippina the Younger. The unusual marriage was probably intended to safeguard the dynasty. Claudius was aging and ill and unlikely to live long enough to see his only son, Britannicus, reach maturity. The other possible heir to the throne was Nero, a son Agrippina had by an earlier marriage. Claudius's union with Agrippina and adoption of Nero joined the surviving branches of the imperial family and created two potential heirs. Because both boys were young, Agrippina was groomed for the role of regent. Claudius gave her the title "Augusta" and minted coins in her honor. Ancient governments used coins to communicate with the masses. As they passed from hand to hand, people absorbed the messages the government had stamped on them. By accustoming the Romans to an Augusta, Claudius prepared them, should it become necessary, for a situation they had never faced before: rule by a woman.

When Claudius died in 54 C.E., Nero (r. 54–68 C.E.), the senior heir, was 17 years old. He, like Caligula, has often been dismissed as a madman, but that may be too simplistic an interpretation of the ancient sources. On the one hand, he is accused of wanton murder of countless persons (including his half-brother, his mother, and his wife) and absurdly self-indulgent, self-deluding behavior. But on the other hand, Suetonius, an ancient Roman historian who never heard a scurrilous rumor he was not eager to repeat, claims that after Nero's death people raised statues to him in the Forum, annually decked his grave with flowers, circulated his edicts, and even claimed that he was not dead but would someday reappear to reclaim his throne.

The Roman concept of leadership was essentially military, but Nero was no soldier and was unwilling to pose as one. His strange behavior may have been an attempt to establish a new kind of authority over Rome. An imperator was a general, a warrior who led by intimidating his subjects. Nero, a poet, may have embraced the romantic idea that an artist could lead by inspiring his followers. His education convinced him that Greek civilization set the standards to which Romans should aspire. He adopted Greek dress, promoted Greek customs, and tried to persuade the Roman mob to accept Greek athletic competitions in place of Roman gladiatorial combats. The more the Romans resisted his efforts to convert their tastes, the more extreme his behavior became.

In 64 C.E. Nero proved that he was capable of governing effectively. When news reached him that a fire had destroyed 10 of Rome's 14 city districts, he hastened to Rome to supervise relief efforts. He then drew up plans for rebuilding Rome on a grander scale and issued new construction codes to make it a safer city. He also confiscated a large tract of land at the eastern end of the Forum on which to build a new palace-garden complex, the Golden House. His enthusiasm for these projects prompted rumors that he had started the fire to clear the way for them. Fires often swept through crowded ancient cities, and Rome's fire was doubtless accidental. However, suspicion of arson fell on a band of Christians, follow-ers of a new eastern religion that preached the imminent destruction of the world. In the midst of Rome's holocaust, some Christians had probably taken to the streets to celebrate the apparent fulfillment of their prophecies and urge last-minute conversions. Nero seized on this circumstantial evidence and made Rome's Christians scapegoats for the fire. It is important to note, however, that it was their alleged arson, not their faith, that led to their persecution and that only the small group of Christians in the city was affected. The Chris-tian movement was not yet large enough to exert much influence on the course of Western history or attract much attention from the imperial government.

Nero's neglect of the army finally brought him down. In 68 C.E. the governor of one of the Gallic provinces organized a revolt that spread by fits and starts. Nero had no idea how to respond, and his confusion soon turned to panic. Assuming that all was lost, he ordered one of his servants to slit his throat.

The Flavian Dynasty   Nero was the last of the Julio-Claudians. Rome had become dependent on an emperor, but because it had created no constitutional machinery to govern succession to its throne, it had no legal way to fill the power vacuum left by the extinction of its first dynasty. The crisis reignited the civil war, but Rome was lucky. Three generals won and lost the city in rapid succession, and the fourth, Vespasian (r. 69–79) restored order and established a new dynasty, the Flavian.

The Julio-Claudians were aristocrats of ancient lineage, but the Flavian family had a far less exalted equestrian background. The new emperor was a 60-year-old career sol-dier with a lifetime of command experience acquired from postings to every corner of the empire. He was a tough, pragmatic man who spoke plainly and cracked crude jokes. The trappings of power did not seduce him into taking himself too seriously. On his deathbed he mocked the Roman custom of deifying dead emperors by quipping, "I think I'm becoming a god!"

Vespasian helped the empire recover from the colorful excesses of the Julio-Claudians. He had used his army to seize power, but he was careful not to revive the soldiers' political aspirations. He broke up dangerous concentrations of troops and transferred men frequently so that they did not put down roots and develop greater loyalties to specific regions and commanders than to the empire. Augustus had envi-sioned an empire run by Italians, but Vespasian (and later rulers) bridged the gap between Italy and the provinces. He encouraged Romanization of the provinces, pro-moted provincials to the Senate, and added them to his administration. He estab-lished a budget for his government based on a census that estimated income from taxes. He funded the construction of roads, bridges, and public buildings through-out the empire and gave Rome a new temple to Jupiter on the Capitoline hill and its famous amphitheater, the 50,000-seat Colosseum.

Vespasian's successor was his elder son Titus (r. 79–81 C.E.), whom he had groomed for the responsibilities of the imperial office. Titus was a seasoned general. At the start

Ruins of Herculaneum   Pompeii is the most famous site devastated by the eruption of Vesuvius on August 24, 79 C.E., but it was not the only place that suffered that day. Pompeii was covered with ash, while the nearby coastal town of Herculaneum was inundated by volcanic mud. The mud hardened into stone, with the result that many of the more perishable materials, such as wood or other organic substances, that burned or rotted away at Pompeii have been preserved at Herculaneum. Excavation there is very difficult, but it has yielded such unexpected things as the contents of an ancient Roman library.

of his father's reign, he had put down a rebellion by Jews seeking independence for Judea. A triumphal arch at the eastern end of the Forum commemorates his victory and depicts the treasures the Romans sacked from Jerusalem's temple. Titus died before he could do much, but his reign was marked by a memorable event. In August of 79 C.E., Vesuvius, a volcano near Naples, erupted and (to the delight of generations of archaeologists and tourists) buried the towns of Pompeii and Herculaneum.

Titus's heir was his younger brother Domitian (r. 81–96 C.E.), an arrogant autocrat. The splendid residence he built on Rome's Palatine hill gave us the word *palace*. He lived in constant fear that plots were being hatched against him, and his wanton executions of suspects ensured that they were. Thanks to his wife's cooperation, one of these conspiracies finally succeeded.

Order and Continuity: The Elective Option

Domitian had no obvious heir, and his assassins had no candidate of their own whom they wished to see succeed him. Instead, they asked the Senate—Rome's most prestigious political assembly—to legitimate what they had done by appointing a new emperor. By now there was no question of reestablishing a true republic, and the Senate knew that if it did not act to fill the throne, the army would.

PEOPLE IN CONTEXT   The Imperial Aristocracy: Pliny the Elder and Pliny the Younger

The Roman Republic had belonged to the aristocratic families that monopolized its political offices, commanded its armies, confiscated its wealth, and charted its destiny. The empire diminished their power. Emperors utilized a few men of senatorial rank as advisors, provincial governors, heads of departments of state, and military officers, but they kept a close eye on them. Association with the court or a too successful military career could be dangerous for a man from a prominent family. Most of the blood shed by Rome's "bad" emperors was the blue blood of upperclass men who were suspected of plotting against the throne or who simply had fortunes their ruler wanted to confiscate. Given the risks of exposure, wealthy men often preferred the security of their country villas to life in Rome. Shut out from the world of politics, they devoted themselves to the safer pursuits of literature and to entertaining one another. Those who published took care not to write anything that might offend their emperor.

Prominent among the literary lights of the day were an uncle and a nephew, both named Pliny. The uncle, Pliny the Elder (c. 23–79 C.E.), was a close friend of Vespasian's, who found time in a busy military career to write poems, histories, and a huge encyclopedia of the ancient world's scientific and pseudoscientific lore. His passion for research led to his death. He was living near Pompeii when Vesuvius erupted. The temptation to view the mountain up close was simply too great, and he was killed by a surge of volcanic

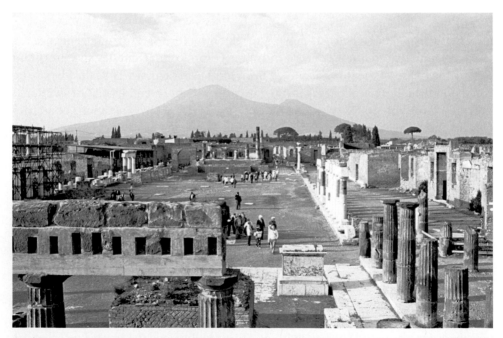

The Ruins of Pompeii   Pliny the Younger has left us an eyewitness account of the eruption of Mount Vesuvius that buried the city of Pompeii in 79 C.E.

gas. His nephew, Pliny the Younger (c. 61–113 C.E.), has left us a description of the eruption and the circumstances of his uncle's death.

Pliny the Younger studied rhetoric with Quintillian (35–95 C.E.), the author of
Rome's leading text on the art of oratory. By the age of 18 he was representing clients
in Rome's courts. He did not follow his uncle into the military, but he held a few prestigious offices. He was briefly a consul (a largely empty honor by his day), and the
emperor Trajan (r. 98–117 C.E.) appointed him governor of Bithynia, a province on the
southwestern coast of the Black Sea.

Pliny was an enthusiastic correspondent who was proud of his literary style and who
edited his letters for publication. He wrote to and about many important people, among
whom was his emperor. An emperor's servant was well advised to show deference and
proceed with caution, and Pliny took no chances. As governor of Bithynia, he referred
every decision about which he had the least doubt to the emperor, for, as he explained
to Trajan, who "could better guide my ignorance." If every Roman governor did likewise,
Trajan's flow of paperwork must have been overwhelming. Among the issues that puzzled Pliny was what to do with some practitioners of a new religion called Christianity.
His letters reveal how little the Roman authorities knew (or cared) about the faith that
would one day transform Western civilization.

Question: How might a society's concern to maintain order affect the work of its
artists and intellectuals?

The "Good Emperors"   Not surprisingly, the new emperor the Senate chose was
one of its own, an elderly man named Nerva (r. 96–98 C.E.). Nerva knew that there was
little chance that the army's generals would allow a senatorial appointee to deprive them
of the opportunity to make a bid for the throne, but he had a strategy for ensuring his
survival. Nerva had no children and at age 66 was not likely to produce any. So like Julius
Caesar, he adopted an heir. In this case the choice was not a teenaged relative, but a
45-year-old man named Trajan. Trajan commanded the legions along the Rhine, and he
was the general who was most likely to win should a battle for Rome break out. The
adoption set a valuable precedent. From 96 to 180 C.E. no emperor had a son, so each
was free to choose his own successor. All chose wisely, and the result was the longest
period of consistently excellent rule that the empire enjoyed.

Trajan (r. 98–117 C.E.) was eager to expand the empire. He created a new province
called Dacia north of the Danube—a Latin-speaking enclave that lay a cultural foundation for the modern nation of Romania. His other campaigns humbled Parthia; conquered Armenia, Assyria, and Mesopotamia; and brought the Roman Empire to its
height (see Map 6–2).

Italy was the preferred recruiting ground for Trajan's legions, and his government
implemented an ingenious program to boost its population. Italy's small farmers and
artisans suffered as producers in the empire's western provinces began to compete with
Italian products on the world market. To enable poorer Italians to raise more children,
Trajan established the **alimenta**, an endowment that provided food and education for

Map 6–2 The Pinnacle of the Roman Empire Augustus conquered territory that he thought would provide the empire with defensible frontiers. Claudius added Britain, but the major and final additions to the empire were the work of Trajan. Hadrian, his successor, concluded that some of the land Trajan had won was too difficult to defend, and he relinquished it.

Question: What portions of Rome's frontier were most vulnerable to attack?

impoverished children of both sexes. The money came from interest that landowners paid on loans the government provided to help them improve their estates. Instead of handing out money, Rome funded its welfare program from investments that promoted economic growth.

Trajan was succeeded by a distant relative, Hadrian (r. 117–138 C.E.), who spent most of his reign away from Rome, touring the provinces and cultivating close ties with his troops. He was popular with his army even though he fought few wars. He concentrated on strengthening the empire's frontiers by retreating to defensible positions. Where terrain offered no help, he built elaborate fortifications (the largest of which was a 72-mile-long wall backed up by a string of forts that spanned northern Britain).

Hadrian was a multifaceted person, a soldier and athletic outdoorsman as well as an aesthete and a scholar. He reformed Roman law to reflect Stoic principles of justice and protect slaves from abuse. He reorganized the empire's administrative system and held its bureaucrats accountable to high standards. He had such a passion for Greek literature and art that he was nicknamed "the Greek." He studied architecture, experimented with novel designs, and lavished buildings on provincial cities. The only major ancient temple still standing in Rome is one of his: the Pantheon, a drum-shaped hall roofed by a dome 141 feet in diameter.

Hadrian's last years were spent wrestling with a painful illness, but he outlived the first man he chose as his heir. When he finally died in 138, he commended the empire to the care of a senatorial aristocrat known for his cultivation of the Roman virtues of dignity, sobriety, and simplicity: Antoninus Pius (r. 138–161 C.E.). Rome faced no wars or other crises throughout Antoninus's long reign, but the quiet was deceptive. Beyond the empire's northern frontiers, hostile German tribes were training in the use of Roman arms and tactics. Shortly after Antoninus passed the reins of government to his successor, Marcus Aurelius (r. 161–180 C.E.), the storm broke.

Marcus Aurelius was 17 when Hadrian arranged for Antoninus Pius to adopt him, but he did not inherit the throne until he was 40. He was serious-minded and drawn to the study of philosophy—particularly Stoicism. Over the period of a decade he composed a series of essays reflecting on life from the Stoic perspective. Collected into a book now entitled *Meditations*, they have been variously praised as exhortations to duty and self-discipline and condemned as the musings of an unrealistic dreamer and dilettante. But whatever their possible shortcomings as philosophy, as history, they provide modern readers their only opportunity to engage a Roman emperor through his own words.

Marcus Aurelius's Stoic detachment was severely tested, for his reign was a long series of crises: plagues, earthquakes, floods, famines, and wars. When he ascended the throne, he anticipated the practice of later emperors by sharing the imperial honor with a colleague, Lucius Verus. The long frontiers of the empire were threatened in the west by Germans and in the east by Parthians, and there was plenty of work for two emperors. Verus's army succeeded in stabilizing the eastern frontier, and in 166 he returned to Rome to celebrate a triumph. Unfortunately, among the spoils his men brought back to Rome was a plague that spread throughout the empire.

After Verus's death in 169 C.E., Marcus Aurelius ruled alone. He spent most of the remainder of his reign campaigning against the Germans on the Danube frontier. He was largely successful, but at the time of his death in Vindobona (Vienna) there was still work to be done. Unfortunately, responsibility for that task passed into incompetent hands.

Alone among the five men whom history remembers as the "Good Emperors," Marcus Aurelius sired a son, Commodus (r. 180–192 C.E.). He was the only male to survive from the 13 children the emperor and his wife Faustina had in 30 years of marriage. Commodus's defects may have been apparent to his father, but Roman traditions of family and the inheritance rights of sons were strong. An attempt to deny him the throne might well have invited a succession struggle and civil war. Commodus spent his reign in dissipation and may have descended into madness. When those around him began to fear for their lives, they assassinated him and, like Domitian's killers, asked the Senate to appoint his successor. This maneuver had inaugurated the era of the Good Emperors, but this time it did not work. The armies mutinied, and the empire was again torn by civil war.

Military Rule   The winner of the civil war was Septimius Severus (r. 193–211 C.E.), commander of the Danube legions. He restored order, but his methods augured poorly for Rome's future. He increased the army's size and nearly doubled its pay. His deathbed advice for his heirs was, "Enrich the troops, and despise everyone else."

The army may always have been the basis of an emperor's power, but it was dangerous for an emperor to acknowledge this too openly. Once the soldiers realized that they were in control, it was impossible to maintain their discipline. They killed the officers who tried to keep them in line and supported those who promised to do their bidding. Of the five emperors of the Severan dynasty, only one died of natural causes. The others were killed by their own men.

Following the murder of the last Severan emperor in 235, the army spun out of control. Over the next 50 years, approximately 25 men claimed the imperial title. They have been called the "**Barracks Emperors**," for most began their careers as common soldiers. The administration of the empire languished while military factions fought among themselves, and large blocks of territory in both the east and west seceded and

The Imperial Dynasties
JULIO-CLAUDIANS (31 B.C.E.–68 C.E.)
Octavian Augustus (31 B.C.E.–14 C.E.) Tiberius (14–37 C.E.) Caligula (37–41 C.E.) Claudius (41–54 C.E.) Nero (54–68 C.E.) "The Year of the Four Emperors" (68–69 C.E.)
FLAVIANS (69–96 C.E.)
Vespasian (69–79 C.E.) Titus (79–81 C.E.) Domitian (81–96 C.E.)
"THE GOOD EMPERORS" (96–180 C.E.)
Nerva (96–98 C.E.) Trajan (98–117 C.E.) Hadrian (117–138 C.E.) Antoninus Pius (138–161 C.E.) Lucius Verus (161–169) & Marcus Aurelius (161–180 C.E.) [Commodus (180–192 C.E.)]
SEVERANS (193–235)
Septimius Severus (193–211) Caracalla (211–217) [Macrinus (217–218)] Elagabalus (218–222) Alexander Severus (222–235)
"THE BARRACKS EMPERORS" (235–285)

set up governments of their own. From 267 to 272 the eastern rim of the Mediterranean from Asia Minor to Egypt was ruled by a woman, Zenobia, queen of the desert city of Palmyra.

Life in an Imperial Environment

Geography helped make Rome's empire, the ancient world's largest and most enduring, a viable entity. Although the empire's frontier was long, much of it needed minimal defense. The Atlantic Ocean protected the west, and the Sahara the south. There were wars with the Parthian Empire in the east, but most trouble on that front was stirred up by the Romans themselves. The frontier that needed the largest military investment was the northern line defined by the Rhine and Danube rivers. Communication, travel, and trade for the people who lived within these boundaries were facilitated by the empire's numerous rivers and its great central sea.

An Imperial Economy   Once the Romans secured the empire's frontiers, swept pirates from the Mediterranean, and began to spread urban institutions throughout their territory, the stage was set for the West's economy to thrive. The empire was abundantly supplied with natural resources. Most regions could provide themselves with fundamental necessities, but once secure trade routes were established, some districts began to specialize in what they could do best. Olive oil was exported from Spain, grain from North Africa and Egypt, and wine from Gaul and Greece. Metal ores were mined in Britain, Spain, Dacia, and Cyprus, and manufacturing centers sprang up in many places. Glass was shipped from Egypt and the Rhineland. A popular line of red-glazed pottery was mass produced in northern Italy. Textiles came from Asia Minor, and bronze work from Italy. Despite the success of some of these enterprises, shipping problems forced most industries to remain small and to produce for local markets. Water offered the only economical means for transporting goods. Wine brought from Gaul to Rome by sea (about 450 miles) was less expensive than wine carted to the city from Italian vineyards only 50 miles away.

The economies of inland districts lagged far behind those of regions on coasts and waterways, and the empire's overall economy began to show signs of weakness as early as the Flavian period. Romans imported large quantities of luxury goods from India and the Far East and paid for them with gold and silver. This drained bullion from the West, and as the productivity of its mines decreased, emperors were hard pressed to find the precious metals they needed to mint an adequate supply of coins. The empire's success in suppressing war also had an economic downside. It diminished the supply of cheap slaves, an important element in its workforce.

Social Developments   Romans were generous in freeing slaves, and many of Rome's citizens were freedmen and their descendants. This may have given some of them sympathy for slaves. Philosophers urged respect for the humanity of slaves, and some emperors passed laws to protect them. But ideals and laws were difficult to enforce.

The gap that steadily widened between rich and poor in the Roman world blurred the line between freedom and slavery. Many of the free poor became **coloni**, tenant farmers who took over the work of slaves on the *latifundia* (large estates) of the rich. Lack of opportunity made them a virtually captive workforce. Large numbers of the indigent and unemployed also flooded into the empire's major cities and eked out livings on the public dole.

The distinction between Italy and the provinces that Augustus wanted to maintain steadily eroded. By the end of the Julio-Claudian period, most of the old republican families were dying out and a new aristocracy, drawn increasingly from the provinces, was taking their place. The settlement of Roman veterans on the frontiers, their intermarriage with local women, and the acquisition of citizenship by non-Italians who served in the auxiliaries all helped to create a larger, more inclusive class of people who identified with the empire. In 212 the Severan emperor Caracalla granted citizenship to all the free residents of the empire. Stoic philosophers preached a doctrine of universal brotherhood, and Roman jurists posited the existence of a natural law that gave equal rights to all men. Roman law is one of the great legacies of the empire, for the principles of justice it articulated have had tremendous influence on the development of Western thinking about courts, the rights of accused people, and the proper use of evidence in determining guilt and innocence.

Although citizenship and legal rights were usually viewed from a male perspective, women were not passive pawns in Roman society. They were required to have guardians to handle their legal affairs, but this had already become a mere formality by the end of the republic. Aristocratic women had great power and influence, and despite Augustus's attempt to revive some version of the patriarchal family of the early republican period, women added to their rights. Romans had long regarded marriage as a private matter that did not involve the state. Tradition had established two kinds of marriage—one that transferred the bride entirely to her husband's *familia* and another that preserved her relationship with her father's household. The second kind of marriage made divorce easier, for the bride and her family retained more power over her dowry. By the beginning of the empire, it had become the standard form of marriage, and divorce and remarriage, at least in aristocratic circles, were common. Augustus believed that this contributed to the decline of the Roman family, and he tried to reverse it by increasing the state's power over marriages. Legal procedures were instituted for divorces, and adultery became a crime prosecuted by the state. A sexual double standard was accepted. Husbands had nothing to fear from the law so long as they did not debauch another man's wife or conspire in the misconduct of their own mate. Because men could safely conduct affairs with women who were licensed as prostitutes, some aristocratic women, who wished to continue their amorous dalliances in safety, got around the law by registering as prostitutes. Augustus's laws had little effect, and his successors made few attempts to legislate morality until the fourth century, when Christian emperors began to impose the moral principles of their faith on society.

Intellectual Life   Virgil, Horace, Ovid, and Livy—Augustus's contemporaries—ended the dependence of Roman authors on Greek sources by providing them with

Latin models for the composition of poetry and prose. However, the growing power of Rome's emperors created an intellectual environment that prevented later authors from writing in the same spirit as the giants of the Golden Age. The *Romanitas* that inspired them was a vision of an idealized republican Rome, and this dream of liberty faded as the reality of life under autocratic emperors became clear. Scholars did not have to wait long for a warning about the danger of speaking too freely. Tiberius, Augustus's successor, convicted the author of a history of the civil wars of treason and burned his books. Elections and popular assemblies also lost much of their meaning during Tiberius's reign as the imperial bureaucracy took over more and more functions of government. This struck at the heart of Roman literary education—the study of rhetoric. Without opportunities to debate real issues and influence important decisions and elections, rhetoric became a pointless exercise. Students continued to be trained in the techniques of debate, but debate became not a means to an end but an end in itself. People wrangled over abstract hypothetical problems that had no connection with contemporary politics. As style came to be more important than substance, formal writing became increasingly elaborate, convoluted, and verbose.

Things temporarily improved when the scholarly Claudius took the throne and appointed the Stoic philosopher Seneca the Younger (c. 4 B.C.E.–65 C.E.) tutor to his heir, Nero. Literary activity revived and began what historians refer to as Rome's Silver Age. The empire produced many good writers, but none as influential as those whom Augustus had encouraged. Many of the new voices came from the provinces—a testimony to Rome's success in spreading Hellenistic civilization.

The first flush of the Silver Age was brief. During the course of his long literary career, Seneca produced plays, essays on Stoic philosophy, treatises dealing with ethical issues, and a book on natural science. Although he tried to tread carefully, his Stoic moralism needled the libertine Nero, and the emperor finally ordered him to commit suicide. Seneca's nephew, Lucan (39–65 C.E.), joined him in self-murder, leaving unfinished a passionately republican epic poem dealing with the war between Caesar and Pompey. Petronius (d. 66 C.E.), another of Nero's victims, wrote a novel, *The Satyricon*, from which only fragments survive. It wittily mocked the falsity, pretentiousness, and crass self-indulgence of wealthy Romans and their sycophants. Satire appealed to a generation of cynical, disillusioned artists. The *Epigrams* of Martial (c. 40–104 C.E.) commented ironically on a wide spectrum of Roman society, and the *Satires* of Juvenal (c. 55–130 C.E.) are as amusing as they are filled with anger and scorn.

Nero's sensitivity to criticism and paranoia suppressed literary activity, and conditions did not improve much under later emperors. The Flavians funded libraries and schools, but silenced philosophers of whose teachings they disapproved. A few historians thrived, however, despite the politically sensitive nature of their material. Tacitus (c. 55–120 C.E.) reflected on the empire from the hostile perspective of the senatorial aristocracy. His elegant prose is replete with pithy, memorable phrases that sum up (often pessimistic) insights into human character. Josephus (c. 37–95 C.E.), a Jewish author, wrote to provide the Romans (and his Flavian patrons) with background

The Roman Forum The city of Rome acquired a number of forums, but the first and most famous was the swampy lowland beside the Palatine hill that the Etruscan kings drained. Over the years it filled with temples, public buildings, and monuments. This view is from the western end looking east to the Arch of Titus. The forum reverted to swamp and pastureland during the Middle Ages, and its buried ruins were not completely excavated until the twentieth century.

on his people. Biblical scholars have found his work an invaluable source of information on the period between the testaments and the environment into which Jesus of Nazareth was born. Suetonius (c. 69–135 C.E.), the most colorful of the era's historians, wrote biographies of Rome's rulers from Julius Caesar to Domitian. He relied heavily on amusing tales and titillating gossip. Plutarch (c. 45–120 C.E.), a Greek author, produced a large set of biographies in which he compared Greek and Roman leaders whom he thought had similar careers. His work is as accurate, or inaccurate, as the literary sources on which he relied, and it reflects the belief of his age that the purpose of history was to provide lessons in morality.

The Decline of Rome

A famous historian has said that the question that should be asked about the Roman Empire is not why it fell, but how it managed to last as long as it did. His point is that the empire was inherently fragile, and to speak of its fall may be misleading. It did not come to a sudden end, and no single thing brought it crashing down. The way of life that Rome represented was incrementally transformed until the world had changed so much that it no longer made sense to call it Roman. The western provinces of the empire were economically weaker, less populous, less urbanized, and more exposed to invasion than the eastern, and by the fifth century the empire was fast becoming for them more a memory than a reality. But a region of vacillating size in the eastern Mediterranean continued to be ruled by a line of Roman emperors for another thousand years.

Rome's Weakness   Like most ancient societies, the Roman Empire's resources barely sufficed to meet its routine needs, and crises caused by invasions, civil wars, plagues, or crop failures could push it to the brink of collapse. Rome's longevity owed much to the absence of a major foreign enemy who might have taken advantage of the empire's internal problems. Parthia was the only civilized state with which Rome shared a border, and it seldom posed a threat. Rome's most vulnerable front was its 1,500-mile-long Rhine–Danube frontier. Occasional localized campaigns were enough to hold this line until the third century, when the German tribes began to consolidate and adopt Roman military practices.

The Roman Empire was handicapped by the ancient world's failure to make more technological progress. The empire was an agrarian state supported by fairly primitive methods of cultivation. Some plantations and manufacturing industries produced products for the world market, but waterways provided the only cost-efficient transportation. The residents of coastal districts and regions near navigable rivers could trade profitably, but people who lived inland had to be self-sufficient. Wheat brought by sea from Egypt and southern Gaul, for instance, sold more cheaply in Rome than did Italian grain raised 50 miles from the city.

Some of the empire's trade depressed its economy. Romans had an appetite for luxury goods from the Far East, but the West produced little that India and China could not provide for themselves. The West, therefore, had to pay with gold and silver for the silks and spices it imported. The bullion this drained from the empire undermined its monetary system. By the second century, the West's mines were being worked out, and gold and silver from which to mint coins were becoming scarce. Emperors stretched the shrinking money supply by debasing coins (that is, by mixing gold and silver with cheaper metals), but this backfired. Because these coins had less innate value, sellers demanded more of them for their goods. Prices rose, and the empire faced the problem of inflation. Overall, the costs of administering and defending the Roman Empire steadily increased, while the economy that sustained the empire declined.

From a modern perspective, the ancient world's failure to grow its economy may appear perplexing. Hellenistic scholars made scientific breakthroughs that, if they had been exploited, could have transformed the ancient way of life. Physicists worked out the principles of levers, gears, and pulleys, and they built working models of steam turbines. Some slave-staffed businesses utilized assembly-line techniques. The Romans possessed key ingredients for an industrial revolution, but somehow they never put them together. Slavery and an aristocratic intelligentsia preoccupied with literary and philosophical pursuits probably contributed to the absence of any motivation to find ways to make work easier and more productive.

Diocletian and the *Dominate*   The rapid turnover of leaders during the half cen-tury (235–285) when the Barracks Emperors squabbled over the throne created such confusion that Rome's imperial government lost control of huge stretches of territory. But the last of the Barracks Emperors, Diocletian (r. 285–305), restored the empire's unity and stability. His policies preserved the empire for another century, but at the cost of many aspects of its traditional way of life. Augustus's title of *princeps* ("first citizen") acknowledged his commitment to civilian government. But Diocletian was called *dominus* ("lord"). He ruled as a divine king over the **dominate,** a system of government ruled with the power of a military autocrat.

Diocletian's first priority was to secure the person of the emperor, for the empire could not function if its leaders continued to be frequently overthrown. To reduce the number of potential competitors for the imperial office, Diocletian divided and dispersed political authority. He doubled the number of the empire's provinces and gave each both a civilian and a military governor. This greatly diminished the strength of the provincial commanders, but at the cost of quadrupling the size of the imperial bureaucracy.

It was too dangerous to divide the army, so Diocletian consolidated an elite, mobile force under his direct command and settled a class of militarized peasants along the em-pire's frontiers. These farmer-soldiers were supposed to fend off attacks on their home districts long enough for the emperor to bring up the main army and restore order. Generous pay and preferential treatment (such as special legal privileges and exemption from taxes) ensured the loyalty of the emperor's troops, his *comitatenses* ("compan-ions"). Diocletian may have had half a million men under arms, and their maintenance imposed a tremendous burden on his treasury.

Similarly costly was Diocletian's court. A *dominus* ruled by intimidation—by projecting an aura of awe-inspiring majesty. He was a remote being insulated from contact with his subjects by court functionaries and elaborate protocols. When he appeared in public, he wore elaborate robes, jewels, and the golden diadem of the sun-god.

Diocletian concluded that one emperor was not enough to defend Rome's fron-tier, and he shared the empire with a colleague named Maximian (286–305). He sta-tioned himself in Asia Minor to watch the Parthian and lower Danube borders, and Maximian established a base in northern Italy from which to guard the upper Danube and the Rhine.

Having no son to inherit his throne, Diocletian tried to revive the practice of adopt-ing successors that had worked so well throughout the second century. He decreed that each "augustus" (the emperor's title) was to choose a "caesar" (a second-in-command) to assist him, and at the end of a 20-year term, the augustus was to retire and the caesar ascend to his office. This tetrarchy ("four-man rule") gave four powerful men a vested interest in working together and it promised an orderly transmission of power to expe-rienced, competent successors (see Map 6–3).

Map 6–3   The Divisions of the Late Roman Empire   Diocletian's creation of separate governments for the eastern and western halves of the Roman Empire forecast a division that became permanent.

Question: Why were all the empire's administrative centers (Trier, Milan, Sirmium, and Nicomedia) on its northern rim rather than in a central location?

The Transformation of Roman Society

Government policies often have unintended consequences. Diocletian's innovations certainly did, for they all increased Rome's economic difficulties. Diocletian quadrupled the size of the empire's bureaucracy, built a larger and more expensive army, and established four imperial courts. Rome could not afford the burdens this imposed, for its simple agrarian economy may have required the labor of six farmers to support each soldier, bureaucrat, and court functionary who did not till the soil.

Diocletian tried to deal with this problem by careful budgeting. He conducted censuses at five-year intervals to estimate the wealth of the empire and set tax rates. He debased the coinage to increase the money supply and encourage economic activity. He tried to halt the inflation that resulted by issuing an Edict of Prices, which decreed what could legally be charged for about a thousand items and services. All this did, however, was to force goods onto a black market that the government could not regulate.

Diocletian was finally driven to confiscate the property of his subjects to meet the expenses of his government, and this transformed the empire's social structure. Its wealthier citizens fled its cities, where they were too exposed to its tax collectors, and took up permanent residence on their rural estates. It was impossible for the government to track them all down, and to do so could be dangerous for tax collectors. This migration had a devastating impact on the empire's cultural institutions, for urban life was the dynamo that powered classical civilization. Without their rich and powerful citizens, cities went rapidly downhill.

Lesser individuals had fewer options for protecting their resources than the wealthy. When government confiscations bit into the working capital of farmers and artisans, they had little choice but to abandon their fields, close their shops, and resort to banditry or go on the public dole. Each year the number of productive individuals declined. This increased the burden on those who remained and drove yet more people out of business. The state tried to maintain production of essential goods by taking over industries and conscripting laborers to work on state plantations. To maintain the workforce, men were required to teach their trades to their sons, and sons were forced to take up their father's professions. What had been, theoretically at least, a free society became a caste system. As masses of peasants (*coloni*) were bound to the lands they worked for the state and wealthy aristocrats, the empire began to break up into quasi-independent rural fiefdoms.

KEY QUESTION | Revisited

The Romans often faced the unhappy choice between freedom and order. Theirs was never a democratic, egalitarian society in which everyone enjoyed the same liberties, but they honored ideals of citizenship and patriotism. These ideals have had a positive influence on the development of Western nations, but Roman history also illustrates what happens to such values when societies are under stress or delivered into the hands of unscrupulous or inept leaders. The insecurity of life in Rome's turbulent republic induced its citizens to submit to a powerful imperial government. For a long time, that government maintained stability and prosperity, and the majority of its subjects may have been content with the balance it struck between freedom and order. It is important to realize that its eventual decline into oppressive autocracy was neither inevitable nor accidental. It was the outcome of decisions that the Romans convinced themselves they were compelled to make.

Review Questions

1. Why was the Roman Republic unable to govern an empire?
3. Did Augustus save the Roman Republic or destroy it?
3. How did relationships between the military and the civilian elements in society change during the era of the empire?
4. Why might residents of the provinces and ordinary Romans have disagreed with the Roman Senate on which of Rome's emperors were good and which bad?
5. Could the Roman Empire have been saved?
6. Is government by the people a luxury that only relatively secure societies can afford?

Please consult the Suggested Readings at the back of the book to continue your study of the material covered in this chapter. For a list of documents on the Primary Source DVD-ROM that relate to topics in this chapter, please refer to the back of the book.

Part 3
The Division of the West 300 to 1300

Muslims and Christians playing chess, ca. 1300, Mallorca, Spain.

During the ancient phase in the history of the West, the peoples whose homelands encircled the Mediterranean shared cultural influences and grew closer together, and for several centuries the whole of the Western civilized world was united under one government: the Roman Empire. There were significant differences among the subjects of that empire. They spoke a variety of languages, practiced numerous religions, and preserved some ethnic distinctions, but at least for the governing classes, the things they shared were more important than the things that divided them. The Mediterranean Sea lay at the center of "a world" that was politically unified, economically interconnected, and intellectually in agreement.

The decline of Rome's empire was more than the end of a political system, for it inaugurated an epoch in Western history in which the ancient trend toward unification reversed. The Mediterranean ceased to tie civilized peoples together, and the West divided against itself. During the ensuing Middle Ages, three distinct civilizations appeared: Latin Catholic Europe, Greek Orthodox Byzantium, and the Arab-Persian Muslim empire. Although all three shared common legacies from the ancient world, they were more alert to their differences than to their similarities. The defensiveness, misunderstanding, and hostility that came to characterize their relationships have yet to be overcome.

	ENVIRONMENT AND TECHNOLOGY	SOCIETY AND CULTURE	POLITICS
c. 300	Urban decay	Christian persecution	Diocletian: the Dominate (305)
	Coloni	Edict of Toleration (311)	Constantine (306–337)
	Two-field cultivation	Council of Nicaea (325)	Visigoths at Adrianople (378)
		Monastic movement begins	
		Christianity mandated (395)	Roman Empire divided
c. 400	Heavy, wheeled plows	Augustine (354–430)	Sack of Rome (410)
			Rhine frontier (406)
			Attila the Hun (d. 454)
			Romulus Augustulus (476)
		Comitatus	German kingdoms
c. 500		Benedictine Rule (ca. 529)	Clovis (d. 511) fds. the Merovingian dynasty
	Hagia Sophia	Byzantine civilization	Justinian (d. 565)
c. 600			Muhammad (570–632)
		Islam and the *umma* (622)	Caliphate (est. 632)
		Shi'ite Islam (660)	Umayyad dynasty (660–750)
c. 700			Isaurian dynasty (fd. 717)
			Charles Martel (d. 741)
			Abbasid dynasty (fd. 750)
	Stirrup and heavy cavalry		Carolingians (fd. 751)
	Mold board plow	*Capitularies*	Charlemagne (768–814)
c. 800	Three-field cultivation system	Carolingian Renaissance	
	Minuscule	Feudalism	Viking–Magyar invasions
	Byzantine *theme*	Manorialism	Macedonian dynasty (fd. 867)
c. 900			Fatimid caliphate (fd. 909)
	Horseshoe	Ottonian Renaissance	Saxon dynasty (fd. 919)
		Cluniac Reform (910)	Capetian dynasty (fd. 987)
c. 1000	Capitalism		Spanish crusade begins
		Towns and trade revive	Salian dynasty (fd. 1024)
			Seljuk sultanate (fd. 1060)
			William the Conqueror
		Investiture Controversy (1075)	Battle of Manzikert (1071)
			Kingdom of Sicily (fd. 1092)
			I Crusade (1095–1099)
c. 1100		Twelfth-Century Renaissance	II Crusade (1144)
			Hohenstaufen dynasty
	Scholastic method	Peter Abelard (1079–1142)	Henry II (1154–1189)
	Romanesque architecture	University of Bologna (1158)	III Crusade (1189–1192)
	Gothic architecture		Philip Augustus (1180–1223)
			Innocent III (1198–1216)
c. 1200		University of Paris (1200)	IV Crusade (1204)
		troubadour lyric, romance	*Magna Carta* (1215)

7 The West's Medieval Civilizations

We were sentenced to be thrown to the beasts, and we returned rejoicing to prison. . . .
A few days later the prison warden realized that we had a great power within us, and he
began to treat us with respect.

—**Vibia Perpetua**, *Memoir*

For all the differences that exist among the world's many peoples . . . there are only two
kinds of societies, which . . . we have accurately characterized as two "cities." One is
the "city of men," inhabited by people who are governed by the appetites of the flesh.
The other is [the city of God], composed of people who live according to the spirit.
Each of these communities decides what will make it happy, and when each gets what
it wants, it lives with the consequences of its choice.

—**Augustine of Hippo**, *The City of God*

KEY | Question

Should freedom of religion be limited?

Religion is often a major contributor to the shared identity that defines a people as a people.
But for this reason it also divides the human community—inspiring controversy, persecution,
and warfare. The ancient world had not had to wrestle much with the divisive potential of religion, for the pagan gods were not jealous. Their polytheistic worshipers welcomed new deities
to the pantheon as they became aware of them. With the spread of monotheistic faiths, such
as Christianity and Islam, however, the situation changed. Early Christians like Vibia Perpetua,
a 22-year-old Roman matron who dictated a memoir shortly before her martyrdom in 203,

Emperor Constantine This bust of the Roman emperor Constantine may be a fragment from a gigantic statue that was raised in Rome during his lifetime to commemorate a battle that won him control of the western Roman Empire.

believed that they alone had the truth. They willingly courted death in the confidence that their sacrifice would be rewarded and vindicated by a higher power. There was, they believed, no room for compromise in matters of faith. Certain of her righteousness, Vibia almost eagerly abandoned a new-born son; turned a deaf ear to the desperate pleas of her aged, loving father; and spurned the traditions and institutions of her people.

By the time that Augustine (354–430), bishop of the North African city of Hippo, was born a century and a half later, Christianity was no longer a religion of martyrs. It had become the state religion and had begun to persecute its pagan predecessors. In this changing world, faith was assumed to require hard choices between clear alternatives. Augustine did not become a Christian until midlife, and he wrestled with the decision to convert for a long time. To be true to the Christian faith, he felt that he had to give up his flourishing secular career, break off a socially advantageous engagement to marry, separate from a mistress with whom he had lived for years and by whom he had a son, take a vow of celibacy, and embrace a life of ascetic self-denial. Halfway measures would not do, for Augustine believed that people had to decide whether their allegiances lay with the "city of God" or the "city of man." There was no middle ground. Those who trusted in Christian revelation were destined for eternal life in communion with God. Unbelievers were damned beyond hope of redemption. These two groups mingled on Earth, but ultimately God would sort them out—and the consequences would be eternal.

The Roman Empire unified the West and held it together for about three centuries. But as the empire came apart, three new civilizations, whose identities were largely shaped by religion, staked claims to Rome's territorial and cultural legacies: Latin Christian Europe, Greek Christian Byzantium, and an Arab-Islamic empire that extended from Spain across North Africa and the Middle East to India. Each of these civilizations championed different (if related) faiths, and their respective religions profoundly influenced their internal politics and their foreign relations.

The pagans of the ancient world were generally predisposed to religious tolerance, for they believed that divinity was a multifaceted reality that manifested itself in many ways. As polytheists, they were open to the discovery and veneration of new gods. Their governments might go to war to win control of shrines and their treasures, or they might outlaw cults that inspired what they viewed as immoral or treasonous behavior. But they did not usually regard religion as a source of contention. This changed as the West entered the Middle Ages (the fifth through fifteenth centuries), for the religions to which the three medieval civilizations were committed were monotheistic faiths. The exclusive allegiance that each demanded to its own understanding of God created the potential for disagreements that escalated into bloody conflicts. Given that religion can divide a people as well as unite them, how should societies handle it?

The Christian Element

The steps that Diocletian took to save the Roman Empire changed it so much that it is reasonable to wonder if the empire he saved was still Roman. Its government was headed by a god-king and staffed by soldiers. Barter began to replace the use of money in its economic transactions. Many of its cities were declining. In some regions, powerful landlords were carving out quasi-independent domains, and people everywhere were being subjected to the restraints of a rigid caste system. Most of this was probably unintentional, for Diocletian did not set out to separate Rome from its past. However, his successor, Constantine (312–337), struck a purposeful blow at the roots of classical civilization by shifting his allegiance from paganism to Christianity.

The Origin of the Christian Faith   Jesus of Nazareth, arguably the most influential individual in Western history, lived and died virtually unnoticed by his contemporaries. His brief career as the leader of a small band of Jewish disciples ended when he was crucified in Jerusalem during the reign of Emperor Tiberius. After his death, some of his acquaintances claimed that he had risen from the grave and that he was the **messiah** (or, in Greek, "the Christ," "the anointed"), a savior whose appearance the Jews had been anticipating. Their proclamation of this *gospel* ("good news") was not met with instant success. As late as the fourth century, when Emperor Constantine legalized Christianity, scholars estimate that only 5% (or perhaps as few as 1%) of his subjects were Christians.

Jesus never strayed far from Galilee, a rural district north of Jerusalem that was populated by conservative Jewish peasants. Nothing is known about his activities until, at about the age of 30, he began to wander about Galilee, preaching and healing. He continued this work for one to three years before going to Jerusalem to die on a Roman cross.

Jesus' history remains elusive. He wrote nothing, and no firsthand reports of his activities have come down to us. The oldest Christian writings are the letters of Paul (the former Saul of Tarsus) that form part of the New Testament, the Christian scriptures. Paul was a Jew from Asia Minor who came to Jerusalem sometime after Jesus' crucifixion. He never met Jesus personally, but was converted to faith in Christ by a mystical experience. He could have learned much about Jesus' earthly ministry from people who had been Jesus' companions, but this apparently did not interest Paul. His letters focus on the resurrected Christ, not the historical Jesus. The major sources of information about Jesus' life are the New Testament's four Gospels: Matthew, Mark, Luke, and John. They were written between 30 and 65 years after Jesus' death, and none of their authors claims to have been an eyewitness of the events he narrates. The Gospels were testimonials of faith, not objective histories. They were written, as the Gospel of John (20:31) says, to persuade those who read them to believe that Jesus is the Christ.

Jesus and his disciples were all Jews, and Jesus is never said to have sanctioned a break with Judaism. His brother James, the head of the Christian community in Jerusalem, was well known for his scrupulous observation of Jewish religious law. As Jews, the first Christians seem to have assumed that gentiles (non-Jews) who wished to join their community ("the **church**," from Greek for "lord's house") would convert to Judaism. If gentile Christians did not become Jews, Jewish Christians could not associate with them without transgressing Jewish religious law. Paul, although he too was a Jew, saw things differently. He condemned any effort to impose Judaism on the church's gentile converts, and his position ultimately prevailed.

Although missionaries like Paul believed that the messiah's appearance meant that the era governed by Jewish religious law had come to an end, they clung to the Hebrew scriptures. The witness of this "Old Testament," as Christians began to call it, was needed to understand the Christ, for the messiah was the fulfillment of the promise God had made to Abraham. God had said that Abraham's descendants would someday become a great nation. For generations the Jews had assumed that this meant that they would acquire land and political power. However, by the second century B.C.E. their expectations had changed. They concluded that on their own they were too few and weak ever to triumph over the great gentile empires. God, therefore, would fulfill His promise by intervening in history on their behalf. He would send them a messiah, an agent who was commissioned (anointed) to act with His authority. Some Jews expected the messiah to resemble the prophets, kings, or priests who had led them in the past. Others claimed that he would be an angel, a supernatural manifestation of God's power. No one anticipated a messiah like Jesus—a humble laborer who was crucified as a common criminal and whose passing left the world apparently unchanged.

Many Jews were shocked by the Christian claim that the transcendent and majestic deity of their faith had incarnated His power in a man like Jesus. Gentiles, on the other hand, were less likely to find this implausible. Pagan religious mythology was full of stories of gods who appeared as all-too-human men and women—and of human beings who became gods. Jesus' crucifixion was, in Paul's words, a "stumbling block" to the faith of both Jew and gentile. However, all things considered, conversion may have been easier for gentiles than for Jews.

The Church's Reception   As the first century C.E. unfolded, Judaism and Christianity grew further and further apart. Jewish leaders condemned Christianity as a distorted version of their faith, and the political situation in Palestine made Christians eager to distinguish themselves from Jews. Palestine was restive under Roman control, and a radical Jewish faction, the Zealots, incited riots against the Roman authorities. (The Romans may have executed Jesus on the assumption that he was a Zealot.) Full-scale war finally broke out in 66 C.E. It took Rome seven years to suppress the Jewish revolt, and in the process Jerusalem was stormed and its temple destroyed. Given these circumstances, Christians were eager to assure the Roman authorities that they were on the empire's side in the conflict. The Gospels were written in this context, and that may explain their eagerness to place as much responsibility as possible for Jesus' crucifixion on the Jews and to shift it from the Romans who actually carried it out.

Rome's objectives in the Jewish conflict were political, not theological, for the Roman practice was to adopt religions rather than suppress them. Romans worshiped simultaneously on multiple levels. The state honored numerous gods: classical mythology's Greco-Roman Olympians, foreign deities such as Asia Minor's Magna Mater and Egypt's Serapis and Isis, and, of course, the emperors themselves. Countless localities had sacred caves, groves, and springs. Families maintained household shrines for their own private guardian spirits, and many individuals were devotees of mystery cults. A mystery cult was a secret society that initiated its members. Its doctrines and rituals were inspired by the story of a divine savior who defeated the forces of evil and opened the way for human beings to obtain personal immortality. These cults sometimes required converts to be baptized before admitting them to the key ritual: a shared meal that united worshipers with one another and their god.

Christianity's resemblance to the popular mystery cults doubtless helped it to grow, but it also had unique features that gave it advantages over these competitors. Its savior was not a fantastic being from a mythic past, but a real man from recent history. It accorded women and slaves the same spiritual standing as free men, and its conviction that the appearance of the Messiah heralded the imminent end of the world motivated it to proselytize with unusual zeal. The chief source of the young religion's friction with Roman society was its commitment to Hebrew monotheism—its insistence that its God was the only god.

Pagans feared that Christian blasphemy against the gods would anger the gods and prompt them to punish everyone. If a disaster occurred, the people affected might spontaneously rise up and attack their Christian neighbors. But there was no empire-wide effort to eradicate Christianity until the reign of Decius (r. 249–251), one of the Barracks Emperors. Decius was fighting to save an empire that was on the verge of collapse, and he had no patience with disloyalty. Christians incited suspicion because they refused to perform a simple patriotic ritual—the sacrifice of a pinch of incense before the statue of the emperor. Their apocalyptic preaching, which maintained that the world (including Decius's empire) was soon to come to an end, also did little to assure the emperor that they supported his efforts to save civilization.

Some Christians may have courted persecution, for **martyrs** were honored as heroes of faith whose salvation was assured. The earliest account of a Christian martyrdom is a description of the death by burning of Polycarp of Smyrna (c. 69–155), a bishop who was said to have been a disciple of Jesus' apostle John. It says that his followers recovered his charred bones and treated them like precious jewels. The medieval church vigorously promoted this kind of piety, and the veneration of relics—of anything that had been associated with a martyr or saint—became a staple of Christian worship. People made arduous pilgrimages to visit places where relics were enshrined, for these sacred objects were believed to work miracles.

The Church's Organization   Persecution of the church was counterproductive. The willingness of Christian martyrs ("witnesses") to go to their deaths rather than compromise their allegiance to their deity made the strongest possible argument for the uniqueness and power of Christian faith. The threat of persecution also weeded out the weak, recruited the strong, and forced Christian communities to organize and work together.

Many religions fragment as they spread, but Christian congregations resisted this tendency. An increasing threat of persecution encouraged them to work together, but so did a sense of mission that was part of their faith from its beginning. Early Christians believed that the messiah's appearance meant that the end of the world was near. Christ would soon come again, and every human being would face God's final judgment. Christians believed that God, in His mercy, was granting them a brief period in which to take this message to the world. The urgency of the situation forced them to invest their limited time where it promised to do the most good. They ignored the people who were scattered thinly across the countryside and focused their attention on those who clustered in cities. Consequently, Christianity became an urban religion, and paganism, the religion of pagani ("rural villagers"), lingered for a long time in the countryside.

As Christianity spread, the organization of the church began to mirror that of the empire. The empire was divided into territorial units centered on cities. The Christian missionaries who worked in these cities created ties among them. When a church in one town sponsored a mission to another, it forged an enduring link between them.

Gradually, a network of such ties spread across the empire. It had no center, but it could diffuse information and financial aid widely. As the number of congregations grew in a town, a **bishop** (*episcopus*, "overseer") would be elected to coordinate their work. Bishops of neighboring communities corresponded and occasionally convened meetings (synods or councils) to discuss doctrinal and disciplinary issues. This helped create and maintain some consistency of faith and practice. Inevitably, the bishops of the larger and more important towns came to dominate their lesser brethren, and an administrative hierarchy began to evolve. No single bishop was ever recognized as the head of the whole church, but one had a unique claim to distinction. Peter, the chief of Jesus' disciples, was said to have been Rome's first bishop and to have been martyred in Rome. In the Gospel of Matthew (16:18–19) Jesus calls Peter "the rock" on which the church is founded and promises that whatever Peter does on Earth will be ratified in heaven. Rome's bishops insisted that, as Peter's successors, his status passed to them, but it was a long time before they could lay exclusive claim to the title pope (*papa*, an affectionate word for a father) or any other privilege.

Constantine and Imperial Christianity

Diocletian launched the empire's most concerted attack on the church. However, his successor, Constantine (r. 312–337), reversed course, embraced Christianity, and encouraged the process of converting the empire. Constantine was not supposed to be Diocletian's successor. He became emperor by the tried and true method of persuading a portion of the army to help him eliminate other candidates for the office. Early Christian historians claim that he was converted by a vision on the eve of the battle that won him control of the western half of the Roman Empire. His faith was doubtless sincere, but it was also politically motivated. Persecution had been a conspicuous failure, and Constantine thought that the shaky empire might gain more by winning the church over than by continuing to oppose it. He did not go so far as to declare Christianity the empire's sole religion, but his policies made his intentions clear. He poured money into the construction of great basilicas, welcomed bishops into councils of state, and gave favorable treatment to Christians in the imperial bureaucracy. After he won control of the whole empire, he took a dramatic step that indicated his expectations for the empire's religious future. He moved its capital east to a new city called Constantinople, which was modeled after Rome. However, where Rome had pagan temples, Constantinople had Christian churches.

The church benefited greatly from Constantine's patronage, but it did not do as much to shore up the empire as he might have hoped. Once the threat of persecution was removed and church offices became stepping stones to wealth and power, Christians began to fight among themselves. The young faith had yet to resolve many theological questions, and now that it was safe for Christians to air their differences, fissures widened in the Christian community. Factions accused one another of promulgating heresy (false teaching), and each claimed that, as the sole arbiter of orthodoxy (correct belief), it ought to lead the church. Mobs took up the cause of one party against another, and religiously inspired violence erupted on the streets of Roman cities.

Constantine's first impulse was to use the power of the state to resolve theological disputes, but his experience with the Donatists, a group of North African Christians

The Arch of Constantine   By Constantine's day Rome had not been the administrative capital of the empire for decades. The seats of imperial government had moved to places that had better communications with chronic trouble spots. However, Rome still had enough importance as a symbol of the empire that emperors continued to adorn it with monuments. Constantine followed the tradition of erecting an arch to celebrate his victory over his competitors for the throne, but his monument suggests that the glory of the ancient world was fading. Its best components were looted from earlier buildings, and its new elements are of inferior quality.

who had withstood Diocletian's persecution, taught him that this was unwise. The Donatists claimed that priests who had yielded to Diocletian's demands had forfeited the power to perform valid sacraments (the sacred rites that imparted God's grace to believers). The only valid priests who remained, therefore, were the Donatists' own. Their opponents disagreed, for, as they saw it, a priest's powers derived from his office, not from his personal merit as a Christian. A sinful priest could forgive other sinners their sins, for a priest did not act on his own authority. He was an agent of the church and therefore of God. Constantine's judges accepted this argument and ordered the Donatists to stop making trouble. The Donatists, however, refused and rejoiced that the state was again giving them the opportunity to validate their faith through martyrdom. Constantine's efforts to heal the split within the African Christian community had only made things worse.

When an Egyptian priest named Arius (c. 250–336) initiated a furious debate over the relationship between Christ the Son and God the Father, Constantine was ready with a different strategy. At issue was whether the Son was the Father's equal or His first creation— a subordinate agent through whom the Father had created the world. Constantine decided to force the church to take responsibility for working this out for itself. In 325 he invited all the bishops of the empire to a council in the city of Nicaea (near Constantinople) and ordered them to resolve the dispute. The bishops hoped to unify the church by providing it with a creed (a statement of essential beliefs) that all Christians could profess. The council ratified a creed, but it failed to bring the warring factions together. Each group interpreted the creed as affirming its position, and the squabbling continued. The exasperated emperor finally resorted to force and even tried switching from one side of the argument to the other, but the Arian debate raged on and spawned other doctrinal controversies.

The church did not unify Rome's crumbling empire, but it rescued much from the empire's decline. The eastern half of the empire survived longer than the western half, and Constantinople's powerful emperors treated the eastern church much like a department of state. The situation was different in Rome's western provinces, where fading imperial governments thrust freedom and responsibility onto the church. Each Roman city had a secular administration staffed by civil magistrates and an ecclesiastical administration headed by a Christian bishop. But as the empire declined in the west, the agents of secular government disappeared. Christian bishops, who were supported by the church's endowments, were the only public officials left in many cities. People inevitably looked to them for leadership. Cities came under the control of bishops, and they labored to preserve some of the administrative machinery of the former Roman state. When new kingdoms eventually began to rise from the ruins of the western empire, their rulers turned to the church's bishops for help in organizing them.

The church that bishops led served "the world"—the realm where men and women raised families and struggled to survive. As the empire declined, however, a kind of church within the church sprang up. It was populated by religious ascetics who wanted nothing to do with the worldly concerns of ordinary people. They believed that by disciplining their flesh, they could strengthen their spirits and draw closer to God. This was not exclusively a Christian impulse. The secular philosophies of the era also tended to be world-denying, and the speed with which the ascetic movement spread suggests that it matched the mood of the age.

The church's first ascetics were hermits—people who fled human company to live alone in remote, desolate places. This idea seems to have struck fire first in Egypt, and a biography of an Egyptian hermit named Anthony (c. 250–355) helped to publicize it. Religious asceticism spread rapidly through the eastern empire, but was somewhat slower to find a foothold in the west. It soon became so popular, however, that large numbers of hermits began to cluster in some places. They were often drawn by the fame of a holy man (like Anthony) from whom they hoped to receive spiritual counseling. Practical concerns forced these spontaneous gatherings to organize themselves, and they evolved into institutions called monasteries—communities of **monks** (from a Greek word meaning "solitary"). The earliest monasteries were set up by one of Anthony's younger contemporaries, a former Egyptian soldier named Pachomius (292–346).

The growth of monasticism accelerated after Constantine legalized Christianity and made the faith both safe and popular. Early Christians expected the world to resist their call for repentance and their warning of an imminent apocalypse. When the world suddenly capitulated and embraced their faith, some Christians were unsure how to respond. Many believed that faith required a witness against the world, and they were shaken when the world not only refused to martyr them, but offered them wealth and power. Fearing seduction, they literally fled into the wilderness and substituted voluntary ascetic disciplines for martyrdom. They became the spiritual heroes of the post-Constantinian church, and crowds of pilgrims sought their prayers and advice. Church officials saw this as a potential problem. Few hermits and monks were ordained priests, and their religious enthusiasm was not a reliable substitute for training in theology. To prevent them from drifting into heresy, church leaders devised rules to govern their communal lives. A **rule** penned by Basil of Caesarea (330–379) won wide acceptance in the eastern empire, and a century later an Italian hermit named Benedict of Nursia (480–542) wrote the rule adopted by most of western Europe's monks. Western monasticism emphasized ascetic disciplines less than eastern monasticism and focused more on a precisely regulated regimen of work and prayer.

Although the hermit's flight from the human community ended with the formation of new communities, the monks who set up these communities still sought to isolate themselves from the world. They raised their own food and established schools to give their recruits the educations they needed to read the scriptures and chant the liturgies of worship. As the empire declined, its urban classes faded away—taking with them the schools and libraries that depended on their patronage. Monasteries survived, however, for they were largely self-sufficient, and the schools they maintained became, by default, the primary institutions keeping literacy alive in the West. Paradoxically, the men and women who fled the civilized world saved its civilization.

The German Element

Constantine was survived by three sons who divided the empire he had spent much of his life uniting. One of these men, Constantius (r. 337–360), outlived his brothers, reunited the empire, and passed it on to his cousin Julian (r. 360–363). Early Christian historians dubbed Julian "the Apostate," for he withdrew state support from Christianity and tried to reform and revive paganism. Julian's reign was too brief to enable him to reverse the tide of events, and his successor, a soldier named Jovian (363), restored the church's privileged status. Jovian reigned for only eight months, and at his death a coalition of military and civilian officials elevated another Christian soldier, Valentinian I (r. 364–375), to the throne. Valentinian divided the empire, taking the western half for himself and assigning the government of the east to his brother Valens (r. 364–378). Valens made a decision that precipitated a crisis from which the empire never recovered.

Invaders and Immigrants   The Germans who began to flood into the western Roman Empire in the fourth century have been called barbarians, but the term is misleading. They were not primitive people or strangers with an alien culture who suddenly appeared to threaten Rome. They had been the empire's neighbors for centuries and were thoroughly familiar with its civilization. They traded with Romans, worked inside the empire, and moved peacefully back and forth across the empire's vague boundaries. Roman diplomats even helped some German chiefs consolidate their tribes, for this stabilized turbulent regions and raised up kings with whom Rome could negotiate treaties. Roman merchants and Christian missionaries worked among the Germans, and some tribes converted to Christianity (albeit to the heretical Arian version) while still outside the empire. Germans envied Rome's wealth and power, and many were attracted to the empire in hopes of sharing the benefits of its civilization. Unfortunately, they came so quickly and in such numbers that the fragile, poorly governed empire could not absorb them.

The Germans were not only drawn to Rome; they were pushed against its frontiers by the migration of the Huns. The Huns had long preyed on China from their homeland in Mongolia. But when an aggressive dynasty arose in China and stiffened its defenses, the Huns were deflected to the west. They were formidable warriors whose equestrian skills were legendary, and they had invented a technique for making powerful bows that were small enough to be shot from horseback. In the mid-fourth century, they reached the lands north of the Black Sea, where they encountered and subdued their first Germans, the Ostrogoths (East Goths). In 375 they routed the Ostrogoths' neighbors, the Visigoths (West Goths), who then fled to the Roman border and begged permission to enter the empire.

This forced Valens, the eastern emperor, to make a difficult decision. As many as 80,000 Visigoths were massed on his frontier. No ancient government could handle that many refugees, but if Valens refused the Visigoths entry, they were likely to attack and cost him soldiers he needed to fend off the Huns. Valens admitted the Visigoths to the empire (hoping perhaps to use them to bolster its defenses), but things did not work out well for the eastern empire. The Visigoths soon faced starvation in their refugee camps, and they were infuriated by the Roman profiteers who tried to exploit them. In desperation, they began to forage for supplies in the region north of Constantinople. Valens pursued them, and on August 9, 378, he blundered into an ambush near the city of Adrianople. He and Rome's eastern army were slaughtered. By then, the western half of the empire had passed to Valentinian I's son, Gratian (r. 375–383). He gave Theodosius, a family friend, the job of restoring order in the eastern empire. Theodosius made peace with the Visigoths and enlisted them as **foederati**—independent allies resident within the empire and pledged to defend it.

By 394 various usurpers had overthrown Gratian and his brother Valentinian II (r. 378–392), and Theodosius (d. 395) had emerged as sole emperor. He was the last man to govern the whole empire and the first to proclaim Christianity its state religion (392). At his death, the empire was divided between his sons. The west passed to Honorius (r. 395–423), who was only 10 years old, and the east to Arcadius (r. 395–408), who was 18. The shortsighted policies of their inept administrations were soon to extinguish the last vestiges of Roman power in the western half of the Mediterranean world.

The Decline of the Western Empire About the time of Theodosius's death, the Visigoths acquired an ambitious young leader named Alaric (c. 370–410). When he began to press Constantinople for new opportunities for his people, the eastern empire took the easy way out. It rid itself of the Visigoths by urging them to move west into Italy. Italy's defense was managed by Stilicho (c. 365–408), a German general who commanded Emperor Honorius's army. He repulsed Alaric's initial assaults, but fear of the Visigoths caused Honorius's government to make some fateful decisions. Milan, the seat of the western empire, seemed too vulnerable to siege, so the court moved to Ravenna, a small port on the Adriatic. Ravenna owed the honor of becoming the last capital of the western Roman Empire to swamps that protected it from landward assault and to its proximity to the sea. The emperor wanted to be able, if need be, to take to his ship and flee Italy. Honorius's advisors also chose to beef up Italy's defenses by recalling the troops that guarded the Rhine and Danube frontiers. This cleared the way for large numbers of Germans from several tribes to cross the Rhine unopposed on the last day of year 406 and begin to loot their way through Gaul.

In 408 the bad situation grew worse. Honorius became suspicious of Stilicho's ambitions and ordered the general's execution. This disrupted the defense of the western empire and gave the Visigoths a chance to break into Italy. Ravenna's swamps prevented Alaric from assaulting Honorius directly, but Alaric had a plan for putting pressure on the western emperor. He ordered the Visigoths to march on Rome. Honorius could not ignore this assault on the symbol of his authority. He opened negotiations with Alaric, but when he failed to implement their agreements, Alaric lost patience and made good his threat. On August 24, 410, he sacked Rome. This was of little practical consequence, for the city was no longer the seat of the western empire. However, Rome's humiliation was a blow to the morale of the ancient world. It had been 800 years since the city last fell to an enemy, and its defeat was an ominous portent. Pagan intellectuals blamed the disaster on the rise of Christianity and the empire's neglect of the gods that had long protected it. The western empire's leading Christian thinker, Augustine (whose words are quoted at the head of this chapter), defended Christianity by putting the event in the broadest possible historical context. It was, he claimed, not all that significant, for it was simply one in a long series of painful consequences of humanity's sinful rebellion against God (see Chapter 8).

The Visigoths did little serious damage to Rome. They were Arian Christians who respected the city's churches, and after three days of looting, they left Rome and marched south along Italy's coast. Their plan was to collect ships and eventually to sail to North Africa. When a storm destroyed the flotilla they had gathered, they turned around and headed north to Gaul. Alaric died somewhere near Naples and was buried in a grave hidden beneath the bed of the Busento River.

Once the Visigoths were out of Italy, Honorius recognized them as *foederati*, and they settled in southern Gaul and Spain. They were far from the only Germans to stake claims to parts of the western empire. Many tribes had entered Roman territory in 406, when Honorius stripped troops from the Rhine frontier. The Vandals were part of the vanguard. As they looted their way across Gaul, others followed in their wake. Scattered bands of Franks occupied northern Gaul, and the Burgundians founded a kingdom in eastern Gaul. When the Visigoths pushed into southern Gaul, the Vandals wandered into Spain. In 429 they crossed the Straits of Gibraltar, conquered North Africa, established a capital for a kingdom at Carthage, and built a navy with which to raid Sicily and Italy. In 455 they sacked Rome. By then, Britain, whose defense Honorius had abandoned in 410, was being taken over by Angles and Saxons. Many other less significant tribes also grabbed bits and pieces of what was still, in theory at least, Rome's empire (see Map 7–1).

The western empire prolonged its existence as a legal entity by recognizing many of the Germans who settled within its boundaries as *foederati*. Rome had little power over these allies, but they responded to its calls for help when it was in their interest to do so. The last major occasion on which they served Rome was in 451, when Attila (c. 406–453),

Map 7–1 Migrations into the Roman Empire Between 376 and 406, the western Roman Empire let down its defenses, and German tribes wandered freely throughout its territory. Constantinople blocked them from spreading into the eastern empire, but in the eighth century the east had to contend with invaders from Arabia and the rise of Islam.

Question: Did geography pose different challenges for the defenders of the eastern and western halves of Rome's empire?

king of the Huns, led his people into Gaul. Aëtius (c. 390–454), a Roman general who served the emperor Valentinian III (r. 425–455), met the Huns at Châlons, south of Reims. With the aid of his German allies, he fought the Huns to a draw, and Attila retreated to Germany. The following year, when the Huns struck south into Italy, Rome was abandoned by its allies. They fought only when their own lands were threatened. Papal diplomacy or a timely outbreak of malaria in Attila's army saved the city of Rome from another sack. The Huns withdrew to Germany's healthier environment, and Attila died the following winter. His empire did not survive him, but its sudden collapse did not guarantee Rome's security. It only freed Germans whom the Huns had enslaved to seek their fortunes in Roman territory.

By now, the western emperors controlled little more than Italy, and that was often only nominally theirs. The real power had passed to generals who were usually of German descent. In 476 one of these, Odovacer (c. 493), deposed the last of the west's figurehead emperors, a 15-year-old boy who bore the name of Rome's founder, Romulus, and who was mockingly called Augustulus ("Little Augustus"). The eastern emperor championed another claimant for the western throne, but he was powerless to seat his candidate.

After Attila's empire fell, the Ostrogoths advanced on Constantinople, and it dealt with them as it previously had the Visigoths—by diverting them to the west. In 489 the eastern emperor commissioned the Ostrogothic king Theodoric (r. 489–526) to invade Italy as his agent and restore it to the empire. Although Theodoric theoretically served the eastern emperor, he was an independent monarch who gave Italy a few decades of peace, during which attempts were made to rescue the West's faltering civilization. Two notable scholars, Boethius (c. 480–524) and Cassiodorus (c. 490–580), worked at his court, and the books they produced became staples of education throughout Europe during the early Middle Ages. Theodoric gave Italy a valuable, if brief, respite from the confusion of a chaotic era. An attempt by an eastern emperor to regain control of Italy after Theodoric's death inflicted far more damage on the heartland of the ancient empire than anything the German "barbarians" had done.

The Byzantine Empire of Constantinople

When people speak of the fall of the Roman Empire, they are usually thinking only of its western half. The eastern Roman Empire, with its seat at Constantinople, was relatively undisturbed by the German invasions, and its succession of emperors continued until 1453, when the city was conquered by the Ottoman Turks and renamed Istanbul. However, once the western Roman Empire was gone, Roman elements in the eastern empire diminished. It became an ardently Christian state with a largely Greek-speaking population and a partially Persian culture. Historians distinguish this emerging medieval civilization from its Roman predecessor by referring to it as the Byzantine Empire (from the Greek name for the site of its capital).

Justinian   In 518 a military coup elevated Justin (r. 518–527), an illiterate soldier of peasant origins, to the eastern throne. He governed with the assistance of a gifted and well-educated nephew named Justinian. Justinian (r. 527–565) eventually succeeded his uncle and assembled a team of remarkable people to help him run his empire. Chief among them was his wife and virtual co-regent, Theodora (c. 500–548).

As the only surviving Roman emperor, Justinian believed that it was his duty to recover the western territories that had been lost to the Germans. The empire had previously come apart on several occasions and been restored. Justinian had no reason to assume that history could not repeat itself. In 533 his loyal general, Belisarius (c. 505–565), made a promising start by quickly overwhelming the fragile Vandal kingdom and restoring North Africa and Sicily to Justinian's control. Diplomatic negotiations then persuaded some places along the coasts of Gaul and Spain to submit, but the Ostrogoths vigorously resisted Justinian's efforts to gain control of Italy. War there raged on until 552, when the Ostrogoths finally gave in and agreed to evacuate Italy. Justinian's victory was, however, Pyrrhic. His war had devastated Italy. The city of Rome suffered great damage, particularly to the aqueducts that supplied its water. During the sixth century it lost nine-tenths of its population. The Byzantine Empire was left so exhausted by the struggle that it could not hold the prize it had won. In 568 another wave of Germans, the Lombards, swept into Italy from the north, and the Byzantines retreated to Ravenna and outposts in southern Italy. Rome's bishop defended his city and preserved its independence. But most of Italy was divided up among Lombard chieftains. The peninsula was to remain politically fragmented for the next 1,293 years.

Justinian could not concentrate all his attention on his western wars. Slavs, Germans, and various Asiatic peoples flooded into his Balkan provinces, and he faced a formidable opponent on his eastern frontier. Khusro I (r. 531–579), the Persian shah of the Sassanid Empire, devoted much of his reign to preying on Byzantine territory. Justin-

ian kept him at bay, but the fight drained both Byzantium and Persia, and made them easy targets for Arab Muslim armies in the seventh century.

The eastern half of Rome's empire had always been more prosperous, populous, and urbanized than the western, and the east was not disrupted, as was the west, by the migrations of German tribes. The eastern emperors, therefore, still had formidable resources at their disposal—as Justinian's reign demonstrates. In addition to his costly wars, he had the wealth to fund so many building

The *Hagia Sophia* Justinian's palace church is one of the world's architectural and engineering masterpieces. The walls and domes of its great hall, which is nearly as long as a football field, were originally covered with colorful mosaics. These were destroyed or covered when the building was converted to a mosque in the fifteenth century. Today it is a museum, and some of its original art has been restored.

projects that his court historian, Procopius, devoted an entire book to describing this aspect of his employer's reign. The most famous of his monuments is the massive Church of Holy Wisdom (the *Hagia Sophia*) that he erected next to his palace in Constantinople. It is an engineering marvel—a vast rectangular hall roofed by a system of interconnected domes, the greatest of which soars to a height of about 180 feet. Its innovative design and skillful construction prove that the eastern Roman Empire was capable of highly original and significant achievement during the era of the ancient world's "fall."

Byzantine Culture   Constantine designed Constantinople to make it a worthy successor to Rome as the capital of a renewed empire. From the city's site on the waterway that connected the Aegean Sea and Black Sea, its rulers could watch both of the late Roman Empire's trouble spots: the German and Persian frontiers. Its location was also economically advantageous, and it became a focal point for major international trade routes. It had access to Mediterranean markets through the Aegean Sea. Via the Black Sea and the Russian rivers that emptied into it, the city had a route to the Baltic region. Goods reached it along "the Silk Road" from China, from India up the Persian Gulf and the Mesopotamian rivers, and from Africa through the Red Sea and the empire's Egyptian ports.

Constantinople's virtually invulnerable fortifications added to its attractions. As conditions in the western empire deteriorated, many of the empire's wealthy families moved themselves, their art collections, and their libraries to the new capital. Emperors stripped other cities to adorn their new seat, and a steady stream of valuable records and objects flowed to "New Rome."

Among the things that Justinian's government inherited was a mountain of legal documents—judicial records, imperial and senatorial edicts, and lawyers' commentaries—that had been accumulating in the imperial archives for centuries. Justinian set up a commission to comb through this material, organize it, and distill from it the essence of Roman law. The result was a set of volumes, the *Corpus juris civilis* (*Body of Civil Law*), that was to have a major influence on the formation of Europe's medieval kingdoms and subsequently on some modern European nations.

Byzantine scholars produced encyclopedias and library inventories that make fascinating, if depressing, reading. They document how much ancient literature once existed and how much has been lost. Byzantine intellectuals are not remembered for much original work, but a few of them made significant contributions to history and theology.

Religion was at the heart of Byzantine civilization, and it both strengthened and stressed the eastern empire. A declining level of education and literacy in the west had the effect of diminishing theological disputes, but arguments over faith flourished in the more highly cultivated east and divided Christians against themselves. There was such an insatiable appetite for theological debate among Byzantines of all classes that it was said that a man could not get his hair cut without receiving a lecture on an obscure doctrinal point from his barber. It is hardly surprising that Constantinople dedicated its most important church to the wisdom (or intellect) of God. Byzantines were fascinated by the intellectual challenge of making sense of the mysteries of faith. They pursued

their arguments with such passion, however, that their rulers concluded that maintenance of a viable empire required them to stamp out dissent (heresy) and enforce conformity of religious opinion (orthodoxy). This preoccupation with purity of doctrine
led to the characterization of eastern Christianity as the Orthodox tradition. The Roman Catholic Church that emerged in western Europe evolved differently, and the eastern and western versions of Christianity formally separated in the eleventh century.

As the western half of the empire sank into confusion and the authority of its emperors faded, the power of their eastern colleagues increased. The eastern emperors
were able to build on the foundation Diocletian had laid for autocratic government and
the command Constantine had acquired over the church. A vast gulf separated the emperor of Constantinople from his subjects, but an elaborate governmental bureaucracy
kept him fully informed and fully in charge. The emperor was the source of all authority, and his agents had a hand in managing (and taxing) all industry and commerce. His
army was recruited from self-sustaining rural peasant villages that dealt directly with
him rather than through a hierarchy of aristocratic overlords. And there was no sepa-
ration of church and state in the eastern empire. The clerical head of the eastern church
was the "patriarch" of Constantinople, but he reported to the emperor, who was him-

Byzantine Art   Byzantine artists excelled in the production of mosaics, pictures executed in tiny
pieces of colored stone and glass. This panel from the Church of San Vitale in Ravenna, Italy, depicts
the empress Theodora, attended by splendidly costumed courtiers, presenting a chalice to the
church. A companion scene shows her husband Justinian offering bread for the mass. By setting the
figures in two-dimensional space, the Christian artist has lifted them from the ordinary world and
placed them in a spiritual environment. He has minimized their human corporeal natures and set
them in a timeless, heavenly realm.

self a quasi-clerical figure. The emperor presided at church councils, and on occasion he took part in liturgies, representing Christ. Such role-playing was consistent with the tendency of eastern Christianity to try to incarnate the divine and make it part of human experience. The overwhelmingly lavish decorations and elaborate services of the Orthodox churches were intended to give worshipers a foretaste of heaven. The desire for a physical link between the realms of heaven and earth, such as Jesus had provided during his earthly existence, found expression in powerful devotion to sacred objects called icons. Icons were usually paintings representing figures from scripture or saints. (Sculptures in three dimensions were less common, doubtless because of their association with pagan idols.) Icons were not worshiped in themselves, but were seen as a medium through which the spiritual realities they represented could be contacted. In this they functioned much like the sacred relics that were eagerly collected and passionately venerated by all medieval Christians.

Islam

About five years after Justinian died, a man named Muhammad ("Highly Praised," c. 570–632) was born in Arabia. At about the age of 40, he began to have religious experiences that transformed his life and the history of the world. He became "the Prophet," the man chosen to reveal the will of Allah, to found the religion known as Islam, and to set in motion events that rapidly created an empire larger than Rome's.

The Arabian Context   At the start of the seventh century, no one could have predicted that the next great world power would arise from Arabia. Most of the million-square-mile Arabian peninsula, with the exception of some oases and coastal districts, was desert inhabited by primitive nomads called Bedouins (*badw*, "desert"). Although Arabia was exposed to civilizing influences from Egypt and Mesopotamia, none of the ancient world's empires paid it much attention. The land was too barren to be worth the cost of conquest. Geography, however, gave Arabia some economic significance. Trade routes that connected the markets of the Mediterranean with those of India and east Africa passed around or through Arabia. As herdsmen wandered from place to place with their flocks, they could easily form caravans and move goods through their territory. Trade brought them into contact with Jews, Christians, Persians, Greeks, and Romans, and enhanced the importance of Mecca, Muhammad's birthplace.

Pre-Islamic Arabia was a politically chaotic country. It had no central government and no coordinated leadership. Arabs acknowledged few loyalties beyond those to blood kin. Scarcity of resources forced them to prey on one another and live by harsher codes than those that governed life in wealthier regions. Such order as existed in Arabia was maintained by fear of vendettas—by the knowledge that a man's kinsmen would avenge any harm done to him.

Trading was risky in a country where there was no governmental protection and in a culture where to display valuable items was to challenge others to try to take them from you. Fortunately, religion helped to compensate for the weakness of political institutions. Awe motivated people to restrain their behavior at sacred sites. Acts of violence or bloodshed were often believed to pollute holy ground, and those who commited them risked divine punishment. Mecca was one of Arabia's sacred places, the site of a rectangular stone building of ancient, but uncertain, origin called the Ka'aba ("cube"). Various Arab tribes had deposited some 300 holy images in the Ka'aba, and they venerated a black stone in its eastern corner. It was said to have been placed there by the Hebrew patriarch Abraham from whom the Arabs, like the Jews, claim descent. The Arabs believe that their ancestor was Ishmael, Abraham's son by his maid Hagar, and that their cousins, the Jews, descend from Isaac, the son Abraham had with his wife Sara. Respect for the Ka'aba created a space around Mecca where a powerful taboo forbade the kinds of fights that were routine elsewhere. Mecca was therefore a good place to trade.

Muhammad's tribe, the Kuraish, bore special responsibility for Mecca and the Ka'aba, but Muhammad was not born to a life of rank and privilege. He was orphaned at a young age, raised by a grandfather and then an uncle, and compelled as a youth to make his own way in the world. He worked on caravans, and about 595 he married a wealthy widow named Khadija, who was his elder by a decade or more. She may have borne her husband seven children, but only one lived: a daughter named Fatima. After Khadija's death Muhammad acquired a harem of nine wives, but Fatima was his only descendant. The lack of a male heir may have confirmed his conviction that he was meant to be God's final prophet.

The Origin of Islam   In 610, when Muhammad was about 40, he began to receive visions that conveyed the precepts of a new faith. An angel (said to be Gabriel, the messenger who had previously inaugurated Christianity by announcing the news of Christ's birth to Mary) ordered him to speak, and he was inspired to recite the first of the 114 **suras**, or divine messages, that compose Islam's sacred book, the Qur'an (the "Recitation"). Muhammad's Arab audiences were stunned by the poetic beauty of his utterances, and they committed them to memory and circulated them as an oral tradition. About 20 years after Muhammad's death, the *suras* were collected, and an authorized text of the Qur'an was compiled. A collection of **hadiths**, "traditions" about the Prophet handed down by his acquaintances, provided additional religious guidance.

In the beginning Muhammad's visions alarmed him, and he was reluctant to make them public. He had good reason. When he began to preach in 615, he set himself on course to collide with the Meccan authorities, the leaders of his tribe. Muhammad was disturbed by the growing materialism of the Meccan merchants, and he called for a return to traditional social values. He insisted that the rich had a duty to care for the poor. He personally had no taste for wealth or luxury and lived so frugally that he repaired his own clothing and helped his wives with household tasks. He advocated egalitarianism. All his followers were to be on the same footing, and no one was to claim superior social or spiritual status. None of this struck Mecca's leaders as new or alarming, but in 616 Muhammad crossed the line. He repudiated the polytheistic beliefs of his ancestors and embraced a radically consistent monotheism. This was an attack on the Ka'aba, and an attack on the Ka'aba was a blow at the foundation of Mecca's economy.

Muhammad claimed that his revelations came from *al-Ilah*, "the God," an ancient Arab term for a remote high god. Muhammad, however, declared Allah the sole deity—a unique, all-encompassing, transcendent divine power that defied human comprehension. Human beings could not hope to understand this ultimate reality; they could only surrender to it. Muhammad's core message was a call to submit (*salama,* "islam") to God's will. Muhammad repudiated every doctrine or image that might compromise Allah's unity or transcendence. He was acquainted with Judaism and Christianity, and he accepted their validity to a point. He said that the Hebrew prophets and Jesus were true spokesmen for God, but that their messages had been misinterpreted. He honored Jesus as a major prophet, but insisted that he was only a man and not an incarnation of God. He also forbade his own followers to pay him divine honors, and he claimed no miraculous powers. He was "the Prophet," God's final messenger, but that did not make him anything other than a mortal man.

By 620 the Prophet's situation in Mecca was deteriorating rapidly. As Muhammad pondered what to do, he had a vision in which he was carried to Jerusalem to the mountain where the Jewish temple had stood. From there he rose into heaven to meet the earlier prophets and to enter the presence of Allah. This experience confirmed his faith—as did a development that marked the turning point in his fortunes. He made six new converts from Yathrib, an oasis 200 miles north of Mecca. Yathrib subsequently came to be called Medina ("city" of the Prophet), but it was not an urban community. It was a 20-square-mile patch of arable land inhabited by tribes of both Arabs and Jews. The people of Yathrib were having a hard time living together. They needed an outsider to mediate their disputes, and in 621 they offered Muhammad the job. Having found a safe haven, Muhammad instructed his followers to prepare for the **hijra** ("departure"). The *hijra* was a spiritual as well as a literal journey, for it meant a break with the tribe of one's birth and a commitment to a new **umma** ("community"), whose members were bound by faith, not blood.

Umma **to Empire**   Because the *hijra* of 622 marked the start of Islam as an independent religious movement, it became the pivot point for Muslim historiography—the event from which all other events are dated. However, it took more than a move to Yathrib to secure Islam's survival. At first, life in Yathrib was as challenging for Muhammad as it had been in Mecca. Some of the oasis's inhabitants were not happy about his arrival, and he had to find some way to support himself and his people. Yathrib's location near the caravan routes that served Mecca solved the latter problem. Muhammad ordered his men to prey on Mecca's trade, and he may have led as many as 25 raids in person. Christians find it hard to imagine Jesus doing such a thing, but Jesus lived in a different world. Muhammad's situation was more like the one that Moses faced as he forged the Jews he had led out of Egypt into a people and helped them to survive by waging wars with competing tribes.

In 627 Mecca dispatched a large army to evict Muhammad from Yathrib, but the campaign backfired. The Prophet won a stunning victory over Mecca's superior forces, and as the news spread, converts to Islam multiplied. In 630 the Meccan authorities came to terms with the man whose spiritual vocation they had ridiculed. It was agreed that all pagan shrines throughout Arabia would be destroyed except Mecca's Ka'aba. The Ka'aba would be purged of its idols, but the building itself would be honored as marking the most sacred place on Earth.

Muhammad's insistence that loyalty to Allah superseded all other allegiances provided a way for the Arabs to transcend their tribal divisions and come together as a people. The

PEOPLE IN CONTEXT A'isha (614–678), Wife of the Prophet

In 620 a girl named A'isha was informed that her father had arranged for her to marry his best friend and spiritual mentor, Muhammad. She was 6 years old, and her future husband was about 50. The wedding took place three years later, and despite the gap in age between the bride and groom, the marriage was a great success. A'isha bore her husband no children, and he had other wives, but she became his favorite. He may have been intrigued by her independent spirit and her audacious sense of humor. (She once told him that she was amazed at how willing Allah was to do his will!) She narrowly avoided divorce when she blundered into a misadventure that raised doubts about her sexual fidelity, and on another occasion she led a harem revolt that brought Muhammad to the brink of repudiating all his wives. Despite occasional conflicts, the Prophet's affection for his feisty wife never waned, and when he was overtaken by his final illness, he asked to be taken to her room. He died with his head in her lap and was buried beneath her bed.

Muhammad's death committed A'isha, at the young age of 18, to perpetual widowhood, for the Prophet proclaimed his wives "Mothers of Believers" and forbade them to remarry. A'isha did not, however, sink into obscurity. As the only one of Muhammad's wives in whose presence he had received revelations from Allah, the leaders of the Muslim community turned to her when they were uncertain what to do. Her memories of what Muhammad had said and done served as precedents for deciding difficult questions. Tradition credits her with some 2,210 *hadiths*, the quasi-scriptural verses that supplement the Qur'an. A'isha knew how to make the most of her situation. She amassed wealth, dispensed influence, and intervened in the struggles that broke out for control of the Islamic community. At the start of Islam's first civil war, she raised an army and was captured on the battlefield when her men were defeated. Her reputation as the Prophet's beloved protected her, and she remained a force to be reckoned with until her death in 678. Clearly the early Islamic community was not exclusively a man's world.

The Prophet's Mosque, Medina, Arabia
Muhammad spent the later portion of his life in Medina, and he died and was buried there.

Question: Given that priestesses were common in the ancient world, why did female religious leadership decline when the medieval West embraced Christianity and Islam?

new faith that the Prophet revealed founded a new community, but Muhammad had little time to turn the *umma* into a state. He died in Medina on June 8, 632. His death did not shake the faith of his followers, for he had never denied his own mortality. It did, however, pose a problem. Muhammad had insisted that there would be no more prophets after him, and he had said nothing about choosing a new leader for the *umma*. Some tribes concluded that their allegiance had been to Muhammad, and that his death dissolved their ties to the *umma*. However, Abu Bakr (632–634), the first of Muhammad's prestigious converts and a long-time friend, stepped in and prevented Islam's dissolution. Muhammad had sometimes chosen Abu Bakr to stand in for him and lead the *umma*'s communal prayers. The precedent that this had established and Abu Bakr's close association with the Prophet made him the logical choice to become Islam's first **caliph** ("successor"), the heir to Muhammad's duties as leader of the *umma*.

Abu Bakr, being about the same age as Muhammad, outlived him by only a few years, but this was long enough to secure the *umma*'s future. Faith helped preserve its unity, but so also did material success. Under Abu Bakr's leadership, Muslim raiding parties thrust into the lands of the Persians and Byzantines that bordered Arabia. Their timing was excellent, for both these empires had been locked in combat for decades and were reeling with exhaustion. Raids quickly became conquests, and Islam began to acquire an empire (see Map 7–2).

Muhammad had forbidden his people to fight among themselves and decreed instead that they devote their energies to waging *jihad* ("holy struggle"). The word is difficult to

Map 7–2   Expansion of the Muslim Empire   This map shows the stages by which Islam spread (in little more than a century) from the interior of Arabia west to the Atlantic, north into France, and east to India and the frontiers of China.

Question: Given that Islam originated on the periphery of the Roman Empire and Muslims claimed much of Rome's former territory, was the Islamic empire a "Western" empire?

translate and has often been misunderstood by non-Muslims and abused by Muslims. It asserts the *umma*'s right to defend itself, but it also extends to the religious duty to fight for a just society and do whatever is necessary to defeat evil in one's own character. It can involve taking up arms against others, but it also entails the difficult spiritual struggle that all believers are called to wage against their darker impulses. There was no strain of pacifism in Muhammad's teaching, but he insisted that wars be fought only for just causes, that they be as brief as possible, and that they cease as soon as opponents offer honorable terms. He did not send his people forth to convert the world at the edge of a sword. Islam's rapid spread owed little to compulsion and much to its innate appeal.

Islam and Christianity   The church, in its various forms, had virtually captured the West by the seventh century. Then, Islam suddenly emerged to challenge Christianity's religious monopoly. The result was a division in Western and world civilization that has had—and continues to have—troubling consequences.

A history of conflict obscures the fact that Islam and Christianity have much in common. Both claim Hebraic ancestry. Both are monotheistic, and both have relied on Greek philosophy for help in developing their theologies. Many of the individuals who appear in the Bible are also found in the Qur'an. More is even said about some Christian figures (Jesus' mother, the Virgin Mary, for example) in the Qur'an than in the New Testament. The Qur'an praises Jesus as a highly respected prophet. It affirms his virgin birth (but not his role as an incarnation of God) and describes him performing some miracles that are not mentioned in the Bible.

It is extremely difficult to summarize the faith and practice of a major religion with fairness and accuracy, but the traditional scheme for highlighting the fundamentals of Muslim belief is something called the "Five Pillars of Islam":

1. Affirmation of a monotheistic creed: "There is no god but Allah, and Muhammad is his prophet";
2. Prayer at fixed times during the day;
3. Contribution to charities that care for the poor;
4. Observation of a season of fasting during the month of Ramadan;
5. At least one pilgrimage to Mecca in a lifetime.

What is too seldom noticed is that medieval Christianity can be described in similar terms. Medieval Christians affirmed monotheistic creeds—although theirs tended to be much longer and more detailed. Christian monks prayed at fixed times during the day, and churches rang their bells at certain hours to encourage laypeople to pause in their labors and pray. The medieval church, like the Muslim state, had the power to levy taxes to support charitable works. Christians observed Lent, a longer period of fasting (40 days) than the Muslim month of Ramadan. Medieval Christians were also enthusiastic pilgrims, many of whom endured great hardship to fulfill the dream of visiting the Holy Land, the birthplace of their faith.

The most blatant contrasts seen today between the practices of Muslims and Christians reflect the gulfs that have widened between secular cultures in different parts of the modern world. There are also some significant differences between the faiths that reflect the particular environments in which their founders worked. The Christian church arose within the Roman Empire. This meant that responsibility for protecting and policing the society within which the church operated belonged to Rome's secular government and that the church could confine itself to a narrowly defined religious mission. As the empire declined, the church was sometimes forced to fend for itself and take on political responsibilities. This created problems during the Middle Ages. Kings and popes sometimes disagreed as to which powers belonged to which leader, but the church and state were still assumed to be different entities. The *umma*, on the other hand, was a religious community that sprang up in a place where there was no state. It had to provide itself with the services of secular government. Consequently, the distinction between sacred and secular authority was far less clear in Muslim than in Christian societies. Islam did not create a priesthood at the head of an independent religious organization. It has no sacraments that require priestly intermediaries, and its mosques (*masjid*, "place of worship") have no altars. In this, Islam resembles Judaism. Mosques, like synagogues, are places for prayer, preaching, and study, and the duties of Islam's imams ("leaders" of prayers) are similar to those of Jewish rabbis. Islamic clergy interpret sacred texts and define **shari'a** ("required path"), laws for the *umma*. The rules for governing a Muslim society reflect a belief that Muhammad shared with the Hebrew prophets and Jesus—that God cares about how people treat one another and that He holds communities and individuals accountable to standards of social justice. Muhammad taught that God's justice would ultimately be revealed by a final judgment. Good people would be separated from bad, and individuals would receive the eternal reward or punishment their conduct merited. Many Muslims are convinced that because human actions have such transcendent significance, *shari'a*, or religious law, should govern every aspect of life and determine the policies of states.

The Muslim World   The Byzantine Empire was in bad shape when Muslim armies erupted from Arabia in the mid-seventh century. Justinian's costly projects had driven taxes so high that some of Constantinople's subjects in Syria and Egypt welcomed the Arabs as liberators. Plagues had depopulated much of Asia Minor, and wars with Slavic invaders of Byzantium's Greek and Balkan provinces had drained the Byzantine Empire's resources. Fights over the throne and palace coups added to the confusion, and in 611 the Persians pushed through Byzantine territory to the Mediterranean coast, cut the empire in half, and sacked Jerusalem (614).

The Byzantine Empire's decline was reversed when an army from its North African province staged a military coup and placed its commander, Heraclius (r. 610–641), on the throne. By 627 Heraclius had driven the Persians back to their capital at Ctesiphon (near ancient Babylon), and regained the empire's lost provinces. He then, however, had to face the Muslims who were surging out of Arabia. In 636 they routed his army at the battle of Yarmuk and occupied Syria, Egypt, and Armenia. Constantinople then enjoyed a respite, for the Muslims shifted their attention to Persia. After the Persian Empire collapsed in 651, Constantinople's days also appeared to be numbered. Dynastic squabbles and brief reigns crippled the Byzantine Empire for the rest of the seventh century. The Muslim threat temporarily diminished, however, for divisions emerged within the *umma*.

As close associates of Muhammad's, the early caliphs were obvious choices for their office. But after Muhammad's generation died out, agreement had to be reached on a system for passing down the leadership of the *umma*. On November 4, 634, Umar (r. 632–634), the man to whom Abu Bakr had bequeathed the caliphate, was stabbed by an assassin. He lived just long enough to charge a committee with responsibility for choosing his successor. Two candidates emerged, each representing different political philosophies. Ali, Fatima's husband and father of the Prophet's grandsons, was the favorite of those who believed that the caliphate should descend in Muhammad's family. Uthman, his opponent, was the head of the prestigious Umayyad family, the first of the great Meccan clans to convert to Islam. Wealth and connections won Uthman (r. 644–656) the prize, but he had little aptitude for the office. In 656 a company of disgruntled soldiers from Egypt besieged his residence in Medina and killed him.

Uthman's assassins tried to save themselves from punishment by claiming that Uthman was unworthy of the caliphate and by offering it to Ali. Ali's acceptance infuriated Mu'awiya, governor of Syria and leader of the Umayyad family. Fighting broke out, and a schism developed within the *umma* that has never been bridged. In 660 a panel of judges declared that Mu'awiya was the legitimate caliph, and he inaugurated an Umayyad dynasty that monopolized the caliphate for a century (660–750). The **Shi'a** (the "party" of Ali), however, refused to acknowledge the Umayyad caliphate. When its leader, Ali, was killed in 661, the *Shi'a* split into factions that championed the rights of various individuals who claimed connections with Muhammad's family. Some Shi'ites insisted that the true caliph was a "hidden imam," an unknown messianic figure who would eventually emerge from obscurity to unite the *umma*. Today, *Shi'a* Islam is centered in Iran and Iraq, but the larger Muslim community, the Sunnis ("orthodox" believers), accepts the legitimacy of Islam's historic dynasties.

The Umayyads settled in Damascus, a far more convenient location for running an empire than the remote religious centers of Mecca and Medina. Once in power, they resumed Islam's wars of conquest. The North African port of Carthage fell in

The Lion Court, the Alhambra Palace, Granada, Spain   Pre-Islamic Arabs were nomads who did not burden themselves with works of art, but as the empire of their Muslim descendants grew, Islam drew from a multitude of cultures to develop a unique artistic tradition. For some time, beginning in the eighth century, artists were forbidden to represent living things, for this was considered a mockery of God's creative powers. The art and architecture of this period explored the aesthetic potentials of geometric abstraction and elaborate calligraphy. Muslim aesthetics reached a high point of grace and refinement in the construction of the palace for the rulers of Spain's last Islamic state, Granada.

698, and by 714 most of Spain was under their control. Muslim navies patrolled the western Mediterranean, and in 718 Muslim armies pushed into France. Islam's eastward expansion was equally rapid. In 711 the Muslims reached the Indus River Valley and began the conquest of what is now Pakistan. In 714 a Muslim expeditionary force probed the frontiers of China.

The Umayyads' empire was too large, given the technologies of its day, to be administered by a central government. Local officials had considerable discretionary authority, and some of them established independent states. Arab rule was not unpopular. Muslims did not force conversions to Islam. Jews and Christians were respected as "People of the Book." They were viewed as inferiors and paid a special tax (*jizya*) to acknowledge that position, but they enjoyed *dhimma* status (that is, recognition as a tolerated religious community). They could practice their faiths (with some limitations) and have a degree of autonomy under their own religious leaders, but they could not bear arms. The Umayyads, indeed, thought of Islam as a privilege Allah bestowed on Arabs. They did allow non-Arabs to convert, but often regarded such converts as second-class Muslims. Separate mosques were provided for them. They paid taxes from which Arabs were exempt, and Arabs were discouraged from intermarrying with them. This discrimination created tensions within the Muslim community that eventually unseated the Umayyads.

In 747 a family that claimed descent from Muhammad's uncle, Abbas (d. 653), rallied non-Arab Muslims and launched a revolution that nearly exterminated the Umayyads. The Abbasid dynasty left Damascus for a new capital called Baghdad ("Gift of God") near the ruins of Ctesiphon, the seat of the former Persian Empire. Baghdad's Abbasid court became legendary for its luxury and sophistication, and the civilization it represented was the most progressive of the early Middle Ages. The caliphs supported scholars who collected and built on the works of the Greeks, Persians, and Indians. As a consequence, the Islamic world began to make significant progress in philosophy, mathematics, and science.

The Abbasid dynasty survived for a long time, but its power steadily eroded. Initially (in 750) it failed to destroy all its Umayyad competitors, and one Umayyad prince escaped to Spain, where his descendants established a rival caliphate. Another sprang up later in North Africa and Egypt. The Abbasid caliphs, like the last of the western Roman emperors, became figureheads for governments run by their soldiers, and the dynasty was finally extinguished in 1258, when a Mongol army destroyed Baghdad.

KEY QUESTION | Revisited

By bringing the peoples of the Mediterranean region and Europe together, the Roman Empire helped to create a unified "Western" civilization. As that empire declined, however, the political and cultural ties that held this "West" together weakened. Differences among regions became more pronounced than things held in common, and fissures widened in the fabric of the empire. Communication between Latin- and Greek-speaking districts diminished. The economy of the western half of the empire declined as it struggled with political upheaval and invasion. Meanwhile, the east, which suffered less from the changing situation, turned in on itself. Religion added a new level of complexity to the situation.

The Three Medieval Civilizations		
EUROPE	**BYZANTIUM**	**ISLAM**
Romulus Augustulus (476) *Merovingian dynasty* (fd. 481) Clovis (d. 511)		
	Justinian (d. 565) Heraclius (610–641)	Muhammad (570–632) Abu Bakr (632) Omar (632–634) Uthman (644–656) Ali (d. 661) *Umayyad dynasty* (fd. 660) Mu'awiya (d. 680)
[Charles Martel (d. 741)]	*Isaurian dynasty* (fd. 717) Leo III (d. 740)	
Carolingian dynasty (fd. 751)		*Abbasid dynasty* (fd. 750)
Pepin III (d. 768) Charlemagne (r. 768–814)		
		Harun al Rashid (786–809)

Constantine had hoped that religion would strengthen the state by compensating for the weakening of other ties. His predecessors had never questioned their right and duty to promote and oversee the religious practices of their people. And given the tolerant attitudes and widespread moral consensus fostered by classical paganism, religion seldom conflicted with state policies. But Christianity had evolved in opposition to the state (and to the world, which Christians regarded as doomed by sin to destruction), and it saw no virtue in tolerating other faiths. Doctrinal disputes among Christians added to the tensions with which the empire had to deal, and Constantine's effort to maintain order created a precedent for the church to claim a degree of autonomy from the state.

The Christian church triumphed over its competitors and was recognized by the empire as the West's sole legitimate faith. As such, it exercised overwhelming influence on the development of Western civilization. It acquired a monopoly over education and literacy, and its precepts were written into law. The result, however, was not universal concord and agreement. Although Christians professed the same faith, they did not all understand that faith in the same way. It divided as well as united them. Quarrels over heresies continued, and as the eastern Roman Empire became the Byzantine Empire, it evolved a Christian culture distinct from, and sometimes opposed to, that of the Latin west. In both east and west, serious disputes arose over the division of powers between secular and religious leaders.

Islam's experience was somewhat similar. Muhammad's preaching unified the Arab peoples and kept them working together long enough to build a huge empire. But like Christianity, Islam soon developed internal divisions—both cultural and theological—

that spawned intense hatred among persons who professed allegiance to the same faith. Islam's spread into territory occupied by Christians created another cause for war and for the fragmentation of the world that Rome had united.

The fact that Islam, Christianity, and Judaism all spring from the same tradition and all honor many of the same sacred figures and shrines has often, paradoxically, made it difficult for them to tolerate one another or even dissident members of their own faith communities. As monotheistic faiths, they share a tendency to assign people to opposing categories: the saved versus the damned, the sheep versus the goats, the citizens of the city of God versus the inhabitants of the city of man, true-believers versus heretics—some version of "us versus them." The West's three great religions saved its civilization. They trained and supported its scholars. They commissioned and inspired its arts, and they provided the ideologies that helped to integrate its political communities—but at the cost of great bloodshed.

Religion has not invariably promoted justice, tolerance, and moral progress. It has a history of provoking wars, pogroms, and lesser conflicts. In light of the current international situation, some commentators have insisted that the world would be better off without religion. Their opponents argue that civilization would be impossible without the grounding that religion provides for values. Religion is not likely to disappear, and much of value would be lost if it did. Freedom of conscience and of religion are fundamental Western values, but can such liberties exist without accountability?

Review Questions

1. Edward Gibbon, an important British historian of the eighteenth century, said that the fall of the Roman Empire was brought about by the triumph of barbarism and religion. Is this a fair assessment of Rome's decline?
2. How did the eastern half of Rome's empire come to differ from the west? Why did the two have different fates?
3. How does Jesus' career compare with Muhammad's?
4. How does Christianity compare with Islam? How is the church different from the *umma*?
5. Why did religion become the most powerful cultural influence shaping Western societies in the early Middle Ages?
6. Are Islam and Christianity both Western religions?

Please consult the Suggested Readings at the back of the book to continue your study of the material covered in this chapter. For a list of documents on the Primary Source DVD-ROM that relate to topics in this chapter, please refer to the back of the book.

8 The Emergence of Europe

I am convinced that no one can describe these deeds [of Charlemagne's] more accurately than I can, for I was there when they transpired and, as people say, witnessed them with my own eyes. What is more, I cannot know for sure that anyone else will record these things. Therefore, I have concluded that it would be better to produce an account myself . . . rather than permit the amazing life of this most remarkable king, the leading man of his generation, to fade from memory.

—Einhard, *Life of Charlemagne*

KEY | Question

How did Europe build on its legacies from the ancient world?

The explanation Einhard (c. 770–840) gave for his decision to pen an account of the life of his king, Charlemagne, reveals how different his world was from ours. In our abundantly documented age, it is unthinkable that a man like Charlemagne, who ruled much of Europe, might be forgotten. Einhard, however, was right to be concerned. He was a member of Charlemagne's inner circle from 793 until the emperor's death in 814, but he had no information about his subject's birth and youth. There were no public records, and no one who knew Charlemagne as a boy was still alive. Only a few years had passed, but already part of the great man's history was lost. Under such circumstances, even the memory of extraordinary events could fade quickly. This worried Einhard, for he believed that his generation had witnessed one of history's turning points—the emergence of Europe as a world power.

Although Einhard and his contemporaries had a very limited knowledge of history, the past was a potent force in their lives. No emperors had reigned in the western half of the Roman Empire after the deposition of Romulus Augustulus in 476, but on Christmas Day 800, the people of Rome had ended a 324-year-long interregnum by reviving the imperial title and bestowing it on Charlemagne. Charlemagne bore little resemblance to Rome's previous emperors, and

Emperor Charlemagne No contemporary portraits of Charlemagne, one of the greatest medieval kings, survive. However, this small bronze figure from the ninth century might have been intended to represent him. *Musee du Louvre/RMN Reunion des Musees Nationaux, France. SCALA/Art Resource, NY*

his lands were not coterminous with those of their empire. His domain extended from the Pyrenees (the mountains between France and Spain) to the Oder River in eastern Germany and from the North Sea to Naples. Much of the territory that Rome had formerly governed, from Spain in the west across North Africa to Egypt and Syria in the east, had come under Muslim control. The Balkans, Greece, and Asia Minor were ruled from Constantinople, whose emperors' line of succession stretched back to the Roman Caesars.

The Greeks coined the word *Europe* (perhaps from an Assyrian term meaning west), but they knew little about the region to which it referred. Much of the land that lay to the north and west of Greece was of peripheral importance to the civilized world even after the Romans added Gaul, Britain, and part of Germany to their empire. This changed following the western empire's collapse. Rome's former northwestern provinces began to expand, coalesce, and develop a sense of identity. Their emerging self-awareness is reflected in the title that one of Einhard's colleagues, Alcuin (c. 737–804), bestowed on Charlemagne: *Europae pater* ("father of Europe").

Charlemagne believed that the great continental state he had created entitled him to the prestige that the imperial title conferred. His coronation was also meant to put the world on notice that Europe was emerging from the decline into which it had slipped in the fifth century and was asserting its claim to the civilization that was Rome's legacy. Charlemagne's subjects were culturally inferior to the ancient empire's other heirs, the Byzantines and Muslims, but history more than vindicated Charlemagne's confidence in his people's future. Rightly or wrongly, Europeans would one day regard themselves as the sole guardians of Western civilization.

When the Roman Empire broke up, what had been a politically unified territory with a veneer of common culture split into regions with ever more diverging identities. As distinctions between east and west—and north and south—increased, shared traditions diminished, and memories of common origins faded. Initially, the inhabitants of the lands along the eastern and southern shores of the Mediterranean, the Byzantines and Muslims, did the best job of preserving and building on the foundations laid by the ancient world. But by the end of the Middle Ages, the peoples who lived north and west of the Mediterranean had taken the lead (thanks in no small measure to help they had received from their eastern and southern neighbors) and were poised to spread the West's civilization around the globe. Much of the modern world, therefore, has experienced Western civilization in a form mediated by Europe. Because Europe's physical and cultural environments were different from those of the ancient Mediterranean region, Europeans had both continued and diverged from the legacies of the ancient world to create a version of its Western civilization appropriate to their context.

The Merovingian Kingdom: Europe's Nucleus

When the Franks, for whom France is named, first appeared in history, they were a gaggle of German tribes inhabiting the eastern bank of the lower reaches of the Rhine River. Emperor Constantine's father, Constantius I, settled some of them (the Salian, or "Saltwater," Franks) in the Netherlands to create a buffer between the empire and wilder folk to the north. Some of the Franks who remained in the Rhineland (the Ripuarian, or "River," Franks) also entered Rome's service. In 406, after Honorius (r. 395–423) recalled Rome's legions to Italy to fight the Visigoths, the Franks tried to hold the Rhine frontier for the empire. Franks were part of the army with which the Roman general Aëtius blocked the Huns' advance into Gaul in 451. Thirty years later, a Frankish chief named Clovis united his people and founded a dynasty that turned Roman Gaul into medieval Francia.

Clovis and the Franks   Clovis (c. 466–511) was about 10 years old when the last western Roman emperor was deposed, and he was still in his teens when he succeeded his father as one of many Frankish tribal chiefs. His people lived near Tournai in Austrasia ("Eastern Lands"), a region between the Rhine and Somme rivers. Clovis's early campaigns extended his power south beyond Paris to the Loire Valley. The Franks called this territory Neustria ("New Lands"). Clovis pushed the Visigoths south to the Garonne River, eliminated rival Frankish chiefs, brought much of Germany under his control, and married to form an alliance with the Burgundians, whose kingdom lay on his southeastern border.

Two decades after Clovis's death in 511, the Byzantine Emperor Justinian still dreamed of regaining control of what had been the western Roman Empire. He succeeded in temporarily occupying Italy, but by then, much of western Europe was firmly established on the road to independence. This was thanks in large part to Clovis, who did more than conquer territory. He helped unify a world that had been culturally fragmented by the events that brought down the western empire. Germans, such as Clovis's Franks, constituted a small minority of the population of the new lands their kings aspired to rule. Most of Gaul's residents were Romanized Celts, Catholic Christian descendants of the subjects of the old empire. Religion was especially important to them, for their leaders were their bishops. The clergy had inherited responsibility for Rome's *civitates* (the city-states that composed the old empire) when the empire's secular government crumbled. Clovis's Gaul was a loose association of regions headed by Catholic bishops from powerful aristocratic families, and German kings, like Clovis, had to come to terms with these native magnates.

This could be difficult for several reasons. Some Germans, Clovis and the Franks among them, were pagans who worshiped ancient tribal gods. Others, such as the Visigoths and Burgundians with whom the Franks competed for control of Gaul, were heretics—Arian Christians. The Catholic clergy despised the Arian faith as a perversion of their religion, but they viewed pagans more positively as candidates for conversion. Clovis, therefore, had a slight advantage in negotiations. Like Constantine a century and a half earlier, he understood the political advantages of conversion, and like Constantine, he justified abandoning his ancestral gods by claiming that the Christian God gave him victory in a crucial battle. The church, which welcomed him as its defender and patron, had much to offer him. It supported him in his wars with the Arian kings and helped him create a more effective monarchy by utilizing what was left of the imperial tax and administrative systems.

Many of the German tribes remained aloof from the peoples whose lands they occupied, but not the Franks. The conversion of the Franks made it possible for them to intermarry with the Romano-Celts and join them in developing a common culture. This required compromises on both sides. The Christian religion and Roman practice altered some German traditions—particularly those governing marriage, the status of women, inheritance, and property rights. Frankish customary law influenced courts and enforcement of justice—the prosecution and punishment of crime becoming a private matter rather than the duty of the state. Government's function was primarily to restrain the vendettas that threatened to break out among quarreling families. Accused persons could clear their names by undergoing physical ordeals or by compurgation (that is, finding a number of individuals who would swear to their innocence). The guilty could avoid physical punishment by paying **wergeld** ("man money"), monetary compensation. Amounts were determined by the nature of the injury and the status of the person who had been harmed. As more formal governmental procedures evolved under Roman influence, the German laws, which had been preserved as an oral tradition, were translated into Latin and written down. Latin survived as the language of scholarship and formal documents, but the "street" Latin spoken by the majority of Gaul's residents was gradually transformed into the Romance ("Roman") dialects that are the ancestors of modern French. As the Frankish and Romano-Celtic peoples fused, Gaul's cultivated, literate nobility disappeared, and the new aristocracy that emerged at the top of society adopted the lifestyle of the German warrior elite. In short, the features of a new medieval civilization began to appear in western Europe.

The Merovingian Succession   Clovis's kingdom was a collection of separate regions that he kept together by force. He did not think of his domain as a state, a political entity to be handed down intact from generation to generation. He understood it to be a private estate—the property of his family, the **Merovingians** (descendants of a quasi-mythical Merovech). This had major consequences for the future of Francia. German tradition dictated that private property be divided among all a man's heirs. Consequently, the Frankish kingdom was repeatedly divided and recombined—giving each generation of Merovingian princes an excuse to fight among themselves and fatally weaken their dynasty (see Map 8–1).

Clovis divided his kingdom among four sons. Fortunately, they were more interested in wars of conquest than in fighting among themselves. One of the boys outlived the others and briefly reunited the realm, but he divided it again for his heirs. From about 570 to 613, civil war raged between the two original Merovingian courts, Austrasia and Neustria. The survivor of the conflict laid claim to all of Francia, but by then the power base of the Merovingian kings was seriously eroded.

The Franks viewed their kings less as administrators of territorial states than as tribal leaders. Their king was a warlord who was supposed to settle disputes among his followers and lead them on profitable raids. A Frank expected his loyalty to his king to be rewarded by a steady stream of gifts. This custom had developed when the Franks were bands of semi-nomadic warriors who made their livings by dividing up the cattle and movable goods they captured from their neighbors. But once they settled down and land became the source of their wealth, their kings had difficulty meeting their expectations. A king who acquired new lands through conquest was able to enrich himself and reward his men. But when conquests ceased, kings sometimes had to give away their own lands to maintain the support of their followers. Over time, important nobles greatly enriched themselves at the expense of the royal family, and the balance of power shifted to them and away from their impoverished monarch.

A proliferation of heirs also helped to weaken the Merovingians and encourage their tendency to fight among themselves. Royal marriages were fluid, and the distinction between a wife and a concubine vague. Kings often had children by many women, and because there was no tradition of primogeniture ("first born") mandating that the whole kingdom pass to a king's eldest son, every male with a bit of Merovingian blood could claim a share of the royal estate. This played into the hands of the Frankish nobles, for rival can-

Map 8–1   Western Europe in the Merovingian Era   Clovis and his descendants assembled what might have become the core territory for a continental state, a united Europe. But they failed to overcome centers of regional power and develop a stable monarchy.

Question: Did geography work for or against Francia's development into the country of France?

didates had to offer them gifts in exchange for their support. The last significant Merovingian monarchs were Chlotar II (d. 629) and his son Dagobert (d. 638). After them, the throne passed to youths and weaklings whose fortunes steadily diminished until the last Merovingian kings were reduced to living modestly on a small farm outside of Paris.

The Franks' Neighbors

The Franks were not the only Germans to try to build new states amid the ruins of Rome's western empire. Other groups made promising starts, but like the Franks, they suffered reversals. The political contours of a new Europe were slow to emerge.

Italy and the Lombards   While Clovis was building a Frankish domain in Gaul, the Ostrogoths, under the leadership of their king Theodoric (r. 489–526), were taking control of Italy. Theodoric restored political stability to Italy, protected its Roman inhabitants, and safeguarded its classical culture. After his death, the Byzantine emperor, Justinian (r. 527–565), invaded Italy, and the peninsula was devastated by a war that dragged on to

552. The Ostrogoths ultimately yielded and left Italy to join the Visigoths in Gaul and Spain (see Chapter 7).

In 568 the exhausted Byzantines fell back as another wave of German invaders, the Lombards, descended on Italy. Alboin, their king, established his seat at Pavia (south of Milan) in what came to be known as Lombardy. The Lombard kingdom was weak, and it failed to impose its authority throughout Italy. Lombard chiefs carved out independent duchies, and the Byzantines hung on to Ravenna and a few outposts in southern Italy. The peninsula was divided up among small states that preyed on one another and kept the region in turmoil.

Spain: The Visigoths and the Muslims

After sacking Rome in 410, the Visigoths settled in southern France and began to spread into Spain. Fighting among factions kept them weak, and in 507 Clovis and the Franks seized much of the land they had occupied in Gaul. Their hold on Spain was not much more secure. The Visigothic nobles elected their kings, and their preference was often for a weak candidate who posed no threat to their independence. The Visigoths' Arian religion was also a problem, for it drove a wedge between them and their Catholic subjects. The Visigoths finally converted to Catholicism in 589, but the continuing reluctance of the Visigoths to marry native Spaniards kept Spain's two peoples divided. The Visigoths spent much of their time fighting among themselves, and in 711 a group of rebels asked Tarik, the Muslim governor of North Africa, to help them overthrow their king. The army that Tarik landed at "Tarik's Mountain" (Jebel el-Tarik, or Gibraltar) chose instead to conquer Spain. Spain's Christians lost everything but the tiny state of Asturias in the northwest corner of the Iberian Peninsula. Spain became, and was for a long time to remain, a Muslim country.

In 720 the Muslims crossed the Pyrenees bent on the conquest of Francia. By then the authority of the impoverished Merovingian kings had all but disappeared, and the Franks found a new leader in Charles Martel, the head of a powerful noble family. In 732 he halted the Muslim advance near the city of Tours. The Muslims retreated but retained control of a strip of France's Mediterranean coast until about 750. In that year the Abbasids overthrew the Umayyad caliph. He and most of the members of his family were slaughtered, but one Umayyad prince escaped and fled to Spain. He waged a bloody struggle that culminated in Spain's repudiation of the Abbasids and the establishment of a rival caliphate with its seat at Córdoba.

England

The Franks and Goths who founded kingdoms in Gaul and Spain got their starts as *foederati* (allies) of Rome's empire. They were influenced by Roman culture, and they tried to save some of the empire's institutions. The situation in the Roman province of Britain was different. The cities the Romans founded in Britain failed to flourish, but the rural villas they scattered about the countryside thrived. During the fifth century, when the migrations of the Germans disrupted production on the continent, demand for British goods soared and Britain's economy prospered. The island's Romano-Celts, the Britons, were understandably dismayed when, about 406, Rome withdrew its troops and told the people of Britain that they would have to defend themselves. Their situation was precarious. They faced raids from Ireland and Scotland, and the wall that the emperor Hadrian had built across northern England was useless without an army to back it up.

Local strongmen emerged to fill the political vacuum left by Rome's departure, and some of them raised armies by recruiting German mercenaries from the tribes of Angles and Saxons who roamed the continent's North Sea coast. These soldiers-for-hire turned on their employers, and by 450 the homeland of the Britons was becoming Angleland (England).

The Anglo-Saxons, in contrast to other Germans, had been little exposed to Rome's civilizing influence, and the Britons gave them no help. The Germans who established the new kingdoms on the continent came from tribes that had a history of involvement with Rome, and when they settled in their new territories, they had the advantage of mixing with Rome's former subjects. But as the Anglo-Saxons moved into Britain, the native Britons either fled or were exterminated. So many emigrated to northwestern Gaul that the area came to be called Brittany. Others moved to Ireland and Spain. Few stayed behind to try to convert the Anglo-Saxons to Christianity or instruct them in the arts of civilization. This period in England's history is largely undocumented, but the memory of at least one battle in which Britons triumphed over Anglo-Saxons survived into the twelfth century. It inspired a cycle of romantic tales about a King Arthur and a legendary land of Camelot. Scholars have proposed various Latin and Celtic roots for the name Arthur, but Camelot's king is a creature of mythology.

Ireland   As civilization declined in Britain, it began to flourish in Ireland, a land that had never been part of the Roman Empire or had much contact with its civilization. Ireland was divided into clan territories headed by petty kings. It had no cities and no literate culture until a chance event set in motion a chain of events that fundamentally altered its way of life.

In the fourth century Irish raiders sacked the coast of Britain and abducted a youth named Patrick, the son of a Roman official. Patrick spent six years as a slave in Ireland before escaping to the continent. For two decades, he studied in various monasteries, and about 432 he was consecrated a bishop and sent back to Ireland. He was phenomenally successful at converting the Irish to Christianity, and the new faith promoted the spread of monasticism and literacy.

Because Ireland was, for some time, cut off from the rest of the Christian world, it evolved some unique religious customs. Ireland did not have cities like those that provided seats for bishops in former

The Book of Kells   This page from an illuminated (decorated) text of the gospels was probably created about 750 at Iona, an Irish monastery on the western coast of Scotland. It lavishly ornaments the Greek letters that begin a verse from the first chapter of the Gospel of Matthew. Celtic and Germanic arts featured complex designs that utilized abstract geometrical forms.

■ ■ ■ ■ ■ ■   ■   ■   ■   ■   ■   ■   ■   ■   ■   ■   ■   ■ ■ ■

PEOPLE IN CONTEXT Brunhild (d. 613) and Fredegund (d. 597): Powers Behind the Throne

I n 567 Sigibert, king of Austrasia, made a prestigious marriage that threatened the balance of power in Francia. He wed Brunhild, daughter of the Visigothic king of Spain. This gave him a major ally in his competitons with his brother, Chilperic, king of Neustria. But Chilperic quickly checked Sigibert's move by winning the hand of Brunhild's sister, Galswinth. For some unknown reason, Chilperic then turned against his bride, murdered her, and returned to a former wife, Fredegund (d. 597), a woman of humble origin with whom he was apparently infatuated.

Merovingian princes often wed commoners to avoid the troublesome entanglements associated with aristocratic marriages, but a match with Fredegund did not make life any easier for Chilperic. She became a power at his court and cleared the way to the throne for her children by eliminating his sons by other women. The only one of her boys to outlive Chilperic was an infant named Chlotar II. Although his paternity was questioned, Fredegund successfully defended his claim to the throne and served as regent during his minority.

War erupted between Austrasia and Neustria after Galswinth's murder, but no contemporary source claims that it was caused by Brunhild's desire for vengeance. Dynastic ambitions may be enough to explain the bloody conflict that raged between her and Fredegund and Chilperic. In 575 Fredegund engineered the assassination of Brunhild's husband, Sigibert. Childebert II, Brunhild's young son by Sigibert, retained control of Austrasia with the help of an uncle, but Brunhild fell into Chilperic's hands. She tried to recoup her fortunes by marrying Merovech, one of Chilperic's sons who was attempting to unseat his father. When their coup failed, Merovech committed suicide, and Brunhild escaped to her son's court. Two of Fredegund's agents, both clergymen, then tried but failed to assassinate Brunhild and Childebert.

Gold Fibula This pin for a cloak was cast for a wealthy Merovingian who lived in the seventh century.

Although one of the Merovingian queens was a foreigner and the other a commoner, both wielded great power. The sources depict them as scheming behind the scenes, but both were highly visible figures. Fredegund's assassination of Sigibert reversed the course of a war, and the queen dominated her husband's successor until her death in 587. Brunhild received flattering letters from Pope Gregory the Great (r. 590–604), who assumed that she had the power to reform the Merovingian church, and her husband and her son were both accused of being under her thumb.

Brunhild manipulated the feuds that divided Francia's aristocratic families, and by 585 she and her son Childebert were firmly in control of Austrasia and busily eliminating their opponents. In 584 Brunhild avenged Fredegund's assassination of Sigibert (Brunhild's husband) by murdering Fredegund's husband, Chilperic I. By 589 Brunhild and Childebert had become the dominant powers in Francia, and the death of an uncle in 592 allowed Childebert to add Burgundy to his possessions. Childebert died four years later, and Brunhild ruled as regent for his sons, Theudebert II and Theuderic II.

When Theudebert reached his majority (c. 600), a coalition of Austrasian nobles forced Brunhild to flee to Burgundy, Theuderic's territory. She then announced that Theudebert was the bastard child of a palace gardener and that Theuderic was the legitimate heir to Austrasia. Her influence over her grandson increased as she encouraged his sexual affairs and dissuaded him from a marriage that would have raised up a rival queen. Reform-minded clergy were scandalized, and declared Theuderic's offspring illegitimate. Brunhild then had the kingdom's bishops denounce the reformers.

In 612 Brunhild finally persuaded Theuderic to attack Austrasia. Theuderic killed Theudebert and his son, and he was on the verge of invading Neustria to unseat Fredegund's son Chlotar II when he died of dysentery. Brunhild prevented the division of Theuderic's estate among his sons, and arranged for the eldest, her great-grandson Sigibert II, to inherit a unified kingdom. At that juncture, a block of aristocrats defected to Neustria and helped Chlotar II capture Brunhild and Sigibert. Chlotar claimed that Brunhild had been responsible for the deaths of ten kings, and he condemned the elderly woman to be torn apart by wild horses.

Question: What do the careers of Brunhild and Fredegund suggest about the roles that other less well-documented aristocratic women may have played in medieval politics?

Roman territory. Its church was organized around monasteries established in the territories of the Irish clans. The abbots who presided over these houses were more important leaders of Ireland's church than its bishops.

Christianity brought literacy to the Irish, and Irish monks became renowned for their superior scholarship at a time when learning was declining on the continent. Irish monasticism also placed a great deal of emphasis on ascetic self-denial. Some monks embraced self-exile as an ascetic discipline. Some became missionaries to England and the continent. They helped to convert the Anglo-Saxons. They planted monastic outposts as far afield as Gaul and Italy, and one of them even tried to reform the morally lax court of the Merovingian queen Brunhild.

The Carolingian Era

In 751 the last of the Merovingians was deposed, and the Franks transferred their allegiance to the family of the **Carolingians**, whose most famous king was Charlemagne (a contraction of the French for "Charles the Great").

A Transition of Dynasties   The Carolingian family was formed by the intermarriage of the heirs of the two most powerful men at the Austrasian court of the Merovingian king Dagobert (d. 638). The Carolingians controlled the office of "mayor of the palace," a kind of prime ministry, and were more powerful than the rulers they theoretically served. In 679 Pepin of Heristal, the Carolingian mayor of Austrasia, extended his authority over Neustria and united both Frankish homelands under a Merovingian puppet king. When he died in 714, his illegitimate son, Charles Martel, dispossessed his half-brothers, who were minors, and assumed control of the family's enterprises. It was Martel (c. 688–741) who repulsed the Muslim invasion of Francia in 732. Further military successes won him the submission of Aquitaine and Burgundy, and new lands in Germany.

Some of Martel's contemporaries called him *rex* ("king"), but this was only a courtesy or flattery. It was Martel's son and heir, Pepin III, "the Short" (r. 741–768), who formally elevated the Carolingian family to royal status. He might simply have appropriated the Merovingians' title, but that would have diminished its worth. Titles are only significant when people believe that they are legitimate, and it was hard for Pepin to challenge the Merovingians' legitimacy. Because the Franks had no memory of a time when they had not been ruled by Merovingians, the Merovingians' right to the throne appeared to be part of the divine order of creation.

Given that the Franks had embraced Christianity and no longer worshiped the gods who had reigned at the start of the Merovingian era, Pepin reasoned that they would accept a change of dynasties if it were approved by the Christian God. The difficulty, of course, lay in finding someone who could speak for God. The bishop of Rome claimed that right, and it was in Pepin's interest to support his claim.

The Christian community had never acknowledged a supreme leader. The emperor dominated the church in Constantinople, and the groups of Christians that were scattered and cut off inside the Muslim empire attended to their own affairs. The church in western Europe was far from unified, but one of its bishops could make a case for precedence over the others. The bishop of Rome (the pope) headed the only diocese in the region that had been founded by one of Jesus' apostles, and its founder, Peter, was a very special apostle. Jesus (in the sixteenth chapter of Matthew's Gospel) had granted him the "power of the keys." Jesus had said that whatever Peter "loosed" or "bound" on Earth would be "loosed" or "bound" in heaven. Catholic dogma holds that this authority passed to Peter's successors in Rome—giving them the right to speak and act for God. A wide gap existed, however, between the powers the early medieval popes claimed and the powers they actually exercised.

The church came of age as one of the institutions of the Roman Empire, and its leaders clung to the empire as long as they could. After the line of western emperors ceased in 476, the bishops of Rome looked to the eastern emperors for protection. But this was not a satisfactory arrangement. Byzantine emperors and popes quarreled over doctrine, and the military assistance that Constantinople could offer Rome steadily diminished as the Lombards moved into Italy. Rome's Senate is not recorded as meeting after 579, and as the city's secular government faded away, responsibility for defending and administering Rome fell to its bishop. During the seventh century, some popes had courted Frankish rulers in hopes of winning their help, but the Franks were reluctant to be drawn into a war with the Lombards.

In 751 the Lombards conquered Ravenna, Constantinople's major base in Italy, and the danger they posed to Rome increased. Pope Zacharias (r. 741–752) made a desperate appeal to Pepin for help. Pepin was willing to negotiate, for the pope now had something of value to offer a Frankish leader. Zacharias endorsed Pepin's argument that the man who had the responsibility of king ought also to have the title, and he urged the Franks to elevate Pepin to their throne according "to their custom." Pepin, supported by the clergy, deposed the last Merovingian king and confined him to a monastery. Pepin was then crowned in a ceremony that included a new ritual—an anointing, a spiritual consecration. This added dignity and awe to the new dynasty, but it raised troubling questions. Did it give kings clerical status and authority over the church? Or did it imply that the church, because it consecrated kings, also had the right to depose them? A serious struggle between church and state was to break out in the distant future, but in Pepin's day kings were so much stronger than popes that the possibility of a conflict between secular and spiritual authorities may not even have occurred to them.

Pepin's sons were both married to Lombard princesses, and his reluctance to offend his Italian allies delayed repayment of his debt to the papacy. In 754 a desperate Pope Stephen II (r. 752–757) came to Paris to plead with Pepin in person—and to reconsecrate him as king. Pepin finally took his army to Italy, drove the Lombards back from Rome, and ceded the lands that he liberated to the pope. This "**Donation of Pepin**" confirmed the existence of a papal kingdom (the Papal States). The pope had conferred spiritual status on Pepin, and Pepin had reciprocated by shoring up the pope's secular power. The pope doubtless needed a base of his own so that he could resist domination by lay lords and kings, but the papacy's temporal interests inevitably conflicted with its spiritual role—at considerable cost to both church and state.

Charlemagne Builds an Empire   When Pepin died in 768, his throne was well established. However, his decision to divide his kingdom between his two sons, Carloman (r. 768–771) and Charles (Charlemagne, r. 768–814), cast doubt on its future. Carloman's premature death in 771 prevented the outbreak of civil war, for Charlemagne quickly deprived Carloman's young sons of their inheritance and reunited the Frankish kingdom. He then set about building an empire.

Charlemagne's first acquisition was the Lombard kingdom in northern Italy. Its ruler, Desiderius, was Charlemagne's father-in-law, but that did not prevent Charlemagne from responding to another appeal from the papacy (in 774) for help against the Lombards. He defeated Desiderius, imprisoned him, and appropriated the Lombard crown. This removed one threat from the papacy, but posed another. With much of France, Germany, and Italy under the control of the Frankish king, the pope had little latitude for independent action.

The papacy's concern for its independence may account for the appearance in the eighth century of a forged document called the "**Donation of Constantine**." In fairness, the forging of documents was not the crime then that it is today. The decline of literacy meant that many people lacked documents confirming rights to which they were entitled. Often the forger's motive was to create records that should have existed but did not. The popes believed that, as the only officials of the Roman Empire left in western Europe, they took precedence over the new German monarchs. The Donation of Constantine made their case by appealing to a popular, but groundless, legend that claimed that Pope Sylvester I (r. 314– 335) had cured the emperor Constantine of leprosy. The grateful emperor had supposedly repaid the pope by ceding the empire to the church, but the pope had graciously decided to allow Constantine to continue to rule the eastern half. The medieval popes did not claim, on the basis of this story, to be emperors. As early as the fifth century, Pope Gelasius I (d. 496) had declared the church and state to be separate and equal partners. He said that kings, like popes, were established by God. The former was given a secular, and the latter a spiritual, "sword." Ideally, each was to assist the other without transgressing on his colleague's turf. In practice, however, popes had a difficult time preventing royal encroachments on the church, and the Donation of Constantine was an attempt to intimidate kings by implying that popes were the final arbiters of the legitimacy of the West's monarchs.

The Donation of Constantine complicated disputes between popes and kings until it was proved to be a forgery in the fifteenth century. Charlemagne was far too powerful to worry about its implications for church-state relations, and he may actually have found it useful in improving his position. His father, Pepin, wanted to become a king, and Charlemagne sought recognition as an emperor. The church helped both men reach their objectives.

If any German leader deserved recognition as an emperor, it was Charlemagne, for he came to control most of western Europe. Following his victory over the Lombards, he turned his attention to Muslim Spain. Spain seemed vulnerable, for the Muslims were fighting among themselves. But as soon as the Franks appeared, the Muslims closed ranks and forced Charlemagne to withdraw. As his army retreated over the Pyrenees, the native Basques attacked its rearguard. This was an inconsequential event that did not alter history, but for some reason it captured the popular imagination. Stories began to be told about a Roland, an alleged duke of Brittany and favorite of Charlemagne's, who died in the encounter. In the late eleventh century these inspired the first major piece of French literature, an epic poem entitled *The Song of Roland*.

Although Charlemagne's first Spanish campaign failed, he continued to probe Muslim territory, and by 801 he had taken Barcelona and created the Spanish **march** (a frontier military district). The march provided Christians with a base south of the Pyrenees from which they launched crusades in the eleventh century to reconquer Spain (see Map 8–2).

Most of Charlemagne's wars were aimed at winning German territory. From 772 to 804 he waged annual campaigns in Saxony (the region south of the Danish peninsula). Mass executions and deportations were needed to pacify Saxony, which became one of Germany's stronger duchies. In 787 Charlemagne put down a rebellion in Bavaria, and a subsequent campaign culminated in the founding of the East March (Ostmark, or Austria). Next, he drove down the Danube Valley into the territory of the Avars, invaders from the Russian steppes who had grown wealthy extorting tribute from Constantinople and the Balkans. In 796 the Franks secured Germany's eastern border by defeating and dispersing the Avars, and Charlemagne returned home with massive amounts of treasure.

Charlemagne wanted the imperial title as a recognition of his achievement in uniting much of western Europe, but its quest confronted him with the same problem his father Pepin had faced. If the title was to be more than a presumptuous affectation, he could not simply assume it. His right to it had to be confirmed by an appropriate au-

Map 8–2 Growth of the Carolingian Empire   By spreading their civilization and government across much of Europe, the Romans created a tradition of European unity that was never forgotten. It inspired repeated efforts to reunite the peoples of Europe under a single political authority.

Question: Does geography work for or against the formation of a continental European state?

thority. The most obvious authority was the surviving Roman emperor who ruled in Constantinople, and in 780 Charlemagne began to negotiate with the Byzantine Empire for recognition as the eastern ruler's western colleague.

To bolster his claim to the imperial title, Charlemagne embarked on a program that would make him look as imperial as possible. German kings tended not to have fixed, permanent seats for their governments. They found it easier to feed their court by moving it from one royal estate or monastery to another than by shipping food from distant farms to a central location. Poor communications also meant that the king had to travel to stay in touch with his subjects. The lifestyle of Roman and Byzantine emperors was different.

Charlemagne's Chapel at Aachen   The palace complex at Aachen was laid out as a rectangle covering an area of about 50 acres. Charlemagne's palace occupied one side of the rectangle, and the church the other. A long covered gallery connected the two. The church was rebuilt and added on to by later generations, but the center portion remains much as Charlemagne knew it.

They resided in capital cities ornamented with monuments testifying to their power. Charlemagne, therefore, decided to construct a grand palace complex as a permanent seat for his court. The site he chose revealed, however, that his capital was to be more a symbol than a center of government. Charlemagne settled in Aachen (Aix-la-Chapelle), an old Roman spa. Its appeal was not its potential as a center for a communications network, but a pool fed by hot springs in which the king enjoyed swimming. The centerpiece of the new capital was a church in Byzantine style. It was as magnificent as the best European artists could make it. They looted Ravenna, the old capital of the western Roman empire, for architectural elements to use in its construction, but the finished building fell far short of the splendors of Constantinople's *Hagia Sophia.*

Charlemagne's negotiations with Constantinople dragged on for over 20 years without making much progress. The delay was due in part to political confusion in the eastern empire. In 797 the eastern emperor's mother, Irene, overthrew him and became the first woman to assert a claim of her own to either a Roman or a Byzantine throne. Because there was doubt about the legitimacy of a female emperor, a case could be made that the office was vacant and therefore available for someone else to claim. The situation might have had some influence on Charlemagne's decision to go to Rome in 800 to extricate Pope Leo III (r. 795–816) from some political difficulties. He stayed on to celebrate Christmas, and at the holiday mass the pope and the Roman populace hailed him as emperor. Einhard, Charlemagne's biographer, claims that the pope did this without Charlemagne's prior knowledge and that it infuriated Charlemagne. That seems unlikely. Leo was on shaky ground and could hardly have risked taking such a momentous step without Charlemagne's approval. It is also hard to imagine how he could have carried out a coronation ceremony without Charlemagne's cooperation. The story of Charlemagne's displeasure may have been circulated to smooth things over with Constantinople. It provided diplomatic cover for Charlemagne by shifting responsibility for the event to the papacy.

The patriarch of Jerusalem acknowledged Charlemagne's status as an international Christian leader of the first rank by sending him the keys to the Church of the Holy Sepulcher, the site of Christ's tomb. Harun al-Rashid (r. 786–809), the Abbasid caliph of

Baghdad, addressed him as an equal and sent him a gift befitting an emperor, a war elephant. Constantinople grumbled, but in 813 it accepted the *fait accompli* in exchange for resolving a dispute over some Balkan territories. A few months after Byzantine ambassadors hailed Charlemagne as an emperor (but not explicitly a Roman emperor) in Aachen, he shared his title with his son and heir in a ceremony that pointedly excluded the clergy. Charlemagne did not want his coronation to set a precedent for the papacy to claim an exclusive right to crown emperors. However, his successor undid his work by subsequently seeking papal confirmation of the title, and thereafter it was firmly established that the imperial title was assumed only with a papal blessing.

The Nature of the Carolingian Empire

Charlemagne's empire was held together by personal relationships that were maintained by the judicious use of carrots and sticks. The emperor was a daunting man who could physically intimidate his subordinates or seduce them with gifts, as the situation warranted. Their loyalty was essential to the functioning of his government, for primitive communications prevented Charlemagne from knowing much about what was occurring in his far-flung domain. Because he had to grant his officials a great deal of discretionary authority, he bound them to him with oaths and personal obligations. He filled most key offices with Austrasian nobles whose families had ties with his. He required all his male subjects over the age of 12 to swear personal oaths of loyalty to him, and he persuaded his leading men to take oaths of vassalage. His father was the first to impose vassalage on the nobility as a sign of their subservience to their king. *Vassus* (or *vassallus*) was a Celtic term for a servant or slave, but by the end of the eighth century, it had come to designate a far more exalted status.

The empire had seven marches (militarized frontier districts) and about 300 counties. A duke (*dux*, "general") or count (*comes*, "companion") headed each of the territorial divisions of the empire, and he was responsible for all aspects of the government and defense of his district. Left largely on his own, he was, in effect, a mini-king, but there were safeguards to prevent him from abusing his power. A man was usually assigned to a region where he did not have influential relatives to back him up, and he was moved from time to time to prevent him from building a power base that he might use against his emperor. Charlemagne frequently summoned his officials to court to remind them of their dependent status, and an annual mustering of the army at the beginning of the campaigning season (the Mayfield) gave him another chance to reinforce ties with them. He circulated open letters called capitularies to establish guidelines for good government, but it was difficult for him to know if his orders were followed. About 779 he began to send out teams of auditors (**missi dominici**, "emissaries of the lord") to check up on his governors and hear complaints against them, but it is doubtful that this did much to stem corruption or halt abuse of power. Most of Charlemagne's subjects thought of their emperor as a remote figure who had little to do with their lives. Their fates were decided locally.

The Division of the Empire

Charlemagne's empire was held together by the vigilance and energy of its leader, and as age sapped his strength, it too declined. The emperor had a bevy of wives, concubines, and children. He avoided some dynastic complications by refusing to allow his daughters to marry, but he planned to divide his realm among his sons. The civil war that this invited was avoided when he outlived all but one of them. Unfortunately, the survivor, Louis the Pious (r. 814–840), may have been the heir least suited to be an emperor.

Louis was a well-educated man who, had he not been destined for a throne, probably would have chosen a life in the church. In childhood he had been dispatched to the French region of Aquitaine to serve as its titular king. Raised there under the tutelage of a monk, he became a sober man who was appalled by the moral laxity of his father's court. One of his first acts upon becoming emperor was to purge the court of everyone (including his sisters) whose conduct was not up to his strict standards. He believed that the church was also in need of reform, but he was overly deferential to his clerical advisors. When his vassals realized that their lord was as weak-willed as he was pious, they began to take liberties. His own sons ultimately turned on him and on one another. After Louis died in 840, his three surviving sons fought for another three years before agreeing to a settlement of their father's estate. In 843 the Treaty of Verdun, which ended their war, foreshadowed the emergence of Europe's major nations. The youngest of Louis's sons, Charles the Bald, became king of western Francia. His brother, Louis the German, got the empire's eastern territories, and the oldest of the three princes, Lothair, claimed the imperial title and a long, narrow kingdom that ran between his brothers' realms from the North Sea down the Rhineland to Italy. The new kingdoms represented regions that were already evolving separate ethnic cultures. Evidence for this is preserved in a chronicle that describes a meeting between Louis and Charles at Strasbourg in 842. Each swore an oath in a tongue that the other's followers could understand, and the text of Louis's oath is the earliest specimen of a Romance language.

Lothair's kingdom was divided among his heirs and eventually disappeared. The rulers of Francia and Germany appropriated parts of it. (France and Germany were still quarreling over Lorraine—Lotharingia—as late as the mid-twentieth century.) No new royal dynasty appeared in Italy, and the imperial title itself was allowed to lapse in 924. By then it meant little.

Invasions and Fragmentation

The western Roman Empire had fallen to the migrations of Charlemagne's German ancestors, and now a similar fate was to befall his empire. Signs of what was to come appeared during the closing years of his reign.

In the second half of the eighth century, Viking fleets began to sally forth from

A Viking Ship   Viking chiefs were sometimes buried in their ships, and well-preserved specimens have been excavated and preserved in Norway's museums. This vessel dates to about 820. *Frits Solvang © Dorling Kindersley, Courtesy of the Universitetets kulturhistoriske museer/Vikingskipshuset.*

Scandinavia, driven by overpopulation or by opportunities for pillage. These Norsemen (Northmen, or Normans) had developed the best seafaring technology of their day. Viking ships could handle the high seas, but their shallow drafts also enabled them to navigate Europe's many rivers and strike deep inland.

While the Vikings attacked from the north, the Muslims renewed their assault from the south. In 800 the Abbasid caliphate ceded Algeria to the Aghlabids, a dynasty of local princes. The Aghlabids ended a long fight between Berber and Arab Muslims in North Africa by diverting their quarreling subjects to Christian targets. In 827 they began the conquest of Sicily, which was still Byzantine territory. From Sicily they raided Europe's Mediterranean coasts. They assaulted Rome in 846, and in 888 they established bases in the south of France from which they attacked traders who used the Alpine passes.

By then, a third threat to the Carolingian kingdoms had appeared on Germany's eastern frontier. The Magyars migrated westward from the Russian steppes and began to push up the Danube Valley into the heart of Europe (see Map 8–3).

The Carolingian states were poorly equipped to counter simultaneous attacks on multiple fronts, for they had little infrastructure to support centralized government. Some paved roads existed in those parts of Europe that had once belonged to Rome, but neither information nor troops could travel quickly. A king could not respond rapidly enough to fend off raids to his realm that might come from any direction or hit different places simultaneously. It made more sense to disperse resources and command authority, for every part of a kingdom needed a strong leader who was permanently in residence and prepared to defend it. Kings did not disappear, but power shifted decisively to their military vassals. Kings became firsts-among-equals who reigned rather than ruled. Their status was superior to that of their vassals, but their primary responsibility, like that of an ordinary lord, was to govern and defend their own estates.

Retrenchment and Reorganization

The medieval era in Western history is one of the most difficult to understand, for it had no central focus—no city like Athens or leaders like the Roman emperors to give structure to its narrative. The radical political fragmentation of Europe that followed the invasions of the ninth century confronts students of history with a special challenge. Scholars rely on models and generalizations to create an overview that helps to make sense out of the past, but the people they study actually lived in particular situations. They were concerned with survival, not conforming to a theory. They did whatever they deemed best to adapt to the specific circumstances they confronted. The European continent has many diverse environments, and its medieval inhabitants had a rich legacy of traditions and customs to draw on when exploiting them. Consequently, it is difficult for historians to say much that is equally true of all medieval people—particularly during the years of their most extreme political and cultural fragmentation.

In the Early Modern Era (post-sixteenth century), scholars sought explanations for the institutions and conventions of European society by delving into the medieval past. Untold numbers of legal documents were preserved in their countries' archives, and many of these dealt with rights to a piece of property or revenue called a **feudum** or fief. This led to the

Map 8–3 The Ninth-Century Invasions The invaders who descended on Europe in the ninth century did not coordinate their attacks and did not have a common objective. Europeans also had no single strategy for opposing them. Rather than the invasions inspiring Europeans to unite to mount a defense, the people of Europe opted to divide their forces.

Question: What challenges did geography pose for the defense of the European continent?

belief that a coherent "feudal system" had structured the lives of medieval people. But over the years, scholars have defined feudalism in so many different ways and found so many exceptions to its supposed "system" that the current trend is to dispense with the term entirely.

Medieval societies did, however, have some distinguishing features, and some generalizations about them can be useful as points of reference and comparison. Students should always keep in mind, however, that generalizations are only approximations of reality. Local and regional studies of medieval peoples will continue to turn up innumerable variations in the ways they arranged their lives, for people are pragmatists when it comes to the struggle for survival. They do what works, not what a theory or the pursuit of rational consistency may dictate.

Political Model   A *feudum* or fief was a resource (often land) given to a vassal to support him while he served his lord. The minting of coins dwindled drastically following the decline of the Roman Empire, and there was little money in circulation. Therefore, rulers in early medieval Europe did not collect most of their taxes in coin and pay their officials' salaries from a public treasury. Most financial transactions involved exchanges of consumable or otherwise desirable items. Because it was too cumbersome to collect all the goods produced on the state's lands for redistribution to the state's servants, governments parceled out the land itself. A lord paid his vassals by giving them the use of fiefs (usually farmland equipped with laborers). They did not own the lands that supported them while they served their lord. They owned only the right to the income from those lands—and that, technically, only so long as they rendered the services that their fiefs were meant to fund.

Once a vassal had a fief in his possession, however, it was hard for his lord to reclaim it. If the vassal had an heir who could perform the tasks for which his fief had been granted, the easiest thing was to pass it to him. But this risked creating precedents that might give the vassal's family a hereditary claim on its fief. To remind an heir of who owned the fief, when he received his inheritance the heir was required to pay his lord "relief" (*relever*, "to pick up again"), a fine that might amount to the first year's income from the fief. If there was no competent mature male heir, a compromise between the rights of the lord and the family had to be worked out. The fief's purpose was to support a soldier. If the heir was a minor, the lord obtained his soldier by making the boy the ward of a man who could provide knight service for him. If the heir was a female (either a daughter or widow), the lord could require her to marry a man of his choice. If the family died out, the fief returned to the lord who originally granted it.

Because a vassal enjoyed all the income from his fief, it made sense that he (not his lord) bore the costs of providing government services for the people who lived on it. As the individual on the scene, he was also much better situated to do this than a distant lord. Land ownership, therefore, came to entail "jurisdiction" (the right to enforce justice and to rule) over those who lived on one's land. There were, however, some restraints on the authority of a fief's owner. In simple, illiterate societies, custom acquires the force of law, and traditions could be quite explicit about the rights and duties of all members of society.

Medieval political and social arrangements had deep roots in the Roman and German pasts. Both the Roman patron-client system and the German warrior band, the **comitatus,** had used oaths of allegiance to structure society, and personal arrangements of this kind were fundamental to the organization of early medieval society. Citizenship had no meaning once the Roman Empire ceased to provide protection for legal rights. Without a state to rely on, individuals had to make private arrangements to ensure their survival. This usually involved commending oneself to the service of a protector. To commend oneself was to surrender some autonomy in exchange for help. Commendation applied to every rank on the social scale from lord and vassal down to the level of serf (a peasant farmer bound to the land). These categories of people had different functions in society, but their legal status was the same. None was free, for freedom was not a desirable condition in a chaotic world where power was more important than right. Free persons had failed to find a niche in society. They had no claim on a protector.

Reliance on oaths was a way of organizing society by means of contracts. Contracts were promises of mutually beneficial exchanges—for example, land for military service. The preservation and enforcement of these promises required special arrangements in what was in the early Middle Ages a largely illiterate world. Most of the contracts that military men and the lords entered into were probably oral agreements that existed only in the memories of witnesses. It was important, therefore, that witnesses understood the precise meaning of the events they were called on to witness. This led to development of rituals and symbolic actions that were widely understood to have specific meanings. Texts describing these ceremonies have survived. They often involved a lord enclosing within his hands the hands of a man doing homage to him. That man would swear an oath of fealty (fidelity) and then be given a clod of earth or some object to "invest" him with his fief.

In the early medieval world as in the modern one, birth often determined a person's options. Children of vassals had the chance to become vassals and those of serfs usually remained serfs. Individuals did, however, personally have to take the oaths their roles required, and there was some social mobility. Noble families could lose their wealth and standing, and talented people of humble origins might rise to great heights, particularly if they pursued careers in the church. Not every man born to a knightly family and trained for military service received a fief. The number of fiefs was limited, and if a fief was divided among all a vassal's sons, the portions soon became too small to support a knight, which defeated the purpose of the fief. This encouraged inheritance rules that passed the fief intact to one son, usually the eldest. His brothers had to find heiresses to marry or employment as mercenaries. There was a large number of career military men who survived by finding employment with a lord rich enough to maintain them as part of his household. They helped to man the private armies that proliferated as royal government declined. These armies provided protection, but they were also often disruptive elements in medieval society.

Militarized local governments took control throughout Europe as Carolinigian rule weakened, but they did not assume the same form everywhere. What worked in the rich grain-growing districts of northern France may not have made as much sense in the different cultural and economic environments of southern France, Germany, or central Europe. In unique regions, such as Switzerland, the terrain may have provided enough protection to minimize the need for much political and military organization at all.

Many places, however, witnessed the rise of a professional military class that enjoyed significant political authority. This class owed its origin to the increasing importance of a new kind of warrior, a heavily armed cavalryman called a knight (*cniht,* "boy" or "servant"). He was the product of medieval inventions that exploited the military potential of the horse in new and highly effective ways. Scholars debate when these inventions took hold in Europe and when the fully developed knight appeared. At the start of the Middle Ages, Frankish soldiers appear to have used horses for transportation to the field of battle, but then to have dismounted for combat. Saddles were in use in the West prior to the first century, but they had no stirrups. This made it hard for a rider to thrust a spear or swing a sword without lofting himself off his horse. The Koreans had stirrups by the fifth century, and the Byzantines were using them by the sixth century. They had certainly reached Francia by the eighth century, but it took time for their potential to be recognized—and other things were needed before that potential could be realized. Larger, stronger horses that could withstand the rigors of battle had to be bred. These animals needed the protection provided by horseshoes, which may not have appeared until the late ninth century. New weapons and armor had to be designed, and men had to devise and master new methods of combat. The fully equipped medieval knight may, therefore, not have charged onto the battlefield much before the late ninth century.

A lance driven by the combined weight and momentum of a charging horse and rider delivered a lethal blow, and a knight could slice through a company of foot soldiers like a tank. The knight marked an advance in military technology that every lord who wanted to remain competitive had to match. The process of making the transition to the new technology was, however, not easy, for knights were extraordinarily expensive. One knight might represent an investment equivalent to the cost of about 20 plow teams. As early as the generation of Charlemagne's grandfather, Charles Martel, Frankish leaders had begun to mobilize the resources of their society for the support of their expensive armies. The church, as well as holders of secular property, was compelled to provide lands for the maintenance of soldiers, and the use of land for this purpose created an association in some places of landownership with military service. It also signaled a change in the status of the ordinary man. The peasant foot soldier ceased to be of much importance as cavalry came to dominate infantry in medieval warfare. Hordes of men on foot might still be marshaled to attend the knights, but fighting—the politically empowering function of providing protection—was increasingly a job for professionals.

Economic Model   Given the economic burden that the new military technology imposed on medieval society, transition to the new kind of warfare would not have been possible if advances in agriculture had not been made to support it.

The methods used to work the thin, dry soils of the Middle East and the Mediterranean's shores did not translate well to northern Europe. Farmers in Francia, Britain, and Germany had to contend with heavy, wet soil and short growing seasons. A simple "scratch plow" (a pointed stick) worked well in southern regions where the ground was easy to break up, and farmers wanted to conserve the moisture it contained by disturbing the land as little as possible. A much heavier, animal-drawn wheeled plow was needed to cultivate northern Europe's fields, and plowshares had to be invented that did not merely break the soil but turned it over to promote drainage. It may have been the sixth century before such farming equipment was widely available.

Draft animals and metal plowshares were expensive. In regions where they were use-ful, farmers banded together to afford them. They established what have been called **manors** (*manere*, "to dwell"), medieval agricultural cooperatives. Manors differed from most modern communes in that they combined private ownership of land with common ownership of the tools that worked the land. Each serf (*servus*, "servant") who was com-mended to a manor held title to certain fields on the manor. He did not receive a percent-age of the total production of the manor, but was entitled only to the crops that grew on the fields designated for his maintenance. Furthermore, his holdings were not concen-trated in one part of the manor, but divided up into strips that were scattered throughout its arable land. This "open-field" system helped spread the risk involved in farming with communal equipment. It prevented fights over who got to use the plow first and ensured that everyone had a bit of land in whatever part of the manor plowing began and ended. This was important, for growing seasons were short in northern Europe. Serfs who had to sow their crops late ran a greater risk of starvation than those who could plant early.

Medieval farmers developed new methods as well as new tools to enhance their pro-ductivity. They understood the use of fertilizers (chiefly, lime and animal manure), but these were in short supply. The common method for maintaining the fertility of fields was fallow farming—plowing, but not planting, land, so that it "rested" for a season. An-cient farmers and medieval farmers in the Mediterranean regions employed a two-field system. That is, they plowed all their land, but planted only half of it—alternating halves annually. The kind of land worked by many of medieval Europe's farmers could support more intensive cultivation by a three-field system that combined fallow farming with crop rotation. They divided their land into thirds and planted one-third in the fall with a grain crop, another in the spring with beans and peas (that restored nitrogen to the soil), and left the third fallow. This reduced the amount of nonproductive plowing, provided some protection in case one of the crops failed, and increased harvests. Farmers made no major improvements on these early medieval techniques until the eighteenth century.

Serfs were not free people. In 332 an edict of Emperor Constantine, which was de-signed to counter the shrinking of the empire's workforce, had required agricultural la-borers to stay on the lands they worked. But the ancient Roman *coloni* and the medieval serfs were not slaves. They had rights. They could not be separated from the land and sold like chattel. They were better off than many free people, for they were at least guaranteed a chance to earn a living. They also had a good deal of autonomy in the conduct of their affairs, for a vassal to whom a manor was given as a fief did not supervise his serfs' work. He was a soldier, not a farmer. His serfs managed their own affairs (guided by the cus-toms of their manors). The vassal was supported in the same way as his serfs. He received whatever grew on his **demesne** (domain), the fields assigned to him. The serfs' chief ob-ligation was to work those fields for him. His serfs might also have to pay for the use of a mill and oven he provided, and he profited from fines levied by his manorial court. Serfs were sometimes assessed a head tax as a sign of their inferior status. Payments from their estates were due to their lords when they died, and they were taxed for the support of the church. In some regions they may have had to forfeit half their annual income.

It is important to remember that not all medieval peasant farmers lived on manors and that many owned property outright. In some regions, the land was best worked by scattered, individual farmsteads, and many of Europe's peasants may have continued the ancient custom of working fields until their fertility declined and then moving to new locations. It might not have been until the eleventh century that the ruling classes began to force them into more stable, permanent village communities.

The Culture of Europe's Dark Age

Some people mistakenly assume that the whole medieval era was a dark age—and many Hollywood movies have depicted the Middle Ages as literally dark and dismal. A dark age, however, is so-called because it is dark to historians, not to those who lived it. It is a period that left few, if any, written records to inform later generations about its history. By this standard Europe's early medieval period might best be described as shady rather than dark. Literacy declined in what had been the western Roman Empire, but it did not disappear. Scholarly work continued in scattered places, and there were even flashes of creative genius.

Scholarship in a Period of Transition
The fifth century produced a trio of great Latin intellectuals who laid the foundation for medieval Europe's Christian culture. Augustine (d. 430), bishop of the North African city of Hippo, remains one of the West's most important theologian-philosophers, a figure who is studied today not just for his historical significance but for the continuing relevance of his ideas. Bishop Ambrose of Milan (c. 340–397), who converted Augustine, shaped the preaching and liturgical practices of the Latin church. Jerome (c. 340–419), an ascetic scholar, produced the Vulgate, the Latin translation of the Bible that was used throughout the Middle Ages.

During the years immediately following the deaths of these men, the confusion created by the migrations of the Germans into the western empire peaked, and intellectual activity in the Latin world declined. Whenever German kings restored a bit of stability, however, scholarly work resumed. The 30 years of order that Theodoric the Ostrogoth (r. 489–526) maintained in Italy gave Boethius (480–524) and Cassiodorus (490–580) the opportunity to create translations and textbooks that influenced education in Europe for centuries (see Chapter 7). Benedict of Nursia (c. 480–543), their contemporary, was no scholar, but he was largely responsible for the survival of schools and libraries in Europe. The rule that Benedict wrote for the monastery he founded in southern Italy at Monte Cassino spread throughout Europe and was ultimately mandated by the Carolingian monarchs for all the monasteries in their empire. The rule owed its success to the skillful balance it struck between the radical asceticism of the eastern hermits and monks and the more pragmatic values of western Europeans. Benedict's monks did not just strive for individual, personal salvation. Their vocation, they believed, was to pray and intercede with God for the sinful world while caring for its poor and needy. Benedict believed that monks should support themselves, so he divided their day into periods for work as well as worship, recreation, and rest. Although Benedictine monks, in the early years, did manual labor, many of their working hours were eventually devoted to the study and production of books.

Turmoil returned to Italy following Theodoric's death in 526, but by then his contemporary, Clovis (c. 466–511), had founded Francia's Merovingian dynasty. Over the

---

Cultural Leaders of the Early Middle Ages

TRANSMITTERS OF CLASSICAL CULTURE

Ambrose of Milan (c. 340–397)
Jerome (c. 340–419)
Augustine of Hippo (354–430)
Patrick (c. 380–c. 461)
Benedict of Nursia (c. 480–c. 550)
Boethius (c. 480–524)

MEROVINGIAN ERA

Columba (521–597)
Fortunatus (c. 535–605)
Gregory of Tours (c. 538–594)
Gregory the Great (c. 590–604)
Bede (c. 672–735)
Isidore of Seville (c. 570–636)
Augustine of Canterbury (d. 604)
Cassiodorus (c. 490–c. 580)

CAROLINGIAN RENAISSANCE

Alcuin (c. 735–804)
Paul the Deacon (c. 720–c. 800)
Peter of Pisa (744–799)
Theodulf of Orleans (c. 750–821)
Einhard (c. 770–840)

---

years, several scholars surfaced at, or corresponded with, the Merovingian courts. The elegant Latin poetry of Fortunatus (535–605), an Italian who was supported by Merovingian patrons, proves that excellent literary educations could still be obtained in Europe. Fortunatus's Frankish contemporary, Bishop Gregory of Tours (c. 538–594), complained, however, that standards of literacy had declined dramatically in his part of the world. The Latin of his *History of the Franks* supports this, but scholars debate whether the obscurity that plagues the text is the fault of its author or of the copyists who transmitted it to us. Despite its literary weaknesses, Gregory's book is a major achievement. In his day, the writing of history was a nearly forgotten art. Had he not revived it, we would know very little about the Merovingians.

Gregory of Tours had a contemporary, also named Gregory, who was one of Rome's most important popes. Gregory I, the Great (r. 590–604), defended Rome from the Lombards, laid a foundation for the Papal States, and still found time for literary work that earned him the title "Europe's schoolmaster." Gregory became pope at a time when the church in the Latin world was in near total disarray. His correspondence with bishops throughout Europe during an era of great confusion helped sustain them and retain a semblance of Christian unity. In addition to his many letters and sermons, he wrote several influential books. *Dialogues,* the most popular of his works, is a collection of stories about saints and miracles that had a tremendous impact on medieval preaching and spirituality. Gregory struggled to raise the standards of the church and further the spread of Christianity. He tried to interest the Merovingian queen Brunhild in church reform, and in 597 he sent missionaries to England to convert the pagan Anglo-Saxons. Augustine (d. 604), the Benedictine monk who led the mission, set up headquarters in Canterbury, the capital of the Anglo-Saxon kingdom of Kent. The archbishops who head England's church today still have their cathedral there.

By the time the pope's emissaries arrived in England, Irish missionaries were already at work. About 565, a monk named Columba (521–597) had established a monastery on the island of Iona, off the coast of Scotland, and launched a mission that spread into northern England. The schools that the Irish and Roman missions established in England produced some of the era's greatest scholars. The most notable of these was a remarkably original thinker named Bede (672–735). His interests ranged from natural science to theology and history. His major contribution to history, *The Ecclesiastical History of the English People*, is noteworthy for research methods that were far ahead of its time. Bede searched out evidence to document historical events and carefully critiqued his sources. He also helped establish the custom of dating historical events from the birth of Christ.

Visigothic Spain produced a notable scholar in this period, Isidore of Seville (c. 570–636), a contemporary of Pope Gregory. Isidore's major work, *Etymologiae* (or *Origines*), was a cross between an encyclopedia and a dictionary. It drew material from many ancient sources to suggest explanations for the meanings of words, and it provided medieval readers with an immense amount of useful information and dubious speculation. Typical was Isidore's claim that the word *medicine* derived from "moderation" because excess causes disease.

Spain's intellectual life received a great boost about 75 years after Isidore's death. The Muslim conquest of the Iberian Peninsula exposed Spaniards to influences from the Islamic world, the seat of the most dynamic of the early medieval civilizations. Muslims, Christians, and Jews rubbed shoulders in Spain. They learned each other's languages, traded literatures, and engaged in learned conversations. The vibrant intellectual life that evolved in Spain eventually drew students from northern Europe and stimulated Europe's recovery from the cultural slump into which it fell at the end of the Roman era.

The Carolingian Renaissance

About the time that Bede died (735) another scholarly Englishman was born. His name was Alcuin, and the excellent training he received at the cathedral of York from a student of one of Bede's students prepared him to become

Bust of Charlemagne No contemporary portraits of Charlemagne survive—if indeed, any were ever made. But in the medieval literary tradition he was honored as a model king, and artists imagined him as the embodiment of majesty.

Europe's most prominent educator. Charlemagne persuaded him to move to Francia and undertake the leadership of a project that historians call the Carolingian Renaissance.

Charlemagne knew that the level of civilization in Europe had declined dramatically since the days of the Roman Empire. The church was in a particularly lamentable condition, for many clergy were illiterate. Village priests, who were often peasants without formal educations, could not chant the mass accurately. Even some bishops could not read and found preaching a challenge. Charlemagne hoped to correct this by ordering monasteries and cathedrals to establish schools. To provide these institutions with teaching materials, curricula, and a model, he asked Alcuin to set up a school at court, and he combed Europe for scholars to staff its faculty. Italy yielded a historian, Paul the Deacon, and a Latin grammarian, Peter of Pisa. Spain sent Theodulf, a poet. A couple of Irish scholars were in residence, and the most prominent Frank was Charlemagne's biographer, architect, and master of the palace works, Einhard (who was quoted at the beginning of this chapter).

The Carolingian Renaissance did not aspire to much original work. Its objective was to rescue literacy so that Europeans could access the intellectual legacy of the ancient world. Given the situation Charlemagne's scholars faced, their achievement was considerable. Following the example set by Roman textbooks, they designed an educational curriculum divided into seven liberal arts, the areas of knowledge needed by a *liber* ("freeborn man"). A liberal arts education emphasized literary skills. It began with the study of the **trivium** (grammar, dialectic, rhetoric), instruction in reading and writing Latin. The **quadrivium** (arithmetic, geometry, astronomy, and music), which followed, taught clergy what they needed to know to manage estates, calculate dates for church feasts, and sing liturgies.

Alcuin and his colleagues wrote textbooks for their schools. They sought out manuscripts of neglected works to build library collections, and they published improved editions of ancient texts. They even reformed the mechanics of writing. So many different scripts had evolved in so many places in Europe that it was difficult for scholars from one region to read what those in another had written. Charlemagne's schools standardized shapes for the letters of the alphabet and taught students to leave spaces between words to make reading easier and more efficient. Our system of writing is based on this Carolingian "minuscule."

The Carolingian Renaissance had some notable successes. It reformed the liturgy of the church by building on Roman customs that it believed went back to the generation of Pope Gregory the Great. The tradition of Gregorian chant, which the renaissance promoted, thrived for centuries and produced music that still moves worshipers. Charlemagne's scholars also halted the loss of books and rescued what was left in Europe of the literary legacy of the ancient world. Few major works exist today in copies older than those made by Carolingian scribes. Primarily, the renaissance's claim to be a decisive moment in European intellectual history rests on the fact that it halted the cultural decline that began with the passing of the Roman Empire and put western Europe back on the road to recovery. The political confusion that broke out after Charlemagne's death was a setback, but things were never again to be as bad as they had been before Charlemagne.

Charlemagne may have hoped for more than he got from his investment in Europe's re-education. The schools that he ordered monks and bishops to establish were not always able to fulfill their missions. His nobles ignored his call to educate themselves, and he may secretly have empathized with them. Einhard says that Charlemagne learned to read but that he started too late in life to master the motor skills that writing requires. He did not give up trying, however. He kept a slate under his pillow and practiced the alphabet before falling asleep.

KEY QUESTION | Revisited

Despite a healthy dose of barbarian ancestry, the inhabitants of early medieval Europe believed that they were legitimate heirs to the civilization of the ancient Mediterranean world, and they were determined to assert their claim to their legacy. They revered Rome's memory, the shreds of classical literature that had survived in their shrunken libraries, and the Christian religion. But they struggled with harsher and more primitive conditions than had faced most of the subjects of Rome's Mediterranean empire. They survived by innovating new technologies. They integrated information from their tribal oral traditions with classicism's literary legacy and their understanding of the Christian faith. They adapted to a challenging physical environment, to an economy that offered little more than basic sustenance, and to a society that had nearly lost all order and structure. Their unique needs and resources shaped what they did with their inheritance from the past. For a long time, the culture they were pioneering remained inferior to the civilizations of Islam and Byzantium, but they were slowly feeling their way toward a great future.

Review Questions

1. When did the northwestern provinces of the Roman Empire cease to be Roman and become European? What changes mark the transition between the two eras?
2. How did the problems that brought down the Merovingian dynasty differ from the problems that caused the fall of Rome's dynasties?
3. How did Charlemagne's empire differ from the realm of the Roman emperors whose title he claimed?
4. Why were medieval Europeans unable to sustain progress toward a continental empire?
5. How did Europeans adapt politically and economically to the Carolingian empire and its decline?
6. How did the civilization of early medieval Europe differ from the classical civilization of the ancient Greeks and Romans? Was it at all similar?

Please consult the Suggested Readings at the back of the book to continue your study of the material covered in this chapter. For a list of documents on the Primary Source DVD-ROM that relate to topics in this chapter, please refer to the back of the book.

9 Europe Turns Outward

You Franks, the beloved of God whom He has chosen (as your many victories prove) and set apart from other peoples by the location of your country, your Catholic faith, and your respect for the church—on you we call! There is grievous news from Jerusalem and Constantinople. A race from Persia—an accursed people who are totally opposed to God—has stormed Christian lands and depopulated them by looting and burning. . . . On whom does the task of avenging these crimes fall . . . if not on you, you on whom God has conferred—more than on any other nation—outstanding military valor, great courage, vigor, and strength with which to overwhelm all who oppose you?

—Pope Urban II

KEY | Question

Was conflict among the medieval civilizations inevitable?

On November 27, 1095, Pope Urban II (r. 1088–1099) allegedly addressed the words quoted above to a crowd of knights assembled on a field at Clermont in central France. The knights who heard him may have been surprised to find themselves exhorted to fight, for they had come to Clermont to pledge themselves to the Truce of God. The Truce of God and an earlier movement called the Peace of God were efforts by the church to persuade feudal warriors to exercise self-restraint. The Peace, which originated in 989 at a council at Charroux in Aquitaine, decreed that knights should do no harm to noncombatants (clergy, women, and peasants). The Truce further curtailed bloodshed by declaring that no fighting should take place on sacred days: Sundays, religious festivals, and during the penitential seasons of Advent and Lent. Urban's call for a holy war was not, however, inconsistent with the objectives of the Peace and Truce. One way to pacify the home front was to divert Europe's military resources to foreign campaigns.

Cathedral of Cordoba This interior view of the cathedral of the Spanish city of Cordoba testifies to the cultural complexity of the medieval world. Now a Christian church, it was at one time the world's second largest mosque.

Urban's war is now known as the First Crusade, but the word **crusade** ("war of the cross") did not exist in his day. In fact, it was not coined until the thirteenth century. Urban called his holy warriors pilgrims. Pilgrims were not supposed to bear arms, and the church had always said that it was a sin to shed blood, but Urban assured the knights who responded to his call that his was a new kind of war that merited new rules. The enemy Christians faced was so heinous—and such an anathema to God and civilization—that killing him was an act of self-sanctification. The crusader's sword purified a warrior's soul, for by wielding it against the enemies of the faith, he fulfilled the mission for which God had created him.

Urban believed—correctly, as it turned out—that Europe had reached a turning point in its history. God, he claimed, had kept the Franks in reserve, tucked away from other peoples on the edge of the world. He had given them the true faith and the superior military virtues needed to defend that faith. The time had come, the pope said, for Europe's soldiers to be loosed on the enemies of God. For centuries Europeans had been in retreat and on the defensive. They had lost territory and suffered humiliating raids and invasions. Finally, however, they were ready to realize their destiny—to take the offensive and destroy all that they regarded as alien.

Urban's crusade was an early manifestation of the European impulse to thrust outward, both territorially and culturally. The descendants of his pilgrim-soldiers would one day build globe-spanning colonial empires and attempt to make their civilization universal. In the process, they divided the world between "the West" and "the Other" and spawned resentments and misunderstandings with which modern nations still struggle. Viewing events simplistically as a battle between the virtuous and the vicious seldom produces an adequate picture of reality. In the case of warring cultures, it absolutizes their differences and makes it difficult to build on whatever common ground they might share.

Islam's Crest and Byzantium's Resurgence

The pan-European empire that Charlemagne hoped to build did not materialize. Europe lacked the infrastructure and cultural ties needed to support political unification, and the invasions of the Vikings, Magyars, and Muslims forced it to decentralize its governments and defenses. The tendency toward political fragmentation was, however, not confined to Europe. The momentum of conquest preserved the Muslim empire until the mid-eighth century, but once expansion ceased, the Muslim world, like Christian Europe, came apart.

Caliphs and Sultans   The Muslim empire was torn by ethnic tensions, new and old. The Umayyad caliphs did not impose Islam on all their subjects or even encourage them to come together to form a single people. They viewed Islam as a gift God intended primarily for Arabs, and they wanted Arabs to remain aloof from the natives of the lands they conquered. Umayyad "racism" had fiscal as well as cultural motives. The empire's non-Muslim subjects paid taxes from which Muslims were exempt. Many non-Arabs were, however, sincerely drawn to Islam. Although it was impossible to deny their wish to convert, Arabs often discriminated against them, and this created tensions within the *umma* (the Muslim community).

In 739 fighting erupted between Berber and Arab Muslims in North Africa, and in 750 Persian converts helped the Abbasids overthrow the Umayyad caliphate. In 756 Abd al-Rahman (731–788), an Umayyad prince who had survived the coup, wrested control of the Iberian Peninsula from the Abbasid caliphs and declared Spain an independent emirate. In 788 a Shi'ite leader won over the Berber Muslims and founded the Aghlabid dynasty in North Africa. In 800 the Abbasids acknowledged its virtual autonomy. The Aghlabids clashed with Spain's Umayyad emir, and they kept their Arab and Berber followers from feuding among themselves by sending them to raid southern Europe. In 902 they drove the Byzantines from Sicily and brought Islam to the island. Sicily, like Spain, developed a thriving Muslim society that eventually helped to stimulate a revival of intellectual life in Europe by acquainting Europeans with the fruits of Muslim scholarship.

In 909 the Aghlabids were overthrown by a Berber faction that supported a Shi'ite who claimed to be a descendant of Muhammad's daughter, Fatima. The Fatimid dynasty that he founded established a Shi'ite caliphate in opposition to the Sunni Abbasids. In 929 Spain's Umayyad emir rallied the Sunni Muslims in the western Mediterranean to his side by declaring himself their caliph. Baghdad's response was weak, for by then the political authority of the Abbasid caliphs was fading (see Map 9–1).

The Abbasid dynasty had reached its peak during the reign of Charlemagne's contemporary, Harun al-Rashid (r. 786–809). Harun al-Rashid's court in Baghdad was probably the most splendid and sophisticated of its day, but ominous developments shadowed the future of his empire. He had lost Spain to the Umayyads, and in 800 he relinquished North Africa to the Aghlabids. Wars between Harun al-Rashid's sons cost the Abbasid dynasty more territory, and in 820 a Persian prince wrested the eastern province of Khurasan from its control.

In the mid-ninth century, the beleaguered Abbasid caliphs tried to secure their position by creating an army of Turkish slaves. The theory was that foreign slaves, who had no powerful families or local allies to support them, would be totally dependent on, and loyal to, the caliph. The Turks, however, rallied behind leaders of their own and wrested territory in Persia, Syria, and Egypt away from their caliph. Some Abbasids put up a good fight, but in 945 Baghdad's caliph submitted to the Persian Buyids. While the Buyids brought Persia and Iraq under control, the Fatimids moved across North Africa to Egypt. In 969 they evicted a Turkish ruler from Egypt and relocated the seat of their caliphate to a new city, which they named Cairo (al-Kahira, "Victorious"). Sporadic warfare raged inconclusively between the Buyids and Fatimids for about a century, and in the end, both succumbed to a third Muslim power, the Seljuk Turks.

The Turks, like the early Germans, were an assortment of nomadic tribes that spoke related languages. They first made contact with Islam about 653, when the Arab armies that were sweeping across the Persian Empire reached the Oxus River. The Turks' relationship with Islam's new empire resembled the one the Germans had with Rome's old empire. They absorbed its religion and were attracted by its wealth, power, and culture. Some immigrated and integrated peacefully. Some were enslaved, and some set up their own states on its territory. During the tenth century, Islam's eastern lands were overrun by Turks. Some of these planted Islam in northern and central India, and others, the Seljuks, took over Persia.

The Seljuks came from the region of the Jaxartes River and converted to Islam in the second half of the tenth century. After occupying Khurasan, they set their sights on the Buyids, and in 1060 they took Baghdad. The Seljuks allowed the Abbasid caliph to serve as a religious figurehead, but their **sultan** (*shultana*, "governor") assumed responsibility for running Baghdad's empire and defending Sunni Islam against its primary enemies, the Shi'ite Fatimids and the Christian Byzantines.

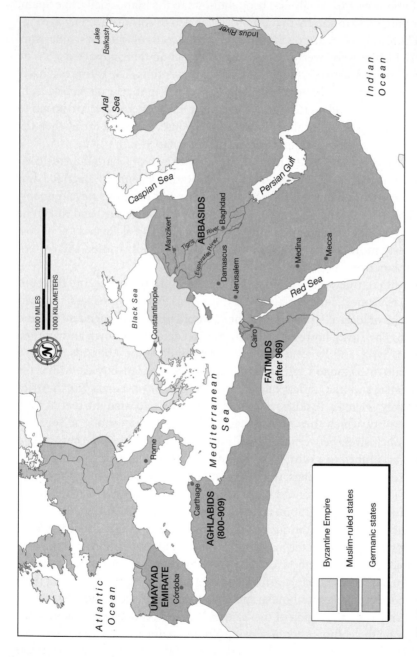

Map 9–1 The Medieval Muslim World The Muslim Empire grew so quickly that it had little opportunity to consolidate before it began to break up into a variety of states with different religious, ethnic, and political identities. The three caliphates that emerged (Umayyad Spain, Fatimid Egypt, and Abbasid Baghdad) created tensions within the Muslim world similar to those that divided the Christian region between the Orthodox and Catholic traditions.

Question: Today the "Muslim world" is sometimes contrasted with "the West." Does that description make historical or geographical sense?

Harun al-Rashid's Court   The magnificence of Harun al-Rashid's Baghdad is hinted at by this gift of an ewer that the caliph sent to Charlemagne. Its lavishly embossed gold surface is studded with jewels and decorated with vividly colored enamels in a technique called cloisonne.

The Fatimid dynasty was the lesser threat. Although Fatimid Egypt had been a strong state with a powerful navy, it had failed to make much progress against the Buyids, the Byzantines, or even rival Shi'ite groups. The Fatimids' early victories had raised unrealistic expectations among their Shi'ite followers. The Shi'ite faith was apocalyptic. It awaited a messiah—the revelation of a secret descendant of the Prophet who would miraculously reunite the *umma* and complete Islam's triumph. As the tenth century dragged on, hope diminished that the Fatimid caliphate would produce such a savior. Wealth and privilege gradually had a corrupting effect on Fatimid rulers, and by the eleventh century, internal power struggles and inept caliphs were costing the Fatimids both followers and territory. The dynasty survived until an unexpected event altered political arrangements throughout the Muslim world. Constantinople triggered an invasion of the Middle East by western Europeans.

Constantinople   When the Arab armies first erupted from their homeland, they descended on a Byzantine Empire that had been weakened by a long war with Persia. In 636 the Byzantine emperor Heraclius (r. 610–641) lost a major battle to the Muslims, and by the time of his death, his empire had been reduced to Asia Minor, parts of Greece and the Balkans, and nominal authority over Sicily, North Africa, and a few outposts in Italy. Then things got worse. Arabs annually raided throughout Asia Minor—sometimes threatening Constantinople itself. They challenged the Byzantine navy's power at sea, and in 670 they began a triumphal march through the Byzantine province of North Africa. Then things got much worse. In 679 the Slavs, who had long posed a threat to Constantinople's possessions in the Balkans, were joined by the Bulgars, a people similar to the Huns. Byzantium's efforts to deal with all these external threats were complicated by internal fights over its throne.

In 717 (just as Charles Martel was laying the foundations for Europe's Carolingian Empire) a great general, Leo III (r. 717–740), seized power in Constantinople and drove the Muslims back from the city. Leo and his heirs, the Isaurian dynasty, restructured Byzantine government and society to mobilize support for a stronger military. They divided the empire into regions called **themes.** A regiment of soldiers was assigned to each, and each was governed by the commander of its regiment. Some soldiers were salaried; however, many were supported, like Europe's vassals, by grants of land. Repeated Muslim raids had broken up many of the great estates and undercut the institution of serfdom. By redistributing lands among free peasants, the Isaurian dynasty created a class of independent farmers from which to recruit stalwart defenders for its empire.

Leo issued a new code of civil law—in Greek instead of Latin, the official language that had been used since Constantinople's origin as the capital of the Roman Empire. He also forced through a controversial religious reform that marked another break with tradition. In 726 he promulgated the first in a series of edicts that forbade the use of icons in worship. Repugnance for religious art was widespread in the Middle East, for both Muslims and Jews regarded it as a temptation to idolatry. Leo apparently believed that veneration of icons was indistinguishable from blasphemous worship of icons, but he also had political motives for ordering their destruction. He wanted to diminish the influence of overly powerful monasteries whose sacred images attracted devotion and support from the masses. Leo's iconoclasm ("destruction of sacred images") sparked revolts among his subjects and was roundly denounced by theologians who believed that a ban on religious images was tantamount to the denial of Christ's humanity. If, as the iconoclasts claimed, material images could not mediate spiritual realities, then Christ could not have been truly incarnated as a human being. Church councils in western Europe also objected to Leo's policy, and opposition to iconoclasm was probably a factor in the papacy's decision to distance itself from the Byzantines and strengthen its ties with the Frankish kings. The issue continued to make trouble for Constantinople until its rulers gave in and repudiated iconoclasm in 843.

In 867 Basil I (r. 867–886), who had risen from slavery to become an imperial advisor, assassinated his emperor and seized the Byzantine throne. The Macedonian dynasty he founded restored the glory of Constantinople and reclaimed territory the Byzantines had lost to the Muslims and Bulgars. The ruthless Basil II (r. 963–1025), "the Bulgar-slayer," brought Russia within the orbit of Constantinople and Christianity. Vikings who worked the river systems that linked the Baltic Sea with the Black Sea joined the Slavs of central Europe to form a people called the Rus ("Russians"), after Ruric, a Viking who ruled Novgorod about 862. Dominance of the region passed to the city of Kiev, whose ruler, Vladimir I (r. 980–1015), accepted baptism in exchange for the hand of Basil's sister. The marriage forged strong commercial and cultural ties between Constantinople and Russia and began the spread of Orthodox Christianity and Byzantine civilization to Russia.

In 1057 a coalition of Byzantine aristocrats and clergy overthrew the last of the Macedonian emperors. Their coup was ill-timed, for it weakened Constantinople's defenses just as the Seljuk Turks were beginning to revive Islam's martial spirit. In 1071 the Byzantine emperor Romanus IV Diogenes (r. 1068–1071) lost a decisive battle with the Seljuks near an Armenian fortress called Manzikert, and the victorious Seljuks seized most of Asia Minor—the region from which Constantinople recruited its armies. The city survived, for it had strong fortifications and continued to prosper as a depot for international trade. The Seljuk threat also quickly receded, for the Turks began to fight among themselves for shares of the lands they had conquered.

The Reorganization of Europe

Europe, which had borne the brunt of the devastation caused by the German invasions that brought down the Roman Empire, lagged behind the Byzantine and Muslim worlds for centuries. Charlemagne had tried to close the gap, but the invasions of the

Vikings, Magyars, and Muslims in the ninth and tenth centuries set Europe back once again. Charlemagne's successors were weak kings whose effective authority did not extend far beyond their own estates. However, once the invasions ended and things began to settle down, the surviving monarchs began to give some attention to building centralized governments and consolidating the states that were to become the nations of modern Europe. This was a difficult project that did not always meet with success. By the end of the Middle Ages, England and France had emerged as stable, unified countries under different kinds of royal authority, but Germany and Italy remained politically fragmented until late in the nineteenth century.

England and France   England was a small country (only a little larger than the state of New York) situated on an island, but geography was not enough to guarantee its political unification. The Anglo-Saxons, who occupied it in the fifth century, may have divided it among as many as seven kingdoms. The Viking invasions of the eighth and ninth centuries obliterated all but one of these—the kingdom of Wessex, England's southwest corner. A young heir to the throne of Wessex, Alfred the Great (r. 871–899), pushed the Vikings (Danes) back and confined them to the Danelaw (the northeastern half of England). The strong Anglo-Saxon state he founded endured for about a century. Alfred, like Charlemagne, was a patron of scholars and a sponsor of a palace school. He was particularly eager to promote Anglo-Saxon literature, and was better educated than the Frankish emperor. He translated a number of books into Anglo-Saxon, updating some of them with information about his part of the world.

In 954 one of Alfred's successors brought all of England under his control and converted the Vikings who had settled on the island to Christianity. Churches and monasteries were restored, but the opportunity to rebuild and consolidate was brief. At the end of the century King Ethelred the Unready (r. 978–1016) confronted a second wave of Viking invaders. He tried to buy them off with the proceeds of a national tax called the **Danegeld**, but in 1013 a Danish army forced Ethelred to flee England (see Map 9–2).

England then became part of a North Sea empire headed by a king who also ruled Denmark, Norway, and parts of Sweden. The island's new ruler, Cnute (r. 1016–1035), was no unlettered barbarian. He visited Rome to consult with the pope and earned a reputation as an able monarch. Europe's history might have been quite different had his empire survived, but fights among his potential heirs destroyed it. Once England regained its independence, Edward the Confessor (r. 1042–1066), the Anglo-Saxon heir to its throne, returned from exile.

Edward, England's last Anglo-Saxon king, had Viking blood. His mother was the sister of a French duke, who was a descendant of a Viking chief named Rollo. In 911 the French king, Charles the Simple (r. 893–929), had tried to limit his losses to the Vikings by coming to terms with Rollo. Rollo swore an oath of fealty to Charles in exchange for the title of duke and a fief consisting of the lower Seine Valley and much of the French side of the English Channel. The king hoped that Rollo's Vikings, the barons of the newly created duchy of Normandy (from Norsemen or Normans), would prevent other Vikings from raiding farther into French territory. The Normans acculturated quickly—adopting Christianity, the French language, and the heavily armed cavalry fighting techniques that

Map 9–2 England and the Viking Migrations The sea can protect an island country or render it vulnerable to attack depending on the technologies its enemies possess. Invaders with minimal sailing skills could cross the narrow channel between the continent and England, but so long as the island was vulnerable along only parts of its coast it was relatively easy to defend. The Viking migration was, however, much broader in scope and relied on something more closely resembling true marine forces than anything Western Europeans had previously confronted.

Question: Given that the Mediterranean Sea had bound much of the Roman Empire together, could a northern empire have developed around the North Sea?

were evolving on the continent. Normandy produced a remarkable number of famous soldiers and adventurers who spread the duchy's influence from Ireland to the Holy Land.

Edward the Confessor had spent most of his life in Normandy and had no personal power base in England. He wed the daughter of the most influential man in his kingdom, an earl (an English title of nobility) named Godwin, but sired no heir. He achieved little, and his death in 1066 set off a three-way race for England's vacant throne. The native Anglo-Saxon candidate was Edward's brother-in-law, Harold Godwinson. Harold Hardrada, king of Norway (r. 1045–1066), asserted the Viking claim. Edward's distant relative, William, duke of Normandy, also entered the lists. In September 1066 Harold Godwinson defeated Harold Hardrada in northern England. But his involvement there gave William a chance to ferry the Norman army across the English Channel and land unopposed in southern England. Harold Godwinson dashed from one campaign to another, and England's fate was decided by a battle fought near the port of Hastings. Godwinson and most of the Anglo-Saxon leaders were killed, and Duke William became King William I, "the Conqueror" (r. 1066–1087).

William—as a conqueror, not a native king—was not bound by English tradition. He was free to impose any kind of government he wanted on his new subjects. He built on institutions with which he was familiar in Normandy, but he wisely preserved some unique English customs that strengthened the monarchy. Medieval kings not only had to work at keeping the masses in line, but also had a struggle to control the men through whom they governed. The nobles who served in a king's government often preferred him to be weak. The less power he had, the more they could appropriate for themselves. But England's new Norman aristocracy found itself in a different situation. It consisted of a small number of French-speaking foreigners who were unpopular with the masses of their Anglo-Saxon subjects. It needed the support of a powerful monarch. William limited the number of castles his nobles were allowed to build, lest they be used against him. He also preserved the Anglo-Saxon division of his kingdom into shires supervised by non-noble officials called shire-reeves (sheriffs). They were responsible for collecting a national tax (which had begun as the Danegeld ransom) and marshaling a peasant army called the **fyrd**. Unlike continental states, England had continued the German tribal custom of requiring all adult males to bear arms should they be needed to defend their country. Sheriffs and the *fyrd* freed the king from having to rely exclusively on the nobles as agents of his government.

William succeeded in establishing a Norman ruling class in control of England, but his victory led to a struggle between the kings of England and France that dragged on for 400 years. If William's estate had been divided as he ordered, however, the problem might have been avoided. At William's death, the duchy of Normandy passed by right of inheritance to his eldest son, Robert "Curthose." Robert showed little promise as a leader, and this may have entered into William's decision to separate the duchy he had inherited from the kingdom he had won. England needed a strong king, and the best candidate was William's second son, William II, "Rufus" (r. 1087–1100). In 1095 Robert pawned Normandy to his brother to raise the money he needed to join the First Crusade. He survived that adventure, but he lost his duchy and his freedom to William's successor, their younger brother Henry. The duchy's reunification with the English crown might have seemed like good policy at the time, for many Norman lords owned lands on both sides of the English Channel. However, it created a diplomatic situation rife with confusion. Henry, as duke of Normandy, was the vassal of the king of France, but as king of England, he was the French monarch's equal.

William the Conqueror's third son became Henry I (r. 1100–1135), king of England, under suspicious circumstances. His brutal and unpopular brother, William Rufus, died in what was represented as a hunting accident but may well have been an assassination. Few lamented his death, but his demise by no means assured Henry's succession. His surviving older brother Robert had the stronger claim to England's throne. Henry therefore set about courting support. He dismissed William's unpopular officials, and at his coronation he issued a Charter of Liberties in which he pledged not to abuse his power. The proclamation had little effect at the time, but it set an important precedent.

The church maintained that a king's power derived from God, not his subjects, and that subjects therefore had no right to sit in judgment on kings. Henry's pledge, however, implied that a monarch was accountable to his people for how he governed them. A century later the famous Magna Carta reaffirmed this principle. Other events helped to keep it alive, but until the English Parliament was firmly established, there was no way to enforce it. Efforts to limit the power of England's monarchs faded during the reigns of strong kings and revived when weak rulers mismanaged the country. As fate would have it, throughout the medieval period strong kings tended to alternate with weak ones in England—leading ultimately to modern Britain's parliamentary government headed by a powerless royal figurehead.

The power that the Conqueror and his sons, William and Henry, had carefully guarded was nearly lost in a struggle for succession to their throne. The only one of Henry's legitimate children to survive him was a daughter, Matilda (1102–1167). Henry forced his reluctant vassals to promise to accept her as his heir. But the idea of a reigning queen was so unconventional that it was easy to rationalize breaking such a pledge. A medieval king was a warlord, and few people thought that a woman could do his job. Some of England's nobles repudiated Matilda (and her French husband, the count of Anjou) and declared her cousin Stephen the rightful heir to Henry's throne. Matilda had the advantage of descent from the Conqueror through the male line, but she was a woman. Ordinarily, Stephen's claim would have been weak or nonexistent, for his link with the Conqueror was through his mother, William's daughter. However, Stephen was a male, and his supporters argued that this tipped the balance in his favor.

Civil war erupted, and for 20 years the nobles had the advantage of being able to play one royal claimant off against another. Stephen finally offered Matilda a compromise. In exchange for her recognition of his right to live out his life in peace as England's king, he acknowledged her son, Henry, as his heir. Stephen died a year later, and England's battered crown passed to a man who had the skill and resources to refurbish it.

Henry II (r. 1154–1189) was the right man in the right place at the right time—intelligent, well educated, crafty, physically vigorous, and charismatic. His family connections positioned him to make the most of his gifts. His uncle bequeathed him the kingdom of England. His mother and father left him duchies and counties covering much of northern France, and his wife, Eleanor (c. 1122–1204), brought him the duchy of Aquitaine, a large portion of southern France. Henry's sprawling Angevin (from Anjou) Empire made him a more powerful man in France than France's king (see Map 9–3).

The English monarchy began strong and was forced by circumstances to accept limits to its authority. The French monarchy headed in the opposite direction. France's early kings were weak, but by the end of the Middle Ages, they were well on their way to becoming absolute monarchs.

Map 9–3   Medieval France   For much of the Middle Ages, France was less a unified country than a collection of separate entities. Each of its regions had a distinct dialect and culture, and the kinds of nationalistic sentiments that seem natural to modern people had not yet appeared to bind them together.

Question: Did geography make the unification of France easy or difficult?

William, as England's conqueror, had the freedom and power to get his dynasty off to a strong start, but the French monarchy had a very different beginning. The invasions of the ninth and tenth centuries cost its kings considerable power and prestige. Because France was four times the size of England and exposed to attack on multiple fronts, a king could not offer as much protection as a strong local lord, and the competition France's kings faced from powerful landed nobles rendered them extremely weak.

In 987 the French nobles switched their allegiance from Charlemagne's ineffectual descendants to Hugh Capet (r. 987–996), count of Paris. Hugh's county was the front line in the war with the Viking invaders, and it was in the self-interest of his fellow nobles to help him defend his small estate. The early kings of the Capetian dynasty, which Hugh founded, had no power to compel obedience from France's nobles, many of whom controlled much more territory than their monarch. The Capetians also had to be careful not to offend their vassals by trying to assert their rights as kings. They were not born kings with a hereditary claim to the crown. They were elected kings by men who could, whenever they wanted, shift their allegiance to someone else. Little could be done to strengthen the monarchy in France until the Capetians established an unchallengeable right to the throne. To do this, they simply had to prolong their possession of the prize. For generations, they threatened no one and always had a viable candidate (an adult son) ready for election before his father's death. Because the Capetians seemed a safe choice and none of the powerful lords wanted a competitor to have the royal title, the Capetians were repeatedly elected kings. Eventually, the succession of a Capetian became a foregone conclusion, and the nobles dispensed with pointless elections. Vassals, who based title to their fiefs on generations of family occupancy, could hardly challenge the Capetians' right to lay claim to the crown on the same grounds.

The first member of the Capetian dynasty who was secure enough to assert his authority was Louis VI, "the Fat" (r. 1108–1137), a contemporary of England's powerful Henry I. Louis did little more than exercise the rights that all lords were traditionally understood to have over their vassals, but he also cultivated allies who wanted a stronger monarchy. France's nobles preferred a weak king who could not threaten their autonomy, but its clergy and many of its ordinary people wanted a king who could restrain its marauding lords and their private armies of knights. The residents of the new towns that sprang up in France in the eleventh and twelfth centuries were particularly eager to promote the development of centralized government. Townspeople depended on trade, and they wanted a king who could make the countryside safe for travelers and limit the tolls local lords imposed on merchants.

A medieval monarchy was inherently weak because it ruled through subordinates whose self-interest was to make it weak. If a king hoped to increase his effectiveness, he had to find an alternative to working through the landed nobility. Townspeople and clergy could help him by giving him money with which to hire salaried officials. It was hard to evict a vassal from his manors, but it was easy to cut off a salary. Salaried officials therefore tended to be more loyal than vassals, and they wanted a strong employer. The stronger the king, the more secure their wages.

Louis VI used the customary privileges of an overlord to tip the balance of power in France decidedly in his dynasty's favor. When the huge duchy of Aquitaine passed to an heiress, Eleanor of Aquitaine, Louis exercised his prerogative to choose her husband.

He wed her to his son and heir Louis VII (r. 1137–1180). The young king was, however, never able to compel his bride or her duchy to submit to his authority. In 1152 the flagrantly incompatible couple persuaded the pope to annul their union, and Eleanor immediately chose as her second husband the man who posed the greatest threat to her first. She wed Henry of Anjou who, in 1154, became King Henry II of England, the architect of the Angevin Empire. Louis spent the rest of his life in an unequal struggle with Henry, but in the next generation the tide turned in the Capetians' favor. Henry's sons, Richard I, "the Lionhearted" (r. 1189–1199), and John (r. 1199–1216), were no match for Louis's heir, Philip II, "Augustus" (r. 1180–1223). Philip recovered many French fiefs from the English kings and kept much of what he won for the royal domain. He bequeathed his heirs a much stronger throne than the one he had inherited, but he did not resolve France's problems with England.

Germany, Italy, and the Papacy

The medieval monarchy that made the most promising start (and the most dismal finish) was Germany's. In 911 the last of Germany's Carolingian rulers died, and the German dukes chose Conrad, duke of Franconia (r. 911–918), to be their king. His primary achievement was to pass the crown to a more viable candidate, Henry I, "the Fowler" (r. 919–936), duke of Saxony. Saxony was a much larger and more powerful duchy than Franconia. Thanks to its location in northwestern Germany, it had been spared the Magyar raids that had weakened the rest of the country. Germany's dukes submitted to Henry's authority because they needed the help he could give them in their fight with the Magyars. In 955 Henry's son and successor, Otto I, "the Great" (r. 936–973), decisively defeated the invaders and reestablished Austria (Charlemagne's Ostmark) as a buffer state protecting Germany's eastern frontier. This contained the Magyars in a land of their own and encouraged them to settle down. Missionaries, whom Otto sponsored, quickly converted them, and in the year 1000 the pope recognized the existence of the new Christian kingdom of Hungary by sending its leader, Stephen (r. 997–1038), a crown.

As Europe's most powerful monarch and the ruler of its largest kingdom, Otto saw himself as picking up where Charlemagne had left off. In 951 he began a war to bring Italy under his control, and in 962 the pope revived the imperial title and bestowed it on Otto. Romantic visions of Roman and Carolingian empires were not the only reasons for Otto's interest in Italy. His home duchy was in northern Germany, and he would have had difficulty holding his kingdom together if the leaders of either of its southern duchies, Swabia and Bavaria, had crossed the Alps and added Italy to their possessions. Otto and most of his successors believed that Germany and Italy (where monarchy had died out) had to be united, but some Italians saw things differently. The papacy and the wealthy towns that flourished in northern Italy feared German domination and put up stiff resistance (see Map 9–4).

Constantinople was persuaded to accept Otto's coronation as emperor, and in 972 a marriage was arranged between his heir, Otto II (r. 973–983), and a Byzantine princess named Theophano. She and her cosmopolitan entourage elevated life at the German court, and the close ties with Constantinople that the marriage established stimulated a burst of artistic and literary activity, which historians call the Ottonian Renaissance.

Map 9–4 Medieval Germany and Italy Although the Roman Empire had never extended far into German territory, medieval Germany was haunted by the memory of the empire. German monarchs claimed the Roman title and believed that it gave them the right to rule Italy. Italians disagreed and viewed the Germans as invaders. The failure of Germany's kings to overcome the combined resistance of the Italian towns, the papacy, and their own feudal nobles sapped their authority and led to the political fragmentation of both Germany and Italy.

Question: Did geography encourage or hamper the attempts of the German kings to unify their country and join it with Italy?

In the process of creating his empire, Otto had acquired a lot of territory for the crown, but he knew that kings often had difficulty hanging on to the lands they won. Land made a king powerful by giving him the resources he needed to support his agents and soldiers. But when he granted land as fiefs to those who served him, it became more theirs than his. Men who possessed land also controlled the source of their income. Economic independence meant that they might not remain as loyal as men who were totally dependent on the king's favor. Otto hoped to solve these problems by granting the bulk of his lands to the church. The church, like a secular lord, owed the king military service for its lands. The advantage was that the leaders of the church could not marry and pass their offices down to their sons. Germany's bishops and abbots were appointed by its king. He could therefore make sure that the lands he gave the church remained in the hands of men he trusted. His power was safe so long as his authority over the church was unquestioned, but in the late tenth century challenges began to be mounted to the power laity had over clergy.

In 910, shortly before Otto's Saxon dynasty was founded in Germany, the duke of Aquitaine funded an ecclesiastical experiment in France. He endowed a new Benedictine monastery called Cluny and gave its monks the privilege of choosing their own abbot and managing their own affairs. This was unusual, for the wealthy families that donated to ecclesiastical institutions usually assumed that they had the right to appoint the clergy who were supported by their gifts. The reformers who sponsored Cluny claimed that this practice had resulted in the corruption and weakening of the church, for a lay patron who had a church office to give away tended to be more influenced by applicants' political connections than by their spiritual qualifications. The result was a lot of unworthy appointments and a general decline of religion. Things would improve, the Cluniacs insisted, if clergy were freed from secular interference and allowed to decide for themselves who was suited for a religious post. Cluny bore this out, for it quickly became the most respected monastery in Europe. Other cloisters asked Cluny to reorganize them, and before long Cluniacs were spearheading a drive to reform the whole church, a movement known as the **Cluniac Reform**.

The Saxon dynasty died out in 1024 before the Cluniac movement had become powerful enough to cause kings much trouble. The Salian dynasty (1024–1125), which succeeded the Saxon, was not so lucky. In 1049 its king, Henry III (r. 1039–1056), appointed his cousin, Leo IX (r. 1049–1054), to the papacy. Leo was a vigorous reformer. He traveled throughout Europe, convening councils to encourage spiritual renewal, and he improved the machinery of papal government by making more use of the cardinals ("primaries," the Roman clergy who reported directly to him). By the time Henry III's son, Henry IV (r. 1056–1106), came to the throne, the German king faced an ecclesiastical hierarchy that was determined to establish the papacy's independence of secular monarchs and to end the tradition of laymen appointing clergy.

Henry was crowned king at a young age, and the regents who governed for him were weak. This gave Pope Nicholas II (r. 1059–1061) an opportunity to establish a new procedure for papal elections that would exclude interference by kings. No formal procedure for choosing popes had ever existed. Some men had been elevated to the papal throne by political factions in the city of Rome. Others had been chosen by whatever emperor, king, or lord had sufficient influence in Rome at the time. Nicholas decreed that

■ ■ ■ ■ ■ ■

PEOPLE IN CONTEXT   Hroswitha of Gandersheim (fl. 935–1002)

The most original of the Ottonian Renaissance's authors was a Benedictine nun, Hroswitha of the Benedictine cloister at Gandersheim. Her personal history, beyond the little that can be inferred from her works, is a blank. She was probably an aristocrat, for Gandersheim was an elite house to which women from the royal family occasionally retreated.

Hroswitha was deeply grateful for the education she received at Gandersheim, and her teachers must have been women of considerable erudition. Hroswitha wrote excellent Latin and was a student of classical literature. Some of her works were what one might expect from a nun: saints' legends, apocryphal tales about the life of the Virgin Mary, and an account of the foundation of her cloister. But Hroswitha also ventured into unusual literary territory. She tried her hand at a history of Otto I's reign (the first attempt, as far as we know, by a medieval woman to write secular history). But her crowning achievement was a set of six plays that she said she wrote to counter the negative image of women found in the comedies of Terence, a playwright from the era of the Roman Republic. Hroswitha's plays are surprising because we might not anticipate that anyone in remote medieval Saxony would know of Terence, that a nun would be drawn to his work, that she would write fine Latin, that she would decide to write plays, and that she would use theater to rehabilitate the image of women. Hroswitha is the only

The Magdeburg Ivories Hroswitha of Gandersheim tried her hand at writing a history of the reign of Otto the Great. This is one of a series of ivory plaques executed in Italy for Otto. It depicts the king presenting the church of Magdeburg to the enthroned Christ. "The Emperor Otto I (912–73) Presenting a Model of His Church at Magdeburg to the Enthroned Christ in the Presence of Saints Peter and Mauritius (?) and Other Saints." One of a series of 17 ivory plaques known as the Magdeburg Ivories, possibly carved in Milan c. 962–68. Ivory, 5" × 4 1/2" (12.7 × 11.4 cm). The Metropolitan Musuem of Art, NY. Bequest of George Blumenthal, 1941 (41.100.157). Photograph © 1986 The Metropolitan Museum of Art playwright known to have worked in the long period between the fall of Rome and the gradual emergence of religious drama from the liturgy of the church in the twelfth century. It is unclear whether she intended her plays to be staged or simply read, but at least one of them seems to call for comic action to flesh out its dialogue.

Hroswitha was that rarest of medieval authors, a woman who wrote about women. Her world offered women only three roles: wife and mother, consecrated virgin, and whore. Hroswitha's plays illustrated how women in each of these situations could become spiritual heroines. She believed that females were physically and mentally inferior to males, but this, she argued, gave them a spiritual advantage over men. In her opinion, the male's strengths of body and intellect subject him to powerful temptations that women find easier to resist. The male is also likely to succumb to sin unless women, with God's help, courageously guard their virtue. Hroswitha's ingenious reinterpretation of the common gender stereotypes of her era challenged medieval religious tradition by placing women at the center of humanity's struggle for salvation.

Question: On what did women base their self-respect in the male-dominated medieval world?

---

henceforth only clergy could participate in a papal election. Because it was impossible to poll clergy throughout Europe, Rome's cardinal clergy were given the job of choosing popes. In 1073 they elected an avid Cluniac reformer who took the name Gregory VII (r. 1073–1085). The new pope immediately made his position perfectly clear. He claimed that popes were the highest authorities on Earth, that no one had the right to judge how they used their office, and that they even had the right to depose secular rulers.

It was some time before Henry IV was able to respond to the papacy's challenges to his authority, for the Salian dynasty had difficulty bringing Germany's landed nobility under control. Once the king had Germany more or less in hand, however, he turned his attention to Italy and to Gregory. The result was the **Investiture Controversy**, a major episode in the ongoing struggle between church and state.

In 1075 Gregory ordered laymen to discontinue the practice of "investing" clergy (that is, appointing candidates to church offices). Henry promptly called the pope's bluff by investing an archbishop for Milan, a major Italian see. This inaugurated a series of escalating events. Gregory denounced Henry. Henry then convened a council of German bishops that declared Gregory deposed, and Gregory reciprocated by excommunicating and deposing Henry. Gregory's deposition decree posed a real threat to Henry, for it gave Germany's nobles an excuse to repudiate a king whose growing strength threatened their freedom. The nobles asked Gregory to come to Germany to give their rebellion an aura of legitimacy, but Henry forestalled this by crossing the Alps in midwinter and ostentatiously begging the pope's forgiveness. Gregory had no choice but to reconcile with a king who made such a flamboyant public show of regret. But when he did so, the German nobles concluded that he had betrayed them, and they turned on him. Henry recovered his hold on Germany, and in 1084 he descended on Rome and forced the pope to flee.

Gregory was humiliated and died in exile, but this did not end the Investiture Controversy or solve the problem of church–state relations. The church was endowed with about one-third of the land in Europe, and kings would not relinquish the right to a say in the choice of the clergy who administered so much territory within the boundaries of their kingdoms. The church therefore settled for a face-saving compromise. Kings agreed not to take part in the ceremonies that invested clergy, but candidates for investiture had first to take oaths of homage to kings for the secular services they owed for the church's land. This gave kings a chance to veto candidates whom they did not like without seeming to violate the church's independence. The resolution of the Investiture Controversy was an example of the strategy the church pursued throughout the Middle Ages. By consistently claiming more power in theory than it settled for in practice the church was able slowly to make practice catch up with theory.

The Salian dynasty did not long survive Henry's victory over Gregory. The death of its last king in 1125 nearly extinguished the monarchy in Germany, and a generation passed before a new dynasty was established. Despite the advantage of an early, strong start, Germany's kings were still a long way from providing their subjects with effective, centralized government.

The Eleventh-Century Turning Point

The shift of resources from centralized monarchies to local lords had succeeded in helping Europe weather the invasions of the ninth and tenth centuries. The fragmented government that resulted tended to be chaotic, but it provided enough security to prevent the loss of the cultural gains made during the Carolingian era. In addition, as the situation slowly stabilized, Europeans returned to the world stage. Europe had largely been on the defensive since the fall of the western Roman Empire, but in the eleventh century that changed. Europe took the offensive, expanded territorially and economically, and developed an environment in which artists and intellectuals flourished.

The Spanish and Sicilian Crusades   The most obvious sign that the eleventh century marked the start of a new phase in Europe's history was the threat Europeans began to pose to their neighbors. After centuries of being invaded, Europe became the invader. It waged crusades—holy wars motivated (at least in part) by a fervent desire to destroy persons whom it regarded as enemies of its church. Crusades primarily targeted Muslims in foreign lands, but they also triggered pogroms in Europe—massacres of Jews that continued to erupt sporadically well into the twentieth century. The hatreds, misunderstandings, and suspicions the crusades nurtured still complicate international relationships.

Europe opened its first front against the Muslim world in Spain, the point of closest contact between western Christendom and Islam. In the middle of the tenth century, the Umayyad caliph of Córdoba united Spain's Muslims and attacked the tiny Christian states on the northern rim of the Iberian Peninsula. In 997 alarm spread throughout Europe when the caliph's vizier, al-Mansur, sacked Compostela, a pilgrimage center that ranked in importance only behind Jerusalem and Rome. Al-Mansur died in 1002, and no comparable Muslim leader was found to take his place. This created an opportunity for Sancho III, "the Great" (r. 1000–1035), the ruler of Navarre, a kingdom on the slopes of the Pyrenees. He appealed to Europe's Christian knights for help in mounting a counteroffensive. The church blessed his campaign as a holy war, and the monks of Cluny vigorously promoted it. The Christian forces advanced steadily, and in 1085 they captured the old Visigothic capital of Toledo in the heart of Spain. At this point, their Muslim opponents received reinforcements from North Africa, and the war bogged down. The Christian reconquest of Spain dragged on for four more centuries, for neither the Muslims nor the Christians could resist fighting among themselves.

Europe's Christians launched their second offensive against Islam in the central Mediterranean. In 1017 a group of Norman knights stopped off in southern Italy on their way back from a pilgrimage to Jerusalem. The Normans discovered that Italy's petty wars provided plentiful employment for mercenaries, and as word spread, recruits poured in from France. Among these were Robert Guiscard ("Cunning") and his brother Roger, two of the numerous sons of Tancred de Hauteville, a minor Norman nobleman. They subdued or evicted the native lords of southern Italy and drove the Muslims from Sicily. In 1130 the pope conferred a royal title on Roger's son, Roger II (r. 1105–1154), and recognized the existence of a Norman monarchy (the future Kingdom of the Two Sicilies) ruling Sicily and southern Italy. Robert Guiscard also tried to conquer Byzantine possessions in the Balkans and Greece, but his dream of building a Mediterranean empire proved too ambitious. Still, the recovery of Sicily greatly strengthened Christian Europe's position in the Mediterranean region. The ports of Italy profited especially from enhanced security and opportunities for trade.

The Crusades to the Holy Land   While the first crusades were altering the balance of power in the western Mediterranean, the situation in the Middle East was also changing. Constantinople had ceded most of Asia Minor to the Seljuk Turks after its defeat at Manzikert in 1071. A decade later, however, it saw a chance to recoup its losses. The Seljuks had broken up into mutually hostile states, and a competent military man, Alexius Comnenus (r. 1081–1118), had ascended the Byzantine throne. Alexius's diminished empire was short on manpower, but there were plenty of Christian knights in western Europe. Alexius therefore asked Pope Urban II (r. 1088–1099) to use the church's communication network to help him recruit soldiers.

Alexius's goal was the recovery of the Byzantine territory that had been lost in 1071, but Urban decided to represent the emperor as proposing something much grander— nothing less than the eviction of Muslims from Jerusalem, a city they had held for almost 500 years. Urban had several motives for endorsing and expanding the scope of Alexius's project. He hoped that by assisting Constantinople, he could heal a **schism** that had erupted between the eastern and western churches in 1054. (They had quarreled over a doctrinal issue—the nature of the relation of the Holy Spirit to the Father and to the Son in the Trinity.) Urban further reasoned that by rallying an international army to wage a universal holy war, the pope would strengthen his claim to be Christendom's supreme leader. The diversion of Europe's soldiers to foreign lands also might help to pacify European society, a cause for which the church had been working for over a century.

By Urban's day, an abundance of underemployed soldiers was posing a threat to the stability of European society. Europe's population was increasing, and the number of

The Three Medieval Civilizations: Leaders and Events		
MUSLIM WORLD	**BYZANTIUM**	**EUROPE**
	Leo III (717–740) Iconoclasm Controversy (726–843)	Pepin III (741–768)
Abbasid dynasty (750) Umayyad Emirate of Spain (756)		
Aghlabids (800)	Macedonian dynasty (867)	Charlemagne (768–814) Vikings attack (860) *England-France-Germany* Alfred the Great (871–899)
Fatimid dynasty (909)		Cluny founded (910) Saxon dynasty (919)
Umayyad caliphate of Spain (929)		
Buyids take Baghdad (945)	Schism: Greek and Latin churches (1054)	Capetian dynasty (987) Cnute (1016–1035) Salian dynasty (1024)
Seljuks take Baghdad (1060)	Manzikert battle (1071)	William I (1066–1087) Investiture Controversy (1075) Toledo reconquered (1085) Sicily reconquered (1092)
	First Crusade (1095–1099)	

knights exceeded the number of fiefs available to support them. A knight did not just train his heir. He trained all his sons to be knights. Lacking other educational opportunities, medieval men usually learned their fathers' professions. By the eleventh century, primogeniture (the right of the eldest male to inherit the whole estate) was becoming the preferred method for preserving both fiefs and a family's fortune and status. It, however, forced the younger brothers of heirs to leave home and fend for themselves. They might find heiresses to marry, enter the church, become soldiers of fortune, or take to the road as brigands. Many found employment in the private armies of local lords. Given that there was little point in a lord supporting knights if he did not use them, these companies of professional soldiers were a standing threat to the peace and order of the countryside.

The church, partly out of self-interest and partly out of a sense of duty, looked for ways to pacify the unruly military elements that threatened to destabilize society. One

The Medieval Knight This page from an illuminated manuscript illustrates episodes from the medieval epic poem *The Song of Roland*. It depicts knights in action, and the slaughter that could result. The soldiers wear chain mail and surcoats, wield spears and long swords, and carry shields that taper to a point (and provide protection for the legs of a man on horseback). Chain mail guarded against sword cuts, but it was vulnerable to penetration by missiles (e.g., arrows or spears). Bit by bit, metal plates were added to reinforce chain mail until, by the end of the Middle Ages, a knight could be entirely encased in a suit of steel.

of its strategies was to persuade knights that honor required them to discipline themselves. The Peace of God and Truce of God movements (see Key Question) appealed to the idealism of young soldiers by declaring knighthood a sacred vocation—a divine commission to protect others. To drive this point home, the church urged that quasi-religious dubbing ceremonies be used to admit men to knightly status. This was helpful, but Urban's plan to divert western Europe's excess soldiers to wars outside Europe was a more direct way of promoting peace in their homelands.

On November 27, 1095, Urban preached a wildly successful sermon at a church council held at Clermont, France. It urged Europe's knights to go to the aid of the east's Christians and offered them all the spiritual and practical assistance the church could provide—primarily, full forgiveness for all their sins and protection for their property at home. The pope toured France for eight months, whipping up enthusiasm for the campaign, and numerous preachers were dispatched to fan the fires he lit. The result was not just a crusade, but a crusading movement that continued for the rest of the medieval era to inspire repeated European assaults on the Muslim world. Historians recognize seven or eight major crusades, but many more European armies departed for the Middle East before the impulse finally died out.

No European king, at the end of the eleventh century, could risk leaving home for an adventure in the Holy Land, and the First Crusade did not have a supreme commander. It was managed (or mismanaged) by a committee of nobles who put themselves at the head of about 4,000 knights, 26,000 foot soldiers, and a horde of pilgrims and camp followers. Some who enlisted hoped to make new lives for themselves in the east, but most planned to return home once the campaign was over. The families of crusader knights endured financial hardship to equip them, and few seem to have made money from the venture.

Before the official crusade got underway, a charismatic preacher called Peter the Hermit led a horde of soldiers and pilgrims to Constantinople. The passions they inspired as they marched across Europe excited Christian mobs to slaughter their Jewish neighbors. Jews were lumped together with Muslims as infidels—as were, in the opinion of some Europeans, the Orthodox Christians of the Middle East. Peter's so-called Peasants' Crusade suffered a disastrous defeat as soon as it crossed into Asia Minor. It was not what Alexius had expected, nor were the French barons, who arrived later with their armies. They did not want to work for him; they had plans of their own (see Map 9–5).

If the Muslims had ceased fighting among themselves and joined forces to defend their territory, the First Crusade could never have succeeded. The Europeans knew little about the Middle East, and they were poorly equipped to deal with its geography and climate. They suffered from heat, thirst, hunger, and disease. Their leaders quarreled. Units defected from the main army to grab lands for themselves. But despite horrific blunders and misadventures, a remnant of the army reached Jerusalem on June 7, 1099. On July 15 they forced their way into the city and slaughtered everyone they found—including Jews and eastern Christians. An eyewitness reported that on the Temple Mount the knights' horses waded up to their bellies in blood and gore.

The crusaders declared Jerusalem the seat of a new Latin kingdom and established a string of crusader states along the Palestinian coast. These fragile European outposts owed their brief survival to the fact that the Muslims continued, for some time, to fight among themselves. In 1144, however, the Muslims recovered Edessa, the first state that the crusaders had claimed. The loss so alarmed Europe that two kings "took the cross" (that is, they wore the image of a cross that marked a man as having made a crusader's vow). The Second Crusade set out under the leadership of Louis VII of France and Conrad III

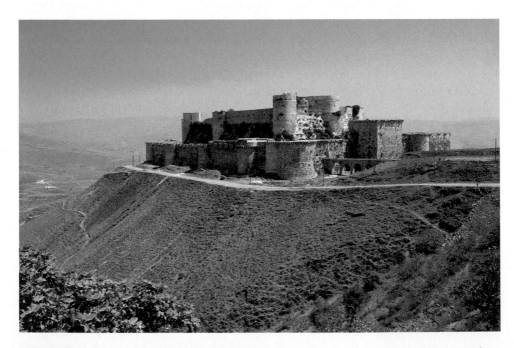

Krak des Chevaliers   To preserve their tenuous hold on their conquests, Europe's crusaders invested heavily in the construction of massive stone fortresses. This castle, which dates to the twelfth century, belonged to an order of crusader monks called the Hospitalers. Sites such as this have kept memories of the crusades alive in the Middle East to a degree that might surprise a European or American.

Map 9-5 Crusade Routes The earlier crusaders marched overland to Constantinople. The faster and easier sea route did not become popular until the twelfth century—after Sardinia and Sicily were in Christian hands and Italy's commercial cities had begun to wrest control of the Mediterranean from the Muslims.

Question: Why did the Mediterranean unite the Roman Empire but separate the medieval civilizations?

(r. 1138–1152) of Germany. Louis's strong-willed wife, Eleanor of Aquitaine, insisted on accompanying them on what proved to be a costly and embarrassing debacle. This crusade and the ones that followed are distinguished primarily by the ways in which they failed.

The Cultural Environment   It is often assumed that if people from different cultures are given a chance to mingle, they will become more understanding and tolerant of one another. This, alas, is not always the case. However, Europeans learned a great deal from the Muslims who became their subjects in Spain and Sicily and their neighbors in the Holy Land. Muslims introduced Europeans to Arabic, Greek, and Hebrew texts that revolutionized intellectual life in the Latin west. Arab poets inspired the knightly **troubadours** ("inventors"), who appeared in the wake of the First Crusade and invigorated European literature, music, and popular culture. The monastery of Cluny was curious enough about the Christian world's rival faith to sponsor a Latin translation of the Qur'an, but none of this made Europeans any more sympathetic toward Islam.

An eleventh-century epic poem, *The Song of Roland*, assumed that Muslims worshiped an odd trinity of gods that included the Greek deity Apollo. The ludicrous picture of Islam it paints reveals how ignorant many Europeans were of Islam on the eve of the crusades. A generation or two later, they were better informed but, if anything, less tolerant. They could not connect the Muslim scholars whose books they admired with the Muslim faith that they regarded as the enemy of truth. Some Europeans were exceptions to this rule, of course, but their generous attitudes could, paradoxically, deepen prejudices against Islam. The longer Latin Christians lived in the Holy Land, for example, the more their lifestyles came to resemble those of their Muslim neighbors. This horrified visitors from Europe and confirmed their suspicion that Islam was an insidious heresy that had to be exterminated to prevent the spread of its infection. Some Europeans took Muslim texts and practices out of context and unfairly used them to create the impression that Islam was a religion of carnal self-indulgence and wanton blood lust. The many things that encouraged Europeans to fear that their Christian faith was engaged in a life-and-death struggle with Islam submerged the pacific elements in Christ's teachings. European Christianity became a militant faith that mirrored the violence that it imagined to be a characteristic of its enemy.

Europe's Economic Revival   The collapse of the western Roman Empire had sent Europe into an economic decline that dragged on for centuries. Rome's western provinces had never been as wealthy or productive as its eastern ones, and although trade across the Mediterranean continued after Rome's fall, the west produced little that the east wanted. The repeated waves of attackers and migrants that swept across Europe disrupted commercial activity, and people adapted to the chronically chaotic environment by becoming as self-sufficient as possible. They never entirely abandoned trade, for vital supplies (salt and metals, for example) were not available in every locality. The church and the wealthy also wanted luxuries (such as spices, silks, and incense) that had to be imported from the east.

When the Viking, Magyar, and Muslim invasions passed and commercial activity began again to revive, two foci for international trade appeared at opposite ends of Europe. Trade flowed into the continent from the city of Venice in the southeast and from the region of Flanders in the northwest.

At the start of the Middle Ages, Christians had ceded most of the Mediterranean to Muslims, but they retained control of the Adriatic Sea. This gave Venice, at the head of the Adriatic, an early advantage over other Christian cities. It commanded a sea route to Constantinople, and the goods it imported could be shipped over nearby Alpine passes to markets in northern Europe. Most of Italy's other ports were on the western coast of the peninsula. Pisa and Genoa began trading along the French and Italian coasts in the tenth century, and in 1016 they drove the Muslims from Sardinia. A half century later, the Norman conquest of Sicily (1072) secured more of the Mediterranean for Italian sailors, and the success of the First Crusade created bases for them in the Middle East.

Flanders, the northern hub of economic activity, developed in response to the voyages of the Vikings. While some Vikings sailed west to raid England and the coast of France, others headed east across the Baltic Sea and down Russia's rivers. Navigable river systems nearly converge in Russia, so that with a little portage overland from one to another, it was possible to sail from the Baltic to the Black Sea. The Vikings established bases at Novgorod and Kiev. From the latter, they sailed down the Dnieper River to the Black Sea and Constantinople. By the eleventh century, Kiev was, after Constantinople, Christendom's largest city. Goods could flow profitably between the Byzantine capital via Scandinavia and the North Sea to Flanders.

Constantinople's merchants were primarily interested in western Europe's raw materials and agricultural products, but Europe had at least one industry that served both foreign and domestic markets. Europe's climate produced a superior quality of wool, and the manufacturers who turned it into cloth played an economic role in the Middle Ages analogous to that of the makers of automobiles in twentieth-century America. Cloth was an ideal product for trade under medieval conditions. Everyone needed it, but not everyone could produce it. It was lightweight and could be transported over long distances without excessively increasing its cost to consumers. Europe's major cloth-producing centers were the cities of Flanders and northern Italy.

Commercial activity built slowly in the early Middle Ages, for merchants faced many obstacles. Their customers were widely scattered. There was little money in circulation to serve as a medium of exchange, and workers produced little surplus with which to trade. So long as opportunities to trade were limited, people had no motivation to produce surpluses. If a community produced more of something than it could consume and it had no way to sell the excess, it had uselessly expended its labor. The goal of an economically isolated community, therefore, was self-sufficiency, not increasing productivity. If commerce was to grow, merchants had to change the way Europe's laborers thought about their work and their economic goals.

In the tenth century nature began to make things a bit easier for Europeans. Europe's climate entered a warming phase that lengthened growing seasons and extended the ranges of some crops. The improving environment and the spreading use of new farming techniques (the three-field system) and tools (collars and shoes that allowed horses to be used as draft animals) encouraged agricultural productivity. Europe began to expand internally by bringing more of its land under the plow. Forests were cleared, wetlands drained, and farmland was even reclaimed from the sea. More food and increasing political stability encouraged population growth. Between 1000 and 1300 Europe more than doubled its population, and the expanding pool of producers and consumers greatly stimulated economic activity.

Europe's economy did not just grow; it changed. Originally, Europeans had assumed that wealth was a finite resource and that the fundamental economic challenge was to figure out how to share it. That belief governed the thinking of the medieval craft **guilds** that monopolized production for local markets. Only members of a guild were allowed to manufacture and sell its product in its market area. The guild limited production to prevent saturation of its market. It regulated prices so that each guild member could make a living, but it also policed manufacturing to ensure that shoddy goods did not alienate its customers. A wise manufacturer understood the necessity of maintaining a healthy market of satisfied consumers.

Guilds could not establish monopolistic control over international markets, and the producers who traded internationally behaved more like capitalists. Capitalism maintains that wealth is not a finite resource, but something that can be increased by human effort. Capitalists try to maximize the production of surplus goods and then find markets in which to sell them at a profit. This profit becomes capital when, instead of being consumed, it is invested in the production of more goods to be sold to generate more profits. Scholars debate whether true capitalism appeared in Europe during the Middle Ages, but the medieval cloth industry was at least a forerunner of the system. Its investors employed a salaried workforce supervised by managers who ruthlessly served "the bottom line." When competition among them led to overproduction and market saturation, they simply fired their workers and ceased business until demand returned. One product of the commercial revolution of the eleventh century was a proletarian underclass of industrial workers who were vulnerable to such exploitation. During economic downturns, these hungry masses threatened social upheaval.

The Rise of Towns and the Middle Class   The early medieval merchant had to search far and wide for customers. The cities that had survived Rome's passing were ghosts of their former selves, and Europe's reduced population was thinly dispersed about the countryside. Few places had enough people to support a permanent market. Many medieval merchants were therefore simple peddlers who wandered about looking for people to buy their goods.

Commercial activity increased as peddlers learned to entice customers to meet them part way. Life in the medieval countryside offered little excitement. Most Europeans lived in small, isolated communities or farmsteads where the arrival of an itinerant merchant would have been a major event. He offered a new face, desirable merchandise, and news from abroad. Peddlers gradually figured out how to exploit this. They discovered that if they let it be known that they would be in a certain place at a certain time, people would travel some distance to meet them. They also discovered that by working together, they could create greater excitement and draw larger crowds. For safety's sake, they preferred to display their merchandise near a castle or monastery that offered them protection, and the best time to appear was when the people who lived nearby congregated at these places to celebrate a holiday, a **fair** (*feria*, "feast day"). Fairs were exciting events that provided entertainment as well as opportunities to stock up on goods that were otherwise unattainable. Medieval people shopped by the calendar, not by whim, and annual cycles of fairs constituted medieval Europe's primary distribution system. Some fairs served retail customers. Others—particularly those of the French county of Champagne, which was a convenient place for traders from Venice and Flanders to meet—primarily provided opportunities for merchants to restock their wares.

As population grew and the customer base increased, fairs in some places stretched out for longer and longer periods of time. By the eleventh century, some merchant encampments were becoming permanent. If merchants wanted to settle down, however, they had to come to an agreement with the lord on whose land they were squatting. To do so, they formed a commune (a kind of corporation) and sought a charter from the lord that gave them title to land and legal freedom to manage their own affairs. The founders of a *bourg* (a fortified settlement), the **bourgeoisie**, sometimes took up arms to win their privileges, but often they simply purchased their land and rights.

Medieval merchant communes reinvented urban life. Some of Europe's new towns occupied the same sites as old Roman cities, but they bore little resemblance to their predecessors. Most ancient cities served military or administrative purposes, but medieval towns owed their origin to commerce. They were created by traders and craftsmen who had no power over anyone but themselves. Their inhabitants were, in the opinion of the scholars of the day, exceptions to the divinely ordained social order. God,

Carcassonne, France   A few medieval towns have survived in Europe. Their walls, buildings, and twisting streets give modern people some impression of what medieval urban life was like, but a visitor who wants to avoid romantic misconceptions should keep in mind that medieval cities had no sewage systems. Their streets were clogged with people, animals, and refuse, and their air was tainted with fumes from ubiquitous cooking and heating fires. They were neither comfortable nor healthy places.

it was alleged, had (with consummate efficiency) created three kinds of people to perform the three tasks essential to human survival. Protection was the work of knights, provision was the duty of serfs and peasants, and prayer was the responsibility of clergy. There was no place in this system for artisans and merchants, but ultimately they grew so powerful that they could not be ignored. Because their wealth and influence placed them somewhere between the lords and knights of the upper class and the agricultural laborers of the lower class, they became the "middle class."

Townspeople may never have accounted for more than 10% of the population of medieval Europe, but they drove the evolution of medieval society by injecting a new kind of freedom into the social order. Free persons were legal outsiders, for they had not commended themselves to the service of a lord nor been bound to the land. Townspeople, however, found ways to make their freedom of movement and self-determination profitable, and their self-governing towns gave people in the surrounding countryside options that had not previously existed. Lords who wanted to keep the serfs who cultivated their fields had to be careful how they treated them, for oppressed serfs might flee into a town. Because a town was an independent entity, a lord had no right to enter it to retrieve fugitives from his lands. Tradition decreed that if a serf stayed in a town for a year and a day, he became legally free. If a serf opted to remain on his lord's land, a town in the neighborhood could still give him a chance to improve his lot. Townspeople did not raise their own food. Serfs who produced surpluses could sell them in a town's market and use the profits to buy privileges from their lords. Lords were inclined to negotiate, for they wanted to keep their workers—and they needed money. Conspicuous consumption was essential to maintaining a lord's aristocratic status, and the expanding economy created a rising standard of living that put him in a bind. He lived on a fixed income, for his serfs owed him only what grew on his *demesne*, the fields assigned him on his manors. As his expenses increased, it made sense for him to give up his rights to labor services and simply rent his lands to his serfs. Tradition limited labor services, but rents were negotiable. As the new economy took hold, serfdom faded away, and other kinds of ties began to take the place of commendation as a way to organize society.

KEY QUESTION | Revisited

By the end of the eleventh century, a newly assertive Europe was preparing to take on the world. As the weakest of the West's three medieval civilizations, it had come to regard its cultural inferiority as a sign of moral superiority. It spurned the Greeks as devious quasi-heretics and the Muslims as enemies of God. It saw itself as the defender of true faith and authentic civilization—of the real West.

Today, the expression "the West" is usually reserved for European-American cultures, but limiting its use in this way obscures the memory of the West's historical development. The European institutions and attitudes that were transplanted to the Americas had deep roots in the ancient Middle East where the Christian religion was born from the much older Hebrew faith. The classical components of Western civilization also owed much to the ancient Middle East. Islamic, Byzantine, and medieval European cultures were all nurtured by the same Hebraic and classical sources. Medieval

Europe would also have had a much more difficult time rebuilding its version of Western civilization if it had not had the help of Muslim and Byzantine scholars.

The people who inhabited the Roman Empire were culturally and ethnically diverse, but they were aware of a common identity, a shared understanding of what constituted civilized life. However, after the empire was split into eastern and western sections and the culture of its western portion went into steep decline, the contrast between east and west was magnified. The rapid rise of a dynamic Muslim empire did more to turn difference into division. The result was that the peoples who lived at opposite ends of the Mediterranean in the early Middle Ages became more aware of things that separated them than of things they shared.

Cultural contrasts became grounds for cultural opposition in the eleventh century as Europeans evolved a stronger sense of identity and acquired the resources to assert themselves. The crusades they inaugurated widened fault lines into gulfs. The kind of future that might have been built on the friendly exchanges that had taken place between Emperor Charlemagne and Caliph Harun al-Rashid no longer seemed possible or desirable. Economic, political, and military contacts among Europeans, Muslims, and Byzantines multiplied during the second half of the Middle Ages, but they did not bring these peoples closer together. At the end of the Middle Ages, when Europe shifted its attention from the Mediterranean to the Atlantic, they grew even further apart. The result is a legacy of alienation, resentment, and misunderstanding that may constitute the most serious threat to the peace of the modern world. For people who do not understand the history of the development of the concepts of a "Christian West" and an "Islamic East," war between them may seem unavoidable. War is always an option, but it is also always a choice. Better alternatives may occur to those who question the inevitability of conflict and understand the origins of cultural differences.

Review Questions

1. How did the European environment differ from that of the Islamic world during the early Middle Ages?
2. Why were the Christians of medieval Europe suspicious of their fellow Christians in Byzantine and Muslim regions?
3. What things did the three medieval civilizations of the Mediterranean world have in common?
4. Were the political struggles faced by the English, French, and German monarchies unique to Europe or similar to developments elsewhere in the medieval world?
5. Why were the crusades launched? How did they affect the three medieval civilizations?
6. What developments made the eleventh century a turning point for western Europe?

Please consult the Suggested Readings at the back of the book to continue your study of the material covered in this chapter. For a list of documents on the Primary Source DVD-ROM that relate to topics in this chapter, please refer to the back of the book.

10 Europe's High Middle Ages

Bernard of Chartres used to say that we resemble dwarfs riding on the shoulders of giants in so far as we see more and farther than they do—not because we are physically or intellectually their superiors, but because their greatness lifts and supports us.

—John of Salisbury, *Metalogicon*

KEY | Question

Why are some societies more open to change than others?

Although John of Salisbury (c. 1115–1180) was an Englishman, he became bishop of Chartres, a diocese southeast of Paris. It would be unusual today for a man who was not French to occupy a major ecclesiastical office in France, but such appointments were common in the Middle Ages. Two of the medieval archbishops of Canterbury, the heads of England's church, were Italians recruited from a French monastery. When a job is important enough to a community, talent outweighs almost any objection that might otherwise be made to an individual's employment. Following World War II, for instance, the United States eagerly embraced the German scientists who had developed rockets for Nazi Germany—ignoring not only the indiscriminate slaughter their weapons had caused, but the vicious exploitation of slave labor that had occurred in the facilities they ran. Because modern Western societies give science and technology the kind of priority that religion had in the medieval world, our scientific institutions are more likely to be staffed by persons with diverse backgrounds than our places of worship.

The remark quoted above, which John of Salisbury credited to his teacher Bernard of Chartres, captures the combination of humility and self-assertion that characterized scholars of John's generation. They were by no means prepared to claim equality with the great thinkers

Chartres Cathedral   The great church of the small town of Chartres, just south of Paris, is one of the earliest and best examples of Gothic architecture. Its architect is unknown, but he was a pioneer in the use of the "flying buttresses" that are a hallmark of Gothic style.

of the ancient world, but they were also no longer constrained by excessive respect for them. They assumed that by studying the works of their predecessors they could pick up where "the giants" had left off, make more progress, and even correct the mistakes of the past.

As the intellectuals of the twelfth century shifted from merely assimilating the past to critiquing it, ideas and disagreements proliferated. Instead of recoiling in fear that this might lead to confusion and undermine traditional values and institutions, they scrambled to develop techniques of analysis and inference that would reconcile conflicting opinions. Some warned about the risks of doubt and skepticism, but most had faith that they could work through the tangle and arrive at a more adequate and comprehensive understanding of life and the world. The dream that motivated many of the period's scholars was the creation of a **summa**—a rationally consistent summation of all truths.

Medieval civilization hit its stride in the twelfth and thirteenth centuries, the High Middle Ages. States evolved more sophisticated instruments of law, justice, and government. Architects conceived radically new designs, and awe-inspiring buildings of a type never before seen rose all across Europe. New kinds of schools promoted a new kind of learning, and innovation in the arts and vernacular literatures flourished. These advances required some painful adjustments, for some of them challenged traditional beliefs and institutions. Critics feared that heresies would multiply, respect for authority would diminish, and confidence in truth itself would be lost. But overall, the positives were deemed to outweigh the negatives, and the pioneers forged boldly and rapidly ahead.

The Renaissance of the Twelfth Century

Europe's intellectual history is studded with renaissances—eras when a surge of interest in ancient Greek and Roman literature promoted cultural advances. Most Greek literature had disappeared from western Europe by the twelfth century, but there were enough Latin classics available to sustain a renaissance. The intellectuals of the twelfth century took Virgil and Cicero as their mentors. They wrote elegant poems, letters, and treatises studded with allusions to Greco-Roman myth and history, and the artistic programs they designed to decorate churches spread their esoteric learning to the unlettered masses.

The twelfth-century renaissance was also stimulated by a flood of scientific and philosophical information from Arabic sources. Muslim scholars had made significant advances in science and philosophy, and Latin translations introduced Europeans to their work and important Greek and Hindu thinkers. Muslims also produced commentaries on ancient texts that helped Europeans understand what they were reading and acquire the intellectual tools they needed to strike out on their own.

Christian Europe was preoccupied with theology, but it was the lure of science that first drew its scholars to Muslim libraries (the nearest of which were in Spain). Constantine the African (d. 1087) specialized in translating Arabic medical texts. Adelard of Bath (d. 1126), an Englishman, made a Latin translation of an Arabic version of Euclid's *Elements of Geometry*. He also published an edition of the astronomical tables of the Arab mathematician al-Khwarizmi (d. 850) that introduced Europeans to trigonometry. About 1145 another Englishman, Robert of Chester, translated al-Khwarizmi's *On the Restoration and Opposition of Numbers*—a text that was so fundamental to the study of mathematics that it came to be known simply as "algebra" (*al Gebra*, "the book"). A generation later, Italian mathematician Leonardo Fibonacci (1170–1230) introduced

Europeans to "Arabic" numerals and the concept of zero, both of which Muslims had appropriated from Hindu sources.

The Popularity of Dialectic   The intellectuals of the High Middle Ages exalted **dialectic** (the craft of constructing logical arguments) over the other liberal arts that structured the medieval educational curriculum. This was due in part to the influence of Gerbert of Aurillac (c. 940–1003), who was reputed to be the most learned man in Europe. Gerbert rose from humble origins in a French monastery to become the head of an influential school, tutor to an emperor, and (despite allegations of witchcraft) a pope (Sylvester II, r. 999–1003). He studied mathematics and astronomy in Barcelona, Córdoba, and Seville; constructed scientific instruments; and revived the use of the abacus (the ancient and medieval world's premier calculating device).

The great thinkers of the Middle Ages, which included Gerbert, turned language into a tool for scientific research. Scientific breakthroughs in the modern era are often the result of new data provided by instruments or techniques that improve on the human senses. Researchers can now look more closely at the world and more deeply into the universe than ever before in history. Medieval scholars did not have this option. Because they could not improve on the information simple observation provides, their only hope for progress lay in improving what their minds did with that information—on refining the language they used to describe it and think about it. They defined terms with technical precision and then explored the logical implications of their words. They focused on a task that scientists still acknowledge to be important: understanding how the mind represents the world to itself.

Gerbert taught his students dialectic with the help of what came to be called the Old Logic, the philosophical treatises that Boethius (see Chapter 8) had assembled and translated in the sixth century. This was familiar material, but it inspired a change of attitude for Gerbert's generation. Earlier scholars had been taught that truth rested on authority—that something was true because a respected source said that it was true. The most important source of truth was revelation (enlightenment by God). The study of dialectic prompted men like Gerbert, however, to suspect that truth needed the support of nothing beyond itself. A true belief appeared to have an inherent rationality that made its validity self-evident.

A famous debate between two eleventh-century theologians, Berengar of Tours (d. 1088) and Lanfranc of Bec (d. 1089), encouraged dialectic's advocates. At issue was what happened when a priest consecrated bread and wine in the sacrament of the mass. The church had not yet taken a stand, but it was widely believed that consecration turned the bread and wine into Christ's body and blood (the Roman Catholic Church's doctrine of transubstantiation). Berengar claimed that this could not be so, for human senses could discern no difference between consecrated and unconsecrated bread and wine. The traditional method for dealing with skeptics like Berengar was to remind them that human understanding was limited and that because some truths could only be grasped by faith, they had to be accepted on the authority of the church. Lanfranc, however, opted to use dialectic to argue for the rationality of faith. Philosophers, Lanfranc noted, distinguish between substance and attribute. A *substance* is the essential nature of a thing, while an *attribute* is a feature of that thing that can change without affecting its identity. (A cloak, for example, remains a cloak no matter what color it is dyed.) In ordinary experience, Lanfranc argued, attributes change but substances do not. Logic dictates, however, that an omnipotent God could make an exception in the case of the mass—changing the substances of consecrated bread and wine but not their attributes. Lanfranc did not claim to have proved that this was the case, but only to have shown that what faith believed was not a logical absurdity.

Lanfranc's reconciliation of faith with reason had a significant implication. If the truths that come from revelation are, as he suggested, compatible with those acquired by ordinary human experience, the universe must be fundamentally intelligible and its mysteries should yield to dialectical analysis. Theologians quickly discovered, however, that reason was a two-edged sword that required skillful handling.

Reason and Authority   Europe's dialecticians were fascinated by a problem that the Old Logic raised but left unresolved: the status of words that refer to classes of things versus those that refer to individual things. Nominalists maintained that a word that referred to a category of objects (*chair*, for example) was a mere *nomen* ("name") that the mind invented for its own convenience. Their opponents, the realists, insisted that the fact that the mind can assign individual things to classes (that is, identify this particular thing as "a chair") means that it perceives something that transcends the separate existences of things—something that is really in them. Chairs can be designed in many ways and made of many different materials, but we recognize them all as chairs because there is an eternal reality (an essential "chairness") that defines them as chairs. Both these positions had unfortunate theological implications. **Nominalism** suggested that the Trinity was only a name for a group of three deities: the Father, the Son, and the Holy Spirit. **Realism**, in contrast, led to the heresy of pantheism (the belief that God is simply the sum total of everything that exists—pure being, the pinnacle of a hierarchy of increasingly general and comprehensive classes). Neither of these alternatives was acceptable to Christians, and the search for a rational alternative to them inspired exploration of the subtleties of logic.

The dialectical method's most famous advocate was Peter Abelard (1070–1142), the eldest son of a minor Breton nobleman. Abelard relinquished his patrimony to a younger brother and, freed of family obligations, left home to seek an education. He drifted from school to school immersing himself in the debate between the nominalists and the realists and soon began to challenge prominent spokesmen for both sides. As his brilliantly constructed critiques revealed the flaws in the arguments of one famous scholar after another, he earned enemies, followers, and (in 1115) a position as a teacher at Ste. Geneviève in Paris. Abelard was a brilliant, charismatic educator who enthralled his students with poetry as well as dialectic. The crowds of scholars who flocked to Paris to hear him established the city's reputation as Europe's premier center of intellectual activity. At the height of his popularity, however, Abelard made a serious blunder.

One of Paris's prominent clerics had a niece named Heloise (d. 1163). He sent her to a convent school where she mastered Latin, Greek, and (possibly) Hebrew and earned a reputation as an intellectual prodigy. Because it was impossible for a girl to mix with the rowdy adolescent males who populated Paris's schools, Heloise's uncle was at a loss as to how to continue her education—until it occurred to him to ask Abelard to tutor her privately. Abelard was intrigued by her intellect (more than her looks, he said), and she fell passionately in love with him. They became sexually involved. After she became pregnant, he persuaded her (although she argued against it) to marry him. His plan was to keep the marriage secret. Medieval scholars were considered clergy, and the rewards they aspired to were appointments to well-funded offices in the church. Because clergy had to be celibate, an acknowledged wife would have ended Abelard's career. Heloise's uncle, however, concluded that Abelard was sacrificing Heloise's reputation to protect his own, and he took drastic steps to avenge her and his family's honor. He hired thugs who broke into Abelard's rooms and castrated him.

Abelard sought refuge in a monastery, and Heloise (for love of him and not God, as she explained to him in her letters) entered a convent. The cloister, however, brought Abelard no peace. New controversies arose, and his situation became precarious when his enemies accused him of attacking the church. Abelard had written a book called *Sic et Non* (*Yes and No*) which listed conflicting opinions on points of doctrine ("yes" affirming and "no" negating) cited from the works of famous theologians. By showing that authorities sometimes disagreed, the book was intended to demonstrate that scholars had to do more to establish the truth of an opinion than quote respected thinkers. Abelard urged his contemporaries to use dialectical methods to critique all opinions, even those of the most revered fathers of the church. The church hierarchy, however, saw this as an attack on traditional beliefs that would result in the proliferation of heresy, and in 1141 a council of clergy condemned Abelard. He immediately set out for Rome to appeal to the pope, but he died on the way. His career might have been less stormy if he had been less brash, for the spirit of the age was with him. Dialectic was in the ascendancy, and his younger contemporary, Peter Lombard (d. 1160), produced a book (*Sentences*) similar to *Sic et Non* that became one of the medieval world's standard student texts.

Universities and Scholasticism

Monasteries dominated education in the early Middle Ages, but during the twelfth century leadership passed to cathedral towns (the seats of bishops). The move reflected a fundamental change in the nature of education. Monks were taught to respect authority and tradition and to sacrifice individuality to a communal ideal. Twelfth-century Europe, however—with its flourishing economy, rising towns, more complex institutions, and increasing contacts with the wider world—needed men who were trained to innovate, solve problems, and take individual initiative. The urban schools that trained church administrators and that had access to the wealth and the new information flowing into Europe were better situated than monasteries to meet this need.

The Academic Guild   Universities developed from local schools that became famous enough to attract an international clientele. The situation in which this clientele found itself prompted its organization as a university. The medieval world had no embassies or consulates and no international agreements to assist travelers and protect resident aliens. Foreign students and faculty had no legal rights in the towns where they studied and taught. They were, therefore, vulnerable to exploitation by landlords and abuse by government authorities. To strengthen their position, they banded together to form a guild or union—a *universitas* ("university"). Together, they had considerable leverage in negotiations with local leaders, for students were a source of income for a town. They rented rooms and bought food and other supplies. Because schools had no campuses or buildings, students and faculty could easily pack up and threaten to take their business to another community. Many of Europe's famous universities were created by migrations of disgruntled academics.

The earliest known charter according legal recognition to an academic *universitas* was issued in 1158 to a school in Bologna, Italy, that was governed by students. The student council employed the university's professors, oversaw its curriculum, and even regulated methods of instruction. Bologna emphasized the study of law and attracted older, career-driven students. Most medieval universities, such as the famous one chartered in Paris in 1200, were faculty guilds.

Teachers and students in the first medieval universities made do with whatever facilities they could find. A man who was licensed by a university guild to teach would set up a lectern (reading desk) in the side aisle of a church or some other public building. His students would stand or sit on the floor around him. Latin was used for instruction and much casual conversation, for it was the only language that all members of the academic community had in common. Many students had no books or writing materials, for these things were expensive. They might use wax-covered boards for taking notes, but medieval scholars trained themselves to memorize what they heard and read. They carried prodigious amounts of information in their heads. Professors (*profiteor*, "to educate") taught by glossing texts. That is, they read a passage from a book and then commented on it, explaining its meaning and spelling out its implications. There were no course exams and no grading system. Students (sometimes as young as 10) were completely on their own. They drifted from teacher to teacher and school to school until they felt that they were ready to apply for membership in the teachers' guild. As with any guild, those who aspired to join (that is, become "masters") were required to produce a masterpiece that demonstrated their command of their craft. An aspiring master shoemaker, for instance, submitted a pair of shoes for examination by the officials of the shoemakers' guild. Candidates for academic guilds submitted theses—propositions that they were prepared to defend in public debate before the whole university community. Graduate programs in modern universities perpetuate this custom. Candidates for degrees conduct original research, write theses or dissertations, and then defend their ideas before committees composed of experts in their fields.

Entry level students in medieval universities were "bachelors of arts," young males who were learning the basics of medieval education, the seven liberal arts of the *trivium* and the *quadrivium* (see Chapter 8). The members of the guild who taught these subjects were "masters of arts." A lengthy course of advanced study in a specialized field earned a scholar the highest academic title, *doctor* ("teacher"). The most prestigious degree was the doctorate in theology. Medieval society was organized hierarchically, and people dressed to reflect their social rank. Academics wore gowns appropriate to their place within the university, and on ceremonial occasions faculty and students of American universities still don the

Medieval Scholar   This miniature from a fifteenth-century manuscript illustrates a twelfth-century scholar, Matthaeus Platearius, at work writing a medical text. It is likely idealized, for few medieval scholars may have been able to afford such comfortable quarters and expensive clothing.

robes and hoods that served their medieval predecessors as overcoats and head coverings.

Scholasticism and the Influence of Aristotle
Medieval scholars never completely threw off their respect for the authority of ancient texts. They took it for granted that the Bible, the church fathers, and the great ancient philosophers all spoke the truth, and they sometimes trusted what these sources said more than the evidence of their own eyes. Universities, however, promoted a more liberal way of thinking that diminished reliance on authority and valued independent investigation. Their scholars were struggling to organize a flood of information from Muslim and Byzantine sources, and rational critiques seemed to offer the best hope for reconciling the diversity of opinions found in their sources. The medieval university nurtured the open-minded spirit of inquiry that characterizes modern Western civilization at its best.

The men who worked at the new schools are called Scholastics. Modern students may find their dialectical methods and arguments tedious, but the great Scholastics were exciting, original thinkers. Although some of them wrote beautiful poetry, their scholarly interests were in the use of language as science, not art. They sought solutions to problems by refining definitions of terms and spinning out incredibly subtle logical arguments. They used language with the precision of mathematics.

The Scholastics owed much to the arrival in Europe during the second half of the twelfth century of the New Logic, previously unknown treatises on logic by the ancient Greek philosopher Aristotle. Europeans' appetite for Aristotle had been whetted by their study of the works of his great Muslim interpreters Avicenna (Abu ali ibn Sina, 980–1037) and Averroës (Ibn-Rushd, 1126–1198). During the thirteenth century, all of Aristotle's works that had survived from antiquity gradually became available to European scholars in Latin versions taken directly from the original Greek. Their impact was revolutionary. Aristotle was the fulfillment of a medieval scholar's dream. He was the primary authority on the rules for constructing logical arguments, and he wrote on a huge range of subjects.

The church was initially alarmed by the enthusiasm scholars manifested for Aristotle, for some of his ideas were incompatible with Christian theology. Aristotle, for instance, maintained that the universe had to be eternal and uncreated, for the alternative (i.e., something arising from nothing) was a logical absurdity. In 1210 a church council tried to protect faith by censoring Aristotle's works and limiting their use, but it was impossible to force the Aristotelian genie back into his bottle. Aristotle quickly became required reading for every serious scholar. Some medieval thinkers simply accepted the conflict between his philosophy and the church's teachings and declared that there were two kinds of truth—one of faith and one of reason. But the era's greatest thinkers—notably, Albertus Magnus (1193–1280) and his student Thomas Aquinas (1225–1274)—devoted their lives to reconciling Aristotle's insights with Christian doctrine. Aquinas did such a masterful job that the Roman Catholic Church has endorsed his theological *summae* as definitive explications of its faith. Aquinas believed that reason and faith were complementary methods for understanding reality. Reason began a journey that only faith could complete. Some medieval scholars attacked Aquinas's work, but the logic of his *summae* was so compelling that they were difficult to undermine. The *summae* were also so comprehensive that Aquinas's followers had little left to do but to comment on and explicate his insights.

Not all medieval intellectuals were equally enthusiastic about dialectic and the influence of Aristotle. John of Salisbury, among others, complained that dialectic substituted narrow vocational training for true education. He championed a broader humanist curriculum based on the study of classical literature. Even at the peak of **Scholasticism**'s popularity, there were critics who used the tools of dialectic to counter what they regarded as the Scholastics' excessive rationalism.

Religious Revival and Diversity of Opinion

A surge of religious enthusiasm energized the cultural creativity of the High Middle Ages by creating a constructive intellectual tension between feeling and reason. The passionately faithful stressed the importance of experience and intuition and cautioned against the era's drift toward excessive rationality. Curiously, however, the religious enthusiasts' exaltation of the practice of faith and direct experience of God over mere speculation about divine mysteries sometimes inspired challenges to traditional beliefs and institutions similar to those that the rationalists posed.

Monastic Innovations   The religious fervor of the High Middle Ages sparked a renewal of interest in monasticism. But recruits did not flock to the older Benedictine houses that Cluny had reformed in the tenth century. They were drawn to new, stricter orders that restored the asceticism and simplicity of the original Benedictine Rule.

The emergence of new monastic ideals was forecast by a hermetical movement at the end of the eleventh century that was officially recognized (about 1130) as the Carthusian Order. Carthusians worshiped as a community but lived alone as hermits in isolated cells where they worked with their hands and practiced rigorous self-denial. Their order was too strict to attract large numbers, but it was so disciplined that it never needed reform. Far more popular was the Cistercian order that sprang up in the first half of the twelfth century. Cistercians eschewed the richly ornamented sanctuaries and elaborate rituals characteristic of the old Benedictine houses. They refused gifts of rich estates worked by serfs and established their houses on wasteland where they labored to support themselves. Many survived by herding sheep and supplying wool to Europe's thriving cloth industry. They were such successful developers that the barren lands to which they fled in pursuit of simplicity and spirituality made them rich and powerful.

So many monastic orders appeared during the twelfth century that the papacy finally decided to authorize no more. But in the early thirteenth century, it made an exception for some orders that redefined the monastic vocation. Monks traditionally withdrew from the world to devote themselves to prayer. Their vocation was to beseech God's mercy and forgiveness for the world's sins, but not to change a world that God had destined for final judgment and destruction. The confident atmosphere of the High Middle Ages, however, nurtured a greater sense of responsibility for working to improve the world. Some people who felt called to devote their lives totally to God wanted to embrace traditional monastic asceticism but not retreat to a cloister. They wanted to stay in the work-a-day world and engage in a struggle to ease suffering and save souls. A man who embraced this new kind of religious vocation was called a **friar** (*frater*, "brother"). The pattern for the life of a friar was set by the son of a prosperous Italian cloth merchant, Francis of Assisi (1181–1226).

Francis initially immersed himself in all the pleasures life offers handsome, wealthy young men. But at some point a religious conversion convinced him that God was calling him to model his life on the example set by Jesus and the Apostles. Francis believed that Jesus and his companions had no possessions and trusted entirely to God to provide for them while they went about preaching and healing. He, therefore, gave away everything he had and became a mendicant, a wandering beggar. Francis drifted about preaching and doing what he could for the poor. He ordered his followers never to keep anything in reserve for the future, but immediately to share everything they were given or earned with the needy. His radical vision of a religious fellowship that pinned its survival entirely on a constant stream of charitable offerings was soon moderated by church authorities. They devised a legal fiction that allowed the friars to enjoy the kinds of endowments that supported traditional monasteries while still claiming not to own any property. Endowments were forthcoming, for the friars' highly visible work among the laity made them the most popular and respected of medieval clergy.

In 1216 a second order of friars was founded by a Spanish priest named Dominic de Guzmán (1170–1221). Dominic was attracted to evangelism, and his plan was to become a missionary. The pope, however, sent him to southern France to deal with another product of the religious revival of the twelfth century—heresy. The Dominicans—officially, the Order of Preachers (or Black Friars, from the color of their robes)—were educators. They were trained to preach and to supplement the limited religious instruction and pastoral care the laity received from parish priests. They hoped that by engaging people's intellects and by setting them an example of Christ-like living, they could combat religious error. The Franciscans' founder was a poet who imbued their order with a deep appreciation for the emotional, mystical aspect of faith. The Dominicans, in contrast, appealed to people who preferred a cooler, more intellectual religion. Although the Dominicans recruited some of the era's most important scholars, others were drawn to the Franciscans, and both orders played major roles at the medieval universities. Their work and popular appeal may have served to mitigate, but it did not halt, criticism of the regular clergy and the spread of heresy.

PEOPLE IN CONTEXT William IX, Duke of Aquitaine and Count of Poitou (1071–1127)

S aints and scholars were not the only contributors to the robust civilization of the High Middle Ages. The era had a thriving popular culture that produced innovative art, music, and literature. Early medieval entertainers had chanted epic poems featuring stolid, one-dimensional warrior-heroes, such as Beowulf and Roland. But the audiences of the High Middle Ages had a taste for something more individual, passionate, and intimate. They were attracted to lyric poetry, music, and romance. Students at universities composed Latin lyrics (on both sacred and profane themes), but the pioneers of vernacular poetry were the troubadours (*trovar*, "inventor") who appeared first in southern France. The names of about 460 troubadours (some of whom were women) have survived.

Troubadours were either aristocrats or artists who depended on the nobility's patronage. Prominent among the early notables was a lord of exalted rank, Duke William IX of Aquitaine. As duke of Aquitaine and count of Poitou, he presided over about one-third of France. His domain was not only large, but it boasted a uniquely rich and sophisticated culture—thanks, in part, to contact with Muslim Spain (whence the inspiration for the new poetry may have come). William was a worldly man who was more inclined to enjoy this life than prepare for the next. The great adventure for noblemen of his generation was the crusade, and the success of the First Crusade prompted him to raise an army and set off for Jerusalem. Unfortunately, he blundered into an ambush while crossing Asia Minor and lost most of his men. He and similarly ill-fated, free-lance campaigners were blamed for restoring the confidence of the crusaders' Muslim opponents.

William was not a man to dwell on setbacks. His poetry is enlivened by a sense of humor, self-mockery, and sheer physical joy at being alive. The songs he composed celebrate the pleasures of rides through the sunny Provençal countryside and his delight in the company (apparently intimate) of beautiful women. The troubadour's primary theme was love—a passionate emotion but one to be governed by elaborate etiquette. Modern literary critics call the fad that troubadour poetry began "**courtly love**," an elegant game of courtship played by

Troubadours   This illustration from a medieval manuscript depicts a band of entertainers: a singing troubadour accompanied by a viol and a flute player.

medieval aristocrats (courtiers). The courtly lover placed the woman he adored "on a pedestal." He praised her as a paragon of beauty and virtue and pledged to endure any hardship in exchange for the slightest sign of her favor. His love for her drove him to realize the best in himself. William's granddaughter, the Eleanor of Aquitaine who became England's queen, continued the duke's tradition of providing patronage for poets, and the troubadour culture that she and her daughters spread through Europe did much to turn its rude feudal warriors into civilized, cultivated gentlemen.

Question: Would the kind of praise that troubadours heaped on women have contributed to the empowerment of women in medieval society?

■ ■ ■ ■ ■ ■ ■

Return of Heresy   The general decline of European culture during the early Middle Ages had reduced the threat of heresy by diminishing intellectual speculation of all kinds. But as levels of education and literacy rose in the twelfth century, heresy returned. People who learned to read could access the Scriptures and decide for themselves what they believed God required from the church and its clergy. Inevitably, some concluded that the conduct of the religious establishment fell far short of Christ's standard. Glaringly obvious was the fact that the lives of the popes, who claimed to be Christ's vicars on Earth, and many of the clergy bore little resemblance to those of Christ and his disciples. The Franciscans and Dominicans were able implicitly to criticize the church on these grounds without breaking with it, but others were less successful at steering such a delicate course.

In the 1170s (a decade or more before Francis of Assisi's birth) a merchant from the French city of Lyons named Peter Waldo heard the Scriptures' call to live the Christ-like life and responded in ways that anticipated Francis and the friars. He gave away his property and devoted himself to serving the poor. When local clergy objected to what they regard as Peter's transgression on their turf, he and his followers became more radical. Like the Protestants produced by the Reformation of the sixteenth century, the Waldensians insisted that the Bible was the only authority binding on Christians. They repudiated the pope and the priesthood and claimed that faithful lay people could administer the sacraments (the Christian rituals that mediate God's saving grace) for themselves. The pope condemned the Waldensians in 1184, but the movement spread and survived. Waldensian churches can be found today in Europe, South America, and the United States.

A more extreme form of religious dissent rooted itself in the south of France. Some historians believe that the religion of the Cathars ("the Pure") or Albigensians (from Albi, a town that a contemporary may have unfairly branded as a center of the heresy) spread into western Europe from the Balkans with the trade that surged in the eleventh century. The Cathars preached a dualistic faith similar to the Gnostic cults that had competed with Christianity during the last centuries of the Roman Empire. They claimed that an evil demon, not the true God, had created the material world and imprisoned souls in flesh. They taught that extreme asceticism could free the soul from a cycle of reincarnation and return it to the realm of pure spirit where God reigned. The Cathars attracted a large following, for their ascetics were more admirable spiritual exemplars than many of the church's clergy. When preaching and threats failed to counter the heresy, the church resorted to force. In

1208 the pope called for a crusade to root out the Cathars, and the lords of northern France seized on it as an excuse to grab rich lands for themselves in the south. The war raged for 20 years and devastated what had been one of Europe's most culturally advanced regions.

Mysticism and the Limits of Reason   Mystical currents have always coursed through Christianity, but they flowed with great vigor at the start of the twelfth century. Mystics have experiences of God that transcend reason and understanding and that give them, in the opinion of other Christians, a kind of prophetic authority. The twelfth-century renaissance produced one of the greatest of the medieval mystics, Bernard of Clairvaux (1090–1153). Although he was abbot of a Cistercian monastery, he was no recluse. He advised kings and popes and was the driving force behind the Second Crusade (see Chapter 9). He devoted some of his considerable energy to destroying the pioneering scholar, Abelard, and to opposing the kind of dialectical approach to theology that Abelard advocated. Bernard believed that knowledge of God came from an encounter with God—that it was mediated by love, not reason.

Many of Bernard's contemporaries shared his passionate approach to faith, and mysticism was not confined to monks and clergy. It influenced the pious practices of the laity. It inspired artists, motivated reform movements, and helped some women escape the constraints that medieval society imposed on their gender. Female mystics and visionaries were particularly plentiful during the second half of the Middle Ages. Some earned such respect that kings, popes, and prominent male intellectuals sought their advice. Bernard held women in low regard, but even he made an exception for two: the Virgin Mary and Hildegard of Bingen (1098–1179). The latter was a visionary nun, a poet, a composer, a physician, and an astute dialectician who carried on a large correspondence with the leading men of her day. In recent years, modern audiences have rediscovered the pleasures of the music she wrote for her sisters to perform.

Mysticism was not willful ignorance. Some of the great thinkers of the High Middle Ages were mystics who used dialectical methods to argue their positions. Bonaventure (1221–1274), a Franciscan scholar and faculty colleague of Thomas Aquinas's, was one of the most influential of these. He, like the early Latin theologian Augustine of Hippo (354–430), believed that human reason is untrustworthy because it, like the rest of human nature, is corrupted by original sin. Reason, he argued, describes the surface of things and provides superficial knowledge unless it is enlightened by love and divine grace. Only an individual who has had an experience of transcendence can intuit truth—the ultimate divine reality that the created world merely symbolizes. Aquinas himself may have come around to Bonaventure's point of view. Toward the end of his life Aquinas is said to have had a mystical experience that so overwhelmed him that he ceased to write.

The Artistic Vision of the High Middle Ages

For medieval mystics such as Bonaventure, the world was filled with visible things that symbolized the invisible truths of faith. That was the purpose of much ecclesiastical architecture, and nothing better captured the spirit of Europe's medieval civilization than the great churches that were erected during the High Middle Ages.

New churches sprang up everywhere during the twelfth and thirteenth centuries. In France, where much of the era's architectural innovation took place, more than 80 cathedrals and thousands of lesser churches were built. A town of 5,000 people might have as many as 50 parish churches, and some cities built cathedrals large enough to house their entire populations. The sheer volume of construction was remarkable, but so were its products. The new churches of the High Middle Ages so perfectly expressed Christianity's transcendent faith that even today they continue to influence the design of Christian houses of worship.

Origin of Christian Architecture   Early Christianity had no architecture of its own. The first Christian congregations were small, poor, and met in the homes of their members or in the open air. So long as persecution threatened, it was not safe for Christians to design buildings that advertised their presence. Only after Emperor Constantine legalized the faith in the fourth century were conditions right for Christianity to evolve an architectural vocabulary of its own.

The church grew so rapidly after Constantine endorsed it that there was no time to invent a new kind of space to house its proliferating congregations. Bishops simply appropriated and consecrated existing public buildings. The Roman Empire's standard

The Basilica of Santa Maria Maggiore   Rome's Church of Santa Maria Maggiore dates to the fifth century and is a splendid example of an early Christian basilica. Its lavish decoration tends to obscure the simplicity of its design—a flat-ceilinged rectangular building consisting of a nave, apse, and side aisles.

multipurpose building was the basilica, a simple rectangular hall (nave) with a rounded bay (apse) at one end to house the office of the building's administrator. Additional floor space was sometimes created by running parallel corridors (aisles) down the side-walls of the building. Basilicas had low-pitched roofs and were lit by windows cut in the wall above the level of the aisles (the clerestory).

The basic basilican design evolved to serve the needs of Christian worship. When more room was needed for the increasing number of clergy who chanted the liturgy, the apse was pushed out to create a space called the choir. Altars multiplied along the walls of the nave, and some expanded into side chapels. When large chapels appeared on op-posing sides of a nave, they created a transept or "crossing" that gave the floor plan of a church the shape of a cross. The blank walls and flat ceilings of basilicas were often en-livened with frescoes, mosaics, or other kinds of decoration.

In addition to rectangular basilicas, a circular church design also appeared in the late Roman period. It probably evolved from shrines built over the graves of saints. The design was particularly popular in the Middle East, and its association with some of the lavish sanctuaries of the Byzantine Empire may explain why Charlemagne chose it for his great church at Aachen. It appealed to the crusaders as well. The Templars, one of the orders of warrior monks, often built round churches.

Romanesque Style   Basilican churches spread to northern Europe in the early Middle Ages, but they were not well adapted to its environment. Their low-pitched wooden roofs were prone to rot in climates damper than those of the sunny Mediter-ranean. The weight of northern snows stressed them, and they were vulnerable to fires. A pious desire to honor Christianity's eternal God with eternal buildings may also have motivated the search for ways to replace wooden roofs with vaults of stone, the most durable building material then available.

Medieval architects began by copying the vaulting techniques used by the Romans. Roman buildings employed round arches. The simplest way to vault a nave was to line up lots of these arches, one next to another like slices of bread. This created a barrel vault, a tunnel-like room that was difficult to light. Because each part of the vault was supported by the wall immediately beneath it, it was risky to cut holes in the walls for windows. Walls also had to be very thick to counterbalance the lateral thrust from the arches that rested on their tops. The use of round arches also imposed design limita-tions. The ratio between the span and the height of a round arch was fixed. The only way to make a barrel-vaulted nave wider was to make it higher, but a point could soon be reached where the weight of the vault became too great to manage.

The medieval architect's **Romanesque** style featured round arches, thick walls, and small windows. It was popular in Italy, Spain, and southern France, for hot, sunny regions welcomed the shelter of dark, cave-like buildings. Romanesque churches continued to be erected in southern Europe long after the north had switched to the later **Gothic** style.

Romanesque architects tried to make their heavy buildings look less ponderous by covering them with elaborate decoration. False arcades were cut into walls to lighten their appearance, and blank spaces were filled with paintings, mosaics, and sheets of colored stone arranged in geometric patterns. But the Romanesque's fortress-like ap-

Romanesque Interior   This view of the nave of the early twelfth-century Church of St. Sernin, Toulouse, France, illustrates the environment typical of a Romanesque church. Its effect is imposing, but also dark and, despite the height of its vault, somewhat oppressive.

pearance fit the defensive mood of the early Middle Ages, and it served well for monastic retreats from the world. The confident, expansionist spirit that pervaded the towns of the high Middle Ages, however, called for something more open and audacious.

Gothic Style

Gothic Style   The first church in the Gothic style (the supreme achievement of the medieval architect) was erected about 1140 at France's royal monastery, St. Denis, near Paris. It was the work of the cloister's abbot, Suger (1081–1151), chief counselor to King Louis VI (r. 1108–1137) and King Louis VII (r. 1137–1180). (For their reigns, see Chapter 9.) By integrating a series of structural innovations, some of which dated back to the eleventh century, Suger invented a new kind of sacred space—one designed to maximize light as a symbol of God's presence. The inscription Suger placed on the door to his new church explained the purpose of the artistry that went into its creation: "Meditation on material things lifts the intellect from lethargy and enables it to grasp the truth."

The most distinctive feature of Gothic architecture is the pointed or broken arch. Gothic architects escaped the limitations imposed by the geometry of the Romanesque's round arch by "breaking" it at its apex. A pointed arch has no fixed ratio between its height and span—its apex can be pitched at any height. It serves as a kind of hinge for halves of an arc that can be widened or narrowed as a builder wants.

By combining pointed arches with rib-vaulting (a technique that Romanesque architects developed), Gothic architects could erect vaults over rectangular or irregular spaces. Rib-vaulting was a significant improvement over the simple barrel vault. If the nave of a church was divided into squares, each square could be vaulted by running round arches not from side to side, but between diagonal corners. These arches (the ribs) intersected over the center of the square and light masonry was used to fill in the spaces between them. They functioned as a built-in scaffolding that bore much of the vault's weight. They also gave an architect more control over the thrust from a vault, for ribs focused the weight they carried on the points where they intersected with the walls. Walls had to be buttressed (thickened) at these places to compensate for that weight, but the reduction of pressure on the wall between the buttresses meant that more of the wall could be cut away to create a window.

Gothic architects allowed even more light into their churches by preventing buttresses from shading the windows near them. They planted buttresses some distance from their

Gothic Interior   Paris's Sainte-Chapelle illustrates how effective Gothic architects could be at lighting the interior of their buildings. Here walls have been replaced by a nearly continuous circuit of window.

buildings and used arches to link them to the pressure points where ribs intersected with walls. These "flying buttresses" turned a Gothic building into a kind of stone tent. The sheet of stone (the vaulting) that roofed it was held in place by stone "ropes" (arches) anchored to stone "pegs" (buttresses) around its perimeter. Because the ribs and buttresses carried most of the weight of the building, its walls could be replaced by vast expanses of window. Well-designed Gothic churches were so filled with light that medieval people called them glass houses.

During the second half of the twelfth century, the Gothic style spread rapidly from its birthplace in northern France throughout Europe. Towns spent phenomenal sums to construct ever larger, brighter, and more awe-inspiring sanctuaries. The record was set by the builders of the cathedral at Beauvais who, after several failed attempts, pitched a vault at the height of 157 feet—high enough to shelter a 14-story building.

The Gothic style captivated medieval people because it was so congruent with their faith and spiritual experience. The easiest way to understand this may be to compare Gothic churches with the temples of the ancient Greeks. Classical architecture reflected the belief that the world centered on the human being. A Greek temple, like Athens' Parthenon, was meant to assure people that the world was an intelligible place that affirmed human nature. The principles of its construction were not intended to be mysterious and awe-inspiring, but immediately obvious and comfortable. Vertical pillars supported horizontal lintels. Stone did what stone was expected to do.

A Gothic church creates the opposite impression. To convey Christianity's faith in a transcendent reality quite different from our own, it offers an experience of a supernatural world. A Gothic church encloses a divine space where nature's laws appear to be transcended. The Gothic architect conceals the principles of his building's construction so that the logic of its design is hidden from those who enter it. Vertical lines dominate the interior and pull the eye upward. The ribs of the vault seem to converge at infinity, and far overhead tons of rock apparently float on walls of light. There are windows on every side. However, their tinted glass prevents the worshiper from connecting the interior with the ordinary world outside and fills the sanctuary with unnatural light. From the engineering point of view, a Gothic church is a supremely rational structure, but one that uses reason to create the experience of irrational space. It is a place where nature, by seeming to behave supernaturally, fulfills Suger's mandate and turns the intellect from the seen to the unseen. A Gothic church is not just a place to hear about God's transcendence; it is a place to experience it.

The Nation-States of the High Middle Ages

The High Middle Ages witnessed decisive events leading to the formation of modern Europe. Carolingian dreams of empire receded, but so did the radical political fragmentation that set in with the decline of the Carolingian dynasty. As powerful states emerged and ethnic enclaves consolidated, Europeans' growing awareness of their diverse political and culture identities struggled with their heritage of a common religious faith.

England   A pattern of alternating strong and weak reigns helped define the institutions of the English monarchy. William the Conqueror (r. 1066–1087) and his sons, William Rufus (r. 1087–1100) and Henry I (r. 1100–1135), exploited the opportunity that conquest gave them to lay the foundations for a powerful royal government in England. Their work was undermined by the 20-year-long civil war (1135–1154) that raged between Matilda (1102–1167), Henry's daughter and only surviving legitimate child, and her cousin Stephen (r. 1135–1154). The truce that ended that war and brought Matilda's son, Henry II (r. 1154–1189), to the throne reversed England's course once again and restored the authority of its throne.

The French lands that Henry II inherited from his parents and acquired by marrying Eleanor of Aquitaine (c. 1122–1204) gave him immense resources, but he was no autocrat. His grandfather, Henry I, had implicitly conceded that England's king was accountable for the use of his powers, and Henry II affirmed the "liberties" that Henry I had promised the English people. Henry's attention was not focused exclusively on England. He had not been raised there and, like many of medieval England's kings, he did not speak English. He ruled a vast Angevin Empire (see Chapter 9) that included about half of France, and he was eager to expand his holdings on the continent.

Although Henry was often abroad, he did not neglect England. He stabilized its frontier with Scotland, brought parts of Wales under control, and invaded Ireland to win recognition of his lordship over the outposts that enterprising Norman warriors had taken the initiative to establish there. In 1172 the pope recognized the English king's claim to Ireland, but the Irish and English are still disputing their relationship.

Henry I greatly improved his kingdom's machinery of government, and Henry II continued his grandfather's work. William I had got off to a strong start by claiming all the land in England by right of conquest and requiring all property owners to contribute to the support of the crown. By preserving the Anglo-Saxon system of shires administered by sheriffs (commoners whom the king appointed), William also freed England's king from total dependence on landed aristocrats to carry out his will. Henry II staffed his government with professional bureaucrats who were trained in Europe's new schools, and he raised enough money to salary most of the men who worked for him. Instead of fighting in the king's army, his vassals were encouraged to pay scutage ("shield money"). This gave the king funds with which to hire professional soldiers, and it had the added benefit of pacifying noble warlords by turning them into a class of tax-paying landowners.

Henry courted support for the monarchy by increasing the services his subjects received directly from the crown. A king was expected to protect his people. This involved not only guarding frontiers from invasion, but preserving internal order by enforcing justice. The right to hold a court and administer justice was a privilege landowners coveted, for the fees and fines a court levied were a significant source of income. Henry took business away from the courts of his vassals by reserving some categories of crimes to the royal justice system. To make it easier for people to access the king's justice, he ordered judges to ride circuits about England. He also expanded the use of writs, documents that people could purchase to order royal officials to take action on their behalf.

The royal courts imposed a "common law," a single standard of justice, in England and developed procedures that are still used today. Henry's courts empaneled two kinds of juries. In order to ferret out criminals, grand (large) juries put local men under oath and ordered them to report any crimes that might have occurred in their communities. This created business for petit (small) juries, which heard cases and rendered verdicts. Juries could usually settle disputes about property, for local people could provide evidence about who owned what and for how long. It was often impossible, however, to gather evidence in criminal cases, so other methods were used to resolve them. **Compurgation** allowed the accused to clear their names by finding a certain number of people who would swear to their integrity. By identifying the most trustworthy party in a dispute, it increased the probability of rendering a just verdict. Sometimes suspects were forced to undergo ordeals—physical tests that risked injury or death. The theory was that God would protect the innocent, but by Henry's day enlightened governments were reducing their reliance on ordeals. In 1215 the pope contributed to the demise of the ordeal by prohibiting priests from receiving the oaths of innocence that ordeals supposedly tested.

As royal governments became more effective and assumed broader responsibilities, the potential for conflict between the church and the state increased. In England, the fight was triggered by Henry's efforts to improve enforcement of justice. In 1164 Henry's **Constitutions of Clarendon** clarified the relationship between his courts and those of the church. Two years earlier he had thrust priesthood and the office of archbishop of Canterbury on his friend, Thomas Becket (1118–1170), a commoner who was serving as England's chancellor (chief minister). Ordination changed Becket's loyalties and led him, in the opinion of some of his fellow bishops, to make extreme claims for the church. At issue was the treatment of clergy who were accused of crimes. Henry did not dispute the church's right to judge their cases, but he insisted that the guilty should be stripped of their clerical status and turned over to the state for punishment. This would ensure that lay and clerical criminals received the same penalties for the same crimes. Becket refused to accept this, fled England, and spent six years trying to turn international opinion against Henry. In 1170 he and Henry declared a truce. But when Becket returned to England, he infuriated Henry by excommunicating some royal officials. When Henry received this news, he made an intemperate remark that a few of his men interpreted as an order to kill Becket. On December 29, 1170, they forced their way into the cathedral of Canterbury and profaned its sanctity by slaughtering its archbishop. The scandalized medieval world instantly hailed Becket as a martyr. Miracles were credited to him, and three years after his death he was officially declared a saint. His tomb at Canterbury became a major pilgrim shrine, and Henry submitted to a whipping by Canterbury's monks as a penance for his part in Becket's murder.

The Becket defeat was humiliating, but the greatest threat to Henry came from his family. Queen Eleanor bore him five sons, and she and they plotted against him. Henry placed Eleanor under house arrest in 1174, and he managed to outlive three of their boys. But the remaining two (with the help of the French king) disrupted the last years of his reign.

Henry's heir was Richard I "the Lionhearted" (r. 1189–1199), a king whose popularity in English literature and folk memory far exceeds his achievements. Richard spent only eight months of his reign in England, and he was interested in his kingdom primarily as a source of revenue for foreign wars. Chief among these was the Third Crusade. In 1187 Saladin (1137–1193), a warrior of Kurdish descent, united the Muslims of the Middle East and retook Jerusalem. The people of Europe clamored for a new crusade, and Richard eagerly responded. He compelled France's young king, Philip II, "Augustus" (r. 1180–1223), to take the cross with him. Frederick I, "Barbarossa" (r. 1152–1190), Germany's aging emperor, agreed to go as well. The venture yielded little for all that was invested in it. Barbarossa drowned on his way to the Holy Land, and Philip Augustus withdrew as soon as possible. Richard lingered in the east, while Philip and Richard's brother, John, worked to undermine his position at home. In 1193 Richard tried to hurry back to his kingdom through the territory of a German enemy and was captured. Eleanor raised a huge ransom to win his release, and he spent his remaining years fighting to regain the French lands he had allowed to slip from his control. He died from a wound received in a skirmish with one of his own vassals.

Richard's successor was his disloyal brother, John (r. 1199–1216). John was neither stupid nor cowardly, but he was headstrong and had a talent for alienating people. He was also no match for Philip Augustus, who took Normandy from him. After he picked a needless quarrel with Pope Innocent III over the appointment of an archbishop for Canterbury, the pope closed all the churches in England and excommunicated John. John held out for six years, but in 1213, when the pope threatened him with deposition, he suddenly reversed course and took an oath of vassalage to the pope. John was developing an elaborate plan for winning back his French lands, and he did not want his vassals to use his quarrel with the church as an excuse to repudiate him.

In 1214 John, his cousin Otto of Brunswick, and the count of Flanders joined forces to invade France. Philip Augustus decisively defeated them at the Battle of Bouvines, and John fled back to England where his disgusted vassals were finally on the brink of revolt. He met them at Runymeade, west of London, and agreed to terms spelled out in the famous Magna Carta ("Great Charter"). Within two months, the document was a dead letter. The pope absolved John from his oath to honor it, for the pope believed subjects had no right to limit the authority of the kings God gave them. John's barons, however, believed that they could persuade God to give them a new king by inviting Philip Augustus's son, Louis, to invade England, depose John, and claim his throne.

The **Plantagenet** dynasty was saved by John's timely death. His heir was his 9-year-old son, Henry III (r. 1216–1272). England's rebellious barons, who preferred a weak child king to a powerful French prince, promptly switched their allegiance back to the English royal family. Henry's reign was one of the least successful in England's history, but its weakness had the effect of inching England further toward limited monarchy. Henry mismanaged England so badly that civil war broke out under the leadership of the king's brother-in-law, Simon de Montfort. In 1264, when the rebels captured Henry, Simon decided to convene a council to rally national support for an act that technically was treason. He invited the barons and church leaders who usually attended such meetings, but he also included representatives of England's shires and boroughs (towns). The result was the first session of what the French-speaking English court called **Parliament** (parler, "to speak").

Henry's son Edward, who was far more competent than his father, rallied the royalist forces, killed Simon (d. 1265), restored his father to the throne, and reversed the monarchy's decline. Edward was open to learning from his enemies. Although the first Parliament had been a rebel organization, Edward continued to convene parliaments for purposes of his own. England's kings were expected to meet the costs of government from their own incomes. If they needed more money, they had to ask their subjects for it. Parliament was an expedient way to do this. Medieval Parliaments were weak. Only the property-owning classes were represented in them, and they met only at the king's pleasure. But they survived, grew in importance, and ultimately became a model that has influenced the design of institutions of popular government throughout the modern world.

Edward I (r. 1272–1307) accomplished a great deal. He brought Wales under his control. He strengthened England's hold on parts of Ireland, and he was on the brink of subduing Scotland when he died. On the civilian front, he promulgated so much legislation that he has been called "the English Justinian." His interest in law and justice did not prevent him from raising money by expelling the Jews from England and confiscating their property. He also destroyed Italian banks by failing to repay the money he borrowed from them.

France   France's Capetian dynasty made slow progress, for its kings were often opposed by powerful English rulers and their own vassals. But the French monarchy reached a turning point in 1214, when Philip Augustus (r. 1180–1223) defeated England's King John at the Battle of Bouvines. Philip's victory secured his hold on northern France and tripled the royal estates and income. In 1208, when the pope called for a crusade against the Cathar heretics of southern France, Philip's soldiers answered and extended his influence into that region.

Philip reorganized royal government to enhance its ability to administer the lands he won. One of his major reforms was an improved method of tax collection. Earlier kings had relied on tax farmers to collect their dues. These men paid the treasury a fixed sum in exchange for the right to collect what was owed to the crown. Whatever additional money they extracted, they kept for themselves. Philip ended the corruption, abuse, and cheating this system invited by replacing tax farmers with salaried government officials.

When Philip died and passed the crown to his mature, experienced son, Louis VIII (r. 1223–1226), the future of the Capetian dynasty seemed secure. Philip had dispatched Louis to protect the crown's interests in the crusade against the Cathars, and Louis had extended royal influence to the shores of the Mediterranean. Despite this strong start, Louis

Caernarfon Castle   To secure his hold on the British Isles, Edward I invested heavily in the construction of castles. His most imposing were built in newly conquered Wales. To encourage the Welsh to accept the legitimacy of English rule, he arranged for his wife to give birth to his heir in Wales and dubbed the boy "Prince of Wales," the title the first in line to Britain's throne still bears.

ended by doing two things that endangered the future of his dynasty and the French monarchy. He died young—leaving the throne to a minor (a first for the Capetians), and his will carved out appanages (quasi-independent territories) from the royal estates for the boy king's three younger brothers.

Louis IX (r. 1226–1270) was only 12 years old when he inherited the throne. He faced a horde of powerful nobles who relished the opportunity a weak regency government gave them to cripple a monarchy that had become too strong for their tastes. Fortunately, the young king had an able defender—his mother, Blanche of Castile (1188–1252), grand-daughter of Eleanor of Aquitaine and England's Henry II. Her job was made easier by the tendency of France's nobles to squabble among themselves. England was small enough that its barons knew one another and sometimes agreed to form a common front against their king. This was less likely in France, which was four times England's size. Regional-ism was strong in France, and awareness of common interests developed slowly among nobles from different districts.

Louis IX grew up to become the most popular and respected of France's kings, and his reputation obliterated whatever doubts remained about the Capetians' divine right to the throne. Twenty-seven years after his death, the church declared him a saint. Louis was pious and inclined to personal asceticism, but these traits did not diminish his effective-ness as a king. He was a strong, courageous military man who sincerely believed that it was a Christian monarch's duty to protect the poor and weak and deliver justice. Louis re-strained France's nobles and limited the private warfare that ravaged its countryside. He made himself accessible to the humblest of his subjects and acted to right their grievances.

He sent out *enquêteurs* ("investigators") to audit the accounts of his officials and hear complaints against them. He relied on the *Parlement* of Paris (a group of legal advisors) to help him improve the professionalism of his administration. He settled territorial squabbles with neighboring kingdoms by making generous concessions, and his reputation for fairness was so great that other countries asked him to adjudicate their internal disputes.

France flourished under Louis's leadership, but the Christian principles that inspired his virtues as a leader also clouded his judgment. He persecuted Jews and persons accused of heresy, and he squandered his country's resources on two crusades that had little likelihood of success. In 1249 he led an elaborately equipped expedition into Egypt. The Muslims cut off his supply lines. Disease broke out in his army, and it was forced to surrender. A huge ransom had to be paid to win Louis's release, but even then he was reluctant to give up and return to France. He never relinquished the dream of winning back Jerusalem, and in July of 1270 he set out on a second crusade. This time he attacked Tunis, intending to work his way across North Africa and Egypt to the Holy Land. Seven weeks into this campaign, he died of a disease that ravaged his army.

Louis had prepared his son, Philip III (r. 1270–1285), for the duties of kingship, but Philip lacked his father's talent and charisma. Philip was overawed by his forceful uncle, Charles of Anjou (1227–1285), who was determined to carve out a kingdom for himself in Italy and Sicily. Philip died shortly after leading a futile expedition into Spain in support of his uncle. The throne then passed to Philip's much more competent son, Philip IV, "the Fair" (r. 1285–1314)(see Chapter 11).

Germany and Italy

France, like Germany, was tempted to try to expand into Italy, but the German experience should have warned the French of the risks of such a policy. Two strong German dynasties, the Saxon and the Salian, tried to join Italy to Germany, and both were defeated by the combined efforts of popes, Italian cities, and truculent German nobles.

The premature death of Henry V (r. 1105–1125) ended the Salian dynasty and began a quarter-century-long tug of war for the German throne. Two factions contended: the Welfs (**Guelfs**) who backed the duke of Saxony-Bavaria, and the Waiblingens (**Ghibelline**s) who supported the duke of Swabia. Kings were chosen, but none was more than a figurehead.

In 1152 the Waiblingen candidate, Frederick I, "Barbarossa" ("Red Beard"), won out over the young Welf duke, Henry the Lion (1129–1195). Frederick (r. 1152–1190), whose mother was Henry the Lion's aunt, was a compromise candidate, and it was hoped that his ties to both ducal factions would persuade them to work together. Frederick established his authority and broke up some of the German duchies. But whereas France's Capetian kings added the lands they conquered to the royal domain and ruled them directly, the German nobles forced Frederick to grant his acquisitions as fiefs. Germany, therefore, remained a fragmented collection of baronies over which the king had only indirect control.

The Hohenstaufen dynasty that Frederick founded pinned its hopes on Italy. Its base, the duchy of Swabia, in the southwestern corner of Germany, was poorly situated to be the capital of a German kingdom, but it was ideally located to become the center of a Roman Empire that united Germany and Italy. Frederick expanded his control of territory on Italy's northern frontier by marrying the heiress to the kingdom of Burgundy, which lay west of his duchy. In 1161 he forced the rich towns of northern Italy (Lombardy) to come to terms. However, as soon as he turned his attention back to Germany, they and the pope colluded against him. In 1176 he lost a battle to the Lombards and was forced to compromise. The cities recognized his overlordship, but retained the right of self-government. A decade later a bit of luck tipped the balance of power in Italy in the Hohenstaufens' favor. Frederick's daughter-in-law, Constance, inherited the kingdoms of Sicily and Naples from her nephew, William II (r. 1166–1189). This surrounded the Papal States with Hohenstaufen territory and opened the way for Frederick to consolidate his hold on Italy. At this point, however, the Third Crusade distracted the aging king, and he headed for Constantinople at the head of the greatest crusading army ever assembled. He drowned before reaching the Holy Land.

Frederick's son, Henry VI (r. 1190–1197), was a competent king, but his reign was brief. His heir (another Frederick) was only 2 years old when he died. The Hohenstaufens' enemies seized the opportunity this gave them to try to topple the dynasty. The young heir's claim to the throne was ignored. He was shunted aside in Sicily while Philip of Swabia, his uncle, and Otto of Brunswick (c. 1174–1218), the head of the Guelf party, battled each other for control of Germany. Pope Innocent III (r. 1198–1216), whose reign began just as their war was breaking out, tried to prolong the fight in order to keep them out of Italy. This worked until Philip was assassinated in 1209. When the victorious Otto then staked a claim to Italy, the pope remembered Frederick, the forgotten Hohenstaufen heir.

Frederick II (r. 1215–1250) was such a remarkable man that his contemporaries nicknamed him *Stupor Mundi,* "Wonder of the World." The young king was an athlete, a warrior, and an intellectual. He was fluent in six languages. He sponsored scientific research, wrote a book on the art of falconry (which survives), founded a university, and gave Sicily a constitution that was a model of centralized monarchy. Frederick believed that a king's duties extended beyond policing and protecting his people. Frederick managed Sicily's economy and even issued environmental regulations to protect air and water quality.

In exchange for the church's support, Pope Innocent elicited a promise from Frederick that he would not rule both halves of Italy, but Frederick had no intention of keeping his word. He grew up as a Sicilian and had little experience of, or interest in, Germany. After defeating Otto and claiming the crown, he allowed the German barons to do as they wished in order to be free to concentrate on Italy. In hopes of distracting Frederick from Italy, the pope persuaded him to go on crusade. But he was so slow to act on his crusader vow that by the time he finally sailed for the Holy Lands in 1228, the pope had excommunicated him. When he arrived in the Middle East, he negotiated with the Muslims and persuaded them to hand Jerusalem over to him without a fight. The pope was appalled that an excommunicate had succeeded where so many faithful crusaders had failed and responded by declaring war on Frederick. Frederick spent the rest of his life battling with the papacy and the Lombard cities. He forced the pope to flee Italy, and its cities would probably have yielded to him had he been a bit more compromising. In the end, his opponents were saved when the king contracted dysentery and died.

Frederick had so alarmed his enemies that they joined forces, tracked down his heirs, and exterminated his dynasty. Germany's empty throne once again became a prize for which many were eager to compete. However, the German barons, who fattened on bribes from candidates, were in no hurry to choose a new king. From 1254 to 1272 the throne remained in dispute, and without a strong king, there was no hope of countering Germany's drift toward political fragmentation.

As Germany retreated, a new threat to Italy's cities and the papacy appeared. Louis IX's brother, Charles of Anjou, invaded and seized control of southern Italy and Sicily. In 1282 the Sicilians drove the French out and offered themselves to one of Spain's monarchs, the king of Aragon. The French held on to Naples, but instead of focusing on Italy, they invested their resources in futile attempts to conquer Hungary and the Balkans.

The progress that artists and intellectuals made during the High Middle Ages was only partially matched by kings and politicians. Rulers sought and received help from scholars and university-trained lawyers that enabled them to construct and staff the most effective governments Europe had seen since the passing of the Roman Empire. But the results were mixed. The English and French monarchies flourished and advanced the consolidation of their realms, but the story was very different in Italy and Germany.

KEY QUESTION | Revisited

A society consists of many things (economic, political, and social) that must work together if it is to remain viable. A change in any one of them forces the others to adjust. Because coordination and accommodation can be difficult and outcomes can be uncertain, people tend to fear change. When their traditional institutions and values begin to fail, their first impulse may not be to try something new, but to reaffirm the past—to try harder to make the old ways work. Familiar things are reassuring, for they have a record of success. A new thing often stirs up anxiety, for it has not been tested. Commitment to it requires an act of faith. Ideally, this faith is an informed belief that has grounds for probable success. But a society's attitude toward change is always determined to some degree by how much it is willing to trust—by how much confidence it has in its ability to understand the world and rise to its challenges.

The dominant intellectual faith that gave thinkers of the High Middle Ages the courage to innovate was a belief that existence would ultimately be discovered to be a rationally coherent, unified system—that everything that human beings learned from experience or received by revelation and faith could be integrated into an intelligible, universal order.

This faith was encouraged by progress toward rationalization and integration on numerous fronts. An international intellectual community appeared, using a common language and training itself in similar schools. It developed methods of research that enabled it to organize, analyze, and exploit the flood of information from Muslim and Byzantine sources that threatened to inundate Europe in the twelfth and thirteenth centuries. The radical fragmentation that had overtaken governments and societies in the wake of the invasions of the Vikings, Magyars, and Muslims began to be reversed—at least in parts of Europe. Clearer rationales for institutions and policies were developed. More sophisticated governments provided a wider range of services. Artists and poets created new forms of entertainment that stimulated the popular imagination and encouraged new codes of conduct. New kinds of religious vocations earned new respect for the clergy and

Political Leaders of the High Middle Ages

ENGLAND	FRANCE	GERMANY	THE PAPACY
Henry I (1100–1135)	Louis VI (1108–1137)	Henry V (1106–1125)	
Stephen (1135–1154)	Louis VII (1137–1180)	[Civil War, 1125–1152]	
Henry II (1154–1189)		Frederick I (1152–1190)	
	Philip II (1180–1223)		
Richard I (1189–1199)		Henry VI (1190–1197)	
John (1199–1216)		Philip & Otto (1198–1214)	Innocent III (1198–1216)
Henry III (1216–1272)	Louis VIII (1223–1226)	Frederick II (1215–1250)	
Edward I (1272–1307)	Louis IX (1226–1270)	[Interregnum 1254–1273]	
	Philip III (1270–1285)		
Edward II (1307–1327)	Philip IV (1285–1314)		

focused some of the church's resources on dealing with social ills. And architects created environments that had never before been experienced—churches in which the rational skills of engineers superbly served the transcendent visions of religious faith.

Bernard of Chartres's "dwarfs" had much of which they could be proud, but their *summae* remained incomplete. The presumed coherence of the world proved frustratingly difficult to capture in a simple rational model. Dialecticians fought among themselves and with mystics. Skeptics questioned reason's ability to search out truth. Reformers and heretics rebelled against traditional institutions and authorities. Consolidation of states led to larger wars, not peace, and promising crusades ended in defeat. None of this, however, persuaded Europeans to alter course. Their faith in their ability to master a changing world was, however, soon to be severely tested.

Review Questions

1. How did intellectual life change in Europe with the appearance of universities?
2. What was dialectic? Why were the scholars of the High Middle Ages preoccupied with it?
3. How did religious enthusiasm affect the cultural and political environments of the High Middle Ages? Were its effects positive or negative?
4. How did Romanesque architecture differ from Gothic? Did theology influence the differences between the two styles?
5. How did the development of the French and English monarchies differ?
6. Why did German kings persist in trying to conquer Italy?

 Please consult the Suggested Readings at the back of the book to continue your study of the material covered in this chapter. For a list of documents on the Primary Source DVD-ROM that relate to topics in this chapter, please refer to the back of the book.

Part 4
Challenges, Conflicts, and Departures
1300 to 1700

The World in 1570. *Dagli Orti (A)/Picture Desk, Inc./Kobal Collection*

■ Throughout the Middle Ages, Europeans believed that they were tucked away in the northwestern corner of the world. People had known at least since the time of the ancient Greeks that the world was round, but geographers argued that nature blocked avenues for exploration. They assumed that the Arctic wastes limited movement north and that it was impossible to sail far west across the trackless Atlantic. They also believed that because temperatures grew warmer as one headed south, a zone of intolerable heat formed a barrier between the northern and southern hemispheres. Europe's only access to the lands of the Far East (the source of exotic silks and spices it desired) was therefore through Russia and the Middle East, journeys of thousands of miles across hostile territory. A few European merchants and missionaries made the trip, but direct contact with these fabled places was rare.

All of this changed at the end of the fifteenth century when Europeans discovered that the Atlantic was not a barrier to their exploration of the wider world, but a highway providing them with access to lands both known and unknown. They were amazed to discover that the world was much larger than they had ever imagined, and the initiative they took in exploring it gave them a new sense of their place in it. The Mediterranean and the Middle East became less important to them, as they began to envision a new world order centered on their western European homelands.

	ENVIRONMENT AND TECHNOLOGY	SOCIETY AND CULTURE	POLITICS
c. 1200	Marco Polo (1254–1324) Dante (1265–1321)	Western Europe: Population Growth and land clearance	Ayyubid Empire Mamluk sultanate Mongol invasions *German Interregnum* (1254–1273) Habsburg dynasty
c. 1300	Giotto (1226–1337) **Italian Renaissance** Petrarch (1304–1374) Chaucer (1340–1400)	"Little Ice Age" commences The Great Pestilence (1347–1350) First appearance of Cannons	Estates General (1302) Avignese papacy (1305–1377) Timur the Lame (1336–1404) Hundred Years' War (1337–1453) Golden Bull (1356) Great Schism (1378–1415) Ottoman dynasty
c. 1400	Conciliarism Joan of Arc (1412–1431) da Vinci (1452–1519) Erasmus (1466–1536)	Portuguese explorations (1430) Printing press (1446)	Council of Constance (1415) Constantinople falls (1453) Ottoman Empire Tudor dynasty
c. 1500	Michelangelo (1475–1564) Martin Luther (1483–1546) **Protestant Reformation** Diet of Worms (1521) English Reformation (1534) Council of Trent (1545–1563) Edict of Nantes (1598)	Columbus's first voyage (1492) Disease ravages the Americas Global circumnavigation (1522) Exports from the Americas change Europe	Safavid dynasty Aztecs fall (1519) Charles V (1519–1556) Süleyman (1520–1566) Incas fall (1529) Habsburg-Valois Wars (1525–1544) St. Bartholomew's Day Massacre (1572) Spanish Armada (1588)
c. 1600	Shakespeare (1564–1616)		Thirty Years' War (1618–1648) English Civil War (1642–1646) Puritan Republic (1649–1660)

11 Challenges to the Medieval Order

Age of sorrow and temptation, of tears, jealousy and torment,
Time of exhaustion and damnation, declining to extinction,
Era filled with horror and deception, lying, pride and envy,
Time without honor and meaning, full of life-shortening sadness.

—Eustache Deschamps

KEY | Question

What did the crises of the late medieval era reveal about the strengths and weaknesses of Europe's civilization?

The verses quoted above are from a poem by Eustache Deschamps (c. 1346–1406) in which he laments the dismal prospects of his generation. His disillusionment is understandable. He trained for the law at a university, won royal patronage, traveled in the service of his king, and held a series of important political offices. But his career unfolded against a background of disasters that would have undercut the confidence of the most determined optimist. Deschamps was born about the time that a great plague carried off a third of the population of Europe, and those who survived were never free of the threat of its return. A devastating war between England and France also disrupted his life. He endured sieges, his home was burned, and he lost his job. From his perspective, the world was drifting toward anarchy, and he had no confidence in the leaders whose duty it was to maintain order and provide justice.

During the twelfth and thirteenth centuries, Europe had expanded on all fronts. Population grew. Commerce, cities, arts, and intellectual life flourished. Then, early in the fourteenth century, things began to go wrong—some suddenly and dramatically, others

grans seignis que chun voulort
monstuer sa puissance Si nest
mul homme combien ql fust
present a la rōnee qui sceut
ne peust ymaginer ne recor
der la verite Especaalement
de la partie des francois tant
y eut poure arroy et petite
ordonnance en leurs grans
contoys qui estorent sans
nombze Et ce que ie scay
de leurs besomgnes et ordon
nances etce que ie deuise
ray et determinera y en ce

laire Ie lay sceu et aprins
le plus par moult vaillans
sommes dingleterre sages
et dyscretz tant chualiers
comme aultres qui moult
ententifuemet auiserent
leur contenant Et aussi
par les gens de mess. iehū
de huynault qui furent
tousiours delez le Roy
phle de france Cy parle de la
bataille de crecy entre le roy de
france et le roy dingleterre.

Battle of Crécy This painting, an illustration for a medieval manuscript, depicts the Battle of Crécy, the first major engagement in the Hundred Years' War between England and France.

slowly and insidiously. Food shortages became common. Epidemics spread. Europe was threatened with invasion. The leadership of the church broke down, and the efforts of government leaders to cope with these crises often made them worse.

People of Deschamps' generation had reason to believe that their world was in decline, but it would be inaccurate and unfair to accuse their civilization of having failed them. The stresses of the fourteenth and fifteenth centuries certainly forced Europeans to make painful adaptations, but many of their problems were signs of evolving circumstances more than cultural failure. Some were the dark side of the achievements of the twelfth and thirteenth centuries, and others were the result of natural and historical processes that were beyond human control.

Historians have rightly described the late medieval period as the Age of Anxiety, a time characterized by pessimism, skepticism, and self-doubt. But the fourteenth century also witnessed the flowering of Italy's Renaissance, a movement associated with a surge of optimistic humanism (see Chapter 12). Some of Deschamps's contemporaries shared his belief that they were sorely afflicted, but they also anticipated the dawn of a glorious new era. It was their destiny to be born at a time of testing for the institutions that the dynamic High Middle Ages had created. The crises they weathered revealed weaknesses in Western civilization but also signs of future strengths.

Challenges from Nature

Because most modern people live in artificial environments, they forget how dependent even an advanced civilization is on the processes of nature. Such forgetfulness is dangerous, for scientists have discovered that the natural environment that sustains all life is not fixed and stable. Earth has experienced such drastic shifts in climate that tropical plants have flourished in what is today the arctic, and glaciers once reached the Mediterranean. The whole history of civilization has unfolded during an unusually warm and stable period in Earth's cycle of climates. This is a sobering fact, for even minor shifts in climate can threaten the viability of human institutions. And consensus is building among scientists that the energy consumption associated with twenty-first-century civilization is accelerating the rate of climate change.

Climate Change   From 1000 to 1300 Europe enjoyed a benign climate, but then the Little Ice Age, an era of slowly diminishing average temperatures, set in and continued into the nineteenth century. This had a serious impact on medieval Europe's largely agrarian economy. Weather patterns changed. Precipitation increased. Growing seasons shortened, and in some places, crops that had once thrived would no longer grow.

Much of Europe lies at the latitude of Canada. (Paris is farther north than Nova Scotia.) Western Europe's climate is moderated by the Gulf Stream and warm seasonal winds from Africa. Any change in these phenomena can have serious repercussions for all forms of life in Europe.

Sporadic famines had always been a part of medieval life, but in the fourteenth century they came more frequently and affected larger areas. In 1309 there was a continent-wide famine, the first in 250 years. Crops failed throughout northern Europe in 1315, 1316, and 1317, and there was another widespread famine in the 1330s. Death by starvation was not unusual. People ate dogs, cats, and rats, and there were even rumors of cannibalism. Medieval governments could do little to respond to such crises. Even if they found supplies of food, they lacked the distribution systems to get emergency relief to afflicted regions.

Food supplies were critical, for increasing political stability and economic growth had allowed Europe's population to triple between the eleventh and the fourteenth centuries. Although population density was not great by modern standards, it reached previously unprecedented heights. There were perhaps 80 million Europeans in 1300 compared with 732 million today. But given the available agricultural technologies, Europe began, by the fourteenth century, to exceed the carrying capacity of its land. During the eleventh, twelfth, and thirteenth centuries, Europeans had brought more and more land into production. They drained swamps, reclaimed fields from the sea, and cleared so much forest that Europe may have more trees today than it did then. Europeans eventually reached the limit of their arable land. And when the climate began to cool, the poorer land stopped producing, and society's agricultural base started to shrink. The demand for food outstripped supply, and people went hungry.

Wealth was unevenly distributed in medieval societies, and there was no social safety net. In any age, economic depressions can trigger migrations from the starving countryside into cities by people who are desperate for food and work. But as large numbers of destitute, chronically malnourished people crowded into Europe's medieval towns, they increased their vulnerability to the second blow that nature struck the West in the fourteenth century: plague.

Plague   Between 1347 and 1350 a great epidemic spread across the world and carried off between 30% and 50% of Europe's population. Medieval people called it simply "the pestilence." The name Black Death appeared in the sixteenth century, and the term *Bubonic Plague* only describes one symptom of the disease. A bubo is a swollen, infected lymph node, usually in the groin or armpit. Plague can rupture blood vessels, causing bleeding from bodily orifices and subcutaneous bleeding that turns the skin black with bruised blotches. It can also infect the lungs and assume a form spread by coughs and sneezes.

The diseases that afflicted the ancient and medieval world are hard to identify, for the records describing symptoms are often inadequate. Diseases also mutate over time, and modern diseases may differ from their earlier versions. For a long time, historians have assumed that the pestilence that afflicted Europe in the fourteenth century was caused by a bacterium called *Yersinia pestis*. It is indigenous to parts of China and Africa and lives in the digestive tracts of fleas that infest certain species of rats. When the bacteria multiply excessively, they block their host flea's digestive track. The starving insect then begins indiscriminately to bite other warm-blooded creatures, and its bite injects them with infected material from its blocked gut. Recent research has raised doubts about the cause of the great medieval pandemic, for it did not conform in many ways to modern plague. Its behavior bore some resemblance to the virulent strain of influenza that swept the globe in 1918.

The fourteenth century was not the first to confront an epidemic. Smallpox spread through the Roman Empire about 180. Measles erupted in 251. *Yersinia pestis* may have spread from Africa north through the Byzantine Empire and into western Europe around 540 and burned itself out by the eighth century. From then until the fourteenth century, Europeans suffered few epidemics, for once the pool of diseases to which they were regularly exposed stabilized, their immune systems were able to adapt. So long as no new infectious agents appeared, they were reasonably secure.

If the fourteenth-century plague was a version of *Yersinia pestis*, the global climate shifts that were taking place at that time may help to explain its arrival in Europe. Humidity and temperature affected the activity of the fleas that were the plague's hosts. As Europe's climate grew wetter, central Asia suffered drought, and flea-infected rodent populations migrated into regions inhabited by nomadic tribes of Turks and Mongols. The medieval epidemic began in China in approximately 1330 and reached Samarkand in 1339, the Crimea in 1345, and Sicily in October 1347. Within months the disease had spread throughout Europe as well as the Islamic world. Muslim countries may also have lost 30% to 50% of their populations. The rapidity with which the epidemic spread, however, is one of the reasons for doubting that it was caused by *Yersinia pestis.*

Modern people are all too familiar with acts of genocide and natural disasters that devastate limited regions, but it is hard to imagine what it was like to experience a universal onslaught of a mysterious, lethal illness. Medieval people were baffled. They knew that the pestilence was infectious, but they did not know how it spread. There were no effective treatments for it, and it was almost always fatal. There seemed to be no logic to its behavior. It struck unevenly, decimating some places and skipping others. Thousands of villages disappeared. Tightly packed communities such as monasteries and nunneries were obliterated. The general upheaval reduced the number of universities from about 30 in 1349 to 10 in 1400. Disease and deteriorating climate led to abandonment of the country of Greenland, and Europe did not recoup its population losses until the mid-sixteenth century.

Social Consequences   Frightened people often turn on one another, and the plague prompted persecution of Europe's resident outsiders, the Jews. Despite the fact that they were dying along with everyone else, rumors spread that Jews were causing the plague by poisoning wells. The physicians who taught at the universities of Paris and Montpellier dismissed this, and Pope Clement VI (r. 1342–1352) ordered the clergy to protect the Jews. However, panicked mobs destroyed over 200 Jewish communities.

Lacking any earthly explanation, university scholars fell back on astrology and attributed the disease to an unfortunate alignment of planets. It was widely assumed that God had sent the plague to chastize humanity for its sins. In desperation, people

The Last Judgment   In the early fourteenth century, Giotto di Bondone, a pioneering Italian artist, covered the entrance wall of the Arena Chapel in Padua with his vision of the final judgment. The condemned occupy the lower right quadrant of the composition.

fasted and made pilgrimages. They increased their acts of charity, and some tried to appease God by tormenting their flesh. Processions of flagellants whipped one another into bloody, ecstatic frenzies. The church condemned such excesses, but it had no effective alternatives to propose for dealing with the crisis. It may have lost 40% of its clergy in the first onslaught of the epidemic, and there was no evidence that sacraments, intercessions, and traditional acts of piety did much good. Some Christians responded to the crisis by turning inward and cultivating a private faith that helped them come to terms with their mortality. This and other developments in late medieval societies accustomed people to assuming more personal responsibility for their spiritual lives.

The era was preoccupied with death. Artists covered the walls of churches with depictions of the Last Judgment, and they lavished imagination on devising horrid punishments for the damned. Grave monuments warned about the tenuous frailty of earthly life. Earlier generations had favored tomb effigies that represented the deceased in the full bloom of youth and vigor, but now the dead were depicted as corpses in an advanced state of decay. The intent was to abase pride and affirm that this life was dust and ashes compared to what awaited the faithful beyond the grave.

Every cloud is said to have a silver lining, and this held true even for the fourteenth-century epidemic. Many of those who survived it found their prospects improved. The disease potentially reduced pressure on Europe's food supply by shrinking its population. The deaths of so many property owners freed up land for the landless, and enabled small holdings to be combined as larger, more viable farms. Wages rose, for a diminished population created a labor shortage that put workers in a good position to bargain. Prior to the epidemic, overpopulation had glutted the labor market and driven wages down. Now, as the process was reversed, employers had to give their workers better terms to keep them. In western Europe the wage-laborer replaced the serf, but in central Europe, where towns and strong kings were few, serfdom spread. The powerful landowners of that region were able to exploit their peasants, for they had no place to flee to and no alternative sources of employment.

The propertied classes did not want to pay the higher wages that workers on their lands demanded, and they had political power that they could use to restore what they regarded as the status quo. The poor had no representation in government, for medieval governments paid attention only to those whom they tapped for money. The rich, therefore, were able to pass laws designed to prevent the poor from profiting from the situation the plague had created. Sumptuary laws preserved class distinctions by regulating how people were allowed to dress and by limiting indulgence in certain luxuries to the aristocracy. More galling, no doubt, were ordinances that kept wages low by imposing caps.

People tolerate bad situations if they assume that misery is inevitable. The dangerous time for a society is when improving conditions raise hopes that are subsequently dashed. Europe was little troubled by popular uprisings so long as its economy was flat or slowly improving. But the economic adjustments necessitated by the plague and the political class's response to them prompted a series of peasant revolts. In 1358 the first of a number of Jacquerie rebellions (named for a kind of cheap leather jacket the poor wore) erupted in France. In 1381 the English throne was shaken by the Peasants' Revolt in which a mob occupied London and executed some royal officials. Similar uprisings took place later in Spain and Germany. Although the commoners, especially in England, sometimes won concessions, the upper classes remained in control. The aristocracy was, however, not a closed order. Wars, feuds, dangerous sports, and political executions put medieval male nobles at great risk. The average life expectancy of a male born into an English ducal family in the fourteenth and fifteenth centuries, for instance, was only 24 years. His sister could anticipate living into her thirties. Aristocratic families had difficulty preserving their male lines for more than a few generations, which created opportunities for new families to climb the social ladder. Commoners broke into the upper class by intermarriage and by acquiring fortunes with which to purchase titles and estates.

Turmoil in the Middle East

During the thirteenth century, a series of events disrupted the Byzantine and Muslim worlds, but few western European leaders may have grasped the dire significance of what these developments portended. They did try to take advantage of the situation to regain footholds in the Middle East, but their interventions backfired disastrously. They weakened Constantinople to the point where it could no longer protect Europe's eastern frontiers from Muslim incursions. The Muslim region was temporarily thrown into a state of upheaval by invaders from the east. But the newcomers converted, reenergized Islam, and set it on the road to building a new empire. The Middle Ages were to end as they had begun—with Muslim and Christian powers contending across the Mediterranean Sea. The crusaders' repeated thrusts into Muslim territory were all repulsed, but Islam's late medieval counteroffensive partially succeeded. Muslim armies seized Greece, the Balkans, and parts of central Europe, and held them for centuries.

Constantinople   The crusades cast a lengthy shadow over Europe's relations with its eastern neighbors. Byzantine emperor Alexius Comnenus (r. 1081–1118) had unintentionally launched the Holy Land crusades by asking Pope Urban II (r. 1088–1099) to help him recruit soldiers for Constantinople's wars (see Chapter 9). What seemed a good idea at the time proved in the long run to be a disaster for Alexius's empire. Constantinople lost trade as the crusaders took control of ports on the eastern coast of the Mediterranean, and Constantinople itself became a target for Europe's crusaders.

In 1202 the armies of the Fourth Crusade gathered in Venice. They planned to sail to the Holy Land. But when they could not raise the money to pay for their passage, they agreed to earn their way by selling their services to Venice. Venice diverted them to Constantinople to support an exiled Byzantine prince's bid for the imperial throne. Once the Venetian candidate was in power, Venice expected to control trade with Constantinople. The intimidated Byzantines crowned the prince, but he soon fell victim to a plot. A series of palace coups increased the confusion and frustrated the crusaders, who finally stormed the city and took it by force on April 13, 1204. The Christian city that for centuries had withstood multiple attacks by barbarian and Muslim armies fell for the first time—and not to its religious enemies, but to soldiers who fought in the name of Christ. The crusaders sacked Constantinople, claimed it for themselves, and enthroned a Latin emperor. Many of the treasures the city had preserved from antiquity were lost in the fires and looting that ensued.

The triumphant crusaders forgot about Jerusalem and rushed to stake claims to Byzantine territory. However, a rival Greek emperor established a base in Asia Minor and rallied resistance to the Catholic Latins, who were loathed by their Orthodox subjects. The Latin Byzantine Empire, like the earlier crusader states, was a weak kingdom whose ruler had little power and few resources. The last of Constantinople's Latin emperors was so desperate for money that he hawked relics from the city's churches and sold the lead that roofed his palace. In 1261 Venice's competitor, the Italian city of Genoa, helped the Greek emperor, Michael Palaeologus (r. 1261–1282), regain control of a depopulated and impoverished Constantinople. Michael's Byzantine Empire was a shadow of its former self, and it faced a world in turmoil. Europe's crusaders had set in motion events that were to lose Christians their last outpost in the eastern Mediterranean. For centuries, Constantinople had blocked Muslim advances into Europe, but its ability to do so was now seriously compromised. However, the city survived in Christian hands for almost another two centuries, for the Muslims had more important matters to attend to.

The Islamic Middle East   The First Crusade succeeded because the Muslims of the Middle East were fighting among themselves. They continued to squabble until a Kurdish warrior named Saladin (1138–1193) brought them under his control. In 1174 he terminated the Fatimid caliphate and occupied Egypt. Syria and Mesopotamia were his by 1186, and in 1187 he took Jerusalem. After he repulsed Richard the Lionhearted's Third Crusade (see Chapter 10), he built an empire that stretched from Tunisia in

North Africa to Armenia and the Caspian Sea. His Ayyubid dynasty reigned over a loose federation that posed no threat to the Christian West. It wanted good trade relations with Italy's cities and was primarily interested in maintaining stability.

The Muslim lands east of the Ayyubid Empire (roughly modern Iran) passed from the Seljuk sultans to the shahs of Khwarazm, the region south of the Aral Sea. There, in 1218, the Muslims first encountered a threat that renewed hope in Europe for their ultimate defeat. The shah's lands were invaded by the Mongols, nomadic tribes who roamed the vast stretch of grasslands bordering northern China. The Mongols were not Muslims. European leaders thrilled at the prospect of converting them to Christianity and enlisting them in a joint effort to exterminate Islam.

Mongols   The Mongols owed their entrance onto history's stage to the leadership of Temujin (c. 1167–1227), who is better known by his well-deserved title, Genghis Khan ("Universal Lord"), and to a unique and highly effective military technology. Mongol craftsmen bonded different materials together to make powerful bows that were small enough for use by mounted soldiers. Mongol bowmen were able to cut opponents to pieces before their enemies' weapons got within striking range. Temujin created an army with a unified command and trained it to execute strategic maneuvers on the battlefield. This enabled him to rout much larger opponents who had little grasp of tactics and who lacked the mobility of Mongol bowmen. Temujin focused his attention on northern China while his generals made progress on other fronts. In 1221 a Mongol army overthrew the shah of Khwarazm and then split into two branches. One headed north of the Aral and Caspian Seas into Russian territory, and the other moved south across Persia (see Map 11–1).

In 1258 the Mongols took Baghdad (in a siege of only four days) and slaughtered all its inhabitants—including the last Abbasid caliph. They met no effective resistance until they reached the shores of the Mediterranean, where the Mamluks, Turkish slave soldiers who had overthrown Egypt's Ayyubid ruler in 1250, made a successful stand. After the Mongols withdrew to Baghdad, the Mamluks emerged as the dominant Muslim power in the Middle East. In 1291, they took the last crusader outposts on the Palestinian coast.

The pope and France's crusader king, Louis IX, tried to establish contact with the Mongols in hopes of converting them and allying with them against the Muslims. In 1245 they dispatched a Franciscan friar, John of Piancarpino, to Mongolia. He returned two years later, bringing Europeans their first eyewitness account of the exotic Far East. In 1255 a second Franciscan, William of Ruybroek, repeated his feat. Late in the century another Franciscan, John of Montecorvino, established a Christian bishopric in Peking. The most famous account of the Mongol Empire derived, however, from the autobiography of a Venetian merchant named Marco Polo (1254–1324). He claimed to have visited the Mongol court with his father and uncle in 1275, to have spent 17 years in China, and even to have been an official in the Mongol government. Some historians question whether Marco Polo ever visited the East and suggest that he may only have cobbled together stories about China that sifted back to Venice along its trade routes. Their doubts arise not so much from what he said about China

Map 11–1   The Mongol Empire   The Mongols resembled the Huns, Avars, Bulgars, and Magyars who had earlier emerged from the Russian steppe to threaten Europe, but their military organization was much more sophisticated than that of their predecessors.

Question: How did Eurasian geography facilitate the Mongol invasions?

but from prominent Chinese customs (tea drinking and foot binding, for example) that he failed to mention.

European hopes for a Mongol alliance were dashed late in the thirteenth century when the Mongols converted to Islam. By then, Europeans had come to view the Mongols more as potential enemies than friends. The northern branch of the Mongol army had charged almost unopposed through the territory north of the Black and Caspian Seas. In 1238 the Mongols sacked the Russian cities of Vladimir and Moscow, and in 1240 they took Kiev. By 1241 they were nearing Cracow in Poland and pushing up the Danube to the gates of Vienna, Austria. Here their momentum was broken by Vienna's Christian defenders and by the confusion that followed the death of their khan.

The Mongols organized the territory north of the Black and Caspian Seas as the khanate of the Golden Horde (named for the color of its ruler's tent). They commissioned the prince of Moscow to collect the tribute their Russian subjects owed them, and this gave him a chance to establish his authority over the Russians. In 1480 Moscow's Ivan III, "the Great" (1462–1505), threw off the Mongol yoke and laid the foundation for a Russian state.

In the late fourteenth century, another Mongol army under the command of a Timur "the Lame" (Tamerlane, 1336–1404), who claimed to be a descendant of Temujin, erupted from the east. He raided across Russia as far as Lithuania, struck south into India, leveled the city of Delhi, and then occupied Baghdad, Damascus, and much of Asia Minor. Europe, with a population diminished by plagues and famines, had reason to anticipate the worst. But when Tamerlane suddenly died, his numerous descendants fell to fighting among themselves for the spoils of his empire.

Far from assisting Europe's Christians in the destruction of Islam, the Mongols added vigorous new blood to the ranks of Muhammad's followers. Their advance thrust

---

The Crusading Movement

The Iberian Crusade (1015–1492)—Spain
The Sicilian Crusade (1059–1091)—Kingdom of the Two Sicilies

First Crusade (1095)—Holy Land
"The Peasants' Crusade"
Conquest of Jerusalem (1099)
Establishment of the Crusader States
{Fall of Edessa, 1144}

Second Crusade (1145)—Holy Land
Louis VII, king of France
{Fall of Jerusalem, 1187}

Third Crusade (1187)—Holy Land
Richard I, the Lionhearted, king of England
Philip II, king of France
Frederick I, Barbarossa, emperor of Germany
"The Northern Crusades" (1193–c. 1300)
Finland, Estonia, Lithuania

Fourth Crusade (1204)—Holy Land
Diverted to the conquest of Constantinople
"The Albigensian Crusade" (1209–1229)
"The Children's Crusade" (1212)

Fifth Crusade (1218)—Holy Land
Cardinal Pelagius, Papal Legate
Fought in Egypt
"The Prussian Crusade" (1226–c. 1300)
Teutonic Knights
Crusade (1229)—Holy Land
Frederick II, excommunicated emperor of Germany, regained Jerusalem by negotiation

Sixth Crusade (1249)—Holy Land
Fought in Egypt
Louis IX, king of France

Seventh Crusade (1270)—Holy Land
Fought at Tunis
1453 {Fall of Constantinople}
1464 Final call for a crusade to the Holy Land fails
Pope Pius II

Europe back on the defensive and raised the specter of yet another charge by eastern peoples into the heart of the continent. A weakened Constantinople, disillusionment with crusades, and loss of the initiative in foreign affairs added to what plague, famine, and social unrest did to make the late medieval era truly an Age of Anxiety.

Spiritual Crises

Even in the modern world, where religion is far more marginalized than it was in medieval society, people often look to religious institutions for help in stressful times. Unfortunately, when the Europeans of the late Middle Ages turned to their church, they found an institution that was in disarray. Instead of offering aid and comfort, it added to the problems of an anxious age.

Innocent III and Papal Monarchy   The pope who most successfully exercised the exalted rights that medieval pontiffs claimed for their office was Innocent III (r. 1198–1216). Innocent was a Roman aristocrat with relatives in the papal court. He studied law at the University of Bologna and theology at Paris. He wrote several books, one of which was a piece of devotional literature that enjoyed great popularity. He was only 37 when he became pope, and in addition to youth, he had the advantage of good timing. For most of his reign, the Germans were too busy with a civil war to intervene in Italy and threaten the papacy's independence.

The text on which Innocent preached at his coronation made plain his understanding of the powers of his office: "I have set you today over nations and kingdoms" (Jeremiah 1:10). Innocent maintained that all Christians, including kings, were subject to the spiritual authority of the pope. He agreed that kings derived their power directly from God. However, as Christ's representative on Earth, the pope was charged with holding kings accountable for how they used the office God entrusted to them. Innocent urged Europe's kings to become his vassals. This would not have made him Europe's ruler, but as overlord of Europe's kings, he would have had the right to adjudicate their disputes. Innocent wanted the church to become a kind of high court in which nations could resolve their difficulties without resorting to war.

Few kings accepted the pope's invitation to become his vassals, but Innocent, on several occasions, challenged great monarchs and forced them to back down. He owed his success to the care with which he chose his fights. He confronted kings when they blundered and made themselves vulnerable. His victories had the effect of making the papacy look stronger than it was.

Like his predecessors, Innocent hoped that by sponsoring crusades, he could strengthen the pope's role as Christendom's supreme leader. This was the least successful of his undertakings. The first army he intended for the Holy Land (the Fourth Crusade) ended by sacking Christian Constantinople in 1204. The crusade he called against the Cathar heretics in 1208 devastated southern France. The Fifth Crusade (1218–1221), an attack on Egypt that he was planning at the time of his death, was a debacle.

Innocent III and St. Francis Although Pope Innocent III was opposed to the proliferation of monastic orders, he showed remarkable wisdom in making an exception for the friars. This fresco from the Basilica of St. Francis in Assisi depicts the pope endorsing the work of St. Francis. *Dagli Orti/Picture Desk, Inc./Kobal Collection*

Innocent's greatest achievement was the strengthening of papal authority over the church and its clergy. In 1215 his Fourth Lateran Council affirmed that the church was a papal monarchy, endorsed the doctrine of transubstantiation as the explanation of the Eucharist (see Chapter 10), enforced clerical celibacy, and imposed new pious duties on the laity. Innocent bluntly asserted that the state had no power over the church and denied kings the right to tax or exercise judicial authority over the clergy. Given the growing strength of some of Europe's monarchies, Innocent committed his successors to a position that they were ill-equipped to defend, and their failure produced a century-long crisis for the church.

Humiliation of the Papacy In 1295 France's powerful king, Philip IV (r. 1285–1314), informed the French clergy that he was imposing taxes on the church. The clergy appealed to Pope Boniface VIII (r. 1296–1303), and the pope informed Philip that the church (as the Fourth Lateran Council had made clear) was totally independent of the state and not subject to taxation by kings. When Philip responded by blocking funds flowing from France to the papal treasury, the financially strapped Boniface tried to make a face-saving retreat. He explained that although kings had no right to tax the church, the church would, of course, help out a king in an emergency—and that a king had the right to decide when an emergency existed.

Having won de facto taxing authority, Philip next challenged the pope's claim that clergy did not fall under the jurisdiction of the state's courts. In 1301 he charged a French bishop with treason and threw him into prison. Boniface fired off a letter to Philip, warning him of the spiritual penalties awaiting him if he continued to attack the church. Philip circulated a distorted version of the letter to inflame his subjects against the pope, and then (in 1302) he convened a national assembly to see where they stood. This first meeting of France's Estates General, like England's Parliament, represented only a minority of the population—the higher clergy, nobility, and townspeople. But with its assurance that France was solidly behind him, Philip dispatched troops to Italy to arrest Boniface. The French held the pope captive for three days, and he died a few weeks later.

The cardinals who met to elect a new pope had learned a hard lesson. If people were forced to choose between their king and their pope, they were likely to side with the king. It was also clear that Europe's leaders would not unite and take action to punish a king who assaulted the head of their church. The cardinals therefore concluded that they had to make peace with France. Boniface's short-lived successor, Benedict XI (r. 1303–1304), lifted the spiritual penalties Boniface had imposed on Philip. At the end of his brief reign, a French archbishop was elected pope.

Clement V (r. 1305–1314) was in France at the time of his election, and he stayed there to negotiate with Philip. There was much for him to do, for he hoped to head off a war that was looming between France and England, and in 1307 Philip attacked the Knights Templar, one of the richest and most prestigious of Europe's military orders. The king arrested as many Templars as he could and tortured them to force them to confess to everything from witchcraft to sexual deviance. The pope, powerless to defend them, acquiesced to the order's dissolution, but did what he could to minimize the king's appropriation of its property.

Clement established what was supposed to be a temporary residence at Avignon, a city in southern France on the border of Philip's territory, but he never had an opportunity to go to Rome. At his death, the College of Cardinals, which was now largely French, elected another French pope who opted to remain in Avignon. The pattern repeated itself, and for more than 70 years (1305–1377) the bishop of Rome never visited the city of Rome. Lavish facilities were built for the papal court at Avignon, and it began to appear that the pope had no intention of ever returning to Rome.

Critics branded the papacy's sojourn in Avignon a "**Babylonian captivity**," a reference to the Bible's account of the Chaldaeans carting the Jews off to exile in ancient Babylon. They accused France of having abducted the papacy. French influences were strong at Avignon, but the Avignese popes were no one's puppets. Many were excellent executives who improved the power and efficiency of the church's central government. Having lost control of the Papal States, they were ingenious at finding other sources of income. They claimed the right to appoint candidates to all major clerical offices, to collect the revenues of those offices during periods when they were vacant, and to hear appeals from all ecclesiastical courts. They created an elaborate bureaucracy dedicated to attracting as much business as possible to the papal court, and they collected fees (and bribes) for all services. The papal administration at Avignon became a model of efficiency for Europe's secular governments, but the popes' fiscal skills hardly enhanced their reputations for sanctity. Holy men were not supposed to be so preoccupied with—and good at—raising money.

As the crises of the fourteenth century mounted, the church on which Europeans depended for spiritual comfort seemed to become ever more worldly and materialistic. Saints—notably Bridget of Sweden (1302–1372) and Catherine of Siena (1347–1380)—begged, and reformers demanded, that the popes return to Rome before they irreparably damaged the church. In 1378 Pope Gregory XI (r. 1370–1378) yielded to the pressure and took the cardinals back to Rome.

Papal Schism   The Papal States were out of control, and the Roman buildings that housed the papacy had been neglected for 70 years. Gregory and the cardinals, who were accustomed to the comforts of their elaborate palace in Avignon, soon concluded that Rome was not livable. Gregory decreed a return to Avignon, where the papal bureaucracy was still headquartered. Death, however, intervened, and Gregory's demise forced the cardinals to stay in Rome until they had chosen his successor. This proved difficult, for the College of Cardinals split in support of rival French candidates. To break the stalemate, the cardinals decided to placate the Roman people by elevating an obscure Italian, Urban VI (r. 1378–1389), to the papacy. The cardinals expected to be able to dominate Urban, and prior to his election they required him to promise to take them back to Avignon. Once seated on the papal throne, however, Urban changed his mind. He knew that in Avignon, as a lone Italian in a sea of Frenchmen, he would have little power.

When Urban informed the cardinals that they would stay in Rome, they refused and returned to Avignon without him. In Avignon they declared his election invalid and chose a new pope, Clement VII (r. 1378–1394). Urban responded by appointing a new College of Cardinals in Rome. Europe suddenly had two papal courts, and because there was no way to decide which one was valid, kings simply supported the pope who best suited their political agendas. France and its allies endorsed Avignon. England, France's enemy, favored Rome, and other states lined up accordingly.

This division of the papacy—the **Great Schism** (1378–1415)—plunged a generation of Europeans into spiritual confusion. Catholic doctrine maintained that allegiance to the true pope was essential for salvation, but there was no way to determine which of Europe's rival popes was Christ's authentic representative. A Christian's salvation depended upon receiving valid sacraments, but a sacrament—the power to act in God's name—was something delegated by Christ to the clergy through their superior, the pope. If the pope was really an anti-pope, the clergy who served him had no authority to act for God. Because the sins they forgave were not truly forgiven, the souls of the best intentioned and most obedient of Christians could be in great danger. A divided papacy posed a major threat to medieval Christian faith and practice.

Prominent Europeans pressed the popes to settle the issue between themselves. But neither man was willing to resign and sacrifice himself for the good of the church. Attention next shifted to the cardinals. They were urged to repudiate both popes and unite behind a new one. The cardinals welcomed this plan, for it confirmed their belief that they were the arbiters of papal legitimacy. In 1409, when they met in the Italian city of Pisa and chose a new pope, the popes they had forsaken in Rome and Avignon appointed new Colleges of Cardinals. Ironically, the strategy for resolving the schism multiplied the number of popes.

Conciliarism and Popular Government   The Avignese papacy and the Great Schism forced Europeans to think seriously about the nature of authority—secular as well as sacred. To end the schism, they needed a justification for forcing popes, who claimed to be accountable only to God, to do what they did not want to do. More was at stake here than restoration of the church's unity. The development of a rationale for sitting in judgment on a pope would have wide-ranging political ramifications, for the same argument could easily be adapted to apply to kings.

William of Ockham (1285–1349), an English Franciscan philosopher, insisted that because popes were human, they were as prone to error as anyone else. The most reliable way for fallible human individuals to determine the truth about an issue, he insisted, was to seek a consensus of opinion from all persons qualified to comment. Ockham warned, however, that even experts make mistakes and that it was important, therefore, that minorities be listened to and coercion minimized.

Marsiglio of Padua (c. 1278–1342), an Italian philosopher, claimed that the church was not some supernatural entity, but only a name for groups of Christians. It should be subordinate to the state, for the state was charged with responsibility for defending the peace on which life itself depends. Furthermore, given that Aristotle had logically demonstrated that whatever affected the whole should be decided by the whole, both the church and the state should be subject to the will of the people—or at least to the will of the more responsible element in the general population.

The Englishman John Wyclif (d. 1384) offered a different justification for empowering the masses. He admitted that dominion (the right to rule) had long been believed to be a sacred power delegated to men by God. But he argued that this logically implied that dominion was to be used for the purpose God intended—for the welfare of God's creatures. If popes (and kings) failed to use the authority God gave them for the good of their subjects, they forfeited legitimacy. The subjects of an ungodly ruler, therefore, had a duty to replace him, for he had no right to dominion over God's people. Wyclif also denied that the pope had sole authority to interpret the Scriptures. He urged that the Bible be translated from Latin into the vernacular languages so that laypeople could study it and make up their own minds about what it taught. The church had forbidden vernacular translations, for it claimed that simple folk, who were not trained in theology, would misread the text and fall into error. Wyclif's championing of the rights of ordinary people may have contributed to the Peasants' Revolt that erupted in 1381. Despite the fact that his theories were inherently revolutionary, a powerful patron protected him until his death. Ultimately, however, the church branded him a heretic and condemned his writings. This drove the popular preachers and religious dissidents whom he inspired (the Lollards) underground, but their movement may have endured and helped to prepare the way for England's break with the papacy in the sixteenth century.

Critiques of papal authority and arguments justifying action by the masses led to the proposal that finally ended the Great Schism. A group of scholars known as the Conciliarists argued that a universal church council would have the authority to end the schism. **Conciliarism**, their theory, held that final authority in spiritual matters belonged to the whole community of Christians as represented by a general church council, not the pope alone. Church lawyers objected that only a pope could summon a council and that no council had exercised power over a pope, but the Conciliarists found ways around these obstacles. They pressured the weakest of the

Council of Constance A fifteenth-century chronicle compiled by Ulrich of Richental provides valuable insight into the work of the Council of Constance. This miniature, which decorates the manuscript, represents Pope Martin V sitting with cardinals and other members of the council. *Dagli Orti/Picture Desk, Inc./Kobal Collection*

popes, the one in Pisa, to convene their council, and they argued that if an essential institution (such as the church) breaks down, logic gives its members the right to do whatever is necessary to save it. The alternative would be to ignore the natural right beings have to exist and to claim that they have no choice but irrationally to will their own destruction.

In 1415 the Swiss city of Constance hosted a council at which most of the powers in Europe—kings, cardinals, bishops, abbots, lawyers, and prominent scholars—were represented. The council had a number of items on its agenda. To demonstrate that it was staunchly orthodox, the council violated a safe conduct it had given to a religious dissident named John Hus and tried him for heresy. Hus had been inspired by John Wyclif's arguments to raise a popular revolt against the papacy in his homeland, Bohemia. His execution at Constance only served to inspire his followers, the Hussites, to take up arms. They defeated the imperial armies sent against them, and peace was restored only after the church made major concessions to satisfy their demands.

The chief business at Constance was the resolution of the Great Schism. This proved to be easy once all the European powers agreed to withdraw their support from the rival popes and unite behind one chosen by the cardinals at the council. The new pope, Martin V (r. 1417–1431), was eager for the meeting to adjourn, for the Conciliarists wanted the delegates next to debate reforming the reunited church. Martin feared that if this happened, the council would replace the pope as the ultimate authority over the church.

Once the schism was healed, much of the excitement went out of the meeting, and its members were eager to go home. Before the council disbanded, however, it passed two potentially revolutionary decrees. The first, *Sacrosancta*, declared that the church was to be governed by councils—implying that popes were simply the church's chief executive officers, agents who were accountable to councils and subject to their supervision. The second decree, *Frequens*, ordered popes to summon councils at regular intervals. If these decrees had succeeded, the church would have become an institution governed by a representative assembly. This did not happen, because kings knew that what was done to popes might be done to kings. In 1431 a council that met in Basel, another Swiss city, made a fatal mistake. It quarreled with the pope, deposed him, and elected a rival. To prevent a new schism from developing, Europe's kings withdrew their support for councils and did not object when popes ignored the schedule for convening them. In 1460 Pope Pius II (r. 1458–1464) declared it a heresy to claim that anyone or any council has authority over a pope. In 1870 Pope Pius IX (r. 1846–1878) confirmed this at the First Vatican Council by promulgating the doctrine of papal infallibility. The church emerged from the crises of the fourteenth century with the claims it made for the authority of its leader intact, but its reputation as a spiritual institution tarnished.

Private Faith, Mysticism, and Skepticism   The medieval church claimed to be the sole intermediary between God and His people. Pope Boniface VIII had clearly stated to King Philip IV of France (and to the world) that there was no salvation outside the communion of the church. Yet for much of the fourteenth century, the church did not inspire trust as a mediator between God and sinners. Rival popes excommunicated one another and insisted that their opponents' sacraments were invalid. Faithful Christians had no way to determine the truth. They were therefore thrust back on their own spiritual resources: private prayer, study, and meditation. Laypeople took the initiative and invented new kinds of religious communities and disciplines that had little to do with the church and clergy. The mystical element in medieval religion thrived, for mysticism was an avenue to a direct, personal communion with God. The breakdown of the church forced people to assume more responsibility for themselves, and the autonomy to which they became accustomed in the religious sphere spilled over into other areas of their lives.

Even the authority of reason, the standard in which medieval dialecticians placed their greatest trust, was questioned by late medieval philosophers such as William of Ockham. Ockham denied that reason could be used to support faith. He argued that the only realities of which the mind can be certain are the things of which the body's senses make it aware. Ockham was a philosophical nominalist (see Chapter 10) who believed that the mind infers classes and abstractions from the specific bits of data that the senses provide. In his opinion, there was no evidence that classes and abstractions actually exist outside the human mind. Reasoning from particular things to general abstractions helped people understand how the natural world operates, but it did not lead to an understanding of God or of ultimate spiritual truths. The truths of faith are not deduced by reason, he insisted, but grasped by intuition. The fact that God created a rational universe does not mean that God is bound by the rules of logic. If God were, logic would be greater than God. Faith in the Bible's omnipotent Creator transcends reason and understanding. Ockham's skepticism severely limited what human beings could hope to know. But by separating faith from reason, he created a justification for liberating science from constraints imposed by theology.

Political Responses: The Burdens of War

The governments of the young states that were taking shape in the late Middle Ages faced the challenge of managing populations unsettled by plague and famine. The tools available to them were as limited as their experience. Kings were still primarily warlords, but war was an unlikely cure for the problems of their unstable world.

France and England   England and France were late medieval Europe's most fully formed states. Both had well-established dynasties and at least a start toward a central-ized bureaucratic government. Unfortunately, however, they also had an unresolved ter-ritorial dispute. Ever since 1066, when the Norman dukes became kings of England, the jurisdictions of the French and English monarchies had overlapped. Henry II of En-gland had ruled about half of France. His son, John, lost much of his father's Angevin Empire (see Chapter 9), and by the fourteenth century, England's holdings on the con-tinent had been reduced to Gascony, the region around Bordeaux in southwestern France. England's kings were, however, not yet ready to give up hope of recouping their losses on the continent.

Edward I (r. 1272–1307), the warrior-king who conquered Wales and nearly sub-dued Scotland, reopened war with France to support his allies in Flanders. Flanders and England had close economic ties, for English wool merchants supplied the Flemish cloth industry. France evened the odds by helping the Scots fend off the English king. In 1308 the French and English dynasties agreed to a truce, and a royal marriage was arranged to seal peace between the two kingdoms. Edward's son and heir, Edward II, married Isabella, daughter of Philip IV of France. The union was supposed to ensure future good relations between France and England, but instead it created grounds for a conflict between them called the **Hundred Years' War**.

Edward II (r. 1307–1327) was as weak a king as his father had been strong. He led his army to disastrous defeat in Scotland, and his excessive devotion to a few un-worthy friends alienated his barons and his wife, Isabella. In 1325 she traveled to Paris on a diplomatic mission to her brother's court, and there she began an affair with an exiled English nobleman, Roger Mortimer, the Earl of March. Isabella and Mortimer raised an army, returned to England, and forced Edward to abdicate in the name of his son, Edward III (r. 1327–1377). The ex-king died, or most likely was murdered, a few months later, and Isabella and Mortimer governed England as re-gents for his son. In 1330 Edward III overthrew them and at age 18 began his inde-pendent rule.

Edward II had seriously damaged the prestige of the monarchy, but Edward III was just the man to restore it. He was a handsome, athletic young man who looked like a king, and he had a gift for what the modern world would call public relations. Enthu-siasm for the Arthurian romances was at its height when Edward came to the throne, and he encouraged his subjects to think of him as a new Arthur. He hosted feasts and tournaments at which he and his friends played at being knights of the round table, and in 1348 he founded the Order of the Garter, a fraternity of knights like the one that the legendary King Arthur had assembled at Camelot.

Hundred Years' War: Opening Phase   Although ceremonies help build a royal image, a medieval king who aspired to glory had to win his spurs as a warrior. Edward led several forays into Scotland, but his men were not excited by the prospect of plundering such a poverty-stricken land. Much more tempting were the rich provinces of their traditional enemy, France. Moreover, Edward believed that he had a justification for a war with France He claimed to be the rightful heir to the French throne.

Ever since its founding in the tenth century, France's Capetian dynasty had enjoyed remarkable biological success. Whenever a king died, there was always a son to take his place. Philip IV had seemingly ensured the future of the dynasty by siring three sons: Louis X (r. 1314–1316), Philip V (r. 1316–1322), and Charles IV (r. 1322–1328). Each succeeded to the throne, but surprisingly, none produced a male heir who survived his father. When Charles died in 1328, the senior line of the Capetian house died with him. The Capetian family, however, did not die out. It had a collateral branch founded by Philip IV's brother, Duke Charles of Valois (1270–1325), who had a son named Philip. When Charles IV died, the throne passed to his cousin Philip of Valois, France's King Philip VI (r. 1328–1350).

Edward did not protest when Philip was crowned in 1328. However, in 1337 the English king's eagerness for an excuse to invade France prompted him to claim that the French throne should have come to him. Philip VI was only Philip IV's nephew. Edward was Philip IV's grandson, a more direct heir. The French disagreed. They pointed out that Edward's link with the Capetian line was through his mother, Isabella, and they claimed that ancient Frankish tradition—the so-called Salian Law—barred women from occupying France's throne or transmitting title to it. This legal wrangling was only a smoke screen. Edward hardly expected France to turn itself over to him. Nor was he likely to conquer it with the resources of a kingdom that was one-quarter its size. His claim to France's throne, however, provided the English with a high-minded justification for looting and pillaging the French.

Edward could do little more than harass the French by staging quick raids on their territory, but in 1346 one of his forays turned into a major battle. A large French army surprised Edward while he was charging across Normandy and forced him to take a stand near the village of Crécy (see Map 11–2). The English were outnumbered, but an unconventional strategy saved them. Edward took up a defensive position and waited for the French to charge him. Archers armed with a uniquely English weapon, the longbow, were stationed on both wings of his army. Their arrows reduced the heavily armored French cavalry to a flailing heap of wounded horses and men before its charge reached the English lines. Edward's knights then dashed in, completed the rout, and won a victory that was as complete as it was unexpected.

The lesson of Crécy was that the era of cavalry's dominance on medieval battlefields was coming to an end, and the reluctance of the French feudal aristocracy to accept this explains why the Hundred Years' War dragged on for so long. Small English armies using new methods repeatedly defeated larger French forces that insisted on

Map 11–2 The Hundred Years' War   France was politically divided at the start of the Hundred Years' War not only between the kings of England and France, but among France's powerful nobles. One of the effects of the war was to increase the power of the French king within his own realm.

Question: What role did geography play in determining the outcome of the Hundred Years' War?

fighting with outmoded techniques. England, however, did not have the strength to exploit its victories and occupy France. All the English could do was go home and celebrate their victories while the French prepared for the next round. The result was periods of combat separated by periods of peace, but no progress toward a resolution of the war.

The medieval aristocracy owed its social and political supremacy to its military technology, but by the fourteenth century new weapons were making expensive aristocratic training and equipment anachronistic. Minimal training was needed to teach a man how to shoot a crossbow—a small bow that was bent by a crank and released by a trigger—and it was so lethal that the church tried to outlaw its use. It cost little to arm large numbers of men with longbows. Their six-foot length gave them great range and power, but a lot of practice was needed to master them. They were therefore used primarily by men from Wales and England who grew up with them. The Swiss developed a weapon called a pike—a combination long-handled spear, axe, and grappling hook. With it, a company of infantrymen could halt a cavalry charge in its tracks, pull knights off their mounts, and slaughter them. By the fourteenth century, gunpowder was also bringing primitive cannons and small arms onto battlefields—although these weapons were not yet very effective. Knights defended themselves against the new weapons by increasing their armor, but heavier armor meant less mobility and therefore vulnerability of a different kind.

Infantry had dominated the battlefields of the ancient world. At the start of the Middle Ages, inventions such as the stirrup had permitted cavalry to gain the upper hand. By the fourteenth century, new inventions were again reversing the balance of power. This was clear to objective observers, but people are reluctant to abandon behaviors that are fundamental to their sense of identity and way of life. France's knights resisted acknowledging that the hard-won traditional military skills of their class were no longer effective, and their obduracy nearly cost France its independence.

As Edward aged, his son and heir apparent, Edward "the Black Prince" (1330–1376), took over the reins of government. In 1356 at Poitiers the prince won a second major victory over the French that was nearly a repeat of his father's triumph at Crécy. He captured the French king, John II, "the Good" (r. 1350–1364), and carted him off to captivity in England. John was a dubious prize. The rules of chivalry required that his English hosts foot the bill for maintaining him in a style appropriate to his rank until his French subjects ransomed him. After an appropriately kingly sum was promised to the English, John went back to France. But when he discovered that it could not be paid, he decided that honor required him to return to captivity in England. He died there a few months later.

During John's absence, France was governed by his far more competent son, Charles V, "the Wise" (r. 1364–1380). Charles earned his reputation for wisdom by giving up pitched battles with the English and turning conduct of the war over to a guerilla fighter, Bertrand du Guesclin (1320–1380). Bertrand's army was composed of mercenaries who valued victory and survival more highly than chivalry. The long war multiplied the numbers of men who fought for pay, and this added to the problems of the Age of Anxiety. Governments hired mercenaries for specific campaigns and then discharged them. Between bouts of employment, these professional soldiers, who had no other sources of income, supported themselves by freelance looting and raping.

■ ■

PEOPLE IN CONTEXT Christine de Pizan (c. 1364–1430), Professional Writer

In 1368 France's King Charles V (r. 1364–1380) offered Tommaso di Benvenuto da Pizzano, a professor of medicine and astrology at the University of Bologna, the post of royal astrologer, and Tommaso moved his family to Paris. His daughter Christine surely absorbed much from the conversations of the learned men who were her father's colleagues and friends, but her only formal education was the elementary training that medieval society gave middle- and upper-class girls.

Christine anticipated a conventional life. At about the age of 16 she married Etienne de Castel, one of the king's secretaries. The couple produced two sons and a daughter, and then the family's fortunes began to fail. Charles V died, leaving the throne to a more frivolous monarch, Charles VI (r. 1380–1422), who provided little patronage for the scholars who had adorned his father's court. Christine's father died in poverty about 1387, and three years later her husband followed his

Christine de Pizan This late medieval manuscript illumination depicts Christine de Pizan in the act of writing one of her popular works. For companionship she has a lap dog, a pet associated with aristocratic ladies.

father-in-law to the grave. Christine, at the age of 25, was left alone to support herself, three young children, a mother, and a niece.

Christine had no training for a trade or profession, but she was literate. She appears, at first, to have maintained her household by working as a copyist. In the days before the printing press, book sellers got their wares from scribes who wrote them out by hand. One benefit of being a copyist was the opportunity the job provided for self-education. A copyist was lent books to work with that otherwise might have been hard to come by, and copying a book meant reading it. This provided Christine with sufficient education to become an author herself.

In 1402 Christine published her first collection of poems, and she soon established herself as one of France's more popular and prolific writers. Some of her works dealt with the theme of love and drew on the romances that were staples of late medieval popular literature. But she also treated more serious themes. She discussed politics and education and advised kings, dukes, and princes. She was particularly interested in the condition of women. She wrote extensively about the roles they had played in history and offered them advice on how to make the best of their current opportunities. Fittingly, Christine's last poem was a celebration of the deeds of a female contemporary who vindicated her faith in the potential of women: Joan of Arc.

Question: What does the career of a woman like Christine de Pizan suggest about the role of women in late medieval society?

There was a long lull in the Hundred Years' War in the second half of the fourteenth century while England struggled with internal problems. The Black Prince, who had been raiding France from his base in Gascony, diverted his attention to civil wars in Spain. By 1367 his overtaxed Gascon subjects were in revolt, and he was suffering from an illness that slowly killed him. Edward turned his duties over to his brother, John of Gaunt, the Duke of Lancaster (1340–1399). He then retired to England, where he died in 1376. By then, the aging Edward III was mentally incompetent. Because the Black Prince's son Richard (his heir) was still a minor, John of Gaunt (the boy's uncle) governed England as a regent. But given the anomalous situation, he was barely able to restrain the quarrelsome English nobility.

When Richard II (r. 1377–1399) reached maturity, he was determined to exercise what he believed was his God-given right to autocratic power. This necessitated the destruction of some of England's great noblemen—particularly Henry of Lancaster, John of Gaunt's son and Richard's cousin. Richard's attempt to strip Henry of his estates was a major mistake. England's barons realized that if Richard succeeded in humiliating the powerful Duke of Lancaster, none of them would be safe. Therefore they rallied to Henry's side and forced Richard to abdicate. Given that Richard had no son, the campaign cleared the way for Henry to claim his cousin's crown.

The Hundred Years' War: Concluding Phase   There were other English nobles with royal ancestry who could have claimed Richard's crown. Consequently, the new Lancastrian monarch, Henry IV (r. 1399–1413), was forced to spend his reign shoring up support for a somewhat shaky throne. His son, Henry V (r. 1413–1422), decided that the best way to promote the young dynasty's popularity with its subjects was to revive the war with France. In 1415, in what was virtually a repeat of Crécy and Poitiers, a large French army cornered the English invaders at Agincourt and was decimated by the English longbow. This time, however, the aftermath of the battle was different, for the situation in France had changed.

In 1392 France's king, Charles VI (r. 1380–1422), began to suffer violent bouts of insanity that required him to be restrained and confined. His uncle Philip, Duke of

Burgundy, and his brother Louis, Duke of Orléans, contested control of the regency for the disabled king. In 1407 Philip's heir, John "the Fearless," assassinated Louis, and war broke out between the Burgundian and Orléanist (or Armagnac) factions. The army that Henry V defeated at Agincourt was Orléanist. After their loss, the Orléanists tried to heal the breach with the Burgundians, but at the peace conference a disgruntled Orléanist avenged Louis's death by assassinating the Burgundian duke. The infuriated Burgundians promptly allied with Henry and gave Agincourt's victor the help he needed to occupy Paris and capture Charles VI. Henry married Charles's daughter, Catherine, and in due course the union produced a male infant—the future Henry VI—who was declared heir to both England and France.

There was another claimant to the French throne, Charles VI's son, Charles "the Dauphin" (the title of the heir to the French throne). As the English advanced, the Dauphin fled to safety in a region that was still controlled by Orléanists, but his sup-

Joan of Arc The art of portraiture began to be revived in the late Middle Ages. One of the earliest reliable royal portraits is one painted of France's King John the Good about 1350. This picture of Joan of Arc is found in a manuscript from the late fifteenth century. Although it dates to Joan's era, no one can know if its artist had any idea of what she looked like. *Marc Charmet/Picture Desk, Inc./Kobal Collection*

porters were too dispirited and disorganized to put up much of a fight. Their prospects improved in 1422, when both Charles VI and Henry V died. The regents who governed for the infant King Henry VI (r. 1422–1461) were his two English uncles. Although it was soon apparent that they were not working well together, another seven years passed before the Dauphin's party took advantage of England's weakness. The Orléanists were finally prodded to action by a 17-year-old peasant girl, Joan of Arc (c. 1412–1431). On her own initiative she made her way to Charles's court to inform him that God had sent her to save France. Charles was skeptical, but he had little to lose by backing her. His soldiers responded enthusiastically to her confident assertion that God was with them, and they began to roll back the poorly led English. In 1429 they regained Reims, the city in whose cathedral France's kings were crowned, and the Dauphin was enthroned as King Charles VII (r. 1429–1461). Confident that England's defeat was now only a matter of time, Charles concluded that Joan had served her purpose, and he began to shunt her aside. When the Burgundians captured her in 1430, he declined to ransom her, and her captors sold her to the English. England hoped to demoralize the French by convicting Joan of heresy. After a lengthy trial, they burned her at the stake, but her death did not improve their situation. (The pope declared Joan's innocence in 1455, but the church did not canonize her until 1920.)

In 1435 Duke Philip "the Good" of Burgundy sealed England's fate by making peace with Charles VII. England had no hope of resisting a united France, and by 1453, it had lost everything on the continent but the port city of Calais (which it retained until 1558). The French monarchy emerged from its humiliation stronger than ever. The long war, which was fought entirely on French territory, convinced the French that they needed a strong royal defender. The king's subjects knew that he had to have the power to act quickly and decisively. Therefore, they did not resist his efforts to tax them or force him to consult with them on major decisions. Wartime conditions prevented the Estates General from aspiring to the kind of political and fiscal authority the English Parliament sought and promoted development of absolute monarchy in France.

The situation in England was different. After a century of famous victories, the English king had to admit to his subjects that he had won the battles but lost the war. This damaged the prestige of the crown, and Henry VI lacked the talent to rebuild it. He was a weak, distracted ruler, and in 1453 he suffered a mental breakdown. A powerful faction formed in support of his more competent cousin, the Duke of York, and in 1455 civil war erupted. The heraldic symbol of the king's Lancastrian family was a red rose, and that of his Yorkist cousins was a white rose. The conflict between them has therefore been dubbed the **War of the Roses**.

The Yorkists triumphed over the Lancastrians, but their tenure on the throne was brief. Edward IV (r. 1466–1483), who deposed Henry, left a 13-year-old heir who disappeared shortly after his father's death. The boy and his brother had been entrusted to an uncle who claimed their inheritance and declared himself King

Richard III (r. 1483–1485). Richard's title was quickly challenged by the exiled leader of the Lancastrian faction, Henry Tudor. Henry invaded England, and Richard died in battle, deserted by his followers. With Richard, the Plantagenet dynasty and England's medieval era came to an end. The new king, Henry VII (r. 1485–1509), founded the Tudor dynasty and began to rebuild the battered monarchy. Much was yet to happen, however, before England settled on what kind of royal government it would have.

KEY QUESTION | Revisited

Periods of stress pose challenges that reveal the weaknesses and prove the strengths of individuals and institutions. The civilization that blossomed in Europe in the twelfth and thirteenth centuries was tested by the crises of the fourteenth and fifteenth. The church did not fare well. But the lapses in its performance gave the faithful the freedom to assume more responsibility for themselves and motivated scholars to think deeply about the nature of legitimate authority. Plagues and economic difficulties confronted states with problems that were beyond their understanding and control, and the use to which they put the tools of government—legislation and war—probably made bad situations worse. The outcome, however, may have been progress toward a stronger, more open society. Economic opportunities improved for the masses. Wars decimated the ranks of the aristocracy, and popular uprisings hinted at new assertiveness on the part of ordinary people. Few persons outside of university circles were probably familiar with the philosophical treatises that developed rationales for individual autonomy, free inquiry, and representative government, but these characteristic features of modern Western civilization were beginning to have some effect on people's lives.

Review Questions

1. What environmental and geographical factors helped make Europe vulnerable to plague?
2. Was religion the only source of medieval Europe's hostility to Islam?
3. How did the problems Europe faced in the late Middle Ages affect its traditional institutions, the church and state?
4. How did reformers justify sitting in judgment on popes (and kings) who were believed to be established on their thrones by God?
5. Why was tiny England able to win so many victories and sustain such a long war with the much larger nation of France?
6. Was Europe strengthened or weakened by the crises of the Age of Anxiety?

Please consult the Suggested Readings at the back of the book to continue your study of the material covered in this chapter. For a list of documents on the Primary Source DVD-ROM that relate to topics in this chapter, please refer to the back of the book.

Topics in This Chapter

The Context for the Renaissance • The Culture of the Renaissance • The Northern
Renaissance • The Middle East: The Ottoman Empire • Europe and Atlantic Exploration

12 Renaissance and Exploration

God gives man the power to have whatever he wants and become whatever he
decides to be. At birth animals have—from their mothers' wombs—all that they will
ever have. At the Creation (or shortly thereafter) the angels became what they will
forever be. But when man appeared, God the Father bestowed on him all of life's
possibilities. Therefore, whatever each individual cultivates will mature and bear fruit
as his nature.

—**Giovanni Pico della Mirandola,** *Oration on the Dignity of Man*

KEY | Question

How should a society use its history?

Giovanni Pico della Mirandola had high ambitions for himself and for all humanity. The
youngest son of the ruler of a tiny state in Italy's Po Valley, he studied at the universities of
Bologna, Padua, and Paris, where he was particularly attracted to Hebrew literature. Pico
believed that the insights of major thinkers from all the ancient Western civilizations—
Greek, Latin, Hebrew, and Arabic—could be reconciled, and at the young age of 23 he set
out to prove this by defending some 900 theses. When the church condemned 13 of his
propositions as heretical, Pico fled to France. A powerful patron interceded for him, and he
was allowed to return to Italy to live out the remainder of his short life in Florence, the capital of the Renaissance.

Pico's celebration of human potential—his faith in the power of people to shape their
own destinies—signaled a shift in European intellectual history. Early medieval thinkers,
such as Augustine of Hippo (354–430), claimed that sin rendered human nature impotent
and turned the world into a worthless realm doomed to extinction. They denigrated earthly
life as something from which people waited to be rescued by God's grace. There was much

Michelangelo's *David* This photo is of a replica of one of the most famous statues from the era of the Italian Renaissance, Michelangelo's *David*. When the original was moved indoors, the replica took its place on Florence's Piazza della Signoria.

in both pagan philosophy and sacred literature to support their view, but Renaissance optimists like Pico believed that these thinkers had missed a more fundamental truth. The Bible's Creator-God had declared His Creation good, imparted His image to the people He made, and ordered them to go forth to populate and subdue the world. God's prime directive was a command that human beings share the divine work of perfecting Creation—themselves included.

Pico was not alone in proclaiming the "dignity" and "excellence" of humanity. The architect Leon Battista Alberti (1404–1472) spoke for many when he asserted that "man can do everything that he sets his mind to." This, the Renaissance's proponents argued, was not a groundless faith but a truth taught by Scripture and the Greek and Roman sages. What set men like Pico and Alberti apart from their medieval predecessors and made them "modern" men, they believed, was their rediscovery of this ancient wisdom.

Some clergy and conservative scholars of the Renaissance era urged caution. They warned that it was a mistake to put too much trust in human virtue, rationality, and self-sufficiency, for the true ancient wisdom was that history offered little support for the kind of confidence in human nature that Pico and Alberti preached. In light of the human record therefore, bold departures from tradition and attacks on the status quo were unwise.

Western civilization has repeatedly reengaged its own history. Sometimes the past has served as a "dead hand," a legacy that caps what people permit themselves to think and do. It inspires a kind of religious fundamentalism, a belief that certain ideas or institutions transcend history. They are eternal absolutes that never change and must not be challenged. Veneration for the past can retard development, but it can also provide security during turbulent times. Conversely, a revival of interest in a historical era can prompt people to think about the present in new ways. It can inspire critiques of received truths and launch reform movements. Either way, the past shapes the present and the future. Much depends on what people do with their history.

The Context for the Renaissance

The Renaissance is a controversial period for historians. They debate when it began, how it should be defined, and even its importance. Some scholars stress the Renaissance's role in ending the medieval era and launching the modern world. Others emphasize its continuity with the Middle Ages and note that its effects were limited. There is, however, widespread agreement that its origin is to be found in medieval Italy's unique urban institutions.

Formation of City-States in Italy   The commercial activity that flourished during the High Middle Ages scattered towns across the map of Europe, but city life flourished more vigorously in Italy than elsewhere. Most of Europe's trade via Mediterranean routes passed through Italy's ports and generated employment for large urban populations. By 1400, four of Europe's five largest cities (Genoa, Florence, Milan, and Venice) were to be found in Italy. Only Paris (at about 80,000) was their equal. Italy had about 20 cities in the second rank with populations of about 25,000. In the rest of Europe, there were only four.

Size and number were not all that made Italy's cities noteworthy. In most parts of Europe a city's jurisdiction ended at its walls, and a city was an isolated island of special political privilege operating inside a larger governmental entity such as a kingdom or the domain of a noble. Italy's cities, however, acquired power over the lands around them and became city-states. The territory a town controlled was often small. Its farthest frontier might be only a day's ride from its urban center. But wealth from trade and industry gave some Italian city-states influence comparable to the much larger countries of northern Europe.

Geography—a mix of mountains, valleys, and plains—encouraged the political division of the Italian peninsula, and some of its city-states had their origin as *civitates* of Rome's former empire. Others, however, owed their rise to medieval Italy's unique political situation. The division of the Carolingian Empire in the ninth century was followed by the rise of royal dynasties in France and Germany, but not in Italy. The Italians had no native king around which central government could coalesce, and at least one Italian power was determined to prevent the establishment of a secular monarchy in Italy. Rome's bishop, the pope, ruled an Italian state, but he also claimed jurisdiction over all Europeans. If a secular ruler succeeded in uniting Italy, the pope would have come under his control and lost credibility as a universal religious leader. He was convinced therefore that the only way to preserve the church was to prevent Italy's political unification. (Popes are still the heads of a state—the 105-acre Vatican City—that is independent of Italy's government.)

For much of the medieval period, it was Germans and not Italians who sought unification of Italy. When Germany's kings assumed the imperial title and invaded Italy, Italy's landed aristocracy had no native king behind whom to rally in defense of their estates, but they had allies close at hand. The urban communities that flourished as trade began to revive in the eleventh and twelfth centuries shared the nobility's opposition to German domination. In addition to political objectives, town and country also had economic concerns in common. Townspeople bought the food raised on the nobles' rural estates, and nobles bought the products manufactured and imported by towns. Over time, self-interest brought urban and rural leaders closer and closer together. Nobles moved into town, intermarried with bourgeois families, and integrated into urban life. As the families and properties of merchants and landowners intermingled, the town's authority spread over the countryside, and it became a city-state.

Many of Italy's city-states began as communes—associations of tradespeople who voluntarily banded together for mutual benefit. A commune was often governed by a town council (of a hundred or more members) assisted by a pair of executive officers. Checks and balances and short terms in office were relied on to prevent individuals or political parties from monopolizing power, but these strategies were not very effective. Family and clan groups competed for dominance. They built fortified towers inside towns and sallied forth to battle one another in the streets. Trade and merchant guilds and various kinds of fraternities also jockeyed for advantage. Consequently, a commune's leaders were engaged in a never ending struggle to persuade numerous self-interested groups to work together. If a hopeless stalemate developed, it became common by the second half of the twelfth century for a town to suspend its constitution and temporarily turn itself over to a *podestà*. A **podestà** was an outsider who was empowered to govern a town for a limited period of time. Because he was a neutral stranger, factions trusted him to arbitrate their disputes and get their community back on track. The danger, of course, was that a *podestà* might make his lordship permanent.

This happened frequently, for republics were far less efficient and less able to defend them-selves than states ruled by autocrats. Sometimes the autocrats openly reveled in their power, as did the Visconti and Sforza despots who ruled Milan. Sometimes they masquer-aded behind a republican facade, as did Florence's Medici family. The exception was the "Serene Republic" of Venice. It was governed by a small number of families who alone had hereditary right to political office, but a constitution that headed off suicidal factional fighting among these families and an adequate distribution of wealth prevented the kind of internal upheaval that brought strongmen to power in many of Italy's states.

Italy's Political Development   The Italian peninsula was divided into political zones of different types (see Map 12–1). A kingdom centered on Naples governed the southern portion of the peninsula. Its rulers won and lost Sicily several times and occa-sionally crossed the Adriatic to try to conquer portions of the Balkans. The popes' realm, the Papal States, spanned the center of Italy and extended up the Adriatic coast into the former Byzantine exarchate of Ravenna. It was a large, but inherently unstable, entity. Entrenched aristocratic families fought among themselves for control of the pa-pacy, and popes, who were often elderly men with short reigns, had difficulty maintain-ing order. Northern Italy was divided among major and minor city-states that experimented with different kinds of governments. Some (primarily Venice, Florence, Genoa, Lucca, Pisa, and Siena) called themselves republics. Others (Milan, Ferrara, Mantua, and Modena) were duchies. Functionally, all were oligarchies dominated in different ways by wealthy minorities.

International trade gave the Italian city-states more wealth and influence than small territories might be expected to possess. Milan, a large northern duchy, lacked ac-cess to the sea but controlled approaches to vital passes through the Alps. Genoa, Mi-lan's western neighbor, was a small coastal republic controlled by a powerful merchant oligarchy. It had a large navy and was one of Italy's richest ports. Venice, a city built on lagoons and islands at the top of the Adriatic, was Genoa's chief competitor for Mediter-ranean trade. Its wealth derived from its commercial ties with Constantinople and the Byzantine Empire. Venice, like Genoa, was formally a republic and functionally an oli-garchy. With the exception of Venice, factionalism plagued the Italian city-states—none more than Florence, the cultural capital of the Renaissance.

Florence was an inland town on the Arno River that traded through the port of Pisa (which it conquered in 1406). Its wealth, which derived from textile manufacturing, banking, and international finance, was immense, but unevenly distributed. A few Flo-rentine families amassed huge fortunes, which they used to fight among themselves. Lesser persons were drawn into their disputes, and unruly factions formed behind the major contestants. Social and economic conditions periodically increased the volatility of the situation. Well over half the city's residents were wage laborers whose economic condition was perilous. Their employment depended on the wildly fluctuating interna-tional cloth market. When it boomed, they worked. When it crashed from overproduc-tion or was otherwise disrupted, they starved. The Great Pestilence that spread through Europe in 1347 created a major crisis. It may have reduced the city's population by more than a third in a few months. Florence, along with the rest of the world, was thrown into

Map 12–1 Renaissance Italy This map simplifies the complicated political geography of Italy during the era of the Renaissance. The boundaries of its states shifted with their military fortunes, and alliances and leagues further altered the configuration of the political landscape.

Question: How did geographical features divide the Italian peninsula? What were the political implications of its division?

economic confusion. By 1350 Florence's first banks, those of the Riccardi, Frescobaldi, Peruzzi, and Bardi families, had all failed—due in large part to the refusal of kings to repay their loans. The city's government was unprepared to deal with the situation. It was controlled by trade and merchant guilds that looked out for the interests of the propertied classes. Humble laborers had no representation. In 1378 poverty and frustration with an unresponsive system triggered a rebellion by the city's wool workers. Their so-called "Ciompi Revolt" was put down, and political infighting among the great families continued.

A new era began in 1434 with the ascendancy of Cosimo de Medici (1389–1464). The bank his father, Giovanni de Medici (1360–1429), founded laid the foundation for a staggering fortune that Cosimo used to oust his opponents and bring the republic under his control. After Francesco Sforza, a **condottiere** (commander of a mercenary army), came to power in Milan in 1450, Cosimo ended a war with the duchy. This was followed in 1454 by a treaty, the Peace of Lodi, that established a balance of power among Italy's greater states: Florence and Milan on one side and Venice and Naples on the other.

Florence owed much of its cultural as well as its political influence to Cosimo de Medici, who began his family's custom of providing patronage for scholars and artists. His grandson, Lorenzo "the Magnificent" (1449–1492), attached some of the period's greatest artists (the young Michelangelo, for example) to his household. Medieval artists often labored in anonymity as humble craftsmen, but the Medici broke with tradition and treated the artists and intellectuals they supported more as honored guests than as servants. The Renaissance highly esteemed talented individuals, no matter what their origin, and the princes who competed for their services believed that their own reputations were enhanced by the genius of the people they attracted to their courts.

The Italian cities' willingness to agree to the Peace of Lodi in 1454 may have owed something to an event that occurred in May of 1453. Constantinople fell to the Ottoman Turks, who had previously moved into the Aegean, Greece, and the Balkans. They were eventually to occupy Hungary, besiege Austria, attempt a direct assault on Italy, and replace Venice as the dominant naval power in the eastern Mediterranean. The fear they inspired was ultimately, however, not great enough to persuade the Italian states to form a united front and cease squabbling among themselves. In 1494 the Papacy joined Naples and Florence in an alliance aimed at Milan, and Milan sought aid from France. The armies of King Charles VIII (r. 1483–1498) swiftly swept through Italy, and the French laid claim to Naples. The Pope and Venice responded by appealing to Germany's Holy Roman Emperor for help. The conflict among Italy's city-states grew to include France, Germany, and Spain. The event that is sometimes seen as marking the end of the Renaissance was a sack of the city of Rome by German forces in 1527 (see Chapter 13).

Italy's troubles during this period prompted the composition of one of the most influential books ever written about politics: *The Prince* by Florentine historian Niccolò Machiavelli (1469–1527). It purports to be a primer for the instruction of a young Medici heir in the arts of government. The lesson Machiavelli draws from history is that a ruler should allow nothing—religion, morality, law, or conscience—to stand in the way of the pursuit of power. The "Machiavellian methods" the book so bluntly advocates (manipulation, brutality, hypocrisy, and treachery) are so extreme in their ruthlessness and amorality that some readers believe that Machiavelli intended his book as a joke. It is likely, however, that Italy's turbulent history convinced the Florentine scholar that nothing mattered more than the establishment of a government strong enough to maintain order.

In 1516 (three years after *The Prince* appeared), Machiavelli's English contemporary, Thomas More, published a witty satire that was similarly pessimistic in its assessment of politics. More called his book and the mythical society it described *Utopia* (Greek for "No-place"). More's Utopians behaved completely rationally. The contrast between their customs and those of More's contemporaries revealed that Europeans clearly did not. Like Machiavelli, More was acutely aware of the painful gap between what human beings are and what they might aspire to be.

Italy's Economy and the Renaissance   The leaders of the Renaissance broke with the ascetic, world-denying ideals of the Middle Ages by stressing the nobility of human existence and the legitimacy of earthly pleasures. They gloried in the creation of beautiful things, the possession of rare objects, esoteric scholarship, courtly refinements, and various forms of conspicuous consumption. All of this was supported and encouraged by the great wealth that accumulated in Italy. Much of that wealth came from Italy's dominance of trade between Europe and the Middle East. Profits from this commerce provided capital to fund banks, and Italy's bankers multiplied their wealth by becoming Europe's leading financiers, industrialists, and (what today would be called) venture capitalists.

Much of the wealth that Italians earned stayed in Italy, for they had to spend little of it abroad. Italy had sufficient raw materials to supply its home industries, enough agricultural production to feed its population, and monopolies on the manufacture of many (but certainly not all) of the luxury goods its people consumed. More money entered Italian markets with invading German, French, and Spanish armies, and the papal treasury in Rome siphoned funds from every corner of Europe.

Political fragmentation prevented any one ruler or government from monopolizing these resources. Wealth was always concentrated in the hands of small elites, but Italy's chronic instability—shifting political fortunes, economic crashes, and onslaughts of plague—kept society open and provided opportunities for some social mobility. Italy, in short, had an ideal environment for the growth of an entrepreneurial middle class of pioneering capitalists who respected talent, industry, and ambition. The Renaissance was, in many ways, an affirmation of the politically engaged, family oriented, secular lifestyle of a prosperous, powerful, and self-aware bourgeoisie.

The Culture of the Renaissance

Most people today associate Italy's Renaissance with the arts—sculpture, painting, and architecture. But the Renaissance was above all a literary movement devoted to the study of ancient Greek and Latin texts. Its scholars searched out forgotten manuscripts, and they found some long-disregarded works in Europe's libraries. Cicero's letters and Tacitus's histories were significant additions to the Latin corpus. A surge in Greek studies also made texts by Homer and Plato widely available to western Europeans. But the Renaissance owed less to the discovery of new documents than to the development of a new way of reading familiar ones. Medieval scholars had long mined classical literature for useful ideas. But Renaissance scholars valued this literature for its own sake and did their best to grasp the original intent of its authors. As they read, they were excited to discover what they thought was an ancient way of life that confirmed their own.

Most historical eras are named by later generations looking back at the past, for it usually takes time for the significance of events to become clear. But the Renaissance was an era named by the people who lived it. The poet and scholar, Petrarch (1304–1374), witnessed a world convulsed by plague, war, and the breakdown of the church, but he was convinced that his generation was on the brink of a glorious new age—that it was emerging from a long dark period during which civilization had languished. Petrarch defined civilization as the way of life pioneered by the ancient Greeks and Romans, and he believed that it was being reborn in Italy's city-states, in communities that he assumed resembled ancient Athens and Rome. For Petrarch, the previous millennium had been "the middle ages," a period of cultural retreat and retrenchment between the ancient and modern worlds, the eras of true civilization.

The Humanist Agenda   The intellectual leaders of the Renaissance were called humanists, for they advocated the study of humanity (**studia humanitatis**). This should not be taken to imply that they embraced what some Americans have called "secular humanism," an atheistic ideology. That the Renaissance was far from hostile to religion is demonstrated by the abundance of religious paintings from the era that can be found in the collection of any major museum. The humanists did, however, value the material world and secular life more highly than many of their medieval predecessors.

Renaissance humanists were often professional scholars who specialized in rhetoric, the study of language—particularly the works of ancient orators such as Cicero and Seneca. Their more traditional faculty colleagues, the scholastic dialecticians who worshiped Aristotle, believed that the function of language was to construct logical arguments. The humanists, in contrast thought of language as an instrument for persuasion. Reason was all that mattered for the scholastics. But humanists maintained that will and passion were also important, for people were more than reasoning machines. Logic and detached contemplation were not enough; to be convinced of truths and fulfilled as individuals, people needed action, empathy, and engagement with the world.

The humanists' philosophy of life affirmed the values of Italy's urban classes. Humanists believed that people should marry, have families, shoulder political responsibilities, develop their individual talents, and enjoy the beauties and pleasures of the material world. They maintained that a fully human life was packed with action and achievement, and that a fully developed human being was a multifaceted individual who was interested in everything and able to do all things well. This was more than a theory; it was a reasonably accurate description of some of the giants of the Renaissance.

Poets and Prose Writers   Early signs of the Renaissance appear in the work of the poet Dante Alighieri (1265–1321) and emerge more clearly in the writings of two of his fellow Florentines of the next generation: the aforementioned Petrarch and Boccaccio

(1313–1375). All three, as was the medieval custom, wrote in Latin when addressing the scholarly community, but their fame derives in large part from what they wrote in Italian. Humanists were enthusiastic students of the classical languages, but they understood that Latin and Greek had been the speech of ordinary people in the ancient world. They concluded therefore that poets and serious thinkers ought to use the tongues common to the eras in which they live.

Dante's thought was deeply rooted in the Middle Ages, but he lived like a Renaissance intellectual. Most medieval scholars took clerical orders, but not Dante. He married, had a family, and pursued a political career. He became a professional man of letters after his party's fall from power forced him to leave Florence and spend the rest of his life in exile.

Among Dante's Latin works was a treatise (*De vulgari eloquentia*) that urged scholars to break with tradition and write in the vernacular so that a wider audience might profit from their work. Dante practiced what he preached—with phenomenal success. About 1293, while he was still living in Florence, he finished *La Vita Nuova* (*The New Life*), a cycle of lyric poems and prose narratives celebrating his passion for a woman called Beatrice. She was not his wife or mistress, but a woman whom he adored as a feminine ideal—like a medieval courtly lover—from afar. His masterwork was a huge poem written during his years in exile. He called it *Comedia*, not because it was funny, but because—unlike a tragedy—it was a story with a happy ending. *The Divine Comedy*, the title Dante's readers gave his poem, purports to describe a dream in which the poet journeys through Hell and Purgatory to Heaven, where he is granted a vision of God. Dante's guide during the first stages of his trip is the pagan Roman poet Virgil (70–19 B.C.E.). Because medieval scholars interpreted one of Virgil's poems as a prediction of Christ's birth, Virgil served Dante as a symbol for the truths that reason can intuit without the help of faith. Because reason does not require Scripture or revelation to grasp society's need for laws and the enforcement of justice, Virgil can lead Dante through the realms where sinners are punished—Hell and Purgatory. But because reason cannot grasp the mysteries of divine grace, Virgil turns back at the gates of Heaven. Beatrice, Dante's love, then appears to lead him into Paradise. *The Divine Comedy*'s cosmology and theology are medieval, but its respect for the dignity of human nature and human love hints at the emerging Renaissance. Dante has a higher opinion of some of the sinners whose punishments he describes in Hell than of spiritless people who go to their graves having done nothing either good or bad.

Petrarch studied at a university, was ordained a priest, and sought ecclesiastical stipends to support his work. At first glance therefore, his scholarly career looks more conventional than Dante's, but the two men had much in common. Although he did not marry, Petrarch formed an attachment with a woman and was a family man with a son and daughter. He shared Dante's interest in the poetry of courtly love, and his equivalent of Dante's Beatrice was an unidentified woman whom he called Laura. The sonnets she inspired him to write in Italian are his most popular compositions.

The Renaissance shines more clearly in Petrarch's work than Dante's primarily because of the role Petrarch played in sparking the Renaissance's passion for classical literature. He has been called "the father of humanism." Petrarch believed that intellectual darkness had descended on Europe after Rome's fall, but that the light of civilization was being rekindled for his generation. Progress, he argued, required an educational reform based on a curriculum that polished literary skills (Latin grammar, rhetoric, and poetry) and promoted moral edification (Roman history and Greek philosophy). He urged scholars to comb through libraries for forgotten works by ancient authors, and he believed that he and his contemporaries could train themselves to pick up where these giants of the past had left off. He encouraged the use of classical Latin rather than the ecclesiastical Latin that had evolved during the Middle Ages. His most ambitious attempt to honor the classical tradition was a poem entitled *Africa*, a Latin epic on the life of the Roman republican general, Scipio Africanus (237–183 B.C.E.) which dealt with the struggles leading to the Roman Republic's victory over Carthage. In 1341 the people of Rome gathered on the Capitoline Hill to award Petrarch the ancient symbol of achievement, a crown of laurel. Petrarch's love for the classics persuaded him that fame was a noble pursuit, but it did not override his Christian concern for the sin of pride. He took his pagan trophy to the Vatican and dedicated it to God. The people of Rome were less deferential to traditional religious authority. They rose up in 1347, took control of the city, and tried until 1351 to govern it as a new Roman Republic.

Boccaccio, the illegitimate son of a Florentine banker, was Petrarch's devoted disciple. Petrarch's influence persuaded Boccaccio to abandon the poetry and storytelling of his youth and take up classical studies. He wrote a number of books in Latin that served his contemporaries as useful compendia of information culled from ancient sources. The most popular of these were a genealogical encyclopedia of the pagan gods and collections of biographies of famous men and women. His more well-known compositions, however, are his earlier vernacular works, the most famous of which is a collection of bawdy and serious tales entitled *Decameron* (a combination of Greek words for ten and day). It is a fictive record of a hundred stories that ten young Florentine men and women allegedly told to entertain themselves while they hid from the plague in the comfort of a luxurious country house. Like Dante and Petrarch, Boccaccio was inspired to write poetry by love for a woman. But unlike Dante and probably Petrarch, he had a physical relationship with Fiammetta, the lady whom he idolized. When she deserted him, he poured out his anguish in his poetry. The intimacy and personal nature of these poems illustrate the humanist's confidence that the emotions and interior life of the individual are worthy of study and documentation.

Boccaccio's contemporary, the English author Geoffrey Chaucer (c. 1340–1400), shared this faith. Chaucer, like many of the great Renaissance artists and scholars, was a son of the middle classes with a background in business and experience in politics. He is not usually thought of as a Renaissance figure, but he read Italian and modeled some of his poems on Boccaccio's work. Italy's Renaissance would not have spread so readily to the rest of Europe if cultures north of the Alps had not, on their own, been evolving similar values and interests. Chaucer's most popular work, *The Canterbury Tales*, describes a company of pilgrims en route to the shrine of St. Thomas Becket at Canterbury. Chaucer introduces each pilgrim and then narrates the stories each tells to amuse the others. In this way the book resembles Boccaccio's *Decameron*. The characters in *The Canterbury Tales* are not the kinds of abstract or allegorical types found in much medieval literature. They are unique, memorable persons, and Chaucer bestows individuality on his pilgrims by matching descriptions of them with the stories they tell.

Sculptors   Vernacular literature helped to spread the Renaissance beyond the narrow circle of humanist scholars, but literature was not the only thing that helped the Renaissance extend its influence. Artists and architects created urban environments that exposed ordinary men and women to the spirit of the new age.

Artifacts of Roman civilization were more abundant in late medieval Italy than they are today, and their influence on Italy's sculptors was apparent as early as the thirteenth century. Real bodies seem to exist beneath the classical robes with which the sculptors Nicola Pisano (c. 1220–1284) and his son Giovanni (c. 1250–1320) draped their figures. Renaissance artists did not, however, simply copy ancient models. They combined the idealism of classical art with a new realism that reflected the humanists' emphasis on the individual. Many ancient Greek statues have a detached, timeless quality that renders them static. Renaissance sculptors tried to convey a greater sense of their subjects existing not in timeless eternity, but in a particular moment. They portrayed ideal types, but with a novel vibrancy. Their medieval predecessors had conceived of statuary as architectural ornament and subordinated it to the lines of the buildings it decorated. But the Florentine sculptor Donatello (1386–1466) revived the art of carving statues that, like many of those in the ancient world, were meant to stand alone and be viewed in the round. They were so natural and imbued with life that some people found them shocking. The early work of Michelangelo (1475–1564), particularly the gigantic *David* he created to stand in front of Florence's town hall, represents the humanist ideals of the Renaissance at their best. *David*'s heroic nudity proclaims the glory of an idealized human body, but the statue's proportions were not dictated by slavish imitation of nature or some mathematical theory about ideal form. The statue's outsized head and hands impart tension to its design, and the intense look on David's face hints at the youth's thoughts as he heads into his unequal contest with the giant, Goliath (I Samuel 17).

Architects   The Gothic style that originated in France in the twelfth century had some influence in Italy, but the Mediterranean region clung to the older Romanesque tradition and the elements of classical style which it preserved. The Renaissance's architects drew both inspiration and, unfortunately, building materials from Italy's abundant Roman ruins. Marble, columns, bronze ornaments, and simple bricks were plundered from the remains of ancient buildings for use in new structures. A book on architecture by Vitruvius, a first-century B.C.E. Roman engineer, that came to light in the fifteenth century also helped spread knowledge of the principles underlying classical designs.

Donatello's *David*   Cosimo de Medici, the banker and leader of Florence, built a magnificent palace for his family, and in 1430 commissioned the sculptor Donatello to create a statue for its courtyard. Donatello's subject was the biblical account of the fight between David and Goliath. He represented David as a very young man, nude except for elaborate boots, and standing over the head of his slaughtered enemy. *David*, the first free-standing nude human figure to be sculpted since the end of the Roman Empire, is sometimes said to be the first true Renaissance sculpture. *Bargello National Museum, Florence/Canali PhotoBank, Milan/SuperStock*

■ ■

PEOPLE IN CONTEXT   Elisabetta Gonzaga (1472–1526)

Feminist historians have pointed out that the Renaissance did not affect men and women in the same way. The respect the period accorded individual talent and achievement in the secular realm—in politics, business, and family life—opened doors for some men. But the ancient Greek and Roman societies that the Renaissance admired were thoroughly patriarchal, and their attitude influenced the humanist perspective on the family. It gave new currency to the ancient belief that women (despite the independence some of them enjoyed in the Roman era) should be confined to the domestic sphere and subordinated to the male heads of their households. Economic reality had more to do with the status of women in most poor and middle-class families than did humanist ideology. These women had to work to help support their families, while the upper class could afford to curtail the activities of its women. This deprived aristocratic women of some of the rights and opportunities they had enjoyed during the medieval era. Their fate ultimately affected their lesser sisters, for the upper class set the standards that the middle class adopted whenever it could afford to. This gave Elisabetta Gonzaga's life an importance she could never have anticipated.

Elisabetta's family, the Gonzaga, ruled the tiny Italian state of Mantua. At the age of 16, Elisabetta wed Guidobaldo da Montefeltro, the duke of Urbino. Her husband was a friend of humanists, an art collector, and the owner of one of the larger libraries in Italy. As the duchess of Urbino, Elisabetta presided over a court famous for its refinement and elegance.

Baldassare Castiglione (1478–1529), the count of Novellata and a distinguished papal diplomat, spent his early career in the service of Urbino's duke. Near the end of his life, Castiglione drew on his extensive experience with court life to write *The Book of the Courtier*, a kind of guidebook to the upper reaches of Renaissance society. The volume, which was translated into numerous languages and remained a best seller for over a century, made Elisabetta famous.

The Book of the Courtier purports to be an account of conversations at Elisabetta's court. It describes a kind of salon

Elisabetta Gonzaga   The art of portrait painting flourished during the Renaissance, for it was consistent with the era's celebration of the value of the individual. Scholars have tentatively identified the subject of this painting as Elisabetta Gonzaga. *Dagli Orti (A)/Picture Desk, Inc./Kobal Collection* where Elisabetta and her guests debate the nature of gentility and, not surprisingly, come to the conclusion that their hostess is the ideal Renaissance lady. Elisabetta is praised for her humanist education—for a knowledge of literature, art, and music that ensures that cultured men find her conversation worthy of their time. But her special vocation as a woman is to keep her court running smoothly and, by her charm and elegant behavior, elevate its tone. The physical activities in which men indulge—riding, hunting, and warfare—are beneath her. She attends to the domestic sphere and serves the wider world by civilizing the men who run it.

Some of Elisabetta's aristocratic female acquaintances were cut from different cloth. They governed states and did not shrink from violence and bloodshed. She, however, actually appears to have been the kind of gracious, but submissive, woman that Castiglione described as the period's ideal. Thanks to the success of his book, generations of Europeans thought of her as the embodiment of a model that all women should aspire to emulate.

Question: To what extent are a society's theories about gender roles an accurate guide to how its people actually behave?

The first of the great Renaissance architects was Filippo Brunelleschi (1377–1446). The dome he designed for Florence's cathedral is an engineering marvel, and it still dominates the city's skyline. Brunelleschi intensively studied Roman buildings, but, like the sculptors of the Renaissance, he did not merely copy his models. He admired their symmetry, simplicity, and proportions, and he used their standard design elements (pillars and round arches). However by the way in which he manipulated these things, he mated Renaissance energy with classical stability.

The most ambitious of the Renaissance's building projects was the reconstruction of Europe's largest church, St. Peter's at the Vatican. The first St. Peter's was a basilican church that Emperor Constantine built for the popes in the fourth century. By the fifteenth century it had deteriorated so badly that Pope Nicholas V (r. 1447–1455) was determined to tear it down and replace it with an entirely new building. The work dragged on for two centuries and involved over a dozen architects, the most

Church of St. Andrea   The facade of the Church of St. Andrea, Mantova, Italy, illustrates the conventions of Renaissance architecture: classical motifs, symmetry, and abstract geometrical forms. It was designed about 1470 by Leon Battista Alberti.

important of whom were Donato Bramante (1444–1514), Michelangelo (1475–1564), and Gianlorenzo Bernini (1598–1680). Michelangelo was not only a superb sculptor, but also a brilliant architect, an extraordinary painter, and a competent poet. The frescoes he created for the vault and altar wall of the Vatican's Sistine Chapel (named for its builder, Pope Sixtus IV, r. 1471–1484) are a miracle of design and execution.

Painters   Unlike sculptors and architects, Renaissance painters had few ancient examples of their art to study. They were inspired by classical sculpture. But to imitate it, they had to invent the techniques to represent three-dimensional figures on the flat surfaces of their paintings.

Medieval artists thought of paintings as pages of text. They drew two-dimensional figures against blank backgrounds and suggested depth and distance simply by painting one figure in front of another. They often combined different scenes from a story in the same composition. A single painting of the Virgin Mary might, for instance, depict the Annunciation, the birth of Jesus, and the Virgin's ascent to heaven. Its overall design could be aesthetically pleasing, but its meaning only became clear when its elements were separated and read like words on a page. Renaissance paintings were not pages, but windows. They framed a scene—a view of a realistic, three-dimensional world into which a spectator could imagine stepping.

The Florentine painter Cimabue (c. 1240–1302) worked in a style that was heavily influenced by Byzantine frescoes and mosaics, but he anticipated the Renaissance by experimenting with ways to suggest three-dimensional space and by giving the faces of his subjects individuality and emotional intensity. Giotto di Bondone (1267–1337), his student, had greater success in achieving these objectives. His human subjects manifest strong feelings and move in real space—like actors in theatrical scenes. The plague that began to spread through Europe in 1348 may explain why Giotto (like his younger contemporary, the poet Dante) had no immediate successor. Eventually, however, a Florentine called Masaccio (1401–1428) picked up where Giotto left off, and an extraordinary number of great artists appeared over the course of a few generations.

Perspective   This painting by Piero della Francesca was executed for the ducal palace in Urbino, Italy. It represents an idealized city-scape and illustrates how Renaissance artists created the illusion of space and depth. The rigor of the composition compels viewers to see the scene from the artist's perspective and is consistent with the humanist's vision of a rationally ordered world. *Piero della Francesca (c. 1420–1492). Italian (Piero della Francesca?). View of an Ideal City. Galleria Nazionale delle Marche, Urbino, Italy. Photo credit: Scala/Art Resource, NY*

Research into how to represent **perspective** (that is, create the illusion of three-dimensional space) began with the study of vision and a search for mathematical formulae that would describe how light enters the eye. Brunelleschi's research into the design of architectural space led to the discovery that if lines are traced along the profiles of buildings and extended as far as possible, they all converge at one point on the horizon. Renaissance artists quickly began to orient their compositions around this so-called "vanishing point." Another architect, Alberti, worked out and published the mathematics governing the projection lines that meet at a vanishing point.

Renaissance painters added a new medium to their art. Medieval and early Renaissance painters usually worked in tempera—that is, with pigments mixed with a binder such as egg yolk. They painted on wooden boards or walls covered with wet plaster.

Leading Artists and Authors of Italy's Renaissance

ca. 1220 Nicola Pisano . . .1284
   1240 Cimabue 1302
   1250 Giovanni Pisano . . .1320
   1265 Dante 1321
   1267 Giotto 1337
   1295 Andrea Pisano 1348
   1304 Petrarch 1374
   1313 Boccaccio 1375
   1377 Brunelleschi 1446
   1378 Ghiberti 1455
   1386 Donatello 1466
   1395 Fra Angelico 1455
   1399 Della Robbia 1482
   1400 Jacopo Bellini 1470
   1401 Masaccio 1428
   1406 Filippo Lippi 1469
   1407 Lorenzo Valla 1457
   1415 Piero della Francesca 1492
   1429 Gentile Bellini 1507
   1430 Giovanni Bellini 1516
   1431 Mantegna 1506
   1435 Verrocchio 1488
   1444 Bramante 1514
   1445 Botticelli 1510
   1452 da Vinci 1519
   1457 Filippino Lippi 1504
   1469 Machiavelli 1527
   1475 Michelangelo 1564
   1475 Giorgione 1510
   1483 Raphael 1520
   1485 Titian 1576
   1500 Cellini 1571
   1518 Palladio 1580

Tempera was a restrictive medium, for it dried quickly and its colors did not blend well. Northern European painters were the first to discover that these difficulties could be overcome by mixing their pigments with oils. Oils dried slowly, and translucent oil-based paints could be applied in multiple layers to produce an infinite variety of intense, glowing colors. There is literary evidence for oil painting as early as the twelfth century, but the first great practitioners of the art were the Netherlanders, Hubert (c. 1366–1426) and Jan van Eyck (c. 1390–1441) and Dirk Bouts (1415–1475). They filled their pictures with a wealth of detail—precisely describing the physical world and representing the gleam or texture of all kinds of materials. Northerners also pioneered landscape painting. Medieval artists had sometimes sketched landscapes as background for human activities, but the respect that Renaissance humanists had for the material world made that world a fit subject for study and description in its own right.

Artists working in Venice introduced oil painting to Italy in the late fifteenth century, along with a second northern invention: the use of a canvas on stretchers as a surface for a painting. This expanded the market for art by reducing the cost of pictures and improving their portability. The church's dominance of patronage declined as the prospering urban classes began to commission paintings, and artists found plenty of work producing decorative objects to satisfy the Renaissance's taste for luxury and self-promotion. The era's renewed respect for the individual created a strong demand for a kind of art that had languished during the Middle Ages: portraiture.

The Northern Renaissance

Germany and the Politics of the Holy Roman Empire   Frederick II had largely ignored Germany as he struggled vainly to win control of Italy. After his death and the extermination of his Hohenstaufen dynasty, the German nobles were slow to seat a new king. The German throne remained vacant from 1254 to 1274. In the interim, the country's hundreds of political entities enjoyed independence. Some regions were governed as hereditary duchies, some were ruled by the church, and many were tiny feudal baronies or urban republics and oligarchies. The most interesting political organization that emerged to counter the confusion of the era was a powerful league of cities.

The German merchants who operated in the Baltic region compensated for the absence of a royal protector by forming a corporation (Hanse) and working together to defend themselves. The cities that established the **Hanseatic League** in 1359 did not occupy contiguous territories, but the army and navy they maintained policed the land and sea routes that connected them. At the league's peak, it had about 170 members and exercised a virtual monopoly over Baltic and North Sea commerce. The league dominated the Scandinavian kingdoms, and England and France treated it as if it were a sovereign state. The development of Atlantic trade routes eventually eroded its economic clout, but it survived into the seventeenth century.

A development with more significance for Germany's future took place on the region's eastern borderlands. In 1248, when the family that ruled Austria died out, the duchy of Austria should have returned to its overlord, the Hohenstaufen emperor, Frederick II. However, he was too preoccupied with wars in Italy to assert his claim. A year after Frederick II died, Ottokar II (r. 1253–1278), heir to the kingdom of Bohemia (the region around Prague), annexed Austria. So long as Germany had no king, there was no one to challenge his usurpation of lands that doubled the size of his kingdom.

The situation changed in 1273 when Pope Gregory X (r. 1271–1276) persuaded the German barons to end the squabbling over their vacant throne by electing a king. They chose a minor nobleman, Rudolf of Habsburg (r. 1273–1291) and assumed he would pose no threat to their independence. Because Rudolf's barons feared the powerful king of Bohemia more than their new Habsburg leader, they agreed to help Rudolf reclaim the duchy of Austria for the crown. When the Bohemians withdrew, Rudolf left his tiny ancestral barony on the Aar River east of the Swiss city of Bern and moved his family to Vienna. The Habsburgs reigned there until 1918, when World War I ended their regime.

The German monarchy was elective, and the nobles' preference for weak rulers turned them against the rapidly rising Habsburg family. After Rudolf's death, the electors transferred the royal title to less consequential men. However, in 1310 their attempt to preserve the weakness of their king was frustrated when history repeated itself. Ottokar of Bohemia's family died out, and the Bohemians offered their throne to the son of Germany's king, Henry VII (r. 1308–1313). Henry's family, the Luxemburgs, followed the example set by the Habsburgs and relocated to their new Central-European domain. In 1347 Charles IV (r. 1347–1378), the Luxemburg ruler of Bohemia, became Germany's Holy Roman Emperor. In 1356 he issued a decree that virtually guaranteed that his descendants would keep the imperial title. Charles's Golden Bull (from *bullum*, the seal that ratifies a document) helped to stabilize Germany by limiting participation in imperial elections to the heads of seven great principalities (four secular lords and three archbishops). This established a rough balance of power among the German magnates and ended the pope's meddling in Germany's affairs. Because Charles recognized the independence of the electors, they felt safe in allowing the crown to remain with the Luxemburg family.

In 1440 the Luxemburgs died out and the throne passed to the Habsburgs with whom they had intermarried. By then, the imperial title was largely an empty honor, and the Habsburgs were far less interested in Germany and Italy than in an empire they were building in Central Europe. On their eastern frontier, they faced the rising power with whom the Italians were attempting to come to terms in the late fifteenth century: the Ottoman Turks. As the Ottomans charged up the Danube valley—the route that the Huns, Avars, and Magyars had taken into the heart of western Europe—Habsburg Vienna was the primary obstacle in their path.

The Arts   Political confusion was no more antithetical to cultural progress north of the Alps than it was to their south. But a vibrant medieval tradition lingered in the north that affected how northerners appropriated aspects of Italy's Renaissance. Gothic architecture was far from dead in the late fifteenth century, particularly in England where a refined and delicate "Perpendicular Gothic" style flourished. The minutely detailed realism that characterized the work of northern oil painters (such as Hubert and Jan van Eyck) owed more to the tradition of medieval manuscript illumination than to Renaissance classicism.

Albrecht Dürer (1471–1528) was the first major northern artist to intensively study Italy's Renaissance. He was a citizen of Nuremberg, an independent German city that had extensive commercial ties with Italy. Many of Italy's Renaissance artists were trained in the shops of goldsmiths. Dürer's father was a goldsmith, and Dürer practiced one of the goldsmith's arts: engraving. His interest, however, was not in ornamenting objects, but in the artistic potential of one of the great technological breakthroughs of the era— the printing press, which Johannes Gutenberg had perfected about 1455. Dürer made a name for himself not only as a painter but as an engraver of plates for printing pictures. It was probably a desire to study the works of the Renaissance artists who were pioneering techniques for drawing in perspective that drove him to make several trips to Italy. Dürer immersed himself in the rapidly growing literature dealing with the laws of perspective, and his reading of classical authors and study of ancient statuary convinced him that art should be informed by a close, scientific study of nature. He filled files with detailed sketches of plants, animals, and people and worked these elements into superbly executed woodcuts and engravings. Prints from his blocks and plates were inexpensive enough that, for the first time, people of modest means could purchase the work of an important artist. The printing press not only encouraged the growth of literacy in early modern Europe, but it also acquainted an ever widening spectrum of European society with the arts of the Renaissance.

Northerners came to Italy to study the Renaissance firsthand, but some Italian artists also migrated to northern regions. Leonardo da Vinci (1452–1519), whose *Mona Lisa* may be the most famous portrait from the Renaissance era, was employed by King Francis I (r. 1515–1547) of France. Francis's political aspirations probably explain why he was the first of northern Europe's kings to become a patron of the Renaissance. Whenever the Germans retreated from Italy, the French were tempted to move in. After the extermination of Frederick II's Hohenstaufen dynasty, Charles of Anjou (brother of France's King Louis IX) had seized the kingdoms of Naples and Sicily. Sicily rebelled and broke free in 1282, and France's attempt to establish an outpost in southern Italy eventually came to nought. But in 1525 Francis mounted another expedition in the hope that acquisition of Italian territory would help him balance the growing power of the Habsburgs. He failed spectacularly, but even futile military ventures were culturally significant, for the hordes of foreign soldiers they brought into Italy absorbed Italy's Renaissance culture and took it home.

Northern Humanism   The environment of northern Europe shaped the kind of interest that northerners took in the Renaissance. Northern Europe had few inspiring Roman ruins to remind people of the grandeurs of classical civilization. Unlike Italy's powerful urban communities, its towns did not see themselves as successors to the classical world's great city-states, and it was not the pagan past that drew northern scholars to the work of Italy's humanists. The northerners were intrigued by another of the ancient civilization's legacies: the Bible and the church.

The northern Renaissance was energized by a religious revival—the **Modern Devotion**—that originated in the Netherlands in the fourteenth century. It inspired the foundation of quasi-monastic organizations dedicated to charitable work and education. The schools maintained by the most famous of these, the Brethren of the Common Life, were noteworthy for the training they provided in the ancient languages. Italy's humanists had pursued the study of classical Latin and Greek in order to better understand the civilization of ancient Rome and Greece. The northern humanists sought the same linguistic competence, but applied it to intensive study of the Bible.

Desiderius Erasmus (1466–1536), the most prominent of the northern humanists, was the illegitimate son of a learned priest who developed an interest in humanism while visiting Italy. Erasmus was educated by the Brethren of the Common Life and entered the church, which was the traditional way for a scholar to further his career. He became a monk and was ordained a priest, but soon realized he had made a mistake. He found monastic life stultifying, and he was no happier when his superiors sent him to study theology at the University of Paris. The medieval scholasticism that still held sway in Paris repulsed Erasmus and drove him into the humanists' camp.

Erasmus's greatest achievement was a superior edition of the Greek New Testament based on a critical analysis of ancient manuscripts, which scholars used to improve the accuracy of Latin and vernacular translations. Erasmus was, however, much more than an arid philologist whose studies were ends in themselves. Like others of the Renaissance period, he believed that intellectuals should not keep their work to themselves, but rather should use it to benefit the masses. His close examination of the Scriptures inspired him with a vision of early Christianity, and he urged the church to jettison much of the baggage it had accumulated during the Middle Ages and revert to the simplicity of the New Testament era. Authentic Christianity, he believed, was a charitable and selfless way of life guided by a personal experience of God. The best way to restore and build faith, he argued, was to give ordinary people a Bible they could read for themselves. He had little sympathy for clergy who wanted to keep their congregations ignorant and subservient. One of his most popular books, *Praise of Folly*, was a social satire that targeted the clergy. Erasmus was such an outspoken critic of medieval Catholicism that his contemporaries joked that he laid the "egg" that the Protestant reformers hatched. When the Reformation broke out, however, Erasmus—like his friend, the English humanist Thomas More (1478–1535)—was unwilling to leave the Catholic Church. He agreed with the Protestants that the church should be reformed to bring it in line with the New Testament model. However, as a humanist, he preferred a more tempered and rational faith than the leading Reformers preached (see Chapter 13).

The Middle East: The Ottoman Empire

The states that the Seljuk Turks had established in the Middle East in the eleventh century were undermined by the Mongol invasion in the thirteenth century. As they crumbled, other Turks who were pushed west by the Mongol advance took their place. The Ottoman Turks were named for Osman (r. 1299–1326), a chief who settled them in Asia Minor close to the Byzantine city of Nicaea. In 1301 he defeated a Byzantine army, and he and his successors steadily detached territory both from Constantinople's crumbling empire and from neighboring Turkish chiefdoms. The Ottomans' location on the frontier of the Byzantine Empire enabled them to recruit men for a popular holy war with Islam's Christian opponents. In 1331 they took Nicaea. By 1340 they had brought most of Asia Minor under their control and had crossed the Dardanelles into Europe. In 1354 a contender for the Byzantine throne, who wanted their help, allowed them to establish a base at Gallipoli, a fortress commanding a choke point on the channel that links the Black and Aegean Seas. From there they moved into the Balkans and began to encircle Constantinople. In 1389 they defeated the Serbs at the first battle of Kosovo, and a year later the remaining parts of Asia Minor as far east as the Euphrates submitted to them.

Expansion of Ottoman Power   In 1402 Timur the Lame (Tamerlane), the greatest Mongol conqueror since Genghis Khan (see Chapter 11), routed an Ottoman army and killed the sultan Bayezid I (r. 1389–1402). However, the Mongols soon turned their attention elsewhere and left the Ottomans to fight among themselves. A decade of confusion ensued until Mehmed I (r. 1413–1421) finally won the upper hand and began to restore Ottoman unity and territory. His son, Murad II (r. 1421–1451), conquered Greece and the Balkans, and pushed into Hungary. The defeats he gave the Hungarians at the battle of Varna in 1444 and at the second battle of Kosovo in 1448 crippled the Christian state and opened the way for the Ottomans to drive deep into Catholic territory.

Murad's son, Mehmed II, "the Conqueror" (r. 1451–1481), secured the Ottomans' position by winning a prize that had eluded Muslim armies for nearly 800 years. On May 29, 1453, the 20-year-old Turkish sultan took the city of Constantinople—with the help of some European technology. In 1452 a Hungarian gunsmith offered to construct a huge cannon for the last Byzantine emperor, Constantine XI (r. 1448–1453). When Constantine failed to raise the money for the project, the Hungarian approached the Ottomans, who commissioned several pieces of artillery. The largest was a cannon 26 feet long that fired missiles weighing 800 pounds. With weapons like this, it took only a few weeks to pound the impoverished and depopulated capital of eastern Christendom into submission. Venice and Genoa might have helped Constantinople, but they did not want to do anything that risked harming the good commercial relations they wanted to establish with the Ottomans.

The Turks renamed Constantinople Istanbul and turned its great church, the Hagia Sophia, into a mosque. The loss of the last great Christian outpost in the Middle East was a shock to Europe, but it had little practical significance. Constantinople had ceased to protect the eastern frontiers of Christendom, and its new Muslim rulers had no intention of severing its mutually profitable commercial ties with Europe. In fact, Italy actually profited from the disaster that befell Constantinople. Greek scholars fleeing the Ottomans sought refuge in Italy, and their linguistic expertise and libraries helped fuel the Renaissance. Cultural influences also flowed in the opposite direction. Mehmed employed Italian artists and architects. Despite Islam's occasional hostility to representational art, he sat for portraits by one of Italy's great Renaissance painters, Gentile Bellini (1429–1507).

Several things contributed to the Ottomans' success. For one, they never seem to have considered dividing their conquests to provide domains for all a ruler's sons. The sultanate passed intact to only one heir (not inevitably the eldest), and to ensure safety and stability his brothers were killed. Mehmed II formalized this tradition as the Ot-

Mehmed II   This portrait of the conqueror of Constantinople is ascribed to the Italian Renaissance artist, Gentile Bellini. The classical style of the arch with which the painter has framed his subject may seem somewhat at odds with Mehmed's eastern dress and appearance, but he obviously would not have thought so. Istanbul and Venice had a long history of close association, and the Ottomans were well informed about developments in Italian politics and culture.

toman law of fratricide. Unique customs also governed how sultans sired their heirs. Their marriages were celibate, and they had their children by concubines. Once a concubine had borne a son, the sultan ended relations with her. This motivated her to focus on the care and preparation of her son to be the winner in the life-and-death struggle for succession to the throne. The relationship that this built between a woman and her son meant that a sultan's mother could become an extremely powerful influence on his government. Once the Ottoman royal house settled in Constantinople and built its lavish residence, the Topkapi Palace, its princes were confined to quarters and raised in luxurious seclusion. This, of course, meant that heirs came to the throne with very little experience of the world. In 1603, due to concerns for the survival of the dynasty, the execution of its princes ended. It then became customary for the throne to pass to the eldest Ottoman prince—often the brother of the previous sultan.

The Ottoman Empire had an extremely diverse population. Although the Ottomans were Muslims, they were exposed to multiple religious influences, for there were different kinds of Islam just as there were different kinds of Christianity. Given that the Ottomans first expanded into Byzantine territory, more of their subjects may initially have been Greek Orthodox Christians than Muslims. Many of the former preferred Muslim rule to domination by the Latin Catholics who had staked claims to Byzantine lands after the Fourth Crusade sacked Constantinople in 1204. Europe's Christians viewed eastern Christians as near heretics and pressed them to submit to the papal church. The Ottomans, by contrast were tolerant of both Christians and Jews. They continued the long-standing Muslim practice of according "the people of the book" a kind of second-class citizenship. Christians and Jews paid special taxes, but were protected and allowed a limited degree of autonomy. Among the taxes they paid, however, was a unique kind of human tribute. Christian boys were taken at a young age, converted to Islam, and educated for special military and governmental service in the corps of Janissaries ("new troops"). Murad I (r. 1362–1389) was said to have founded the Janissaries to counter the influence of the Turkish cavalry. The horse soldiers were supported by grants of land which gave them a degree of independence from the sultan, but Janissaries were the sultan's slaves. Slave armies had a long history in the Middle East. The Seljuk and Mamluk regimes had been founded by formerly enslaved soldiers. The trust the Ottoman sultan placed in the Janissaries led to their occupying many of the posts in his government. The result was a Muslim empire largely managed by recent converts from Christian families.

Mehmed and his successors did not concentrate all their attention on European targets, for they had much to do in the divided Muslim world. In 1502 Shah Ismail I (r. 1502–1524) founded the Safavid Empire in Persia (Iran). Religion complicated the situation, for the Ottomans were Sunni Muslims and the Safavids were Shi'ites (see Chapter 7). Each empire regarded the other as heretical and tried to purge its territory of inhabitants who professed its opponent's faith. In 1514 Selim I (r. 1512–1520) routed a Safavid army and took control of Egypt and the Muslim holy cities of Mecca and Medina. This brought the Arab homeland into the Ottoman Empire, and in 1517 Selim was hailed as caliph, a title implying religious as well as governmental authority (see Map 12–2).

The Ottoman Empire reached a peak of power and magnificence during the reign of Selim's successor, Süleyman (r. 1520–1566). His domain extended east into Iraq and north and west to Hungary and the walls of Vienna, which he besieged in 1529. In 1522 he drove the Knights of St. John from the island of Rhodes and established the dominance of his navy in the eastern Mediterranean. The Ottoman juggernaut rolled on without serious reverses until 1565, when a great armada failed to take the island of Malta south of Sicily.

Ottoman Civilization   The civilization of the Ottoman Empire was shaped by the Turks' devotion to Islamic religious law, the Shariah. Muslims believe the Qur'an literally records God's words. As such, it is a source of immutable laws for human conduct. All such laws are, in theory, already revealed in the life and teachings of the Prophet Muhammad. Additions to the law are therefore impossible, but religious scholars can interpret the law to deal with new situations. The Ottoman ruler's function was not to make law but to enforce the divine law with the help of **muftis** (religious jurists). Islam has no priests, for it has no sacraments. Its religious leaders, like Jewish rabbis, are specialists in the interpretation of sacred texts and laws. Muslim faith in a revealed code of divine laws did not stifle change, but it did make change problematic. New things had to be justified as extensions of Islamic principles.

Paradoxically, the Ottomans' concern for Muslim orthodoxy did not lead to intolerance. The Ottoman Empire was, in fact, far more religiously tolerant than most contemporary European states. The empire had many Jewish, Christian, and even some Shi'ite Muslim subjects, and there were variations within its official Sunni faith. Muslims who found the legalism and formal liturgies of their state religion emotionally unfulfilling turned to Sufism. Sufis were mystics who used music, song, poetry, and dance to cultivate ecstatic trances and visions.

Culturally, the Ottoman Empire was sandwiched between two quite different peoples: the Shi'ite Safavids in the east and the Catholic Europeans in the west. Both were enemies, but the Ottomans absorbed influences from both. Protection and promotion of commercial relations was a priority of Istanbul's government, and the empire allowed Europeans to establish residency in its ports and to travel within its boundaries.

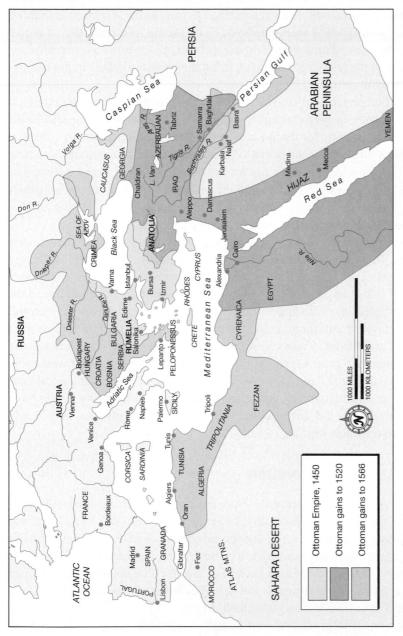

Map 12–2 The Ottoman Empire After the conquest of Constantinople, the Ottoman sultan maintained, as his Byzantine predecessors had, that he stood in a line of rulers that began with Rome's emperors. The lands he controlled included and exceeded those of the ancient eastern Roman Empire.

Question: Given the amount of European territory and Mediterranean shoreline within the Ottoman Empire, should it be classified as a western or an eastern state?

Few Muslims, however, toured Europe. The empire's trade outposts in Europe were usually manned by its Jewish or Christian subjects.

The Ottoman Empire survived into the twentieth century. Its longevity is proof of its ability to evolve and adapt, but whether such adaptation should be viewed as success or decline depends very much on one's perspective. As early as the seventeenth century, some Turkish historians judged their empire to be in decline. The fault, they claimed, lay with sultans who allowed unworthy favorites and corrupt servants to usurp their authority. The power of the central government, if not the empire, did fade in the late sixteenth and seventeenth centuries.

In 1571 the Ottoman navy suffered a major defeat in a battle off Lepanto in the Gulf of Corinth. Although the fleet was rebuilt, the nature of naval warfare changed. The era of great armadas and struggle for dominance of the Mediterranean came to an end as the European states shifted their attention to the Atlantic and global exploration. New and faster kinds of ships, designed for use on the oceans, replaced heavy galleys. The poorly policed Mediterranean was infested by pirates, privateers, and enterprising buccaneers. Ottoman merchants faced problems of a different kind in the Red Sea and Indian Ocean where Portuguese traders were beginning to compete.

The Ottomans continued military activity on some fronts. In 1669 they took over Crete, and in 1683 they staged their final assault on Vienna. But the strain of fighting wars on two fronts (Europe and Persia) sapped the empire's resources. Manpower shortages lowered standards of training, and even the organization and discipline of the elite Janissaries suffered. Warlords appeared in the provinces, raised private armies, and compelled Istanbul to grant them greater degrees of autonomy. The bullion that flooded through Europe from its colonial outposts contributed to inflation. The sultan's government scrambled to meet expenses and resorted to tax farming. The weakening of centralized government did not, however, lead to the fall of the empire. Local governments strengthened and assumed greater responsibility for preserving peace, prosperity, and stability. Rebels did not seek the overthrow of the empire but only to win greater freedom to operate within it.

Europe and Atlantic Exploration

The rise of the Ottoman Empire meant that once again western Europe was under siege from the east. By the late sixteenth century, however, the anxiety this initially created was receding (except perhaps in central Europe, which was directly threatened by Ottoman armies). Europeans had discovered that the Atlantic was not, as their ancestors assumed, an impassable obstacle at their backs. For the first time in history, they shifted their attention from the Mediterranean and the Middle East to the Atlantic and to a much larger world than they had ever imagined existed.

A long tradition of technological and scientific invention lay behind the ships, weapons, and tools that equipped Europeans to embark on the adventures that ultimately spread the influence of their civilization around the globe. Many of the inventions that enabled them to explore and to transform their world were made by eastern peoples and diffused across the Eurasian continents. New farming tools and techniques appeared early in the medieval era. By the eleventh century, the horse's potential for use on the farm and on the battlefield was being fully realized for the first time. The Romans had watermills, but medieval people may have improved on them with ideas from the Chinese. They also harnessed the winds and tides and invented crankshafts and camshafts to improve on machines driven by these powers of nature. They built sawmills to make lumber and water-powered hammers to pulverize ore and full cloth. By the fourteenth century, water-powered bellows—which the Chinese had developed as early as the first century C.E.—were easing the work of ore smelting and forging.

Some societies resist learning from others, but medieval Europeans readily appropriated (and improved on) ideas from many sources. They learned paper-making from the Muslims, and then created a product that competed successfully on the world market. The Chinese or Koreans pioneered printing with inked blocks of wood. The earliest Chinese printed book dates to the ninth century. Europeans adapted ink, paper, metal casting, and die cutting, and Johannes Gutenberg combined these things with a press similar to those used to crush grapes and olives to begin a revolution in European literacy. There may have been only about 100,000 books in all of Europe in 1450, but by 1500, there were probably nine million. Gutenberg may have been preceded in the invention of movable type by the Chinese. But if so, the Chinese did not find the innovation as useful as did the Europeans (perhaps because the Western languages could be printed with a handful of letters, while the Chinese script employed thousands of characters). The Chinese invented gunpowder, perhaps as early as the ninth century, and they may have cast the first metal cannon in the late thirteenth century. These weapons appeared in Europe in the early fourteenth century and led to the armaments that gave later generations of Europeans unsurpassed success in building colonial empires. A Chinese astronomer of the eleventh century is believed to have constructed a mechanical clock. However, his invention, like the model steam turbines built by the Hellenistic Greeks, initially had little impact. Yet, when the clock appeared in Europe at the start of the fourteenth century, it revolutionized human behavior. Once time could be accurately measured, the activities of whole communities could be coordinated and work planned with unprecedented efficiency. Towns all across Europe began to erect clock towers as a public service. The Chinese discovered the properties of magnetized needles and used them as compasses. Compasses and the astrolabe, an ancient Greek invention for making celestial measurements that was improved by medieval Muslims, made voyages easier for sailors. By the thirteenth century, Europeans had ships that relied entirely on sails (not oars). By the fourteenth, they had large vessels with multiple masts and lateen rigging—a Muslim invention that permitted a ship to sail against the wind. A host of innovations that improved sailcloth, rope, carpentry, metals, and navigational instruments contributed to the creation of the ships that enabled Europeans to undertake global exploration late in the fifteenth century.

Portuguese Explorations   The tiny Iberian state of Portugal pioneered European Atlantic exploration. It was highly motivated, for its only access to the Mediterranean (the center of the medieval world's trade network) was through the Straits of Gibraltar, which were controlled by Spanish and Muslim competitors. In 1415 Prince Henry "the Navigator" (1394–1460), third son of Portugal's king, John I (r. 1385–1433), earned his knight's spurs in a battle that won Portugal the Muslim port of Ceuta on the African coast opposite Gibraltar. Henry's subsequent military campaigns were inconsequential, but his sponsorship of voyages of Atlantic exploration paid huge dividends.

The Portuguese initially worked their way down the Atlantic coast of Africa, searching for the source of the gold that Muslim caravans brought across the Sahara Desert from Africa's interior. By 1432, they had discovered the Atlantic islands: the Canaries, Azores, and Madeiras. When these proved suitable for growing sugar, the nearby African continent was raided for slaves to work island sugar plantations. (Slaves were to be found in Renaissance Europe employed as household servants, but it was in regions where plantation systems were profitable that slavery truly flourished.) Successive expeditions inched farther and farther down the African coast until Bartolomeu Dias (c. 1450–1500) rounded the southern tip of the African continent in 1488. In 1498 Vasco da Gama (c. 1460–1524) explored the east coast of Africa and, with the help of Muslim sailors, charted a sea route across the Indian Ocean that linked Portugal to the port of Calicut. News of his return with a cargo of spices (particularly pepper) sent shock waves through the markets of Europe. By importing directly from India, the Portuguese could compete with merchants who used the older overland routes. The Portuguese wasted no time in exploiting their advantage. They dispatched a fleet of ships, negotiated access to Indian ports, and then pushed farther east to Indonesia, China, and Japan.

However, Vasco da Gama was not the first to sail around the African continent. An ancient Carthaginian may have done so, and Arab and Chinese vessels had worked their way down the eastern coast of Africa and into the Atlantic before the Portuguese charted the continent's western coast. One of the puzzles of world history is why Europeans rather than Chinese exploited the sea route between the West and the Far East. The third emperor of the Ming dynasty (1386–1644) built ships that were many times larger than any that his European contemporaries were capable of constructing, and between 1405 and 1433, he dispatched fleets of 60 or more vessels to Africa's eastern coast. His successors, however, terminated the project, and China ceased to explore. What the Chinese had learned of the outside world evidently did not intrigue them, and they may have concluded that the costs of exploration outweighed its potential profits. China did not withdraw from trade and contact with the outside world, but to bolster the claims of its emperor to a unique mandate from heaven, foreign trade was officially described as tribute.

Spanish Explorations   Italy, with centuries of seafaring experience to draw on, produced excellent navigators and cartographers, some of whom were eager to take part in the Atlantic adventure. About 1478 Christopher Columbus (1451–1506), a Genoese sailor and map maker, emigrated to Portugal, where he married the daughter of a ship's captain who had sailed for Prince Henry.

Columbus's study of the geographical information available in his day led him to grossly underestimate the size of the globe. Otherwise, he never would have proposed trying to reach the Far East by sailing west across the Atlantic. Had the Americas and certain Pacific islands not been where they are, no ship of Columbus's day could have survived a journey directly from Europe to the other side of the world. Columbus tried to persuade the Portuguese government to fund an expedition to prove his theory that the shortest route to the Far East lay west. However, Portugal decided that its African explorations, which were just beginning to pay off, were a better investment.

Columbus considered going to France next, but he finally decided to try his luck at the Spanish court. Spain was a new nation, which had been formed in 1469 by the marriage of Queen Isabella I of Castile and King Ferdinand V of Aragon (joint reign, 1474–1504). The royal couple was intrigued by Columbus's proposal, but the time was not propitious for a new project. In 1484 Ferdinand and Isabella had set out to conquer Granada, Spain's sole remaining Muslim state. Until that costly campaign was resolved, they were not prepared to take on anything else. Granada finally surrendered on January 2, 1492. Thereafter, things moved quickly. Columbus received his commission on April 17, set sail with a fleet of three small ships on August 3, and 70 days later planted Spain's standard on what was probably one of the Bahamian islands—although he was certain that it was not far from Japan. Columbus had been lucky. By striking south to avoid the Portuguese, he had discovered the prevailing winds that offered the easiest passage across the Atlantic.

Columbus's largest ship ran aground in the Caribbean, and he was forced to leave half his crew (44 men) behind when he hastened back to Spain to announce that he had reached outlying portions of India and contacted "Indians." He received a hero's welcome, a title of nobility, and a much larger fleet for a return to what he claimed, until the end of his days, was the perimeter of Asia. The four expeditions Columbus led explored the Caribbean and the coast of Central America, but they never found the passage to Japan that their admiral was certain had to be in the vicinity.

England occupied the extreme western end of the lengthy medieval trade routes that linked Europe with the Far East. The shorter Atlantic passage that Columbus claimed to have found promised to be an economic godsend for England. News of his discoveries therefore persuaded King Henry VII (r. 1485–1509) to fund an expedition by another Genoese explorer, whose anglicized name was John Cabot (1450–1498). In 1497 Cabot reached islands off the coast of Canada and returned to England to inform the king that he had made contact with Asia somewhere north of Japan. A second voyage in 1498 took Cabot as far south as Labrador.

The Discovery of the New World   This woodcut is from a series created (c. 1493) to publicize Columbus's discoveries. Columbus was never shaken in his belief that he had reached the outer rim of the orient. The exotic look of the boat and the eastern costumes of the men who are exchanging items with the naked natives may have been intended to support this claim.

England's financiers contemplated more expeditions, but because Cabot had found nothing of value aside from some furs, investors and plans were slow to materialize.

In 1500 a Portuguese fleet bound for India via the African route went off course and sighted a land its leader named Brazil (for a species of tree that grew there). A year later, the Portuguese dispatched a follow-up expedition piloted by Amerigo Vespucci (1454–1512), one of Columbus's associates. Vespucci was among the first to suggest that what the Europeans were exploring was not the outer reaches of Asia, but a "New World"—new to Europeans that is, but obviously not to its indigenous peoples. The geographers who used his reports labeled the continent whose outline was emerging on their maps "the discoveries of Amerigo" ("America"). Any lingering doubts about the place America occupied on the globe were resolved in 1522 when the remnants of a Spanish fleet that had set out under the command of Ferdinand Magellan (1480–1521) completed the first circumnavigation of the Earth (see Map 12–3).

Columbus never found the gold he promised his Spanish sponsors, but in 1519 the longed-for wealth finally began to flow. Hernán Cortés (1485–1547) invaded Mexico and looted the treasures of the Aztec Empire. Ten years later Francisco Pizarro (c. 1475–1541) overthrew the New World's other major civilization, the empire of Peru's Inca. Small companies of Spanish soldiers subdued large native populations with surprising ease, for the invaders had advantages that more than compensated for their inferior numbers. Their weapons were vastly superior, and they had horses—animals that were new to the Americas, which had no comparable indigenous species. Native armies had never before confronted anything as formidable as a force of mounted warriors with guns. But an unanticipated development further tipped the scales in favor of the Europeans. Whether they intended to or not, they became practitioners of germ warfare. Migration and trade among the peoples of Asia, Africa, and Europe had exposed the inhabitants of these regions to many diseases. Over time, their descendent's evolved the ability to minimize the effects of what became familiar infections. Lack of similar exposure meant that the peoples of the western hemisphere had different immune systems that left them defenseless against diseases that were minor childhood afflictions for Europeans. Smallpox, chicken pox, measles, and other illnesses swept ahead of the European invaders and cleared the way for their conquests. Native populations were quickly reduced to such a low level that the European entrepreneurs who established plantations and mines in the New World had to reconstitute its workforce by importing slaves from Africa—people who shared the Old World immunities. It is difficult to reconcile the brutality with which Columbus and Europe's later explorers treated Native Americans with their sincere desire to baptize them and bring them into the Christian community. Some missionaries did protest the Europeans' excesses and abuses, but the profits to be made from slave labor in mining and plantation agriculture proved too tempting even for the church to forego.

In 1494 the pope presumed, as Christ's vicar on Earth, to draw a longitudinal line that divided the globe into Portuguese and Spanish spheres of influence. Territories east of his "**Line of Demarcation**" (which ran through Brazil) were declared Portuguese, and anything to the west was declared to be Spain's property. Other European

Map 12-3 Europe's Initial Global Explorations This map shows the routes taken by the Portuguese, Spanish, English, and French explorers as they ventured into the Atlantic and beyond.

Question: What effect would the increasing attention that Europe gave to global exploration have on relations between the Christian and Muslim worlds?

nations with access to the Atlantic refused to be restrained by the papal decree. Three years after the pope's proclamation, John Cabot staked England's claim to the New World, and in 1534 France sent out the first of its explorers, Jacques Cartier (1491–1557). He made four trips to a land he thought the natives called Canada (their word actually meant "village"). Cartier searched for a waterway through the Americas to the Far East and a rumored North American kingdom that was said to be as rich in gold as Mexico's Aztec Empire. Although he found neither, France sent out more explorers and added the Mississippi watershed and some Caribbean islands to the American territories it claimed. In 1595 tiny Holland established bases in the East Indies to compete with the Portuguese. England and France eventually followed. As Europeans moved out into the world, they spread their civilization and the power of their colonial empires around the globe. The twenty-first century is still struggling to come to terms with the consequences.

KEY QUESTION | Revisited

A handful of European explorers needed only a few decades to change the course of world history. They cleared the way for Europe's civilization and the political and economic power of its colonial empires to transform life for peoples around the globe. European society was as profoundly affected as any of the alien cultures its colonizers encountered. The gold, silver, and raw materials that poured into Europe greatly expanded its economy. Luxury consumables, such as sugar, rice, and spices, became much more affordable. The new plants that explorers brought back for cultivation in Europe revolutionized society at every level. Europeans tasted maize, squash, and tomatoes for the first time and discovered the pleasures of tobacco and chocolate. They eagerly took to coffee, an Ethiopian beverage that spread through the Muslim world in the fifteenth century. Tea from the Far East likewise entered the European market in the sixteenth century. The potato, which was indigenous to Peru and Chile, flourished in Europe's cool, wet climate and began to replace wheat as the staple food of the poor. This eased famines and encouraged population growth. The national cuisines for which European countries are famous today feature foods, drinks, and flavors that were unknown to Europeans until relatively recently.

The New World's creation of a new Europe caused Europeans some anxiety. The flood of information that suddenly became available to them about peoples, places, and things whose existence they had not previously suspected posed immense challenges. For the first time, they became aware of viable alternatives to their way of life, and this forced them to rethink the fundamental assumptions of their civilization and religion. There was no hint in their histories and traditions of anything that would prepare them for what they were discovering and experiencing. The past, therefore, began to seem less reliable as a guide for comprehending the present and plotting the future. Europeans were, however, accustomed to dealing with change. Their late medieval Renaissance, despite its name, was less a rebirth of the past than a creative response to it. It revived beliefs and institutions of an earlier age, but treated these things as the beginning, not the end, of its search for understanding and a better life.

There was always, however, a tempting alternative that has never lost its appeal for some people. Change is costly. What one person counts as gain another experiences as loss. The common strategy for opposing change is to insist that all essential truths have been revealed and are already known. The responsible thing to do, therefore, is to cling firmly to traditional beliefs and values and reject anything that might challenge them. There is wisdom in warning people not to let an appetite for novelty obscure the hard-won lessons of earlier generations. However, excessive reverence for the past diminishes curiosity about the world, acquiesces when limits are placed on intellectual freedom, and hampers experimentation and exploration. It can lead to stagnation and ultimate irrelevance. What people do with their past—their history—goes a long way toward determining their future.

Review Questions

1. Why did the Renaissance originate in Italy before spreading elsewhere?
2. What is humanism? What medieval ideas and values did it challenge?
3. What features do the different arts of the Renaissance—sculpture, architecture, and painting—have in common? How do they relate to humanism?
4. How did the Renaissance change as it moved into northern Europe?
5. Is the history of the Ottoman Empire and Islam part of Western history?
6. How did the discovery of the New World change the way Europeans thought about themselves?

Please consult the Suggested Readings at the back of the book to continue your study of the material covered in this chapter. For a list of documents on the Primary Source DVD-ROM that relate to topics in this chapter, please refer to the back of the book.

13 Reformation, Religious Wars, and National Conflicts

Why should we tear the world apart arguing over obscure things which are incomprehensible or arguable or useless? The world is filed with anger, hostility, and strife.

—**Desiderius Erasmus,** *Sponge to Wipe Away the Aspersions of Hutten*

KEY Question

How do civilized societies justify war?

The humanist scholar Erasmus (c. 1466–1536) was dismayed to witness the unintended fruits of his labors. His critical studies had revealed errors in the traditional Latin text of the Bible, and his witty satires had lampooned corrupt clergy. But he had intended to promote reform, not rebellion, and his expectation was that rational debate would lead to a new and better consensus on matters of faith. Instead, he found himself witnessing the birth of an era of warfare in the name of religion. Wars are not rare in human history, but a congruence of forces (rivalry among monarchies, the class struggles of a capitalistic economy, opposing belief systems, and a host of other things) made them especially abundant in sixteenth- and seventeenth-century Europe. People in almost every era have grievances that might lead to war, but they do not always act on their sense of wrong or always find the same issues worth fighting for. Therefore, it is important for them to learn what history can teach about motivations for shedding blood. How can it be that a war that seems senseless to some is, to others, worth the sacrifice of life itself?

The Reformation of the sixteenth century ended the medieval church's monopolistic control over the practice of the Christian faith in Europe. Confronted for the first time with religious pluralism, Europeans reacted violently. Wars flared on all sides as they took up arms to defend one variety of Christian faith from another. Catholics warred with Protestants,

Queen Elizabeth I England's first Queen Elizabeth (1533–1603) struggled to navigate the currents of an extremely turbulent era. She was about 47 when she sat for this portrait by the Italian painter Federico Zuccari (c. 1542–1609).

but sometimes Protestants sided with Catholics against other Catholics or other kinds of Protestants. Sometimes the leaders of opposing factions made suspiciously opportunistic conversions. Wars fought for sincerely held religious reasons could obviously also have other causes.

The explanations that people give for their quarrels are not always accurate or sufficient. Because civilized people have consciences that require them to justify violent acts, they prefer to think that when they commit mayhem, they do so for a noble purpose. The personal advantage a victory may bring is only a pleasant (if well-deserved) byproduct of their action. The most exalted of motivations is fidelity to God or, in secular terms, commitment to an ultimate value. Although the West's major religions—Judaism, Christianity, and Islam—urge people to live together in love and peace, they have often inspired hatred and slaughter. Secular ideologies, such as communism, fascism, nationalism, and democracy, have done the same. It is reasonable, therefore, to ask whether faith (in either a sacred or secular ideal) is a cause for war, a pretext for war, a precondition for war, or a preventative of war. A civilized state promotes specific religious and secular ideals to provide its people with a context that gives their lives meaning. Sometimes, however, a society resorts to barbarism in the name of its civilizing ideals. It is vitally important to understand how human beings come to terms with this morally ambiguous situation.

The Lutheran Reformation

The Reformation sprang from ground tilled by the humanists of Italy's Renaissance. The humanists believed that Western civilization and Christian faith had been corrupted over the centuries, but that their original natures could be restored by studying ancient texts. Humanism was, however, largely confined to an intellectually elite segment of society, while the Reformation was a mass movement—something that would not have been possible before the invention of the printing press and the subsequent rapid spread of literacy. The Reformation's theologians shared the humanists' belief that ancient wisdom would correct the errors of the recent past. But their enthusiasm was not for paganism's classical culture. It was for the "apostolic" Christianity of the early church.

Luther   Martin Luther (1483–1546), the man whose personal religious struggle became a catalyst for the Protestant Reformation, was not inclined to rebellion by either nature or education. Until middle age, he led a very conventional life, and he never abandoned a certain fundamental conservativism. Although he claimed peasant origins, his father was actually an upwardly mobile member of the middle class who could afford to give his son a good education. Luther completed his arts degree at the University of Erfurt in 1505 and then began to study law in preparation for a secular career. But after a few months, a growing anxiety for the state of his soul led him to do what highly motivated medieval Christians had been doing for centuries. He turned his back on the world, dropped out of school, and entered a monastery. He completed the novitiate, took the vows of an Augustinian monk, and in May 1507 was ordained a priest. He earned a doctorate in theology, and his order assigned him to lecture at the University of Wittenberg in Saxony.

Luther was 34 years old before anything caused him to question his medieval Catholic faith. He had been taught to think of himself as a sinner destined for judgment by a righteous and angry God. Fear of God and of eternal punishment had driven him to take monastic vows, but the fasts, prayers, and disciplines of the monastic life failed to bring him an assurance of salvation. Sometime after 1512, however, he had a kind of conversion experience—a burst of insight prompted by reading the letters of the Apostle Paul (particularly the Epistle to the Romans). Paul, according to the New Testament's Book of Acts, had not wanted to become a Christian and was actively persecuting the church when God suddenly intervened, bestowed faith on him, and made him a Christian. Luther concluded that what had been true for Paul was true for all Christians. They did not earn salvation by doing good works; salvation was a gift God freely gave them while they were still sinners. It could not be earned, and human beings could not comprehend God's motives in bestowing it.

Luther's resolution of his personal crisis of faith did not turn him into a reformer or a critic of the church, for he did not believe that he had discovered anything revolutionary. He had only understood what was plainly laid out for everyone in the Bible. Therefore, he settled back into his routine as a college professor and might never have been heard of had it not been for a chance encounter in 1517 with a Dominican friar named Johann Tetzel (c. 1465–1519).

In 1514 an ambitious German clergyman, Albert of Brandenburg, sought a favor from the pope. At the age of 23, Albert was already bishop of two dioceses, but now he wanted a third: the archdiocese of Mainz, one of Germany's most important sees. Pope Leo X (r. 1513–1521) agreed to sell Albert the office and to license a sale of indulgences in Germany (by men like Tetzel) to help raise the money to pay for it. An **indulgence** was a dispensation from the need to do penance for one's sins. Church doctrine held that while God freely forgave the guilt of sin, sinners still owed compensation for the moral damage caused by their sin. The souls of the dead who had not fully atoned for their sins in life were sent to Purgatory to complete their penances before being admitted to heaven. Originally, the church granted indulgences as an act of mercy or as a reward for self-sacrificial service. An indulgence would release a Christian from a penance that proved too severe or protect a crusader who died fighting for the faith in a foreign land without receiving absolution. In 1343, however, a pope opened the way for indulgences to be granted with unprecedented liberality. He declared that the church possessed an infinite "treasury of merit," a vast spiritual reservoir of grace, that it could draw on to pay the debts of individual sinners—both dead and alive. The temptation for the church was then to begin to grant indulgences from this inexhaustible source for more and more reasons. When it showed its gratitude to generous donors by dispensing them from the penalties of their sins, it opened itself to the charge that it was selling salvation.

Martin Luther certainly believed that Johann Tetzel was doing this, for Tetzel devised a thoroughly modern marketing campaign to sell Pope Leo's indulgences. He dispatched advance men to whip up customer demand. He organized parades with banners and songs, and composed what may be history's first advertising jingle: "When a coin in my coffer rings, a soul from Purgatory springs!" Luther's understanding of the Christian faith rested not only on the tradition of the church but on his study of the New Testament. He believed that Tetzel, by claiming to be able to sell what God freely gave, was committing fraud and endangering souls. He also believed that it was his duty as a pastor to expose Tetzel, whom he assumed was operating on his own initiative without sanction from the church. Following medieval scholastic tradition, he proposed debating 95 propositions relating to indulgences. Tradition holds that he nailed them to the door of his Wittenberg church. If he did, this was not an attack on the church. Church doors served as community bulletin boards, and all sorts of notices were posted on them. The fact that Luther wrote his 95 theses in Latin suggests that they were intended for his fellow scholars and not meant to rouse the populace.

When the debate Luther stirred up began to hurt the sale of indulgences, Archbishop Albert asked the pope to silence the annoying monk. The pope was willing, but there was a complication. Luther's overlord was Frederick the Wise, the Elector of Saxony (r. 1486–1525), one of the princes who chose the Holy Roman Emperor. Frederick was no proto-Protestant. (He had one of the largest collections of holy relics in Europe.) He was, however, not about to let the pope compromise his sovereignty by intervening in his territory. He took Luther under his wing, and Luther suddenly found himself in a theological dispute that was also a high-stakes political struggle.

The Political Context   In June 1519 the election of the Habsburg heir, Charles V (r. 1519–1556), as Holy Roman Emperor created a situation that gave men like Frederick reason to be protective of their sovereignty. The 19-year-old emperor's sprawling domain included Austria, Hungary, Bohemia, the Netherlands, Spain, Sicily, Sardinia, the Kingdom of Naples, and overlordship of Germany and Italy (see Map 13–1). Charles posed a threat to every ruler in Europe, and Germany's lords were particularly worried about maintaining their independence. The Reformation provided them with an excellent justification for challenging the authority of the Catholic emperor.

In 1521 Charles summoned Luther to appear before a **diet** (Germany's equivalent of England's Parliament and France's Estates General) in the city of Worms. Luther had never intended to break with the church, but a series of pamphlets he wrote to explain his beliefs argued for positions that were at odds with medieval Catholic tradition. They articulated three principles common to most forms of Protestantism. The first was that salvation is by faith alone—that it is a gift from God that cannot be earned by human effort. The second was that the Bible (not the pope or the tradition of the church) is the primary authority a Christian must obey. And the third maintained that every Christian has a direct relationship with God that does not depend on the church and mediation by its priests. When the church ordered Luther to recant these beliefs, he refused. To do so, he claimed, would be to violate his conscience, the highest court to which each individual is ultimately accountable.

The emperor and the diet condemned Luther as a heretic, but Frederick the Wise saved him by spiriting him away to a remote castle. He passed his time in hiding by translating the New Testament into colloquial German. His insistence at Worms that private conscience and the Bible were the highest authorities to which a person should be held accountable implied that ordinary men and women were entitled to have Bibles they could read for themselves. Vernacular translations of the Scriptures already existed,

Map 13–1   The Empire of Charles V   Charles's empire was the product of a series of carefully plotted dynastic marriages that made him the heir to lands scattered across Europe.

Question: Can an empire consist of scattered states, or must it consolidate its territory in order to survive?

but they were based on the Vulgate, the Latin translation of the Greek text that Saint Jerome had made in the early fifth century. The Renaissance humanists had labored to recover and improve the accuracy of the ancient texts that were the primary sources of Western civilization, and Luther built on their work. He based his translation on the best Greek text available—an edition that Erasmus published in 1516. Luther's German New Testament appeared in print in 1522, and it was an instant success. Within a decade, nearly 200,000 copies had been sold. A companion version of the Old Testament did not appear until 1534, however, for its preparation required delving into Hebrew manuscripts with the assistance of other scholars. Luther's German Bible had tremendous influence on the development of the German language.

During Luther's absence from the public stage, the Reformation proceeded without him. Events took an alarming course. Luther's opponents had warned him that his insistence on the autonomy of each individual's conscience threatened the breakdown of society by undermining respect for authority, and Luther feared that they might be right. Some of his self-proclaimed followers vandalized churches and monasteries, seized their property, and made radical changes in traditional religious practices.

In the spring of 1524 the situation threatened to spin completely out of control. A peasant uprising spontaneously erupted in southwestern Germany. It found leaders among the mercenary soldiers employed by the empire and rapidly spread. The authorities were caught off guard, for many of their regular troops had been committed to campaigns in Italy. Early in 1525 negotiators considered a multiple-point plan for restoring order. The peasants wanted the abolition of serfdom and burdensome dues and taxes, and they also wanted the right to choose their own clergy. Luther had justified his rebellion against the church by an appeal to Scripture, and the peasants seized on his arguments to ground their revolt against the state. They even offered to submit their demands to Luther and a board of mediators and relinquish any that were proven to be contrary to Scripture.

The uprising was initially restrained, but became increasingly violent as it spread. A particularly radical faction materialized around Thomas Müntzer, a university-educated man whom Luther had recommended for a pastorate. Müntzer challenged the authority of scholars like Luther by claiming that the inspiration of the Holy Spirit could give simple people religious knowledge in addition to that derived from the study of Scripture. He urged his followers to seize control of towns, drive out their opponents, and establish communities governed by leaders who were directly inspired by God. Müntzer preached the imminence of the Apocalypse and the bloody struggles that were prophesied to precede Christ's return. Luther initially tried to steer a middle course between the peasants and Germany's princes, but he became alarmed as the increasing radicalism of Müntzer and the rebels threatened to undermine support for the Reformation. In 1525 he published an intemperately worded pamphlet, *Against the Robbing and Murdering Hordes of Peasants*, that urged the German nobles to "smite, slay, and stab" the peasants—claiming that nothing is more "devilish than a rebellious man." God had empowered princes, he said, to maintain order and they were justified in doing whatever was necessary to stamp out rebellion. As their troops began to return from Italy in mid-1525, the princes quickly put down the divided and poorly led rebels. Müntzer was executed, and thousands of peasants were hunted down and killed.

Luther's fundamental instincts were conservative. He feared disorder, and there was much about the medieval church to which he was emotionally attached. Seeing no other option, he concluded that the head of the state, whom he believed was charged by God with maintaining order in society, had the right to decide what kind of church he would tolerate and to use force to require his subjects to conform to its practices. Luther therefore filled the void of leadership he had created when he repudiated the pope by endorsing state control of the church.

Luther had inadvertently unleashed disorder and instability on the world. As he aged and struggled with illness, he became increasingly intolerant of opposition and continuing conflicts. He refused to compromise with other Reformers, and he turned against the Jews, who he had once hoped would convert to his renewed version of Christianity. In 1543 he published a series of harshly worded pamphlets, with such titles as *The Jews and Their Lies*, that have caused some people to brand him, fairly or unfairly, as an anti-Semite.

The power to suppress rebellion that Luther said God gave to secular leaders might have been used by Emperor Charles V to squelch the Reformation had crises on other fronts not distracted him. However, a decade passed before Charles could give his full attention to events in Germany. In the interim, Lutheranism spread widely, particularly in urban areas. Its empowerment of the individual appealed to humanist scholars and their students at universities, and these men scattered through Germany preaching and leading public discussions of Luther's call to return to the religious practices described in the New Testament. Luther had poetic gifts, and the hymns he composed were effective instruments for proselytizing the masses. He authored a flood of pamphlets that poured off the new presses, which also issued woodcut prints and cartoons—a new form of highly effective propaganda. Some rulers were attracted to Protestantism by the excuse the Reformation provided for confiscating church property and setting up state-controlled churches. In the 1530s, the king of Sweden—the dominant Scandinavian monarch—established Lutheranism as his country's official religion, and Denmark and Norway soon followed suit.

In 1530 Charles convened a diet at Augsburg and gave the Lutherans a year in which to return to the Catholic faith or face dire consequences. This prompted some of the Lutheran states to form the Schmalkaldic League, a military alliance named for the town where its leaders met. Civil war was averted when problems elsewhere in Charles's sprawling empire prevented him from acting on his threat. He was not able to return to Germany until 1546. A year later, he defeated the armies of the Schmalkaldic League, but Catholic France helped the Lutherans recover. Catholic rulers were no more eager for Charles to unite and control Germany than were their Lutheran colleagues.

Charles finally concluded that his huge empire could not be governed by one person. When he retired in 1556, the eastern Habsburg territories were being administered by his brother Ferdinand (r. 1558–1564), and he assigned responsibility for his western possessions—including Spain and the Netherlands—to his son Philip II (r. 1556–1598). In 1555 another diet that met at Augsburg arranged a truce between Lutherans and Catholics. On the assumption that people of different faiths could not live together, it decreed that each prince should decide for himself whether his state would be Catholic or Lutheran. His subjects would then have to either conform or emigrate to a place where their faith was legal. The **Peace of Augsburg** lasted until 1618, but by polarizing Germany, it created the conditions for one of Europe's most devastating conflicts, the **Thirty Years' War** (1618–1648).

The Swiss Reformation

Martin Luther was neither the first nor the only person to challenge the authority of the papacy on the basis of a reading of the Scriptures. Peter Waldo had done so in the twelfth century. A group of Franciscan friars, the Spirituals, had done so in the thirteenth century. The English theologian, John Wyclif, had followed suit in the fourteenth century, and his writings inspired the Bohemian reformer, John Hus, to launch a successful reform movement in the early fifteenth century. It was, however, one thing for the church's critics to agree that Christians should be guided by Scripture and another for them to agree on what the Scripture said. Luther's conservative practice was to allow traditional customs that were not mentioned in the New Testament to continue in use so long as they did not contradict Scripture. However, an independent

Martin Luther   The printing press made leading figures of the Reformation, such as Martin Luther, the first media stars. This likeness of the reformer is from the workshop of Lucas Cranach the Elder (1472–1553), painter to the court of Luther's protector, Duke Frederick of Saxony. It may have been executed about 1529. Oil portraits were sometimes copied in engravings or woodcuts to produce inexpensive prints for distribution to the masses.

reform movement that began in Switzerland was more radical. It insisted on wiping the slate clean and restoring only what the Bible mandated, but even this rigorous approach failed to produce consensus.

Zwingli   Ulrich Zwingli (1484–1531), the first major figure of the Swiss Reformation, became a reformer thanks in large part to the humanist education that prepared him for the Catholic priesthood. Like the great humanist biblical scholar Erasmus, he believed that the study of the New Testament would sweep away medieval superstition and bring about the moral regeneration of Christian society. Zwingli was a powerful orator, and his gifts served him well when, in 1519, he was assigned to fill the pulpit of the chief church in the Swiss city of Zurich.

Zwingli used sermons that explicated biblical texts to persuade his congregation to embrace reform. His study of the New Testament led him to question traditional pious customs (such as fasting and priestly celibacy) that had no scriptural basis. It also led him to the conclusion that churches should be purged of art and musical instruments, for there was no New Testament precedent for the presence or use of such things. Zwingli could also find no support for the Catholic doctrine of transubstantiation. He argued that the Eucharist, the ritual meal that Jesus directed his disciples to celebrate, was not a sacrament (a divine mystery in which people literally partook of the body and blood of Christ) but only a symbol, a ritual commemoration that reminded the faithful of Christ's work. Luther passionately disagreed, and his opposition to Zwingli hampered the attempts of Protestant leaders to cooperate against their enemies. In 1529 Philip of Hesse (r. 1509–1567), the leader of the Lutheran princes, arranged a meeting between Luther and Zwingli. Charles V was preparing to attack Germany's Lutherans. (They had begun by then to be called Protestants because of their protestations against Charles's policies.) Philip hoped that a united front would strengthen the Protestant cause, but it was not to be. Luther insisted that Christ's flesh and blood were in some sense truly present in the Eucharist, and he was appalled by Zwingli's reduction of the central Christian mystery to a mere symbol. Swiss and German Protestants declined to work together, and in 1531 Zwingli died in a war with Swiss Catholics. Luther did not lament his passing.

The Anabaptists   Luther considered Zwingli a radical, but some of Zwingli's fellow Swiss did not think that he was radical enough. Zwingli convinced them that the Bible was the sole authority in faith, but they were frustrated by his cautious approach to enforcing its precepts. In 1523 they took matters into their own hands and alarmed the authorities by smashing religious art and demanding an immediate end to the Roman mass. When they met resistance, they withdrew from society into communities of their own. They called themselves the Swiss Brethren, but their opponents dubbed them Anabaptists (Rebaptizers). They insisted on baptizing adult converts who had been baptized as children because they considered infant baptism to be unbiblical and therefore invalid.

The Anabaptists advocated separating from society and establishing elite communities of "saints" governed solely by Scripture. Their eagerness to recreate biblical societies led some of them to endorse practices, such as polygamy and communal ownership of property, that are in the Bible but that were out of step with the widely held convictions of their contemporaries. A literal reading of the Bible's apocalyptic passages also convinced some Anabaptists that the end of the world was at hand, and this prompted more radical behavior. In 1534 a group of Anabaptists seized the German city of Münster and purged it of all people who did not profess their faith. Lutherans and Catholics joined forces to retake the city, and the determination of the authorities to suppress the Anabaptist movement caused some Anabaptists to moderate their behavior. They gave up hope of mastering the world and retreated to parts of Europe where they could live unmolested. Some (the Mennonites, Hutterites, and Amish) eventually emigrated to North America and established communities that have endured and that still continue the way of life that their founders decreed to be godly.

Calvin and the Reform Tradition   Lutheranism did not spread as widely as the brand of Protestantism named for John Calvin (1509–1564), a Frenchman who eventually settled in Geneva. Like Luther, Calvin was the son of a family newly risen to the middle class, raised a Catholic, and educated for the priesthood. At the University of Paris, he made the acquaintance of humanists, but in 1528 his father ordered him to give up his theological studies and enter the law school at the University of Orléans. Unlike Luther, he completed his degree, and legal training shaped his work as a theologian and reformer.

On May 21, 1534, at the age of 25, Calvin took a step that radically altered his circumstances. Having been persuaded of the truth of Protestantism by an experience that he described as a burst of insight, he resigned the posts in the Catholic Church that provided his income. His change of mind owed much to humanism, but he did not share the humanists' optimism about human nature. Like Luther, the Apostle Paul, and the early Latin theologian Augustine of Hippo, he believed that human beings were captive to sin and lost unless God intervened to save them.

Calvin was a subject of the French monarch, Francis I (r. 1515–1547). Francis was a patron of the Renaissance and was sympathetic with aspects of humanism, but he had no motive for backing the humanists' push for radical church reform. The papacy had ceded the French king virtual control over the Catholic Church in France, and Francis did not want anyone to interfere with an institution that had become one of the instruments of his power. In October 1534, after militant reformers plastered Paris with posters attacking the mass, the king struck hard at suspected Protestants.

Calvin fled and found asylum in the Swiss city of Basel, and there, in August 1535, he published a rigorously rational explication of Protestant faith, *The Institutes of the Christian Religion.* The book was immediately popular and influential. Luther was a brilliant polemicist who dashed off thoughts in response to specific situations. This resulted in some gaps and inconsistencies in his writings that make their interpretation difficult. Calvin, however, was a systematic thinker who, in lawyerly fashion, developed a complete, succinct, and tightly reasoned case for Protestantism. Catholics, with centuries of scholarship to draw on, were well-prepared for theological debates; Calvin suddenly leveled the playing field by providing Protestants with cogent arguments for their beliefs.

Calvin and Luther agreed that the Bible was the sole guide to faith and that salvation was entirely a gift from God. Both endorsed **predestination**—the idea that humans could not affect God's decision about their ultimate fate. But they differed on the implications of this principle. Luther believed that God's laws were meant to convince people of the depth of their sin and the impossibility of earning salvation by their own efforts. Once they accepted that salvation was God's gift, they were freed from all concern for themselves and able to do good works. Only then were they truly able to devote themselves to serving others. Luther believed that if the church imposed rules governing behavior, people would slip back into thinking that obedience to these rules would earn them salvation. Calvin disagreed. He claimed that God's law was eternally valid. It did not earn anyone salvation, but it was binding on everyone (the damned as well as the saved) simply because it was God's law. It had to be enforced because God is God and human beings are His creatures.

Catholics insisted that the Protestant doctrine of salvation by faith undercut the motive for moral striving. Why, they asked, should anyone be good if good deeds are not rewarded? Contrary to Catholic expectation, however, Calvinist doctrine did not turn Calvinists into amoral libertines. It tended instead to produce dour moralists and ascetics—people who embraced "the Protestant work ethic," the sober lifestyle of the pleasure-averse laborers who, some scholars claim, have been major contributors to the success of the West's capitalist economy. The Calvinists' behavior makes some sense when viewed from a psychological perspective. If people believe that the most important decision that could ever be made about their lives has already been made, they will want desperately to know what this decision is. Calvin warned that no one could be certain that he or she is among the "elect" whom God had chosen for salvation. But it was reasonable to assume that those whom God had saved would do His will, and the Bible promised that "you will know them by their fruits" (Matthew 7:16). The desire to assure themselves that they were saved encouraged Calvinists to be moralistic and hardworking—and introspective. To see into their own hearts, they began to compile diaries in which they recorded their deeds and analyzed their motives.

In 1527 the people of Geneva expelled their Catholic bishop, and in 1534 they invited Calvin to reorganize their churches. The rigorous discipline he imposed was not popular, and the town's governing councils refused fully to empower the Consistory, a board of clergy and lay elders that Calvin set up to police public morals. Calvin was dismissed in 1538, but in 1541 Geneva recalled him and submitted to his reform program. With Calvin in charge, Geneva quickly became a haven for Protestant refugees from every corner of Europe. About 5,000 of them entered the city between 1549 and 1559—a huge number for a town that originally had about 12,000 inhabitants. When it was safe for them to go home, the Calvinism they absorbed in Geneva went with them. John Knox (1513–1572), Scotland's reformer, claimed that Geneva was "the most perfect school of Christ that ever was in the earth since the days of the Apostles."

The lessons people learned in Calvin's "school" extended beyond the practice of faith to the realm of politics. Luther endorsed a state church which submitted to the authority of a secular government. However, **Reform** (Calvinist) congregations followed what they believed was the custom of the early church. They elected councils of presbyters ("elders"), consisting of both clergy and laity, to lead them. The bodies of representatives that ran their churches increased pressure on states to accommodate a similar form of popular government.

The emphasis that Calvin placed on individual conscience and participatory decision making did not lead him (any more than it had Luther) to sanction rebellion against established authority. He drove those who opposed him from Geneva and even burned a Spanish refugee, Michael Servetus (1511–1553), at the stake for denying the doctrine of the Trinity and the divinity of Christ. However, when the shoe was on the other foot and Calvinists were the persecuted rather than the persecutors, they readily rationalized revolution—as England and France soon learned (see Map 13–2).

The Catholic Reformation

At the start of the Reformation, most of Europe's Christians belonged to a church that was—at least in their frame of reference—literally catholic ("universal"). But within a few years of Luther's excommunication, the church headed by Rome's pope was Catholic only in name and struggling to defend traditions and institutions that previously had seemed unassailable. Its response to the Protestant challenge has been characterized as a Counter-Reformation. However, it would be more accurate to call it a Catholic Reformation, for it was more than a reaction to the rise of Protestantism. It owed much to a reform movement that was active within the church before Martin Luther spoke out. In 1517, the year in which Luther attacked indulgences, an organization called the **Oratory of Divine Love** was established in Rome to promote religious renewal among both clergy and laity. Its influential members advocated reform, but they faced a serious obstacle in the Renaissance papacy.

The Renaissance Popes   In the years leading up to the Reformation, the papacy was preoccupied with rebuilding its power. The Great Schism (1378–1417) had lessened respect for popes, and the Conciliarist movement had questioned the basis for

Map 13–2 Religious Diversity in Post-Reformation Europe By the middle of the sixteenth century the region that medieval people thought of as Christendom was no longer united in allegiance to a single church. This affected the policies of the states that were emerging in many parts of the continent.

Question: Does the map suggest any explanation for where the various kinds of Protestantism spread?

their authority (see Chapter 12). Secular governments were also limiting a pope's right to operate within the boundaries of the emerging territorial states. The popes responded to these challenges abroad by building up their home base, the Papal States. Many of the popes were members of the aristocratic families that jockeyed for power in Italy, and they were well-schooled in the use of the tools of Renaissance governments: bribery, deception, assassination, and war. Their eager participation in Italy's convoluted politics made it difficult to distinguish them from the secular lords with whom they contended.

Popes, like the Renaissance's secular rulers, used patronage of the arts to bolster their image, and therefore their power. Pope Nicholas V (r. 1447–1455), the founder of the Vatican library, launched a program for reconstructing Rome that continued for generations. The city filled with buildings designed to bestow majesty on the papacy. Churches multiplied. Cardinals erected lavish palaces, and the old Vatican basilica, which Emperor Constantine had given to Rome's bishops, was pulled down to make way for construction of what was intended to be the grandest ecclesiastical building in Christendom. Kings embarked on similar programs of conspicuous display to nurture similar claims to status and respect, but behavior acceptable for a king was less so for a spiritual leader. The schemes popes devised to fund their pursuit of power earned them a reputation for greed and worldliness.

The worst popes had few aspirations beyond living like kings and enriching their relatives. Sixtus IV (r. 1471–1484) devoted most of his energies to the wars that raged among the Italian states. He was even implicated in a plot to assassinate the Medici family during mass in Florence's cathedral. The ironically named Innocent VII (r. 1484–1492) had 16 children, whom he richly rewarded from the spoils of the papal office. Alexander VI (r. 1492–1503) won the papacy by bribing the cardinals and used the church's wealth to fund wars that he hoped would win an Italian duchy for his son, Cesare Borgia (1476–1507). Julius II (r. 1503–1513) was determined—as he made clear by the name he chose when he became pope—to emulate the conquests of Julius Caesar. He donned armor and personally led troops in battle. But he was also a knowledgeable patron of the arts who commissioned Raphael to decorate the papal apartments and Michelangelo the Sistine Chapel. It fell to a Medici prince, Leo X (r. 1513–1521), to deal with Martin Luther. Not surprisingly, the aristocratic Italian pope failed to take the ranting of an obscure German monk seriously.

The papacy did not begin to mount a serious offensive against Protestantism until the reign of Paul III (r. 1534–1549). Paul appointed reforming cardinals and established a commission to draw up a plan for renewing the church. In 1537 his agents issued a report that documented many of the abuses of ecclesiastical authority of which Protestants complained. Three years later, Paul authorized the establishment of the Society of Jesus (the Jesuits), a religious order dedicated to serving the papacy and winning converts for the church. In 1542 he gave the Court of **Inquisition** authority to hunt down heretics everywhere in Europe, and in 1545 he convened the body that was primarily responsible for rebuilding the Catholic Church, the **Council of Trent**.

The Council of Trent worked with the Society of Jesus to effect the Catholic Reformation. The Jesuits were founded by Ignatius Loyola (1491–1556), a Basque soldier who discovered his spiritual vocation while recuperating from a war injury. The order accepted only the most gifted men, and it subjected candidates for admission to a 12-year-long course of study and testing that prepared them for the church's toughest assignments. Jesuits reversed gains the Reformation initially made in southern Germany, Poland, and Hungary. They spread the Catholic religion to the Americas, the East Indies, Japan, and China, and they founded hundreds of schools, colleges, and universities to provide Catholics with a firm intellectual grounding in their faith.

The Council of Trent, which met intermittently from 1545 to 1563, set the church on the path that it has (with some adjustments) followed ever since. The council affirmed that faith was based not only on Scripture, as Protestants claimed, but also on the traditions of the church. It rejected the idea that salvation was by faith alone and asserted the importance of good works. It reaffirmed transubstantiation as the explanation for the mystery of the Eucharist and asserted that each mass was an offering of Christ's sacrifice on the cross. The council's decrees were not meant to invite a dialogue that would lead to reconciliation with Protestants. They were intended to strengthen the Catholic cause by making it perfectly clear where the church stood in opposition to Protestantism. Having decided on its position, the church vigorously defended it. The Inquisition weeded out dissenters, and in 1559 the papacy imposed censorship. It forbade the reading of vernacular translations of the Bible and published an Index of Prohibited Books. So strict were the Index's standards that it condemned works by Erasmus, the loyal humanist biblical scholar who had opposed the Reformation.

The success of the Reformation should not be assumed to imply that sixteenth-century Catholicism was a moribund faith. While the Reformation spread in some parts of Europe, elsewhere a surge of enthusiasm for monastic vocations and passionate, mystical piety reflected renewed devotion to traditional religious life. Commitment to the defense and advancement of Catholicism was strongest in Spain, where Ferdinand and Isabella, "the Catholic kings," presided over the last phase in the long Iberian crusade. They crowned their conquest of Granada, Spain's last Islamic state, by banishing Jews as well as Muslims from Spain and by establishing an Inquisition that mercilessly policed the Catholic orthodoxy of their subjects. Spain's inquisitors were so alert to any whiff of heterodoxy that they briefly incarcerated the Jesuit's founder, Ignatius Loyola, and cast a wary eye on Teresa of Ávila (1515–1582), a Carmelite nun who was the era's leading mystic. Loyola's *Spiritual Exercises* and the works of Teresa and her disciple, John of the Cross (1542–1591), have become classics of Christian mystical literature. All three of these influential authors were eventually canonized (that is, acknowledged to be saints).

The Habsburg-Valois Wars

The Protestant and Catholic reformers did not work in a social vacuum. Because it was widely assumed that peoples of different faiths could not live together, one's allegiance to a religion implied one's support for—or opposition to—a government and the faith that it endorsed. This made religious and political issues inseparable.

The collapse of the German monarchy that followed the death of the Hohenstaufen emperor Frederick II in 1250 (see Chapter 12) cleared the way for France to move into Italy. Charles of Anjou, brother of Louis IX of France, conquered the Kingdom of Naples and founded a dynasty that survived until 1435. In 1494 King Charles VIII of France (r. 1483–1498) led an army into Italy to reclaim Naples for France, but a league of Italian states defeated him. In 1499 his successor, Louis XII (r. 1499–1515), occupied the duchy of Milan. However, by 1512 the French had once again been forced to retreat from Italy.

The election of Charles V as Holy Roman Emperor in 1519 made control of Italian territory a high priority for France's king, Francis I (r. 1515–1547). Charles held lands on every side of France, and Francis hoped that by occupying Italy he could avoid encirclement by the Habsburg Empire (see Map 13–1). Francis's first campaign ended in 1525 with his defeat and capture by Charles. No sooner was the king free, however, than he began a second war that also ended disastrously—particularly for his ally, Pope Clement VII (r. 1523–1534). In May 1527 Charles's imperial army broke out of control and sacked Rome—making the pope a virtual prisoner. Francis still refused to give up. In 1533 he strengthened his ties with the pope, who was eager to get out from under Charles's thumb. Francis arranged for Clement's niece, Catherine de Medicis (1519–1589), to marry his heir, Henry II (r. 1547–1559). Francis then shocked Europe by establishing diplomatic relations with the Ottoman sultan, Süleyman the Magnificent (r. 1520–1566), who had occupied most of Hungary and besieged Habsburg Vienna in 1529 with 200,000 men. Süleyman attacked Vienna again in 1532, and Francis wanted him to keep up the pressure on Charles V while the French navy assisted the Turkish fleet against the Habsburgs in the Mediterranean.

Francis began a third war with Charles in 1535. Fighting erupted in Italy, southern France, and the Habsburg Netherlands and dragged on until 1538. A fourth war broke out in 1542. Francis invaded Spain, and Charles thrust into France nearly to the gates of Paris. But by 1544 mutual exhaustion forced the opponents to agree to a truce. Both men were dead by the time the Treaty of Câteau-Cambrésis established peace between France and Spain in 1559.

England's Ambivalent Reformation

Apart from the Scandinavian states, England was the only major country to break with the papacy. Its decision to do so owed more to politics than to religion. As nation-states consolidated in the late medieval era, their governments increasingly regarded the papacy as a foreign power whose right to intervene in their affairs had to be curtailed. In the mid-fourteenth century, the English Parliament limited the pope's authority to fill offices in the English church and hear appeals from English courts. In 1438 the **Pragmatic Sanction of Bourges** declared that the French clergy (actually their king) would choose the bishops who headed the French church. Even the Court of Inquisition that the papacy established to root out heretics in Spain in 1477 served the interests of Spain's rulers, Ferdinand and Isabella. The decision to break with the papacy and make England a nominally Protestant country was similarly inspired by a desire to secure the kingdom by ensuring the future of its Tudor dynasty (1485–1603).

Henry VIII   England's civil war, the War of the Roses, ended in 1485, when Henry Tudor, a Welsh noble, defeated Richard III, the last Plantagenet king, and ascended the throne (see Chapter 11). England did not yield easily to its new ruler, Henry VII (r. 1485–1509). He spent much of his reign suppressing rebellions, but his clemency, intelligent government, and sound fiscal policies laid a solid foundation for his Tudor dynasty.

England had long cultivated alliances with the Spanish kingdoms against France, and in 1501 Henry reaffirmed this foreign policy. He obtained the hand of Catherine of Aragon (1485–1536), daughter of Spain's Ferdinand and Isabella, for Arthur (1486–1502), his son and heir. When Arthur died less than six months after the wedding, Henry decided to maintain the tie with Spain by obtaining papal permission for

Catherine to wed his new heir, his second son, the future Henry VIII (r. 1509–1547). A dispensation from canon law was required, for a biblical text (Leviticus 20:21) forbade a marriage between a man and his brother's widow.

Catherine endured many pregnancies, but only one of her children survived, a daughter named Mary. Henry doubted that England would accept a female heir to his throne and feared that after his death, the country would lapse back into the civil war from which it had recently emerged. He believed that the security of his kingdom depended on his having a son. When Catherine, who had not had a pregnancy in seven years, turned 40 in 1525, Henry—who was 34—decided that his only hope for a son lay in obtaining a younger wife.

Henry hoped that the pope would void his marriage on the principle that God had rendered sterile a marriage that the Bible had forbidden. The church had a long history of finding reasons to dissolve inconvenient marriages for influential people, but Clement VII, the pope to whom Henry appealed, was in no position to oblige England's king. Catherine opposed Henry's petition, and her nephew, Charles V—whose troops had recently sacked Rome—dominated Italy. When the pope prolonged the negotiations to buy time, Henry turned to Parliament for help in pressuring Rome. Parliament obliged by enacting a series of laws that began to sever ties between England and the papacy.

Events came to a head in 1533. Henry had fallen in love with Anne Boleyn (1504–1536), the daughter of one of his courtiers. Near the close of 1532 Anne became pregnant. Henry, who was desperate to assure the legitimacy of her child, secretly wed her in January 1533. In May his compliant archbishop of Canterbury, Thomas Cranmer (1489–1556), declared that he had never been validly married to Catherine and that Anne was therefore his legal wife. To the king's great disappointment, however, Anne bore him another daughter, Elizabeth.

In 1534 the pope came to Catherine's defense and declared her to be Henry's legitimate wife. Parliament responded by passing the **Act of Supremacy**, which severed ties with the papacy and recognized the king as the head of England's church. The break with Rome was not motivated by any royal sympathy with Protestantism. Henry had made his antipathy to the Reformation clear in 1521 by publishing an attack on Luther. The pope had been so grateful for Henry's support that he had awarded him the title: "Defender of the Faith." England's monarchs still list this among their titles although the faith they defend has changed.

A few prominent individuals, most famously the humanist Thomas More (the king's former chancellor), refused to swear allegiance to the new church and were executed. Although some modern scholars believe that anticlericalism was on the rise in England, most of Henry's subjects considered themselves to be Catholics. In 1536, when Henry began to suppress England's monasteries and confiscate their vast properties, there was a rebellion (the Pilgrimage of Grace) in the north of England. However, this was not solely a religiously motivated protest. It was also a reaction by the numerous tenants who lived on monastic estates to Henry's disruption of their lives. The strongest support for reforming England's church came from the merchant class, which had close commercial ties with those parts of Europe where Protestantism was spreading. This segment of English society was well represented in the Parliaments that met in 1536, 1537, 1538, 1539, and 1543 to draw up regulations for the new church. However, apart from suppressing monasteries and endorsing the use of vernacular Scriptures, Henry made few concessions to Protestantism. The Anglican (English) church over which he presided was to be nationalized, but not to depart significantly from its Roman Catholic model. It was to be ruled by bishops (whom the king appointed) and staffed by a celibate clergy who celebrated seven sacraments, and continued most medieval liturgical practices.

The king had risked much to marry Anne, and when her second pregnancy miscarried, he lost faith in her. He accused her of adultery, beheaded her, and took a third wife, Jane Seymour (1509–1537). On October 12, 1537, she died not long after giving birth to the long-sought male heir, the future Edward VI. Henry's next bride, a German Lutheran named Anne of Cleves (1515–1557), was chosen to forge an alliance between England and Germany's Lutheran princes. Thomas Cromwell (c. 1485–1540), Henry's chief minister, had argued that this would dissuade France and Spain from heeding the pope's call for a crusade against England. Henry, however, disliked Anne so much that their (allegedly unconsummated) marriage was annulled. In 1540 he wed Catherine Howard, a sprightly young niece of the duke of Norfolk. Her flagrant promiscuity with young men at court prompted her execution in 1542. A few months later, Henry married his sixth wife, Catherine Parr (1512–1548), a sensible widow with strong Protestant sympathies. She provided her aging husband with domestic comforts and took charge of the education of his children.

The Tudor Succession   When Henry died in January 1547, his 9-year-old-son, Edward VI (r. 1547–1553), ascended the throne. Edward was afflicted with chronic ill health but was intellectually precocious and (thanks to his stepmother and the Lutheran tutors she provided) a sincere Protestant. The chief monument of his brief reign was a new liturgy for the Anglican Church, *The Book of Common Prayer*. It tried to reconcile the various religious factions that were developing in England by being ambiguous on contentious issues.

The course of the English Reformation was nearly reversed when the young king died. His father's will named his half-sister Mary, Catherine of Aragon's Catholic daughter, next in line to the throne. Edward's Protestant advisors persuaded the dying boy to disinherit Mary, but the English people refused to accept this and rallied to her side.

Mary I (r. 1553–1558) shared her Spanish mother's conservative Catholic faith and was eager to restore England's allegiance to the papacy. She imprisoned some prominent Protestant clergy at the start of her reign but preferred to rid England of Protestants by urging them to reconvert or emigrate. Hundreds fled to the Netherlands, Germany, and Switzerland. There, under the influence of Calvinism, many became **Puritans**—sober, but passionate, Protestants who were filled with contempt for Catholicism and dedicated to "purifying" England's church of every taint of "Romanism."

Mary's first Parliament revoked some of her brother's religious legislation but balked at rebuilding England's monasteries. This would have necessitated the restoration of their confiscated lands, many of which had been acquired by members of Parliament. The thing that alarmed Parliament most about its new queen was not religion but her intended marriage. Mary was 37 years old, and she was desperate to bear an heir who would guarantee a Catholic succession to the English throne. The mate she chose was Charles V's son, Philip II, heir to Spain and the western half of the Habsburg Empire. Premarital agreements could limit the rights of the queen's husband over her kingdom, but not those of any child she and her spouse might have. It would have inherited both their thrones and made England, the weaker country, a Spanish dependency.

Four months after she became queen, Mary swept Parliament's objections aside and married Philip by proxy. Nine months later Philip arrived in England to meet a bride who was 11 years his senior. With Philip's encouragement, Mary sought formal reconciliation with Rome, which was granted on November 30, 1554.

Fear of Spain undercut support for Mary and encouraged her Protestant opponents. She reacted by searching out and executing Protestant sympathizers. She may have burned about 280 men and women at the stake (the standard punishment for heretics), which caused later Protestant historians to blacken her reputation. Some scholars point out that she was responsible for fewer deaths than her successor, her Protestant sister Elizabeth, but Elizabeth's record as an executioner was compiled over a much longer reign.

After less than a year of marriage, Philip left England. He did not give Mary a child, but he did draw her into the Habsburgs' wars with France. This misadventure cost England its last continental possession—the French port of Calais. Mary, isolated and disillusioned, lost touch with reality. When she died on November 17, 1558, Elizabeth—Mary's hated half-sister and the daughter of Anne Boleyn, whose marriage to Henry VIII had humiliated Mary and her mother—ascended her throne.

Convergence of Foreign and Domestic Politics: England, Spain, and France

The religious diversity the Reformation created greatly complicated political life in Europe, for it was widely assumed that a state could not survive unless all its citizens shared the same faith. Subjects who differed with the religion of their ruler were suspected to be traitors, particularly when wars broke out between Catholic and Protestant states.

Elizabeth's Compromises   In 1558 John Knox (c. 1505–1572), a Protestant exile from Scotland who found refuge in Geneva, published *The First Blast of the Trumpet Against the Monstrous Regiment of Women*. Knox blamed the ills of his generation on the women who, contrary (he claimed) to the laws of God and nature, were presuming to govern kingdoms. Mary Tudor, an ardent opponent of Protestantism, ruled England. In addition, Mary of Guise (1515–1560), a daughter of a powerful French Catholic family, governed Scotland as regent for her daughter, Mary Stuart (r. 1542–1567). What Knox considered a bad situation was destined, from his point of view, to get worse. France soon came under the thumb of its queen mother, Catherine de Medicis, and in 1558 England's throne passed to its second female heir. There were, however, no more blasts from Knox's trumpet, for timing made his book something of an embarrassment for his Protestant allies. The *First Blast* was intended to deafen a Protestant enemy, Mary Tudor, but it actually grated on the ears of Europe's most important Protestant monarch, Mary's sister Elizabeth I (r. 1558–1603).

Because Catholics did not recognize the validity of the marriage between Henry VIII and Anne Boleyn, they believed that Elizabeth's birth was illegitimate and that she therefore had no right to England's throne. But political objectives could trump religious scruples, and Europe's Catholic powers did not immediately attack the new queen. The pope held out hope for her conversion, and Philip II, Mary's widower, considered proposing to her. Elizabeth's position was precarious. England was nearly surrounded by Catholic states, and there was a Catholic claimant to her throne: Mary Stuart, a granddaughter of a sister of Henry VIII's who had married the king of Scotland. She was Scotland's hereditary queen and, as spouse of France's short-lived King Francis II (r. 1559–1560), briefly queen of France. Religious divisions were also increasing among Elizabeth's subjects. Some opposed her father's Reformation, and some—particularly the radicalized Puritans who returned to England from exile after Mary Tudor's death—believed that his Reformation had not gone far enough.

Elizabeth survived by making it difficult for everyone to figure out where she stood. She was adept at depriving potential opponents of clear targets and keeping alive their hopes for reconciliation. She flirted with, but never committed to, the many men who sought her hand in marriage. She endorsed some Catholic practices and some Protestant ideas. Gradually, she eased her country toward a "settlement" of religion—a church with a Catholic hierarchical structure and ritual and a partially Protestant theology. This did not end religious conflict in England, but it postponed a showdown until the 1630s.

Philip II and Spain's Golden Age
Elizabeth hoped to maintain England's alliance with Spain against France, but Spain's ruler had other plans. Philip II (r. 1556–1598) inherited the western half of Charles V's empire: Spain, Spain's New World possessions, and the Habsburg Netherlands (modern Belgium, Holland, and Luxembourg). Control of the commercially rich Netherlands and a steady flow of gold and silver from America gave Philip great resources, and he was willing to spend whatever it took to bring more of Europe under his control.

The weakest point in Philip's empire was the Netherlands, a small but highly urbanized and wealthy country whose independent townspeople were notoriously difficult to govern. The Netherlands was a loose collection of culturally diverse provinces. The ten southern provinces were French or Flemish, and the seven northern ones were linked by the Rhine River to Germany and Switzerland. Protestant influences (predominantly Calvinistic) spread to the Netherlands and there, as elsewhere, appealed to urban populations. Townspeople had, throughout the Middle Ages, been predisposed to self-government, and they responded to Luther's defense of the rights of the individual and Calvin's arguments for representative institutions. Philip concluded, therefore, that to strengthen his hold over the highly urbanized provinces, he had to purge them of Protestantism. This only increased the determination of some Netherlanders to resist Spanish domination.

El Escorial   The greatest monument from Spain's Golden Age is the huge palace-monastery complex that Philip II erected in honor of St. Lawrence, El Escorial. The structure reflects the wealth, power, and ardent faith of its builder. Philip's austere quarters were placed next to its great church and featured a window through which the king, who was sometimes bedridden, could witness the celebration of mass.

In 1567, after lesser measures had failed, Philip sent an army into the Netherlands to compel conformity to his religious policies. This heavy-handed action roused nationalistic passions, and a resistance movement formed around a native nobleman, William of Orange (1533–1584). William tried to unite all the provinces, but religious disputes doomed his efforts. In 1579 the largely Franco-Catholic southern provinces sided with Spain, while the north's more easily defended Dutch-speaking provinces formed a Protestant alliance (the United Provinces) and continued the fight for independence. Because the United Provinces received help from England's Protestant queen, Philip decided to try to subdue both these enemies in a single campaign. Developments seemed to favor his success. William of Orange was assassinated in 1584. A pro-Spanish faction won ascendancy at the French court, and a plot unfolded in England to place Mary Stuart on Elizabeth's throne.

England's Henry VIII had tried to win Mary Stuart's hand for his son and successor, Edward. But the Scots, who had long relied on France's help to maintain their independence from England, preferred that their queen wed the heir to the French throne. As a young child, Mary (1542–1567) was sent to France to be educated for her future role as its queen. Her mother, Mary of Guise (a member of an extremely powerful and ardently Catholic French noble family), governed Scotland as her regent. Although some Scots favored the French alliance, others feared French dominance. In 1559 a cadre of nobles, with an agenda that mixed religion and politics, overthrew Mary of Guise and recalled a native son, John Knox, from exile in Geneva. Knox, a former Catholic priest who had embraced Calvinism, was charged with reforming Scotland's church. A year later, Mary Stuart's husband, Francis II, died. The young widow of the French king was then sent back to Scotland to govern a country she had not seen since early childhood. Mary, who was accustomed to the luxury and sophistication of the elegant French court, was ill-prepared for life in a much poorer and less urbane society. Her manner offended men like Knox, and she was soon at odds with powerful members of her court. She worsened her situation by conducting an affair with—and ultimately marrying—the man suspected of killing her second husband, a great-grandson of England's Henry VII. In 1566 she gave birth to a son (Scotland's James VI and England's future James I), and a year later she was compelled to abdicate her throne to him. She then fled to England to ask for help, despite the fact that she was a strong potential rival for its Protestant queen's throne. Elizabeth was uncertain what to do with her. Not wanting to kill her or trusting what she might do if she were free, the English queen kept Mary in confinement for 20 years. Rumors of plots to overthrow Elizabeth and enthrone Mary multiplied, and in 1587 evidence for Mary's involvement in one of Philip II's schemes persuaded Elizabeth to order her beheading.

Elizabeth had good reason to fear for her throne, for Philip was assembling a great fleet for an invasion of England. His plan was to sail to the Netherlands with an army, pick up additional troops there, and then cross the channel to England. Various setbacks delayed the departure of the so-called **Spanish Armada** until the summer of 1588, and then the expedition was undone by a combination of bad planning, worse weather, and the skills of English sailors. After the Armada's destruction, Philip continued to threaten England, but his resources were diminishing as his problems were multiplying. The struggle in the Netherlands continued, and in 1589 he attacked France. The English also devised an effective way to undermine him. Privateers (government-licensed, privately funded pirates) raided Spanish shipping. The queen herself invested in these highly profitable ventures, over a hundred of which sailed in some years. England did not yet have a navy, but it was on its way to becoming a major sea power.

After Philip's death in 1598, Spain entered a long period of gradual decline. The gold and silver that Spaniards had extracted from the Americas had not been invested in building a productive economy. Instead, the bullion had flowed through Spain to fund Philip's numerous wars. The church controlled about half the land in Spain and supported a huge number of clergy. Most of the rest of the country was in the hands of an entrenched aristocracy that clung to its medieval prerogatives. Portraits of Spain's grandees by the artist El Greco (c. 1541–1614) proclaim their sense of entitlement, and the paintings by Velázquez (1599–1660), a generation later, suggest a royal court that had drifted into the realm of fantasy. In addition to major artists, Spain's Golden Age also framed the career of its greatest writer: Miguel de Cervantes Saavedra (1547–1616). Cervantes' groundbreaking novel, *Don Quixote,*

Mary, Queen of Scots   This portrait is the work of Nicholas Hilliard (1547–1619), the leading painter of miniatures at the court of Elizabeth I. A number of prominent figures from the Elizabethan age, including the queen herself, had likenesses drafted by Hilliard.

affectionately lampooned his countrymen's romantic devotion to an archaic way of life that was dooming them to irrelevance.

France's Wars of Religion   Spain was not Elizabeth's only concern. A war between Catholic and Protestant factions raged in France for much of her reign and complicated her foreign policy. In France, as elsewhere, the Reformation attracted people who were critical of established authority and who saw religious change as part of a broader program of reform. Many of these came from the professional and middle classes and the lower nobility—educated people who chafed under the restraints of institutions that they regarded as outmoded. France's Protestants were Calvinists called Huguenots. Scholars are uncertain of the origin of their name.

For most of the sixteenth century, France's royal government left much to be desired. Francis I used the French Catholic Church as a source of political patronage and squandered his country's resources in futile wars with his Habsburg rival, Charles V. Francis's son, Henry II (r. 1547–1559), achieved little before an accident in a tournament bout ended his life and delivered France into the hands of his Italian wife, Catherine de Medicis (1519–1589). Catherine was the power behind a throne that passed in succession to three of their sons. Francis II (r. 1559–1560) survived his father for only a year. He was succeeded by his 10-year-old brother, Charles IX (r. 1560–1574). The third brother, Henry III (r. 1574–1589), was an adult when he became king, but debauchery subverted his effectiveness as a ruler.

It was all that Catherine could do simply to preserve the Valois dynasty, for France was less a unified kingdom than a league of powerful principalities. Whenever its kings were weak, aristocratic factions led by great noblemen fought for dominance at court. During the sixteenth century, religious differences defined the opposing camps. The Catholic party was led by the dukes and cardinals of the Guise family and the Protestants by the Bourbons, a cadet branch of the royal house. In 1562 the duke of Guise began a war with the Protestants by slaughtering 70 Huguenots whom he surprised at worship. In 1572 Catherine's attempt to reconcile France's Catholic and Protestant factions backfired and led to a mass murder that shocked Europe. The French aristocracy gathered in Paris for the wedding of Catherine's daughter, Margaret, to Henry of Navarre, the Bourbon head of the Huguenot faction. The marriage was intended to bring Catholics and Protestants together, but on the eve of the ceremony someone tried to assassinate one of the Huguenot leaders. Fear of Protestant reprisals prompted the crown to act quickly and with great force. Early on the morning of August 24, the feast of St. Bartholomew, the king's army fell on the unsuspecting Huguenots. The slaughter spread to other cities, and some 70,000 Protestants may have perished before the purge ended. The **St. Bartholomew's Day Massacre** poisoned relationships between Protestants and Catholics throughout Europe and diminished hope that the faiths could coexist peacefully.

Spain and England encouraged civil war in France by providing aid to the combatants, and the bloodshed continued until 1589, when a monk extinguished the Valois dynasty by assassinating Henry III. This cleared the way to the throne for the Bourbon heir, the Protestant Henry of Navarre, France's King Henry IV (r. 1589–1610). After a prolonged struggle, Henry concluded that his largely Catholic country would not accept a Protestant king, and he converted—allegedly quipping, "Paris is worth a mass." Henry IV, a nominal Catholic with Protestant credentials, had enough credibility with both sides to negotiate a truce between them. In 1598 he issued the **Edict of Nantes**, which declared France a Catholic country but designated places where Huguenots could worship and ceded some towns to their control. Since 1555, a similar arrangement (the Peace of Augsburg) had maintained order in Germany, but events there were about to demonstrate that religious segregation was not a permanent solution.

The Final Religious Upheavals

By the end of Elizabeth's reign (1603), a lull was developing in Europe's conflicts. England was fairly secure. Spain's struggles in the Netherlands were winding down, and France was recovering from its long internal bloodletting. There were, however, problems on the horizon. Despite all the killing, Europe's population had increased by

■ ■

PEOPLE IN CONTEXT William Shakespeare (1564–1616)

Literature flourished in Elizabethan England as never before, and the period's greatest author was, as one of his contemporaries put it, "not of an age, but for all time." He might have added "and for all cultures," for William Shakespeare's plays have been translated into many tongues, staged as operas and Broadway musicals, and produced as commercially successful films. Given their fame, it is surprising that so little is known about their author.

Shakespeare, for all his talent, seems to have led a fairly conventional life. John Shakespeare, his father, was a glove maker, money lender, and commodity trader in the town of Stratford-on-Avon. He and his wife, Mary Arden, had eight children. Will, the eldest of their four sons, was born in a terrifying year in which about 250 of Stratford's 800 inhabitants died of the plague. John served a term as mayor of Stratford and applied for a coat-of-arms to bolster his social aspirations. But by the time Will was 11, his father was suffering serious financial reverses and could do little to help his son make a start in life.

Shakespeare's formal education appears to have been in Stratford's free school. Unlike other famous playwrights of his generation, there is no evidence that he studied at one of England's universities. His plays testify to his familiarity with the major classic authors (Ovid, Plutarch, Seneca, etc.) but do not suggest that he was unusually well read. This background has caused some to doubt that he could have written the works ascribed to him. Various more distinguished individuals (including noblemen and rival poets) have been proposed as writers for whom he fronted. Although his works have been minutely combed for clues to the identity of an anonymous author, there is no convincing evidence that Shakespeare did not write the plays and poems his contemporaries credited to him. Genius such as he displayed is not unprecedented, but it usually seems inexplicable.

At the age of 18 Shakespeare married Anne Hathaway, a woman eight years his senior. Six months after the wedding, their daughter Susanna was baptized, and three years later they had twins—a boy and a girl. No one knows how young Shakespeare supported his family or what drew him to London and the theater in the late 1580s.

William Shakespeare This portrait of William Shakespeare is from an engraving that was made for a 1623 edition of his work.

Somehow he learned to act and to write plays, and by 1592 his work was attracting envious notice from his competitors. By 1597, he was rich enough to purchase the second largest house in Stratford, and by 1599, he was part owner of a new London theater called "The Globe."

Shakespeare's family may have secretly clung to the old Catholic faith, but Shakespeare was no propagandist or overt advocate for a cause. He was a professional playwright whose goal was to please his audiences without overtly taking sides in contentious political or religious debates. He dealt with universal themes of perennial human concern: love, jealousy, ambition, deceit, treason, and the meaning of life. He wrote to make a living, and when he could afford to (in 1613), he laid down his pen and devoted the rest of his life to managing his business interests. He appears to have given little thought to preserving his work for posterity. He died on April 23, 1616, and seven years passed before a group of admirers gathered up scattered manuscripts of his plays and edited them for publication.

Shakespeare wrote exclusively for his own company at the rate of about two plays a year. Scholars credit him with 154 sonnets, several longer poems, and about 40 plays. The latter span the genre of theater: comedies, tragedies, histories, romances, and fantasies. The great characters he created for the stage—Romeo, Juliet, Hamlet, Macbeth, Lear, Othello, Falstaff, and many others—have become prototypes in world literature. Lines from his plays (e.g., "Neither a borrower nor a lender be," *Hamlet*) are commonplace quotations that are sometimes mistaken for verses from Scripture. It is likely no other single author has had more influence on the development of the English language and its literary canon.

Question: Does Shakespeare's work support the common assumption that artists reflect the dominant values and concerns of the eras in which they live?

about 40% during the sixteenth century. The gold and silver that had flooded in from the New World had caused inflation to soar. Widespread poverty and unstable economies inspired riots and rebellions. Governments strained to control their subjects, and some failed conspicuously.

The Thirty Years' War   By separating Germany's Lutherans and Catholics, the Peace of Augsburg diminished opportunities for the two faith communities to learn to trust one another. Some people were also determined to undermine Augsburg's arrangements. The Jesuits reclaimed much of southern Germany for the Catholics. The Calvinists, who were rivals of the Lutherans and who had not been accorded legal recognition in the Augsburg agreement, were equally aggressive in their recruiting. In 1608 the Calvinist ruler of the Palatinate, Frederick IV (r. 1592–1610), established the Protestant Union, an alliance of Protestant states. Duke Maximilian of Bavaria (1573–1651) countered by recruiting members for what was called the Catholic League. France, England, and Holland supported Frederick, and the Habsburgs—both Spanish and Austrian—backed Maximilian.

The only thing needed for war to break out was an incident to trigger hostilities. That was provided by a colorful event that took place in Prague in 1618 in the wake of the ascension to the Bohemian throne of the Austrian archduke Ferdinand (1578–1637), the Catholic heir to the Holy Roman Empire (as Ferdinand II). The kingdom of Bohemia had accommodated religious heterodoxy at least since the early fifteenth century, when the followers of John Hus fought for and won a degree of independence from the papacy (see Chapter 11). Bohemia had subsequently provided refuge for Anabaptists, and Calvinism had spread in some aristocratic circles. The Jesuit-educated Ferdinand, however, had no sympathy with his new kingdom's tradition of tolerance, and he broke pledges he had made to his Protestant subjects by mandating their return to Catholicism. The Bohemian nobles reacted to the orders he sent them by tossing his messengers out a window onto a dung heap. Ferdinand treated this "Defenestration of Prague" as a declaration of war and prepared to invade Bohemia. The Bohemians responded by turning to the son and successor of Frederick IV of the Palatinate, Frederick V (r. 1610–1632), for help. The German states quickly chose sides—not allowing their religious preferences to stand in the way of their political interests. Some Lutherans, who despised Calvinists, supported Ferdinand. In contrast, some Catholics, who did not want the Catholic Habsburgs to grow stronger, sided with Frederick.

In the first phase of the war, the Catholic forces swept through Germany and routed Frederick, but that only widened the conflict. The possibility of a Germany united under a Catholic monarch so alarmed Germany's neighbors that they intervened on the Protestant side. Denmark was the first to attack, but its campaign foundered and enabled the Catholics to seize additional ports on the Baltic. That, however, brought Sweden into the fray. In 1630 Sweden's great warrior king, Gustavus Adolphus (r. 1611–1632), forced Ferdinand to retreat from northern Germany. Catholic France then allied with Lutheran Sweden. After Gustavus Adolphus was killed in battle, France directed the course of the war against the Catholic emperor. France was governed by Cardinal Richelieu (1585–1642), chief minister for Henry IV's son, Louis XIII (r. 1610–1643). Richelieu was a sincere Catholic and a "prince" of the papal establishment, but he put the interests of his country above those of his church. The last thing France wanted was to face a unified Germany along its eastern frontier. Therefore, Richelieu had little choice but to help Germany's Protestants fend off their Catholic emperor. The intervention of foreign powers turned Germany into an international killing ground. By the time the war ended, battles, raids, plagues, massacres, and famines had resulted in the deaths of about eight million people, roughly 40% of Germany's population.

The **Peace of Westphalia** that concluded the war in 1648 ensured that Germany would remain an impotent collection of hundreds of tiny states and that the Holy Roman Empire would be an empire only in name. The victors rewarded themselves with bits of German territory, and the Habsburg defeat cleared the way for the Swiss cantons and the Dutch Republic to be recognized as independent states. Germany's collapse and Spain's humiliation also meant that France now had a chance to dominate the continent (see Map 13–3).

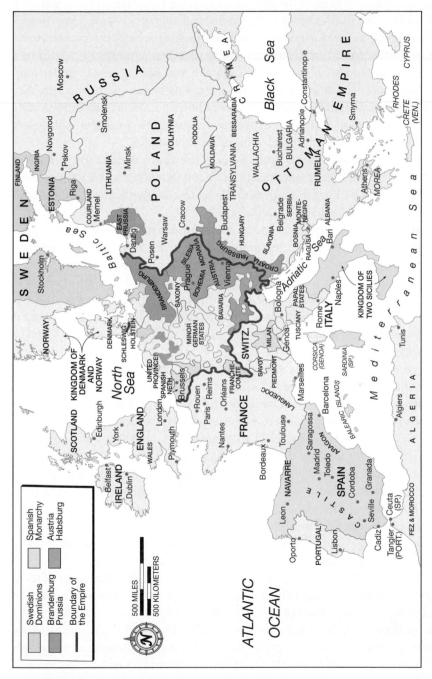

Map 13-3 Europe After the Peace of Westphalia The Treaty of Westphalia redrew the map of Europe. France and Sweden acquired additional territory. The United Provinces and the Swiss cantons were recognized as independent states, and Germany's political fragmentation was assured to continue.

Question: To what extent were the political borders that the treaty drew on the map of Europe determined by geography?

England's Civil War   By the time Westphalia brought the continent's religious wars to an end, a conflict between Puritans and Anglicans was raging in England. England's religious factions had different political visions for both their country's church and its government. The Puritans wanted a church consisting of self-governing congregations overseen by a national synod to which congregations elected representatives. The secular equivalent for this ecclesiastical organization was a monarchy headed by a king who ruled in consort with Parliament. Elizabeth and her successors understood the political implications of Protestant church order, which was one reason why they insisted on an Anglican Church modeled on the traditional Catholic hierarchy. A state church governed by bishops appointed by the crown was more consistent with strong monarchy than the alternatives favored by England's Protestants.

Elizabeth never married, and her death brought the Tudor dynasty to an end. Her heir, James I (r. 1603–1625), was Mary Stuart's son, Scotland's King James VI. Ironically, centuries of war waged by English kings who hoped to conquer Scotland ended with Scotland's king ascending England's throne.

James's experience with Presbyterians in Scotland did not inspire him with enthusiasm for either Protestantism or representative government. In 1598 he published a book, *A True Law of Free Monarchies*, that clarified his stance. It firmly embraced the medieval principle that God appointed kings and that kings were accountable only to God, which was out of step with recent trends in English history. The Tudor dynasty had needed Parliament's help to effect the Reformation and manage its consequences, and Parliament had come to think of itself as a partner with the monarch in governing England.

Parliament met only when the monarch called it, and what kept its tradition alive was its control of taxation. England's kings could not levy taxes without parliamentary approval. To avoid calling a Parliament that might try to limit his authority, a king had to find other ways to meet the expenses of government, and James was ingenious in devising these. He imposed customs duties, sold titles of nobility, licensed monopolies for a fee, and did everything he could think of to fill the royal coffers without resorting to Parliament. He had no sympathy with any aspect of Puritanism and even sponsored a national campaign to encourage the recreations, games, and sports that the Puritans condemned as frivolous and ungodly pastimes. His major concession was to commission a new vernacular translation of the Scriptures. The result was the eloquent Authorized Version (or as it is popularly known, the King James Version) of the Bible.

James's policies and dissolute court were so offensive to Puritans that some of them gave up hope for England's reformation and decided to make fresh starts elsewhere. In 1593 a small group of radical Puritan separatists left London for the Netherlands, and in 1620 they emigrated again to found a colony called Plymouth in North America. They were the vanguard of a much larger migration that eventually brought thousands of more mainstream Puritans to New England and the islands of the West Indies. As it turned out, they were somewhat premature in anticipating the decline of the Puritan cause in their homeland.

Leaders of the Reformations and the Wars of Religion

RELIGIOUS LEADERS	POLITICAL LEADERS	EVENTS
Luther (1483–1546)	Charles V (1519–1556)	Diet of Worms (1521)
Leo X (1513–1521)	Süleyman (1520–1566)	
Zwingli (1484–1531)	Francis I (1515–1547)	Habsburg-Valois Wars (1521–1544)
Clement VII (1523–1534)	Henry VIII (1509–1547)	
Calvin (1509–1564)	Catherine of Aragon (1485–1536)	English Reformation (1534)
		Geneva reformed (1541)
Ignatius Loyola (1491–1556)	Edward VI (1547–1553)	Peace of Augsburg (1555)
Paul III (1534–1549)	Mary Tudor (1553–1558)	Council of Trent (1545–1563)
Knox (1505–1572)	Philip II (1556–1598)	Scotland reformed (1559)
Theresa of Avila (1515–1582)	Elizabeth I (1558–1603)	Spanish Armada (1588)
	Mary Stuart (1542–1567)	
	Catherine de Medicis (1485–1536)	French Wars of Religion (1562–1589)
	Henry IV (1594–1610)	Edict of Nantes (1598)
	James I (1603–1625)	
	Frederick V (1596–1632)	
	Ferdinand II (1578–1637)	Thirty Years' War (1618–1648)
	Gustavus Adolphus (1611–1632)	
	Richelieu (1585–1642)	
	Charles I (1625–1649)	English Civil War (1642–1646)
	Cromwell (1599–1658)	English Republic (1649–1660)

James's son and successor, Charles I (r. 1625–1649), shared his father's determination to rule without interference from his subjects. After a Parliament early in his reign forced him to acknowledge that he had no unilateral right to levy taxes, he avoided convening another session for 11 years (1629–1640). He was even less willing than his father to compromise with Protestants, and the Puritans suspected him of being a Catholic at heart. His French wife enjoyed the privilege of hearing mass at court, and his archbishop of Canterbury, William Laud, had his support in promoting liturgical reforms that Puritans regarded as a reversion to Roman worship.

Puritans who criticized him in print or from their pulpits were dragged into court, speedily convicted, and harshly punished. What precipitated his fall, however, was not his quarrel with England's Puritans but his determination to force Scotland's church to conform with Anglican practice. In 1637 Charles ordered Scotland's Presbyterian clergy to use the Anglican prayer book. When the Scots refused, Charles took up arms against them. The small army he was able to raise without Parliament's assistance failed to do anything but goad the Scots into invading England in 1640. This forced Charles to call a Parliament, but that only worsened his situation. When members of Parliament insisted that he carry out extensive governmental reforms before they granted new tax levies, he dissolved the meeting (the "Short Parliament"). A few months later, a victory by the Scots forced him to reconvene Parliament. This meeting passed a law to the effect that a parliamentary session could only be ended by vote of its members. Given that no resolution for adjournment was passed for the next 20 years, this became the era of the "Long Parliament." The Long Parliament moved rapidly to curtail the power of the king. It dismissed his archbishop, punished some of his councilors, repealed his taxes, and decreed that the king had to call future Parliaments at regular intervals. Charles believed that Parliament was vastly overstepping its boundaries and curtailing his royal prerogatives. The reforms it demanded were in fact similar to those that later limited the powers of the throne and established Parliament as the dominant body in Britain's government. In 1642 the exasperated king made the mistake of sending soldiers to break up Parliament. When Parliament's leaders resisted and London rose to support them, the king left London and began to rally his supporters in the west and north of England.

This was the prelude to a civil war that raged for four years (1642–1646). Its turning point came in 1645 with Parliament's institution of the **New Model Army**, a reorganized military recruited from committed Protestants called "Roundheads." (Their closely cropped hair contrasted with the flowing locks of the king's courtiers, the "Cavaliers.") Unlike earlier armies, the New Model Army was commanded not by aristocrats, but by experienced officers who advanced by merit. Its men were strictly disciplined, passionate about their

Oliver Cromwell This unfinished miniature is a likeness of the enigmatic Puritan leader, Oliver Cromwell. He allegedly had a religious experience in his youth that convinced him that he was one of God's elect—a man destined to serve God in unique ways. His confidence in his calling may explain the forceful means he often employed to impose his will on others.

cause, and respected for their moral rectitude. They routed armies larger than their own and did not indulge in the rape and pillage that had traditionally been the prerogatives of victorious soldiers. Parliament was also fortunate in finding a brilliant military strategist among its members. Oliver Cromwell (1599–1658), a member of the House of Commons, was an obscure individual from the ranks of the country gentry. He raised a company of cavalrymen whose spirit and discipline spread through the parliamentary forces, and he quickly rose in the chain of command.

The king's army was broken at the Battle of Naseby in June 1645, but Charles eluded capture and survived as a fugitive in his own country for a year. In May 1646 he surrendered to the Scots who held him for eight months before turning him over to the English.

Parliament was better at winning wars than governing England, for victory cleared the way for its numerous religious factions to begin to fight among themselves. A rift also opened between politicians and soldiers when Parliament attempted precipitously to disband the army. Parliament's Presbyterian majority was more conservative than many of the soldiers. A faction known as the Levelers demanded that the current Parliament be dissolved and that every adult male citizen be given the right to vote for a new Parliament that would govern without restraint by a king or House of Lords. Freedom of religion was also to be guaranteed.

In November of 1647 the king escaped, and the war flared up again. This had the effect of strengthening the army and draining whatever respect the soldiers still had for the monarchy. The army recaptured the king, occupied London, and purged Parliament of its Presbyterian majority. The much reduced "Rump Parliament" then convicted the king of treason and—on January 30, 1649—beheaded him. The monarchy was declared at an end, and England was henceforward to be governed as a republic. In reality, Cromwell became the new head of state. His support derived in large part from his ability as a military leader to restore order to a country that was desperate for stability. He stuck to a Puritan middle path—suppressing both the radical Levelers and the Anglo-Catholics. He dealt harshly with critics and opponents, and mounted new military campaigns. He put down revolts in Ireland, brought Scotland back under England's control, and waged war at sea with the Dutch. The taxes he imposed were more onerous than those that Charles had levied, and in 1653 this prompted Parliament to consider disbanding his army. He prevented this by using the army to disband the Rump Parliament. Cromwell wanted to rule in cooperation with a Parliament, but when debates in the meetings he subsequently convened grew too radical for his tastes, he sent their delegates home. He leaned heavily on the army to maintain himself in power and in May of 1657 he assumed the title of hereditary Lord Protector—a king by a new title. He survived for another year, dying on September 3, 1658.

Cromwell's son, Richard, briefly assumed his father's office, but he was unable to maintain control of a divided army and a country that had been disillusioned by both Republicanism and Puritan extremism. A period of confusion ensued in which civil war again threatened. Finally, a powerful general arranged for the election of a new Parliament. In April of 1660 it invited Charles I's son, Charles II (r. 1660–1685), to return from exile in France and restore the monarchy and the Anglican Church. England embraced its former institutions, but the Puritan revolution had not been a complete failure. Mindful of Charles I's fate, England's kings moderated claims to absolute authority and conceded Parliament a role in their governments. Britain's "constitutional" monarchy was not yet complete, but it was on the brink of the final stage in its development.

KEY QUESTION | Revisited

During the sixteenth and seventeenth centuries, Europeans worked to resolve power struggles of various kinds. Emerging states jousted for advantage. Within states, there were tugs of war between regional and centralized authorities. Nobles resisted the growing power of kings. Social and economic classes and rural and urban areas were in conflict. The long-standing tension between the two visions for Europe—imperial unity and religious homogeneity or political fragmentation and cultural diversity—came to a head.

Religious convictions, both sincere and opportunistic, provided moral justification for decisions to shed blood that was spilled for many other reasons as well. The ethical context for the wars of the Reformation era may have been more complex than for the religious wars of earlier generations. Unlike the crusades, which were wars of foreign aggression waged in defense of European Christianity against what was thought to be a hostile, alien faith, Europe's "wars of religion" were civil wars within European Christendom. Their rationale involved differing views of orthodoxy and heresy—of what constituted fidelity to God and what was to be fought as a perversion of true faith.

Combatants championed different belief systems, but they were sometimes willing to ignore religious differences when it was to their advantage. The determination of the German princes to defend their separate sovereignties had much to do with their decisions to embrace or combat the Reformation. Fear of the potential power of the Catholic Habsburg Empire drove some into the Protestant camp, and the expectation of help from Catholic authorities kept others loyal to the papacy. In France, religion split an aristocracy that had a long history of struggling within its own ranks for ascendancy at court. In England, most openly of all, political motives and perceived national interests lay behind the initial decision to break with Rome.

Opportunism aside, religion had a direct link with politics, for it affected how people thought about authority and legitimate government. The sovereignty that Protestantism claimed for individual conscience predisposed Protestants (particularly Calvinists) to favor some form of popular or representative government. Catholics, who were inclined to the traditional belief that authority was a gift God bestowed on rulers of His choice, supported monarchy and hierarchical systems of administration. Partisans from both camps faced the same dangerous temptation—to equate the defense of particular human institutions with the survival of transcendent principles. When opponents make that leap, they risk disaster. By absolutizing their positions, they persuade themselves that mediation and compromise are equivalent to treachery. All means, no matter what the human cost, seem justified when "the Truth" is at stake.

Review Questions

1. What key beliefs forced Luther to separate from the Catholic Church?
2. How were Calvinists different from Lutherans? From Anabaptists?
3. Was the English Reformation a reformation or a revolution?
4. What effect did the Reformation have on Catholicism and the power of the papacy?
5. What roles did religion play in the wars of the sixteenth and seventeenth centuries?
6. How did religion affect political developments in Spain, France, Germany, and England?

Please consult the Suggested Readings at the back of the book to continue your study of the material covered in this chapter. For a list of documents on the Primary Source DVD-ROM that relate to topics in this chapter, please refer to the back of the book.

Glossary

Act of Supremacy Act passed by the English Parliament in 1534 that severed England's ties with the papacy and established the king as the head of the Church in England.

Alimenta An endowment established by Rome's emperors to support and educate the children of poverty stricken Italians.

Amarna Capital of Egypt during the reign of the pharaoh Akhenaten (1352–1338 B.C.E.); seat of his religious reform and a unique era in the history of Egyptian art.

Areopagus Council of the Areopagus, the oldest political body in Athens, the seat of aristocratic influence before the rise of the Athenian democracy.

Axial Age A characterization of the seventh and sixth centuries B.C.E. as a time of major religious and philosophical developments throughout the ancient world.

Babylonian Captivity Critical characterization of the era (1378–1415) in which the popes left Rome and resided in Avignon; reference to the exile of the ancient Jews from Jerusalem by the Chaldaeans of Babylon.

Barracks Emperors Characterization of the period in Roman history from 235 to 285 C.E. when there was a rapid turnover of claimants to the imperial throne; most were men "from the barracks" (i.e., ordinary soldiers who rose through the ranks).

Bishop The *episcopus* or "overseer," the title given to the religious official who oversaw the clergy working in a district called a diocese.

Boule The representative assembly central to the organization of Athens' democracy; founded by Solon and reorganized by Cleisthenes.

Bourgeoisie Term for the people who lived in a medieval *bourg*, a fortified settlement; a designation for the new middle class that appeared in medieval Europe.

Caliph "Successor," office of the heir to Muhammad's role not as prophet, but as leader of the *umma*.

Carolingians The dynasty of Frankish kings that succeeded the Merovingians; their most famous member, Charlemagne, ruled the territory of modern France, much of Germany, and part of Italy.

Church "Lord's House," term for the communities established by the early Christians.

Cluniac Reform A movement originating at the French monastery of Cluny that sought to elevate the level of conduct of the medieval clergy by establishing the church's independence of the laity.

Code of Hammurabi Collection of laws issued by the Amoritic ruler of Babylon, Hammurabi (1792–1750 B.C.E.); earliest major collection of legal materials.

Coloni Tenant farmers who, late in the history of the Roman Empire, became tied to the lands they worked.

Comitatus A band of German warriors that was created by the oaths of personal loyalty that members took to their leader.

Compurgation A legal procedure by which an accused person could clear his or her name by finding a certain number of people who would swear to his or her integrity.

Conciliarism A legal argument for recognizing universal councils, not popes, as the supreme authorities for determining the faith and practice of the Catholic Church.

Condottiere Commander of an army of mercenaries; when hired to defend one of Italy's towns, the risk was that he would use his soldiers to take over and make his power permanent.

Constitutions of Clarendon A decree issued by England's King Henry II that sought to bring clergy who were convicted of crimes in church courts under the jurisdiction of royal courts for their punishment.

Council of Trent A church council, meeting from 1545 to 1563, that was charged with the responsibility of strengthening the Roman Catholic Church to equip it to respond to the challenge of the Protestant Reformation.

Courtly Love A modern term for a medieval aristocratic fad, a game of courtship in which a man exalted a woman as a paragon of beauty and virtue and pledged to endure any hardship in exchange for a sign of her favor.

Crusade "War of the cross," term commonly applied to the military offensives that medieval European Christians launched against Muslim opponents.

Cuneiform A script or system of writing devised by the Sumerians; its elements were composed of the wedge-shaped impressions that a stylus makes in the surface of a mud tablet.

Danegeld A tax levied by the Anglo-Saxon kings of England to purchase peace from Viking invaders.

Delian League A defensive alliance Athens organized following the Persian Wars; became the basis for the construction of an Athenian Empire.

Demagogue Politician who acquires power and influence by manipulating the emotions of the masses.

Demesne The fields on a medieval manor from which its lord derived his income; the primary obligation of the peasants who lived on the manor was to work these fields for the lord who provided their protection.

Dialectic The academic discipline that, during the Middle Ages, focused on methods for the construction and critique of logical arguments.

Diet A German political assembly.

Dominate A system of government headed by a *Dominus*, lord; the autocratic system that took hold during the reign of the Roman emperor Diocletian.

Donation of Constantine A document forged in the eighth century to enhance the political authority of the papacy; it claimed that the ancient Roman Emperor Constantine had ceded control over the Roman Empire to Pope Sylvester I.

Donation of Pepin Gift to the pope of Italian land that the Frankish king Pepin (r. 741–768) took from the Lombards; a step in the creation of the Papal States.

Dynasty A ruling family; transmission of monarchical authority through lines of descent within a family.

Edict of Nantes A decree that King Henry IV issued in 1598 that established places in France where Protestants could legally worship.

Exodus The pivotal event in the history of the Hebrew people, their departure from Egypt under Moses, their covenant with God, and the beginning of the fulfillment of God's pledge to Abraham.

Fair A regularly scheduled time for merchants and customers to gather at a particular place for the purpose of conducting business; frequently corresponded with a holiday (a *feria*, "feast day").

Fertile Crescent An arc of cultivated land stretching from the Persian Gulf up the Tigris and Euphrates Rivers across Syria to the Mediterranean and south through Palestine to and including Egypt; the seat of the earliest civilizations.

Feudum The income that a medieval government provided to support the agents that served it; in the absence of a monetary economy and a system of taxation, it was often a piece of land.

Foederati "Allies," Latin term for the German tribes that were permitted to occupy land within the Roman Empire in exchange for a pledge to assist with its defense.

Friar A new religious invocation that emerged in Europe in the late twelfth century; a Christian who took monastic vows of poverty and celibacy but who stayed in the world rather than retreat to a monastery.

Fyrd A peasant army unique to Anglo-Saxon England.

Gaugamela The decisive battle, at a site north of Babylon, at which Alexander the Great defeated Darius and went on to consolidate his hold on the Persian Empire.

Ghibelline A medieval political faction founded by the dukes of Swabia that sought to extend the authority of the German kings into Italy.

Gothic A style of medieval architecture that utilized pointed or broken arches and flying buttresses; it emphasized vertical lines and sought to create buildings flooded by light.

Great Dionysia Spring festival in honor of the god Dionysus, origin of the tradition of Greek theater.

Great Schism The period from 1378 to 1415 during which there were multiple claimants to the papacy.

Guelf A medieval political faction founded by the dukes of Saxony and subsequently a movement in Italy that opposed the efforts of German kings to extend their authority into Italy.

Guild A medieval union or corporation that monopolized the production of a product with the intent of sustaining a healthy market.

Hadith "Traditions" handed down about the Prophet Muhammad's acts and teachings; material supplementary to the Qur'an.

Hanseatic League An alliance of cities in northern Germany (established in 1359) that enabled them to dominate commerce in the Baltic and North Seas.

Hieroglyph "Sacred writing," a script or system of writing devised by the ancient Egyptians utilizing pictographs.

Hijra "Departure," Muhammad's relocation from Mecca to Medina and organization of the first Muslim community; the pivot point for the Muslim calendar.

Hoplite Name for a Greek infantryman, derived from his unique bowl-shaped shield; fought in a tightly packed company called a phalanx.

Hundred Years' War An era of occasionally renewed conflict between England and France in the fourteenth and fifteenth centuries that culminated in England's retreat from the continent.

Imperium The authority to command armies during the era of the Roman Republic and Empire.

Indo-European A family of languages that extends from Ireland across Europe and Persia to India; spread by a major migration at the start of the second millennium that established major new peoples in the ancient world (e.g., Greeks, Romans, Hittites, Persians, etc.).

Indulgence A papal dispensation from the obligation to perform a penance.

Inquisition A church court established by the papacy to root out heresy in Catholic countries.

Investiture Controversy A dispute between the papacy and Europe's kings in 1075 over the right of kings to appoint candidates to offices in the church and participate in the ceremonies that invested clergy with their authority and properties.

Latifundia Latin term for a plantation, staffed by slaves and specializing in crops raised for market.

Line of Demarcation A longitudinal line decreed by the pope in 1494 to divide territories in the western hemisphere between Spain and Portugal.

Linear B Script developed by the Mycenaeans following the example of the Minoans (Linear A); earliest recorded specimens of the Greek language.

Manor A medieval agricultural cooperative; it combined private ownership of land with common ownership of the tools that worked the land.

March A frontier district held by an army to provide protection for a country and a base for potential conquest and expansion.

Martyr "Witness," in particular someone who suffers or dies to testify to a religious belief.

Merovingians The descendants of the Frankish king Clovis (466–511 C.E.); the first dynasty of French kings.

Messiah "Anointed"; in Hebrew tradition, an agent commissioned to act for God to bring about fulfillment of God's covenant with Abraham; in Christian tradition, the role that Jesus of Nazareth played in history.

Middle Kingdom The era in Egyptian history (2025–1630 B.C.E.) characterized by public works, literary production, and the shift of the seat of government to Thebes.

Missi dominici "Emissaries of the Lord," title granted to the agents who toured Charlemagne's empire to hear complaints against local governors.

Modern Devotion A religious revival originating in northern Europe during the fourteenth and fifteenth centuries that promoted education and charitable work.

Monist The thesis argued by Thales, the first philosopher (640–546 B.C.E.), and his followers; suggested that the world was a coherent place because everything in it was the product of a single substance.

Monk "Solitary"; a Christian who chose to live apart from family and society in order to devote himself exclusively to prayer and acts of faith.

Mufti A specialist in the interpretation of Islamic religious law.

Neolithic Era "The New Stone Age," the final phase in prehistoric cultural development; characterized by a farming economy, domestication of wild plant and animal species, and semi-permanent village settlements.

New Comedy Popular theatrical genre that thrived during the Hellenistic era; unlike Old Comedy (e.g., the plays of Aristophanes), which usually had a serious message, it was pure entertainment.

New Kingdom "The Egyptian Empire" (1550–1075 B.C.E.), the era when the ancient Egyptians abandoned their traditional isolationism and expanded south into Nubia and east into Palestine and Syria.

New Model Army A Protestant military organization established by Oliver Cromwell in 1645 that enabled the English Parliament to depose King Charles I and govern England as a Puritan republic.

Nominalism The philosophical claim that words for categories of things are only names that people invent for convenience of communication; such words do not correspond to anything that actually exists.

Old Kingdom "The Pyramid Age" (2700–2200 B.C.E.), the formative phase in the development of ancient Egyptian civilization.

Optimates Roman political faction that hoped to stabilize the Roman Republic by preserving traditions that empowered the Senatorial classes.

Oratory of Divine Love An organization of Catholic clergy and laity that was established in the sixteenth century to work for religious renewal.

Ostracism A vote to determine whether any individual should be exiled from Athens as a suspected threat to the city.

Paleolithic Era "The Old Stone Age," the first period in the evolution of human culture; characterized by a hunter-gather economy and pressure-chipped tool manufacture.

Pantheon A roster of the ancient gods, particularly those associated with Zeus-Jupiter.

Parliament The political body that began to evolve in England in the thirteenth century; it brought together representatives of all the propertied classes in England and provided them with an opportunity to negotiate with their king, but it did not represent the peasant majority.

Parthenon Athenian temple on the Acropolis in the Doric style; most famous specimen of Classical Greek architecture.

Patrician Term for a man from one of the politically empowered families that originally controlled the Roman Republic.

Peace of Augsburg A truce that was declared between Protestant and Catholic factions in Germany in 1555 and which prevented religious conflict in Germany until 1618.

Peace of Westphalia The international agreement concluded in 1648 that ended the Thirty Years' War and resolved numerous boundary disputes.

Peloponnesian War A Greek civil war (432–404 B.C.E.) that led to the decline of Hellenic civilization, opposing sides led by Athens and Sparta.

Perspective The techniques developed by painters during the era of the Renaissance to create the illusion of three-dimensional space on a flat surface.

Plantagenet The name by which England's Norman dynasty ultimately came to be known; it derives from the father of King Henry II (r. 1154–1189).

Plebeian Term for a man from a citizen family that originally had no right to participate in the government of the Roman Republic.

Pluralist Term for the ancient Greek thinkers who suggested that the world was a product of a variety of things (e.g., elements or atoms).

Podestà A neutral stranger who was brought in to rule and mediate among factions when conflict caused the government of an Italian town to break down.

Polis A Greek city-state that undertook a program of social engineering to influence the development of its citizens.

Populares Roman political faction that sought influence by appealing to the Roman masses.

Pragmatic Sanction of Bourges An agreement in 1438 between the king of France and the pope that extended the authority of the French monarchy over the Catholic Church in France.

Predestination Belief, primarily associated with the Swiss theologian John Calvin, that the absolute sovereignty of God implies that a person's conduct cannot alter God's decision about his or her ultimate fate.

Pre-Socratics Greek philosophers prior to Socrates (469–399 B.C.E.) who studied the external world and natural science, whereas later Greek thinkers focused on the internal world of human psychology, rationality, and values.

Princeps "First Citizen," title of honor the Romans bestowed on Octavian (63 B.C.E.–14 C.E.) to thank him for his alleged restoration of their Republic.

Ptolemy Friend of Alexander the Great who won control of Egypt after Alexander's death and found the last dynasty of pharaohs to rule that country.

Puritan Name for a radical Protestant faction that drew its inspiration from the Swiss Reformation. It temporarily overthrew the monarchy and established a Republican government in England.

Quadrivium The secondary portion of the medieval student's curriculum; instruction in arithmetic, geometry, astronomy, and music.

Realism The philosophical claim that words for categories of things are not arbitrary conventions of speech, but refer to fundamental metaphysical realities.

Reform Protestantism Protestant churches that trace their origin less to Martin Luther and Germany than to the work of the Swiss reformers Ulrich Zwingli and John Calvin.

Romanesque A style of medieval architecture that utilized round arches, heavy masonry walls, small windows, and attached buttresses.

Romanitas The customs, traditions, and values that the ancient Romans regarded as the source of their unique strengths and virtues as a people.

Rule The name for the constitution that the church approved to govern the lives of an order of monks or nuns.

Schism A split or division within a community or organization.

Scholasticism The dominant philosophy of the High Middle Ages; drew heavily on the teachings of Aristotle and the construction of dialectical arguments.

Sea Peoples Collective term for the wave of invaders who spread throughout the eastern Mediterranean about 1200 B.C.E.

Seleukos Macedonian soldier who seized control of Babylon after Alexander the Great's death; his descendants formed a dynasty that held the central portion of that empire until ousted by the Parthians and Romans.

Shari'a "Required path," the religious law that governs some Muslim communities.

Shi'a "Party," the branch of Islam that springs from the supporters of Ali, Muhammad's son-in-law, in his struggle for the caliphate.

Spanish Armada The great fleet that Philip II launched in 1588 in what proved to be a futile attempt to conquer England and subdue Protestant resistance in the Netherlands.

St. Bartholomew's Day Massacre A surprise attack that the French monarchy launched (August 24, 1572) on Protestants who had gathered in Paris to celebrate the wedding of a daughter of queen regent Catherine de Medicis to Henry of Navarre, a Protestant leader.

Studia humanitas The mission of the intellectual leaders of Italy's Renaissance, a search for methods to discover and realize the potentials of human nature.

Sultan Title of the leader of the Seljuk Turks who rose to power in the domain of the Abbasid caliph in the eleventh century.

Summa An attempt to sum up in a logically coherent system an entire field of knowledge; for example, the works of the medieval theologian Thomas Aquinas.

Suras The divine messages revealed to Muhammad that, taken together, constitute the Qur'an, Islam's sacred text.

Theme A region within the Byzantine Empire assigned to a military commander.

Thirty Years' War A devastating war fought on German territory from 1618 to 1648; originating as a conflict between Germany's Protestants and Catholics, concern for the balance of power ultimately encouraged French and Scandinavian monarchs to intervene.

Tholos Unique pseudo-domed tomb structures erected by the Mycenaeans.

Torah The first five books of the Hebrew Scriptures: Genesis, Exodus, Numbers, Leviticus, and Deuteronomy.

Triumvirate An arrangement among three men to share governmental authority; Rome's First Triumvirate was a private agreement among Julius Caesar, Pompey, and Crassus; Rome's Second Triumvirate was a formal legal arrangement whereby Octavian, Mark Anthony, and Lepidus were to work for the restoration of the Roman Republic.

Trivium The elementary portion of the medieval student's curriculum; instruction in basic literacy: grammar, dialectic, rhetoric.

Troubadour "Inventor," a kind of lyric poet that appeared in Europe in the eleventh century; who departed from the earlier warrior epic tradition by concentrating on themes of love and intimate personal feelings.

Umma "Community," the new principle of unity that Muhammad created to bind people together through faith in his role as prophet.

War of the Roses Civil war in England (1455–1485) in which the families of the dukes of York and Lancaster struggled for the throne; ended with the establishment of the Tudor dynasty.

Wergeld A provision in Germanic law that allowed an individual who harmed someone to pay a fine equivalent to the seriousness of the injury he had inflicted; a method of avoiding socially disruptive vendettas.

Ziggurat A multistory mound of sun-dried brick erected as a platform for a temple by the Sumerians and Babylonians.

Photo Credits

Suggested Resources

Introduction

The increasing interconnectedness of the modern world has produced numerous reflections on the nature of history and the importance of understanding the interrelatedness of global peoples.

J. M. Hobson, *The Eastern Origins of Western Civilization* (2004); D. Landes, *The Wealth and Poverty of Nations* (1998); R. Royal, "Who Put the West in Western Civilization?" *The Intercollegiate Review* (Spring 1998); F. Fukuyama, *The End of History and the Last Man* (1993); J. Roberts, *The Triumph of the West* (1985).

Chapter 1

Scholars who study the transition from the prehistorical to the historical eras must infer a great deal from scanty evidence. Archaeologists have made some lucky discoveries at widely scattered sites, but only a few key locales have been intensively explored. Anthropological studies of modern tribal peoples have suggested theoretical models that might shed light on the remote past. The dramatic progress that ecologists have been making in uncovering information about Earth's climate cycles has also yielded valuable information about the environments to which early human cultures adapted and spawned theories about the demise of some ancient civilizations.

R. Desalle & I. Tattersall, *Human Origins* (2007); C. Zimmer, *Smithsonian Intimate Guide to Human Origins* (2007); C. Gamble, *Origins and Revolutions: Human Identity in Earliest Prehistory* (2007); R. Gabriel, *The Ancient World* (2007); B. Kemp, *Ancient Egypt: An Anatomy of a Civilization*, 2nd ed. (2006); J. Diamond, *Collapse: How Societies Choose to Fail or Succeed* (2005); R. Chadwick, *First Civilizations: Ancient Mesopotamia and Ancient Egypt*, 2nd ed. (2005); J. McIntosh, *Ancient Mesopotamia: New Perspectives* (2005); H. Crawford, *Sumer and Sumerians* (2004); N. B. Hunt, *Historical Atlas of Ancient Mesopotamia* (2004); D. Lambert, *Encyclopedia of Prehistory* (2002); S. Sanderson, *The Evolution of Human Sociality: A Darwinian Conflict Perspective* (2001); M. Isler, *Sticks, Stones, and Shadows: Building the Egyptian Pyramids* (2001); E. Delson et al., *Encyclopedia of Human Evolution and Prehistory* (2000); R. Rudgley, *The Lost Civilizations of the Stone Age* (2000); R. J. Werke, *Prehistory: Humankind's First Three Million Years* (1999); S. Pollock, *Ancient Mesopotamia: The Eden That Never Was* (1999); R. Ardrey, *The Territorial Imperative: A Personal Inquiry into the Animal Origins of Property and Nations* (1997); J. Diamond, *Guns, Germs, and Steel: The Fates of Human Societies* (1997); D. C. Snell, *Life in the Ancient Near East* (1997); C. Freeman, *Egypt, Greece, and Rome* (1996); A. Cherry, *The Socializing Instincts: Individual, Family, and Social Bonds* (1994); A. J. Spencer, *Early Egypt: The Rise of Civilization in the Nile Valley* (1993); J. N. Postgate, *Early Mesopotamia* (1992); M. Ehrenberg, *Women in Prehistory* (1989); D. O. Henry, *From Foraging to Agriculture* (1989); H. W. F. Saggs, *Civilization Before Greece and Rome* (1989); N. Grimal, *A History of Ancient Egypt* (1988); S. Lloyd, *The Archaeology of Mesopotamia* (1984); S. N. Kramer, *History Begins at Sumer* (1959); H. Frankfort et al., *The Intellectual Adventure of Ancient Man* (1946).

Chapter 2

The invention of writing made it possible for human beings to document their lives in unprecedented detail. Ancient peoples produced both intentional and unintentional records—that is, archival documents that they expected to survive and incidental jottings whose survival has been totally fortuitous. From these things it is possible, for the first time, to infer something about the intellectual lives and thought processes of human beings. The following items survey some of this intriguing work.

B. Fagan, *Return to Babylon: Travelers, Archaeologists, and Monuments in Mesopotamia* (2007); R. Gabriel, *The Ancient World* (2007); M. Chavalas, *The Ancient Near East: Historical Sources in Translation* (2006); P. Esler, *Ancient Israel: The Old Testament in Its Social Context* (2006); W. Grajetzki, *The Middle Kingdom of Ancient Egypt* (2006); D. Silverman, *Akhenaten and Tutankhamon: Revolution and Restoration* (2006); M. Van de Mieroop, *King Hammurabi of Babylon: A Biography* (2005); C. Roehrig,

Hatshepsut: From Queen to Pharaoh (2005); M. Smith, *The Memoirs of God: History, Memory, and the Experience of the Divine in Ancient Israel* (2004); C. Scarre & B. M. Fagan, *Ancient Civilizations*, 2nd ed. (2003); V. Matthews, *A Brief History of Ancient Israel* (2002); I. Finkelstein, *The Bible Unearthed: Archaeology's New Vision of Ancient Israel and the Origin of Its Sacred Texts* (2001); J. & D. Oates, *Nimrud: An Assyrian City Revealed* (2001); I. Shaw, *The Oxford History of Ancient Egypt* (2000); O. Eliezer, *The Sea Peoples and Their World: A Reassessment* (2000); B. Brier, *The Murder of Tutankhamen* (1998); K. R. Nemet-Nejat, *Daily Life in Ancient Mesopotamia* (1998); A. Kuhrt, *The Ancient Near East, c. 3000–330 B.C.* (1995); H. W. F. Saggs, *Babylonians* (1995); G. Robbins, *Women in Ancient Egypt* (1993); N. Grimal, *A History of Ancient Egypt* (1988); D. Redford, *Akhenaten* (1987); O. R. Gurney, *The Hittites* (1954/81); S. Moscati & N. Sanders, *The Sea Peoples: Warriors of the Ancient Mediterranean* (1978); S. Moscati, *Ancient Semitic Civilizations* (1960); J. B. Pritchard, *The Ancient Near East: An Anthology of Texts and Pictures* (1958); H. Frankfort et al., *The Intellectual Adventure of Ancient Man* (1946).

Chapter 3

The classical Greek civilization that arose in the Aegean was incredibly inventive and potent. It permanently changed life in the West, and its influence continues to be felt today. Scholars, however, debate explanations for its origin. Some emphasize its originality and others stress its indebtedness to other cultures.

L. Schofield, *The Mycenaeans* (2007); H. A. Shapiro, *The Cambridge Companion to Archaic Greece* (2007); D. Kyle, *Sport and Spectacle in the Ancient World* (2007); P. Cartledge, *Thermopylae: The Battle that Changed the World* (2006); J. Ducat, *Spartan Education: Youth and Society in the Classical Period* (2006); R. Castleden, *Mycenaeans* (2005); M. Schmidt, *The First Poets: Lives of the Ancient Greek Poets* (2005); J. Foley, *A Companion to Ancient Epic* (2005); T. Holland, *Persian Fire: The First World Empire and the Battle for the West* (2005); A. Lloyd, *Marathon: The Story of Civilizations on Collision Course* (2004); T. Figueira, *Spartan Society* (2004); P. Cartledge, *The Spartans: The World of the Warrior-Heroes of Ancient Greece, From Utopia to Crisis and Collapse* (2003); P. De Souza, *The Greek and Persian Wars, 499–386 B.C.* (2003); J. Lesley Fittor, *Minoans* (2002); F. Braudel, *Memory and the Mediterranean* (2002); J. M. Camp, *The Archaeology of Athens* (2002); N. Lunaghi, *The Historian's Craft in the Age of Herodotus* (2001); J. A. MacGillivray, *Minotaur: Sir Arthur Evans and the Archaeology of the Minoan Myth* (2000); S. B. Pomeroy, S. M. Burstein, W. Donlan, & J. T. Roberts, *Ancient Greece: A Political, Social, and Cultural History* (1999); L. G. Mitchell & P. J. Rhodes, Eds., *The Development of the Polis in Archaic Greece* (1997); O. Dickinson, *The Aegean Bronze Age* (1994); R. Drews, *The End of the Bronze Age: Changes in Warfare and Catastrophes, ca. 1200 B.C.* (1993); V. D. Hanson, *The Western Way of War* (1989); J. Boardman, J. Griffin, & O. Murray, *Greece and the Hellenistic World* (1988); R. Drews, *The Coming of the Greeks: Indo-European Conquests in the Aegean and Near East* (1988); W. Bernal, *Black Athena: The Afroasiatic Roots of Classical Civilization* (1987); R. Osborne, *Demos* (1985); A. R. Burn, *Persia and the Greeks: The Defense of the West*, rev. ed. (1984); J. Boardman, *The Greeks Overseas*, rev. ed. (1980); W. Forrest, *A History of Sparta, 950–121 B.C.*, 2nd ed.(1980); J. Griffin, *Homer* (1980); M. I. Finley, *The World of Odysseus*, rev. ed. (1979); J. Chadwick, *The Mycenaean World* (1976); A. C. Brackman, *The Dream of Troy* (1974); A. Andrews, *Greek Tyrants* (1963).

Chapter 4

The artistic and literary monuments of classical Greek civilization were created over the span of only a few generations—and against a background of frequent military activity. Wars tested Greece's institutions but apparently did not divert Greek intellectuals from thinking deeply about the phenomena of the natural world and the mysteries of human self-awareness. The result was the production of a body of philosophical, scientific, and artistic work of unsurpassed importance.

L. Samons, *The Cambridge Companion to the Age of Pericles* (2007); D. Shangke, *Thucydides and the Philosophical Origins of History* (2007); J. Hurwit, *The Acropolis in the Age of Pericles* (2007); L. Navia, *Socrates: A Life Examined* (2007); M. Linck, *The Ideas of Socrates* (2007); J. Warren, *Presocratics: Natural Philosophers Before Socrates* (2007); A. Saxonhouse, *Free Speech and Democracy in Ancient Athens*

(2006); N. Bagnall, *The Peloponnesian War: Athens, Sparta, and the Struggle for Greece* (2006); J. Morrison, *Reading Thucydides* (2006); P. Connolly, *The Ancient City: Life in Classical Athens and Rome* (2006); G. Ley, *A Short Introduction to the Ancient Greek Theater* (2006); V. Hanson, *A War Like No Other: How the Athenians and Spartans Fought the Peloponnesian War* (2005); D. Kagan, *The Peloponnesian War* (2003); J. Annas, *Plato: A Very Short Introduction* (2003); J. Barnes, *Aristotle: A Very Short Introduction* (2000); S. B. Pomeroy et al., *Ancient Greece: A Political, Social and Cultural History* (1999); M. M. Henry, *Prisoner of History: Aspasia of Miletus and Her Biographical Tradition* (1995); A. Shapiro, *Women in the Classical World* (1994); J. K. Davies, *Democracy and Classical Greece* (1993); C. W. Fornara & L. J. Samons, *Athens from Cleisthenes to Pericles* (1991); D. Kagan, *Pericles of Athens and the Birth of Athenian Democracy* (1991); I. F. Stone, *The Trial of Socrates* (1989); J. Boardman et al., *Greece and the Hellenistic World* (1988); S. Woodford, *An Introduction to Greek Art* (1986); Y. Garlan, *Slavery in Ancient Greece* (1988); W. Burkert, *Greek Religion* (1985); J. D. Romilly, *A Short History of Greek Literature* (1985); J. Boardman, *Greek Art* (1985); A. Burn, *Persia and the Greeks: The Defense of the West*, 2nd ed. (1984); K. J. Dover, *Greek Homosexuality* (1978); R. Meigs, *The Athenian Empire* (1972); J. J. Pollitt, *Art and Experience in Classical Greece* (1972); M. Grant, *The Ancient Historians* (1970); G. E. R. Lloyd, *Early Greek Science* (1970); W. K. Guthrie, *History of Greek Philosophy* (1962–1981); E. Hamilton, *The Greek Way* (1930).

Chapter 5

Roman civilization was a Hellenistic civilization. That is, Rome adopted and adapted the cosmopolitan Greek culture that spread throughout the West in the wake of Alexander the Great's conquests. The Romans were, however, also innovators and pioneers—particularly in the arenas of law and politics. America's "founding fathers" were greatly attracted to the study of Roman history, and their idealized visions of ancient Rome influenced the formation of the early American republic.

C. Thomas, *Alexander the Great in His World* (2007); A. Goldsworthy, *Caesar: Life of a Colossus* (2006); N. Cantor, *Alexander the Great: Journey to the End of the Earth* (2005); A. Fraschetti, *The Foundation of Rome* (2005); D. Kleiner, *Cleopatra and Rome* (2005); M. Grant, *Cleopatra* (2004); L. Burn, *Hellenistic Art from Alexander the Great to Augustus* (2004); H. Flower, *The Cambridge Companion to the Roman Republic* (2004); C. Mackay, *Ancient Rome: A Military and Political History* (2004); F. Borrelli, *The Etruscans: Art, Architecture, and History* (2004); G. Irby-Massie, *Greek Science of the Hellenistic Era: A Sourcebook* (2002); R. Seager, *Pompey the Great: A Political Biography* (2002); H. Mouritsen, *Plebs and Politics in the Late Roman Republic* (2001); P. Horden, *The Corrupting Sea: A Study of Mediterranean History* (2000); A. Goldsworthy, *The Punic Wars* (2000); S. Haynes, *Etruscan Civilization: A Cultural History* (2000); A. W. Lintott, *The Constitution of the Roman Republic* (1999); T. J. Cornell, *The Beginnings of Rome: Italy and Rome from the Bronze Age to the Punic Wars* (1995); M. H. Crawford, *The Roman Republic*, 2nd ed. (1993); F. W. Walbank, *The Hellenistic World* (1993); R. A. Bauman, *Women and Politics in Ancient Rome* (1992); P. Green, *Alexander of Macedon* (1991); N. Bagnall, *The Punic Wars* (1990); J. Boardman et al., *The Roman World* (1990); E. N. Borza, *In the Shadow of Olympus: The Emergence of Macedon* (1990); R. E. Mitchell, *Patricians and Plebeians: The Origin of the Roman State* (1990); N. G. L. Hammond & F. W. Walbank, *A History of Macedonia* (1988); A. B. Bosworth, *Conquest and Empire: The Reign of Alexander the Great* (1988); A. D. Long, *Hellenistic Philosophy: Stoics, Epicureans, Skeptics*, 2nd ed. (1986); J. J. Pollitt, *Art in the Hellenistic Age* (1986); G. Alföldy, *The Social History of Rome* (1985); E. S. Gruen, *The Hellenistic World and the Coming of Rome* (1984); H. H. Scullard, *A History of the Roman World, 753–146 B.C.E.*, 4th ed. (1980); M. Pallottino, *The Etruscans* (1975); P. M. Fraser, *Ptolemaic Alexandria* (1972); M. Grant, *Cleopatra* (1972); R. M. Errington, *The Dawn of Empire: Rome's Rise to World Power* (1971); B. H. Warmington, *Carthage*, 2nd ed. (1969); R. Syme, *The Roman Revolution* (1960).

Chapter 6

The Roman Empire was a remarkably successful and long-lived institution. It maintained order and stability throughout the entire Western world for over two centuries, a record that no subsequent government has equaled. The empire was not, however, sustained by a single set of unchanging institutions. To preserve the empire, Rome's leaders had to constantly adapt and reorganize it. Eventually, it changed so much that its core identity was threatened.

W. Eck, *The Age of Augustus* (2007); J. B. Rives, *Religion in the Roman Empire* (2007); D. S. Potter, *A Companion to the Roman Empire* (2006); E. Fantham, *Julia Augusti: The Emperor's Daughter* (2006); J. Osgood, *Caesar's Legacy: Civil War and the Emergence of the Roman Empire* (2006); P. Matyszak, *The Sons of Caesar: Imperial Rome's First Dynasty* (2006); K. Galinsky, *The Cambridge Companion to the Age of Augustus* (2005); J. Malitz, *Nero* (2005); R. Seager, *Tiberius* (2005); E. Speller, *Following Hadrian: A Second-Century Journey Through the Roman Empire* (2004); J. Carcopino, *Daily Life in Ancient Rome: The People and the City at the Height of the Empire* (2003); A. Barrett, *Livia: First Lady of Imperial Rome* (2002); J. Grubbs, *Women and the Law in the Roman Empire* (2002); J. Boardman, *The Oxford Illustrated History of the Roman World* (2001); R. Thomas, *Virgil and the Augustan Reception* (2001); J. C. Coulston, *Ancient Rome: The Archaeology of the Eternal City* (2000); M. Boatwright, *Hadrian and the Cities of the Roman Empire* (2000); K. Galinsky, *Augustan Culture* (1996); M. Grant, *The Antonines: The Roman Empire in Transition* (1994); T. Wiedemann, *Emperors and Gladiators* (1992); H. C. Boren, *Roman Society*, 2nd ed. (1992); D. Shotter, *Augustus Caesar* (1991); A. Ferrill, *Caligula: Emperor of Rome* (1991); R. P. Saller, *The Roman Empire: Economy, Society and Culture* (1987); M. Grant, *The Roman Emperors* (1985); B. Campbell, *The Emperor and the Roman Army* (1984); P. MacKendrick, *The Mute Stones Speak: The Story of Archeology in Italy*, 2nd ed. (1983); T. Barnes, *The New Empire of Diocletian and Constantine* (1982); R. Duncan-Jones, *The Economy of the Roman Empire* (1982); F. G. B. Millar, *The Emperor in the Roman World, 31 B.C.–A.D. 337* (1977); E. N. Luttwak, *The Grand Strategy of the Roman Empire* (1976); E. T. Salmon, *A History of the Roman World, 30 B.C. to A.D. 138* (1968); R. Syme, *The Roman Revolution* (1960).

Chapter 7

As the Roman Empire declined, its eastern and western halves separated. This foreshadowed the split that has emerged in the modern era between a Christian "West" and a Muslim "East." During the Middle Ages, however, the civilization that spread throughout Europe was transformed by surges of influences from the Middle East. The most significant of these was, of course, Christianity. But the brilliant Byzantine and Islamic cultures that also arose in the Middle East were particularly instrumental in helping Europe emerge from its Dark Age and restore its civilized institutions.

S. Mitchell, *A History of the Later Roman Empire, A.D. 284–641: The Transformation of the Ancient World* (2007); A. Casiday, *Constantine to c. 600* (2007); R. van Dam, *The Roman Revolution of Constantine* (2007); M. Kulikowski, *Rome's Gothic Wars:From the Third Century to Alaric* (2007); A. Barbero, *The Day of the Barbarians: The Battle that Led to the Fall of the Roman Empire* (2007); I. Zeitlin, *The Historical Muhammad* (2007); H. Halm, *The Arabs: A Short History* (2007); B. Rogerson, *The Heirs of Muhammad: Islam's First Century and the Origins of the Sunni-Shia Split* (2007); W. A. Goffart, *Barbarian Tides: The Migration Age and the Later Roman Empire* (2006); C. T. R. Hewer, *Understanding Islam* (2006); G. E. M. De Ste. Croix, *Christian Persecution, Martyrdom, and Orthodoxy* (2006); R. Horsley, *Christian Origins* (2005); P. Heather, *The Fall of the Roman Empire* (2005); D. Catchpole, *Jesus People: The Historical Jesus and the Beginning of Community* (2006); M. White, *From Jesus to Christianity* (2004); C. Kelly, *Ruling the Later Roman Empire* (2004); D. S. Potter, *The Roman Army at Bay, A.D. 180–395* (2004); M. Salzman, *The Making of a Christian Aristocracy: Social and Religious Change in the Western Roman Empire* (2002); W. Stagemann, *The Social Setting of Jesus and the Gospels* (2002); P. Southern, *The Roman Empire from Severus to Constantine* (2001); G. Dawes, *The Historical Jesus Quest: Landmarks in the Search for the Jesus of History* (2000); F. E. Peters, *Muhammad and the Origins of Islam* (1994); J. Morehead, *Justinian* (1995); K. Armstrong, *Muhammad: A Biography of the Prophet* (1992); A. Schimmel, *Islam: An Introduction* (1992); A. H. Hourani, *A History of the Arab Peoples* (1992); R. Browning, *The Byzantine Empire* (1992); P. J. Heather, *Goths and Romans, 332–489* (1991); T. Barnes, *The New Empire of Diocletian and Constantine* (1982); W. Goffart, *Barbarians and Romans, A.D. 418–584: The Techniques of Accommodation* (1980); M. Grant, *The Fall of the Roman Empire* (1990); C. H. Lawrence, *Medieval Monasticism*, 2nd ed. (1989); H. St. L. B. Moss, *The Birth of the Middle Ages,*

395–814, 2nd ed. (1972); P. Brown, *The World of Late Antiquity, c.e. 150–750* (1971); G. Ostrogosky, *History of the Byzantine State*, 2nd ed. (1969); P. Brown, *Augustine of Hippo* (1967).

Chapter 8

Early medieval Europe was characterized by a diversity of peoples and cultures. Several attempts were made to overcome its political fragmentation and restore the unity it had enjoyed during the Roman era, but none succeeded for very long. The resulting period in history is difficult to generalize with any accuracy. A rich mix of peoples and movements contributed to Europe's reorganization and its gradual emergence as an original and influential civilization.

R. A. Hall, *The World of the Vikings* (2007); M. Arnold, *The Vikings: Wolves of War* (2007); J. Sypeck, *Becoming Charlemagne: Europe, Baghdad, and the Empires of a.d. 800* (2006); C. Corning, *The Celtic and Roman Traditions: Conflict and Consensus in the Early Medieval Church* (2006); C. McClendon, *The Origins of Medieval Architecture:Building in Europe, a.d. 600–900* (2005); A. Clot, *Harun al-Rashid and the World of the Thousand and One Nights* (2005); A. D. M. Forte, *Viking Empires* (2005); T. Glick, *Islamic and Christian Spain in the Early Middle Ages* (2005); T. Gregory, *A History of Byzantium* (2005); A. Barbero, *Charlemagne: Father of a Continent* (2004); C. Backman, *The Worlds of Medieval Europe* (2003); J. Moorhead, *The Roman Empire Divided, 400–700* (2001); P. Fouracre, *The Age of Charles Martel* (2000); N. Christie, *The Lombards, the Ancient Longobards* (1995); I. N. Wood, *The Merovingian Kingdoms, 450–751* (1994); R. McKitterick, *Carolingian Culture: Emulation and Innovation* (1994); S. Reynolds, *Fiefs and Vassals: The Medieval Evidence Reinterpreted* (1994); R. W. Mathisen, *Roman Aristocrats in Barbarian Gaul: Strategies for Survival in an Age of Transition* (1993); J. P. Ply & E. Bournazel, *The Feudal Transformation, 900–1200* (1991); F. D. Logan, *The Vikings in History*, 2nd ed. (1991); L. Bitel, *Isle of the Saints: Monastic Settlement and Christian Community in Early Ireland* (1990); P. J. Geary, *Before France and Germany: The Creation and Transformation of the Merovingian World* (1988); H. R. Loyn, *The Governance of Anglo-Saxon England, 500–1087* (1984); J. D. Randers-Pherson, *Barbarians and Romans: The Birth Struggle of Europe, a.d. 400–700* (1983); R. McKitterick, *The Frankish Kingdoms under the Carolingians, 751–987* (1983); R. Collins, *Early Medieval Spain: Unity in Diversity, 400–1000* (1983); O. Chadwick, *The Making of the Benedictine Ideal* (1981); J. Richards, *The Popes and the Papacy in the Early Middle Ages, 476–752* (1979); L. White, *Medieval Technology and Social Change* (1972); J. Boussard, *The Civilization of Charlemagne* (1971); P. H. Blair, *The World of Bede* (1970); G. Duby, *Rural Economy and Country Life in the Medieval West* (1968).

Chapter 9

Europe entered the Middle Ages as the weakest of the Mediterranean world's three civilizations. Its Byzantine and Muslim neighbors were far more culturally sophisticated and had richer economies and more thriving urban institutions. Not surprisingly, therefore, Europe languished on the defensive, struggling with successive waves of invasion and migration. By the eleventh century, however, European societies had begun to stabilize, and Europeans were able to reverse course and take the offensive. The wars of conquest—which they inaugurated—and the crusades both signaled and promoted the revival of European civilization, but these wars have left a legacy of hate that continues to the present day.

A. Cameron, *The Byzantines* (2006); C. Tyenman, *God's War: A New History of the Crusades* (2006); D. Horspool, *King Alfred: Burnt Cakes and Other Legends* (2006); S. Friedman, *A History of the Middle East* (2006); R. H. Bloch, *A Needle in the Right Hand of God: The Norman Conquest of 1066 and the Making of the Bayeux Tapestry* (2006); M. Angold, *Eastern Christianity* (2006); N. Oikonomidès, *Society, Culture, and Politics in Byzantium* (2005); R. Huscroft, *Ruling England, 1042–1328* (2005); A. Clot, *Harun al-Rashid and the World of the Thousand and One Nights* (2005); T. Ashridge, *The First Crusade: A New History* (2004); J. P. Berkey, *The Formation of Islam: Religion and Society in the Near East, 600–1800* (2003); K. Armstrong, *Holy War: The Crusades and Their Impact on Today's World*, rev. ed. (2001); M. Gervens, *Tolerance and Intolerance: Social Conflict in the Age of the Crusades* (2001); R. Barber, *Henry Plantagenet* (2001); M. Brett, *The Rise of the Fatimids: The World of the Mediterranean and the Middle East in the 4th Century of the Hijra, 10th Century c.e.* (2001); E. Hallam, *Capetian France, 987–1328*

(2001); G. A. Loud, *The Age of Robert Guiscard: Southern Italy and the Norman Conquest* (2000); R. I. Moore, *The First European Revolution* (2000); D. Crouch, *The Reign of King Stephen, 1135–1154* (2000); J. Haldon, *Byzantium: A History* (2000); R. Hodges, *Towns and Trade in the Age of Charlemagne* (2000); D. Webb, *Pilgrims and Pilgrimage in the Medieval West* (1999); C. Hillenbrand, *The Crusades: Islamic Perspectives* (1999); J. Rathbone, *The Last English King* (1999); J. Riley-Smith, *The First Crusaders, 1095–1131* (1997); J. Riley-Smith, Ed., *The Oxford Illustrated History of the Crusades* (1997); R. Bartlett, *The Making of Europe: Conquest, Colonization and Cultural Change, 950–1350* (1993); W. Roesener, *Peasants in the Middle Ages* (1992); W. Treadgold, *The Byzantine Revival, 780–842* (1988); U. R. Blumenthal, *The Investiture Controversy: Church and Monarchy from the Ninth to the Twelfth Century* (1988); H. Kennedy, *The Prophet and the Age of the Caliphates: The Islamic Near East from the Sixth to the Eleventh Century* (1986); S. Reynolds, *Kingdoms and Communities in Western Europe, 900–1300* (1984); E. M. Hallam, *Capetian France, 987–1328* (1980); E. Ennen, *The Medieval Town* (1979); G. Barraclough, *The Crucible of Europe, the Ninth and Tenth Centuries in European History* (1976); R. S. Lopez, *The Commercial Revolution of the Middle Ages, 950–1350* (1971); B. Hill, *Church and State in the Middle Ages* (1970); R. Jenkins, *Byzantium: The Imperial Centuries, 610–1071* (1969); D. C. Douglas, *William the Conqueror: The Norman Impact Upon England* (1964); S. Runciman, *A History of the Crusades* (1964).

Chapter 10

During the High Middle Ages, the contours of some of Europe's major nation-states began to appear on the map and strides were made toward the development of their characteristic political and cultural institutions. This was a period of intellectual and artistic inventiveness. Great cathedrals— wonders of engineering and architectural vision—were erected. Universities appeared, literacy spread, and Europeans engaged in lively (often contentious) debates that produced breakthroughs in philosophy and science.

C. Lindberg, *A Brief History of Christianity* (2006); R. Horrox, *A Social History of England, 1200–1500* (2006); J. Flori, *Richard the Lionheart: King and Knight* (2006); R. Huscroft, *Ruling England, 1042–1328* (2005); M. McCarthy, *Classical and Gothic: Studies in the History of Art* (2005); P. Strafford, *Romanesque Churches of France; A Traveller's Guide* (2005); R. Begley, *Medieval Education* (2005); R. M. Holt, *The Crusader States and their Neighbors* (2004); J. Brower, *The Cambridge Companion to Abelard* (2004); R. Rubenstein, *Aristotle's Children: How Christians, Muslims, and Jews Rediscovered Ancient Wisdom and Illuminated the Dark Ages* (2003); A. Nichols, *Discovering Aquinas: An Introduction to His Life, Work and Influence* (2002); D. Spoto, *Reluctant Saint: The Life of Francis of Assisi* (2002); D. Burr, *The Spiritual Franciscans* (2001); R. Barber, *Henry Plantagenet* (2001); D. Crouch, *The Reign of King Stephen, 1135–1154* (2000); M. Kitchen, *The Cambridge Illustrated History of Germany* (2000); M. Barber, *The Cathars: Dualist Heretics in Languedoc in the High Middle Ages* (2000); R. Bartlett, *England Under the Norman and Angevin Kings, 1075–1225* (2000); C. H. Berman, *The Cistercian Evolution: The Invention of a Religious Order in Twelfth-Century Europe* (2000); J. Gillingham, *Richard I* (1999); R. N. Swanson, *The Twelfth-Century Renaissance* (1999); L. B. Glick, *Abraham's Heirs: Jews and Christians in Medieval Europe* (1999); M. T. Clanchy, *Abelard: A Medieval Life* (1997); M. D. Costen, *The Cathars and the Albigensian Crusade* (1997); C. H. Lawrence, *The Friars: The Impact of the Early Mendicant Movement on Western Society* (1994); H. Schulze, *States, Nations and Nationalism* (1994); H. de Ridder-Symoens, Ed., *Universities in the Middle Ages* (1992); W. S. Stoddard, *Art and Architecture in Medieval France* (1990); D. Abulafia, *Frederick II: A Medieval Emperor* (1988); M. R. Menocal, *The Arabic Role in Medieval Literary History: A Forgotten Heritage* (1987); J. Marenbon, *Later Medieval Philosophy (1150–1350): An Introduction* (1987); J. B. Baldwin, *The Government of Philip Augustus: Foundations of French Royal Power in the Middle Ages* (1986); S. C. Ferruolo, *The Origins of the University* (1985); S. Reynolds, *Kingdoms and Communities in Western Europe, 900–1300* (1984); J. Bony, *French Gothic Architecture of the Twelfth and Thirteenth Centuries* (1983); E. M. Hallam, *Capetian France, 987–1328* (1980); W. C. Jordan, *Louis IX and the Challenge of the Crusade: A Study in Rulership* (1979); K. J. Conant, *Carolingian and Romanesque Architecture, 800–1200*, 2nd ed. (1979); W. L. Warren, *Henry II* (1973); J. W. Baldwin, *The Scholastic Culture of the Middle Ages, 1000–1300* (1971); J. R.

Strayer, *On the Medieval Origins of the Modern State* (1970); P. Munz, *Frederick Barbarossa: A Study in Medieval Politics* (1969).

Chapter 11

The late medieval world was tested in many ways, and, over all, it confronted its challenges successfully. Despite failures of leadership and what was sometimes an all-consuming preoccupation with a struggle to survive, Europe's cultural creativity was undiminished. Europeans weathered their crises, restored their institutions, and emerged from their trials prepared for a new era of invention and expansion.

J. Aberth, *Disease in Human History* (2007); D. Morgan, *The Mongols* (2007); D. Green, *Edward the Black Prince: Power in Medieval Europe* (2007); D. Spoto, *Joan: The Mysterious Life of the Heretic Who Became a Saint* (2007); R. Blumenfeld-Kosinski, *Poets, Saints, and Visionaries of the Great Schism, 1378–1417* (2006); M. Prawdin, *The Mongol Empire: Its Rise and Legacy* (2006); S. Haw, *Marco Polo's China: A Venetian in the Realm of Khubilai Khan* (2006); M. Livingstone, *The Road to Crécy: The English Invasion of France* (2005); P. Jackson, *The Mongols and the West* (2005); A. Ayton, *The Battle of Crécy* (2005); R. J. Knecht, *The Valois: Kings of France, 1328–1589* (2004); J. Philips, *The Fourth Crusade and the Sack of Constantinople* (2004); J. Byrne, *The Black Death* (2004); A. Curry, *The Hundred Years' War* (2003); J. C. Moore, *Pope Innocent III: To Root Up and to Plant* (2003); K. Fowler, *Medieval Mercenaries, Vol. 1: The Great Companies* (2001); N. Cantor, *In the Wake of the Plague: The Black Death and the World It Made* (2001); J. Larner, *Marco Polo and the Discovery of the World* (1999); J. Moore, *Innocent III and His World* (1999); R. Brown-Grant, *Christine de Pizan and the Moral Defense of Women: Reading Beyond Gender* (1999); J. Poole, *Joan of Arc* (1998); D. Herlihy, *The Black Death and the Transformation of the West* (1997); W. C. Jordan, *The Great Famine: Northern Europe in the Early Fourteenth Century* (1996); R. Frame, *The Political Development of the British Isles, 1100–1400* (1995); J. Schatzmiller, *Jews, Medicine, and Medieval Society* (1994); P. Stump, *The Reforms of the Council of Constance, 1414–1418* (1994); A. Curry, *The Hundred Years' War* (1993); J. H. Burns, Ed., *The Cambridge History of Medieval Political Thought* (1988); C. Allmand, *The Hundred Years' War: England and France at War* (1988); R. Gottfried, *The Black Death: Natural and Human Disaster in Medieval Europe* (1983); N. W. Warner, *Joan of Arc: The Image of Female Heroism* (1981); M. G. A. Vale, *War and Chivalry: Warfare and Aristocratic Culture in England, France, and Burgundy at the End of the Middle Ages* (1981); J. R. Strayer, *The Reign of Philip the Fair* (1980); F. Oakley, *The Western Church in the Later Middle Ages* (1979); T. S. R. Boase, *Death in the Middle Ages: Mortality, Judgment, and Remembrance* (1972); Y. Renouard, *The Avignon Papacy, 1305–1403* (1970); J. P. Morrall, *Political Thought in Medieval Times* (1962).

Chapter 12

Europe's Renaissance and Age of Exploration mark a turning point in global history. Many of the key developments that have shaped life in the modern world can be traced to this era: mass literacy, global exchanges of goods and cultures, widening divergence of Christian and Muslim peoples, and the resurgence of influences from the ancient phase in Western civilization.

C. L. Frommel, *The Architecture of the Italian Renaissance* (2007); R. Jacoff, *The Cambridge Companion to Dante* (2007); N. R. Havely, *Dante* (2007); K. A. Simon Eliot, *A Companion to the History of the Book* (2007); E. Enenkel, *Petrarch and His Readers in the Renaissance* (2006); L. Fusco, *Leonardo de' Medici* (2006); R. Crum, *Renaissance Florence: A Social History* (2006); H. Kamen, *Spain, 1469–1714: A Society in Conflict* (2005); J. Reston, *Dogs of God: Columbus, the Inquisition, and the Defeat of the Moors* (2005); S. Füssel, *Gutenberg and the Impact of Printing* (2005); J. Snyder, *Northern Renaissance Art* (2005); R. Mackenney, *Renaissances: The Cultures of Italy, c. 1300–1600* (2005); H. Thomas, *Rivers of Gold: The Rise of the Spanish Empire, from Columbus to Magellan* (2004); J. C. Smith, *The Northern Renaissance* (2004); J. Najemy, *Italy in the Age of the Renaissance, 1300–1550* (2004); J. Edwards, *Ferdinand and Isabella* (2004); P. Strathern, *The Medicis:Godfathers of the Renaissance* (2003); B. Lewis, *What Went Wrong? Western Impact and Middle Eastern Response* (2002); H. Beinart, *The Expulsion of the Jews from Spain* (2002); P. Russell, *Prince Henry "the Navigator": A Life* (2000); S. Bemrose, *A New Life of Dante* (2000); M. Greene, *A Shared World: Christians and Muslims in the Early Modern Mediterranean* (2000); P. Johnson, *The Renaissance: A Short History* (2000); P. Dollinger, *The German Hansa*

(1999); P. Burke, *The European Renaissance: Centers and Peripheries* (1998); B. Thompson, *Humanists and Reformers* (1996); L. Jardine, *Worldly Goods: A New History of the Renaissance* (1996); C. G. Nauert, *Humanism and the Culture of the Renaissance* (1995); B. G. Kohl & A. A. Smith, *Major Problems in the History of the Italian Renaissance* (1995); J. Hale, *The Civilization of Europe in the Renaissance* (1994); J. Huizinga, *The Autumn of the Middle Ages* (1924/1996); G. Holmes, *Renaissance* (1996); F. Fernandez-Armesto, *Columbus* (1991); M. L. King, *Women of the Renaissance* (1991); G. V. Scammell, *The First Imperial Age: European Overseas Expansion, c. 1400–1715* (1989); L. Martins, *Power and Imagination: City-States in Renaissance Italy* (1989); A. W. Crosby, *The Biological Expansion of Europe* (1986); J. N. Hillgarth, *The Spanish Kingdoms, 1250–1516* (1978); E. L. Eisenstein, *The Printing Press as an Agent of Change* (1978); G. Leff, *The Dissolution of the Medieval Outlook, an Essay on Intellectual and Spiritual Change in the Fourteenth Century* (1976); H. Inalcik, *The Ottoman Empire: The Classical Age, 1300–1600* (1973); D. Waley, *The Italian City Republics* (1969); B. Lewis, *Istanbul and the Civilization of the Ottoman Empire* (1963).

Chapter 13

Despite the confident predictions of many secularists, religion has not faded as a significant factor influencing the behavior of modern peoples and states. The history of the era of Europe's Reformation and religious wars may, therefore, be of special interest to students of current world affairs. It is also important for the study of American history, for the religious ideologies that emerged at this time were transplanted to America and shaped the American way of life.

R. Shaughnessy, *The Cambridge Companion to Shakespeare and Popular Culture* (2007); S. Ronald, *The Pirate Queen: Queen Elizabeth I, Her Pirate Adventurers, and the Dawn of Empire* (2007); R. Rex, *Henry VIII and the English Reformation* (2006); M. Bennett, *Oliver Cromwell* (2006); G. W. Bernard, *The King's Reformation: Henry VIII and the Remaking of the English Church* (2005); P. Oswald, *Mary Stuart* (2005); L. DeLisle, *After Elizabeth: The Rise of James of Scotland and the Struggle for the Throne of England* (2005); M. Holt, *The French Wars of Religion, 1562–1629* (2005); C. V. Wedgwood, *The Thirty Years' War* (2005); L. Picard, *Elizabeth's London: Everyday Life in Elizabethan London* (2004); H. Kleinschmidt, *Charles V: The World Emperor* (2004); H. Kamen, *Golden Age Spain* (2004); P. Collinson, *The Reformation: A History* (2004); M. Mullett, *Martin Luther* (2004); D. McKim, *The Cambridge Companion to Martin Luther* (2003); C. Levin, *Elizabeth I, Always Her Own Free Woman* (2003); B. Pursell, *The Winter King: Frederick V of the Palatinate and the Coming of the Thirty Years' War* (2003); L. Frieda, *Catherine de Medici, Renaissance Queen of France* (2003); A. Levi, *Renaissance and Reformation: The Intellectual Genesis* (2002); G. Parker, *Philip II* (2002); M. Kitchen, *The Cambridge Illustrated History of Germany* (2000); R. J. Knechy, *Catherine de' Medici* (1998); C. Haigh, *Elizabeth I*, 2nd ed. (1998); S. Greenblatt, Ed., *The Norton Shakespeare* (1997); B. Thompson, *Humanists and Reformers: A History of Renaissance and Reformation* (1996); P. Gaunt, *Oliver Cromwell* (1996); C. Lindberg, *The European Reformations* (1996); M. P. Holt, *The French Wars of Religion, 1562–1629* (1995); R. Ashton, *Counter-Revolution: The Second Civil War and Its Origin, 1646–1648* (1995); W. P. Stephens, *Zwingli* (1994); A. McGrath, *Reformation Thought: An Introduction*, 2nd ed. (1993); G. H. Williams, *The Radical Reformation*, 2nd ed. (1992); H. A. Oberman, *Luther* (1992); S. Ozment, *Protestants: The Birth of a Revolution* (1992); J. Wormald, *Mary Queen of Scots: A Study in Failure* (1991); J. McConica, *Erasmus* (1991); H. Kamen, *Spain 1469–1714: A Society of Conflict*, 2nd ed. (1991); S. J. Lee, *The Thirty Years' War* (1991); E. Cameron, *The European Reformation* (1991); R. Bonney, *The European Dynastic States, 1494–1660* (1991); A. McGrath, *A Life of John Calvin: A Study in the Shaping of Western Culture* (1990); P. Caravan, *Ignatius Loyola: A Biography of the Founder of the Jesuits* (1990); A. G. Dickens, *The English Reformation*, 2nd ed. (1989); W. J. Bouwsma, *John Calvin: A Sixteenth-Century Portrait* (1988); P. Collinson, *The Religion of Protestants: The Church in English Society, 1559–1625* (1982); S. Ozment, *The Age of Reform, 1250–1550: An Intellectual and Religious History of Late Medieval and Reformation Europe* (1980); R. S. Dunn, *The Age of Religious Wars, 1559–1715*, 2nd ed. (1979); F. Braudel, *The Mediterranean and the Mediterranean World in the Age of Philip II*, 2 vols. (1976); M. R. O'Connell, *The Counter Reformation, 1559–1610* (1974); P. Gay & R. K. Webb, *Modern Europe to 1815* (1973); A. Wandruszka, *The House of Habsburg* (1965).

Index

DVD Table of Contents

22 World War I: The End of Enlightenment

Text Sources

- Neville Chamberlain, *In Search of Peace*
- Marc Bloch, from *Strange Defeat*
- Heinrich Himmler, "Speech to SS Officers"
- Franklin D. Roosevelt, "Call for Sacrifice"
- Franklin D. Roosevelt and Winston Churchill, "The Atlantic Charter"
- Emmanuel Ringelblum, "Notes from the Warsaw Ghetto"
- Anna Petrovna Ostroumova-Lebedeva, "Leningrad Diary"
- Adolf Hitler, "The Obersalzberg Speech"
- A. Philip Randolph, "A Call to March on Washington"

Visual Sources
- Warsaw ghetto
- U.S. troops before D-Day
- U.S. air bombing of Bologna
- Tokyo shanty town, September 1945
- Tokyo and Nuremberg war crimes trials, I
- Tokyo and Nuremberg war crimes trials, II
- The war in the Pacific
- The internment of Japanese Americans, I
- The internment of Japanese Americans, II
- The internment of Japanese Americans, III
- The Holocaust, I
- The Holocaust, II
- The destruction of Europe
- Summits of the Allied leaders, I
- Summits of the Allied leaders, II
- Rosie the Riveter
- Nazis executing Russian civilians
- Japanese surrender aboard the *USS Missouri*
- Japanese bombing of Pearl Harbor
- Hitler and Chamberlain
- Hiroshima after the dropping of the atomic bomb
- France surrenders to the Germans
- D-Day
- Civilian refugees in Europe
- Atomic bomb mushroom cloud
- American workers at B-17 bomber plant
- American propaganda poster
- American GIs in Holland
- "United We Win" poster
- U.S. and Soviet forces meet, 1945

25 Decolonization and the Cold War

Text Sources
- Winston Churchill, from "The Iron Curtain Speech"

- Helga Schütz, "The Wall in My Back Yard"
- Robert Schuman, "The Schuman Declaration"
- *Ladies Home Journal*, "Young Mother"
- Nikita S. Krushchev, "Address to the Twentieth Congress"
- Joseph Stalin, excerpts from the "Soviet Victory" Speech
- John F. Kennedy, Address Before the General Assembly of the United Nations
- James B. Stockdale, excerpt from *A Vietnam Experience: Ten Years of Reflection*
- Henry A. Myers, "East Berliners Rise Up Against Soviet Oppression"
- Harry S Truman, "The Truman Doctrine"
- George Kennan, "The United States and Russia"
- George C. Marshall, "The Marshall Plan"
- Francois Mitterand, Speech to the United Nations
- United Nations, "Universal Declaration of Human Rights"
- United Nations, "Declaration on the Granting of Independence to Colonial Countries and Peoples"
- Palestinian Declaration of Independence
- Jawaharlal Nehru, "Why India Is Non-Aligned"
- Mohandas Ghandi, from *Hind Swaraj*
- Kwame Nkrumah, from *I Speak of Freedom: A Statement of African Ideology*
- Jomo Kenyatta, from *Facing Mt. Kenya: The Tribal Life of the Gokuyu*
- Jawaharlal Nehru, from *The Autobiography of Jawaharlal Nehru*
- Israel's Proclamation of Independence
- Ho Chi Minh, "Declaration of Independence of the Democratic Republic of Vietnam"
- Gamal Abdel Nasser, Speech on the Suez Canal
- Frantz Fanon, from *The Wretched of the Earth*
- Martin Luther King, Jr., Letter from Birmingham City Jail

Visual Sources
- Bulgarian labor brigade
- Vietnamese refugees
- U.S. and British votes in the UN on the Suez Canal crisis, 1956
- UN sprays DDT over Seoul
- The "Kitchen Debate" between Nixon and Khrushchev

26 Western Civilization and the Global Community

Text Sources

Visual Sources